Java 7 Recipes

A Problem-Solution Approach

Josh Juneau
Carl Dea
Freddy Guime
John O'Conner

Apress®

Java 7 Recipes: A Problem-Solution Approach

ISBN-13 (pbk): 978-1-4302-4056-3

ISBN 978-1-4302-4057-0 (eBook)

President and Publisher: Paul Manning
Lead Editor: Jonathan Gennick
Technical Reviewers: Mark Beaty and David Coffin
Editorial Board: Steve Anglin, Mark Beckner, Ewan Buckingham, Gary Cornell, Morgan Ertel, Jonathan Gennick, Jonathan Hassell, Robert Hutchinson, Michelle Lowman, James Markham, Matthew Moodie, Jeff Olson, Jeffrey Pepper,Douglas Pundick, Ben Renow-Clarke, Dominic Shakeshaft, Gwenan Spearing, Matt Wade, Tom Welsh
Coordinating Editor: Annie Beck
Copy Editor: Nancy Sixsmith
Compositor: Apress Production (Christine Ricketts)
Indexer: SPI Global
Artist: SPI Global
Cover Designer: Anna Ishchenko

Distributed to the book trade worldwide by Springer Science+Business Media New York, 233 Spring Street, 6th Floor, New York, NY 10013. Phone 1-800-SPRINGER, fax (201) 348-4505, e-mail orders-ny@springer-sbm.com, or visit www.springeronline.com.

For information on translations, please e-mail rights@apress.com, or visit www.apress.com.

Apress and friends of ED books may be purchased in bulk for academic, corporate, or promotional use. eBook versions and licenses are also available for most titles. For more information, reference our Special Bulk Sales–eBook Licensing web page at www.apress.com/bulk-sales.

Any source code or other supplementary materials referenced by the author in this text is available to readers at www.apress.com. For detailed information about how to locate your book's source code, go to http://www.apress.com/source-code/.

This book is dedicated to the members of the Java community. The Java platform would not be what it is today without the continued support and contributions from everyone in the community.

Contents at a Glance

Contents

About the Authors

■Josh Juneau has been developing software and database systems for several years. Database application programming has been the focus of his career since the beginning. He became an Oracle database administrator and adopted the PL/SQL language for performing administrative tasks and developing applications for Oracle database. As Josh's skills evolved, he began to incorporate Java into his PL/SQL applications and later began to develop stand-alone applications in Java. He has extended his knowledge of the JVM by learning and developing applications with other JVM languages such as Jython and Groovy. His interest in learning new languages that run on the JVM led to his interest in Jython. Since 2006, Josh has been the editor and publisher for the *Jython Monthly* newsletter. In late 2008, he began a podcast dedicated to the Jython programming language. Josh was the lead author for *The Definitive Guide to Jython* and *Oracle PL/SQL Recipes*, which were published by Apress. He works as an application developer and database administrator at Fermi National Accelerator Laboratory, and is the lead for the *Django-Jython* project (http://code.google.com/p/django-jython/). Josh has a wonderful wife and four great children with whom he loves to spend time and teach about technology. To hear more from Josh, follow his blog, which can be found at http://jj-blogger.blogspot.com. You can also follow him on Twitter via @javajuneau.

■Carl P. Dea is currently a software engineer working for BCT-LLC on projects with high performance computing (HPC) architectures. He has been developing software for 15 years with many clients from Fortune 500 companies to nonprofit organizations. He has written software ranging from mission-critical applications to web applications. Carl has been using Java since the very beginning and he also is a huge JavaFX enthusiast, dating back to when it was called F3. His passion for software development started when his middle school science teacher showed him the TRS-80 computer. Carl's current software development interests include rich client applications, game programming, Arduino, mobile phones, and tablet computers. When he's not working, he and his wife love to watch their daughters perform at gymnastics meets. Carl lives in Pasadena (aka "The Dena"), Maryland, USA.

■**Freddy Guime** has been in the software industry for more than 12 years. He started programming at age 7 and billed his first consulting gig at 15. He has been working with Javafor more than 5 years and is a regular speaker at the JavaOne conference. Freddy currently works for an options trading software company in Chicago, in which sub-millisecond response time in response to market events is paramount. With his experience in multithreading and Java Swing he has managed to create Java clients that can consume tens of thousands of market events per second. He is also the host of `JavaPubHouse.com`, a podcast dedicated to the Java language, on which programming tips and tricks are discussed.

■**John O'Conner** is a husband, father, and sleep-deprived technology enthusiast. Currently the globalization architect at Adobe Systems, John uses a variety of technologies, strategies, and best practices to ensure that Adobe's Creative Media and Marketing products meet the demands of a global customer base. He began his Java career at Sun Microsystems in 1997 and helped develop the internationalization and Unicode support libraries of the core Java SE platform. The common thread running through John's career is his interest in creating globalized, world-ready software platforms. He frequently writes about Java and internationalization topics on his blog at `joconner.com`. You can also follow him on Twitter as `@jsoconner`.

About the Technical Reviewers

■Mark Beaty has been developing in Java since 1998 when he went to work for Sun Microsystems. During his years at Sun, Mark helped to develop and evolve Sun's web presence, in various roles ranging from architect to developer. As a web application developer, Mark has spent a lot of time developing large-scale, multitiered web applications on the server side, but he also enjoys developing rich client applications in the browser. Prior to becoming a Java developer, Mark worked as a software engineer in the defense industry, using a little-known programming language called Ada. During his 10+ years in the defense industry, Mark had a huge amount of fun developing real-time embedded software for military training systems and flight simulators. Mark is currently an independent software consultant focusing on developing mobile web and native applications on Android and iOS. Mark lives in Colorado, where he enjoys cycling, hiking, skiing, and pretty much anything that involves being outdoors.

■**David Coffin** is the author of *Expert Oracle and Java Security*, published by Apress. He is an IT analyst working at the Savannah River Site, a large Department of Energy facility. For more than 30 years, David's expertise has been in multiplatform network integration and systems programming. Before coming to the Savannah River Site, he worked for several defense contractors and served as the technical lead for office and network computing at the National Aerospace Plane Joint Program Office at Wright-Patterson Air Force Base in Ohio. As a perpetual student, David has one master's degree and many hours toward another. As a family man, he has raised eight children. Coffin is a triathlete and distance swimmer who competes in the middle of the pack. He is also a classical guitar player, but he's not quitting his day job.

Acknowledgments

To my wife Angela: you have provided me with the love and support that I need to be successful in my career. Thanks for being there for me always and talking to me about technology even though I know it bores you. You have always been, and will continue to be, my inspiration for success. I am so happy raising our children together; I hope they will turn out to be as kind and loving as you are.

To my children Kaitlyn, Jacob, Matthew, and Zachary: please stop growing up! I love you all so much and enjoy having such wonderful children. We will read through this book together one day, and you, too, can learn the joy of developing successful software. For now, I will enjoy all the time we have together as you continue to grow and learn more each day.

I want to thank my family for their continued support in my career. You have always listened to my lectures on technology and programming, and I appreciate that. It means the world to me. I want to thank my co-workers at Fermilab for allowing me to guide the organization's application development efforts and build successful solutions to keep us moving forward.

To my co-authors Carl Dea, Freddy Guime, John O'Conner, and Mark Beaty: you are excellent authors and experts in Java technology and I am honored to have had the opportunity to work with each of you. I thank you all for working together to produce this excellent book; it would not have been possible without you.

To the folks at Apress, I thank you for providing me with the chance to share my knowledge with others. I especially thank Jonathan Gennick for the continued support of my work and for providing the guidance to produce useful content for our readers. You've become a good friend over the last couple of years and I really enjoy working with you. I thank Annie Beck and Anita Castro for the ability to coordinate the efforts of each author who contributed to this book; you have both done an outstanding job. I also would like to thank Steve Anglin for believing in my abilities to author books on the Java technology for Apress. The technical reviewers, David Coffin and Mark Beaty, have done an excellent job of solidifying the book content. Thanks for your hard work and technical expertise. Lastly, I'd like to thank everyone else at Apress who had a hand in this book.

To the Java community, I thank you all for helping the JVM to become a successful development platform. We all have the privilege of working with a mature and robust platform, and it would not be successful today if it weren't for everyone's continued contributions to the technology. I also thank all the Oracle Java experts: you hit a home run with Java 7 and the roadmap for the future is looking great. I am looking forward to using Java technology for many years to come.

--Josh

I would like to thank my wife,Tracey, and my daughters, Caitlin and Gillian, for their loving support and sacrifices. A special thanks to my daughter Caitlin, who helped with illustrations and brainstorming fun examples. A big thanks to Jim Weaver for recommending me for this project and being so encouraging. I would also thank Josh Juneau for his leadership and guidance throughout this journey. I also want to thank my co-authors, John O'Conner, Freddy Guime, and Mark Beaty for their excellent advice. Thanks also to David Coffin for his uncanny ability to know my intentions and providing great feedback. I want to thank the wonderful people at Apress for their professionalism. A special thanks to Jonathan Gennick for believing in me and whipping me into shape. Thanks to Annie Beck and Anita Castro for keeping me on track when things got rough. Thanks to all who follow me on Twitter, especially the ones who relate to Java Swing and JavaFX. Also, thanks to Stephen Chin and Keith Combs for heading up the JavaFX User Group. Lastly, I want to give a big kudos and acknowledgment to the people at Oracle who helped me (directly or indirectly) as JavaFX 2.0 was being released: Jonathan Giles, Jasper Potts, Michael Heinrichs, Richard Bair, Amy Fowler, David DeHaven, Nicolas Lorain, Kevin Rushforth, Sheila Cepero, Gail Chappell, Cindy Castillo, Scott Hommel, Joni Gordon, Alexander Kouznetsov, Irina Fedortsova, Dmitry Kostovarov, Alla Redko, Igor Nekrestyanov, Nancy Hildebrandt, and all the Java, JavaFX, and NetBeans teams involved. "Whether, then, you eat or drink or whatever you do, do all to the glory of God" (1 Corinthians 10:31).

--Carl

Dedicated to the love of my life (and wife) Gabriela; my three awesome children Jolie, Natalie and Max; and my mom Julia and dad Alberto.

--Freddy

Thanks to my supportive, patient, and loving wife Robyn; and our five children Jackson, Nicholas, Matthew, Tressa, and Ruby. Our greatest success is our wonderful close family. You make life great.

--John

Introduction

The Java programming language was first introduced in 1995 by Sun Microsystems. Derived from languages such as C and C++, Java was designed to be moreintuitive and easier to use than older languages, specifically due to its simplistic object model and automated facilities such as memory management. At the time, Java drew the interest of developers because of its object-oriented, concurrent architecture; excellent security and scalability; and because applications developed in the Java language could be run on any operating system that contained a Java Virtual Machine (JVM). Since its inception, Java has been described as a language that allows developers to "write once, run everywhere" as code is compiled into class files that contain bytecode, and the resulting class files can run on any compliant JVM. This concept made Java an immediate success for desktop development, which later branched off into different technological solutions over the years, including development of web-based applications and rich Internet applications (RIAs). Today, Java is deployed on a broad range of devices including mobile phones, printers, medical devices, blue ray players, and so on.

The Java platform consists of a hierarchy of components, starting with the Java Development Kit (JDK), which is composed of the Java Runtime Environment (JRE), the Java programming language, and platform tools that are necessary to develop and run Java applications. The JRE contains the Java Virtual Machine (JVM), plus the Java application programming interfaces (APIs) and libraries that assist in the development of Java applications. The JVMis the base upon which compiled Java class files run and is responsible for interpreting compiled Java classes and executing the code. Every operating system that is capable of running Java code has its own version of the JVM. To that end, the JRE must be installed on any system that will be running local Java desktop or stand-alone Java applications. Oracle provides JRE implementations for most of the major operating systems, most recently adding Mac OS X to the list. Each operating system can have its own flavor of the JRE. For instance, mobile devices can run a scaled down version of the full JRE that is optimized to run Java Mobile Edition (ME) applications.

The Java platform APIsand libraries are a collection of predefined classes that are used by all Java applications. Any application that runs on the JVM makes use of the Java platform APIs and libraries. This allows applications to make use of functionality that has been predefined and loaded into the JVM and leaves developers with more time to worry about the details of their specific application. The classes that comprise the Java platform APIs and libraries allow Java applications to use one set of classes in order to communicate with the underlying operating system. As such, the Java platform takes care of interpreting the set of instructions provided by a Java application into operating system commands that are required for the machine on which the application is being executed. This creates a façade for Java developers to write code against so that they can develop applications; which can be written once and ran on every machine that contains a relevant JVM.

The JVM and the Java platform APIs and libraries play key roles in the lifecycle of every Java application. Entire books have been written to explore the platform and JVM. This book will focus on the Java language itself, which is used to develop Java applications, although the JVM and Java platform APIs and libraries will be referenced as needed. The Java language is a robust, secure, and modern object-oriented language that can be used to develop applications to run on the JVM. The Java programming language has been refined over several iterations and it becomes more powerful, secure, and modern with each new release. This book covers many features of the Java programming language from those that were introduced in Java 1.0 through those that made their way to the language in Java 7. In 2011,

Oracle Corporation released Java 7, which was a milestone release for the Java ecosystem. Not only is Java 7 the most modern, statically typed, object-oriented language available for development, it also enhances the ability to integrate different languages that run on the JVM, such as Jython, Groovy, JRuby, and Scala to name a handful.

On the heels of the Java 7 release, Oracle also delivered JavaFX 2.0, a breakthrough in desktop application development for the JVM. JavaFX 2.0 can be used for developing rich desktop and Internet applications using the Java language, or any other language that runs on the JVM. It provides a rich set of graphical and media user interfaces to develop extraordinary visual applications. This release is a major update to the JavaFX platform, allowing applications to be written entirely in the Java language. Previous releases of JavaFX mandated the use of JavaFX Script for development of user interfaces for JavaFX. JavaFX 2.0 does away with the mandate for using JavaFX Script and allows developers to use the language of their choice for working with the JavaFX application programming interfaces.

This book covers fundamentals of Java development such as installation of the JDK, writing classes, and running applications.It delves into essential topics such as the development of object-oriented constructs, exception handling, unit testing, and localization. The book also provides solutions for desktop application development using the Swing API, and web-based solutions including servlets and applets. It covers JavaFX 2.0 in depth and is an essential guide for developers beginning to use JavaFX.This book can be used as a guide for solving problems that ordinary Java developers may encounter at some point. A broad range of topics is discussed, and the solutions to the problems that are covered in this book are concise and tothe point.

If you are a novice Java developer, we hope that this book will help you get started on your journey to working with one of the most advanced and widely used programming languages available today. For those of you who have used the Java language for some time, we hope that this book will provide you with updated material that is new to Java 7 and JavaFX 2.0 so that you can further refine your Java development skills. We ensure that advanced Java application developers will also learn a thing or two regarding the new features of the language and perhaps even stumble upon some techniques that were not used in the past. Whatever your skill level, this book will be good to have close at hand as a reference for solutions to those problems that you will encounter in your daily programming.

Who This Book Is For

This book is intended for all those who are interested in learning the Java programming language and/or already know the language but would like some information regarding the new features included in Java SE 7 and JavaFX 2.0. Those who have not yet programmed in the Java language can read this book, and it will allow them to start from scratch to get up and running quickly. Intermediate and advanced Java developers who are looking to update their arsenal with the latest features that Java SE 7 and JavaFX 2.0 make available to them can also read the book to quickly update and refresh their skill set.

Java desktop programmers will find this book useful for its content on developing desktop applications using the Java Swing toolkit and JavaFX 2.0. Developers of Java web applications will find useful content regarding servlets, applets, and more. There is, of course, a myriad of other essential topics that will be useful to Java developers of any type.

How This Book Is Structured

This book is structured so that it does not have to be read from cover to cover. In fact, it is structured so that developers can chose which topic(s) they'd like to read about and jump right to them. Each recipe contains a problem to solve, one or more solutions to solve that problem, and a detailed explanation of how the solution works. Although some recipes may build upon concepts that have been discussed in other recipes, they will contain the appropriate references so that the developer can find other related recipes that are beneficial to the solution. The book is designed to allow developers to get up and running quickly with a solution so that they can be home in time for dinner.

C H A P T E R 1

Getting Started with Java 7

The Java language has been around for quite some time now. It has been labeled a "legacy language," and some say that Java will become outdated and a language of the past. Those who advocate languages that do not run on the Java Virtual Machine (JVM) make these statements, and they are untrue. With each release, the Java language gains new features, adding new capabilities to help developers of the JVM become more productive.

The first major release of Java was distributed in 1996, and since then the language has undergone many changes. Over the years, the language has added features such as inner classes, JavaBeans, regular expressions, generics, enumerations, and so on. With each release, the Java language changes the way in which applications are built and used. The last major update of Java was Java 1.6 (Java 6 Tiger), which was released in late 2006. That release featured updates that offered new features to the Java language, as well as other languages on the JVM. Scripting language support with JSR223 paved the road for integration between Java and other languages to integrate with one another.

The Java 7 release marks one of the most monumental updates to the language in years. Not only does Java 7 offer more features but it also enhances the ability to write other languages for the JVM. Constructs such as the try-with-resources and the diamond operator add productivity to the language. Invoke Dynamic increases the language's ability to offer support for dynamic languages. The new I/O library enhances platform independence and makes I/O easier to use. New graphics features have been added along with new Swing components to make graphical user interfaces (GUIs) better. All these features and more offer one of the largest updates to the Java language in years. The language is better than ever, and it has a user community that rivals any other.

This chapter will introduce newcomers to the Java language. It will help those who are unfamiliar with the language to get started. You will learn how to install Java and configure it for your environment. You will learn basics of Java such as how to create a class and how to accept keyboard input. Documentation is often overlooked, but in this chapter you will quickly learn how to create great documentation for your Java code. In the end, you will quickly get up and started developing with Java 7.

1-1. Downloading and Installing Java 7

Problem

You want to install the Java 7 Development Kit (JDK 7) on your computer workstation or laptop.

Solution

Download the requisite Java 7 distribution for your platform, or download and build OpenJDK. Once downloaded and/or built, run installation scripts as necessary.

To download the binary distribution of the JDK, please visit the Oracle downloads page and choose the correct binary Java SE release for your platform of choice.

■ **Note**   If you are working on Mac OS X, you have a couple of options for working with OpenJDK. To download sources for OpenJDK, please visit `http://openjdk.java.net` and build the sources on your workstation or laptop, or go to the Google Source project `openjdk-osx-build` and download an installer.

How It Works

The JDK is distributed in a binary format via the Oracle Corporation. If interested in obtaining the most recent build of the latest JDK, go to the OpenJDK site, download, and build the sources. Since the binary installer contains an installation wizard, I will not cover the wizard installation in detail. However, there are a few key things to note regarding the installation process. Be sure that you download the JDK and not the Java Runtime Environment (JRE) because you will want to develop with Java. The JRE does not include the tools that are required to develop and compile Java code. Instead, the JRE merely provides the runtime required to load and execute Java applications on the JVM.

When you initiate the installation wizard, you will be presented with a number of different features that can be installed. Specifically, you will be given the choice to install Development Tools, Demos and Samples, and Source Code. I recommend installing everything because you will benefit from looking at the demos and samples, and you may also benefit from looking at the JDK sources. You can specify a default installation location for the JDK. By default, the wizard will want to install to the Program Files area on a Windows machine. I recommend changing this location to another directory that contains no spaces in its name and is made at the root of your OS drive. This will alleviate CLASSPATH issues in the future. I recommend installing to `C:\Java\jdk1.7.0` on a Windows machine. If you have multiple drives, you can install to any of them, although it is not recommended to install the JDK on an external drive.

On all platforms, you can have more than one JDK installed. This allows you to run older Java programs that rely on deprecated or removed Java tools, and at the same time provides the ability to work with the most recent Java platform. Hence, it is a smart choice to install the JDK into a directory containing the JDK release number. In our case, we are installing into the directory `jdk1.7.0`.

If you are working on a Solaris or Linux platform, you will have the same type of wizard that is provided for use with Microsoft Windows. However, if you are working on a Mac OS X platform, you may not be provided with such a wizard. The JDK 7 Developer Preview from Oracle is bundled as a disk image, and the installation involves opening the disk image and dragging the JDK bundle to the designated location within the OS. You also have the option of going to the OpenJDK site and downloading the sources so that they can be built and installed on your operating system. There is also a `dmg` (disk image) available for the latest builds of OpenJDK for OS X hosted on the Google Code repository. Since this is the easier route to take, we choose to install from the disk image.

Go to the openjdk-osx-build project on Google Code (`http://code.google.com/p/openjdk-osx-build/`) and download the most recent OpenJDK disk image. You will want to install the universal disk image if it is available. Once downloaded, you can open the disk image, and run the `Installation.pkg` file. Once you run the installer, a standard OS X installation wizard will begin. Unlike the Microsoft Windows installation wizard, you cannot select the installation path. Once the installation completes, you can go to the Java Preferences utility and see the OpenJDK 7 listed as one of the options. Drag it to the top of the list to ensure that Java 7 will be the default runtime.

■ **Note** If you are running Java applications that are not compatible with Java 7 on OS X, you can use the Java Preferences utility to drag the JDK of your choice to the top of the list of available JDK installations to set as default.

1-2. Configuring the CLASSPATH

Problem

You want to execute a Java program or include an external Java library in the application you are executing.

■ **Note** Would you like to run a "Hello, World" program now that you've installed the JDK as described in the previous recipe? Not to worry. That's the very next recipe. First though, you should configure your CLASSPATH.

Solution

Set the CLASSPATH equal to the directory location of the user-defined Java classes or Java Archive (JAR) files that you need to have access to for executing your application.

■ **Note** It is a good idea to organize your code; it is also good to organize where you place your code on the computer. A good practice is to place all your Java projects within the same directory; it can become your workspace. Place all the Java libraries that are contained in JAR files into the same directory for easier management.

Let's say that you have a directory named JAVA_DEV located at the root of your OS drive, and all the files that you need to have access to are located in this directory. If this is the case then you would do the following at the command line or terminal:

- Setting CLASSPATH on a Microsoft Windows platform:

```
set CLASSPATH=C:\JAVA_DEV\some-jar.jar
```

- Setting CLASSPATH on a UNIX platform:

```
export CLASSPATH=/JAVA_DEV/some-jar.jar
```

Alternately, the javac tool provides an option for specifying resources that need to be loaded for an application. On all platforms, setting the CLASSPATH using this technique can be done as follows:

```
javac –classpath /JAVA_DEV/some-jar.jar
```

Of course, on Microsoft Windows machines the file path will use the backslash (\) instead.

How It Works

In order for the JVM to find the resources that are needed to execute Java applications, there needs to be a specified search path that can be used to find associated files. That being said, the CLASSPATH can be used by the JVM in order to find and load any Java sources or JAR files that may be required. The CLASSPATH is a parameter that tells the JVM where to look for classes and packages, and it can be set using an environment variable or command-line argument.

When executing Java programs, the JVM finds and loads classes as needed using the following search order:

- The classes that are fundamental to the Java Platform and are contained in the Java installation directory

- Any packages or JAR files that are located within the extension directory of the JDK

- Packages, classes, JAR files, and libraries that are loaded somewhere on the specified CLASSPATH

■ **Note** JAR files are a used to package applications and Java libraries into a distributable format.

You may need to load more than one directory or JAR file into the CLASSPATH for an application. This could be the case if your dependencies are located in more than one location. To do so, simply use the delimiter for your operating system (either ; or :) as a separator between the locations specified for the CLASSPATH as such (on UNIX):

```
export CLASSPATH=/JAVA_DEV/some-jar.jar:/JAVA_LIB/myjar.jar
```

or

```
javac –classpath /JAVA_DEV/some-jar.jar:/JAVA_LIB/myjar.jar
```

When loading the resources for a Java application, the JVM loads all the classes and packages that are specified in the first location, followed by the second, and so on. This is important because the order of loading may make a difference in some instances.

In order to add all the JAR files within a specified directory, use the wildcard character (*) after the directory containing the files. You can do so as follows when using the -classpath option of the javac tool:

```
javac –classpath /JAVA_DEV/*:/JAVA_LIB/myjar.jar
```

Specifying a wildcard will tell the JVM that it should be loading JAR files only. It will not load class files that are located in the directory specified with the wildcard character. In order to include Java class files that are located in a directory, do not specify the wildcard. For example, if you want to load all JAR files and class files within the /JAVA_DEV directory, you would specify the following:

```
javac –classpath /JAVA_DEV/*:/JAVA_DEV
```

Subdirectories contained within the CLASSPATH would not be loaded. In order to load files that are contained within subdirectories, those directories and/or files must be explicitly listed in the CLASSPATH. However, Java packages that are equivalent to the subdirectory structure will be loaded. Therefore, any Java classes that reside within a Java package that is equivalent to the subdirectory structure will be loaded.

1-3. Writing an Executable Java Class

Problem

You want to develop an executable Java program that can be run from the command line or terminal.

Solution

Create a Java class that includes a main() method. A class containing a main() method is executable because this method will be loaded when the application is executed. In the following Java class, a "Hello World" message will be printed at the command line when executed.

```
public class MainTest {

public static void main(String[] args) {
    System.out.println("Hello World");
    }
}
```

How It Works

To make a Java class executable, simply add a main() method somewhere within the class that will be executed when the class is run. The main() method should take care of any application setup or instantiations in order to run the program. The main() method is comparable to the "driver" for the application. It should always be specified using the same definition, including the static modifier so that it can be invoked without creating an instance of the class first. The return type of the method should always be void, meaning that nothing will be returned from the method. Lastly, the signature of the main() method should include a String array as an argument. This String array allows arguments to be passed to the program at runtime. Zero or more arguments can be passed to the program using a space to separate them.

In the following example class, the main() method is printing each of the arguments that are passed to the program at runtime:

```
public class MainTestArguments {
    public static void main(String[] args){
        if(args. length > 0){
            System.out.println("Arguments that were passed to the program: ");
            for (String arg:args){
                System.out.println(arg);
            }
        } else {
            System.out.println("No arguments passed to the program.");
        }
    }
}
```

First, the length of the args String array is tested to see whether it is greater than zero. If it is, the method will loop through each of the arguments in the String array using a for loop, printing each out along the way. If there are no arguments passed to the program, the length of the args String array will be zero, and a message indicating as such will be printed.

To learn how to execute this program and pass arguments via the command line or terminal, please see Recipe 1-4.

1-4. Compiling and Executing Java Class

Problem

You have written a Java class and you want to compile and execute it.

Solution

First, if you are planning to make use of the CLASSPATH environment variable, set up your CLASSPATH to include all the required resources to run your Java class. For more information on doing this, please see Recipe 1-2. Next, compile your Java class using the `javac` tool that ships with the JDK. For example, to compile the class named `MainTestArguments.java` that was created in Recipe 1-3, use the following syntax from the command line or terminal:

```
javac MainTestArguments.java
```

■ **Note** In order to compile Java sources, you must be located in the same directory containing the sources, or specify the full path to the sources when issuing the `javac` command. So using the command line enables you to change directories until you are within the same directory that contains the code you want to compile.

As a result of using the `javac` utility, you will see a file named `MainTestArguments.class` that is created in the same directory. In order to execute this class, use the `java` tool that also ships with the JDK:

```
java –cp .org/java7recipes/chapter1/recipe1_03/MainTestArguments
```

Note that you do not include the `.java` suffix after the class name when executing the class. Similarly, you do not include a `.class` suffix after the class name. However, you do append the Java package directory structure to the front of the class name, and use the `–cp` flag to set the CLASSPATH. The preceding command will execute the `MainTestArguments` class, and you should receive the following output when executing this application:

```
No arguments passed to the program.
```

How It Works

In order to compile a Java class, all required classes and libraries must be in the CLASSPATH. This can be accomplished either by setting the CLASSPATH environment variable or by using the `-classpath` option of the `javac` tool, as demonstrated in Recipe 1-2. Once all the dependent resources are specified in the

CLASSPATH, use the javac tool to compile the sources into class files. To use the javac tool, you must either be working from within the command line or terminal unless you are working within an integrated development environment (IDE). The command can be issued from within the directory in which the Java source file resides; otherwise, the entire path to where the source is located must be specified along with the file name. For instance, if the MainTestArguments.java source file resides within the path /JAVA_DEV/org/java7recipes/chapter1/recipe1_03, you must either change directories (cd) to that location, or specify the entire path along with the file name as follows:

```
javac /JAVA_DEV/org/java7recipes/chapter1/recipe1_03/MainTestArguments.java
```

Once the javac tool compiles the code, another file with the same name and a .class suffix will be generated. This resulting file can be run on the JVM by use of the java command. To run any executable Java class file that has already been compiled, issue the java command, followed by the name of the class as you see here:

```
java -cp /JAVA_DEV/org/java7recipes/chapter1/recipe1_03/MainTestArguments
```

To maintain consistency throughout the examples, the command shown here runs the compiled Java class file from a directory different from the one in which it resides. The same rules apply for the java command as with the javac utility, in that you can use the java command from within the same directory of a Java class file if the Java class is not contained within any Java packages or from another directory, and use the –cp flag to include the entire path to the file along with the file name (or the path to the file from the directory in which you are currently located). The –cp flag will set the CLASSPATH for the java command.

As demonstrated in the preceding example, using the java command can become a bit trickier when Java packages are introduced. A *Java package* is basically a directory that can contain a Java source file. Most Java applications use packages for organization of code, and packages are often nested within each other to form an organized file system of code. Because packages are directories, you may think that it is possible to traverse within them in order to get to the same package containing your Java source to issue the java command, but that is not correct. In order to run a Java class that is contained within a Java package, you must traverse to the root of the application source structure (outside of the outermost package) and specify the package path along with the file name. Another option is to include the parent directory of the outermost package within the CLASSPATH, as demonstrated by the example using the –cp flag. To learn more about packages, please see Recipe 1-12.

1-5. Printing Output

Problem

You want to print output from a Java program to the command line or terminal.

Solution

Pass the output in String format to `System.out.println()`from anywhere within the class. For example, suppose that you would like to display the message "I love Java 7" for those running your program. To do so, make use of the `System.out.println()` utility by doing the following:

```
System.out.println("I love Java 7");
```

How It Works

The `System` class acts as a utility for Java application developers. It cannot be instantiated, and it contains a myriad of fields and methods to assist developers in performing commonly used tasks. As such, printing to the command line is a very common way of displaying messages to application users, or printing error codes and messages for debugging purposes.

`System.out` is the standard output stream for the Java language. It is already open by default, so it can be used right away without any setup. What is actually occurring when `System.out.println()` is invoked is that a `PrintStream` object is used, and the `println()` method of that `PrintStream` object displays the text passed into the object.

Using the `System.out` stream to print messages to the command line is essential for any command line–based application. However, often Java applications are not used from within the command line. In such cases, the `System.out` stream is not visible to the user unless the application has been coded so that the stream is presented to the application display. In any case, `System.out` can still be useful for displaying messages because any message sent to it will be printed in the server log for web applications. As for Swing, JavaFX, or other GUI–based applications, `System.out` can still be handy for a myriad of tasks including debugging.

1-6. Passing Arguments via the Command Line

Problem

You want to pass arguments to a Java application via the command line or terminal.

Solution

Run the application using the `java` command-line tool and specify the arguments that you want to pass into it after the application name. For example, suppose you want to pass the arguments "one" and "two" to the `MainTestArguments` class that we created in Recipe 1-3. To do so, you should first traverse into the directory containing the outermost package `org` and then issue the command as follows:

```
java org/java7recipes/chapter1/recipe1_03/MainTestArguments one two
```

You should see the following output:

```
Arguments that were passed to the program:
one
two
```

How It Works

As you know by now, all Java classes that are executable from the command line or terminal contain a main() method. If you look at the signature for the main() method, you can see that it accepts the String[] argument. In other words, you can pass an array of String values into the main() method. Therefore, since the main() method is the first piece of code that is executed when running a Java class, any arguments that you pass to the class will go into this String array so that they can be used from within the application.

Commonly a series of Strings or numbers is passed into an executable Java class, and then the method iterates through the elements of the String array and performs some processing. In the case of the class that was used in the Solution to this recipe, two String values were passed into the main() method and printed out. Much more complex work can be performed with the arguments that are passed in as well. What happens if you try to pass a number into the main() method? It will convert the number to a String automatically and it will be treated as a string of numeric characters rather than as a numeric value. If you attempt to pass the numbers 1, 2, 3, and 4 to the MainTestArguments class, it will simply print those numbers back out. Anything that is passed into the main() method is treated as a String. If you need to work with number values for calculation purposes, String-to-Integer conversions can be performed. You can read more about converting Strings to number values in Recipe 2-6.

1-7. Obtaining and Setting Environment Variable Values

Problem

The application you are developing needs to make use of some OS environment variables. You are also interested in setting the values of environment variables from within the Java application.

Solution

Make use of the Java System class to retrieve any OS environment variable values. The System class has a method getenv(), which accepts a String argument corresponding to the name of a system environment variable. It will then return the value of the given variable. If no matching environment variable exists, a NULL value will be returned.

In the following example, the Java class EnvVars accepts an environment variable name and prints out its value. As noted previously, if there is not a matching variable name, a NULL value will be returned and an error message will be displayed:

```java
public class EnvVars {

public static void main(String[] args) {
        if (args.length > 0) {
            String value = System.getenv(args[0]);
            if (value != null) {
                System.out.println(args[0].toUpperCase() + " = " + value);
            } else {
                System.out.println("No such environment variable exists");
            }
        } else {
            System.out.println("No arguments passed");
        }
    }
}
```

If you are interested in retrieving the entire list of environment variables that is defined on a system, do not pass any arguments to the System.getenv() method. Once you have obtained the Map of variables, you can iterate through them. This technique is demonstrated in the example below. Once the Map of variables is obtained, the program iterates through each of the variables and prints the corresponding value:

```java
public class EnvVarsAll {

    public static void main(String[] args){
        if(args.length > 0){
            String value = System.getenv(args[0]);
        if (value != null) {
            System.out.println(args[0].toUpperCase() + " = " + value);
        } else {
            System.out.println("No such environment variable exists");
        }
        } else {
            Map<String, String> vars = System.getenv();
            for(String var : vars.keySet()){
                System.out.println(var + " = " + vars.get(var));
            }
        }
    }

}
```

How It Works

The System class contains many different utilities that can aid in application development. One of those is the getenv() method, which will return a value for a given system environment variable. Environment variables are stored in a Map, a collection of name/value pairs; the getenv() method is used to pass the name of an environment variable, and it will return that variable's value. If there is no environment variable name that matches the one passed to getenv(), a NULL value is returned.

If you want to obtain an entire list of all environment variables, do not pass any String value to System.getenv(). When no value is passed to System.getenv(), a Map of all system environment variables is returned. Such a Map can be traversed so that the name/value pairs can be read, displayed, and used as necessary.

1-8. Documenting Code with Javadoc

Problem

You want to document some of your Java classes to assist in future maintenance.

Solution

Use Javadoc to place comments before any of the classes, method, and fields that you want to document. To begin the comment, use the characters /** and then begin each subsequent line that you want to add to the comment with an asterisk (*). Lastly, to end the Javadoc comment, close it with the characters */ at the end. The following method is commented with Javadoc:

```
/**
 * Accepts an unlimited number of values and
 * returns the sum.
 *
 * @param nums
 * @return Sum of numbers
 */
public static BigInteger addNumbers(BigInteger[] nums){
    BigInteger result = new BigInteger("0");
    for (BigInteger num:nums){
        result = result.add(num);
    }

    return result;
}
```

Such comments can be added to the beginning of classes and fields the same way. Not only does this assist when looking through the code but it also provides a standard documentation set in HTML format. The JDK provides another useful tool named Javadoc that parses the named Java source file and formulates HTML documentation based upon the defined class elements and Javadoc comments. If no Javadoc comments exist within the source, some default documentation will be produced automatically. The following command will create the Javadoc for a Java source file named DeprecationExample.java. Keep in mind that the same rules apply when using the Javadoc tool as with using javac. You must reside within the same directory as the source file or prepend the name of the file with the path to where it is located.

```
javadoc java7recipes/chapter1/recipe1_08/DeprecationExample.java
```

This command will produce several HTML files containing the documentation for the class, methods, and fields.

How It Works

Generating documentation for applications can be quite tedious. Maintaining documentation can be even more troublesome. The JDK comes packaged with an extensive system for documentation known as Javadoc. Placing some special comments throughout the code source and running a simple command-line tool makes it easy to generate useful documentation and keep it current. Moreover, even if some of the classes, methods, or fields in an application are not commented specifically for the Javadoc utility, default documentation will be recorded for such elements.

To create Javadoc comments, begin the comment line with the characters (/**). Although optional since Java 1.4, a common practice is to include an asterisk as the first character of every line within the comment. Another good practice is to indent the comment so that it aligns with the code that is being documented. Lastly, close the comment with the characters (*/).

Javadoc comments should begin with a short description of the class or method. Fields are rarely commented using Javadoc. The comment can be several lines in length and can even contain more than one paragraph. If you want to break comments into paragraphs, then separate them using the <p>tag. Comments can include several tags that indicate various details regarding the method or class that is being commented. Javadoc tags begin with an asterisk (@), and some of the common tags are as follows:

- @param: Name and description of a parameter
- @return: What is returned from the method
- @see: Reference to another piece of code

You may also include inline links within Javadoc to reference different URLs. To include an inline link, use the tag {@link My Link}, where link is the actual URL that you want to point at and My Link is the text that you want to have appear. There are also many other tags that can be used within Javadoc comments including {@literal}, {@code}, {@value org}, and many others. For a complete listing, please see the Javadoc reference on the Oracle site.

As mentioned in the solution to this recipe, the Javadoc utility is used to create the actual documentation set for a given class. This utility ships along with the JDK and resides within the bin directory of your JDK install. Running the Javadoc utility is much like running javac in that you must either reside within the same directory as the sources you want to run the utility against or prepend the name with the full path to the sources. Once initiated, Javadoc will produce several HTML files that will document all features of the given class. The utility is smart enough to provide some default documentation for each class, method, and field without any Javadoc comments being manually provided. However, it is highly recommended to include Javadoc comments before each class and method to indicate a description of functionality.

The Javadoc tool can also be run against entire packages or source. To do this, simply pass the entire package name to the Javadoc tool rather than individual source file names. For instance, if an application includes a package named org.juneau.beans, all source files within that package can be documented by running the tool as follows:

```
javadoc org.juneau.beans
```

To generate Javadoc for more than one package at a time, separate the package names with spaces as follows:

```
javadoc org.juneau.beans org.juneau.entity
```

Another option is to specify the path to the source files using the -sourcepath flag as follows:

```
javadoc -sourcepath /java/src
```

One thing to note is that by default, the Javadoc tool will generate the HTML and place it into the same packages as the code itself. This can become a cluttered nightmare if you like to have source files separate from documentation like I do. You can set up a destination for the generated documentation by passing the –d flag to the Javadoc tool. There are also a number of other flags that can be passed to the tool in order to customize your documentation. Some of the most commonly used flags are listed in Table 1-1. For a complete listing of the flags, you can issue the Javadoc -help command.

Table 1-1. Javadoc Tool Flags

Flag	Description
-sourcepath	Sets the path for the source files
-d	Sets the destination for the generated documentation
-overview	Provides a file for overview text
-windowtitle	Adds a window title
-doctitle	Adds a document title
-header	Provides a running header text
-bottom	Provides text for the bottom of the generated documentation pages
-use	Adds the "Use" files

The Javadoc tool contains many options, but it is a great way to document application sources. The best part is that if a change is made to the sources, the Javadoc tool can simply be run again to update the documentation. This recipe only touches upon the many options available for use with Javadoc. If you are interested in learning more, please look at the documentation available on Oracle's web site.

1-9. Marking Features as Deprecated

Problem

You want to mark a method in your Java class as deprecated because a newer version of the method has been created, and the older version will be going away in a future release.

Solution

Use the @Deprecated annotation to signify that the method has been deprecated and may be taken out of future versions of your class. Also make sure that you use the @Deprecated Javadoc tag to mark the method as deprecated within the documentation. In the following class, the addNumbers() methods is deprecated in lieu of a newer, more robust application programming interface (API) that has been put into place. The code marks the method as deprecated, and its Javadoc makes use of the @Deprecated tag to inform users that the new API should now be used:

```java
public class DeprecationExample {

    public static void main(String[] args){
        BigInteger[] arr = new BigInteger[2];
        arr[0] = new BigInteger("1");
        arr[1] = new BigInteger("25");
// Use the older, deprecated method
        System.out.println(addNumbers(1, 25));
        // Use the newer, non-deprecated method
        System.out.println(addNumbers(arr));
    }

    /**
     * Accepts two values and returns their sum.
     *
     * @param x
     * @param y
     * @return
     * @deprecated The newer, more robust addNumbers(BigInteger[]) should
     *             now be used
     */
    @Deprecated
    public static int addNumbers(int x, int y){
        return x + y;
    }

    /**
```

```
 * Newer, better method that accepts an unlimited number of values and
 * returns the sum.
 *
 * @param nums
 * @return
 */
public static BigInteger addNumbers(BigInteger[] nums){
    BigInteger result = new BigInteger("0");
    for (BigInteger num:nums){
        result = result.add(num);
    }

    return result;
}

}
```

How It Works

The word *deprecated* has a few different meanings. It can mean that a specified class, method, or field is no longer important and should not be used. It can also mean that the specified item contains a poor programming practice, is insecure, contains bugs, or is highly inefficient. Any feature that has been designated as *deprecated* may or may not be available in a future release.

There are a couple of different ways to designate a class, method, or field as deprecated. First, the @Deprecated annotation was added to the Java language in release 1.5. This annotation can be placed before the signature of a class, method, or field. When the compiler uses a program element marked with the @Deprecated annotation, a warning will be issued. This warning will indicate to the developer that said program element should no longer be used. In the solution to this recipe, you saw that the @Deprecated annotation was used as follows:

```
@Deprecated
public static int addNumbers(int x, int y){
    return x + y;
}
```

When the addNumbers(int x, int y) method is called, the compiler will issue a warning. Many IDEs (integrated development environments) will place a line through the element if a developer tries to use it. Another way to indicate that a class, method, or field is deprecated would be to mark it with the @deprecatedJavadoc tag. By doing so, the Javadoc will add special HTML to any tagged elements so that they can be easily identified. When marking Javadoc with the @Deprecated tag, a space or newline should follow the tag, and a paragraph should be used to explain why the element has been deprecated and what new functionality has been added to replace it. Again, the example in the solution to this recipe showed how this was done:

```
/**
 * Accepts two values and returns their sum.
 *
```

```
 * @param x
 * @param y
 * @return
 * @Deprecated The newer, more robust addNumbers(BigInteger[]) should
 *             now be used
 */
```

Using the @Deprecated annotation will cause a compiler warning if you are compiling a class that calls a deprecated method, and it also automatically marks Javadoc for the element as deprecated. Therefore, it is the preferred method of marking an element as deprecated. The ability to deprecate adds functionality to code in that it allows for a smooth transition to newly developed code in order to phase out older code. It also warns all developers using deprecated code to begin learning the updated API, rather than simply removing functionality and leaving the developer stranded to learn on their own.

1-10. Creating Methods in a Class

Problem

You want to encapsulate some functionality that is contained within a Java class so that it can be reused in other places.

Solution

Abstract the functionality that you want to encapsulate and place it into a method so that it can be reused. Methods reside within Java classes and they encompass a body of code that is used to perform a task. They can accept zero or more parameters, and they may or may not return a value. In the following Java class, the functionality for adding two numbers and displaying the result has been placed inside a method named addNumbers(). Similarly, the functionality for multiplying the same two numbers has been placed inside of a method named multiplyNumbers(). These two methods are called from the main() method.

```java
public class CalculationExampleOne {

    static int num1 = 0;
    static int num2 = 4;

    public static void main(String[] args){
        if (args.length > 1){
            num1 = Integer.valueOf(args[0]);
            num2 = Integer.valueOf(args[1]);
        }
        // Call the addNumbers method
        addNumbers();
        // Call the multiplyNumbers method
```

```
        multiplyNumbers();

    }

    /**
     * Adds num1 and num2, then prints the sum.
     */
    public static void addNumbers(){
        int sum = num1 + num2;
        System.err.println("The sum of num1 and num2 is " + sum);
    }

    /**
     * Multiplies num1 and num2 then prints the product.
     */
    public static void multiplyNumbers(){
        int product = num1 * num2;
        System.out.println("The product of num1 and num2 is " + product);
    }

}
```

As you can see, both methods encapsulate some mathematical functionality, produce a result, and print a value. If the numbers 5 and 6 are passed to the program, the following result will be displayed:

```
The sum of num1 and num2 is 11
The product of num1 and num2 is 30
```

How It Works

Java methods are another one of the fundamental building blocks of a Java application. Any Java application will contain at least one method. In fact, a Java desktop application cannot execute without the main() method. Methods encapsulate functionality so that it can be reused. Methods can be made public, protected, or private depending on the level of access that is required. If a method has a private modifier, it can be invoked only from within the same class in which it is contained. If a method has a protected modifier, any class within the same package can invoke it. Any methods designated with a public modifier are accessible to all classes in the application. Methods can return a value if needed, but they do not have to do so. Methods can accept zero or more arguments, and the data type of each argument that is passed must be denoted within the *method signature*.

The method signature consists of the access modifier, return value, method name, and argument list. Following are two examples:

```
public static void multiplyNumbers()

private int divideBy(int divisor, int dividend)
```

The first example demonstrates a method that has a public modifier. The method with this signature can be invoked without instantiating its containing class because it is marked as static. This method is called multiplyNumbers and it accepts no arguments. The second example demonstrates a private method signature. The method with a signature like the one in the second example is named divideBy, it returns an int value, and it accepts two arguments with int types.

In the solution to this recipe, two class fields with the int data type are declared. When the class is executed, two numbers will be accepted and stored into the class fields. The main() method then calls each method implemented in the class separately to perform calculations on the numbers that are stored within the class fields. As you can see, to invoke a method simply call it by name and pass any arguments that it requires within the parentheses at the end of the name. If no arguments are required, place an empty set of parentheses at the end of the name, as demonstrated by the Solution to this recipe.

```
addNumbers();
```

Methods can accept arguments, such as the divideBy() method that was discussed previously in this section. To learn more about passing arguments to a method, please see Recipe 1-11. Likewise, methods have the ability to return values. Please see Recipe 1-11 for more information on returning values from methods.

1-11. Passing Arguments to Methods and Returning Values

Problem

You want to create a method that accepts arguments and returns a result.

Solution

Declare any method(s) that will accept arguments by naming the specific number of arguments and the data types of the arguments within the method signature. Once declared, only those specified argument types will be acceptable as input for that method. If the method will return a value, list the returning value data type within the method signature prior to the method name. The following class contains the same functionality as the one listed in the solution for Recipe 1-10. However, instead of the program declaring class fields that will hold the value of the integers, two fields are declared within the main() method and then passed to each method when they are called:

```java
public class CalculationExampleTwo {

    public static void main(String[] args){
        int num1  = 0, num2 = 0;

        if (args.length > 1){
            num1 = Integer.valueOf(args[0]);
            num2 = Integer.valueOf(args[1]);
        }
```

```java
        // Call the addNumbers method
        addNumbers(num1, num2);
        // Call the multiplyNumbers method
        System.out.println("The product of num1 and num2 is " +
                multiplyNumbers(num1, num2));

    }

    /**
     * Adds num1 and num2, then prints the sum.
     */
    public static void addNumbers(int num1, int num2){
        int sum = num1 + num2;
        System.err.println("The sum of num1 and num2 is " + sum);
    }

    /**
     * Multiplies num1 and num2 then prints the product.
     */
    public static int multiplyNumbers(int num1, int num2){
        int product = num1 * num2;
        return product;
    }
}
```

Running this class will yield the same result as the class in Recipe 1-10, but instead of each method using global variables, they will use the int arguments that are passed instead.

How It Works

Methods can be very useful for encapsulating logic that performs tasks. This encapsulation can help to make code more readable and reusable. For instance, if you were to code a calculation operation such as one that is demonstrated in the Solution to this Recipe, it makes sense to place it into a separate method. Otherwise, you would have to rewrite that calculation logic each time you wanted to use it.

This Recipe discusses two of the major strengths that methods provide: the ability to accept arguments and to return a value. The ability to accept arguments allows methods to become reusable. If you had to rely on using global variables for work within methods, they would be useful only for the purpose of working with the same data each time they were called. Using the logic of passing arguments allows methods to be coded in a generic manner, so that they can work on the data that has been passed into them instead.

Consider the multiplyNumbers() method demonstrated in the Solution to this recipe. If it were not able to accept parameters then it would only be able to calculate variables that were globally defined within its containing class, such as demonstrated in Recipe 1-10. However, by affording this method the opportunity to accept arguments, it has become a method that can be reused anytime and in any location in order to perform the task of multiplying two values.

The ability to return a value allows for reusability as well. Often methods will need to return a value to the caller so the value can be used by the application in some way. If methods were not allowed to return values, they would be made much less reusable because they'd have to rely on storing any results in the global declaration of some variable within the containing class. The type of any value being returned must match the return type in the method's signature. The following piece of code demonstrates the ability to assign a value of a variable based upon the result that is returned from a method:

```
int multValue = multiplyNumbers(5,4);
```

Any nontrivial Java application will contain methods that can be reused. They are an important part of the language, and they help to promote object-oriented capability in an application codebase.

1-12. Organizing Code with Packages

Problem

Your application consists of a set of Java classes, interfaces, and other types. You want to organize these source files to make them easier to maintain and avoid potential class-naming conflicts.

Solution

Create Java packages and place source files within them much like a filing system. Java packages can be used to organize logical groups of source files within an application. Packages can help to organize code, reduce naming conflicts among different classes and other Java type files, and provide access control. To create a package, simply create a directory within the root of your application source folder and name it. Packages are usually nested within each other and conform to a standard naming convention. For the purposes of this recipe, assume that my organization is named *Juneau* and that my organization makes widgets. To organize all the code for the widget application, create a group of nested packages conforming to the following directory structure:

```
/org/juneau
```

Any source files that are placed within a package must contain the package statement as the first line in the source. The package statement lists the name of the package in which the source file is contained. For instance, suppose that the main class for the widget application is named JuneauWidgets.java. To place this class into a package named org.juneau, physically move the source file into a directory named juneau, which resides within the org directory, which in turn resides within the root of the source folder for the application. The directory structure should look like the following:

```
/org/juneau/JuneauWidgets.java
```

The source for JuneauWidgets.java is as follows:

```
package org.juneau;

/**
 * The main class for the Juneau Widgets application.
 * @author juneau
 */
public class JuneauWidgets {
    public static void main(String[] args){
        System.out println("Welcome to my app!");
    }
}
```

Note that the first line in the source contains the *package statement*, which lists the name of the package that the source file is located within. The entire package path is listed in the statement, and each package name is separated by a dot.

■ **Note** A package statement must be the first statement listed within the Java source. However, there may be a comment or Javadoc listed before the package statement.

An application can consist of any number of packages. If the widget application contains a few classes that represent widget objects, they could be placed within the org.juneau.widget package. The application may have interfaces that can be used to interact with the widget objects. In this case, a package named org.juneau.interfaces may also exist to contain any such interfaces.

How It Works

Java packages are useful for organizing source files, controlling access to different classes, and ensuring that there are no naming conflicts.

■ **Note** When a class resides within a Java package, it is no longer referenced by only the class name, but instead the package name is prepended to the class name, which is known as the *fully qualified name*. For instance, because the class that resides within the file JuneauWidgets.java is contained within the org.juneau package, the class is referenced using org.juneau.JuneauWidgets, not simply JuneauWidgets. An identically named class can reside within a different package (for instance, org.java7recipes.JuneauWidgets).

Packages are represented by a series of physical directories on a file system, and they can contain any number of Java source files. Each source file must contain a package statement before any other statements in the file. This package statement lists the name of the package in which the source file resides. In the solution to this recipe, the source included the following package statement:

```
package org.juneau;
```

This package statement indicates that the source file resides within a directory named `juneau`, and that directory resides within another directory named `org`. Package-naming conventions can vary by company or organization. However, it is important that Java keywords are in lowercase so they do not conflict with any Java class or other type file names. Many companies will use the reverse of their domain name for package naming. However, if a domain name includes hyphens, underscores should be used instead.

Packages are very useful for establishing levels of security as well as organization. By default, different classes that reside within the same package have access to each other. If a source file resides within a different package than another file that it needs to use, an import statement must be declared at the top of the source file (underneath the package statement) to import that other file for use; otherwise, the fully qualified `package.class` name must be used within the code. Classes may be imported separately, as demonstrated in the following import statement:

```
import org.juneau.JuneauWidgets;
```

However, it is often likely that all classes and type files that reside within a package need to be used. A single import statement utilizing a wildcard character (*) can import all files within a named package as follows:

```
import org.juneau.*;
```

Although it is possible to import all files, it is not recommended unless absolutely necessary. As a matter of fact, it is considered a poor programming practice to include many import statements that use the wildcard. Instead, classes and type files should be imported individually.

Type file organization by package can prove to be very helpful. Suppose that the widget application that was described in the Solution to this Recipe includes different Java classes for each different widget object. Each of the widget classes could be grouped into a single package named `org.juneau.widgets`. Similarly, each of the widgets could extend some Java type or interface. All such interfaces could be organized into a package named `org.juneau.interfaces`.

Any substantial Java application will include packages. Any Java library or API that you use includes packages. When you import classes or types from those libraries, you are listing packages that are contained in the library.

1-13. Accepting Keyboard Input from the Command Line

Problem

You are interested in writing a command line or terminal application that will accept user input from the keyboard.

Solution

Make use of the `java.io.BufferedReader` and `java.io.InputStreamReader` classes to read keyboard entry and store it into local variables. In the following example, the user is prompted to enter a username when they run the program. With the help of the aforementioned classes, when users type their usernames into the keyboard, they are saved into a local variable and then printed out:

```java
package org.java7recipes.chapter1.recipe1_13;

import java.io.BufferedReader;
import java.io.InputStreamReader;
import java.io.IOException;

/**
 * Read keyboard entry and print it back out.
 * @author juneau
 */
public class GreetingMessage {
    public static void main(String[] args){
        BufferedReader readIn = new BufferedReader(new InputStreamReader(System.in));
        String username = "";
        System.out.println("Please enter your username: ");
        try{
            username = readIn.readLine();
            System.out.println("Your username is " + username);
        } catch (IOException ex){
            System.out.println(ex);
        }

    }

}
```

After the user is finished typing the username into the command line or terminal, it is read into the program and saved into a `BufferedReader` type variable. Later, that variable is parsed and printed. The output should reflect the entry that was made.

How It Works

Quite often, our applications need to accept user input of some kind. Granted, most applications are not used from the command line or terminal nowadays, but having the ability to create an application that reads input from the command line or terminal helps to lay a good foundation. It can also be useful for developing administrative applications that you or a system administrator may use. The two helper classes that were used in the solution to this recipe are `java.io.BufferedReader`, and `java.io.InputStreamReader`. As you can see from the example, `System.in` is passed into a new instance of the `InputStreamReader`, which is then passed into a new instance of the `BufferedReader`. This *stacking* of statements is very common in Java development.

CHAPTER 2

Strings

Strings are one of the most commonly used data types in any programming language. They can be used for obtaining text from a keyboard, printing messages to a command line, and much more. Given the fact that Strings are used so often, there have been many features added to the String object over time in order to make them easier to work with. After all, a String is an object in Java, so it contains methods that can be used to manipulate the contents of the String. Strings are also immutable in Java, which means that their state cannot be changed or altered. This makes them a bit different to work with than some of the mutable, or changeable, data types. It is important to understand how to properly make use of immutable objects, especially when attempting to change or assign different values to them.

This chapter will focus on some of the most commonly used String methods and techniques for working with String objects. We will also cover some useful techniques that are not inherent of String objects.

2-1. Obtaining a Subsection of a String

Problem

You would like to retrieve a portion of a String.

Solution

Use the substring() method to obtain a portion of the String between two different positions. In the solution that follows, a String is created and then various portions of the String are printed out using the substring() method.

```
public static void substringExample(){
    String originalString = "This is the original String";
        System.out.println(originalString.substring(0, originalString.length()));
        System.out.println(originalString.substring(5, 20));
        System.out.println(originalString.substring(12));
    }
```

Running this method would yield the following results:

```
This is the original String
is the original
original String
```

How It Works

The String object contains many helper methods. One such method is `substring()`, which can be used to obtain portions of the String. There are two variations of the `substring()` method. One of them accepts a single argument, that being the starting index; and the other accepts two arguments: startingindex and endingindex. Having two variations of the `substring()` method makes it seem as though the second argument is optional; if it is not specified, the length of the calling String is used in its place. It should be noted that indices begin with zero, so the first position in a String has the index of 0, and so on.

As you can see from the solution to this recipe, the first use of `substring()` prints out the entire contents of the String. This is because the first argument passed to the `substring()` method is 0, and the second argument passed is the length of the original String. In the second example of `substring()`, an index of 5 is used as the first argument, and an index of 20 is used as the second argument. This effectively causes only a portion of the String to be printed, beginning with the character in the String that is located in the sixth position, or index 5 because the first position has an index of 0; and ending with the character in the String that is located in the twentieth position, the index of 19. The third example specifies only one argument; therefore, the result will be the original String beginning with the position specified by that argument.

■ **Note** The `substring()` method only accepts positive integer values. If you attempt to pass a negative value, an exception will be thrown.

2-2. Comparing Strings

Problem

An application that you are writing needs to have the ability to compare two or more String values.

Solution

Use the built-in `equals()`, `equalsIgnoreCase()`, `compareTo()`, and `compareToIgnoreCase()` methods to compare the values contained within the Strings. The following is a series of tests using different String comparison operations.

As you can see, various if statements are used to print out messages if the comparisons are equal:

```java
String one = "one";
String two = "two";

String var1 = "one";
String var2 = "Two";

String pieceone = "o";
String piecetwo = "ne";

// Comparison is equal
if (one.equals(var1)){
    System.out.println ("String one equals var1 using equals");
}

// Comparison is NOT equal
if (one.equals(two)){
    System.out.println ("String one equals two using equals");
}

// Comparison is NOT equal
if (two.equals(var2)){
    System.out.println ("String two equals var2 using equals");
}

// Comparison is equal, but is not directly comparing string values using ==
if (one == var1){
    System.out.println ("String one equals var1 using ==");
}

// Comparison is equal
if (two.equalsIgnoreCase(var2)){
    System.out.println ("String two equals var2 using equalsIgnoreCase");
}

System.out.println("Trying to use == on Strings that are pieced together");

String piecedTogether = pieceone + piecetwo;

// Comparison is equal
if (one.equals(piecedTogether)){
    System.out.println("The strings contain the same value using equals");
}
```

```
// Comparison is NOT equal using ==
if (one == piecedTogether) {
    System.out.println("The string contain the same value using == ");
}

// Comparison is equal
if (one.compareTo(var1) == 0){
    System.out.println("One is equal to var1 using compareTo()");
}
```

Results in the following output:

```
String one equals var1 using equals
String one equals var1 using ==
String two equals var2 using equalsIgnoreCase
Trying to use == on Strings that are pieced together
The strings contain the same value using equals
One is equal to var1 using compareTo()
```

How It Works

One of the trickier parts of using a programming language can come when attempting to compare two or more values. In the Java language, comparing Strings can be fairly straightforward, keeping in mind that one should *not* use the == for String comparison. This is because the comparison operator (==) is used to compare references, not values of Strings. One of the most tempting things to do when programming with Strings in Java is to use the comparison operator, but you must not because the results can vary.

■ **Note** Java uses interning of Strings to speed up performance. This means that the JVM contains a table of interned Strings, and each time the intern() method is called on a String, a lookup is performed on that table to find a match. If no matching String resides within the table, the String is added to the table and a reference is returned. If the String already resides within the table, the reference is returned. Java will automatically intern String literals, and this can cause variation when using the == comparison operator.

In the solution to this recipe, you can see various different techniques for comparing String values. The equals() method is a part of every Java object. The Java String equals() method has been overridden so that it will compare the values contained within the String rather than the object itself. As you can see from the following examples that have been extracted from the solution to this recipe, the equals() method is a safe way to compare Strings.

```
// Comparison is equal
if (one.equals(var1)){
    System.out.println ("String one equals var1 using equals");
```

```
}
// Comparison is NOT equal
if (one.equals(two)){
    System.out.println ("String one equals two using equals");
}
```

The equals() method will first check to see whether the Strings reference the same object using the == operator; it will return true if they do. If they do not reference the same object, equals() will compare each String character by character to determine whether the Strings being compared to each other contain exactly the same values. What if one of the Strings has a different case setting than another? Do they still compare equal to each other using equals()? The answer is no, and that is why the equalsIgnoreCase() method was created. Comparing two values using equalsIgnoreCase() will cause each of the characters to be compared without paying attention to the case. The following examples have been extracted from the solution to this recipe:

```
// Comparison is NOT equal
if (two.equals(var2)){
    System.out.println ("String two equals var2 using equals");
}
// Comparison is equal
if (two.equalsIgnoreCase(var2)){
    System.out.println ("String two equals var2 using equalsIgnoreCase");
}
```

The compareTo()and compareToIgnoreCase() methods perform a lexicographical comparison of the Strings. This comparison is based upon the Unicode value of each character contained within the Strings. The result will be a negative integer if the String lexicographically precedes the argument String. The result will be a positive integer if the String lexicographically follows the argument String. The result will be zero if both Strings are lexicographically equal to each other. The following excerpt from the solution to this recipe demonstrates the compareTo() method:

```
// Comparison is equal
if (one.compareTo(var1) == 0){
    System.out.println("One is equal to var1 using compareTo()");
}
```

Inevitably, many applications contain code that must compare Strings at some level. The next time you have an application that requires String comparison, consider the information discussed in this recipe before you write the code.

2-3. Trimming Whitespace

Problem

One of the Strings you are working with contains some whitespace on either end. You would like to get rid of that whitespace.

Solution

Use the String trim() method to eliminate the whitespace. In the following example, a sentence is printed including whitespace on either side. The same sentence is then printed again using the trim() method to remove the whitespace so that the changes can be seen.

```
String myString = " This is a String that contains whitespace.    ";
System.out.println(myString);
System.out.println(myString.trim());
```

The output will print as follows:

```
This is a String that contains whitespace.
This is a String that contains whitespace.
```

How It Works

Regardless of how careful we are, whitespace is always an issue when working with Strings of text. This is especially the case when comparing Strings against matching values. If a String contains an unexpected whitespace character then that could be disastrous for a pattern-searching program. Luckily, the Java String object contains the trim() method that can be used to automatically remove whitespace from each end of any given String.

The trim() method is very easy to use. In fact, as you can see from the solution to this recipe, all that is required to use the trim() method is a call against any given String. Because Strings are objects, they contain many helper methods, which can make them very easy to work with. After all, Strings are one of the most commonly used data types in any programming language% so they'd better be easy to use! The trim() method returns a copy of the original String with all leading and trailing whitespace removed. If, however, there is no whitespace to be removed, the trim() method returns the original String instance. It does not get much easier then that!

2-4. Changing the Case of a String

Problem

A portion of your application contains case-sensitive String values. You would like to change all the Strings to uppercase before they are processed in order to avoid any case sensitivity issues down the road.

Solution

Make use of the toUpperCase() and toLowerCase() methods. The String object provides these two helper methods to assist in performing a case change for all of the characters in a given String.

For example, given the String in the following code, each of the two methods will be called:

```
String str = "This String will change case.";
System.out.println(str.toUpperCase());
System.out.println(str.toLowerCase());
```

The following output will be produced:

```
THIS STRING WILL CHANGE CASE.
this string will change case.
```

How It Works

To ensure that the case of every character within a given String is either upper- or lowercase, use the toUpperCase() and toLowerCase() methods, respectively. There are a couple of items to note when using these methods. First, if a given String contains an uppercase letter, and the toUpperCase() method is called against it, the uppercase letter is ignored. The same concept holds true for calling the toLowerCase() method. Any punctuation or numbers contained within the given String are also ignored.

There are two variations for each of these methods. One of the variations does not accept any arguments, while the other accepts an argument pertaining to the locale you want to use. Calling these methods without any arguments will result in a case conversion using the default locale. If you want to use a different locale, you can pass the desired locale as an argument, using the variation of the method that accepts an argument. For instance, if you want to use an Italian locale, you would use the following code:

```
str.toUpperCase(Locale.ITALIAN);
```

Converting Strings to upper- or lowercase using these methods can make life easy. They are also very useful for comparing Strings that are taken as input from an application. Consider the case in which a user is prompted to enter a username, and the result is saved into a String. Now consider that later in the program that String is compared against all the usernames stored within a database to ensure that the username is valid. What happens if the person who entered the username types it with an uppercase first character? What happens if the username is stored within the database in all uppercase? The comparison will never be equal. In such a case, a developer can use the toUpperCase() method to alleviate the problem. Calling this method against both the Strings that are being compared will result in a comparison in which the case is the same in both Strings.

2-5. Concatenating Strings

Problem

There are various Strings that you want to combine into one.

Solution #1

If you want to concatenate Strings onto the end of each other, use the concat() method. The following example demonstrates the use of the concat() method:

```
String one = "Hello";
String two = "Java7";
String result = one.concat(two);
```

The result is this:

```
HelloJava7
```

Solution #2

Use the concatenation operator to combine the Strings in a shorthand manner. In the following example, a space character has been placed in between the two Strings:

```
String one = "Hello";
String two = "Java7";
String result = one + " " + two;
```

The result is this:

```
HelloJava7
```

Solution #3

Use StringBuilder or StringBuffer to combine the Strings. The following example demonstrates the use of StringBuffer to concatenate two Strings:

```
String one = "Hello";
String two = "Java7";
StringBuffer buffer = new StringBuffer();
buffer.append(one).append(" ").append(two);
String result = buffer.toString();
System.out.println(result);
```

The result is this:

```
HelloJava7
```

How It Works

The Java language provides a couple of different options for concatenating Strings of text. Although neither is better, you may find one or the other to work better in different situations. The `concat()` method is a built-in String helper method. It has the ability to append one String onto the end of another, as demonstrated by solution #1 to this recipe. The `concat()` method will accept any String value; therefore, you can explicitly type a String value to pass as an argument if you want. As demonstrated in solution #1, simply passing one String as an argument to this method will append it to the end of the String, which the method is called upon. However, if you wanted to add a space character in between the two Strings, you could do so by passing a space character as well as the String you want to append as follows:

```
String result = one.concat(" " + two);
```

As you can see, having the ability to pass any String or combination of Strings to the `concat()` method makes it very useful. Because all of the String helper methods actually return copies of the original String with the helper method functionality applied, you can pass Strings calling other helper methods to `concat()` (or any other String helper method) as well. Consider that you want to display the text "Hello Java" rather than "Hello Java7". The following combination of String helper methods would allow you to do just that:

```
String one = "Hello";
String two = "Java7";
String result = one.concat(" ".concat(two.substring(0, two.length()-1)));
```

The concatenation operator (+) can be used to combine any two Strings. It is almost thought of as a shorthand form of the `concat()` method. The last technique that is demonstrated in solution #3 to this example is the use of `StringBuffer`, which is a mutable sequence of characters, much like a String, except that it can be modified. The `StringBuffer` class contains a number of helper methods for building and manipulating character sequences. In the solution, the `append()` method is used to append two String values. The `append()` method places the String that is passed as an argument at the end of the `StringBuffer`. For more information regarding the use of `StringBuffer`, please refer to the online documentation: `http://download.oracle.com/javase/7/docs/api/java/lang/StringBuffer.html`.

2-6. Converting Strings to Numeric Values

Problem

You would like to have the ability to convert any numeric values that are stored as Strings into Integers.

Solution #1

Use the `Integer.valueOf()` helper method to convert Strings to `int` data types. For example:

```
String one = "1";
String two = "2";
int result = Integer.valueOf(one) + Integer.valueOf(two);
```

As you can see, both of the String variables are converted into Integer values. After that, they are used to perform an addition calculation and then stored into an `int`.

■ **Note** A technique known as autoboxing is used in this example. *Autoboxing* is a feature of the Java language that automates the process of converting primitive values to their appropriate wrapper classes. For instance, this occurs when you assign an `int` value to an Integer. Similarly, *unboxing* automatically occurs when you try to convert in the opposite direction, from a wrapper class to a primitive. For more information on autoboxing, please refer to the online documentation at

`http://download.oracle.com/javase/1.5.0/docs/guide/language/autoboxing.html`

Solution #2

Use the `Integer.parseInt()` helper method to convert Strings to `int` data types. For example:

```
String one = "1";
String two = "2";
int result = Integer.parseInt(one) + Integer.parseInt(two);
System.out.println(result);
```

How It Works

The Integer class contains the `valueOf()` and parseInt() methods, which are used to convert Strings or `int` types into Integers. There are two different forms of the Integer class's `valueOf()` type that can be used to convert Strings into Integer values. Each of them differs by the number of arguments that they accept. The first `valueOf()` method accepts only a String argument. This String is then converted into an Integer value if possible. If the String does not convert into an Integer correctly, then the method will throw a `NumberFormatExeption`.

The second version of Integer's `valueOf()` method accepts two arguments: a String argument that will be converted into an Integer and an `int` that represents the radix that is to be used for the conversion.

■ **Note** Many of the Java type classes contain `valueOf()` methods that can be used for converting different types into that class's type. Such is the case with the String class because it contains many different `valueOf()` methods that can be used for conversion. For more information on the different `valueOf()` methods that the String class or any other type class contains, please see the online Java documentation (http://download.oracle.com/javase/7/docs/).

There are also two different forms of the Integer class's `parseInt()` method. One of them accepts one argument: the String you want to convert into an Integer. The other form accepts two arguments: the String that you want to convert to an Integer and the radix. The first format is the most widely used, and it parses the String argument as a signed decimal integer. A `NumberFormatException` will be thrown if a parsable Integer is not contained within the String. The second format, which is less widely used, returns an Integer object holding the value that is represented by the String argument in the given radix.

2-7. Iterating Over the Characters of a String

Problem

You want to iterate over the characters within a String of text so that you can manipulate it at the character level.

Solution

Use a combination of String helper methods to gain access to the String at a character level. If you use a String helper method within the context of a loop, you can easily traverse a String by character. In the following example, the String `str` is broken down using the `toCharArray()` method.

```
String str = "Break down into chars";
System.out.println(str);
for (char chr:str.toCharArray()){
    System.out.println(chr);
}
```

The same strategy could be used with the older version of the `for` loop. An index could be created that would allow access to each character of the String using the `charAt()` method.

```
for (int x = 0; x <= str.length()-1; x++){
System.out.println(str.charAt(x));
}
```

Both of these solutions will yield the following result:

B
r
e
a
k

d
o
w
n

i
n
t
o

c
h
a
r
s

■ **Note** The first example using toCharArray() generates a new character array. Therefore, the second example, using the traditional for loop, might perform faster.

How It Works

String objects contain methods that can be used for performing various tasks. The solution to this recipe demonstrates a number of different String methods. The toCharArray() method can be called against a String in order to break the String into characters and then store those characters in an array. This method is very powerful and it can save a bit of time when performing this task is required. The result of calling the toCharArray() method is a char[], which can then be traversed using an index. Such is the case in the solution to this recipe. An enhanced for loop is used to iterate through the contents of the char[] and print out each of its elements.

The String length() method is used to find the number of characters contained within a String. The result is an int value that can be very useful in the context of a for loop, as demonstrated within the solution to this recipe. In the second example, the length() method is used to find the number of characters in the String so that they can be iterated over using the charAt() method. The charAt() method accepts an int index value as an argument and returns the character that resides at the given index in the String.

Often the combination of two or more String methods can be used to obtain different results. In this case, using the length() and charAt() methods within the same code block provided the ability to break down a String into characters.

2-8. Finding Text Matches

Problem

You would like to search a body of text for a particular sequence of characters.

Solution #1

Make use of regular expressions and the String matches() helper method to determine how many matches exist. To do this, simply pass a String representing a regular expression to the matches() method against any String you are trying to match. In doing so, the String will be compared with the String that matches() is being called upon. Once evaluated, matches() will yield a Boolean result, indicating whether it is a match or not. The following code excerpt contains a series of examples using this technique. The comments contained within the code explain each of the matching tests.

```
String str = "Here is a long String...let's find a match!";
// This will result in a TRUE since it is an exact match
boolean result = str.matches("Here is a long String...let's find a match!");
System.out.println(result);
// This will result iin FALSE since the entire String does not match
result = str.matches("Here is a long String...");

System.out.println(result);
str = "True";

// This will test against both upper & lower case "T"...this will be TRUE
result = str.matches("[Tt]rue");
System.out.println(result);

// This will test for one or the other
result = str.matches("[Tt]rue|[Ff]alse]");
System.out.println(result);

// This will test to see if any numbers are present, in this case the
// person writing this String would be able to like any Java release!
str = "I love Java 7!";
result = str.matches("I love Java [0-9]!");
System.out.println(result);
```

```
// This will test TRUE as well...
str = "I love Java 6!";
result = str.matches("I love Java [0-9]!");
System.out.println(result);

// The following will test TRUE for any language that contains
// only one word for a name. This is because it tests for
// any alphanumeric combination. Notice the space character
// between the numeric sequence...
result = str.matches("I love .*[ 0-9]!");
System.out.println(result);

// The following String also matches.
str = "I love Jython 2.5.2!";
result = str.matches("I love .*[ 0-9]!");

System.out.println(result);
```

Each of the results printed out in the example will be TRUE, with the exception of the second example because it does not match.

Solution #2

Use the regular expression Pattern and Matcher classes for a better performing and more versatile matching solution than the String matches() method. Although the matches() method will get the job done most of the time, there are some occasions in which you will require a more flexible way of matching. Using this solution is a three-step process:

1. Compile a pattern into a Pattern object.

1. Construct a Matcher object using the matcher() method on the Pattern.

2. Call the matches() method on the Matcher.

In the following example code, the Pattern and Matcher technique is demonstrated:

```
String str = "I love Java 7!";
boolean result = false;

Pattern pattern = Pattern.compile("I love .*[ 0-9]!");
Matcher matcher = pattern.matcher(str);
result = matcher.matches();

System.out.println(result);
```

The previous example will yield a TRUE value just like its variant that was demonstrated in solution #1.

How It Works

Regular expressions are a great way to find matches because they allow patterns to be defined so that an application does not have to explicitly find an exact String match. They can be very useful when you want to find matches against some text that a user may be typing into your program. However, they could be overkill if you are trying to match Strings against a String constant you have defined in your program because the String class provide many methods that could be used for such tasks. Nevertheless, there will certainly come a time in almost every developer's life when regular expressions can come in handy. They can be found in just about every programming language used today. Java makes them easy to use and easy to understand.

■ **Note** Although regular expressions are used in many different languages today, the expression syntax for each language varies. For complete information regarding regular expression syntax, please see the documentation online at http://download.oracle.com/javase/7/docs/api/java/util/regex/Pattern.html

---

The easiest way to make use of regular expressions is to call the matches() method on the String object. Passing a regular expression to the matches() method will yield a Boolean result that indicates whether the String matches the given regular expression pattern or not. At this point, it is useful to know what a regular expression is and how it works.

A *regular expression* is a String pattern that is used to match against other Strings in order to determine its contents. Regular expressions can contain a number of different patterns that enable them to be dynamic in that they can have the ability to match many different Strings that contain the same format. For instance, in the solution to this recipe, the following code can match several different strings:

```
result = str.matches("I love Java [0-9]!");
```

The regular expression String in this example is "I love Java [0-9]!", and it contains the pattern [0-9], which represents any number between 0 and 9.Therefore, any String that reads "I love Java" followed by the number 0 through 9 and then an exclamation point will match the regular expression String. To see a listing of all the different patterns that can be used in a regular expression, please see the online documentation available at
http://download.oracle.com/javase/7/docs/api/java/util/regex/Pattern.html
A combination of Pattern and Matcher objects can also be used to achieve similar results as the String matcher() method. The Pattern object can be used to compile a String into a regular expression pattern. A compiled pattern can provide performance gains to an application if the pattern is used multiple times. You can pass the same String–based regular expressions to the Pattern.compile() method as you would pass to the String matches() method. The result is a compiled Pattern object that can be matched against a String for comparison. A Matcher object can be obtained by calling the Pattern object's matcher() method against a given String. Once a Matcher object is obtained, it can be used to match a given String against a Pattern using any of the following three methods, which each return a

Boolean value indicating a match. The following three lines of solution #2 could be used as an alternate solution to using the Pattern.matches() method, minus the reusability of the compile pattern:

```
Pattern pattern = Pattern.compile("I love .*[ 0-9]!");
Matcher matcher = pattern.matcher(str);
result = matcher.matches();
```

- The Matcher matches() method attempts to match the entire input String with the pattern.

- The Matcher lookingAt() method attempts to match the input String to the pattern starting at the beginning.

- The Matcher find() method scans the input sequence looking for the next matching sequence in the String.

In the solution to this recipe, the matches() method is called against the Matcher object in order to attempt and match the entire String. In any event, regular expressions can be very useful for matching Strings against patterns. The technique used for working with the regular expressions can vary in different situations, using whichever method works best for the situation.

2-9. Replacing All Text Matches

Problem

You have searched a body of text for a particular sequence of characters, and you are interested in replacing all matches with another String value.

Solution

Use a regular expression pattern to obtain a Matcher object; then use the Matcher object's replaceAll() method to replace all matches with another String value. The example that follows demonstrates this technique:

```
String str = "I love Java 7! It is my favorite language. Java 7 is the "
        + "7th version of this great programming language.";
boolean result = false;
Pattern pattern = Pattern.compile("[0-7]");
Matcher matcher = pattern.matcher(str);
System.out.println("Original: " + str);
System.out.println("Replacement: " + matcher.replaceAll("6"));
```

This example will yield the following results:

```
Original: I love Java 7! It is my favorite language. Java 7 is the 7th version of this great
programming language.
Replacement: I love Java 6! It is my favorite language. Java 6 is the 6th version of this
great programming language.
```

How It Works

The replaceAll() method of the Matcher object makes it easy to find and replace a String or portion of String that is contained within a body of text. In order to use the replaceAll() method of the Matcher object, you must first compile a Pattern object by passing a regular expression String pattern to the Pattern.compile() method. Use the resulting Pattern object to obtain a Matcher object by calling its matcher() method. The following lines of code show how this is done:

```
Pattern pattern = Pattern.compile("[0-7]");
Matcher matcher = pattern.matcher(str);
```

Once you have obtained a Matcher object, call its replaceAll() method by passing a String that you want to use to replace all the text that is matched by the compiled pattern. In the solution to this recipe, the String "6" is passed to the replaceAll() method, so it will replace all the areas in the String that match the "[0-7]" pattern.

2-10. Determining Whether a File Name Ends with a Given String

Problem

You are reading a file from the server and you need to determine what type of file it is in order to read it properly.

Solution

Determine the suffix of the file by using the endsWith() method on a given file name. In the following example, assume that the variable filename contains the name of a given file, and the code is using the endsWith() method to determine whether filename ends with a particular string.:

```
if(filename.endsWith(".txt")){
    System.out.println("Text file");
} else if (filename.endsWith(".doc")){
    System.out.println("Document file");
```

```
} else if (filename.endsWith(".xls")){
    System.out.println("Excel file");
} else if (filename.endsWith(".java")){
System.out.println("Java source file");
} else {
    System.out.println("Other type of file");
}
```

Given that a file name and its suffix are included in the `filename` variable, this block of code will read it and determine what type of file the given variable represents by reading its suffix.

How It Works

As mentioned previously, the String object contains many helper methods that can be used to perform tasks. The String object's `endsWith()` method accepts a character sequence and then returns a `Boolean` value representing whether the original String ends with the given sequence. In the case of the solution to this recipe, the `endsWith()` method is used in an `if` block. A series of file suffixes are passed to the `endsWith()` method to determine what type of file is represented by the `filename` variable. If any of the file name suffixes matches, a line is printed, stating what type of file it is.

CHAPTER 3

Numbers and Dates

Numbers play a significant role in many applications. As such, it is helpful to know how to use them correctly within the context of the work that you are trying to perform. This chapter will help you to understand how to perform some of the most basic operations with numbers, and it will also provide insight on performing advanced tasks such as working with currency. Dates can also become important as they can be used for many different reasons within an application. In this chapter, you will learn how to work with dates and how to perform calculations with them.

This chapter will also cover some new additions to the Java language with the Java 7 release. There have been some minor but important updates to binary literals and numeric literals that will be demonstrated in this chapter. In the end, you will learn how to perform essential tasks with both numbers and dates in order to make your application development easier.

3-1. Rounding Float and Double Values to Integers

Problem

You need to have the ability to round floating-point numbers or doubles within your application to an Integer value.

Solution

Use one of the `java.lang.Math round()` methods to round the number into the format you require. The Math class has two different methods that can be used for rounding floating-point numbers or Double values. The following code demonstrates how to use each of these methods:

```
public static int roundFloatToInt(float myFloat){
    return Math.round(myFloat);
}

public static long roundDoubleToLong(double myDouble){
    return Math.round(myDouble);
}
```

The first method, roundFloatToInt(), accepts a floating-point number and uses the java.lang.Math class to round that number to an Integer. The second method, roundDoubleToLong(), accepts a Double value and uses the java.lang.Math class to round that Double to a Long.

How It Works

The java.lang.Math class contains plenty of helper methods to make our lives easier when working with numbers. The round() methods are no exception as they can be used to easily round floating-point or double values. One version of the java.lang.Math round() method accepts a float as an argument. It will round the float to the closest int value, with ties rounding up. If the argument is NaN, then a zero will be returned. When arguments that are positive or negative infinity are passed into round(), a result equal to the value of Integer.MAX_VALUE or Integer.MIN_VALUE will be returned respectively. The second version of the java.lang.Math round() method accepts a double value. The double value is rounded to the closest long value, with ties rounding up. Just like the other round(), if the argument is Not a Number (NaN), a zero will be returned. Similarly, when arguments that are positive or negative infinity are passed into round(), a result equal to the value of Long.MAX_VALUE or Long.MIN_VALUE will be returned, respectively.

■ **Note** The NaN, POSITIVE_INFINITY, and NEGATIVE_INFINITY values are constant values defined within the Float and Double classes. NaN (Not a Number) is an undefined or unrepresentable value. For example, a NaN value can be produced by dividing 0.0f by 0.0f. The values represented by POSITIVE_INFINITY and NEGATIVE_INFINITY refer to values that are produced by operations that generate such extremely large or negative values of a particular type (floating-point or double) that they cannot be represented normally. For instance, 1.0/0.0 or -1.0/0.0 would produce such a value.

3-2. Formatting Double and Long Decimal Values

Problem

You need to have the ability to format double and long numbers within your application.

Solution

Use the DecimalFormat class to format and round the value to the precision your application requires. In the following method, a double value is accepted and a formatted String value is printed:

```
public static void formatDouble(double myDouble){
```

```
    NumberFormat numberFormatter = new DecimalFormat("##.000");
    String result = numberFormatter.format(myDouble);
    System.out.println(result);
}
```

For instance, if the `double` value passed into the `formatDouble()` method is 345.9372, the following will be the result:

```
345.937
```

Similarly, if the value .7697 is passed to the method, the following will be the result:

```
.770
```

Each of the results is formatted using the specified pattern and rounded accordingly.

How It Works

The `DecimalFormat` class can be used along with the `NumberFormat` class to round and/or format `double` or `long` values. `NumberFormat` is an abstract class that provides the interface for formatting and parsing numbers. This class provides the ability to format and parse numbers for each locale, and obtain formats for currency, percentage, integers, and numbers. By itself, the `NumberFormat` class can be very useful as it contains factory methods that can be used to obtain formatted numbers. In fact, little work needs to be done in order to obtain a formatted String. For example, the following code demonstrates the calling of some factory methods on `NumberFormat` class:

```
// Obtains an instance of NumberFormat class
NumberFormat format = NumberFormat.getInstance();

// Format a double value for the current locale
String result = format.format(83.404);
System.out.println(result);

// Format a double value for an Italian locale
result = format.getInstance(Locale.ITALIAN).format(83.404);
System.out.println(result);

// Parse a String into a Number
try {
    Number num = format.parse("75.736");
    System.out.println(num);
} catch (java.text.ParseException ex){
    System.out.println(ex);
}
```

To format using a pattern, the `DecimalFormat` class can be used along with `NumberFormat`. In the solution to this recipe, you saw that creating a new `DecimalFormat` instance by passing a pattern to its constructor would return a NumberFormat type. This is because DecimalFormat extends the NumberFormat class. Because the NumberFormat class is abstract, DecimalFormat contains all the functionality that NumberFormat contains, plus added functionality for working with patterns. Therefore, it can be used to work with different formats from the locales just as you have seen in the previous demonstration. This provides the ultimate flexibility when working with double or long formatting.

As mentioned previously, the DecimalFormat class can take a String-based pattern in its constructor. You can also use the applyPattern() method to apply a pattern after the fact. Each pattern contains a prefix, numeric part, and suffix, which allows you to format a particular decimal value to the required precision, and include leading digits and commas as needed. The symbols that can be used to build patterns are displayed in Table 3-1. Each of the patterns also contains a positive and negative subpattern. These two subpatterns are separated by a semicolon (;), and the negative subpattern is optional. If there is no negative subpattern present, the localized minus sign is used. For instance, a complete pattern example would be "###,##0.00;(###,##0.00)".

Table 3-1. DecimalFormat Pattern Characters

Character	Description
#	Digit, blank if no digit is present
0	Digit, zero if no digit is present
.	Decimal
-	Minus or negative sign
,	Comma or grouping separator
E	Scientific notation separator
;	Positive and negative subpattern separator

The DecimalFormat class provides enough flexibility to format double and long values for just about every situation.

3-3. Comparing int Values

Problem

You need to compare two or more int values.

Solution #1

Use the comparison operators to compare Integer values against one another. In the following example, three int values are compared against each other, demonstrating various comparison operators:

```
int int1 = 1;
int int2 = 10;
int int3 = -5;

System.out.println(int1 == int2);  // Result:  false
System.out.println(int3 == int1);  // Result:  false
System.out.println(int1 == int1);  // Result:  true
System.out.println(int1 > int3);   // Result:  true
System.out.println(int2 < int3);   // Result:  false
```

As you can see, comparison operators will generate a Boolean result.

Solution #2

Use the Integer.compare(int,int) method to compare two int values numerically. The following lines could compare the same int values that were declared in the first solution:

```
System.out.println("Compare method -> int3 and int1: " + Integer.compare(int3, int1));
// Result -1
System.out.println("Compare method -> int2 and int1: " + Integer.compare(int2, int1));
// Result 1
```

How It Works

Perhaps the most commonly used numeric comparisons are against two or more int values. The Java language makes it very easy to compare an int using the comparison operators (see Table 3-2).

Table 3-2. Comparison Operators

Operator	Function
==	Equal to
!=	Not equal to
>	Greater than
<	Less than
>=	Greater than or equal to
<=	Less than or equal to

The second solution to this recipe demonstrates the Integer compare() method that was added to the language in Java 7. This static method accepts two int values and compares them, returning a 1 if the first int is greater than the second, a 0 if the two int values are equal, and a -1 if the first int value is less than the second. To use the Integer.compare() method, pass two int values as demonstrated in the following code:

```
Integer.compare(int3, int1));
Integer.compare(int2, int1));
```

Just like in your math lessons at school, these comparison operators will determine whether the first Integer is equal to, greater than, or less than the second Integer. Straightforward and easy to use, these comparison operators are most often seen within the context of an if statement.

3-4. Comparing Floating-Point Numbers

Problem

You need to compare two or more floating-point values in an application.

Solution #1

Use the Float object's compareTo() method to perform a comparison of one Float against another. The following example shows the compareTo() method in action:

```
Float float1 = new Float("9.675");
Float float2 = new Float("7.3826");
Float float3 = new Float("23467.373");

System.out.println(float1.compareTo(float3));  // Result: -1
System.out.println(float2.compareTo(float3));  // Result: -1
System.out.println(float1.compareTo(float1));  // Result: 0
System.out.println(float3.compareTo(float2));  // Result: 1
```

The result of calling the compareTo() method is an Integer value. A negative result indicates that the first float is less than the float that it is being compared against. A zero indicates that the two float values are equal. Lastly, a positive result indicates that the first float is greater than the float that it is being compared against.

Solution #2

Use the Float class compare() method to perform the comparison. The following example demonstrates the use of the Float.compare(float, float) method.

```
System.out.println(Float.compare(float1, float3));
```

```
System.out.println(Float.compare(float2, float3));
System.out.println(Float.compare(float1, float1));
System.out.println(Float.compare(float3, float2));
```

How It Works

The most useful way to compare two Float objects is to make use of the compareTo() method. This method will perform a numeric comparison against the given float objects. The result will be an integer value indicating whether the first Float is numerically greater than, equal to, or less than the Float that it is compared against. If a float value is NaN, it is considered to be equal to other NaN values or greater than all other float values. Also, a float value of 0.0f is greater than a float value of -0.0f.

An alternative to using compareTo() is the compare() method, which is also native to the Float class. The compare() method was introduced in Java 1.4, and it is a static method that compares two float values in the same manner as compareTo(). It only makes the code read a bit differently. The format for the compare() method is as follows:

```
Float.compare(primitiveFloat1, primitiveFloat2)
```

The compare() method shown will actually make the following call using compareTo():

```
new Float(float1).compareTo(new Float(float2))
```

In the end, the same results will be returned using either compareTo() or compare().

3-5. Performing Calculations with Complex Numbers

Problem

You have a requirement to perform calculations with complex numbers in your Java application.

Solution

Download the Apache Commons Math library and make use of the Complex class. The Commons Math library makes it easy to work with complex numbers. In the following example code, a Java class including import statements for the Apache Commons Math library demonstrates how to create complex numbers and perform arithmetic operations:

```
import org.apache.commons.math.complex.Complex;

public class ComplexNumberExamples {

    public static void main(String[] args){
        complexArithmetic();
    }
```

```java
public static void complexArithmetic(){

    // Create complex numbers by passing two floats to the Complex class
    Complex complex1 = new Complex(8.0, 3.0);
    Complex complex2 = new Complex(4.2, 5.0);
    Complex complex3 = new Complex(8.7, 13.53);
    Complex result;

    // Find the absolute value of a complex number
    double absresult = complex1.abs();

    // Compute the exponential function
    Complex exp = complex1.exp();

    // Add two complex numbers together
    result = complex1.add(complex2);

    // Subtract two complex numbers
    result = complex2.subtract(complex3);

    // Divide two complex numbers
    result = complex2.divide(complex3);

    // Multiply two complex Numbers
    result = complex1.multiply(complex2);

    // Multiply a complex number and a double
    result = complex1.multiply(absresult);

    // Return the additive inverse of a given complex number
    result = complex1.negate();

    // Return the list of the 5th roots for this complex number
    List nth = complex1.nthRoot(5);

    // Computes complex number raised to the power of another
    Complex pow = complex1.pow(complex2);

    // Computes the square root of the complex number
    Complex sqrt = complex1.sqrt();

    // Retrieve the real and imaginary parts of the result
    double real = result.getReal();
    double imag = result.getImaginary();
```

```
        // Obtain the tangent
        result = complex1.tan();
    }
}
```

This example provides you with a solid foundation on how to use the Apache Commons Math library to work with complex numbers. To learn more about printing out the results of an imaginary number and formatting properly, please see recipe 3-6.

How It Works

Complex numbers consist of two parts: real and imaginary. For the most part, they are used in scientific and engineering fields, and they make it possible to extend the real value of a number so that problems can be solved. The issue with using complex numbers in Java is that there are no classes built into the language for working with them properly. Therefore, many people have worked around this by building their own complex number classes to work with them. As a result, there are hundreds of different Complex.java classes (or some named similarly) that can be found on the Web. In this book, we will use one of the most widely accepted libraries, the Apache Commons Math library, to tackle tasks such as these when possible. This library contains its own set of classes for working with complex numbers. To get started, the first thing you need to do is download the latest JAR files for the Apache Commons Math library from its location on the web (http://commons.apache.org/math/), and place the JAR files in your CLASSPATH. As of this writing, release 2.2 was the most current version. Therefore, the examples in the solution to this recipe might differ if you are using a different version of the library. The Apache Commons Math library will contain at least two JAR files. Version 2.2 contains three JAR files, and these files include the library, sources, and Javadoc. Make sure you place the JAR file that contains the compiled library into your CLASSPATH. This JAR will be named commons-math-2.2.jar, but the version number might differ if you are using another one. If you are using an IDE, you might want to also include the Javadoc JAR file into your CLASSPATH as this will allow the IDE to display the associated Javadoc with a method when you are using auto-completion.

Once the JARs are downloaded and in your CLASSPATH, you need to import the appropriate classes into the class from which you wish to make use of the library. Once imported, you can create complex numbers using the Complex class, perform calculations, and manipulate them as needed. To create a complex number object using the library, pass two double arguments to the constructor. The first double represents the real number part, and the second represents the imaginary part. The following code creates a complex number that includes a real part with a value of 8.0 and an imaginary part with a value of 3.0:

```
Complex complex1 = new Complex(8.0, 3.0);
```

After you've created a complex number object, you can work with it by calling the various methods contained within it. Most of the methods contained within the Complex class are used to perform mathematical calculations, while a handful of helper methods are used to gain access to different parts of the number, see if the number is NaN, and other miscellaneous tasks. The mathematical methods include those that are useful for performing everyday mathematics, as well as those that are useful for working with the numbers in a trigonometric methodology. A summary of the standard mathematical methods can be seen in Table 3-3.

Table 3-3. Complex Class Standard Mathematics Methods

Method	Description
abs()	Returns the absolute value of the complex number
add(Complex num)	Returns the sum of two complex numbers
divide(Complex num)	Returns the quotient of two complex numbers
exp()	Returns the exponential function
multiply(Complex num)	Returns the product of two complex numbers
multiply(double num)	Returns the product of the complex number and a given double
negate()	Returns the additive inverse of the complex number
nthRoot(int num)	Computes and returns the nth roots
pow(Complex num)	Returns the complex number raised to the power of num
sqrt()	Returns the square root
subtract(Complex num)	Returns the difference between two complex numbers

To make use of these methods, you call them against any given complex number object. All the methods that perform a calculation against two complex numbers accept another `Complex` object as an argument. A demonstration of these methods can be seen in the solution to this recipe.

Trigonometric methods can also be called against a `Complex` object, and they do not accept any arguments. They each return a `Complex` object. A summary of the trigonometric `Complex` class methods can be seen in Table 3-4.

Table 3-4. Complex Class Trigonometic Methods

Method	Description
acos()	Computes the inverse cosine
asin()	Computes the inverse sine
atan()	Computes the inverse tangent
cos()	Computes the cosine
cosh()	Computes the hyperbolic cosine
log()	Computes the natural logarithm
sin()	Computes the sine
sinh()	Computes the hyperbolic sine
tan()	Computes the tangent
tanh()	Computes the hyperbolic tangent

You can see some of these trigonometric methods demonstrated in the solution to this recipe. You might have noticed that earlier in this section the NaN symbol was used. This is comparable to a NULL value for a Complex object. The isNaN() method can be called against a Complex object to return a Boolean value stating whether the object is NaN. To test the equality of two Complex objects, simply call the equals() method, as the following code demonstrates: it returns a Boolean value indicating whether the two Complex objects are equal to each other:

```
complex1.equals(complex2);
```

There are a few more methods that can be used on a Complex object, and you can see the documentation for more information on them. As you might have noticed, the solution to this recipe does not print out the values for any of the manipulations that were performed. To learn more about formatting and printing complex number values, see recipe 3-6.

3-6. Formatting and Parsing Complex Numbers

Problem

You have a requirement to format complex numbers with your Java application.

Solution

Download the Apache Commons Math library (refer to recipe 3-5 for more details) and make use of the ComplexFormat class. This class will allow you to properly format the complex number and convert it to a String that represents both the real and imaginary number parts. The following code demonstrates the use of the ComplexFormat class:

```
ComplexFormat format = new ComplexFormat(); // default format
Complex c = new Complex(3.1415, 7.846);
String s = format.format(c);
System.out.println(s); // prints = 3.14 + 7.85i

NumberFormat numformat = NumberFormat.getInstance();
numformat.setMinimumFractionDigits(3);
numformat.setMaximumFractionDigits(3);

ComplexFormat format2 = new ComplexFormat(numformat);
s = format2.format(c);
System.out.println(s); // prints: 3.142 + 7.846i
```

The ComplexFormat class also allows for the parsing of Strings into Complex objects. The code that follows demonstrates parsing a String into a Complex object:

```
ComplexFormat cf = new ComplexFormat();
Complex complexNum = null;
```

```
try {
    complexNum = cf.parse("1.110 + 2.222i");
} catch (ParseException ex) {
    ex.printStackTrace();
}
```

In the previous code, the String is parsed using the ComplexFormat class, and a Complex object, complexNum, is generated.

How It Works

The ComplexFormat class extends the java.text.Format class. Much like other classes that extend java.text.Format, new instances of ComplexFormat can be generated and then different attributes can be set on those instances in order to obtain the required formatting for an application. By default, ComplexFormat will generate a String in the standard complex number format, including the real and imaginary number parts separated by a plus (+) symbol. The ComplexFormat class can also be used to take a complex number in String format and parse it into a Complex object. Doing such conversions can often come in quite handy, especially if you are accepting input from a user.

3-7. Calculating Monetary Values

Problem

You are developing an application that requires the use of monetary values and you are not sure which data type to use for storing and calculating currency values.

Solution

Use the BigDecimal data type to perform calculation on all monetary values. Format the resulting calculations using the NumberFormat.getCurrencyInstance() helper method. In the following code, three monetary values are calculated using a handful of the methods that are part of the BigDecimal class. The resulting calculations are then converted into double values and formatted using the NumberFormat class. First, take a look at how these values are calculated:

```
BigDecimal currencyOne = new BigDecimal("25.65");
BigDecimal currencyTwo = new BigDecimal("187.32");
BigDecimal currencyThree = new BigDecimal("4.86");
BigDecimal result = null;
String printFormat = null;

// Add all three values
result = currencyOne.add(currencyTwo).add(currencyThree);
// Convert to double and send to formatDollars(), returning a String
```

```
printFormat = formatDollars(result.doubleValue());
System.out.println(printFormat);

// Subtract the first currency value from the second
result = currencyTwo.subtract(currencyOne);
printFormat = formatDollars(result.doubleValue());
System.out.println(printFormat);
```

Next, let's take a look at the `formatDollars()` method that is used in the code. This method accepts a double value and performs formatting on it using the `NumberFormat` class based upon the U.S. locale. It then returns a String value representing currency:

```
public static String formatDollars(double value){
    NumberFormat dollarFormat = NumberFormat.getCurrencyInstance(Locale.US);
    return dollarFormat.format(value);
}
```

As you can see, the `NumberFormat` class allows for currency to be formatted per the specified locale. This can be very handy if you are working with an application that deals with currency and has an international scope.

```
$217.83
$161.67
```

How It Works

Many people attempt to use different number formats for working with currency. While it might be possible to use any type of numeric object to work with currency, the `BigDecimal` class was added to the language to help satisfy the requirements of working with currency values, among other things. Perhaps the most useful feature of the `BigDecimal` class is that it provides complete control over rounding. This is essentially why such a class is so useful for working with currency values. The `BigDecimal` class provides an easy API for rounding values, and also makes it easy to convert to double values such as the solution to this recipe demonstrates.

■ **Note** The use of `BigDecimal` for working with monetary values is a good practice. However, it can come at some performance expense. Depending upon the application and performance requirements, it might be worth using `Math.round()` to achieve basic rounding if performance becomes an issue.

To provide specific rounding with the `BigDecimal` class, you should use a `MathContext` object or the `RoundingMode` enumeration values. In either case, such precision can be omitted by using a currency formatting solution such as the one demonstrated in the solution example. `BigDecimal` objects have mathematical implementations built into them, so performing such operations is an easy task. The arithmetic operations that can be used are described in Table 3-5.

Table 3-5. BigDecimal Arithmetic Methods.

Method	Description
add()	Adds one BigDecimal object value to another
subtract()	Subtracts one BigDecimal object value from another
multiply()	Multiplies the value of one BigDecimal object with another
abs()	Returns the absolute value of the given BigDecimal object value
pow(n)	Returns the BigDecimal to the power of n, the power is computed to unlimited precision

After performing the calculations you require, call the doubleValue() method on the BigInteger object to convert and obtain a double. You can then format the double using the NumberFormat class for currency results.

3-8. Randomly Generating Values

Problem

An application that you are developing requires the use of randomly generated numbers.

Solution #1

Use the java.util.Random class to help generate the random numbers. The Random class was developed for the purpose of generating random numbers for a handful of the Java numeric data types. This code demonstrates the use of Random to generate such numbers:

```
// Create a new instance of the Random class
Random random = new Random();

// Generates a random Integer
int myInt = random.nextInt();

// Generates a random Double value
double myDouble = random.nextDouble();

// Generates a random float
float myFloat = random.nextFloat();

// Generates a random Gaussian double
```

```
// mean 0.0 and standard deviation 1.0
// from this random number generator's sequence.
double gausDouble = random.nextGaussian();

// Generates a random Long
long myLong = random.nextLong();

// Generates a random boolean
boolean myBoolean = random.nextBoolean();
```

Solution #2

Make use of the `Math.random()` method. This will produce a double value that is greater than 0.0, but less than 1.0. The following code demonstrates the use of this method:

```
double rand = Math.random();
```

How It Works

The `java.util.Random` class uses a 48-bit seed to generate a series of pseudo-random values. As you can see from the example in the solution to this recipe, the `Random` class can generate many different types of random number values based upon the given seed. By default, the seed is generated based upon a calculation derived from the number of milliseconds that the machine has been active. However, the seed can be set manually using the `Random setSeed()` method. It should be noted that if two `Random` objects have the same seed, they will produce the same results.

It should be noted that there are cases in which the `Random` class might not be the best choice for generating random values. For instance, if you are attempting to use a threadsafe instance of `java.util.Random`, you might run into performance issues if working with many threads. In such a case, you might consider using the `ThreadLocalRandom` class instead. To see more information regarding `ThreadLocalRandom`, see the documentation at http://download.oracle.com/javase/7/docs/api/java/util/concurrent/ThreadLocalRandom.html. Similarly, if you require the use of a cryptographically secure `Random` object, consider the use of SecureRandom. Documentation regarding this class can be found at http://download.oracle.com/javase/7/docs/api/java/security/SecureRandom.html.

The `java.util.Random` class comes in very handy when you need to generate a type-specified random value. Not only is it easy to use but it also provides a wide range of options for return-type. Another easy technique is to use the `Math.random()` method, which produces a double value that is within the range of 0.0 to 1.0, as demonstrated in solution #2. Both techniques provide a good means of generating random values. However, if you need to generate random numbers of a specific type, `java.util.Random` is the best choice.

3-9. Obtaining the Current Date

Problem

You are developing an application for which you would like to obtain the current date to display on a form.

Solution #1

If you only need to obtain the current date without going into calendar details, use the `java.util.Date` class to generate a new `Date` object. Doing so will cause the new `Date` object to be equal to the current system date. In the following code, you can see how easy it is to create a new Date object and obtain the current date:

```
Date date = new Date();

System.out.println(date);
System.out.println(date.getTime());
```

The result will be a Date object that contains the current date and time taken from the system that the code is run on, as shown following. The time is the number of milliseconds since January 1, 1970, 00:00:00 GMT.

```
Sat Sep 10 14:45:57 CDT 2011
1315683957625
```

Solution #2

If you need to be more precise regarding the calendar, use the `java.util.Calendar` class. Although working with the `Calendar` class will make your code longer, you can be much more precise. The following code demonstrates just a handful of the capabilities of using this class to obtain the current date:

```
Calendar gCal = Calendar.getInstance();

// Month is based upon a zero index, January is equal to 0,
// so we need to add one to the month for it to be in
// a standard format
int month = gCal.get(Calendar.MONTH) + 1;int day = gCal.get(Calendar.DATE);
int yr = gCal.get(Calendar.YEAR);

String dateStr = month + "/" + day + "/" + yr;
System.out.println(dateStr);
```

```
int dayOfWeek = gCal.get(Calendar.DAY_OF_WEEK);

// Print out the integer value for the day of the week
System.out.println(dayOfWeek);

int hour = gCal.get(Calendar.HOUR);
int min  = gCal.get(Calendar.MINUTE);
int sec = gCal.get(Calendar.SECOND);


// Print out the time
System.out.println(hour + ":" + min + ":" + sec);

// Create new DateFormatSymbols instance to obtain the String
// value for dates
DateFormatSymbols symbols = new DateFormatSymbols();
String[] days = symbols.getWeekdays();
System.out.println(days[dayOfWeek]);

// Get crazy with the date!
int dayOfYear = gCal.get(Calendar.DAY_OF_YEAR);
System.out.println(dayOfYear);

// Print the number of days left in the year
System.out.println("Days left in " + yr + ": " + (365-dayOfYear));

int week = gCal.get(Calendar.WEEK_OF_YEAR);
// Print the week of the year
System.out.println(week);
```

As demonstrated by this code, it is possible to obtain more detailed information regarding the current date when using the Calendar class. The results of running the code would look like the following:

```
9/10/2011
7
2:45:57
Saturday
253
Days left in 2011: 112
37
```

How It Works

Many applications require the use of the current calendar date. It is often also necessary to obtain the current time. There are a couple of different ways to do that, and the solution to this recipe demonstrates two of them. By default, the `java.util.Date` class can be instantiated with no arguments to return the current date and time. The `Date` class can also be used to return the current time of day via the `getTime()` method. As mentioned in the solution, the `getTime()` method returns the number of milliseconds since January 1, 1970, 00:00:00 GMT, represented by the Date object that is in use. There are several other methods that can be called against a Date object with regards to breaking down the current date and time into more granular intervals. For instance, the Date class has the methods `getHours()`, `getMinutes()`, `getSeconds()`, `getMonth()`, `getDay()`, `getTimezoneOffset()`, and `getYear()`. However, it is not advisable to use any of these methods, with the exception of `getTime()`, because each has been deprecated by the use of the `java.util.Calendar get()` method. When some method or class is deprecated, that means it should no longer be used because it might be removed in some future release of the Java language. However, a few of the methods contained within the Date class have not been tagged as deprecated, so the Date class will most likely be included in future releases of Java. The methods that were left intact include the comparison methods `after()`, `before()`, `compareTo()`, `setTime()`, and `equals()`. Solution #1 to this recipe demonstrates how to instantiate a Date object and print out the current date and time.

As mentioned previously, the `Date` class has many methods that have become deprecated and should no longer be used. In solution #2 of this recipe, the `java.util.Calendar` class is demonstrated as the successor for obtaining much of this information. The Calendar class was introduced in JDK 1.1, at which time many of the `Date` methods were deprecated. As you can see from solution #2, the `Calendar` class contains all the same functionality that is included in the `Date` class, except the `Calendar` class is much more flexible. The `Calendar` class is actually an abstract class that contains methods that are used for converting between a specific time and date, and manipulating the calendar in various ways. The `Calendar`, as demonstrated in solution #2, is one such class that extends the Calendar class and therefore provides this functionality.

In order to obtain the current date with a `Calendar` object, you first need to instantiate a new `Calendar` instance using the `Calendar.getInstance()` method. Once you have created a new `Calendar` object, you can extract the different date and time intervals using the `get()` method and passing one of the `Calendar` object's static `int` values. As seen in solution #2 to this recipe, the current date can be extracted and printed using the following lines of code:

```
Calendar gCal = Calendar.getInstance();

int month = gCal.get(Calendar.MONTH);
int day = gCal.get(Calendar.DATE);
int yr = gCal.get(Calendar.YEAR);
```

For some applications, the `Date` class will work fine. For instance, the `Date` class can be useful when working with timestamps. However, if the application requires detailed manipulation of dates and times then it is advisable to make use of a `Calendar` class, which includes all the functionality of the `Date class` and also adds more features. Both solutions to this recipe are technically sound; choose the one that best suits the need of your application.

3-10. Adding and Subtracting Days, Months, and Years

Problem

You would like to perform date calculations within your application.

Solution

Use the `java.util.Calendar` class to perform date calculations. This class allows you to obtain the Integer representation for a given month, day, or year of a specified date. These Integer values can be used to perform calculations to obtain the desired result.

```java
public static void calculateDates() {
    Calendar cal = Calendar.getInstance();
    String monthStr = null;
    // Note:  month values range from 0 to 11...so add one to the number

    int month = cal.get(Calendar.MONTH);
    int day = cal.get(Calendar.DATE);
    int yr = cal.get(Calendar.YEAR);

    System.out.println("January = " + Calendar.JANUARY);
    System.out.println("June = " + Calendar.JUNE);

    System.out.println("Current Date: " + formatDate(cal));

    // Add two months to current date
    cal.add(Calendar.MONTH, 2);

    System.out.println("Current Date Plus 2 Months: " + formatDate(cal));

    cal = Calendar.getInstance();

    // Subtract 8 months from current date
    cal.add(Calendar.MONTH, -8);

    System.out.println("Current Date Minus 8 Months: " + formatDate(cal));

    cal = Calendar.getInstance();
    cal.add(Calendar.DATE, -8);
    System.out.println("Current Date Minus 8 Days: " + formatDate(cal));

    // Add 15 hours to current date
```

```
        cal = Calendar.getInstance();
        cal.add(Calendar.HOUR, 15);
        System.out.println("Current Date Plus 15 Hours: " + formatDate(cal));
}

/**
 * Date formatting method that accepts a Calendar object and returns
 * a formatted String.
 *
 * @param cal
 * @return
 */
public static String formatDate(Calendar cal) {
    SimpleDateFormat simpleFormatter = new SimpleDateFormat("MMM dd yyyy hh:mm:ss aaa");

    return simpleFormatter.format(cal.getTime());

}
```

The results of running this code will resemble the following:

```
January = 0
June = 5
Current Date: Sep 11 2011 08:03:48 AM
Current Date Plus 2 Months: Nov 11 2011 08:03:48 AM
Current Date Minus 8 Months: Jan 11 2011 08:03:48 AM
Current Date Minus 8 Days: Sep 03 2011 08:03:48 AM
Current Date Plus 15 Hours: Sep 11 2011 11:03:48 PM
```

The Calendar class contains methods that make it easy to perform basic mathematics using date and time values.

How It Works

Performing date calculations can be difficult if they require conversion between dates into time or into other measurements. Such is the case if you use the java.util.Date class to perform calculations. In the early days of Java, a Date object was often converted into hours, minutes, and seconds; and time was used to perform mathematics on a given date. This is no longer the case with the use of the Calendar class. The two basic requirements for date calculations are addition and subtraction. Most often, days, weeks, months, or years need to be added or subtracted from a given date. Via the use of the Calendar add() method, each of these two functionalities can be easily performed. The add() method signature can be displayed as follows:

```
add(int field, int amount)
```

In the preceding signature, the first argument is an int value that represents the field type that will be added to the given date. The second argument is another int value that represents the number of the field type to add to the given date. The `static int` field values that can be passed as the first argument are listed in Table 3-6.

Table 3-6. `static int` *Calendar Fields*

Field	Description
DATE	Field number indicating the day of the month
DAY_OF_MONTH	Field number indicating the day of the month
DAY_OF_WEEK_IN_MONTH	Field number indicating the day of the week in the current month
DAY_OF_YEAR	Field number indicating the day of the year
WEEK_OF_YEAR	Field number indicating the week of the year
HOUR	Field number indicating the hour
HOUR_OF_DAY	Field number indicating the hour of the day
MILLISECOND	Field number indicating the millisecond of the minute
MINUTE	Field number indicating the minute of the hour
MONTH	Field number indicating the month of the year
SECOND	Field number indicating the second of the minute
YEAR	Field number indicating the year

As demonstrated in solution #2, any of the fields in Table 3-6 can be used with the `Calendar.add()` method to perform date arithmetic. When using the `add()` method, pass a negative value for the argument to perform a subtraction. Working with the Calendar class might take a few minutes of use to become familiar with the syntax, but it is flexible and easy to use.

3-11. Finding the Difference Between Two Dates

Problem

You need to determine how many hours, days, weeks, months, or years have elapsed between two dates.

Solution

Use the `java.util.concurrent.TimeUnit` enum to perform calculations between given dates. Using this enum, you can obtain the Integer values for days, hours, microseconds, milliseconds, minutes, nanoseconds, and seconds. Doing so will allow you to perform the necessary calculations.

```
// Obtain two instances of the Calendar class
Calendar cal1 = Calendar.getInstance();
```

```
Calendar cal2 = Calendar.getInstance();

// Set the date to 01/01/2010:12:00
cal2.set(2010,0,1,12,0);
Date date1 = cal2.getTime();
System.out.println(date1);

long mill = Math.abs(cal1.getTimeInMillis() - date1.getTime());
// Convert to hours
long hours = TimeUnit.MILLISECONDS.toHours(mill);
// Convert to days
Long days = TimeUnit.HOURS.toDays(hours);
String diff = String.format("%d hour(s) %d min(s)", hours,
TimeUnit.MILLISECONDS.toMinutes(mill) - TimeUnit.HOURS.toMinutes(hours));
System.out.println(diff);

diff = String.format("%d days", days);
System.out.println(diff);

// Divide the number of days by seven for the weeks
int weeks = days.intValue()/7;
diff = String.format("%d weeks", weeks);
System.out.println(diff);
```

The output of this code will be formatted to display Strings of text indicating the differences between the current date and the Date object that is created.

How It Works

As with most programmatic techniques, there is more than one way to perform date calculations with Java. However, one of the most useful techniques is to perform calculations based upon the given date's time in milliseconds. This provides the most accurate calculation because it works on the time at a very small interval: milliseconds. The current time in milliseconds can be obtained from a Calendar object by calling the getTimeInMillis() method against it. Likewise, a Date object will return its value represented in milliseconds by calling the getTime() method. As you can see from the solution to this recipe, the first math that is performed is the difference between the given dates in milliseconds. Obtaining that value and then taking its absolute value will provide the base that is needed in order to perform the date calculations. In order to obtain the absolute value of a number, use the abs() method that is contained in the java.lang.Math class, shown in the following line of code:

```
long mill = Math.abs(cal1. getTimeInMillis() - date1.getTime());
```

The absolute value will be returned in long format. The TimeUnit enum can be used in order to obtain different conversions of the date. It contains a number of static enum constant values that represent different time intervals, similar to those of a Calendar object. Those values are displayed below.

■ **Note** An *enum type* is a type whose fields consist of a fixed set of constant values. Enum types were welcomed to the Java language in release 1.5.

- DAYS

- HOURS

- MICROSECONDS

- MILLISECONDS

- MINUTES

- NANOSECONDS

- SECONDS

The values speak for themselves with regard to the conversion interval they represent. By calling conversion methods against these enums, `long` values representing the duration between two dates can be converted. As you can see in the solution to this recipe, first the time unit is established using the enum and then a conversion call is made against that time unit. Take, for instance, the following conversion. First, the time unit of `TimeUnit.MILLISECONDS` is established. Second, the `toHours()` method is called against it, and a `long` value that is represented by the `mill` field is passed as an argument:

`TimeUnit.MILLISECONDS.toHours(mill)`

This code can be translated in English as follows: "The contents of the field `mill` are represented in milliseconds; convert those contents into hours." The result of this call will be the conversion of the value within the `mill` field into hours. By stacking the calls to `TimeUnit`, more-precise conversions can be made. For instance, the following code converts the contents of the mill field into hours and then into days:

`TimeUnit.HOURS.toDays(TimeUnit.MILLISECONDS.toHours(mill))`

Again, the English translation can be read as "The contents of the field `mill` are represented in milliseconds. Convert those contents into hours. Next, convert those hours into days."

`TimeUnit` can make time interval conversion very precise. Combining the precision of the `TimeUnit` conversions along with mathematics will allow you to convert the difference of two dates into just about any time interval.

3-12. Formatting Dates for Display

Problem

Dates need to be displayed by your application using a specific format. You would like to define that format once and apply it to all dates that need to be displayed.

Solution

Use the java.util.Calendar class to obtain the date that you require and then format that date using the java.text.SimpleDateFormat class. The following example demonstrates the use of the SimpleDateFormat class:

```
// Create new calendar
Calendar cal = Calendar.getInstance();

// Create instance of SimpleDateFormat class using pattern
SimpleDateFormat dateFormatter1 = new SimpleDateFormat("MMMMM dd yyyy");
String result = null;

result = dateFormatter1.format(cal.getTime());
System.out.println(result);

dateFormatter1.applyPattern("MM/dd/YY hh:mm:ss");
result = dateFormatter1.format(cal.getTime());
System.out.println(result);

dateFormatter1.applyPattern("hh 'o''clock' a, zzzz");
result = dateFormatter1.format(cal.getTime());
System.out.println(result);
```

Running this example would yield the following result:

```
June 22 2011
06/22/11 06:24:41
06 o'clock AM, Central Daylight Time
```

As you can see from the results, the SimpleDateFormat class makes it easy to convert a date into just about any format.

How It Works

Date formatting is a common concern when it comes to any program. People like to see their dates in a certain format for different situations. The SimpleDateFormat class was created so we don't have to perform manual translations for a given date.

■ **Note** Different date formats are used within different locales, and the SimpleDateFormat class facilitates locale-specific formatting.

To use the class, an instance must be instantiated either by passing a String-based pattern as an argument to the constructor or passing no argument to the constructor at all. There are actually four constructors for instantiating an instance of SimpleDateFormat:

```
SimpleDateFormat()
SimpleDateFormat(String pattern)
SimpleDateFormat(String pattern, DateFormatSymbols symbols)
SimpleDateFormat(String pattern, Locale locale)
```

In the solution to this recipe, the second constructor in the preceding list is used. The String-based pattern provides a template that should be applied to the given date and then a String representing the date in the given pattern style is returned. A pattern consists of a number of different characters strung together. Table 3-7 shows the different characters that can be used within a pattern.

Table 3-7. Pattern Characters

Character	Description
G	Era
y	Year
Y	Week year
M	Month in year
w	Week in year
W	Week in month
D	Day in year
d	Day in month
F	Day of week in month
E	Name of day in week
u	Number of day in week
a	AM/PM

H	Hour in day (0–23)
k	Hour in day (1–24)
K	Hour in AM/PM (0–11)
h	Hour in AM/PM (1–12)
m	Minute in hour
s	Second in minute
S	Millisecond
z	General time zone
Z	RFC 822 time zone
X	ISO 8601 time zone

Any of the pattern characters can be placed together in a String and then passed to the SimpleDateFormat class. If the class is instantiated without passing a pattern, the pattern can be applied later using the class's applyPattern() method. The applyPattern() method also comes in handy when you want to change the pattern of an instantiated SimpleDateFormat object, as seen in the solution to this recipe. The following excerpts of code demonstrate the application of a pattern:

```
SimpleDateFormat dateFormatter1 = new SimpleDateFormat("MMMMM dd yyyy");
dateFormatter1.applyPattern("MM/dd/YY hh:mm:ss");
```

Once a pattern has been applied to a SimpleDateFormat object, a long value representing time can be passed to the SimpleDateFormat object's format() method. The format() method will return the given date\time formatted using the pattern that was applied. The String-based result can then be used however your application requires.

3-13. Comparing Dates

Problem

You need to determine whether one date is equal to or greater than another date.

Solution

Use the comparative methods that are part of java.util.Calendar to determine which date is greater. In the following example, two Calendar objects are instantiated, and then they are compared with each other:

```
Calendar cal1 = Calendar.getInstance();
Calendar cal2 = Calendar.getInstance();
```

```
// Set the date to 01/01/2010:12:00
cal2.set(2010,0,1,12,0);

System.out.println(formatDate(cal1) + " before " + formatDate(cal2) + "? " +
cal1.before(cal2));
System.out.println(cal2.compareTo(cal1));
```

The result of this code demonstration would be a String that displays a `Boolean` value indicating whether the first date is prior to the second. The second line returned from this code is an `int` indicating whether the `cal1 Calendar` object is before or after the `cal2 Calendar` object. They would resemble something like the following:

```
Sep 11 2011 09:01:39 AM before Jan 01 2010 12:00:39 PM? false
-1
```

How It Works

Date comparison methods are conveniently included as part of the `java.util.Calendar` class. The comparison methods `after()` and `before()` that are contained within the `Calendar` class accept another `Calendar` object as an argument and return a `Boolean` indicating whether the Date passed as an argument comes after or before the `Calendar` object on which the method is invoked.

The `Calendar` object also has another method named `compareTo()` that accepts another `Calendar` object and returns an `int` indicating if the `Calendar` argument is before or after the `Calendar` object on which the method is invoked. The results of the `compareTo()` method are shown in Table 3-8.

Table 3-8. Calendar Object s compareTo() Result

Result	Description
0	Equal
1	Date argument is less than the object invoking the call
-1	Date argument is greater than the object invoking the call

3-14. Writing Readable Numeric Literals

Problem

Some of the numeric literals in your application are rather long and you would like to make it easier to tell how large a number is at a glance.

Solution

Use underscores in place of commas or decimals in larger numbers in order to make them more readable. The following code shows some examples of making your numeric literals more readable by using underscores in place of commas:

```
int million = 1_000_000;
int billion = 1_000_000_000;
float ten_pct = 1_0f;
double exp = 1_234_56.78_9e2;
```

How It Works

Sometimes working with large numbers can become cumbersome and difficult to read. Because of the release of Java SE7, underscores can now be used within numeric literals in order to make code a bit easier to read. The underscores can appear anywhere between digits within a numeric literal. This allows for the use of underscores in place of commas or spaces to separate the digits and make them easier to read.

■ **Note** Underscores cannot be placed at the beginning or end of a number, adjacent to a decimal point or floating-point literal, prior to an *F* or *L* suffix, or in positions where a string of digits is expected.

3-15. Declaring Binary Literals

Problem

You are working on an application that requires the declaration of binary numbers.

Solution

Make use of binary literals to make your code readable. The following code segment demonstrates the use of binary literals.

```
int bin1 = 0b1100;
short bin2 = 0B010101;
short bin3 = (short) 0b1001100110011001;
System.out.println(bin1);
System.out.println(bin2);
System.out.println(bin3);
```

This will result in the following output:

```
12
21
-26215
```

How It Works

Binary literals became part of the Java language with the release of JDK 7. The types `byte`, `short`, `int`, and `long` can be expressed using the binary number system. This feature can help to make binary numbers easier to recognize within code. In order to use the binary format, simply prefix the number with `0b` or `0B`.

CHAPTER 4

■■■

Data Structures, Conditionals, and Iteration

Java is one of the most capable programming languages in use today. Java powers the desktop, the enterprise, the Web, mobile devices, and much more. As a Java developer, regardless of which space you are working in, there are some parts of the language that you use occasionally as needed, other parts of the language that you use rarely, and those parts of the language that you likely use on a regular basis. In this chapter, we present a variety of recipes covering topics that fall into the latter category. All Java applications require the use of data structures, iteration, and conditional control flow. You will find recipes covering the use of classes from the Java Collections Framework as well as Java arrays. If you are a new Java developer, there is a recipe to get you up to speed quickly on the use of generic types with the `Collection` classes. Regardless of your level of Java experience, be sure to check out this recipe to read about a new Java 7 feature, the diamond syntax, which will make your life easier if you are doing a lot of generics programming. In the iteration category, you may find the recipes on the use of the `Iterable` interface, the enhanced `for` loop, and `Map` iteration useful. There is a recipe that demonstrates a long-awaited addition to the language, finally appearing in Java 7: the ability to use `Strings` in the `switch` statement.

We start off the chapter with a couple of recipes covering what is quite likely one of the most underappreciated and underutilized features of Java: the enum type.

4-1. Defining a Fixed Set of Related Constants

Problem

You need a type that can represent a fixed set of related constants.

Solution

Use an enum type. The following example defines an enum type, called `FieldType`, to represent various form fields you might find on the GUI of an application:

```
// See BasicFieldType.java
public enum FieldType { PASSWORD, EMAIL_ADDRESS, PHONE_NUMBER, SOCIAL_SECURITY_NUMBER }
```

This is the simplest form of an enum type, which will often suffice when all that is needed is a related set of named constants. The next recipe will demonstrate how to use Java enum types in a much more powerful way. First, let's take a look at the capabilities that all enum types possess. In this code, a `field` variable, of type `FieldType`, is declared and initialized to the `FieldType.EMAIL_ADDRESS` enum constant. Next, the code prints out the results of calling various methods that are defined for all enum types:

```
FieldType field = FieldType.EMAIL_ADDRESS;

System.out.println("field.name(): " + field.name());
System.out.println("field.ordinal(): " + field.ordinal());
System.out.println("field.toString(): " + field.toString());

System.out.println("field.isEqual(EMAIL_ADDRESS): " +
                    field.equals(FieldType.EMAIL_ADDRESS));
System.out.println("field.isEqual(\"EMAIL_ADDRESS\"): " + field.equals("EMAIL_ADDRESS"));

System.out.println("field == EMAIL_ADDRESS: " + (field == FieldType.EMAIL_ADDRESS));
// Won!t compile - illustrates type safety of enum
// System.out.println("field == \"EMAIL_ADDRESS\": " + (field == "EMAIL_ADDRESS"));

System.out.println("field.compareTo(EMAIL_ADDRESS): " +
                    field.compareTo(FieldType.EMAIL_ADDRESS));
System.out.println("field.compareTo(PASSWORD): " + field.compareTo(FieldType.PASSWORD));

System.out.println("field.valueOf(\"EMAIL_ADDRESS\"): " + field.valueOf("EMAIL_ADDRESS"));

try {
    System.out.print("field.valueOf(\"email_address\"): ");
    System.out.println(FieldType.valueOf("email_address"));
} catch (IllegalArgumentException e) {
    System.out.println(e.toString());
}

System.out.println("FieldType.values(): " + Arrays.toString(FieldType.values()));
```

Running this code will result in the following output:

```
field.name(): EMAIL_ADDRESS
field.ordinal(): 1
field.toString(): EMAIL_ADDRESS
field.isEqual(EMAIL_ADDRESS): true
field.isEqual("EMAIL_ADDRESS"'): false
field == EMAIL_ADDRESS: true
field.compareTo(EMAIL_ADDRESS): 0
field.compareTo(PASSWORD): 1
field.valueOf("EMAIL_ADDRESS"): EMAIL_ADDRESS
field.valueOf("email_address"): java.lang.IllegalArgumentException: No enum constant
org.java7recipes.chapter4.BasicEnumExample.FieldType.email_address
FieldType.values(): [PASSWORD, EMAIL_ADDRESS, PHONE_NUMBER, SSN]
```

How It Works

A common pattern for representing a fixed set of related constants is to define each constant as an int type or some other type like a String. Often, these constants are defined in a class or interface whose sole purpose is to encapsulate constants. In any case, constants are typically defined with the static and final modifiers:

```
// Input field constants
public static final int PASSWORD = 0;
public static final int EMAIL_ADDRESS = 1;
public static final int PHONE_NUMBER = 2;
public static final int SOCIAL_SECURITY_NUMBER = 3;
```

There are multiple problems with this pattern, the primary one being the lack of type safety. By defining these constants as ints, it is possible to assign an invalid value to a variable that is supposed to only be allowed to hold one of the constant values:

```
int inputField = PHONE_NUMBER;  // OK
inputField = 4;  // Bad - no input field constant with value 4; compiles without error
```

As you can see, there will be no compiler error or warning produced to inform you of this invalid value assignment. Chances are, you will discover this at runtime, when your application tries to use inputField. In contrast, Java enum types provide compile-time type safety. That is, attempts to assign a value of the wrong type to an enum variable will result in a compiler error. In the solution code, the FieldType.EMAIL_ADDRESS enum constant was assigned to the field variable. Attempting to assign a value that isn't of type FieldType naturally results in a compiler error:

```
FieldType field = FieldType.EMAIL_ADDRESS;  // OK
field = "EMAIL_ADDRESS"; // Wrong type - compiler error
```

An enum is just a special type of class. Under the covers, Java implements an enum type as a subclass of the abstract and final `java.lang.Enum` class. Thus, an enum type cannot be instantiated directly (outside of the enum type) or extended. The constants defined by an enum type are actually instances of the enum type. The `java.lang.Enum` class defines a number of final methods that all enum types inherit. In addition, all enum types have two implicitly declared `static` methods: `values()` and `valueOf(String)`. The solution code demonstrates these `static` methods and some of the more often used instance methods. Most of these methods are pretty self-explantory, but the following details should be kept in mind:

- Each enum constant has an ordinal value representing its relative position in the enum declaration. The first constant in the declaration is assigned an ordinal value of zero. The `ordinal()` method can be used to retrieve an enum constant's ordinal value; however, it is not recommended that applications be written to depend on this value for maintainability reasons.

- The `name()` method and the default implementation of the `toString()` method both return a string representation of the enum constant (`toString()` actually calls `name()`). It is common for `toString()` to be overridden to provide a more user-friendly string representation of the enum constant. For this reason, and for maintainability reasons, it is recommended that `toString()` be used in preference to `name()`.

- When testing for equality, note that both the `equals()` method and `==` perform reference comparison. They can be used interchangeably. However, it is recommended that `==` be used to take advantage of compile-time type safety. This is illustrated in the solution code. Performing `equals()` comparison with a `String` parameter, for example, may allow the error to go unnoticed; it will compile, but it will always return `false`. Conversely, attempting to compare an enum with a `String` using the `==` comparison would result in an error at compile time. When you have the choice of catching errors sooner (at compile time) rather than later (at runtime), choose the former.

- The implicitly declared static methods `values()` and `valueOf(String)` do not appear in the Java documentation or the source code for the `java.lang.Enum` class. However, the Java Language Specification does detail their required implementations. In summary, `values()` returns an array containing the constants of the enum, in the order they are declared. The `valueOf(String)` method returns the enum constant whose name exactly matches (including case) the value of the `String` argument, or throws an `IllegalArgumentException` if there is no enum constant with the specified name.

Please refer to the online Java documentation for further details on `java.lang.Enum` and each its methods (`http://download.oracle.com/javase/7/docs/api/java/lang/Enum.html`). You are also encouraged to check out the Enums section of the Java Language Specification for a lot of good information on enum types (`http://download.oracle.com/javase/cmn/spec_index.html`). As the next recipe will demonstrate, enum types, as full-fledged Java classes, can be used to build more intelligent constants.

4-2. Designing Intelligent Constants

Problem

You need a type that can represent a fixed set of related constants, and you would like to build in some state and behavior (logic) around your constants in an object-oriented fashion.

Solution

Use an enum type and take advantage of the fact that enum types are full-fledged Java classes. An enum type can have state and behavior just like any other class, and the enum constants, themselves being instances of the enum type, inherit this state and behavior. This is best illustrated by an example. Let's expand on the example from the previous recipe. Imagine that you need to process and validate all the form fields from an HTML form that has been submitted. Each form field has unique rules for validating its contents, based on the field type. For each form field, you have the field's "name" and the value that was entered into that form field. The FieldType enum can be expanded to handle this very easily:

```java
// See FieldType.java
public enum FieldType {

    PASSWORD("password") {

        // A password must contain one or more digits, one or more lowercase letters, one or
        // more uppercase letters, and be a minimum of 6 characters in length.
        //
        @Override
        public boolean validate(String fieldValue) {
            return Pattern.matches("((?=.*\\d)(?=.*[a-z])(?=.*[A-Z]).{6,})",
                                    fieldValue);
        }
    },

    EMAIL_ADDRESS("email") {

        // An email address begins with a combination of alphanumeric characters, periods,
        // and hyphens, followed by a mandatory ampersand (!@!) character, followed by
        // a combination of alphanumeric characters (hyphens allowed), followed by a
        // one or more periods (to separate domains and subdomains), and ending in 2-4
```

```java
        // alphabetic characters representing the domain.
        //
        @Override
        public boolean validate(String fieldValue) {
            return Pattern.matches("^[\\w\\.-]+@([\\w\\-]+\\.)+[A-Z|a-z]{2,4}$",
                                fieldValue);
        }
    },

    PHONE_NUMBER("phone") {

        // A phone number must contain a minium of 7 digits. Three optional digits
        // representing the area code may appear in front of the main 7 digits. The area
        // code may, optionally, be surrounded by parenthesis. If an area code is included,
        // the number may optionally be prefixed by a !1! for long distance numbers.
        // Optional hypens my appear after the country code (!1!), the area code, and the
        // first 3 digits of the 7 digit number.
        //
        @Override
        public boolean validate(String fieldValue) {
            return Pattern.matches("^1?[- ]?\\(?(\\d{3})\\)?[- ]?(\\d{3})[- ]?(\\d{4})$",
                                fieldValue);
        }
    },

    SOCIAL_SECURITY_NUMBER("ssn") {

        // A social security number must contain 9 digits with optional hyphens after the
        // third and fifth digits.
        //
        @Override
        public boolean validate(String fieldValue) {
            return Pattern.matches("^\\d{3}[- ]?\\d{2}[- ]?\\d{4}$",
                                fieldValue);
        }
    };  // End of enum constants definition

    // Instance members
    //
    private String fieldName;

    private FieldType(String fieldName) {
        this.fieldName = fieldName;
    }
```

```java
public String getFieldName() {
    return this.fieldName;
}

abstract boolean validate(String fieldValue);

// Static class members
//
private static final Map<String, FieldType> nameToFieldTypeMap = new HashMap<>();

static {
    for (FieldType field : FieldType.values()) {
        nameToFieldTypeMap.put(field.getFieldName(), field);
    }
}

public static FieldType lookup(String fieldName) {
    return nameToFieldTypeMap.get(fieldName.toLowerCase());
}

private static void printValid(FieldType field, String fieldValue, boolean valid) {
    System.out.println(field.getFieldName() +
                        "(\"" + fieldValue + "\") valid: " + valid);
}

public static void main(String... args) {

    String fieldName = "password";
    String fieldValue = "1Cxy9";   // invalid - must be at least 6 characters
    FieldType field = lookup(fieldName);
    printValid(field, fieldValue, field.validate(fieldValue));

    fieldName = "phone";
    fieldValue = "1-800-555-1234";   // valid
    field = lookup(fieldName);
    printValid(field, fieldValue, field.validate(fieldValue));

    fieldName = "email";
    fieldValue = "john@doe";   // invalid - missing .<tld>
    field = lookup(fieldName);
    printValid(field, fieldValue, field.validate(fieldValue));

    fieldName = "ssn";
    fieldValue = "111-11-1111";   // valid
    field = lookup(fieldName);
    printValid(field, fieldValue, field.validate(fieldValue));
}
```

```
}
```

Running the above code results in the following output:

```
password("1Cxy9") valid: false
phone("1-800-555-1234") valid: true
email("john@doe") valid: false
ssn("111-11-1111") valid: true
```

How It Works

Notice that our enhanced `FieldType` enum now defines a `fieldName` instance variable and a constructor with a `fieldName String` argument for initializing the instance variable. Each enum constant (again, each constant being an instance of `FieldType`) must be instantiated with a `fieldName`. `FieldType` also defines an `abstract validate(String)` method that each enum constant must implement to perform the field validation. Here, each `FieldType`'s `validate()` method applies a regular expression match against the field value and returns the `boolean` result of the match. Imagine the following form input fields corresponding to our `FieldType` instances:

```
<input type="password" name="password" value=""/>
<input type="tel" name="phone" value=""/>
<input type="email" name="email" value=""/>
<input type="text" name="ssn" value=""/>
```

The value of the input field's "name" attribute is what will be used to identify the `FieldType`; we used this same name when we instantiated each `FieldType` enum constant. When a form is submitted, we have access to each input field's "name" and the value that was entered into thefield. We need to be able to map the field's "name" to a `FieldType` and call the `validate()` method with the input value. The class variable, `nameToFieldTypeMap`, is declared and initialized for this purpose. For each `FieldType` enum constant, `nameToFieldTypeMap` stores an entry with the field name as the key, and the `FieldType` as the value. The `lookup(String)` class method uses this map to look up the `FieldType` from the field name. The code to validate an "email" input field with an input value of "john@doe.com" is quite concise:

```
// <input type="email" name="email" value="john@doe.com"/>
String fieldName = "email";
String fieldValue = "john@doe.com";
boolean valid = FieldType.lookup(fieldName).validate(fieldValue);
```

The `main()` method shows an example validation for each of the `FieldTypes`. The `printValid()` method prints the field name, field value, and the field's validation result.

This recipe has demonstrated that there is a lot more potential in the enum type than just the ability to define a set of named constants. Enum types have all the power of a normal class, plus additional features that allow you to create well-encapsulated and intelligent constants.

4-3. Executing Code Based Upon a Specified Value

Problem

You want to execute different blocks of code based on the value of a singular expression.

Solution

Consider using a `switch` statement if your variable or expression result is one of the allowed `switch` types and you want to test for equality against a type-compatible constant. These examples show various ways to use the `switch` statement, including a new feature of Java 7: the ability to switch on `String`s. First, let's play some Rock-Paper-Scissors! The `RockPaperScissors` class shows two different `switch` statements: one using an `int` as the `switch` expression type, and the other using an `enum` type.

```java
// See RockPaperScissors.java
public class RockPaperScissors {

    enum Hand { ROCK, PAPER, SCISSORS, INVALID };

    private static void getHand(int handVal) {
        Hand hand;
        try {
            hand = Hand.values()[handVal - 1];
        }
        catch (ArrayIndexOutOfBoundsException ex) {
            hand = Hand.INVALID;
        }
        switch (hand) {
            case ROCK:
                System.out.println("Rock");
                break;
            case PAPER:
                System.out.println("Paper");
                break;
            case SCISSORS:
                System.out.println("Scissors");
                break;
            default:
                System.out.println("Invalid");
        }
    }
}
```

```java
private static void playHands(int yourHand, int myHand) {

    // Rock = 1
    // Paper = 2
    // Scissors = 3

    // Hand combinations:
    // 1,1; 2,2; 3,3 => Draw
    // 1,2 => sum = 3 => Paper
    // 1,3 => sum = 4 => Rock
    // 2,3 => sum = 5 => Scissors
    //
    switch ((yourHand == myHand) ? 0 : (yourHand + myHand)) {
        case 0:
            System.out.println("Draw!");
            break;
        case 3:
            System.out.print("Paper beats Rock. ");
            printWinner(yourHand, 2);
            break;
        case 4:
            System.out.print("Rock beats Scissors. ");
            printWinner(yourHand, 1);
            break;
        case 5:
            System.out.print("Scissors beats Paper. ");
            printWinner(yourHand, 3);
            break;
        default:
            System.out.print("You cheated! ");
            printWinner(yourHand, myHand);
    }
}

private static void printWinner(int yourHand, int winningHand) {
    if (yourHand == winningHand) {
        System.out.println("You win!");
    }
    else {
        System.out.println("I win!");
    }
}

public static void main(String[] args) {
```

```
        Scanner input = new Scanner(System.in);
        System.out.println("Let's Play Rock, Paper, Scissors");
        System.out.println("  Enter 1 (Rock)");
        System.out.println("  Enter 2 (Paper)");
        System.out.println("  Enter 3 (Scissors)");
        System.out.print("> ");

        int playerHand = input.hasNextInt() ? input.nextInt() : -99;
        int computerHand = (int)(3*Math.random()) + 1;

        System.out.print("Your hand: (" + playerHand + ") ");
        getHand(playerHand);
        System.out.print("My hand: (" + computerHand + ") ");
        getHand(computerHand);
        playHands(playerHand, computerHand);
    }
}
```

Java 7 added the capability to switch on Strings. The SwitchTypeChecker class demonstrates the use of a String as the switch expression type. The isValidSwitchType() method takes a Class object and determines whether the corresponding type is a valid type that can be used in a switch expression. So, SwitchTypeChecker is using a switch statement to simultaneously demonstrate switching on Strings and to show the valid types for use in a switch expression:

```
// See SwitchTypeChecker.java
public class SwitchTypeChecker {

    public static Class varTypeClass(Object o) { return o.getClass(); };
    public static Class varTypeClass(Enum e) { return e.getClass().getSuperclass(); };
    public static Class varTypeClass(char c) { return char.class; };
    public static Class varTypeClass(byte b) { return byte.class; };
    public static Class varTypeClass(short s) { return short.class; };
    public static Class varTypeClass(int i) { return int.class; };
    public static Class varTypeClass(long l) { return long.class; };
    public static Class varTypeClass(float f) { return float.class; };
    public static Class varTypeClass(double d) { return double.class; };
    public static Class varTypeClass(boolean d) { return boolean.class; };

    public void isValidSwitchType(Class typeClass) {
        String switchType = typeClass.getSimpleName();
        boolean valid = true;
        switch (switchType) {
            case "char":
            case "byte":
            case "short":
            case "int":
```

```
                    System.out.print("Primitive type " + switchType);
                    break;
            case "Character":
            case "Byte":
            case "Short":
            case "Integer":
                    System.out.print("Boxed primitive type " + switchType);
                    break;
            case "String":
            case "Enum":
                    System.out.print(switchType);
                    break;
            default:  // invalid switch type
                    System.out.print(switchType);
                    valid = false;
        }
        System.out.println(" is " + (valid ? "" : "not ") + "a valid switch type.");
    }

    public static void main(String[] args) {
        SwitchTypeChecker check = new SwitchTypeChecker();
        check.isValidSwitchType(varTypeClass('7'));
        check.isValidSwitchType(varTypeClass(7));
        check.isValidSwitchType(varTypeClass(777.7d));
        check.isValidSwitchType(varTypeClass((short)7));
        check.isValidSwitchType(varTypeClass(new Integer(7)));
        check.isValidSwitchType(varTypeClass("Java 7 Rocks!"));
        check.isValidSwitchType(varTypeClass(new Long(7)));
        check.isValidSwitchType(varTypeClass(true));
        check.isValidSwitchType(varTypeClass(java.nio.file.AccessMode.READ));
    }
}
```

How It Works

The switch statement is a control flow statement that allows you to execute different blocks of code based on the value of a switch expression. It is similar to the if-then-else statement, except that the switch statement can only have a single test expression, and the expression type is restricted to one of several different types. When a switch statement executes, it evaluates the expression against constants contained in the switch statement's case labels. These case labels are branch points in the code. If the value of the expression equals the value of a case label constant, control is transferred to the section of code that corresponds to the matching case label. All code statements from that point on are then executed until either the end of the switch statement is reached or a break statement is reached. The break statement causes the switch statement to terminate, with control being transferred to the statement following the `switch` statement. Optionally, the `switch` statement can contain a default label, which provides a branch point for the case when there is no `case` label constant that equates to the `switch` expression value.

The `SwitchTypeChecker isValidSwitchType()` method demonstrates the use of a `String` as the `switch` test expression. If you study closely the `isValidSwitchType()` method, you will see that it is testing whether a `Class` object represents a type that corresponds to one of the valid `switch` expression types. The method also demonstrates how `case` labels can be grouped to implement a logical OR conditional test. If a `case` label does not have any associated code to execute, and no `break` statement, the flow of execution falls through to the next closest `case` label containing executable statements, thus allowing common code to be executed if the result of the `switch` expression matches any one of the grouped `case` constants.

The `RockPaperScissors` class implements a command-line Rock-Paper-Scissors game, where you are playing against the computer. There are two methods in this class that demonstrate the `switch` statement. The `getHand()` method shows the use of an `enum` variable in the `switch` expression. The `playHands()` method simply intends to show that the `switch` expression, although often just a variable, can be any expression whose result is of one of the allowed `switch` types. In this case, the expression is using a ternary operator that returns an `int` value.

4-4. Working with Fix-Sized Arrays

Problem

You need a simple data structure that can store a fixed (and possibly large) amount of same-typed data and provide for fast sequential access.

Solution

Consider using an array. While Java provides more sophisticated and flexible `Collection` types, the array type can be useful data structure for some types of applications. The following example demonstrates the simplicity of working with arrays. The `GradeAnalyzer` class provides a means for calculating various grade-related statistics, such as the mean (average) grade, minimum grade, and maximum grade.

```
// See GradeAnalyzer.java
public class GradeAnalyzer {

    // The internal grades array
    private int[] _grades;

    public void setGrades(int[] grades) {
        this._grades = grades;
    }
```

```java
// Return cloned grades so the caller cannot modify our internal grades
public int[] getGrades() {
    return _grades != null ? _grades.clone() : null;
}

public int meanGrade() {
    int mean = 0;
    if (_grades != null&& _grades.length > 0) {
        int sum = 0;
        for (int i = 0; i < _grades.length; i++) {
            sum += _grades[i];
        }
        mean = sum / _grades.length;
    }
    return mean;
}

public void sort() {
    Arrays.sort(_grades);
}

public int minGrade() {
    int min = 0;
    if (_grades != null && _grades.length > 0) {
        sort();
        min = _grades[0];
    }
    return min;
}

public int maxGrade() {
    int max = 0;
    if (_grades != null && _grades.length > 0) {
        sort();
        max = _grades[_grades.length - 1];
    }
    return max;
}

static int[] initGrades1() {
    int[] grades = new int[5];
    grades[0] = 77;
    grades[1] = 48;
    grades[2] = 69;
```

```java
        grades[3] = 92;
        grades[4] = 87;
        return grades;
    }

    static int[] initGrades2() {
        int[] grades = { 57, 88, 67, 95, 99, 74, 81 };
        return grades;
    }

    static int[] initGrades3() {
        return new int[]{ 100, 70, 55, 89, 97, 98, 82 };
    }

    public static void main(String... args) {

        GradeAnalyzer ga = new GradeAnalyzer();
        ga.setGrades(initGrades1());
        System.out.println("Grades 1:");
        System.out.println("Mean of all grades is " + ga.meanGrade());
        System.out.println("Min grade is " + ga.minGrade());
        System.out.println("Max grade is " + ga.maxGrade());
        ga.setGrades(initGrades2());
        System.out.println("Grades 2:");
        System.out.println("Mean of all grades is " + ga.meanGrade());
        System.out.println("Min grade is " + ga.minGrade());
        System.out.println("Max grade is " + ga.maxGrade());
        ga.setGrades(initGrades3());
        System.out.println("Grades 3:");
        System.out.println("Mean of all grades is " + ga.meanGrade());
        System.out.println("Min grade is " + ga.minGrade());
        System.out.println("Max grade is " + ga.maxGrade());

        Object testArray = ga.getGrades();
        Class testClass = testArray.getClass();
        System.out.println("isArray: " + testClass.isArray());
        System.out.println("getClass: " + testClass.getName());
        System.out.println("getSuperclass: " + testClass.getSuperclass().getName());
        System.out.println("getComponentType: " + testClass.getComponentType());
        System.out.println("Arrays.toString: " + Arrays.toString((int[])testArray));

    }
}
```

Running this code will result in the following output:

```
Grades 1:
Mean of all grades is 74
Min grade is 48
Max grade is 92
Grades 2:
Mean of all grades is 80
Min grade is 57
Max grade is 99
Grades 3:
Mean of all grades is 84
Min grade is 55
Max grade is 100
isArray: true
getClass: [I
getSuperclass: class java.lang.Object
getComponentType: int
Arrays.toString: [55, 70, 82, 89, 97, 98, 100]
```

How It Works

The Java array type is often dismissed for its insuperiority to Java's more sophisticated `ArrayList` (part of the Java Collections Framework). Often this criticism comes from the inflexibility of the array type. Java arrays hold a fixed amount of data. That is, when an array is created, you must tell it how much data it can hold. Once an array has been created, you cannot insert or remove array items, or otherwise change the size of the array. However, if you have a fixed amount (and especially a very large amount) of data that you just need to work on while iterating over it sequentially, an array may be a good choice.

The first thing you need to know about the Java array type is that it is an `Object` type. All arrays, regardless of the type of data they hold, have `Object` as their superclass. The elements of an array may be of any type, as long as all elements are of the same type—either primitive or object reference. Regardless of the array type, the memory for an array is always allocated out of the heap space for the application. The heap is the area of memory used by the JVM for dynamic memory allocation.

■ **Note** It is possible to create an array of `Objects` (`Object[]`) that can hold references to objects of different types, however, this is not recommended as it requires you to check the type of elements and perform explicit type casting when retrieving elements from the array.

There are two steps to completely defining an array object in Java: array variable declaration, which specifies the array element type, and array creation, which allocates the memory for the array. Once an array is declared and the memory allocated, it can be initialized. There are multiple ways to initialize an array, which are shown in the solution code. If you know in advance what data you need to store in the array, you can combine array declaration, creation, and initialization in one step using a shortcut syntax you will see demonstrated in the solution code.

Let's walk through the `GradeAnalyzer` class and examine the various ways to declare, create, initialize, and access arrays. First, notice that our class has one instance variable to hold the grades to be analyzed:

```
private int[] _grades;
```

Like all other uninitialized `Object` reference instance variables, the `_grades` array instance variable is automatically initialized to `null`. Before we can start analyzing grades, we have to set the `_grades` instance variable to reference the grades data we want to analyze. This is done using the `setGrades(int[])` method. Once `GradeAnalyzer` has a collection of grades to analyze, the `meanGrade()`, `minGrade()`, and `maxGrade()` methods can be called to compute their respective statistics. Together, these three methods demonstrate how to iterate over the elements of an array, how to access elements of an array, and how to determine the number of elements an array can hold. To determine the number of elements an array can hold, simply access the implicitly defined, final instance variable, `length`, which is defined for all arrays:

```
_grades.length
```

To iterate over the elements of an array, simply use a `for` loop whose index variable goes through all possible indices of the array. Array indices start at 0, so the last array index is always (`_grades.length` - 1). While iterating over the array, we can access the array element at the current index by using the name of the array variable followed by the current index enclosed in brackets (often called an array subscript):

```
// From the meanGrade() method:
for (int i = 0; i < _grades.length; i++) {
    sum += _grades[i];
}
```

Alternatively, the enhanced `for` loop, also known as the `foreach` loop, could be used to iterate over the array (see recipe 4-7 for more discussion of the foreach loop):

```
for (int grade : _grades) {
    sum += grade;
}
```

Notice that to determine the min and max grade, the grades are first sorted in their natural (ascending) order using the utility `sort` method from the `java.util.Arrays` class. After sorting, the min grade is the simply the first element (at index 0) of the array, and the max grade is the last element (at index length -1) of the array.

The three static class methods, `initGrades1()`, `initGrades2()`, and `initGrades3()`, demonstrate three different ways of creating and initializing the array data we will use to "seed" our `GradeAnalyzer`. The `initGrades1()` method declares and creates an array (using `new`) that can hold five grades, then manually sets the value at each element index to an integer grade value. The `initGrades2()` method combines array creation and initialization in one line using the special array initializer syntax:

```
int[] grades = { 57, 88, 67, 95, 99, 74, 81 };
```

This syntax creates an array with a length of 7 and initializes the elements from index 0 through index 6 with the integer values shown. Note, this syntax can be used only in an array declaration, so the following is not allowed:

```
int[] grades;
grades = { 57, 88, 67, 95, 99, 74, 81 }; // won!t compile
```

The `initGrades3()` method looks very similar to `initGrades3()`, but is slightly different. Here we are creating and returning an anonymous (unnamed) array:

```
return new int[]{ 100, 70, 55, 89, 97, 98, 82 };
```

With this syntax, you use the `new` keyword with the array element type, but the size of the array is not explicitly specified. Similar to the array initializer syntax shown in the `initGrades2()` method, the array size is implied by the number of elements given within the initializer brackets. So, again, this code is creating and returning an array with a length of 7.

After computing the grade statistics for the three sets of grades data, the remainder of the `GradeAnalyzer main()` method demonstrates various methods that can be used to determine array type information and to convert an array to a printable string. You see that we first assign the array returned from a call to the `getGrades()` instance method to an `Object` variable, `testArray`:

```
Object testArray = ga.getGrades();
```

We can make this assignment because, as stated previously, an array is an `Object`. You can also see this by the result from the call to `testArray.getSuperclass()`. The call to `testArray.getClass().getName()` is also interesting; it returns `[I`. The left bracket says "I am an array type", and the "I" says "with a component type of integer". This is also backed up by the result from the call to `testArray.getComponentType()`. Finally, we call the `Arrays.toString(int[])` method, which returns a nicely formatted string representation of the array and its contents. Notice that because `testArray` is an `Object` reference, it must be cast to an `int` array for the `Arrays.toString(int[])` method. (See the Java documentation for the `java.util.Arrays` class for other useful utility methods that can be used with arrays.)

As you have seen, arrays are simple and easy to work with. There will be times when this simplicity works to your advantage. In recipe 4-6 we'll show an alternative to the array type that provides for easy insertion and removal of elements: the `ArrayList` collection class.

4-5. Using Generic Types

Problem

You are a new Java developer and you need to come up to speed quickly on on generics, or you are an experienced Java developer and you want to learn about a new Java 7 feature that will make your generics programming easier.

Solution

You'll likely first encounter generic types when using the interfaces and classes that are part of the Java Collections Framework (http://download.oracle.com/javase/tutorial/collections/). The Collections Framework makes heavy use of Java generics. All collection types are parameterized to allow you to specify, at the time of instantiation, the type of elements the collection can hold. The example code in this recipe will be less of a "recipe" and more of a demonstration of the need-to-know topics of generics that will get you up to speed quickly. The examples will demonstrate the use of generics with Java collections versus showing you how to create generic types. Unless you are developing a library API, you probably won't be creating your own generic types. However, if you understand how generics are used with the Collection interfaces and classes, you will have the knowledge you need to create your own generic types. The source code for this recipe is contained in GenericsDemo.java.

■ **Note** When we talk generally about a *collection* or a *collection type*, you can read this as those types that make up the Java Collections Framework. This includes all the classes and interfaces that descend from the Collection and Map interfaces. Collection types generally refer to types that descend from the Collection interface.

How It Works

The first thing to understand and remember about Java generics is that they are strictly a compile-time feature that aids the developer in creating more type-safe code. All the type information that you specify when you parameterize a generic type gets "erased" by the compiler when the code is compiled down to byte code. You'll see this described as *type erasure*. Let's look at an example of a generic Collection type: the List. List is an interface defined as follows:

```
public interface List<E> extends Collection<E> { ... };
```

To specify the element type for a List (or any Collection type), simply include the type name in angle brackets when declaring and instantiating objects. When you do this, you are specifying a "parameterized type". The following code declares List of Integers. A variable, aList, of the parameterized type List<Integer> is declared and then initialized with the reference obtained from the instantiation of the parameterized type, LinkedList<Integer> (also called a "concrete parameterized type"):

```
List<Integer> aList = new LinkedList<Integer>();
```

Now that we've parameterized these types to restrict the element type to Integers, the List add(E e) method becomes:

```
boolean add(Integer e);
```

If we try to add anything other than an Integer to aList, the compiler will generate an error:

```
aList.add(new Integer(121));
aList.add(42);    // 42 is the same as new Integer(42), due to autoboxing.
aList.add("Java");  // won!t compile, wrong type
```

It's important to note that it's the reference type that is checked at compile time, so the following will also result in a compiler error:

```
Number aNum = new Integer("7");
aList.add(aNum);  // won!t compile, wrong type
```

This is a compile error because aNum could reference any Number object. If the compiler were to allow this, we could end up with a set that contains Doubles, Floats, and so on, which would violate the Integer parameter constraint we specified when we created aList. Of course, a simple type cast could get you around the compiler error, but this would surely cause unintended consequences when casting between incompatible Number objects. Generics were designed to reduce the amount of explicit type casting you have to do in your code, so if you find yourself using explicit type casting when using methods of parameterized types, this is a clue of potentially dangerous code.

```
aList.add((Integer)aNum);  // compiles, but don!t do this.
```

Another thing to watch out for when using generic types is compiler warnings. They may indicate that you're doing something that is not recommended and it usually indicates that your code has a potential runtime error looming. An example can help to illustrate this. The following code will compile but produce two compiler warnings:

```
List rawList = new LinkedList();
aList = rawList;
```

First, we're creating `rawList`, which is a *raw type*, a generic type that isn't parameterized. When generics were introduced into the language, the language designers decided that in order to maintain compatibility with pregenerics code, they would need to allow the use of raw types. However, the use of raw types is strongly discouraged for new (post–Java 5) code, so compilers will generate a raw type warning if you use them. Next, `rawList` is assigned to `aList`, which was created using parameterized types. Again, this is allowed by the compiler (due to generics type erasure and backward compatibility), but an unchecked conversion warning is generated for the assignment to flag potential runtime type incompatibility. Imagine if `rawList` contained `Strings`. Later, if you later tried to retrieve `Integer` elements from `aList`, you would get a runtime error.

Regarding type compatibility, it doesn't apply to generic type parameters. For example, the following is not a valid assignment:

```
List<Number> bList = new LinkedList<Integer>();  // won!t compile; incompatible types
```

Although `Integers` are `Numbers` (`Integer` is a subtype of `Number`), and `LinkedList` is a subtype of `List`, `LinkedList<Integer>` is not a subtype of `List<Number>`. Fortunately, this won't slip by you if you accidentally write code like this; the compiler will generate an "incompatible types" warning.

So you may be wondering whether there is a way to achieve a variant subtyping relationship similar to what we tried to do in the previous line of code. The answer is yes, by using a feature of generics called the *wildcard*. A wildcard is denoted by use of a question mark (?) within the type parameter angle brackets. Wildcards are used to declare parameterized types that are either bounded or unbounded. The following is an example declaration of a bounded parameterized type:

```
List<? extends Number> cList;
```

When a wildcard is used with the `extends` keyword, an upper bound is established for the type parameter. In this example, `? extends Number` means any type that is either a `Number` or a subtype of a `Number`. Therefore, the following would be valid assignments because both `Integer` and `Double` are subtypes of `Number`:

```
cList = new LinkedList<Number>();
cList = new LinkedList<Integer>();
cList = new LinkedList<Double>();
```

So, `cList` can hold a reference to any `List` instance that has an element type that is compatible with `Number`. In fact, `cList` could even reference a raw type. Obviously, this makes it a challenge for the compiler to enforce type safety if it were to allow elements to be added to `cList`. Therefore, the compiler does not allow elements (other than a `null`) to be added to a collection type that is parameterized with `?` `extends`. The following would result in a compiler error:

```
cList.add(new Integer(5));  // add() not allowed; cList could be LinkedList<Double>
```

However, you are allowed to get an element from the list without any problem:

```
Number cNum = cList.get(0);
```

The only restriction here is that the reference we get from the list has to be treated like a `Number`. Remember, `cList` could be pointing to a list of `Integers`, a list of `Doubles`, or list of any other subtype of `Number`.

A wildcard can also be used with the `super` keyword. In this case, a lower bound is established for the type parameter:

```
List<? super Integer> dList;
```

In this example, `? super Integer` means any type that is either an `Integer` or any supertype of `Integer`. Therefore, the following would be valid assignments because `Number` and `Object` are the only supertypes of `Integer`:

```
dList = new LinkedList<Integer>();
dList = new LinkedList<Number>();
dList = new LinkedList<Object>();
```

So, you see that `Integer` is the lower bound. This lower bound now places a restriction on retrieving elements from the list. Because `dList`can hold a reference to any one of the above parameterized types, the compiler would not be able to enforce type safety if an assumption were made about the type of the element being retrieved. Therefore, the compiler must not allow calls to `get()`on a collection type that is parameterized with `? super`, and the following would result in a compiler error:

```
Integer n = dList.get(0);  // get() not allowed; dList.get(0) could be a Number or Object
```

However, now we can add elements to the list, but the lower bound, `Integer`, still applies. Only `Integers` can be added because `Integer` is compatible with `Number` and `Object`:

```
dList.add(new Integer(5));  // OK
Number dNum = new Double(7);
dList.add(dNum);  // won!t compile; dList could be LinkedList<Integer>
```

You will see the use of the wildcard with both `extends` and `super` throughout the collection types. Most often, you will see them used in method parameter types, such as the `addAll()` method, which is defined for all `Collections`. Sometimes you will see the collection types using the wildcard (?) alone as a type parameter, which is called an *unbounded wildcard*. The `Collection removeAll()` method is such an example. In most cases, this usage is self-explanatory. You probably won't be (probably shouldn't be) defining your own parameterized types using an unbounded wildcard. If you try to do this, you will soon learn there isn't much you can do with it. If you understand concrete parameterized types, wildcard parameterized types, and the concept of bounded and unbouned types, as described in this recipe, you have most of what you need to work with the generic collection types, and create your own generic types if you so chose.

Now that we've talked a lot about parameterizing types, we're going to tell you to forget about some of it. With the Java 7 release, there is a nice little new feature called the *diamond* (sometimes seen referred to as the *diamond operator*, although it is not considered to be an operator in Java). The diamond allows the compiler to infer the type argument(s) from the context of the parameterized type usage. A simple example of the diamond usage follows:

```
List<Integer> eList = new ArrayList<>();
```

Notice there is no type argument specified between the angle brackets when instantiating the `ArrayList`. The compiler can easily infer the type to be `Integer`, based on the context of the assignment or initializer. `Integer` is the only type that would work in this context. In fact, the Java 7 compiler (and a Java 7–compliant IDE) will actually warn you if you do not use a diamond where it is possible to use it. Another more complex example shows the benefit even better:

```
Map<Integer, List<String>> aMap = new HashMap<>();  // Nice!
```

The diamond can similarly be used in `return` statements, as well as in method arguments:

```
// diamond in method return
public static List<String> getEmptyList() {
    return new ArrayList<>();
}

// diamond in method argument
List<List<String>> gList = new ArrayList<>();
gList.set(0, new ArrayList<>(Arrays.asList("a", "b")));
```

Note that using the diamond as shown here is not the same as using a raw type. The following is not equivalent to the declaration of `aMap` that uses the diamond; it will result in an "unchecked conversion" warning, and possibly a raw type warning, from the compiler:

```
Map<Integer, List<String>> bMap = new HashMap();   // compiler warnings; avoid raw types
```

The discussion around why this is different than the diamond example is beyond the scope of this recipe. If you remember to avoid the use of raw types, you shouldn't need to worry about this. Use the diamond whenever possible to save yourself some typing, as well as to make your code more robust, readable, and concise.

4-6. Working with Dynamic Arrays

Problem

You need a flexible data structure that can store a variable amount of data and that allows for easy insertion and deletion of data.

Solution

Consider using an ArrayList. The example code for this recipe is the StockScreener class that allows you to screen a list of stocks or a single stock based on a specific screen parameter (P/E, Yield, and Beta) and screen value. An example screen might be "Tell me which of the stocks in this list has a P/E (price-to-earnings ratio) of 15 or less." Don't worry if you're not familiar with these stock market terms. Whatever you do, don't use this class to make your stock investment decisions!

```java
// See StockScreener.java
public class StockScreener {

    enum Screen { PE, YIELD, BETA };

    public static boolean screen(String stock, Screen screen, double threshold) {
        double screenVal = 0;
        boolean pass = false;
        switch (screen) {
            case PE:
                screenVal = Math.random() * 25;
                pass = screenVal <= threshold;
                break;
            case YIELD:
                screenVal = Math.random() * 10;
                pass = screenVal >= threshold;
                break;
            case BETA:
                screenVal = Math.random() * 2;
                pass = screenVal <= threshold;
                break;
        }
        System.out.println(stock + ": " + screen.toString() + " = " + screenVal);

        return pass;
    }

    public static void screen(List<String> stocks, Screen screen, double threshold) {
        Iterator<String> iter = stocks.iterator();
        while (iter.hasNext()) {
            String stock = iter.next();
            if (!screen(stock, screen, threshold)) {
                iter.remove();
            }
        }
    }

    public static void main(String[] args) {
```

```
        List<String> stocks = new ArrayList<>();
        stocks.add("ORCL");
        stocks.add("AAPL");
        stocks.add("GOOG");
        stocks.add("IBM");
        stocks.add("MCD");
        System.out.println("Screening stocks: " + stocks);

        if (stocks.contains("GOOG") &&
            !screen("GOOG", Screen.BETA, 1.1)) {
            stocks.remove("GOOG");
        }
        System.out.println("First screen: " + stocks);

        StockScreener.screen(stocks, Screen.YIELD, 3.5);
        System.out.println("Second screen: " + stocks);
        StockScreener.screen(stocks, Screen.PE, 22);
        System.out.println("Third screen: " + stocks);

        System.out.println("Buy List: " + stocks);
    }
}
```

The output from running this code will vary because it is randomly assigning a stock's screen result value. Here is one sample of output from running the class:

```
Screening stocks: [ORCL, AAPL, GOOG, IBM, MCD]
GOOG: BETA = 1.9545048754918146
First screen: [ORCL, AAPL, IBM, MCD]
ORCL: YIELD = 5.54002319921808
AAPL: YIELD = 5.282200818124754
IBM: YIELD = 3.189521157557543
MCD: YIELD = 3.978628208965815
Second screen: [ORCL, AAPL, MCD]
ORCL: PE = 3.5561302619951993
AAPL: PE = 13.578302484429233
MCD: PE = 23.504349376296886
Third screen: [ORCL, AAPL]
Buy List: [ORCL, AAPL]
```

How It Works

The ArrayList is one of the most often used classes in the Java Collections Framework. The ArrayList class implements the List interface, which, in turn, implements the Collection interface. The Collection interface defines the set of common operations for all Collection types, and the List interface defines the set of operations that are specific to the list-oriented `Collection` types. The Collections Framework makes heavy use of Java generics. If you are new to generics, it is recommended that you read recipe 4-5, which gives a brief summary of generics and their use with collections.

The `StockScreener main()` method starts by declaring a `List` of stocks, and specifying with the generic type parameter, that the stocks list elements will be of type `String`. Notice that the actual list type is an `ArrayList` that is created using the new Java 7 feature, the diamond, which is discussed in recipe 4-5. The stocks list will hold a variable number of stocks, represented by their stock market symbol (a `String`):

```
List<String> stocks = new ArrayList<>();
```

Now that we've specified that our stocks list can only hold `Strings`, all the `List` methods, in turn, get parameterized to only allow `Strings`. So, next, the code makes several calls to the `ArrayList`'s `add(String)` method to add our stocks to the list. After that, a screen is run on GOOG (Google) based on its Beta (a measure of stock risk); if it does not pass the screen, the `List remove(String)` method is called to remove the stock from the stock list. Two more screens are then run on the entire stock list to get a list of stocks that have a P/E of 22.0 or less, and a Yield of 3.5% or more. The `screen()` method used for these screens takes a parameter of type `List<String>`. It has to iterate over the list, run the screen for each stock in the list, and remove those stocks that do not pass the screen. Note that in order to safely remove an element from a `Collection` while iterating over it, you must use iterate using the `Collection`'s `Iterator`, which can be obtained by calling its `iterator()` method. Here, we are showing the use of a `while` loop to iterate over the stocks list (a `for` loop could similarly be used). As long as we're not to the end of the list (`iter.hasNext()`), we can get the next stock from the list (`iter.next()`), run the screen, and remove the element from the list (`iter.remove()`) if the screen didn't pass.

■ **Note**   You may find that calling the list's `remove()` method while iterating the list seems to work. The problem is that it's not guaranteed to work and will produce unexpected results. At some point, the code will also throw a `ConcurrentModificationException`, regardless of whether you have multiple threads accessing the same list. Remember to always remove elements through the iterator when iterating over any `Collection`.

The `ArrayList` is a very useful data structure that should normally be used in place of the array type. It provides much more flexibility than a simple array, in that elements can be added and removed dynamically with ease. While it is true that `ArrayList` uses an array internally, you benefit from optimized `add()` and `remove()` operations that are implemented for you. Also, `ArrayList` implements many other very useful methods. Refer to the online Java documentation for further details (http://download.oracle.com/javase/7/docs/api/java/util/ArrayList.html).

4-7. Making Your Objects Iterable

Problem

You have created a custom collection–based class that wraps (instead of extends) the underlying collection type. Without exposing the internal implementation details of your class, you would like objects of your class to be iterable, especially with the use of a foreach statement.

Solution

Have your class extend the Interable<T> interface, where T is the element type of the collection to be iterated. Implement the iterator() method to return the Iterator<T> object from this collection. The example for this recipe is the StockPortfolio class. Internally, StockPortfolio manages a collection of Stock objects. We would like users of our class to be able to treat StockPortfolio objects as iterable objects using a foreach statement. The StockPortfolio class follows:

```java
// See StockPortfolio.java and Stock.java
public class StockPortfolio implements Iterable<Stock> {

    Map<String, Stock> portfolio = new HashMap<>();

    public void add(Stock stock) {
        portfolio.put(stock.getSymbol(), stock);
    }

    public void add(List<Stock> stocks) {
        for (Stock s : stocks) {
            portfolio.put(s.getSymbol(), s);
        }
    }

    @Override
    public Iterator<Stock> iterator() {
        return portfolio.values().iterator();
    }

    public static void main(String[] args) {

        StockPortfolio myPortfolio = new StockPortfolio();
        myPortfolio.add(new Stock("ORCL", "Oracle", 500.0));
        myPortfolio.add(new Stock("AAPL", "Apple", 200.0));
        myPortfolio.add(new Stock("GOOG", "Google", 100.0));
```

```
        myPortfolio.add(new Stock("IBM", "IBM", 50.0));
        myPortfolio.add(new Stock("MCD", "McDonalds", 300.0));

        // foreach loop (uses Iterator returned from iterator() method)
        for (Stock stock : myPortfolio) {
            System.out.println(stock);
        }
    }
}
```

The main() method creates a StockPortfolio and then calls the add() method to add a number of Stocks to the portfolio. A foreach loop is then used to loop over and print all the stocks in the portfolio. Running the StockPortfolio class results in the following output:

```
50.0 shares of IBM (IBM)
300.0 shares of MCD (McDonalds)
100.0 shares of GOOG (Google)
200.0 shares of AAPL (Apple)
500.0 shares of ORCL (Oracle)
```

■ **Note**   The order of the lines in the output may be different when you run the StockPortfolio class in your environment because the underlying implementation uses a HashMap. A HashMap does not guarantee the order of the elements stored in the map, and this extends to its iterators. If we wanted our iterator to return elements sorted by the stock symbol, we could use one of the sorted collections, such as TreeMap or TreeSet, instead of HashMap.

How It Works

The Iterable interface was introduced in Java 5 to support the enhanced for loop (also known as the foreach loop) which was introduced at the same time. Along with these enhancements to the language, all Collection classes were retrofitted to implement the Iterable interface, thus allowing Collection classes to be iterable using the foreach loop. The Iterable interface is a generic type defined as follows:

```
public interface Iterable<T> {
    Iterator<T> iterator();
}
```

Any class that implements Iterable<T> must implement the iterator() method to return an Iterator<T> object. Typically, the Iteratorreturned is the default iterator of the underlying collection, however, it may also return an instance of a custom Iterator. In the StockPortfolio class, a Map is used to represent thestock portfolio. The key for each map entry is the stock symbol, and the value associated with each key is a Stock object. Maps in Java are not iterable; that is, they are not Collection classes, therefore, they do not implement Iterable. However, both the keys and the values of a map are Collections, and therefore are Iterables. We want our implementation of the Iterable iterator()method to return an Iterator over the values (Stock references) of the portfolio map; therefore, our Iterable implementation is parameterized by the Stock type:

```
public class StockPortfolio implements Iterable<Stock>
```

The Map values() method returns the Collection of map values; in this case, a Collection of Stocks. Our iterator() method implementation can then simply return the Iterator for this Collection:

```
@Override
public Iterator<Stock> iterator() {
    return portfolio.values().iterator();
}
```

With this implementation of Iterable<Stock>, a foreach loop can be used to iterate a StockPortfolio instance and print each Stock:

```
for (Stock s : portfolio) {
    System.out.println(s);
}
```

You will notice that StockPortfolio also contains the add(List<Stock>) method, which allows the portfolio to be populated from a List. This method also uses a foreach loop to iterate through the input List. Again, this is possible because Lists are Iterables. (Note that this method is never called in the code; it exists only for illustration purposes.)

■ **Note** There's one issue with our implementation of StockPortfolio. We have gone to great lengths to not expose the internal implementation details of our class (the portfolio map). This allows us to change the implementation without affecting StockPortfolio client code. However, when we implemented Iterable, we effectively exported the underlying portfolio map through the iterator() method. As was demonstrated in recipe 4-5, an Iterator allows the underlying collection to be modified by calling its remove() method. Unfortunately, Java does not provide an UnmodifiableIterator class that could be used to wrap an Iterator and prevent modification of the underlying Collection. However, it would be simple to implement such a class that forwards the hasNext() and next() calls to the wrapped Iterator, but leaves the remove() method unimplemented (per the Iterator Java documentation, UnsupportedOperationException should be thrown). Alternatively, your iterator() method could return the Iterator from an unmodifiableCollection obtained through a call to the Collections.unmodifiableCollection() class method. You are encouraged to explore these two options. To give you a start, one possible implementation of UnmodifiableIterator has been provided in the source code download (see UnmodifiableIterator.java).

As we have seen in this recipe, the Iterable interface allows you to create iterable objects that are compatible with the foreach loop. This is very useful when you wish to design a custom collection-based class that encapsulates implementation details. Just keep in mind that in order to enforce the encapsulation and prevent modification of your underlying collection, you should implement one of the solutions mentioned in the preceding note.

4-8. Iterating Over a Map

Problem

You are using one of the Map classes, such as HashMap or TreeMap, and you need to iterate over the keys, values, or both. You may also want to remove elements from the map while you are iterating over it.

Solution

There are multiple ways to iterate over a Map. The method you chose should depend on what portions of the map you need to access and whether you need to remove elements from the map while iterating. The StockPortfolio1 class is a continuation of the StockPorfolio class shown in the previous recipe. It adds three methods, summary(), alertList(), and remove(List<String>), that demonstrate alternative methods for iterating over the portfolio map:

```java
// See StockPortfolio1.java
public void summary() {
    for (Map.Entry<String, Stock> entry : portfolio.entrySet()) {
        System.out.println("Stock = " + entry.getKey() + ",
                        Shares = " + entry.getValue().getShares());
    }
}

public List<Stock> alertList() {
    List<Stock> alertList = new ArrayList<>();
    for (Stock stock : portfolio.values()) {
        if (!StockScreener.screen(stock.getSymbol(), StockScreener.Screen.PE, 20)) {
            alertList.add(stock);
        }
    }
    return alertList;
}

public void remove(List<String> sellList) {
    Iterator<String> keyIter = portfolio.keySet().iterator();
    while (keyIter.hasNext()) {
```

```
        if (sellList.contains(keyIter.next())) {
            keyIter.remove();
        }
    }
}
```

How It Works

The `summary()` method uses a `foreach` loop to iterate over the portfolio map's `Entry` set. The `Map` `entrySet()` method returns a `Set` of `Map.Entry` objects. Within the loop, you then have access to the key and value for the current `Map.Entry` by calling the respective methods, `key()` and `value()`, on that entry. Use this method of iterating when you need to access both the map keys and values while iterating, and you don't need to remove elements from the map.

The `alertList()` method uses a `foreach` loop to iterate over just the values of the portfolio map. The `Map` `values()` method returns a `Collection` of the map values; in this case, a `Collection` of `Stocks`. Use this method of iterating when you only need access to the map values and you don't need to remove elements from the list. Similarly, if you only need access to the map keys (again, without the need to remove elements), you can iterate using the `keySet()` method:

```
for (String symbol : portfolio.keySet()) {
    ...
}
```

If you also need to also access the map value while iterating using the key set, avoid the following, as it is very inefficient:

```
for (String symbol : portfolio.keySet()) {
    Stock stock = portfolio.get(symbol);
    ...
}
```

Instead, use the method of iteration shown in the `summary()` method.

The `remove(List<String>)` method takes a list of stock symbols representing the stocks to be removed from the portfolio. This method iterates over the portfolio map keys using the `keySet()` iterator, removing the current map entry if it is one of the stocks specified for removal. Notice that the map element is removed through the iterator's `remove()` method. This is possible because the key set is backed by the map, so changes made through the key set's iterator are reflected in the map. You could also iterate over the portfolio map using its `values()` iterator:

```
Iterator<Stock> valueIter = portfolio.values().iterator();
while (valueIter.hasNext()) {
    if (sellList.contains(valueIter.next().getSymbol())) {
        valueIter.remove();
    }
}
```

As with the key set, the values collection is backed by the map, so calling `remove()` through the values iterator will result in removal of the current entry from the portfolio map.

In summary, if you need to remove elements from a map while iterating over the map, iterate using one of the map's collection iterators, and remove map elements through the iterator, as shown in the `remove(List<String>)` method. This is the only safe way to remove map elements during iteration. Otherwise, if you don't need to remove map elements, prefer the use of a `foreach` loop and use one of the methods of iteration shown in the `alertList()` or `summary()` methods.

CHAPTER 5

Input and Output

On enterprise applications, there is always the need of obtaining and manipulating the I/O terminals. In today's operating systems, that usually means file access and network connectivity. Java has been slow to adopt good file and network framework because when standing true to its roots of write once, read everywhere, a lot of the original file I/O and network connectivity needed to be simple and universal. If any Java developer wanted to get features like folder monitoring or scalable sockets, she would usually go out and create (or use) native code, but since Java 7, the wait is over!

With Java 7, file and network I/O has evolved into a much better framework for handling files, network scalability, and ease of use. By creating the network input output version 2 API (NIO.2), Java now has the capability of monitoring folders, accessing OS-dependent methods, and create scalable asynchronous network sockets. This is in addition to the already robust library for handling input and output streams, and serializing (and deserializing) object information.

STREAMS AND THE DECORATOR PATTERN

I/O streams are the foundation of most of the Java I/O and include a plethora of ready-made streams for any occasion, but it is very confusing on how to use them if some context is not provided. A stream (like a river) represents an inflow/outflow of data. Think about it this way. When you type, you create a stream of characters that the system receives (input stream). When the system produces sounds, it sends them to the speaker (output stream). The system could be receiving keystrokes and sending sound all day long, and thus the streams can be either processing data or waiting for more data.

When a stream doesn't receive any data, it waits (nothing else to do, right?). As soon as data comes in, the stream starts processing this data. The stream then stops and waits for the next data item to come. This keeps going until our proverbial river becomes dry (the stream is closed).

Like a river, streams can be connected to each other (this is the decorator pattern). For the content of this chapter, there are mainly two input streams that we care about. One of them is the file input stream, and the other is the network socket input stream. These two streams are a source of data for our I/O programs. There are also their corresponding output streams: file output stream and the network socket output streams (how creative isn't it?). Like a plumber, we can hook them together and create something new. For example, we could weld together a file input stream to a network output stream to (for example) send the contents of the file through a network socket. Or we could do the opposite and connect a network input stream (data coming in), to a file output stream (data being written to disk). In I/O parlance, the input streams are called *sources*, while the output streams are called *sinks*.

There are other input and output streams that can be glued together. For example, there is a BufferedInputStream, which allows you to read the data in chunks (it's more efficient than reading it byte by byte), and the DataOutputStream allows you to write Java primitives to an output stream (instead of just writing bytes). One of the most useful streams is the ObjectInputStream and ObjectOutputStream, which will allow you to serialize/deserialize object (there is a recipe for that here).

The decorator pattern allows you to keep plucking streams together to get many different effects. The beauty of this design is that you can actually create a stream that will take any input and produce any output, and then can be thrown together with every other stream.

5-1. Serializing Java Objects

Problem

You need to serialize a class (save the contents of the class) so that you can restore it at a later time.

Solution

Java implements a built-in serialization mechanism. You access that mechanism via the ObjectOutputStream class. Look in the following example, in the section **saveSettings**. There you will see ObjectOutputStream being used to serialize the settings object in preparation for writing the object to disk:

```
public class Ch_5_1_SerializeExample {
    public static void main(String[] args) {
        Ch_5_1_SerializeExample example = new Ch_5_1_SerializeExample();
        example.start();
    }

    private void start() {
        ProgramSettings settings = new ProgramSettings( new Point(10,10),  ↵
                                                new Dimension(300,200),  ↵
                                                Color.blue,  ↵
                                                "The title of the application" );
        saveSettings(settings,"settings.bin");
        ProgramSettings loadedSettings = loadSettings("settings.bin");
        System.out.println("Are settings are equal? :"+loadedSettings.equals(settings));


    }

    private void saveSettings(ProgramSettings settings, String filename) {
        try {
            FileOutputStream fos = new FileOutputStream(filename);
```

```
            ObjectOutputStream oos = new ObjectOutputStream(fos);
            oos.writeObject(settings);
            oos.close();
        } catch (IOException e) {
            e.printStackTrace();
        }
    }

    private ProgramSettings loadSettings(String filename) {
        try {
            FileInputStream fis = new FileInputStream(filename);
            ObjectInputStream ois = new ObjectInputStream(fis);
            return (ProgramSettings) ois.readObject();
        } catch (IOException e) {
            e.printStackTrace();
        } catch (ClassNotFoundException e) {
            e.printStackTrace();
        }
        return null;
    }
}
```

How It Works

Java supports *serialization*, which is the capability of taking an object and creating a byte representation that can be used to restore the object at a later time. By using an internal serialization mechanism, most of the setup to serialize objects is taken care of. Java will transform the properties of an object into a byte stream, which can then be saved to a file or transmitted over the wire.

■ **Note** The original Java Serialization framework uses reflection to serialize the objects, so it might be an issue if serializing/deserializing heavily. There are plenty of open source frameworks that offer different trade-offs depending on your need (speed versus size versus ease of use). See https://github.com/eishay/jvm-serializers/wiki/.

For a class to be serializable, it needs to implement the Serializable interface, which is a *Marker interface*: it doesn't have any methods, but instead tells the serialization mechanism that you have allowed the ability of your class to be serialized. While not evident from the onset, serialization exposes all the internal workings of your class (including protected and private members), so if you want to keep secret the authorization code for a nuclear launch, you might want to make the class that contains that information nonserializable.

It is also necessary that all properties (a.k.a. members, variables, or fields) of the class are serializable (and/or transient, which we will get in a minute). All primitives—int, long, double, float (plus their wrapper classes)—and the String class are serializable by design. Other Java classes are serializable on a case-by-case basis. For example, you can't serialize any Swing components (like JButton, JSpinner), and you can't serialize File objects, but you can serialize the Color class (`awt.color`, to be more precise).

As a design principle you don't want to serialize your main classes, but instead you want to create classes that contain only the properties that you want to serialize. It will save a lot of headache in debugging because serialization becomes very pervasive. If you mark a major class as serializable (`implements Serializable`), and this class contains many other properties, you need to declare those classes as serializable as well. If your Java class inherits from another class, the parent class must also be serializable. In that way, you will find marking classes serializable when they really shouldn't be.

A possible solution to not declare a property serializable is to declare it as *transient*. Transient properties tell the Java compiler that you are not interested in saving/loading the property value, so it will be ignored. Some properties are good candidates for being transient, like cached calculations, or a date formatter that you always instantiate to the same value.

By the virtue of the Serialization framework, static properties are not serializable; neither are static classes. The reason is that a static class is supposed to never have any instances at any time. So if we save and then load the static class at the time, we will have loaded another copy of the static class, throwing the JVM for a loop.

The Java serialization mechanism works behind the scenes to convert and traverse every object within the class that you specify to be serialized. If you have objects within objects and you cross-reference objects, the Serialization framework will resolve it and not store two copies of the object—but only one. Each property then gets translated to a `byte[]` representation. The format of the byte array includes the actual class name (for example: com.somewhere.over.the.rainbow.preferences.UserPreferences), followed by the encoding of the properties (which in turn may encode another object class, with its properties, etc., etc., *ad infinitum*).

For the curious, if you look at the file generated (even in a text editor), you can see the class name as almost the first part of the file.

■ **Caution** Serialization is very brittle. By default, the Serialization framework generates a *Stream Unique Identifier (SUID)* that captures information about what fields are presented in the class, what kind they are (public/protected), and what is transient, among other things. Even a perceived slight modification of the class (for example: changing an `int` to a `long` property) will generate a new SUID. A class that has been saved with a prior SUID cannot be deserialized on the new SUID. This is done to protect the serialization/deserialization mechanism, while also protecting the designers.

You can actually tell the Java class to use a specific SUID. This will allow you to serialize classes, modify them, and then deserialize the original classes while implementing some backward compatibility. The danger you run into is that the deserialization must be backward-compatible. Renaming or removing fields will generate an exception as the class is being deserialized. If you are specifying your own serial Serializable on your Serializable class, be sure to have some unit tests for backward-compatibility every time you change the class. In general, the changes that can be made on a class to keep it backward-compatible are found here: `http://download.oracle.com/javase/6/docs/platform/serialization/spec/version.html`.

■ **Caution** Due to the nature of serialization, don't expect constructors to be called. What this means is that if you have initialization code in constructors that is required for your object to function properly, you may need to refactor them out of the constructor to allow to be executed after construction. The reason is that in the deserialization process, the deserialized objects are "restored" internally (not created) and don't invoke constructors.

5-2. Serializing Java Objects More Efficiently

Problem

You want to serialize a class, but want to make the output more efficient, or smaller in size, than that generated by the built-in serialization method.

Solution

By making the object implement the Externalizable interface, one instructs the Java Virtual Machine to use a custom serialization/deserialization mechanism, as provided by the readExternal/writeExternal methods.

```java
public class ExternalizableProgramSettings implements Externalizable {
    private Point locationOnScreen;
    private Dimension frameSize;
    private Color defaultFontColor;
    private String title;

    // Empty constructor, required for Externalizable implementors
    public ExternalizableProgramSettings() {

    }

    @Override
    public void writeExternal(ObjectOutput out) throws IOException {
        out.writeInt(locationOnScreen.x);
        out.writeInt(locationOnScreen.y);
        out.writeInt(frameSize.width);
        out.writeInt(frameSize.height);
        out.writeInt(defaultFontColor.getRGB());
        out.writeUTF(title);
    }

    @Override
    public void readExternal(ObjectInput in) throws IOException, ClassNotFoundException {
        locationOnScreen = new Point(in.readInt(), in.readInt());
        frameSize = new Dimension(in.readInt(), in.readInt());
```

```
        defaultFontColor = new Color(in.readInt());
        title = in.readUTF();
    }
// getters and setters omitted for brevity
}
```

How It Works

The Java Serialization framework does provide the ability for you to specify exactly how to serialize an object. As such, it requires implementing the Externalizable interface in lieu of the Serializable interface. Externalizable has two methods: `writeExternal(ObjectOutput out)` and `readExternal(ObjectInput in)`. By implementing these methods, you are telling the framework how to encode/decode your object.

The `writeExternal()` method will pass in as a parameter an `ObjectOutput` object. This object will then let you write your own encoding for the serialization. The `ObjectOutput` has the methods listed in Table 5-1.

Table 5-1. ObjectOutput Methods

ObjectOutput	ObjectInput	Description
writeBoolean (boolean v)	booleanreadBoolean ()	Read/writes the Boolean primitive.
writeByte(int v)	intreadByte()	Read/writes a byte. **Please note:** Java doesn't have a byte primitive, so an int is used as a parameter, but only the least-significant byte will be written.
writeShort(int v)	intreadShort()	Read/writes two bytes. **Please note:** Only the two least-significant bytes will be written.
writeChar(int v)	intreadChar()	Read/writes two bytes as a char (reverse order than writeShort).
writeInt (int v)	intreadInt()	Read/writes an integer.
writeLong (long v)	intreadLong()	Read/writes a long.
writeDouble (double v)	double readDouble	Read/writes a double.

The reason you might want to implement the Externalizable interface instead of the Serializable interface is because Java's default serialization is very inefficient. Because the Java Serialization framework needs to make sure that every object (and dependent object) is serialized, it will write even objects that have default values or that might be empty and/or null. Implementing the Externalizable interface also allows you more finer-grained control on how your class is being serialized. In our example, the Serializable version created a setting of 439 bytes, compared with the Externalizable version of only 103 bytes!

■ **Note** You will need an empty (no-arg) constructor for classes that implement the Externalizable interface.

5-3. Serializing Java Objects as XML

Problem

While you love the Serialization framework, you want to create something that is at least cross-language-compatible (or human readable). You would like to save and load your objects using XML.

Solution

In this example, one uses the XMLEncoder object to encode our own Settings object, which contains program settings information and writes it to the settings.xml file. The XMLDecoder takes the settings.xml file and read is as a stream, decoding the Settings object.

```
//Encoding

FileSystem fileSystem = FileSystems.getDefault();
FileOutputStream fos = new FileOutputStream("settings.xml");
XMLEncoder encoder = new XMLEncoder(fos);
encoder.setExceptionListener(new ExceptionListener() {
        @Override
        public void exceptionThrown(Exception e) {
        System.out.println("Exception! :"+e.toString());
        }
});
encoder.writeObject(settings);
encoder.close();
fos.close();

//Decoding
FileInputStream fis = new FileInputStream("settings.xml");
XMLDecoder decoder = new XMLDecoder(fis);
ProgramSettings decodedSettings = (ProgramSettings) decoder.readObject();
System.out.println("Is same? "+settings.equals(decodedSettings));
decoder.close();
fis.close();
```

How It Works

The XMLEncoder and XMLDecoder, like the Serialization framework, use reflection to find out what fields they contain, but instead of writing these fields in binary, they are written in XML. Objects that are to be encoded don't need to be serializable, but they do need to follow the Java Beans specification.

Java Bean is the name of any object that conforms to the following contract:

- The object has a public empty (no-arg) constructor.

- The object has public getters and setters for each protected/private property that take the name of get{Property}() and set{Property}().

The XMLEncoder and XMLDecoder will encode/decode only the properties of the bean that have public accessors (get{property}, set{property}), so if you have any properties that are private and have no accessors, they will not be encoded/decoded.

■ **Tip** It is a good idea to register an Exception Listener when encoding/decoding.

The XmlEncoder starts by creating a new instance of the class that you are trying to serialize (remember that they need to be Java Beans, so they must have an empty no-arg constructor). The XmlEncoder then figures out what properties are accessible (via get{property}, set{property}). And if a property of the newly instantiated class is the same value as the property of the original class (i.e., has the same default value), the XmlEncoder doesn't write that property. In other words, if the default value of a property hasn't changed, the XmlEncoder will not write it out. This allows the flexibility of changing what a "Default" value is between versions, but it is something to be aware of, as objects that were persisted when the default of a property was, for example "2", and later decoded after the default property changed from "2" to "4", will contain the new default property of "4" (which might or might not be correct).

The XMLEncoder also keeps track of references. If an object appears more than once when being persisted in the object graph (for example, an object is inside a Map from the main class, but is also as the DefaultValue property), then the XMLEncoder will only encode it once, and link up a reference by putting a link in the xml.

The XMLEncoder/XMLDecoder is much more forgiving than the serialization framework. When decoding, if a property changed its type, or if it was deleted/added/moved/renamed, the decoding will decode "as much as it can" while skipping the properties that it couldn't decode.

The recommendation is to not persist your main classes (even though the XMLEncoder is more forgiving), but to create special objects that are simple, hold the basic information, and don't do a lot by themselves.

5-4. Creating a Socket Connection and Sending Serializable Objects Across the Wire

Problem

You need to open a network connection, and send/receive objects from it. Also, you have heard that the traditional Java 6 way of doing that doesn't scale well, it's a pain, it's blocking, and it holds kittens hostage.

Solution

Why use Java's New Input Output API version 2 (NIO.2), of course! The solution relies on the NIO.2 features of nonblocking sockets (by using Future tasks):

```java
// Server Side
hostAddress = new InetSocketAddress(InetAddress.getByName("127.0.0.1"), 2583);

Future<AsynchronousSocketChannel> serverFuture = null;
AsynchronousServerSocketChannel serverSocketChannel =
AsynchronousServerSocketChannel.open().bind(hostAddress);
serverFuture = serverSocketChannel.accept();
final AsynchronousSocketChannel clientSocket = serverFuture.get(2000, TimeUnit.MILLISECONDS);
System.out.println("Connected!");
if ((clientSocket != null) && (clientSocket.isOpen())) {
        InputStream connectionInputStream = Channels.newInputStream(clientSocket);
        ObjectInputStream ois = null;
        ois = new ObjectInputStream(connectionInputStream);
        while (true) {
                Object object = ois.readObject();
                if (object.equals("EOF")) {
                        connectionCount.decrementAndGet();
                        clientSocket.close();
                        break;
                }
                System.out.println("Received :" + object);
        }
        ois.close();
        connectionInputStream.close();
}
```

```java
// Client Side
AsynchronousSocketChannel clientSocketChannel = AsynchronousSocketChannel.open();
Future<Void> connectFuture = clientSocketChannel.connect(hostAddress);
connectFuture.get();              // Wait until connection is done.
OutputStream os = Channels.newOutputStream(clientSocketChannel);
ObjectOutputStream oos = new ObjectOutputStream(os);
for (int i = 0; i < 5; i++) {
        oos.writeObject("Look at me " + i);
        Thread.sleep(1000);
}
oos.writeObject("EOF");
oos.close();
clientSocketChannel.close();
```

How It Works

At its basic level, sockets require a type, IP address, and port. While sockets literature has consumed whole books, the main idea is pretty straightforward. Like the post office, socket communications relies on addresses. These addresses are used to deliver data. In our example, we picked the loopback (the same computer where the program is running) address (127.0.0.1), and chose a random port number (2583).

The advantage of the new NIO.2 is that it is asynchronous in nature. By using asynchronous calls, you can scale your application without creating thousands of threads for each connection. In our example, we have taken the asynchronous calls and wait for a connection (effectively making it single-threaded for the sake of the example), but don't let that stop you for enhancing this example with more asynchronous calls. (Check the recipes on the multithreaded section of this book.)

For a client to connect, it requires a socket channel. The NIO.2API allows creating asynchronous socket channels. Once a socket channel is created, it will need an address to connect to. The socketChannel.connect() operation does not block; instead it returns a Future object (this is a different from traditional NIO, where calling socketChanne.connect() will block until a connection is established). The Future object allows a Java program to continue what it is doing and just query the status of the submitted task. To take the analogy further, instead of waiting at the front door for your mail to arrive, you go do other stuff, and "check" periodically to see whether the mail has arrived. Future objects have methods like isDone(),isCancelled() that let you know if the task is done or cancelled. It also has the get() method, which allows you to actually wait for the task to finish. In our example, we use the Future.get() to wait for the client connection to be established.

Once the connection is established, we use Channels.newOutputStream() to create an output stream to send information. Using the decorator pattern, we decorate the outputStream with our ObjectOutputStream to finally send objects through the socket.

The server code is a little more elaborate. Server socket connections allow more than one connection to happen, thus they are used to monitor or receive connections instead of initiating a connection. For this reason, the server is usually waiting for a connection asynchronously.

The server begins by establishing the address it listens to (127.0.0.1:2583) and accepting connections. The call to serverSocketChannel.accept() returns another Future object that will give you the flexibility of how to deal with incoming connections. In our example, the server connection simply calls future.get(), which will block (stop the execution of the program) until a connection is accepted.

After the server acquires a socket channel, it creates an inputStream by calling Channels.newInputStream(socket) and then wrapping that input stream with an ObjectInputStream. The server then proceeds to loop and read each object coming from the ObjectInputStream. If the object received's toString() method equals "EOF", the server stops looping, and the connection is closed.

■ **Caution** Using an ObjectOutputStream and ObjectInputStream to send and receive a lot of objects can lead to memory leaks. ObjectOutputStream keeps a copy of the sent object for efficiency. If you were to send the same object again, ObjectOutputStream and ObjectInputStream will not send the same object again, but instead send a previously sent Object ID. This behavior or just sending the Object ID instead of the whole object raises two issues.

The first issue is that objects that are changed in-place (mutable) will not get the change reflected in the receiving client when sent through the wire. The reason is that because the object was sent once, the ObjectOutputStream believes that the object is already transmitted and will only send the ID, negating any changes to the object that have happened since it was sent. To avoid this, don't make changes to objects that were send down the wire. This rule also applies to subobjects from the object graph.

The second issue is that because `ObjectOutputStream` keeps a list of sent objects and their Object ID, if you send a lot of objects the dictionary of sent objects to keys grows indefinitely, causing memory starvation on a long-running program. To alleviate this issue, you can call `ObjectOutputStream.reset()`, which will clear the dictionary of sent objects. Alternatively you can invoke `ObjectOutputStream.writeUnshared()` to not cache the object in the `ObjectOutputStream` dictionary.

5-5. Obtaining the Java Execution Path

Problem

You want to get the path where the Java program is running.

Solution

Invoke the `System` class's `getProperty` method. For example:

```
String  path = System.getProperty("user.dir");
```

How It Works

When a Java program starts, the JRE updates the `user.dir` system property to record from where the JRE was invoked. The solution example passes the property name "`user.dir`" to the `getProperty` method, which returns the value.

5-6. Copying a File

Problem

You need to copy a file from one folder to another.

Solution

From the default `FileSystem`, you create the "to" and "from" paths where the files/folders exist and then use the `Files.copy` static method to copy files between the created paths:

```
FileSystem fileSystem = FileSystems.getDefault();
Path sourcePath = fileSystem.getPath("file.log");
Path targetPath = fileSystem.getPath("file2.log");
```

```
        System.out.println("Copy from "+sourcePath.toAbsolutePath().toString()+" to
"+targetPath.toAbsolutePath().toString());
        try {
            Files.copy(sourcePath, targetPath, StandardCopyOption.REPLACE_EXISTING);
        } catch (IOException e) {
            e.printStackTrace();
        }
```

How It Works

In the new NIO.2 libraries, Java works with an abstraction level that allows for more direct manipulation of file attributes belonging to the underlying operating system.

`FileSystem.getDefaults()` gets the usable abstract system that we can do file operations on. For example, running this example in Windows will get you a `WindowsFileSystem`; if you were running this example in Linux, a `LinuxFileSystem` object would be returned. `AllFileSystems` supports basic operations; in addition, each concrete `FileSystem` provides access to the unique features offered for that operating system.

After getting the default `FileSystem` object, you can query for file objects. In the NIO.2 file, folders and links are all called *paths*. Once you get a path, you can then perform operations with it. In this example, `Files.copy` is called with the source and destination paths. The last parameter refers to the different copy options. The different copy options are file-system dependent so make sure that the one that you choose is compatible with the operating system you intend to run the application in.

5-7. Moving a File

Problem

You need to move a file instead of just copying it around.

Solution

As in Solution 5-6, you use the default `FileSystem` to create the "to" and "from" paths, and invoke the `Files.move()` static method:

```
            FileSystem fileSystem = FileSystems.getDefault();
            Path sourcePath = fileSystem.getPath("file.log");
            Path targetPath = fileSystem.getPath("file2.log");
            System.out.println("Copy from "+sourcePath.toAbsolutePath().toString()+↩
                              " to "+targetPath.toAbsolutePath().toString());
            try {
                Files.move(sourcePath, targetPath);
            } catch (IOException e) {
                e.printStackTrace();
            }
```

How It Works

Same as copying a file, you create the path of source and destination. After having the source and destination path, `Files.move` will take care of moving the file for you. Other methods provided by the Files object are the following:

- `Delete (path)`: Deletes a file (or a folder, if it's empty).

- `Exists (path)`: Checks whether a file/folder exists.

- `isDirectory (path)`: Checks whether the path created points to a directory.

- `isExecutable (path)`: Checks whether the file is an executable file.

- `isHidden (path)`: Checks whether the file is visible or hidden in the operating system.

5-8. Creating a Directory

Problem

You need to create a directory from your Java application.

Solution 1

By using the default `FileSystem`, you instantiate a path pointing to the new directory; then the `Files.createDirectory()` static method creates the directory specified in the path.

```
FileSystem fileSystem = FileSystems.getDefault();
Path directory= fileSystem.getPath("./newDirectory");
try {
    Files.createDirectory(directory);
} catch (IOException e) {
    e.printStackTrace();
}
```

Solution 2

If using a Linux operating system, you can specify the folder attributes by invoking the `PosixFilePermission()` method, which lets you set access at the owner, group, and world levels. For example:

```
FileSystem fileSystem = FileSystems.getDefault();
Path directory= fileSystem.getPath("./newDirectoryWPermissions");
try {
    Set<PosixFilePermission> perms = PosixFilePermissions.fromString("rwxr-x---");
    FileAttribute<Set<PosixFilePermission>> attr =
PosixFilePermissions.asFileAttribute(perms);
```

```
        Files.createDirectory(directory, attr);
    } catch (IOException e) {
        e.printStackTrace();
    }
```

How It Works

The `Files.createDirectory()` method takes a path as a parameter and then creates the directory. By default, the directory created will inherit the default permissions. If you wanted to specify specific permissions in Linux, you can use the `PosixAttributes` as an extra parameter in the `createDirectory()` method.

5-9.Iterating Over Files in a Directory

Problem

You need to scan files from a directory. There are possibly subdirectories with more files. You want to include those in your scan.

Solution

Using the NIO.2, create a `FileVisitor` and visit the folder. For example:

```
FileVisitor<Path> myFileVisitor = new SimpleFileVisitor<Path>() {
    @Override
    public FileVisitResult visitFile(Path file, BasicFileAttributes attrs) ↵
                        throws IOException {
        System.out.println("Visited File: "+file.toString());
        return FileVisitResult.CONTINUE;
    }
};

FileSystem fileSystem = FileSystems.getDefault();
Path directory= fileSystem.getPath(".");
try {
    Files.walkFileTree(directory, myFileVisitor);
} catch (IOException e) {
    e.printStackTrace();
}
```

How It Works

Before NIO.2, trying to traverse a directory tree involved recursion, and depending on the implementation, it could be very brittle. The calls to get files within a folder were synchronous and required the scanning of the whole directory before returning, generating what appears to be an unresponsive method call. With the new NIO.2, one can just tell the VM which folder to start traversing on, and the NIO.2 calls will handle the recursion details on its own. The only thing you provide to the NIO.2 API is a class that tells it what to do when a file/folder is found (SimpleFileVisitor implementation). Also, because NIO.2 uses a Visitor pattern, it doesn't need to prescan the whole folder, but instead processes files as they are being iterated over.

The implementation of the SimpleFileVisitor class as an anonymous inner class includes overriding the visitFile(Path file, BasicFileAttributesattrs() method. When you override this method, you can put the behavior of what do when a file is encountered.

The visitFile method returns a FileVisitReturn enum. This enum then tells the FileVisitor what action to take:

- CONTINUE: Will continue with the traversing of the directory tree.

- TERMINATE: Stops the traversing.

- SKIP_SUBTREE: Stops going deeper from the current tree level (only useful if this enum is returned on the preVisitDirectory() method).

- SKIP_SIBLINGS: Skips the other directories at the same tree level than the current.

The SimpleFileVisitor class, aside from the visitFile() method, also contains the following:

- preVisitDirectory: Called before entering a directory to be traversed

- postVisitDirectory: Called after finished traversing a directory

- visitFile: Called as it visits the file, as in our example code

- visitFileFailed: Called if the file cannot be visited; for example, on an I/O error

5-10. Querying (and Setting) File Metadata

Problem

You need to get information about a particular file, such as file size, whether it's a directory, etc. Also, you might want to mark a file as Archived in the Windows operating system or grant specific POSIX file permissions in the Linux operating system (refer to Recipe 5-8).

Solution

Using Java NIO.2 you can get a lot more information on a file/directory than you could do with the regular NIO. For example:

```
Path path = FileSystems.getDefault().getPath("./file2.log");
try {
    // General file attributes, supported by all Java systems
    System.out.println("File Size:"+Files.size(path));
    System.out.println("Is Directory:"+Files.isDirectory(path));
    System.out.println("Is Regular File:"+Files.isRegularFile(path));
```

```
            System.out.println("Is Symbolic Link:"+Files.isSymbolicLink(path));
            System.out.println("Is Hidden:"+Files.isHidden(path));
            System.out.println("Last Modified Time:"+Files.getLastModifiedTime(path));
            System.out.println("Owner:"+Files.getOwner(path));

            // Specific attribute views.
            DosFileAttributeView view = Files.getFileAttributeView(path,
    DosFileAttributeView.class);
            System.out.println("DOS File Attributes\n");
            System.out.println("-----------------------------------\n");
            System.out.println("Archive  :"+view.readAttributes().isArchive());
            System.out.println("Hidden   :"+view.readAttributes().isHidden());
            System.out.println("Read-only:"+view.readAttributes().isReadOnly());
            System.out.println("System   :"+view.readAttributes().isSystem());

            view.setArchive(false);

        } catch (IOException e) {
            e.printStackTrace();
        }
```

How It Works

Java NIO.2 allows much more flexibility in getting and setting file attributes. NIO.2 abstracts the different operating system attributes into both a "Common" set of attributes and an "OS Specific" set of attributes. The standard attributes are the following:

- isDirectory: True if it's a directory.

- isRegularFile: Returns false if the file isn't considered a regular file, the file doesn't exist, or it can't be determined whether it's a regular file.

- isSymbolicLink: True if the link is symbolic (most prevalent in Unix systems).

- isHidden: True if the file is considered to be hidden in the operating system.

- LastModifiedTime: The time the file was last updated.

- Owner: The file's owner per the operating system.

Also, NIO.2 allows entering the specific attributes of the underlying operating system. To do so, you first need to get a view that represents the operating system's file attributes (in this example, it is a DosFileAttributeView). Once you get the view, you can query and change the OS-specific attributes.

■ **Caution** Please note that the AttributeView will only work for the operating system that is intended (you cannot use the DosFileAttributeView in a Linux machine).

5-11. Monitoring a Directory for Changes

Problem

You need to keep track when a directory's content has changed (for example, a file was added, changed, or deleted) and act upon those changes.

Solution

By using a WatchService, you can subscribe to be notified on events happening on that folder. In this example, we subscribe for ENTRY_CREATE, ENTRY_MODIFY, and ENTRY_DELETE events:

```
    try {
        System.out.println("Watch Event, press q<Enter> to exit");
        FileSystem fileSystem = FileSystems.getDefault();
        WatchService service = fileSystem.newWatchService();
        Path path = fileSystem.getPath(".");
        System.out.println("Watching :"+path.toAbsolutePath());
        path.register(service, StandardWatchEventKinds.ENTRY_CREATE,
StandardWatchEventKinds.ENTRY_DELETE, StandardWatchEventKinds.ENTRY_MODIFY);
        boolean shouldContinue = true;
        while(shouldContinue) {
            WatchKey key = service.poll(250, TimeUnit.MILLISECONDS);

            // Code to stop the program
            while (System.in.available() > 0) {
                int readChar = System.in.read();
                if ((readChar == 'q') || (readChar == 'Q')) {
                    shouldContinue = false;
                    break;
                }
            }
            if (key == null) continue;
            for (WatchEvent<?> event : key.pollEvents()) {
                if (event.kind() == StandardWatchEventKinds.OVERFLOW) continue;
                WatchEvent<Path> ev = (WatchEvent<Path>)event;
                Path filename = ev.context();
                System.out.println("Event detected :"+filename.toString()+" "+ev.kind());
            }
            boolean valid = key.reset();
            if (!valid) {
                break;
            }
        }
    } catch (IOException | InterruptedException e) {
        e.printStackTrace();
    }
```

How It Works

With NIO.2, you now have a built-in poll mechanism to watch for changes in the FileSystem. Using a poll mechanism allows you to wait for events and check them at an interval. Once an event happens, you can process it, and, at the end of processing it, consume it. A consumed event tells the NIO.2 framework that you are ready to handle a new event.

To start watching a folder, create a WatchService that you can use to poll for changes. After the WatchService is created, you should register the WatchService with a path. A path symbolizes a folder in the system. When the WatchService is registered with the path, you define what kinds of events you want to receive (see Table 5-2).

After registering the WatchService with the path, you can then "poll" the WatchService for events. By calling the watchService.poll() method, you will wait for a file/folder event on that path. Using the watchService.poll(int timeout, Timeunit timeUnit) will wait until the timeout specified before continuing. If the watchService receives an event, or if the allowed time has passed, then it will continue execution. If there were no events and the timeout was reached, the WatchKey object returned by the watchService.poll(int timeout) will be null, otherwise the WatchKey object returned will contain the relevant information for the event that has occurred.

Because many events can happen at the same time (say, for example, moving a whole folder or pasting a bunch of files in a folder), the WatchKey might contain more than one event. You can use the watchKey to get all the events that are associated with that key by calling the watchKey.pollEvents() method.

The watchKey.pollEvents() call will return a list of watchEvents that can then be looped through. Each watchEvent contains information on the actual file or folder that the event refers to (for example, a whole subfolder could have been moved or deleted), and the event type (add, edit, delete). The only event types that you will be notified of are the eventTypes registered for when creating the watchService. The event types you can register are listed in Table 5-2.

Once an event has been processed, it is important to call the EventKey.reset(). The reset will return a Boolean value determining whether the WatchKey is still valid or not. A WatchKey becomes invalid if it is cancelled or if its originating watchService is closed. If the eventKey returns false, you should break from the watch loop.

Table 5-2. Types of watchEvents

WatchEvent	Description
OVERFLOW	An event that has overflown (ignore)
ENTRY_CREATE	A directory or file was created
ENTRY_DELETE	A directory or file has been deleted
ENTRY_MODIFY	A directory or file has been modified

5-12. Reading Property Files

Problem

You need to create some settings for your program that needs to be editable either with text or programmatically.

Solution

Using the `Properties` object, we load properties stored in the `properties.conf` file. For certain properties, if not present in the file, we use a default value. Toward the end of the example, we rewrite the `properties.conf` file, saving the properties back to the file:

```
File file = new File("properties.conf");
try {
    if (!file.exists()) file.createNewFile();
} catch (IOException e) {
    e.printStackTrace();
}

Properties properties = new Properties();
try {
    properties.load(new FileInputStream("properties.conf"));
} catch (IOException e) {
    e.printStackTrace();
}

boolean shouldWakeUp = false;
int startCounter  = 100;

String shouldWakeUpProperty = properties.getProperty("ShouldWakeup");
shouldWakeUp = (shouldWakeUpProperty == null) ? false :↵
Boolean.parseBoolean(shouldWakeUpProperty.trim().toLowerCase());

String startCounterProperty = properties.getProperty("StartCounter");
try {
  startCounter = Integer.parseInt(startCounterProperty);
} catch (Exception e) {
    System.out.println("Couldn't read startCounter, defaulting to "+startCounter);
}
String dateFormatStringProperty = properties.getProperty("DateFormatString","MMM dd yy");

System.out.println("Should Wake up? "+shouldWakeUp);
System.out.println("Start Counter: "+startCounter);
System.out.println("Date Format String:"+dateFormatStringProperty);

//setting property
properties.setProperty("StartCounter","250");
try {
```

```
    properties.store(new FileOutputStream("properties.conf"),"Properties Description");
} catch (IOException e) {
    e.printStackTrace();
}
properties.list(System.out);
```

How It Works

The Java `Properties` class helps you manage your program properties. It allows you to manage the properties either by external modification (someone editing a `myapp.conf` file) or internally by using the `Properties.store()` method.

The `Properties` object can be instantiated either without a file or with a preloaded file. The files that the `Properties` object read are in the form of `[name]=[value]` and are textually represented. If you need to store values in other formats, you need to write to and read from a String.

If you are expecting the files to be modified outside the program (the user directly opens a text editor and changes the values), be sure to sanitize the inputs; like trimming the values for extra spaces and ignoring case if need be.

To query the different properties from the `Properties`, you call the `getProperty(String)` method. The method will return null if the property is not found. Alternatively, you can invoke the `getProperty` `(String,String)` method, on which if the property is not found in the `Properties` object, it will return the second parameter as its value. It is a good practice to default values in case the file doesn't have an entry for a particular key.

If you look at the generated property file, you will notice that the first two lines indicate the description of the file, and the date when it was modified. These two lines start with #, which in Java property files is the equivalent of a comment. When starting a line with #, the `Properties` object will skip that line when processing the file.

■ **Caution** If you allow users to modify your configuration files directly, it is important to have validation in place when retrieving properties from the `Properties` object. One of the most common issues encountered in the value of properties is leading and/or trailing spaces. If specifying a Boolean or integer property, be sure that they can be parsed from a String. At a minimum, catch an exception when trying to parse to survive an unconventional value (and log the offending value).

5-13. Uncompressing Compressed Files

Problem

You have to uncompress and extract files from a compressed `.zip` file.

Solution

Using the Java.util.zip package, you can open a .zip file and loop through its entries. If we find a directory entry, we create the directory. If we find a file entry, we write the decompressed file to the file .unzipped.

```
file = new ZipFile("file.zip");
FileSystem fileSystem = FileSystems.getDefault();
Enumeration<? extends ZipEntry> entries = file.entries();
String uncompressedDirectory = "uncompressed/";
Files.createDirectory(fileSystem.getPath(uncompressedDirectory));
while (entries.hasMoreElements()) {
    ZipEntry entry = entries.nextElement();
    if (entry.isDirectory()) {
        System.out.println("Creating Directory:" + uncompressedDirectory ↵
+ entry.getName());
        Files.createDirectories(fileSystem.getPath(uncompressedDirectory ↵
+ entry.getName()));
    } else {
        InputStream is = file.getInputStream(entry);
        System.out.println("File :" + entry.getName());
        BufferedInputStream bis = new BufferedInputStream(is);

        String uncompressedFileName = uncompressedDirectory + entry.getName();
        Path uncompressedFilePath = fileSystem.getPath(uncompressedFileName);
        Files.createFile(uncompressedFilePath);
        FileOutputStream fileOutput = new FileOutputStream(uncompressedFileName);
        while (bis.available() > 0) {
            fileOutput.write(bis.read());
        }
        fileOutput.close();
        System.out.println("Written :" + entry.getName());
    }
}
```

How It Works

By creating a ZipFile object, you get access to the .zip file information. Each ZipFile object will contain a collection of entries, and by looping through the entries you can get information on each of the compressed files in the Zip folder. Each ZipEntry instance will have the compressed and uncompressed size, the name, and the input stream of the uncompressed bytes.

By hooking up to the input stream, we can then read the uncompressed bytes into a byte buffer to then (in our case) write it to a file. Using the fileStream we ask how many bytes we can read without blocking the process. Once we read these many bytes, we then in turn write the read bytes directly into the output file. We keep doing this until we read the number of bytes of the uncompressed file.

■ **Caution** Reading the whole file in memory might not be a good idea if the file is extremely large in size. If you need to work with a large file, it would be best to first write it uncompressed to disk (as in the example) and then open it and load it in chunks. If the file that you are working on is not large (you can limit the size by checking the `getSize()` method) you can probably load it in memory.

CHAPTER 6

Exceptions and Logging

Exceptions are a way of describing exceptional circumstances within a program. They are a way of signaling that something unexpected (exceptional) has happened. For that reason, exceptions are efficient at interrupting the current flow of the program and signaling that there is something that requires attention. As such, programs that judiciously use exceptions benefit from a better control flow and become more robust. Even so, using exceptions indiscriminately can cause performance degradation.

Within Java, exceptions are said to be *thrown* and *caught*. Throwing an exception involves telling the code that you have encountered an exception and involves using the `throw` keyword to signal the JVM to find any code capable of handling this exceptional circumstance within the current stack. Catching an exception involves telling the compiler which exceptions you can handle, and on which part of the code you want to monitor for these exceptions occurring. This is denoted by the `try`/`catch` Java syntax (described in recipe 6-1)

All exceptions inherit from `Throwable`, as shown in Figure 6-1. Classes that are inherited from `Throwable` are allowed to be defined in the catch clause of a `try`/`catch` statement. The `Error` classes are primarily used by the JVM to denote serious and/or fatal errors. According to the Java documentation, applications are not expected to catch `Error` exception as they are considered fatal (think computer being on fire). The bulk of exceptions within a Java program will be inherited from the `Exception` class.

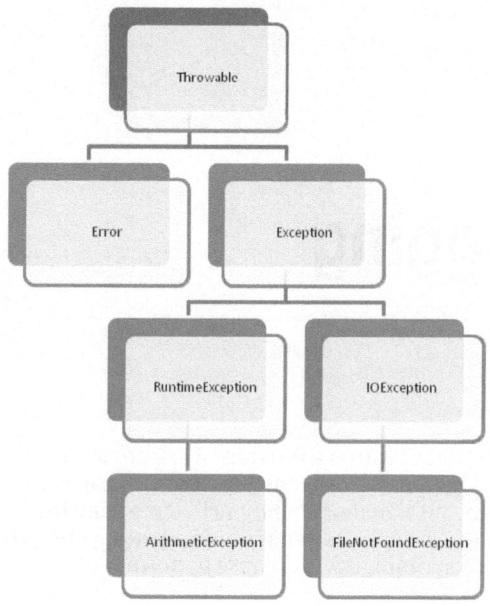

Figure 6-1. Part of the exception class hierarchy in Java

An important aspect of exceptions is that within the JVM there are two types of exceptions: checked and unchecked. Checked exceptions are enforced by methods. In the method signature, one can specify what kind of exceptions the method can throw. This requires any caller of this method to create a `try`/`catch` block that handles the exceptions that the method declared on its signature. Unchecked exceptions don't require such as stringent convention and are free to be thrown anywhere without enforcing the implementation of a `try`/`catch` block. Even so, unchecked exceptions (as described on recipe 6-6) are usually discouraged because they can lead to threads unraveling (if nothing catches the exception) and poor visibility of problems. Classes that inherit from `RuntimeException`are considered unchecked exceptions, whereas classes that inherit directly from `Exception` are considered to be checked exceptions.

Be aware that the act of throwing exceptions is expensive (compared with other language construct alternatives), and as such throwing exceptions makes a poor substitute for control flow. For example, you shouldn't throw an exception to indicate an expected result of a method call (say a method like `isUsernameValid (String username)`. It is a better practice to call the method and return a `boolean` with the result than trying to throw an `InvalidUsernameException` to indicate failure.

Logging within an application helps understand what is happening without the need for debugging the code. This is especially true in production environments where there isn't the opportunity for live debugging. In that sense, logging collects clues on what is happening (most likely what went wrong) and helps with troubleshooting production problems. A solid logging framework with a sound logging methodology will save many late-nights at work wondering "what happened?"

Logging for Java is very mature. There are many open-source projects that are widely accepted as the *de facto* standard for logging. In our recipes we will use Java's Logging framework and the Simple Logging Façade for Java (SLF4). Both of these projects together create a good-enough solution for most logging needs. For the recipes involving SLF4J and Log4j, please download SLF4J (`http://www.slf4j.org/`), and put them in your project's dependency path.

6-1. Catching Exceptions

Problem

You need to catch an exception from code.

Solution

Using the built-in `try`/`catch` language construct allows you to catch exceptions. In this example, there is a function that returns true/false if a string is shorter than five characters long. If the string passed in is null, a `nullPointerException` is thrown by the `length()` method and caught by the catch block.

```
private void start() {
    System.out.println("Is th string 1234 longer than 5↩
chars?:"+isStringShorterThanFiveCharacters("1234"));
    System.out.println("Is th string 12345 longer than 5↩
chars?:"+isStringShorterThanFiveCharacters("12345"));
    System.out.println("Is th string 123456 longer than 5↩
chars?:"+isStringShorterThanFiveCharacters("123456"));
    System.out.println("Is th string null longer than 5↩
chars?:"+isStringShorterThanFiveCharacters(null));

}

private boolean isStringShorterThanFiveCharacters(String aString) {
    try {
        return aString.length() > 5;
    } catch (NullPointerException e) {
        System.out.println("An Exception Happened!");
        return false;
    }
}
```

How It Works

The `try` keyword tells the Java program that the enclosing code segment could raise a potential exception. At the end of the `try` block we add the catch clauses. Each catch clause then specifies what exception they are catching for. If you do not provide a catch clause for a checked exception, the compiler will generate an error. Two possible solutions are to add a catch clause or to include the exception in the throws clause of the enclosing method. Any checked exceptions that are thrown but not caught will propagate up the call stack. If this method doesn't catch the exception, the thread that executed the code terminates. If the thread terminating is the only thread in the program, it terminates the execution of the program.

■ **Caution** When throwing an exception, be sure that you really want to throw it. If the thrown exception is not caught, it will propagate up the call stack; and if there isn't any catch clause capable of handling the exception, it will cause the running thread to terminate (also known as *unraveling*). If your program has only one main thread, an uncaught exception will terminate your program.

6-2. Guaranteeing that Cleanup Code Runs, No Matter What

Problem

You want to write code that executes when control leaves a code segment, no matter whether that control leaves due to an error being thrown or the segment ending normally. For example, you have acquired a lock and want to be sure that you are releasing it correctly. You want to release the lock in the event of an error and also in the event of no error.

Solution

Use a try/catch/finally block to properly release locks and other resources that you acquire in a code segment. In the example, the finally keyword specifies a code block that will always execute, regardless of whether an exception was thrown in the try block. Within the finally block, the lock is released by calling lock.unlock():

```
private void callFunctionThatHoldsLock() {
    myLock.lock();
    try {
        int number = random.nextInt(5);
        int result = 100 / number;
        System.out.println("A result is " + result);
        FileOutputStream file = new FileOutputStream("file.out");
        file.write(result);
        file.close();
    } catch (FileNotFoundException e) {
        e.printStackTrace();
    } catch (IOException e) {
        e.printStackTrace();
    } catch (Exception e) {
        e.printStackTrace();
    } finally {
        myLock.unlock();
    }
}
```

How It Works

By acquiring the lock at the beginning of the function and then releasing it in the `finally` block, you guarantee that the lock will be released at the end of the function regardless of whether an exception (checked or unchecked) is thrown. In all, acquired locks should always be released in a `finally` block. In the example, suppose that the `mylock.unlock()` function call were not in the `finally` block (but at the end of the `try` block); if an exception were to happen, the call to `mylock.unlock()` would not happen because code execution would be interrupted in the location where the exception happened. In that case, the lock would be forever acquired, and never released.

■ **Caution** If you need to return a value on a method, be very careful of returning values in the `finally` block. A return statement in the `finally` block will always execute, regardless of any other return statements that might have happened within the `try` block.

6-3. Throwing Exceptions

Problem

You need to account for an exceptional problem by throwing an exception from within your code. You don't want the execution to continue on the current code path. You want to abort the execution of the current code path by throwing the exception.

Solution

Using the `throw` keyword, one can signal the current thread to look for `try`/`catch` blocks (at the current level and up the stack) that can process the thrown exception. In our example, the `callSomeMethodThatMightThrow` throws an exception if the parameter passed in is `null`.

```
private void start() {
    try {
        callSomeMethodThatMightThrow(null);
    } catch (IllegalArgumentException e) {
        System.out.println("There was an illegal argument exception!");
    }
}

private void callSomeFunctionThatMightThrow(Object o) {
    if (o == null) throw new NullPointerException("The object is null");
}
```

In this code example, the `callSomeMethodThatMightThrow` checks for valid arguments. If the argument is invalid, it then throws an `IllegalArgumentException`, signaling that the caller of this method did it with the wrong parameters.

How It Works

The `throw` keyword allows you to explicitly generate an exceptional condition. When the current thread throws an exception, it doesn't execute anything beyond the `throw` statement and instead transfers control to the catch clause (if there are any) or terminates the thread.

■ **Caution** When throwing an exception, be sure that you really want to throw it. If an exception is not caught as it propagates up the stack, it will terminate the thread that is executing (also known as unraveling). If your program has only one main thread, an uncaught exception will terminate your program.

6-4. Catching Multiple Exceptions

Problem

You want to catch multiple exceptions that might happen within a `try` block.

Solution 1

By using different catch clauses (ordered from the most specific to the most general), you can catch multiple exceptions:

```
try {
    Class<?> stringClass = Class.forName("java.lang.String");
    FileInputStream in = new FileInputStream("myFile.log") ; // Can throw ↙
IOException
    in.read();

} catch (IOException e) {
    System.out.println("There was an IOException "+e);
} catch (ClassNotFoundException e) {
    System.out.println("There was a ClassCastException "+e);
}
```

Solution 2

If the code for the different exceptions is the same, in Java 7 you can use the | operator for catching multiple exceptions (known as Multi-catch exception in Java 7):

```
try {
    Class<?> stringClass = Class.forName("java.lang.String");
    FileInputStream in = new FileInputStream("myFile.log") ;
// Can throw IOException
    in.read();


} catch (IOException | ClassNotFoundException e) {
    System.out.println("An exception of type "+e.getClass()+" was thrown! "+e);
}
```

How It Works

By using different catch clauses you can adjust what gets executed when a particular exception is thrown. Sometimes we are just catching all the checked exceptions that can be thrown in a given code and want to handle it the same way (logging them, for example). In such a case, we can use the new Java 7 construct that allows us to specify all the exceptions to be caught in a catch block (instead of creating one catch block per checked exception.

■ **Note** If catching an exception in multiple catch blocks (Solution 1), make sure that the catch blocks are defined from the most specific to the most general. Failure to follow this convention will prevent an exception from being handled by the more-specific blocks. This is most important when there are catch (Exception e) blocks, which catch almost all exceptions.

Having a catch (Exception e) block% called a catch-all or *Pokémon*® exception handler (gotta catch them all)% is usually poor practice because such a block will catch every exception type and treat them the same. This becomes a problem because the block can catch other exceptions that happen deeper in the call-stack that you may not have intended the block to catch (an OutOfMemoryException).

6-5. Catching the Uncaught Exceptions

Problem

You want to know when a thread is being terminated because of an uncaught exception such as a
NullPointerException.

Solution 1

When creating a Java thread, sometimes you want to catch not only checked exceptions but also any
type of exceptions, at least to properly log them, or to "keep going" and avoid termination of the
executing thread. To that effect, Java allows you to register an ExceptionHandler() either per thread or
globally.

For example, the following code registers a per-thread handler:

```java
private void start() {
    Thread.setDefaultUncaughtExceptionHandler(new Thread.UncaughtExceptionHandler() {
        @Override
        public void uncaughtException(Thread t, Throwable e) {
            System.out.println("Woa! there was an exception thrown somewhere! ↵
"+t.getName()+": "+e);
        }
    });

    final Random random = new Random();
    for (int j = 0; j < 10; j++) {
        int divisor = random.nextInt(4);
        System.out.println("200 / " + divisor + " Is " + (200 / divisor));
    }
}
```

Solution 2

Use the thread's own UncaughtExceptionHandler(). Any exception that happens within the thread and
that has not been caught will be handled by the uncaughtException() method of the
uncaughtExceptionHandler(). For example:

```java
Thread.currentThread().setUncaughtExceptionHandler(↵
new Thread.UncaughtExceptionHandler() {
```

```
    @Override
    public void uncaughtException(Thread t, Throwable e) {
        System.out.println("In this thread "+t.getName()+" an ↵
        exception was thrown "+e);
    }
});

Thread someThread = new Thread(new Runnable() {
    @Override
    public void run() {
        System.out.println(200/0);
    }
});
someThread.setName("Some Unlucky Thread");
someThread.start();

System.out.println("In the main thread "+ (200/0));
```

How It Works

The `Thread.defaultUncaughtExceptionHandler()` will be invoked for each unchecked exception that has not being caught. When the `UncaughtExceptionHandler()` handles the exception it means that there was no try/catch block that was capable of catching the exception and as such bubbled all the way up the thread stack. This is the last code executed on that thread before it terminates. When an exception is caught on either the thread's or the default's `UncaughtExceptionHandler()`, the thread will terminate. The `UncaughtExceptionHandler()` can be used to log information on the exception to help pinpoint the reason of the exception.

In the second solution, the `UncaughtExceptionHandler()` is set up specifically for the current thread. When the thread throws an exception that is not caught, it will bubble up to the `UncaughtExceptionHandler()` of the thread. If this is not present, it will bubble up to the `defaultUncaughtExceptionHandler()`. Again, in either situation, the thread originating the exception will terminate.

■ **Tip** When dealing with multiple threads, it is always a good practice to explicitly name these threads. It makes life easier to know that the exception was caused by the DatabaseThread, instead of Thread-## (the default naming pattern of unnamed threads).

6-6. Managing Resources with try/catch Blocks

Problem

You need to make sure that if an exception is thrown, the resources that are being used in the try/catch block are released.

Solution

By using the new Java 7 Automatic Resource Management (ARM) feature, you can specify a try-with-resources block:

```
try (
        FileOutputStream fos = new FileOutputStream("out.log");
        BufferedOutputStream bos = new BufferedOutputStream(fos);
        DataOutputStream dos = new DataOutputStream(bos)
) {
    dos.writeUTF("This is being written");
} catch (Exception e) {
    System.out.println("Some bad exception happened ");
}
```

How It Works

Before Java 7, managing resources was problematic if an exceptional condition happened. Usually you want to cleanly close/dispose of resources that are acquired within a try/catch block. If a program doesn't close/dispose of its resources or does so improperly, the resources could be acquired indefinitely. Most resources are limited (file handles or database connections) and as such will cause performance degradation (and more exceptions to be thrown). To avoid that, Java 7 provides a way of automatically releasing resources when an exception occurs within a try/catch block. By declaring a try-with-resources block, you are guaranteed that if there is an exception thrown within the block, the resource on which the try block was checked will be closed. Most of the resources that come with Java 7 can be added to the try-with-resources statement (for a full list, see implementers of the java.lang.AutoCloseable interface). Also, third-party implementers can create resources that will work with the try-with-resources statements by implementing the AutoCloseable interface.

The syntax for the try-with-resources block involves the try keyword, followed by an opening parenthesis and then followed by all the resource declarations that you would want to be released in case of an exception, and ending with a closing parenthesis. Please note that if you try to declare a resource/variable that doesn't implement the AutoCloseable interface, you will get a compiler error. After the closing parenthesis, the syntax of the try/catch block is the same as previously used.

The main advantage of the try-with-resources Java 7 feature is that it allows a cleaner release of resources. Usually when acquiring a resource, there are a lot of interdependencies (creating file handlers, which are wrapped in output streams, which are wrapped in buffered streams). Properly closing and disposing of these in exceptional conditions requires checking the status of each dependent resource and carefully disposing of it, and doing that requires that you write a lot of code. By contrast, the `try-with-resources` construct causes the JVM to take care of proper disposal of resources, even in exceptional conditions.

■ **Note** A `try-with-resources` block will always close the defined resources, even if there were no exceptions thrown.

6-7. Creating an Exception Class

Problem

You need to create a new type of exception.

Solution 1

By extending `RuntimeException`, you can create exceptions that are not required to be checked, but instead can happen at any time. For example:

```
class IllegalChatServerException extends RuntimeException {
    IllegalChatServerException(String message) {
        super(message);
    }
}

private void disconnectChatServer(Object chatServer) {
    if (chatServer == null) throw new IllegalChatServerException("Chat server is
empty");
}
```

Solution 2

By extending `Exception`, you create a checked exception that needs to be either caught or rethrown up the stack. For example:

```
class ConnectionUnavailableException extends Exception {
    ConnectionUnavailableException(String message) {
        super(message);
    }
```

```
    }

    private void sendChat(String chatMessage) throws ConnectionUnavailableException {
        if (chatServer == null)
                throw new ConnectionUnavailableException("Can't find the chat server");
    }
```

How It Works

Sometimes you want to create your own exceptions, especially when creating an API. The usual recommendation is to use one of the available Exception classes provided by the JDK. For example, use IOException for IO-related issues or the IllegalArgumentException for illegal parameters. If there isn't a JDK exception that fits cleanly, you can always extend Exception or RuntimeException and implement its own family of exceptions.

Depending on the base class, creating an Exception class is fairly straightforward. Extending RuntimeException allows you to be able to throw the resulting exception any time without requiring anyone to catch it. This is advantageous in that RuntimeException is a more lax contract to work with, but throwing such an exception can lead to thread termination if there isn't anyone catching the exception. Extending Exception instead allows you to clearly force any code that throws the exception to be able to handle it in a catch clause. The checked exception is then forced by contract to implement a catch handler, potentially avoiding a thread termination.

In practice, we discourage extending RuntimeException because it can lead to poor exception handling. Our rule of thumb is that if it's possible to recover from an exception, you should create the associated exception class by extending Exception. If a developer cannot reasonably be expected to recover from the exception (say a NullPointerException), extend RuntimeException.

6-8. Rethrowing the caught Exception

Sometimes you have a multicatch statement, but want to re-throw the original exception with the exception type that was caught. Before Java 7, re-throwing the same exception involves a series of catch statements for each specific exception and then a throw on that exception, making the code verbose. Now with Java 7, the steps are much clearer.

Problem

You need to rethrow the same exception type as you caught.

Solution

Now you can just throw the exception from a catch block, and it will rethrow it on the same type as it was caught:

```
private void doSomeWork() throws IOException, InterruptedException {
    LinkedBlockingQueue<String> queue = new LinkedBlockingQueue<String>();

    try {
        FileOutputStream fos = new FileOutputStream("out.log");
        DataOutputStream dos = new DataOutputStream(fos);
        while (!queue.isEmpty()) {
            dos.writeUTF(queue.take());
        }
    } catch (InterruptedException | IOException e ) {
        e.printStackTrace();
        throw e;
    }

}
```

How It Works

Starting with Java 7, you can simply throw the exception that you've caught, and the JVM will bubble the exception to the appropriate type. Note that if you are throwing a checked exception, then these have to be also defined in the Method declaration.

6-9. Logging Events in Your Application

Problem

You like to start logging events, debug messages, error conditions, and so on in your application.

Solution

Use SLF4J, along with the Java Logging API to implement your logging solution. The following example first creates a logger object with the name of recipeLogger. The example then proceeds to log an informational message, a warning message, and an error message:

```
private void loadLoggingConfiguration() {
    FileInputStream ins = null;
```

139

```
        try {
            ins = new FileInputStream(new File("logging.properties"));
            LogManager.getLogManager().readConfiguration(ins);
        } catch (IOException e) {
            e.printStackTrace();
        }
    }
    private void start() {
        loadLoggingConfiguration();
        Logger logger = LoggerFactory.getLogger("recipeLogger");
        logger.info("Logging for the first Time!");
        logger.warn("A warning to be had");
        logger.error("This is an error!");
    }
}
```

How It Works

The loadLogConfiguration() function opens a stream to the logging.properties file and passes it to the java.util.logging.LogManager(). Doing so configures the java.util.logging framework to use the settings specified in the logging.properties file. Then, within the start method of the recipe, the code acquires a logger object named recipeLogger. The example proceeds to log messages to through recipeLogger. More information on the actual logging parameters can be found in recipe 6-10.

SLF4J provides a common API using a simple façade pattern that abstracts the underlying logging implementation. SLF4J can be used with most of the common logging frameworks, such as the Java Logging API (java.util.logging), Log4j, Jakarta Commons Logging, and others. In practice, SLF4J gives you the flexibility to choose (and swap) your logging framework, and allows projects that use SLF4J to quickly be integrated into your selected logging framework.

To use SLF4J in your application, you first have to download the SLF4J binaries located at http://www.slf4j.org/. Once downloaded, extract their contents and add slf4j-api-1.6.2.jar to your project. This is the main .jar file that contains the SLF4J API (on which your program can call and log information). After adding the slf4j-api-1.6.2.jar file to your project, find slf4j-jdk14-1.6.2.jar and add that to your project. This second file indicates that SLF4j will use the java.util.logging classes to log information.

The way SLF4J works is that at runtime SLF4J scans the classpath and picks the first .jar that implements the SLF4J API. In the example case, the slf4j-jdk14-1.6.2.jar is found and loaded. This .jar represents the native Java Logging Framework (known as jdk.1.4 logging). If for example, you wanted to use another logging framework, you would replace slf4j-jdk14-1.6.2.jar with the corresponding SLF4J implementation for your logger. For example, to use Apache's Log4J logging framework, you would include slf4j-log4j12-1.6.2.jar.

■ **Note** The java.util.logging framework is configured by the properties log file.

Once SLF4J is configured, you can log information in your application by calling the SLF4J logging methods. The methods log information depending on the logging level. The logging level can then be used to filter which messages are actually logged. The ability to filter messages by log level is useful because there might be a lot of informational or debugging information being logged. If there is the need to troubleshoot an application, the logging level can be changed, and more information is visible in the logs without changing any code. The ability to filter messages through their level is called *setting the log level*. Each logging framework reference has its own configuration file that sets the log level (among other things, such as the logging file name and logging-file configurations). In the example case, because SLF4j is using the `java.util.logging` framework to log, one would need to configure the `java.util.logging` properties for logging.

Table 6-1. Logging Levels

Logging Level	Recommendation
Trace	Least important of the logging events
Debug	Use for extra information that helps with debugging
Info	Use for everyday logging messages
Warn	Use for recoverable issues, or where the suspicions of a wrong setting/nonstandard behavior happens
Error	Use for exceptions, actual errors, and things that you really need to know
Fatal	Most important

■ **Note**   When setting the log level, loggers will log at that level and below. So if a logging configuration sets the log level to info, messages at the Info, Warn, Error, and Fatal levels will be logged.

6-10. Rotating and Purging Logs

Problem

You have started to log information, but the information logged keeps growing out of control. You would like to only keep the last 250KB worth of log entries in your log files.

Solution

Use SLF4J with `java.util.logging` to configure rolling logs. In this recipe, we get the logger named `recipeLogger` and log many times into this logger. The output will produce rolled log files with the most recent logged information in the important `Log0.log` file. Here is the recipe code:

```
loadLoggingConfiguration();

Logger logger = LoggerFactory.getLogger("recipeLogger");
logger.info("Logging for the first Time!");
logger.warn("A warning to be had");
logger.error("This is an error!");

Logger rollingLogger = LoggerFactory.getLogger("rollingLogger");
for (int i =0;i < 5000;i++) {
    rollingLogger.info("Logging for an event with :"+i);
}
```

`logging.properties file`

```
handlers = java.util.logging.FileHandler

recipeLogger.level=INFO

.level=ALL

java.util.logging.FileHandler.formatter=java.util.logging.SimpleFormatter
java.util.logging.FileHandler.pattern=importantLog%g.log
java.util.logging.FileHandler.limit=50000
java.util.logging.FileHandler.count=4
```

How It Works

Configure the `java.util.logging` framework and specify rolling log files. Choosing the rolling log files option causes the latest information to be kept in `ImportantApplication0.log`. Progressively older information will be in `ImportantApplication1.log`, `ImportantApplication2.log`, and so forth. When `ImportantApplication0.log` fills to the limit you specify (50,000 bytes in this example), its name will be rotated to `ImportantApplicationLog1.log`, and the other files will have their names similarly rotated downward. The number of log files to keep is determined by the `java.util.logging.FileHandler.count` property, which is set to 4 in this recipe's example.

The `logging.properties` file starts by defining the handlers that the `java.util.logging` framework will use. Handlers are objects that take care of logging messages. `FileHandler` is specified in the recipe, which logs messages to files. Other possible handlers are the `ConsoleHandler` (logs to the `system.output` device), `SocketHandler` (logs to a socket), and `MemoryHandler` (keeps logs in a circular buffer in memory). There is also the possibility of specifying your own handler implementation by creating a class that extends the `Handler` abstract class.

Next comes the defining of logging levels. Within a logging framework there is the concept of separate logger objects. A logger can carry different configurations (for example, different logging levels), and can be identified in the log file. Our example configures the recipeLogger's level to info, whereas the root logger's level is ALL (root loggers in the java.util.logging framework are denoted by not having any prefix before the property).

The next part of the logging.properties file defines the FileHandler configuration. The formatter indicates how the log information will be written to disk. The simpleFormatter writes the information as plain text, with a line indicating the date and time, a line with the logging level, and the message to be logged. The other default choice for the formatter is the XMLFormatter, which will create XML markup containing the date, time, logger name, level, thread, and message information for each log event. You can create your own formatters by extending the Formatter abstract class.

Following the formatter, the fileHandler pattern is defined. This specifies the file name and location of the log files (the %d is replaced by the rolling log number [0 ~ 4]). The Limit property defines how many bytes the log can have before rolling over (50000 bytes ~ 50kb). The count defines the maximum index of log files to keep (in this recipe's case: 4).

■ **Caution** Logging can be expensive; if you are logging a lot of information, your Java program will start consuming memory (as the java.util.logging framework will try to keep all the information that needs to be written to disk in-memory until it can be flushed). If the java.util.logging framework cannot write the log file as fast as log entries are created, you will run into OutOfMemory errors. The best approach is to log only the necessary information, and, if needed, check to see Logger.isDebugEnabled() before writing out debugging log messages. The logging level can be changed from the logging configuration file.

6-11. Logging Exceptions

From the previous recipes you know how to catch exceptions and how to log information. This recipe will put these two recipes together

Problem

You want to be able to record exceptions in your log file.

Solution

By using SLF4J and try/catch blocks you can log exceptions to the error log. For example:

```
private void start() {
    loadLoggingConfiguration();
    Thread.setDefaultUncaughtExceptionHandler(new Thread.UncaughtExceptionHandler() {
        @Override
```

```
        public void uncaughtException(Thread t, Throwable e) {
            rootLogger.error("Error in thread "+t+" caused by ",e);
        }
    });

    int c = 20/0;
}
```

How It Works

The examples use an `UncaughtExceptionHandler` in conjunction with SLF4J to log exceptions to a logging file. When logging an exception, it is good to include the stack trace showing where the exception was thrown. The `applicationLogger` object includes a method that takes a `String` and a `Throwable` as parameters. When you invoke that function, the logger will record the stack trace of the `Throwable` object in the log file.

■ **Note** If an exception is thrown repeatedly, the JVM tends to stop populating the stack trace in the `Exception` object. This is done for performance reasons because retrieving the same stack trace becomes expensive. If this happens, you will see an exception with no stack trace being logged. When that happens, check the log's previous entries and see whether the same exception was thrown. If the same exception has been thrown previously, the full stack trace will be present on the first logged instance of the exception.

CHAPTER 7

Object-Oriented Java

Programming languages have changed a great deal since the first days of application development. Back in the day, procedural languages were state-of-the-art; as a matter of fact, there are still thousands of COBOL applications in use today. As time went on, coding became more efficient; and reuse, encapsulation, abstraction, and other object-oriented characteristics became fundamental keys to application development. As languages evolved, they began to incorporate the idea of using objects within programs. The Lisp language introduced some object-oriented techniques as early as the 1970s, but true object-oriented programming did not take off in full blast until the 1990s.

Object-oriented programs consist of many different pieces of code that all work together in unison. Rather than having a long list of statements and commands, an object-oriented philosophy is to break functionality up into different objects. Programming techniques such as using methods to encapsulate functionality and copying the functionality of another class began to catch on as people noticed that object orientation equated to productivity.

In this chapter, we will touch upon some of the key object-oriented features of the Java language. From the basic recipes such as learning about access modifiers, to the advanced recipes such as inner classes, this chapter contains recipes that will help you understand Java's object-oriented methodologies.

7-1. Controlling Access to Members of a Class

Problem

You want to create some class members that are not accessible from any other class.

Solution

Create `private` instance members rather than making them available to other classes (`public` or `protected`). For instance, suppose you are creating an application that will be used to manage a team of players for a sport. You create a class named `Player` that will be used to represent a player on the team. You do not want the fields for that class to be accessible from any other class. The following code demonstrates the declaration of some instance members, making them accessible only from within the class in which they were defined.

```java
private String firstName = null;
private String lastName = null;
private String position = null;
private int status = -1;
```

How It Works

To designate a class member as `private`, prefix its declaration or signature using the `private` keyword. The `private` access modifier is used to hide members of a class so that outside classes cannot access them. Any members of a class that are marked as `private` will be available only to other members of the same class. Any outside class will not be able to access fields or methods designated as `private`, and an IDE that uses code completion will not be able to see them.

As mentioned in the solution to this recipe, there are three different access modifiers that can be used when declaring members of a class. Those modifiers are `public`, `protected`, and `private`. Members that are declared as `public` are available for any other class. Those that are declared as `protected` are available for any other class within the same package. It is best to declare `public` or `protected` only those class members that need to be directly accessed from another class. Hiding members of a class using the `private` access modifier helps to enforce better object orientation.

7-2. Making Private Fields Accessible

Problem

You would like to create `private` instance members so that outside classes cannot access them directly. However, you would also like to make those `private` members accessible via a controlled method.

Solution

Encapsulate the `private` fields by making getters and setters to access them. The following code demonstrates the declaration of a `private` field, followed by accessor and mutator methods that can be used to obtain or set the value of that field from an outside class:

```java
private String firstName = null;


/**
 * @return the firstName
 */
public String getFirstName() {
 return firstName;
```

```
}

/**
 * @param firstName the firstName to set
 */
public void setFirstName(String firstName) {
    this.firstName = firstName;
}
```

The getFirstName() method can be used by an outside class to obtain the value of the firstName field. Likewise, the setFirstName(String firstName) method can be used by an outside class to set the value of the firstName field.

How It Works

Often when fields are marked as private within a class, they still need to be made accessible to outside classes. Why not just work with the fields directly and make them public then? It is not good programming practice to work directly with fields of other classes because by using accessors and mutators, access can be granted in a controlled fashion. By not coding directly against members of another class, you also decouple the code, which helps to ensure that if one object changes, others that depend upon it are not adversely affected. As you can see from the example in the solution to this recipe, hiding fields and working against public methods to access those fields is fairly easy. Simply create two methods; one is used to obtain the value of the private field, the "getter" or accessor method. And the other is used to set the value of the private field, the "setter" or mutator method. In the solution to this recipe, the getter is used to return the unaltered value that is contained within the private field. Similarly, the setter is used to set the value of the private field by accepting an argument that is of the same data type as the private field and then setting the value of the private field to the value of the argument.

The class that is using the getters or setters for access to the fields does not know any details behind the methods. Furthermore, the details of these methods can be changed without altering any code that accesses them.

■ **Note** Using getters and setters does not completely decouple code. In fact, many people argue that using getters and setters is not a good programming practice because of this reason. Objects that use the accessor methods still need to know the type of the instance field they are working against. That being said, getters and setters are a standard technique for providing external access to private instance fields of an object. To make the use of accessor methods in a more object-oriented manner, declare them within interfaces and code against the interface rather than the object itself. For more information regarding interfaces, refer to recipe 7-6.

7-3. Creating a Class That Can Have Only One Instance

Problem

You would like to create a class for which only one instance can exist in the entire application, so that all application users interact with the same instance of that class.

Solution 1

Create the class using the Singleton pattern. A class implementing the Singleton pattern allows for only one instance of the class and provides a single point of access to the instance. Suppose that you wanted to create a statistics class that would be used for calculating the statistics for each team and player within an organized sport. It does not make sense to have multiple instances of this class within the application, so you want to create the statistics class as a Singleton in order to prevent multiple instances. The following class represents the Singleton pattern:

```
package org.java7recipes.chapter7.recipe7_03;

import java.util.ArrayList;
import java.util.List;

public class Statistics {

// Definition for the class instance
private static final Statistics instance = new Statistics();

private List teams = new ArrayList();

/**
 * Constructor has been made private so that outside classes do not have
 * access to instantiate more instances of Statistics.
 */
private Statistics(){
}

/**
 * Accessor for the statistics class.  Only allows for one instance of the
 * class to be created.
 * @return
 */
public static Statistics getInstance(){

    return instance;
```

```
}

/**
 * @return the teams
 */
public List getTeams() {
    return teams;
}
/**
 * @param teams the teams to set
 */
public void setTeams(List teams) {
    this.teams = teams;
}
```

If another class attempts to create an instance of this class, it will use the getInstance() accessor method to obtain the Singleton instance.

Solution 2

Create an enum and declare a single element named INSTANCE within it. Then declare other fields within the enum that you can use to store the values that are required for use by your application. The following enum represents a singleton that will provide the same abilities as that of solution 1:

```
import java.util.ArrayList;
import java.util.List;

public enum StatisticsSingleton {
    INSTANCE;

    private List teams = new ArrayList();

    /**
     * @return the teams
     */
    public List getTeams() {
        return teams;
    }

    /**
     * @param teams the teams to set
     */
    public void setTeams(List teams) {
        this.teams = teams;
    }
}
```

■ **Note** There is a test class within the `recipe7_03` package that you can use to work with the `enum` Singleton solution.

How It Works

The Singleton pattern is used to create classes that cannot be instantiated by any other class. This can be useful in cases in which you only want one instance of a class to be used for the entire application. The Singleton pattern can be applied to a class by following three steps. First, make the constructor of the class `private` so that no outside class can instantiate it. Next, define a `private static final` field that will represent an instance of the class. Create an instance of the class and assign it to the field. In the solution to this recipe, the class name is `Statistics`, and the field definition is as follows:

```
private static final Statistics instance = new Statistics();
```

Last, implement an accessor method called `getInstance()` that simply returns the instance field. The following code demonstrates such an accessor method:

```
public static Statistics getInstance(){
    return instance;
}
```

To use the Singleton from another class, call the Singleton's `getInstance()` method. This will return an instance of the class. The following code shows an example of another class obtaining an instance to the `Statistics` Singleton that was defined in solution 1 to this recipe.

```
Statistics statistics = Statistics.getInstance();
```

List teams = `statistics.getTeams();`

Any class that calls the `getInstance()` method of the class will obtain the same instance. Therefore, the fields contained within the Singleton have the same value for every call to `getInstance()` within the entire application.

Solution 2 demonstrates a different way to create a Singleton, which is to use a Java enum rather than a class. Using this approach can be beneficial because an enum provides serialization, prohibits multiple instantiation, and allows one to work with code more concisely. In order to implement the enum Singleton, create an enum and declare an `INSTANCE` element. This is a static constant that will return an instance of the enum to classes that reference it. You can then add elements to the enum that can be used by other classes within the application to store values.

As with any programming solution, there is more than one way to skin a cat. Some believe that the standard Singleton pattern demonstrated in solution 1 is not the most desirable solution. Others do not like the enum solution for different reasons. Both of them will work, although you may find that one works better than the other in certain circumstances.

7-4. Generating Instances of a Class

Problem

In one of your applications, you would like to provide the ability to generate instances of an object on the fly. Each instance of the object should be ready to use, and the creator should not need to know about the details of the object creation.

Solution

Make use of the factory method pattern to instantiate instances of the class while abstracting the creation process from the creator. Creating a factory will enable new instances of a class to be returned upon invocation. The following class represents a simple factory that returns a new instance of a `Player` subclass each time its `createPlayer(String)` method is called. The subclass of `Player` that is returned depends upon what `String` value is passed to the `createPlayer` method.

```java
public class PlayerFactory {

    public static PlayerType createPlayer(String playerType){
        PlayerType returnType;
        switch(playerType){
        case "GOALIE":
            returnType = new Goalie();
            break;
        case "LEFT":
            returnType = new LeftWing();
            break;
        case "RIGHT":
            returnType = new RightWing();
            break;
        case "CENTER":
            returnType = new Center();
            break;
        case "DEFENSE":
            returnType = new Defense();
            break;
        default:
            returnType = new AllPlayer();
        }
        return returnType;
    }
}
```

If a class wants to use the factory, it simply calls the static `createPlayer` method, passing a String value representing a new instance of `Player`. The following code represents one of the `Player` subclasses; the others are very similar:

```java
public class Goalie extends Player implements PlayerType {

    private int totalSaves;

    /**
     * @return the totalSaves
     */
    public int getTotalSaves() {
        return totalSaves;
    }

    /**
     * @param totalSaves the totalSaves to set
     */
    public void setTotalSaves(int totalSaves) {
        this.totalSaves = totalSaves;
    }
}
```

Each of the `Player` subclasses is very similar to the `Goalie` class. The most important code to note is the factory method, `createPlayer`, which can be used to create new instances of the `Player` class.

How It Works

Factories are used to generate objects. Usually they are used to abstract the actual creation of an object from its creators. This can come in very handy for cases where the creator does not need to know about the actual implementation details of generating the new object. The factory pattern can also be useful when controlled access to the creation of an object is required. In order to implement a factory, create a class that contains at least one method that is used for returning a newly created object.

In the solution to this recipe, the `PlayerFactory` class contains a method named `createPlayer(String)` that returns a newly created `Player` object. This method doesn't do anything special behind the scenes; it simply instantiates a new `Player` instance depending upon the String value that is passed to the method. Another object that has access to the `PlayerFactory` class can use `createPlayer` to return new `Player` objects without knowing how the object is created. While this does not hide much in the case of the `createPlayer` method, the `PlayerFactory` abstracts the details of which class is being instantiated so that the developer only has to worry about obtaining a new `Player` object.

The factory pattern is an effective way for controlling how objects are created and making it easier to create objects of a certain type. Imagine if a constructor for an object took more than just a handful of arguments; creating new objects that require more than just a couple of arguments can become a hassle. Generating a factory to create those objects so that you do not have to hard-code all the arguments with each instantiation can make you much more productive!

7-5. Creating Reusable Objects

Problem

You would like to generate an object that could be used to represent something within your application. For instance, suppose that you are creating an application that will be used for generating statistics and league information for different sports teams.

Solution

Create a JavaBean that can be used to represent the object that you want to create. JavaBean objects provide the capability for object fields to be declared as `private`, and they also allow the attributes to be read and updated so that an object can be passed around and used within an application. This recipe demonstrates the creation of a JavaBean named Team. The Team object contains a few different fields that can be used to hold information:

```java
public class Team implements TeamType {

    private List<Player> players;
    private String name = null;
    private String city = null;

    /**
     * @return the players
     */
    public List<Player> getPlayers() {
        return players;
    }

    /**
     * @param players the players to set
     */
    public void setPlayers(List<Player> players) {
        this.players = players;
    }

    /**
     * @return the name
     */
    public String getName() {
        return name;
    }
```

```java
/**
 * @param name the name to set
 */
public void setName(String name) {
    this.name = name;
}

/**
 * @return the city
 */
public String getCity() {
    return city;
}

/**
 * @param city the city to set
 */
public void setCity(String city) {
    this.city = city;
}

}
```

As you can see, the object in this solution contains three fields, and each of those fields is declared as private. However, each field has two accessor methods getter and setter that allow for the fields to be indirectly accessible.

How It Works

The JavaBean is an object that is used to hold information so that it can be passed around and used within an application. One of the most important aspects of a JavaBean is that its fields are declared as private. This prohibits other classes from accessing the fields directly. Instead, each field should be encapsulated by methods defined in order to make them accessible to other classes. These methods must adhere to the following naming conventions:

- Methods used for accessing the field data should be named using a prefix of get, followed by the field name.

- Methods used for setting the field data should be named using a prefix of set, followed by the field name.

For instance, in the solution to this recipe, the Team object contains a field with the name of players. In order to access that field, a method should be declared that is named getPlayers. That method should return the data that is contained within the players field. Likewise, to populate the players field, a method should be declared that is named setPlayers. That method should accept an argument that is of the same type as the players field, and it should set the value of the players field equal to the argument. This can be seen in the following code:

```
public List<Player> getPlayers() {
    return players;
}

void setPlayers(List<Player> players) {
    this.players = players;
}
```

JavaBeans can be used to populate lists of data, written to a database record, or used for a myriad of other functions. Using JavaBeans makes code easier to read and maintain. It also helps to increase the likelihood of future code enhancements because very little code implementation is required. Another benefit of using JavaBeans is that most major IDEs will auto-complete the encapsulation of the fields for you.

7-6. Defining an Interface for a Class

Problem

You would like to generate an abstract type that can be used as a common template to expose the methods and constants that a class implements.

Solution

Generate a Java interface to declare each of the constant fields and methods that a class must implement. Such an interface can then be implemented by a class, and used to represent an object type. The following code is a simple interface that is used to declare the methods that must be implemented by a Team object:

```
public interface TeamType {

    void setPlayers(List<Player> players);
    void setName(String name);
    void setCity(String city);
    String getFullName();
}
```

All the methods in the interface are implicitly abstract. That is, only a method signature is provided. It is also possible to include static final variable declarations in an interface.

How It Works

A Java interface is a construct that is used to define the structures, be it variables or methods, that a class must implement. Any class that implements an interface must include implementations for the methods that are declared within the interface unless it is an abstract class (see recipe 7-11 for more details). An interface does not include any method implementations; rather, it only includes method signatures. Interfaces can include variables that are implicitly `static` and `final`.

In the solution to this recipe, the interface does not include any constant variable declarations. However, it includes three method signatures. All the method signatures have no access modifier specified because all declarations within an interface are implicitly `public`. Interfaces are used to expose a set of functionality; therefore, all methods exposed within an interface must be implicitly `public`. As mentioned previously, only method signatures are present within an interface no implementations. Any class that implements an interface will provide the implementation for the methods declared in the interface, with the exception of an abstract class, in which case it may leave the implementation for one of its subclasses.

While the Java language does not allow multiple inheritance, a Java class can implement multiple interfaces, allowing for a more controlled form of multiple inheritance. Abstract classes can also implement interfaces. The following code demonstrates a class implementing an interface: the Team object declaration implements the TeamType interface.

```java
public class Team implements TeamType {

    private List<Player> players;
    private String name;
    private String city;

    /**
     * @return the players
     */
    public List<Player> getPlayers() {
        return players;
    }

    /**
     * @param players the players to set
     */
    public void setPlayers(List<Player> players) {
        this.players = players;
    }

    /**
     * @return the name
     */
    public String getName() {
        return name;
    }
```

```
    /**
     * @param name the name to set
     */
    public void setName(String name) {
        this.name = name;
    }

    /**
     * @return the city
     */
    public String getCity() {
        return city;
    }

    /**
     * @param city the city to set
     */
    public void setCity(String city) {
        this.city = city;
    }

public String getFullName() {
        return this.name + " - " + this.city;
    }

}
```

Of course, an abstract class only contains method signatures. (To learn more about using classes to implement interfaces, see recipe 7-8.) Interfaces can be used to declare a type for an object. Any object that is declared to have an interface type must adhere to all the implementations declared in the interface. For instance, the following variable declaration defines an object that contains all the properties that are declared within the TeamType interface:

```
TeamType team;
```

Interfaces can also implement other interfaces (thus the same type of theory that is provided by multiple inheritance). However, because no method implementation is present in an interface, it is much safer to implement multiple interfaces in a Java class than it is to extend multiple classes in C++.

Interfaces are some of the single most important pieces of the Java language. Although it is possible to create entire applications without using interfaces, they help to promote object orientation and hide class implementation from other classes.

7-7. Constructing Instances of the Same Class with Different Values

Problem

Your application requires the ability to construct instances of the same object, but each object instance needs to contain different values; thereby creating different types of the same object.

Solution

Make use of the builder pattern in order to build different types of the same object using a step-by-step procedure. For instance, suppose that you are interested in creating the different teams for a sports league. Each of the teams need to contain the same attributes, but the values for those attributes vary by team. So you create many objects of the same type, but each of the objects is unique. The following code demonstrates the builder pattern, which can be used to create the teams that are required.

First, you need to define a set of attributes that each team needs to contain. To do this, a Java interface should be created, containing the different attributes that need to be applied to each team object. The following is an example of such an interface:

```java
public interface TeamType {

    public void setPlayers(List<Player> players);
    public void setName(String name);
    public void setCity(String city);
    public String getFullName();

}
```

Next, define a class to represent a team. This class needs to implement the TeamType interface that was just created so that it will adhere to the format that is required to build a team:

```java
public class Team implements TeamType {

    private List<Player> players;
    private String name = null;
    private String city = null;
    private int wins = 0;
    private int losses = 0;
    private int ties = 0;

    /**
     * @return the players
     */
```

```java
    public List<Player> getPlayers() {
        return players;
    }

    /**
     * @param players the players to set
     */
    public void setPlayers(List<Player> players) {
        this.players = players;
    }

    /**
     * @return the name
     */
    public String getName() {
        return name;
    }

    /**
     * @param name the name to set
     */
    public void setName(String name) {
        this.name = name;
    }

    /**
     * @return the city
     */
    public String getCity() {
        return city;
    }

    /**
     * @param city the city to set
     */
    public void setCity(String city) {
        this.city = city;
    }

    public String getFullName(){
        return this.name + " - " + this.city;
    }


}
```

Now that the Team class has been defined, a builder needs to be created. The purpose of the builder object is to allow for a step-by-step creation of a team object. In order to abstract the details of building an object, a builder class interface should be created. The interface should define any of the methods that would be used to build the object as well as a method that will return a fully built object. In this case, the interface will define each of the methods needed to build a new Team object, and then the builder implementation will implement this interface.

```java
public interface TeamBuilder {
    public void buildPlayerList();
    public void buildNewTeam(String teamName);
    public void designateTeamCity(String city);
    public Team getTeam();


}
```

The following code demonstrates a builder class implementation. Although the following code would not create a custom player list, it contains all the features required to implement the builder pattern. The details of creating a more customized player list can be worked out later, probably by allowing the user to create players via a keyboard entry. Furthermore, the TeamBuilder interface could be used to implement different types of sport teams. The following class is named HockeyTeamBuilder, but a similar class implementing TeamBuilder could be named FootballTeamBuilder, and so forth.

```java
public class HockeyTeamBuilder implements TeamBuilder {

    private Team team;

    public TeamBuilder(){
        this.team = new Team();
    }

    @Override
    public void buildPlayerList() {
        List players = new ArrayList();
        for(int x = 0; x <= 10; x++){
            players.add(PlayerFactory.getPlayer());
        }
        team.setPlayers(players);
    }

    @Override
    public void buildNewTeam() {
        team.setName("The Java 7 Team");
    }

    @Override
    public void designateTeamCity(){
        team.setCity("Somewhere in the world");
```

```
    }

    public Team getTeam(){
        return this.team;
    }

}
```

Last, use the builder by calling upon the methods defined in its interface to create teams. The following code demonstrates how this builder could be used to create one team. You can use the Roster class within the sources for this recipe to test this code:

```
public Team createTeam(String teamName, String city){
    TeamBuilder builder = new HockeyTeamBuilder();
    builder.buildNewTeam(teamName);
    builder.designateTeamCity(city);
    builder.buildPlayerList();
    return builder.getTeam();
}
```

Although this demonstration of the builder pattern is relatively short, you can see how it would be valuable by making objects easier to build. You do not need to know the implementation details of the methods within the builder; you only need to call upon the methods.

How It Works

The builder pattern provides a way to generate new instances of an object in a procedural fashion. It abstracts away the details of object creation, so the creator does not need to do any specific work in order to generate new instances. By breaking the work down into a series of steps, the builder pattern allows objects to implement its builder methods in different ways. Because the object creator only has access to the builder methods, it makes creation of different types of objects much easier.

There are a few classes and interfaces that are necessary for using the builder pattern. First, you need to define a class and its different attributes. As the solution to this recipe demonstrates, the class may follow the JavaBean pattern (see recipe 7-5 for more details). By creating a JavaBean, you will be able to populate the object by using its setters and getters. Next, you should create an interface that can be used for accessing the setters of the object that you created. Each of the setter methods should be defined in the interface, and then the object itself should implement that interface. As seen in the solution, the Team object contains the following setters, and each of them is defined in the TeamType interface:

```
public void setPlayers(List<Player> players);
public void setName(String name);
public void setCity(String city);
```

In real life, a team will probably contain more attributes. For instance, you'd probably want to set up a mascot and a home stadium name and address. The code in this example can be thought of as abbreviated because it demonstrates the creation of a generic "team object" rather than show you all the code for creating a team that is true to life. Because the Team class implements these setters that are defined within the TeamType interface, the interface methods can be called upon in order to interact with the actual methods of the Team class.

After the object and its interface have been coded, the actual builder needs to be created. The builder consists of an interface and its implementation class. To start, you must define the methods that you want to have other classes call upon when building your object. For instance, in the solution to this recipe the methods buildNewTeam(), designateTeamCity(), and buildPlayerList() are defined within the builder interface named TeamBuilder. When a class wants to build one of these objects later, it will only need to call upon these defined methods in order to do it. Next, define a builder class implementation. The implementation class will implement the methods defined within the builder interface, hiding all the details of those implementations from the object creator. In the solution to this recipe, the builder class, Hockey TeamBuilder, implements the TeamBuilder interface. When a class wants to create a new Team object then it simply instantiates a new builder class.

```
TeamBuilder builder = new HockeyTeamBuilder();
```

To populate the newly created class object, the builder methods are called upon it.

```
builder.buildNewTeam(teamName);
builder.designateTeamCity(city);
builder.buildPlayerList();
```

Using this technique provides a step-by-step creation for an object. The implementation details for building that object are hidden from the object creator. It would be easy enough for a different builder implementation to use the same TeamBuilder interface for building team objects for different types. For instance, a builder implementation could be written for generating team objects for hockey, and another one could be defined for generating team objects for baseball. Each of the team object implementations would be different. However, both of them could implement the same interface; TeamBuilder, and the creator could simply call upon the builder methods without caring about the details.

7-8. Interacting with a Class via Interfaces

Problem

You have created a class that implements an interface, or class type. You would like to interact with the methods of that class by working with the interface rather than working directly with the class.

Solution

Declare a variable of the same type as an interface. You can then assign classes that implement the interface to that variable and call upon the methods declared in the interface to perform work. In the following example, a variable is declared to be of type TeamType. Looking back at recipe 7-7, you can see that the class Team implements the TeamType interface. The variable that is created in the following example holds a reference to a new Team object.

Because the Team class implements the TeamType interface, the methods that are exposed in the interface can be used:

```
TeamType team = new Team();
team.setName("Juneau Royals");
team.setCity("Chicago");
System.out.println(team.getFullName());
```

The resulting output:

```
Juneau Royals - Chicago
```

How It Works

Interfaces are useful for many reasons. Two of the most important use cases for interfaces are conformity and abstraction. Interfaces define a model, and any class that implements the interface must conform to that model. Therefore, if there is a variable defined within the interface, it will automatically be available for use in the class. If there is a method defined within the interface, then the class must implement that method. Interfaces provide a nice way to allow classes to conform to a standard.

Interfaces hide unnecessary information from any class that does not need to see it. Any method that is defined within the interface is made public and accessible to any class. As demonstrated in the solution to this recipe, an object was created and declared to be the type of an interface. The interface in the example, TeamType, only includes a small subset of methods that are available within the Team object. Therefore, the only methods that are accessible to any class working against an object that has been declared to be of TeamType are the ones that are defined within the interface. The class using this interface type cannot see any of the other methods or constants, nor does it need to. Interfaces are a great way for hiding logic that does not need to be used by other classes. Another great side effect: A class that implements an interface can be changed and recompiled without affecting code that works against the interface. However, if an interface is changed, there could be an effect on any classes that implement it. Therefore, if the getFullName() method implementation changes, any class that is coded against the TeamType interface will not be affected because the interface is unchanged. The implementation will change behind the scenes, and any class working against the interface will just begin to use the new implementation without needing to know.

Finally, interfaces help to promote security. They hide away implementation details of methods that are declared in an interface from any class that may call that method using the interface. As mentioned in the previous paragraph, if a class is calling the getFullName() method against the TeamType interface, it does not need to know the implementation details of that method as long as the result is returned as expected.

The Enterprise JavaBean (EJB) 3.0 model used interfaces for interacting with methods that performed database work. This model worked very well for hiding the details and logic that were not essential for use from other classes. Other frameworks use similar models, exposing functionality through Java interfaces. Interface use has proven to be a smart way to code software because it promotes reusability, flexibility, and security.

7-9. Making a Class Cloneable

Problem

You would like to enable a class to be cloned by another class.

Solution

Implement the `Cloneable` interface within the class that you want to clone; then call that object's clone method to make a copy of it. The following code demonstrates how to make the `Team` class cloneable:

```java
public class Team implements TeamType, Cloneable, Serializable {

    private String name;
    private String city;


    /**
     * @return the name
     */
    public String getName() {
        return name;
    }

    /**
     * @param name the name to set
     */
    public void setName(String name) {
        this.name = name;
    }

    /**
     * @return the city
     */
    public String getCity() {
        return city;
    }

    /**
     * @param city the city to set
     */
    public void setCity(String city) {
        this.city = city;
```

```java
}

public String getFullName() {
    return this.name + " - " + this.city;
}

/**
 * Overrides Object's clone method to create a deep copy
 *
 * @return
 */
public Object clone() {

    Object obj = null;
    try {
        ByteArrayOutputStream baos = new ByteArrayOutputStream();
        ObjectOutputStream oos = new ObjectOutputStream(baos);
        oos.writeObject(this);
        oos.close();

        ByteArrayInputStream bais = new ByteArrayInputStream(baos.toByteArray());
        ObjectInputStream ois = new ObjectInputStream(bais);
        obj = ois.readObject();
        ois.close();
    } catch (IOException e) {
        e.printStackTrace();
    } catch (ClassNotFoundException cnfe) {
        cnfe.printStackTrace();
    }
    return obj;
}

/**
 * Overrides Object's clone method to create a shallow copy
 *
 * @return
 */
public Object shallowCopyClone() {

    try {
        return super.clone();
    } catch (CloneNotSupportedException ex) {
        return null;
    }
}
```

```
    @Override
    public boolean equals(Object obj) {

        if (this == obj) {
            return true;
        }
        if (obj instanceof Team) {
            Team other = (Team) obj;
            return other.getName().equals(this.getName())
&& other.getCity().equals(this.getCity());
        } else {
            return false;
        }
    }
}
```

Next, to make a deep copy of a Team object, the clone() method needs to be called against that object. To make a shallow copy of the object, the shallowCopyClone() method must be called. The following code demonstrates this technique:

```
Team team1 = new Team();
Team team2 = new Team();

team1.setCity("Boston");
team1.setName("Bandits");

team2.setCity("Chicago");
team2.setName("Wildcats");


Team team3 = team1;
Team team4 = (Team) team2.clone();

Team team5 = team1.shallowCopyClone();

System.out.println("Team 3:");
System.out.println(team3.getCity());
System.out.println(team3.getName());

System.out.println("Team 4:");
System.out.println(team4.getCity());
System.out.println(team4.getName());

// Teams move to different cities
team1.setCity("St. Louis");
```

```
team2.setCity("Orlando");

System.out.println("Team 3:");
System.out.println(team3.getCity());
System.out.println(team3.getName());

System.out.println("Team 4:");
System.out.println(team4.getCity());
System.out.println(team4.getName());

System.out.println("Team 5:");
System.out.println(team5.getCity());
System.out.println(team5.getName());


if (team1 == team3){
    System.out.println("team1 and team3 are equal");
} else {
    System.out.println("team1 and team3 are NOT equal");
}

if (team1 == team5){
System.out.println("team1 and team5 are equal");
    } else {
System.out.println("team1 and team5 are NOT equal");
}
```

Although this code does not do very much, it demonstrates how to make a clone of an object. The resulting output would be as follows.

```
Team 3:
Boston
Bandits
Team 4:
Chicago
Wildcats
Team 3:
St. Louis
Bandits
Team 4:
Chicago
Wildcats
Team 5:
Boston
Bandits
team1 and team3 are equal
team1 and team5 are NOT equal
```

How It Works

There are two different strategies that can be used to copy an object: shallow and deep copies. A *shallow copy* can be made that would copy the object without any of its contents or data. Rather, all the variables are passed by reference into the copied object. After a shallow copy of an object has been created, the objects within both the original object and its copy refer to the same data and memory. Thus, modifying the original object's contents will also modify the copied object. By default, calling the `super.clone()` method against an object performs a shallow copy. The `shallowCopyClone()` method in the solution to this recipe demonstrates this technique.

The second type of copy that can be made is known as a *deep copy*, which copies the object including all the contents. Therefore, each object refers to a different space in memory, and modifying one object will not affect the other. In the solution to this recipe, the difference between a deep and a shallow copy is demonstrated. First, `team1` and `team2` are created. Next, they are populated with some values. The `team3` object is then set equal to the `team1` object, and the `team4` object is made a clone of the `team2` object. When the values are changed within the `team1` object, they are also changed in the `team3` object because both object's contents refer to the same space in memory. This is an example of a shallow copy of an object. When the values are changed within the `team2` object, they remain unchanged in the `team4` object because each object has its own variables that refer to different spaces in memory. This is an example of a deep copy.

In order to make an exact copy of an object (deep copy), you must serialize the object. The base `Object` class implements the `clone()` method. By default, the `Object` class's `clone()` method is `protected`. In order to make an object cloneable, it must implement the `Cloneable` interface and override the default `clone()` method. You can make a deep copy of an object by serializing it through a series of steps, such as writing the object to an output stream and then reading it back via an input stream. The steps shown in the `clone()` method of the solution to this recipe do just that. The object is written to a `ByteArrayOutputStream` and then read using a `ByteArrayInputStream`. Once that has occurred, the object has been serialized, which creates the deep copy. The `clone()` method in the solution to this recipe has been overridden so that it creates a deep copy.

Once these steps have been followed and an object implements `Cloneable` as well as overrides the default Object `clone()` method, it is possible to clone the object. In order to make a deep copy of an object, simply call that object's overridden `clone()` method.

```
Team team4 = (Team) team2.clone();
```

Cloning objects is not very difficult, but a good understanding of the differences that can vary with object copies is important.

7-10. Comparing Objects

Problem

Your application requires the capability to compare two or more objects to see whether they are the same.

Solution 1

To determine whether the two object references point to the same object, make use of the == and != operators. The following solution demonstrates the comparison of two object references to determine whether they both refer to the same object.

```
// Compare if two objects contain the same values
Team team1 = new Team();
Team team2 = new Team();

team1.setName("Jokers");
team1.setCity("Crazyville");

team2.setName("Jokers");
team2.setCity("Crazyville");

if (team1 == team2){
    System.out.println("These object references refer to the same object.");
} else {
    System.out.println("These object references do NOT refer to the same object.");
}

// Compare two objects to see if they refer to the same object
Team team3 = team1;
Team team4 = team1;

if (team3 == team4){
    System.out.println("These object references refer to the same object.");
} else {
    System.out.println("These object references do NOT refer to the same object.");
}
```

The results of running the code:

```
These object references do NOT refer to the same object.
These object references refer to the same object.
```

Solution 2

To determine whether the two objects contain the same values, use the equals() method. The object being compared must implement equals() and hashCode() in order for this solution to work properly. Following is the code for the Team class that overrides these two methods:

```
public class Team implements TeamType, Cloneable {

    private List<Player> players;
```

```java
    private String name;
    private String city;
    // Used by the hashCode method for performance reasons
    private volatile int cachedHashCode = 0;

    /**
     * @return the players
     */
    public List<Player> getPlayers() {
        return players;
    }

    /**
     * @param players the players to set
     */
    public void setPlayers(List<Player> players) {
        this.players = players;
    }

    /**
     * @return the name
     */
    public String getName() {
        return name;
    }

    /**
     * @param name the name to set
     */
    public void setName(String name) {
        this.name = name;
    }

    /**
     * @return the city
     */
    public String getCity() {
        return city;
    }

    /**
     * @param city the city to set
     */
    public void setCity(String city) {
        this.city = city;
```

```java
    }

    public String getFullName() {
        return this.name + " - " + this.city;
    }

    /**
     * Overrides Object's clone method
     *
     * @return
     */
    public Object clone() {

        try {
            return super.clone();
        } catch (CloneNotSupportedException ex) {
            return null;
        }
    }

    @Override
    public boolean equals(Object obj) {

        if (this == obj) {
            return true;
        }
        if (obj instanceof Team) {
            Team other = (Team) obj;
            return other.getName().equals(this.getName())
&& other.getCity().equals(this.getCity())
&& other.getPlayers().equals(this.getPlayers());
        } else {
            return false;
        }

    }

@Override
    public int hashCode() {
        int hashCode = cachedHashCode;
        if (hashCode == 0) {
            String concatStrings = name + city;
            if (players.size() > 0) {
                for (Player player : players) {
                    concatStrings = concatStrings
```

```
                        + player.getFirstName()
                        + player.getLastName()
                        + player.getPosition()
                        + String.valueOf(player.getStatus());

            }
        }
        hashCode = concatStrings.hashCode();
    }
    return hashCode;
}
}
```

The following solution demonstrates the comparison of two objects that contain the same values.

```
// Compare if two objects contain the same values
Team team1 = new Team();
Team team2 = new Team();

// Build Player List
Player newPlayer = new Player("Josh", "Juneau");
playerList.add(0, newPlayer);
newPlayer = new Player("Carl", "Dea");
playerList.add(1, newPlayer);
newPlayer = new Player("Freddy", "Guime");
playerList.add(1, newPlayer);
newPlayer = new Player("John", "OConner");
playerList.add(1, newPlayer);
 newPlayer = new Player("Mark", "Beaty");
playerList.add(1, newPlayer);

team1.setName("Jokers");
team1.setCity("Crazyville");
team1.setPlayers(playerList);

team2.setName("Jokers");
team2.setCity("Crazyville");
team2.setPlayers(playerList);

if (team1.equals(team2)){
    System.out.println("These object references contain the same values.");
} else {
    System.out.println("These object references do NOT contain the same values.");
}
```

The results of running this code:

```
These object references contain the same values.
```

How It Works

The comparison operator (==) can be used to determine the equality of two objects. This equality does not pertain to the object values, but rather to the object references. Often an application is more concerned with the values of objects; in such cases, the equals() method is the preferred choice because it compares the values contained within the objects rather than the object references.

The comparison operator takes a look at the object reference and it determines whether it points to the same object as the object reference that it is being compared against. If the two objects are equal to each other, a Boolean true result will be returned; otherwise, a Boolean false result will be returned. In solution 1, the first comparison between the team1 object reference and the team2 object reference returns a false value because those two objects are separate in memory, even though they contain the same values. The second comparison in solution 1 between the team3 object reference and the team4 object reference returns a true value because both of those references refer to the team1 object.

The equals() method can be used to test whether two objects contain the same values. In order to use the equals() method for comparison, the object that is being compared should override the Object class equals()and hashCode() methods. The equals() method should implement a comparison against the values contained within the object that would yield a true comparison result. The following code is an example of an overridden equals() method that has been placed into the Team object:

```java
@Override
public boolean equals(Object obj) {

    if (this == obj) {
        return true;
    }
    if (obj instanceof Team) {
        Team other = (Team) obj;
        return other.getName().equals(this.getName())
&& other.getCity().equals(this.getCity())
&& other.getPlayers().equals(this.getPlayers());
    } else {
        return false;
    }

}
```

As you can see, the overridden equals() method first checks to see whether the object that is passed as an argument is referencing the same object as the one that it is being compared against. If so, a true result is returned. If both objects are not referencing the same object in memory, the equals() method checks to see whether the fields are equal to each other. In this case, any two Team objects that contain the same values within the name and city fields would be considered equal. Once the equals() method has been overridden, the comparison of the two objects can be performed, as demonstrated in solution 2 to this recipe.

The hashCode() method returns an int value that must consistently return the same integer. There are many ways in which to calculate the hashCode of an object. Perform a web search on the topic and you will find various techniques. One of the most basic ways to implement the hashCode() method is to concatenate all the object's variables in String format and then return the resulting String's hashCode(). It is a good idea to cache the value of the hashCode for later use because the initial calculation may take some time. The hashCode() method in solution 2 demonstrates this tactic.

Comparing Java objects can become confusing, considering that there are multiple ways to compare objects. If the comparison that you want to perform is against the object identity, use the comparison (==) operator. However, if you want to compare the values within the objects, or the state of the objects, then the equals() method is the way to go.

7-11. Extending the Functionality of a Class

Problem

One of your applications contains a class that you would like to use as a base for another class. You want your new class to contain the same functionality of this base class, but also include additional functionality.

Solution

Extend the functionality of the base class by using the extends keyword followed by the name of the class that you would like to extend. The following example shows two classes. The first class, named HockeyStick, represents a hockey stick object. It will be extended by the second class named WoodenStick. By doing so, the WoodenStick class will inherit all the properties and functionality that is contained within HockeyStick, with the exception of private variables and those that have the default access level. The WoodenStick class becomes a subclass of HockeyStick. First, the HockeyStick class contains the basic properties of a standard hockey stick:

```java
public class HockeyStick {

    public int length;
    public boolean isCurved;
    public String material;

    public HockeyStick(int length, boolean isCurved, String material){
        this.length = length;
        this.isCurved = isCurved;
        this.material = material;
    }

    public int getlength() {
        return length;
    }
```

```java
    public void setlength(int length) {
        this.length = length;
    }

    public boolean isIsCurved() {
        return isCurved;
    }

    public void setIsCurved(boolean isCurved) {
        this.isCurved = isCurved;
    }

    public String getmaterial() {
        return material;
    }

    public void setmaterial(String material) {
        this.material = material;
    }

}
```

Next, we will look at the subclass of HockeyStick: a class named WoodenStick.

```java
public class WoodenStick extends HockeyStick {

    public static final String material = "WOOD";
    public int lie;
    public int flex;

    public WoodenStick(int length, boolean isCurved){
        super(length, isCurved, material);
    }

    public WoodenStick(int length, boolean isCurved, int lie, int flex){
        super(length, isCurved, material);
        this.lie = lie;
        this.flex = flex;
    }
}
```

How It Works

Object inheritance is a fundamental technique in any object-oriented language. Inheriting from a base class adds value because it allows code to become reusable in multiple places. This helps to make code management much easier. If a change is made in the base class, it will automatically be inherited in the child. On the other hand, if you had duplicate functionality scattered throughout your application, one minor change could mean that you would have to change code in many places. Object inheritance also makes it easy to designate a base class to one or more subclasses so that each class can contain similar fields and functionality.

The Java language only allows a class to extend one other class. This differs in concept from other languages such as C++; which contain multiple inheritance. Although some look at single class inheritance as a hindrance to the language, it was designed that way to add safety and ease of use to the language. When a subclass contains multiple superclasses, confusion ensues.

7-12. Defining a Class Template

Problem

You would like to define a template that can be used to generate objects containing similar functionality.

Solution

Define an abstract class that contains fields and functionality that can be used in other classes. The abstract class can also include unimplemented methods, called *abstract methods*, which will need to be implemented by a subclass of the abstract class. The following example demonstrates the concept of an abstract class. The abstract class represents a team schedule, and it includes some basic field declarations and functionality that every team's schedule will need to use. The Schedule class is then extended by the TeamSchedule class, which will be used to implement specific functionality for each team. First, let's take a look at the abstract Schedule class:

```
public abstract class Schedule {

    public String scheduleYear;
    public String teamName;

    public List<Team> teams;

    public List homeGames;
    public List awayGames;

    Map gameMap;

    public Schedule(){}
```

```java
    public Schedule(String teamName){
        this.teamName = teamName;
    }

    public Map obtainSchedule(){
        if (gameMap == null){
            gameMap = new HashMap();
        }
        return gameMap;
    }

    public void setGameDate(Team team, Date date){

        obtainSchedule().put(team, date);
    }

    abstract void calculateDaysPlayed(int month);

}
```

Next, the TeamSchedule extends the functionality of the abstract class.

```java
public class TeamSchedule extends Schedule {

    public TeamSchedule(String teamName){
        super(teamName);
    }

    @Override
    void calculateDaysPlayed(int month) {

        // Perform implementation here

        throw new UnsupportedOperationException("Not supported yet.");
    }

}
```

As you can see, the TeamSchedule class can use all the fields and methods that are contained within the abstract Schedule class. It also implements the abstract method that is contained within the Schedule class. By the way, do not attempt to figure out what exactly these classes will do in the end because they are provided for this basic example only. I am not a professional sports schedule implementer, nor do I claim to be; these are just a few fields and methods that came to mind when thinking about what it may take to create a team's schedule.

How It Works

Abstract classes are labeled as such, and they contain field declarations and methods that can be used within subclasses. What makes them different from a regular class? Abstract classes can contain abstract methods, which are method declarations with no implementation. The solution to this recipe contains an abstract method named `calculateDaysPlayed()`. Abstract classes may or may not contain abstract methods. They can contain fields and completely implemented methods as well. Abstract classes cannot be instantiated; other classes can only extend them. When a class extends an abstract class, it gains all the fields and functionality of the abstract class. However, any abstract methods that are declared within the abstract class must be implemented by the subclass.

You may wonder why the abstract class wouldn't just contain the implementation of the method so that it was available for all its subclasses to use. If you think about the concept, it makes perfect sense. One type of object may perform a task differently from another. Using an abstract method forces the class that is extending the abstract class to implement it, but it allows the ability to customize how it is implemented.

7-13. Increasing Class Encapsulation

Problem

One of your classes requires the use of another class's functionality. Furthermore, no other class requires the use of that same functionality. Rather than creating a separate class that includes this additional functionality, you'd like to generate an implementation that can only be used by the class that needs it.

Solution

Create an *inner class* within the class that requires its functionality.

```java
import java.util.ArrayList;
import java.util.List;

/**
 * Inner class example. This example demonstrates how a team object could be
 * built using an inner class object.
 *
 * @author juneau
 */
public class TeamInner {

    private Player player;
    private List<Player> playerList;
    private int size = 4;
```

```java
/**
 * Inner class representing a Player object
 */
class Player {

    private String firstName = null;
    private String lastName = null;
    private String position = null;
    private int status = -1;

    public Player() {
    }

    public Player(String position, int status) {
        this.position = position;
        this.status = status;
    }

    protected String playerStatus() {
        String returnValue = null;

        switch (getStatus()) {
            case 0:
                returnValue = "ACTIVE";
                break;
            case 1:
                returnValue = "INACTIVE";
                break;
            case 2:
                returnValue = "INJURY";
                break;
            default:
                returnValue = "ON_BENCH";
                break;
        }

        return returnValue;
    }

    public String playerString() {
        return getFirstName() + " " + getLastName() + " - " + getPosition();
    }

    /**
```

```java
     * @return the firstName
     */
    public String getFirstName() {
        return firstName;
    }

    /**
     * @param firstName the firstName to set
     */
    public void setFirstName(String firstName) {
        if (firstName.length() > 30) {
            this.firstName = firstName.substring(0, 29);
        } else {
            this.firstName = firstName;
        }
    }

    /**
     * @return the lastName
     */
    public String getLastName() {
        return lastName;
    }

    /**
     * @param lastName the lastName to set
     */
    public void setLastName(String lastName) {
        this.lastName = lastName;
    }

    /**
     * @return the position
     */
    public String getPosition() {
        return position;
    }

    /**
     * @param position the position to set
     */
    public void setPosition(String position) {
        this.position = position;
    }
```

```java
        /**
         * @return the status
         */
        public int getStatus() {
            return status;
        }

        /**
         * @param status the status to set
         */
        public void setStatus(int status) {
            this.status = status;
        }

        @Override
        public String toString(){
            return this.firstName + " " + this.lastName + " - "+ this.position + ": " +
this.playerStatus();
        }
    }

    /**
     * Inner class that constructs the Player objects and adds them to an array
     * that was declared in the outer class;
     */
    public TeamInner() {

        // In reality, this would probably read records from a database using
        // a loop...but for this example we will manually enter the player data.
        playerList = new ArrayList();
        playerList.add(constructPlayer("Josh", "Juneau", "Right Wing", 0));
        playerList.add(constructPlayer("Carl", "Dea", "Left Wing", 0));
        playerList.add(constructPlayer("Mark", "Beaty", "Center", 0));
        playerList.add(constructPlayer("Jonathan", "Gennick", "Goalie", 0));
    }

    public Player constructPlayer(String first, String last, String position, int status){
            Player player = new Player();
            player.firstName = first;
            player.lastName = last;
            player.position = position;
            player.status = status;
            return player;
    }

    public List<Player> getPlayerList() {
        return this.playerList;
```

```
        }

    public static void main(String[] args) {
TeamInner inner = new TeamInner();
        System.out.println("Team Roster");
        System.out.println("===========");
for(Player player:inner.getPlayerList()){
            System.out.println(player.playerString());
        }
    }
}
```

The result of running this code is a listing of the players on the team.

```
Team Roster
===========
Josh Juneau - Right Wing
Carl Dea - Left Wing
Mark Beaty - Center
Jonathan Gennick - Goalie
```

How It Works

Sometimes it is important to encapsulate functionality within a single class. Other times it does not make sense to include a separate class for functionality that is only used within one other class. Imagine that you are developing a GUI and you need to use a class to support functionality for one button. If there is no reusable code within that button class, it does not make sense to create a separate class and expose that functionality for other classes to use. Instead, it makes sense to encapsulate that class inside of the class that needs the functionality. This philosophy is one use case for inner classes (also known as *nested classes*).

An inner class is a class that is contained within another class. The inner class can be made public, private, or protected just like any other class. It can contain the same functionality as a normal class; the only difference is that the inner class is contained within an enclosing class, otherwise referred to as an *outer class*. The solution to this recipe demonstrates this technique. The class TeamInner contains one inner class named Player. The Player class is a JavaBean class that represents a Player object. As you can see, the Player object has the capability to inherit functionality from its containing class, including its private fields. This is because inner classes contain an implicit reference to the outer class. It can also be accessed by the containing TeamInner class, as demonstrated within the constructPlayer() method:

```
public Player constructPlayer(String first, String last, String position, int status){
        Player player = new Player();
        player.firstName = first;
        player.lastName = last;
        player.position = position;
        player.status = status;
        return player;
    }
```

Outer classes can instantiate an inner class as many times as needed. In the example, the constructPlayer() method could be called any number of times, instantiating a new instance of the inner class. However, when the outer class is instantiated, no instances of the inner class are instantiated.

Inner classes can reference outer class methods by referring to the outer class and then referring to the method that it wants to call. The following line of code demonstrates such a reference using the same objects that are represented in the solution to this recipe. Suppose that the Player class needed to obtain the player list from the outer class; you would write something similar to the following:

```
TeamInner.this.getPlayerList();
```

Although not very often used, classes other than the outside class can obtain access to a public inner class by using the following syntax:

```
TeamInner outerClass = new TeamInner();
outerClass.Player innerClass = outclass.new Player();
```

Inner classes help to provide encapsulation of logic. Furthermore, they allow inheritance of private fields, which is not possible using a standard class.

CHAPTER 8

Concurrency

Concurrency is one of the toughest topics to handle in modern computer programming; understanding concurrency requires the capacity of thinking abstractly, and debugging concurrent problems is like trying to pilot an airplane by dead reckoning. Even so, with today's Java 7, it has become easier (and more accessible) to write bug-free concurrent code.

Let's start with definitions; *concurrency* is the ability of a program to execute different (or the same) instructions at the same time. A program that is said to be concurrent has the ability to be split up and run on multiple cpus. By making concurrent programs, you take advantage of today's multicore CPUs. You can even see benefit on single-core CPUs that are I/O intensive.

In this chapter, we present the most common need for concurrency tasks% from running a background task to splitting a computation into work units. Throughout the chapter, you will find the most up-to-date recipes for accomplishing concurrency in Java 7.

8-1. Starting a Background Task

Problem

You have a task that needs to be run outside of your main thread.

Solution

Implement a Runnable interface and start a new Thread. For example:

```
private void someMethod()  {
    Thread backgroundThread = new Thread(new Runnable() {
        public void run() {
            doSomethingInBackground();
        }
    },"Background Thread");

    System.out.println("Start");
    backgroundThread.start();
```

```
    for (int i= 0;i < 10;i++) {
        System.out.println(Thread.currentThread().getName()+": is counting "+i);
    }

    System.out.println("Done");
}

private void doSomethingInBackground() {
    System.out.println(Thread.currentThread().getName()+ ": is Running in the
background");
    }
```

How It Works

The Thread class allows executing code in a new thread (path of execution), distinct from the current thread. The Thread constructor requires as a parameter a class that implements the Runnable interface. The Runnable interface requires the implementation of only one method: public void run(). Then the Thread's start() method is invoked. That method will in turn create the new thread and invoke the run() method of the Runnable.

Within the JVM are two types of threads: User and Daemon. User threads keep executing until their run() method finishes, whereas Daemon threads can be terminated if the application needs to exit. An application exits if there are only Daemon threads running in the JVM. When you start to create multithreaded application, you must be aware of these differences and when to use each type of thread.

Usually, Daemon threads will have a Runnable interface that doesn't finish; for example a while (true) loop. This allows these threads to periodically check or perform a certain condition through the life of the program and be discarded when the program is done executing. In contrast, User threads, while alive, will execute and prevent the program from terminating. If you happen to have a program that is not closing and/or exiting when expected, you might want to check the thread types that are actively running (See recipe 9-8 for getting a Thread dump).

To set a thread as a Daemon thread, use the thread.setDaemon(true) before calling the thread.start() method. By default, Thread instances are created as User thread types.

■ **Caution** This recipe shows the simplest way to create and execute a new thread. The new thread created is a User thread, which means that the application will not exit until both the main thread and the background thread are done executing.

8-2. Updating (and Iterating) a Map

Problem

You need to update a Map object from multiple threads, and you want to make sure that the update doesn't break the contents of the Map object and that the Map object is always in a consistent state. You also want to traverse (look at) the content of the Map object while other threads are updating the Map object.

Solution

Use a ConcurrentMap to update Map entries. The following example creates 1,000 threads. Each thread then tries to modify the Map at the same time. The main thread then waits for a second, and proceeds to iterate through the Map (even when the other threads are still modifying the Map):

```
ConcurrentMap<Integer,String> concurrentMap = ↵
                new ConcurrentHashMap<Integer, String>();
for (int i =0;i < 1000;i++) {
    startUpdateThread(i, concurrentMap);
}
try {
    Thread.sleep(1000);
} catch (InterruptedException e) {
    e.printStackTrace();
}
for (Map.Entry<Integer, String> entry : concurrentMap.entrySet()) {
    System.out.println("Key :"+entry.getKey()+" Value:"+entry.getValue());
}
```

////

```
private void startUpdateThread(int i, final ConcurrentMap<Integer, String> concurrentMap) {
    Thread thread = new Thread(new Runnable() {
        public void run() {
            while (!Thread.interrupted()) {
                int randomInt = random.nextInt(20);
                concurrentMap.put(randomInt, UUID.randomUUID().toString());
            }
        }
    });
    thread.setName("Update Thread "+i);
    updateThreads.add(thread);
    thread.start();
}
```

How It Works

ConcurrentHashMap allows for multiple threads to modify the table concurrently and safely. In our example, we have 1,000 threads over a second modifying the Map. The ConcurrentHashMapiterator also allows safe iteration over its contents. When using the ConcurrentMap's iterator, you do not have to worry about locking the contents of the ConcurrentMap while iterating over it (and it doesn't throw ConcurrentModificationExceptions).

■ **Note** ConcurrentMap iterators, while thread safe, don't guarantee that you will see entries added/updated after thre iterator was created.

8-3. Inserting a Key into a Map Only If the Key is not Already Present

Problem

You need to put a key/value pair in a Map only if the key is not present, and the Map is being constantly updated by other threads. You need to check for the key's presence first, and you need assurance that some other thread doesn't insert the same key after you check and before you insert yourself.

Solution

Using the ConcurrentMap.putIfAbsent() method, you can be assured that either the map was modified atomically or not. For example, the following code uses the method to check and insert in a single step, thus avoiding the concurrency problem:

```java
private void start() {
    ConcurrentMap<Integer, String> concurrentMap = new ConcurrentHashMap<Integer,
String>();
    for (int i = 0; i < 100; i++) {
        startUpdateThread(i, concurrentMap);
    }

    try {
        Thread.sleep(1000);
    } catch (InterruptedException e) {
        e.printStackTrace();
    }
```

```
        for (Map.Entry<Integer, String> entry : concurrentMap.entrySet()) {
            System.out.println("Key :" + entry.getKey() + " Value:" + entry.getValue());
        }

    }

    private void startUpdateThread(final int i, ↵
                        final ConcurrentMap<Integer, String> concurrentMap) {
        Thread thread = new Thread(new Runnable() {
            public void run() {
                int randomInt = random.nextInt(20);
                String previousEntry = concurrentMap.putIfAbsent(randomInt, "Thread # " + i ↵
                        + " has made it!");
                if (previousEntry != null) {
                    System.out.println("Thread # " + i + " tried to update it but guess ↵
                                        what, we're too late!");
                    return;
                } else {
                    System.out.println("Thread # " + i + " has made it!");
                    return;
                }
            }
        });
        thread.start();
    }
```

How It Works

Updating a Map concurrently is hard because it involves two operations: a *check-then-act* type of operation. First, the Map has to be checked to see whether an entry already exists in it. If the entry doesn't exist, you can put the key and the value into the Map. On the other hand, if the key exists, the value for the key is retrieved. To do so, we use the ConcurrentMap's putIfAbsent atomic operation. This ensures that either the key was present and the value is not overwritten, or the key was not present and the value is set. For the JDK implementations of ConcurrentMap, the putIfAbsent() method will return null if there was no value for the key or return the current value if the key has a value. By asserting that the putIfAbsent() method returns null, you are assured that the operation was successful and that a new entry in the map has been created.

There are cases when putIfAbsent() might not be efficient to execute. For example, if the result is a large database query, executing the database query all the time and then invoking putIfAbsent() will not be efficient. In this kind of scenario, you could first call the map's containsKey() method to ensure that the key is not present. If it's not present then call the putIfAbsent() with the expensive database query. There might be a chance that the putIfAbsent() didn't put the entry, but this type of check reduces the number of potentially expensive value creation.

See the following code snippet:

```
keyPresent = concurrentMap.containsKey(randomInt);
        if (!keyPresent) {
                concurrentMap.putIfAbsent(randomInt, "Thread # " + i + " has made it!");
        }
```

In this code, the first operation is to check whether the key is already in the map. If it is, it doesn't execute the `putIfAbsent()` operation. If the key is not present, you can proceed to execute the `putIfAbsent()` operation.

If you are accessing the values of the map from different threads, you should make sure that the values are threadsafe. This is most evident when using collections as values because they then could be used from different threads. Having the main map threadsafe will prevent concurrent modifications to the map, but once you get access to the values of the map, you should exercise good concurrency practices around the values of the map.

■ **Note** ConcurrentMaps don't allow `null` keys, which is different from its non threadsafe cousin `HashMap` (which allows `null` keys).

8-4. Iterating Through a Changing Collection

Problem

You need to iterate over each element in a collection, but the collection is always being changed by other threads.

Solution 1

By using a `CopyOnWriteArrayList` you can safely iterate through the collection without worrying about concurrency. In our solution, the `startUpdatingThread()` method creates a new thread, which actively change the `List` passed to it. While `startUpdatingThread()` modifies the list, you iterate through it concurrently by using a `for` loop.

```
private void copyOnWriteSolution() {
    CopyOnWriteArrayList<String> list = new CopyOnWriteArrayList<String>();
    startUpdatingThread(list);
    for (String element : list) {
        System.out.println("Element :" + element);
    }
    stopUpdatingThread();

}
```

Solution 2

Using a `synchronizedList()` allows to atomically change the collection. Also, a `synchronizedList()` provides a way to synchronize safely on the list while iterating through it (which is done in the `for` loop). For example:

```
private void synchronizedListSolution() {
    final List<String> list = Collections.synchronizedList(new ArrayList<String>());
    startUpdatingThread(list);
    synchronized (list) {
        for (String element : list) {
            System.out.println("Element :" + element);
        }
    }
    stopUpdatingThread();

}
```

How It Works

Java comes with many concurrent collection options. The selection of the collection to use depends on how the read operations compare with write operations. If writing happens far and in-between compared with reads, using a `copyOnWriteArrayList` instance is the most efficient collection to use because it doesn't *block* (stop other threads) from reading the list and is threadsafe to iterate over (no `ConcurrentModificationException` being thrown when iterating through it). If there are the same number of writes and reads, using a `SynchronizedList` is the preferred choice.

In solution 1, the `CopyOnWriteArrayList` is being updated while you traverse the list. Because the recipe uses the `CopyOnWriteArrayList` instance, there is not need to worry of threadsafety when iterating through the collection (as is being done in this recipe by using the `for` loop). To note is that the `CopyOnWriteArrayList`, offers a snapshot in time when iterating through it. If another thread modifies the list as one is iterating through it, the changes to the modified list will not be visible when iterating.

■ **Caution** Locking properly depends on the type of collection used. Anything that comes as a result of using `Collections.synchronized` can be locked by using the collection itself (`synchronized (collectionInstance)`), but some more efficient (newer) concurrent collections like the `ConcurrentMap` cannot be used in this fashion because their internal implementations don't lock in the object itself.

Solution 2 creates a synchronized list, which is created by using the `Collections` helper class. The `Collection.synchronizedList()` method wraps a `List` object (it can be `ArrayList`, `LinkedList`, or another `List` implementor) into a `List` that synchronizes the access to the list operations. Every time that you need to iterate over a list (either by using the `for-each` statement or using an iterator) you must be aware of the concurrency implications for that list's iterator. The `CopyOnWriteArrayList` is safe to iterate over (as specified in the Javadoc), but the synchronizedList iterator must be synchronized manually (also specified in the Collections.synchronizedlist.list iterator Javadoc). In the solution, the list can safely be iterated while inside the synchronized(list) block. When synchronizing on the list, no read/updates/other iterations can happen until the synchronized(list) block is completed.

8-5. Coordinating Different Collections

Problem

You need to modify different but related collections at the same time and want to be sure that no other thread see these structures until they are done being modified.

Solution 1

By synchronizing on the principal collection, you can guarantee that collection can be updated at the same time. In the following example, the fulfillOrder needs to both check the inventory of the order to be fulfilled, and if there is enough inventory to fulfill the order it needs to add the order to the customersOrders list. The fulfillOrder() method synchronizes on the inventoryMap map and modifies both the inventoryMap map and the customerOrders list before finishing the synchronized block.

```
    private boolean fulfillOrder(String itemOrdered, int quantityOrdered, String customerName)
{
        synchronized (inventoryMap) {
            int currentInventory  = inventoryMap.get(itemOrdered);
            if (currentInventory < quantityOrdered) {
                System.out.println("Couldn't fulfill order for "+customerName
                            +" not enough "+itemOrdered+" ("+quantityOrdered+")");
                return false; // sorry, we sold out
            }
            inventoryMap.put(itemOrdered,currentInventory - quantityOrdered);
            CustomerOrder order = new CustomerOrder(itemOrdered, quantityOrdered,
customerName);
            customerOrders.add(order);
            System.out.println("Order fulfilled for "+customerName+" of "
                        +itemOrdered+" ("+quantityOrdered+")");
            return true;
        }
    }

    private void checkInventoryLevels() {
        synchronized (inventoryMap) {
            System.out.println("------------------------------------");
            for (Map.Entry<String,Integer> inventoryEntry : inventoryMap.entrySet()) {
```

```
            System.out.println("Inventory Level :"+
                    inventoryEntry.getKey()+" "+inventoryEntry.getValue());↵
        }
        System.out.println("----------------------------------");
    }
}


    private void displayOrders() {
        synchronized (inventoryMap) {
            for (CustomerOrder order : customerOrders) {
                System.out.println(order.getQuantityOrdered()+" "+order.getItemOrdered()+" for
"+order.getCustomerName());
            }
        }
    }
}
```

Solution 2

Using a reentrant lock, you can prevent multiple threads accessing the same critical area of the code. In this solution, the inventoryLock is acquired by calling inventoryLock.lock(). Any other thread that tries to acquire the inventoryLock lock will have to wait until the inventoryLock lock is released. At the end of the fulfillOrder() method (in the finally block), the inventoryLock is released by calling the inventoryLock.unlock() method:

```
Lock inventoryLock = new ReentrantLock();
private boolean fulfillOrder(String itemOrdered, int quantityOrdered,
            String customerName) {
    try {
        inventoryLock.lock();
        int currentInventory = inventoryMap.get(itemOrdered);
        if (currentInventory < quantityOrdered) {
            System.out.println("Couldn't fulfill order for " + customerName +↵
                    " not enough " + itemOrdered + " (" + quantityOrdered + ")");
            return false; // sorry, we sold out
        }
        inventoryMap.put(itemOrdered, currentInventory - quantityOrdered);
        CustomerOrder order = new CustomerOrder(itemOrdered, ↵
                                    quantityOrdered, customerName);
        customerOrders.add(order);
        System.out.println("Order fulfilled for " + customerName + " of " + ↵
                    itemOrdered + " (" + quantityOrdered + ")");
        return true;
    } finally {
        inventoryLock.unlock();
```

```
        }
    }

    private void checkInventoryLevels() {
        try {
            inventoryLock.lock();
            System.out.println("------------------------------------");
            for (Map.Entry<String, Integer> inventoryEntry : inventoryMap.entrySet()) {
                System.out.println("Inventory Level :" + inventoryEntry.getKey()
                        + " " + inventoryEntry.getValue());↵
            }
            System.out.println("------------------------------------");
        } finally {
            inventoryLock.unlock();
        }
    }

    private void displayOrders() {
        try {
            inventoryLock.lock();
            for (CustomerOrder order : customerOrders) {
                System.out.println(order.getQuantityOrdered() +
                    " " + order.getItemOrdered() + " for " + order.getCustomerName());↵
            }
        } finally {
            inventoryLock.unlock();
        }
    }
}
```

How It Works

If you have different structures that are required to be modified at the same time, you need to make sure that these structures are updated atomically. An *atomic* operation refers to a set of instructions that can be expected to be executed as a whole or none at all. The atomic operation is visible to the rest of the program only when it is complete.

In solution 1 (atomically modifying both the inventoryMap map and the customerOrders list), you pick a "principal" collection on which you will lock (the inventoryMap). By locking on the principal collection, you guarantee that if another thread tries to lock on the same principal collection, it will have to wait until the lock on the collection is released by the current executing thread.

■ **Note** Notice that even though `displayOrders` doesn't use the `inventoryMap`, you still synchronize on it (in solution 1). Because the `inventoryMap` is the main collection, even operations done on secondary collections will still need to be protected by the main collection synchronization.

Solution 2 is more explicit, offering an independent lock that is used to coordinate the atomic operations instead of picking a principal collection. *Locking* refers to the ability of the JVM to restrict certain code paths to be executed by only one thread. The way locking works is that threads try to get the lock (locks are provided, for example, by a `ReentrantLock` instance, as shown in the example). The lock can be given to only one thread at a time. If other threads were trying to acquire the same lock, they will be suspended (WAIT) until the lock is available. The lock becomes available when the thread that currently holds the lock releases it. When a lock is released, it can then be acquired by one (and only one) of the threads that were waiting for that lock.

Locks by default are not "fair." What that means is that the order of the threads that requested the lock is not kept; this allows for very fast locking/unlocking implementation in the JVM, and in most situations it is generally okay to have unfair locks. On a very highly contended lock, if you really need to evenly distribute the lock (make it fair), you do so by setting the `setFair` property on the lock.

In solution 2, calling the `inventoryLock.lock()` method will either acquire the lock and continue, or will suspend execution (WAIT) until the lock can be acquired. Once the lock is acquired, no other thread will be able to execute within the locked block. At the end of the block, you release the lock by calling `inventoryLock.unlock()`.

It is common practice when working with `Lock` objects (`ReentrantLock`, `ReadLock`, `WriteLock`) to surround the use of these `Lock` objects by a `try/finally` clause. After opening the `try` block, the first instruction would be a call to the `lock.lock()` method. This guarantees that the first instruction executed is the acquisition of the lock. The release of the lock (by calling `lock.unlock()`) is done in the matching `finally` block. Having the `lock` be unlocked in the `finally` clause allows that, in the event of a `RuntimeException` happening while you have acquired the lock, that one doesn't "keep" the lock and prevent other threads to acquire it.

The use of the `ReentrantLock` object offers additional features that the `synchronized` statement doesn't offer. As an example, the `ReentrantLock` has the `tryLock()` function, which attempts to get the lock only if no other threads have it (the method doesn't make the invoking thread wait). If another thread holds the lock, the method returns `false` but continues executing. It is better to use the `synchronized` keyword for synchronization and use `ReentrantLock` only when its features are needed. For more information on the other methods provided by the `ReentrantLock`, visit http://download.oracle.com/javase/7/docs/api/java/util/concurrent/locks/ReentrantLock.html.

■ **Caution** While this is only a recipe book, and proper threading techniques span their own volumes, it is important to raise awareness of deadlocks. *Deadlocks* happen when two locks are involved (and are acquired in reverse order in another thread). The simplest way to avoid deadlock is to not let the lock "escape." This means that the lock, when acquired, should execute nothing that calls other methods that could possibly acquire a different lock, and if that's not possible, release the lock before calling such a method. See recipe 9-8 for information on finding and troubleshooting deadlocks.

Care should be taken in that any operation that refers to one or both collections needs to be protected by the same lock. Operations that depend on the result of one collection to query the second collection need to be executed atomically; they need to be done as a unit in which neither collection can change until the operation is completed.

8-6. Splitting Work into Separate Threads

Problem

You have work that can be split into separate threads and want to maximize the use of available CPU resources.

Solution

Use a ThreadpoolExecutor instance, which allows you to break the tasks into discrete units. In the following example, you create a BlockingQueue and fill it with Runnable object (which describe what needs to be done). It then is passed to the ThreadPoolExecutor instance. The ThreadPoolExecutor is then initialized, and started by calling the prestartAllCoreThreads() method and then you wait until all the Runnable objects are done executing by calling the shutdown() method, followed by the awaitTermination() method:

```
private void start() throws InterruptedException {
    BlockingQueue<Runnable> queue = new LinkedBlockingQueue<Runnable>();
    for (int i =0;i < 10;i++) {
        final int localI = i;
        queue.add(new Runnable() {
            public void run() {
                doExpensiveOperation(localI);
            }
        });
    }
    ThreadPoolExecutor executor = new ThreadPoolExecutor(10,10,1000,
                                    TimeUnit.MILLISECONDS,        queue);
    executor.prestartAllCoreThreads();
    executor.shutdown();
    executor.awaitTermination(100000,TimeUnit.SECONDS);

    System.out.println("Look ma! all operations were completed");
}
```

How It Works

A ThreadPoolExecutor consists of two components: the Queue of tasks to be executed, and the Executor, which tells how to execute the tasks. The Queue is filled with Runnable objects, on which the method run() contains the code to be executed.

The Queue used by a ThreadPoolExecutor is an implementer of the BlockingQueue interface. The BlockingQueue interface denotes a queue in which the consumers of the queue will wait (be suspended) if there are no elements in the Queue. This is necessary for the ThreadPoolExecutor to work efficiently.

The first step is to fill the Queue with the tasks that need to be done in parallel. This is done by calling the Queue's add() method and passing it a Runnable interface implementer. Once that's done, the executor is initialized.

The ThreadPoolExecutor constructor has many options in its constructor; the one used in the solution is the simplest one. Table 8-1 has a description of each parameter:

Table 8-1. ThreadPoolExecutor s Parameters

Parameter	Description
CorePoolSize	The minimum number of threads that are created as tasks are submitted
MaximumPoolSize	The maximum number of threads that the Executor would create
KeepAliveTime	The time that the waiting threads will wait for work before being disposed (as long as the number of live thread is still more than the CorePoolSize)
TimeUnit	The unit on which the KeepAliveTime is expressed (i.e. TimeUnit.SECONDS, TimeUnit.MILLISECONDS)
WorkQueue	The Blocking queue that contains the tasks to be processed by the Executor

After the ThreadPoolExecutor is initialized, you call the prestartAllCoreThreads(), this method "warms up" the ThreadPoolExecutor by creating the number of threads specified in the CorePoolSize and actively starts consuming tasks from the Queue if it is not empty.

To wait for all the tasks to be completed, you can call the shutdown() method of the ThreadPoolExecutor. By calling this method, you instruct the ThreadPoolExecutor to not accept any new events from the queue (previously submitted events will finish processing). This is the first step in the orderly termination of a ThreadPoolExecutor. To wait for all the tasks in the ThreadPoolExecutor to be done, call the awaitTermination() method. This will put the main thread to wait until all the Runnables in the ThreadPoolExecutor!s queue are done executing.After all the Runnables are executed, the main thread will wake up and continue.

■ **Note** A `ThreadPoolExecutor` needs to be configured correctly to maximize CPU usage. The most efficient number of threads for an executor depends on the types of tasks that are submitted. If the tasks are CPU-intensive, having an executor with the current number of cores would be ideal. If the tasks are I/O-intensive, the executor should have more threads than the current number of cores of threads.How many threads an executor should have depends on how intensive the I/O operations are; the more I/O-bound, the higher the number of threads.

8-7. Coordinating Threads

Problem

Your application requires that two or more threads be coordinated to work in unison.

Solution 1

With wait/notify for thread synchronization you can coordinate threads. In this solution, the main thread waits for the `objectToSync` object until the database loading thread is done. Once the database-loading thread is done, it notifies the `objectToSync` that whomever is waiting on it can continue executing. The same process happens when loading the orders into our system. The main thread waits on the `objectToSync` until the orders loading thread notifies the `objectToSync` to continue by calling the `objectToSync.notify()` method. After ensuring that both the inventory and the orders are loaded, the main thread executes the `processOrder()` method to process all orders.

```
private final Object objectToSync = new Object();

private void start() {
    loadItems();

    Thread inventoryThread = new Thread(new Runnable() {
        public void run() {
            System.out.println("Loading Inventory from Database...");
            loadInventory();
            synchronized (objectToSync) {
                objectToSync.notify();
            }
        }
    });

    synchronized (objectToSync) {
```

```
        inventoryThread.start();
        try {
            objectToSync.wait();
        } catch (InterruptedException e) {
            e.printStackTrace();
        }
    }

    Thread ordersThread = new Thread(new Runnable() {
        public void run() {
            System.out.println("Loading Orders from XML Web service...");
            loadOrders();
            synchronized (objectToSync) {
                objectToSync.notify();
            }
        }
    });

    synchronized (objectToSync) {
        ordersThread.start();
        try {
            objectToSync.wait();
        } catch (InterruptedException e) {
            e.printStackTrace();
        }
    }
    processOrders();
}
```

Solution 2

With a CountDownLatch object, you can control when the main thread continues. In the following code, a countdownLatch with an initial value of 2 is created; then the two threads for loading the inventory and loading the order information are created and started. As each of the two threads finish executing, they call the CountDownLatch's countDown() method, which decrements the latch's value by one. The main thread waits until the CountDownLatch reaches 0, at which point it resumes execution.

```
CountDownLatch latch = new CountDownLatch(2);

private void start() {
    loadItems();

    Thread inventoryThread = new Thread(new Runnable() {
        public void run() {
            System.out.println("Loading Inventory from Database...");
```

```java
                loadInventory();
                latch.countDown();
            }
        });

        inventoryThread.start();

        Thread ordersThread = new Thread(new Runnable() {
            public void run() {
                System.out.println("Loading Orders from XML Web service...");
                loadOrders();
                latch.countDown();
            }
        });

        ordersThread.start();

        try {
            latch.await();
        } catch (InterruptedException e) {
            e.printStackTrace();
        }

        processOrders();

    }
```

Solution 3

By using `Thread.join()`, you can wait for a thread to finish executing. The following example has a thread for loading the inventory and another thread for loading the orders. Once each thread is started, a call to `inventoryThread.join()` will make the main thread wait for the `inventoryThread` to finish executing before continuing.

```java
    private void start() {
        loadItems();

        Thread inventoryThread = new Thread(new Runnable() {
            public void run() {
                System.out.println("Loading Inventory from Database...");
                loadInventory();
            }
        });

        inventoryThread.start();
```

```
    try {
        inventoryThread.join();
    } catch (InterruptedException e) {
        e.printStackTrace();
    }

    Thread ordersThread = new Thread(new Runnable() {
        public void run() {
            System.out.println("Loading Orders from XML Web service...");
            loadOrders();
        }
    });

    ordersThread.start();
    try {
        ordersThread.join();
    } catch (InterruptedException e) {
        e.printStackTrace();
    }

    processOrders();

}
```

How It Works

There are many ways of coordinating threads in Java, and these coordination efforts rely on the notion of making a thread wait. When a thread waits, it suspends execution (it doesn't continue to the next instruction and is removed from the JVM's thread scheduler). If a thread is waiting, it can then be awakened again by notifying it. Within the Java's concurrency lingo, the word *notify* implies that a thread will stop being in its waiting state and resume execution (the JVM will add the thread to the thread scheduler). So in the natural course of thread coordination, the most common sequence of events is a main thread waiting, and a secondary thread then notifying the main thread to continue (or wake up). Even so, there is the possibility of a waiting thread being interrupted by some other event. When a thread is interrupted, it doesn't continue to the next instruction, but instead throws an InterruptedException, which is a way of signaling that even though the thread was waiting for something to happen, some other event happened that needs the thread's attention. This is better illustrated by the following example:

```
    BlockingQueue queue = new LinkedBlockingQueue();
    while (true) {
        synchronized (this) {
            Object itemToProcess = queue.take();
            processItem (itemToProcess);
        }
    }
```

If you look at the previous code, the thread that runs this code would never terminate because it loops forever and waits for an item to be processed. If there are no items in the Queue, the main thread waits until there is something added to the Queue from another thread. You couldn't graciously shut down the previous code (especially if the thread running the loop is not a Daemon thread).

```
BlockingQueue queue = new LinkedBlockingQueue();
while (true) {
    synchronized (this) {
        Object itemToProcess = null;
        try {
            itemToProcess = queue.take();
        } catch (InterruptedException e) {
            return;
        }
        processItem (itemToProcess);
    }
}
```

The new code has now the ability of "escaping" the infinite loop. From another thread, you can now call thread.interrupt(); which throws the InterruptedException that is then caught by the main thread's catch clause. Within this clause you can then return, effectively exiting the infinite loop.

InterruptedExceptions are a way of sending extra information to waiting (or sleeping) threads so that they can handle a different scenario (for example, an orderly program shutdown). For this reason, every operation that changes the state of the thread to sleep/wait will have to be surrounded by a try/catch block that can catch the InterruptedException. This is one of the cases in which the exception (InterruptedException) is not really an error but more of a way of signaling between threads that something has happened that needs your attention.

Solution 1 shows the most common (oldest) form of coordination. The solution requires making a thread wait, suspending execution, until the thread gets notified (or awakened) by another thread.

For solution 1 to work, the originating thread needs to acquire a lock. This lock will then be the "phone number" on which another thread can notify the originating thread to wake up. After the originating thread acquires the lock (phone number), it proceeds to wait. As soon as the wait() method is called, the lock is released, allowing other threads to acquire the same lock. The secondary thread then proceeds to acquire the lock (the phone number) and then notifies (which, in fact, would be like dialing a wake-up call) the originating thread. After the notification, the originating thread resumes execution.

In the solution 1 code, the lock is a dummy object called objectToSync. In practice, the object on which you locks for waiting and notifying could be any valid instance object in Java; for example, you could have used the this reference to make the main thread wait (and within the threads you could have used Recipe 8_7_1.this variable reference to notify the main thread to continue).

The main advantage of using this technique is the explicitness of controlling on whom to wait and when to notify (and the ability to notify all threads that are waiting on the same object; see the following tip).

■ **Tip**   Multiple threads can wait on the same lock (same phone number to be awakened). When a secondary thread calls notify, it will wake up one of the "waiting" threads (there is no fairness about which is awakened). Sometimes you will need to notify all the threads; you can call the notifyAll() method instead of calling the notify() method. This is mostly used if you are preparing many threads to take some work, but the work is not yet done setting up.

Solution 2 uses a more modern approach to notification. It involves a CountDownLatch. When setting up, you say how many "counts" the latch will have. The main thread will then wait (stop execution) by calling the CountDownLatch's await() method until the latch counts down to 0. When the latch reaches 0, the main thread will wake up and continue execution. As the worker thread completes, you call the latch.countdown() method, which will decrement the latch's current count value. If the latch's current value reaches 0, the main thread that was waiting on the CountDownLatch will wake up and continue execution.

The main advantage of using CountDownLatches is that you can spawn multiple tasks at the same time and just wait for all of them to complete (in the solution example, you didn't need to wait until one or the other thread were completed before continuing, they all were started, and when the latch was 0, the main thread continued).

Solution 3 instead offers a solution in which we have access to the thread we want to wait on. For the main thread, it's just a matter of calling the secondary thread's join() method. Then the main thread will wait (stop executing) until the secondary thread finishes.

The advantage of this method is that it doesn't require the secondary threads to know any synchronization mechanism. As long as the secondary thread terminates execution, the main thread can wait on them.

8-8. Creating Threadsafe Objects

Problem

You need to create an object that is threadsafe because it will be accessed from multiple threads.

Solution 1

Use synchronized getters and setters, and protect critical regions that change state. In the following example, you create an object with getters and setters that are synchronized for each internal variable, and you protect the critical regions by using the synchronized(this) lock:

```
class CustomerOrder {
    private String itemOrdered;
    private int quantityOrdered;
    private String customerName;
```

```java
    public CustomerOrder() {

    }

    public double calculateOrderTotal (double price) {
        synchronized (this) {
            return getQuantityOrdered()*price;
        }
    }

    public synchronized String getItemOrdered() {
        return itemOrdered;
    }

    public synchronized int getQuantityOrdered() {
        return quantityOrdered;
    }

    public synchronized String getCustomerName() {
        return customerName;
    }

    public synchronized void setItemOrdered(String itemOrdered) {
        this.itemOrdered = itemOrdered;
    }

    public synchronized void setQuantityOrdered(int quantityOrdered) {
        this.quantityOrdered = quantityOrdered;
    }

    public synchronized void setCustomerName(String customerName) {
        this.customerName = customerName;
    }
}
```

Solution 2

Create an immutable object (an object that, once created, doesn't change its internal state). In the following code, the internal variables to the object are declared final, and are assigned at construction. By doing so it is guaranteed that the object is immutable:

```java
class ImmutableCustomerOrder {
    final private String itemOrdered;
    final private int quantityOrdered;
    final private String customerName;
```

```
    ImmutableCustomerOrder(String itemOrdered, int quantityOrdered, String customerName) {
        this.itemOrdered = itemOrdered;
        this.quantityOrdered = quantityOrdered;
        this.customerName = customerName;
    }

    public String getItemOrdered() {
        return itemOrdered;
    }

    public int getQuantityOrdered() {
        return quantityOrdered;
    }

    public String getCustomerName() {
        return customerName;
    }

    public synchronized double calculateOrderTotal (double price) {
        return getQuantityOrdered()*price;
    }
}
```

How It Works

Solution 1 relies on the principle that any change done to the object is protected by a lock. Using the synchronized keyword is a shortcut to writing the expression synchronized (this). By synchronizing your getters and setters (and any other operation that alters the internal state of your object), you guarantee that the object is consistent. Also, it is important that any operations that should occur as a unit (say something that modifies two collections at the same time, as listed in recipe 8-5) are done within a method of the object and are protected by using the synchronized keyword.

For instance, if an object offers a getSize() method as well as getItemNumber(int index), it would be unsafe to write the following object.getItemNumber (object.getSize()-1). Even though it looks that the statement is concise, another thread can change the contents of the object between getting the size and getting the item number. Instead, it is safer to create a object.getLastElement() method, which atomically figures out the size and the last element.

Solution 2 relies on the property of immutable objects. Immutable objects don't change their internal state, and objects that don't change their internal state (are *immutable*) are by definition threadsafe. If you need to modify the immutable object because of an event, instead of explicitly changing its property, create a new object with the changed properties. This new object then takes the place of the old object, and on future requests for the object, the new immutable object is returned. This is by far, the easiest (albeit verbose) method for creating threadsafe code.

8-9. Implementing Threadsafe Counters

Problem

You need a counter that is threadsafe so that it can be incremented from different execution threads.

Solution

By using the inherently threadsafe `Atomic` objects, you can create a counter that guarantees thread safety and has an optimized synchronization strategy. In the following code, you create an `Order` object, which requires a unique order ID generated by using the `AtomicLong incrementAndGet()` method:

```
AtomicLong orderIdGenerator = new AtomicLong(0);

        for (int i =0;i < 10;i++) {
            Thread orderCreationThread = new Thread(new Runnable() {
                public void run() {
                    for (int i= 0;i < 10;i++) {
                        createOrder(Thread.currentThread().getName());
                    }
                }
            });
            orderCreationThread.setName("Order Creation Thread "+i);
            orderCreationThread.start();
        }

///////////////////////////////////////////////////
    private void createOrder(String name) {
        long orderId = orderIdGenerator.incrementAndGet();
        Order order = new Order(name, orderId);
        orders.add(order);
    }
```

How It Works

`AtomicLong` (and its cousin `AtomicInteger`) are built to be used safely in concurrent environments. They have methods to atomically increment (and get) the changed value. Even if two or hundreds of threads were to call the `AtomicLong increment()` method, their returned value will always be unique.

If you need to make decisions and update the variables, always use the atomic operations that are offered by the `AtomicLong`; for example, `compareAndSet`. If not, your code will not be threadsafe (as any check-then-act operation needs to be atomic) unless you externally protect the atomic reference by using your own locks (see recipe 8-7).

The following code illustrates several code safety issues to be aware of. First is that changing a long value may be done in two memory write operations (as allowed by the Java Memory Model), and thus two threads could end up overlapping those two operaitons in what might on the surface appear to be threadsafe code. The result would be a completely unexpected (and likely wrong) long value:

```
long counter =0;

public long incrementCounter() {
  return counter++;
}
```

This code also suffers from *unsafe publication*, which refers to the fact that a variable might be cached locally (in the CPU's internal cache) and might not be commited to main memory. If another thread (executing in another CPU) happens to be reading the variable from main memory, that other thread might miss the changes made by the first thread. The changed value might be cached by the first thread's CPU, and not yet committed to main memory where the second thread can see it. For safe publication, you must use the `volatile` Java modifier (see http://download.oracle.com/javase/tutorial/essential/concurrency/atomic.html).

A final issue with the preceding code is that it is not atomic. Even though it looks like there is only one operation to increment the counter, in reality there are two operations that happen at the machine language level (a retrieve of the variable and then an increment). There could be two or more threads that get the same value as they both retrieve the variable but haven't incremented it yet. Then all the threads increment the counter to the same number.

8-10. Breaking Down Tasks into Discrete Units Of Work

Problem

You have an algorithm that benefits from using a *divide-and-conquer strategy*, which refers to the ability of breaking down a unit of work into two separate subunits and then piecing together the results from these subunits. The subunits can then be broken down into more subunits of work until reaching a point where the work is small enough to just be executed. By breaking down the unit of work into subunits, you can take advantage of the multicore nature of today's processors with minimum pain.

Solution

The new Fork/Join framework in Java 7 makes applying the divide-and-conquer strategy straightforward. The following example creates a representation of the Game of Life. The code uses the Fork/Join framework to speed up the calculation of each iteration when advancing from one generation to the next:

//

```java
        ForkJoinPool pool = new ForkJoinPool();
        long i = 0;

        while (shouldRun) {
            i++;
            final boolean[][] newBoard = new boolean[lifeBoard.length][lifeBoard[0].length];
            long startTime = System.nanoTime();
            GameOfLifeAdvancer advancer = new GameOfLifeAdvancer(lifeBoard, 0,0,
lifeBoard.length-1, lifeBoard[0].length-1,newBoard);
            pool.invoke(advancer);
            long endTime = System.nanoTime();
            if (i % 100 == 0 ) {
                System.out.println("Taking "+(endTime-startTime)/1000 + "ms");
            }
            SwingUtilities.invokeAndWait(new Runnable() {
                public void run() {
                    model.setBoard(newBoard);
                    lifeTable.repaint();
                }
            });
            lifeBoard = newBoard;
        }
```

//

```java
    class GameOfLifeAdvancer extends RecursiveAction{

        private boolean[][] originalBoard;
        private boolean[][] destinationBoard;
        private int startRow;
        private int endRow;
        private int endCol;
        private int startCol;

        GameOfLifeAdvancer(boolean[][] originalBoard, int startRow, int startCol, int endRow,
int endCol, boolean [][] destinationBoard) {
```

```
            this.originalBoard = originalBoard;
            this.destinationBoard = destinationBoard;
            this.startRow = startRow;
            this.endRow = endRow;
            this.endCol = endCol;
            this.startCol = startCol;
        }

        private void computeDirectly() {
            for (int row = startRow; row <= endRow;row++) {
                for (int col = startCol; col <= endCol; col++) {
                    int numberOfNeighbors = getNumberOfNeighbors (row, col);
                    if (originalBoard[row][col]) {
                        destinationBoard[row][col] = true;
                        if (numberOfNeighbors < 2) destinationBoard[row][col] = false;
                        if (numberOfNeighbors > 3) destinationBoard[row][col] = false;
                    } else {
                        destinationBoard[row][col] = false;
                        if (numberOfNeighbors == 3) destinationBoard[row][col] = true;
                    }
                }
            }
        }

        private int getNumberOfNeighbors(int row, int col) {
            int neighborCount = 0;
            for (int leftIndex = -1; leftIndex < 2; leftIndex++) {
                for (int topIndex = -1; topIndex < 2; topIndex++) {
                    if ((leftIndex == 0) && (topIndex == 0)) continue; // skip own
                    int neighbourRowIndex = row + leftIndex;
                    int neighbourColIndex = col + topIndex;
                    if (neighbourRowIndex<0) neighbourRowIndex = originalBoard.length +
neighbourRowIndex;
                    if (neighbourColIndex<0) neighbourColIndex = originalBoard[0].length +
neighbourColIndex ;
                    boolean neighbour = originalBoard[neighbourRowIndex %
originalBoard.length][neighbourColIndex % originalBoard[0].length];
                    if (neighbour) neighborCount++;
                }
            }
            return neighborCount;
        }

        @Override
        protected void compute() {
```

```
        if (getArea() < 20) {
            computeDirectly();
            return;
        }
        int halfRows = (endRow - startRow) / 2;
        int halfCols = (endCol - startCol) / 2;
        if (halfRows > halfCols) {
            // split the rows
            invokeAll(new GameOfLifeAdvancer(originalBoard, startRow, startCol,
startRow+halfRows, endCol,destinationBoard),
                        new GameOfLifeAdvancer(originalBoard, startRow+halfRows+1, startCol,
endRow, endCol,destinationBoard));
        } else {
            invokeAll(new GameOfLifeAdvancer(originalBoard, startRow, startCol, endRow,
startCol+ halfCols,destinationBoard),
                        new GameOfLifeAdvancer(originalBoard, startRow, startCol+halfCols+1,
endRow, endCol,destinationBoard));
        }
    }

    private int getArea() { return (endRow - startRow) * (endCol - startCol);   }

}
```

How It Works

The first part of the example creates a ForkJoinPool object. The default constructor provides reasonable defaults (such as creating as many threads as there are CPU cores) and sets up an entry point to submit divide-and-conquer work. While the ForkJoinPool inherits from an ExecutorService, it is best suited to handle tasks that extend from RecursiveAction. The ForkJoinPool object has the invoke(RecursiveAction) method, which will take a RecursiveAction object and apply the divide-and-conquer strategy.

The second part of the solution creates the GameOfLifeAdvancer class, which extends the RecursiveAction class. By extending the RecursiveAction class, you can split the work to be done. The GameOfLifeAdvancer class advances the Game of Life board to the next generation. The constructor takes a two-dimensional boolean array (which represents a Game of Life board), a start row/column, an end row/column, and a destination two-dimensional boolean array, on which the result of advancing the Game of Life for one generation is collected.

The GameOfLifeAdvancer is required to implement the compute() method. In this method, you figure out how much work there is to be done. If the work is small enough, the work is done directly (achieved by calling the computeDirectly() method and returning). If the work is not small enough, the method splits the work by creating two GameOfLifeAdvancer instances that process only half of the current GameOfLifeAdvancer work. This is done by either splitting the number of rows to be processed into two chunks or by splitting the number of columns into two chunks. The two GameOfLifeAdvancer instances are then passed to the ForkJoin pool by calling the invokeAll() method of the RecursiveAction class. The invokeAll() method takes the two instances of GameOfLifeAdvancer (it can take as many as needed) and waits until they both are finished executing (that is, the meaning of the -all postfix in the invokeAll() method name; it waits for all of the tasks submitted to be completed before returning control).

In this way, the GameOfLifeAdvancer instance is broken down into new GameOfLifeAdvancer instances that each processes only part of the Game of Life board. Each instance waits for all the subordinate parts to be completed before returning control to the caller. The resulting division of work can take advantage of the multiple CPUs available in the typical system today.

■ **Tip**   The ForkJoinPool is generally more efficient than an ExecutorService because it implements a work-stealing policy. Each thread has a Queue of work to do; if the Queue of any thread gets empty, the thread will "steal" work from another thread queue, making a more efficient use of CPU processing power.

CHAPTER 9

Debugging and Unit Testing

Debugging is a big part of software development. To effectively debug, you must be able to "think" like a computer and dive into the code, deconstructing every step that lead to the logic error that you're working to resolve. In the beginning of computer programming, there weren't a lot of tools to help in debugging. Mostly, debugging involved taking a look at your code and spotting inconsistencies; then resubmit the code to be compiled again. Today, every IDE offers the ability of using breakpoints and inspecting memory variables, making it much easier to debug. Outside the IDE there are other tools that help in daily debugging, building, and testing of your project; and these tools ensure that your code is being continually tested for errors introduced when programming. In this chapter, you explore the different tools that will help aid in debugging, analyzing, and testing Java software. Hopefully these recipes will help you debug faster, and burn less of that midnight oil.

9-1. Understanding Exceptions

Problem

You caught and logged an Exception (as described in solution 6-1), and need to understand what happened.

Solution

Analyze the Exception's StackTrace() method:

```
try {
    int a = 5/0;
} catch (Exception e) {
    e.printStackTrace();
}
```

```
java.lang.ArithmeticException: / by zero
    at org.java7recipes.chapter9.Recipe9_1.start(Recipe9_1.java:18)
    at org.java7recipes.chapter9.Recipe9_1.main(Recipe9_1.java:13)
```

How It Works

In Programming lingo, a *stack* refers to the list of functions that were called to get to a point in your program, usually starting from the immediate (System.out.println()) to the more general (public static void main). Every program keeps track of how it got to a specific part of the code. Stack trace% output refer to the stack that was in memory when an error occurred. Exceptions thrown in Java keep track of where they happened and what code path was taken to when the exception was thrown. Stack trace shows from the most specific place where the exception happened (the line where the exception occurred) to the top-level invoker of the offending code (and everything in-between). This information then allows you to pinpoint what kind of method calls were done, and might shed some light on why the exception was thrown.

In this example, the divide by zero Exception occurred on line 18 of Recipe9_1.java and was caused by a call from the main() method (at line 13). Sometimes, when looking at the Stack trace's output , you will see methods that don't belong to the project. This happens naturally as sometimes method calls are generated in other parts of a working system. It is, for example, very common to see AWT methods in Swing applications when an exception is raised (due to the nature of the EventQueue). If you look at the more specific function calls (earliest),you will eventually run with the project's own code and can then try to figure out why the exception was thrown.

■ **Note** The Stack trace output will contain line number information if the program is compiled with "Debug" info. By default, most IDEs will include this information when running in a Debug configuration.

9-2: Locking Down Behavior of Your Classes

Problem

You need to lock down the behavior of your class and want to create unit tests that verify that behavior in your application.

Solution

Use JUnit to create unit tests that verify behavior in your classes.

To use this solution, you need to include the JUnit dependencies. JUnit can be downloaded from (http://www.junit.org). Once downloaded, add the junit-xxx.jar file and the junit-xxx-dep.jar file to your project (where xxx is the downloaded version number). When JUnit becomes part of your project, you will be able to include the org.junit and junit.framework namespaces.

In this example you create two unit tests for the MathAdder class. It contains two methods: addNumber (int, int) and substractNumber (int,int). These two methods return the addition (or subtraction) of their passed parameters (a simple class). The unit tests (marked by the @Test annotation) verifies that the MathAdder class does, in fact, add and/or subtract two numbers.

```
package org.java7recipes.chapter9;

import junit.framework.Assert;
```

```java
import org.junit.Test;

/**
 * Created by IntelliJ IDEA.
 * User: Freddy
 * Date: 9/15/11
 * Time: 5:36 PM
 * Simple Unit Test
 */
public class Recipe9_3_MathAdderTest {

    @Test
    public void testAddBehavior() {
        Recipe_9_3_MathAdder adder = new Recipe_9_3_MathAdder();
        for (int i =0;i < 100;i++) {
            for (int j =0;j < 100;j++) {
                Assert.assertEquals(i+j,adder.addNumbers(i,j));

            }
        }
    }

    @Test
    public void testSubstractBehavior() {
        Recipe_9_3_MathAdder adder = new Recipe_9_3_MathAdder();
        for (int i =0;i < 100;i++) {
            for (int j =0;j < 100;j++) {
                Assert.assertEquals(i-j,adder.substractNumber(i,j));

            }
        }
    }
}


public class Recipe_9_3_MathAdder {

    public int addNumbers (int first, int second) {
        return first+second;

    }

    public int substractNumber (int first, int second) {
        return first-second;
    }

}
```

How It Works

Unit tests are a way of enforcing expected behaviors on your classes. Having unit tests in your project makes it less likely to break old functionality when adding or refactoring it. When you create unit tests, you are specifying how an object should behave (what is referred to as its *contract*). The unit tests will then test that the expected behavior happens (they do this by verifying the result of a method and using the different JUnit.Assert methods).

The first step to write a unit test is to create a new class that describes the behavior you want to verify. One of the general unit–test naming conventions is to create a class with the same name as the class being tested with the postfix of `Test`; in this recipe's example, the main class is called Recipe9_3_MathAdder, while the testing class is called Recipe9_3_MathAdderTest.

The Unit test class (MathAdderTest) will contain methods that check and verify the behavior of the class. To do so, it annotates the method names. *Annotation* refers to the capability of Java of adding extra information to a class/method that doesn't necessarily change the code. This extra information is not used by the program, but by the compiler/builder (or external tools) to guide the compilation, building, and/or testing of the code. For unit testing purposes, you annotate the methods that are part of the unit test by writing `@Test` before each method name. Within each method, you use `Assert.assertEquals` (or any of the other Assert static methods) to verify behavior.

The `Assert.assertEquals` method instructs the unit testing framework to verify that the expected value of the method call from the class that we are testing is the same as the actual value returned by its method call. In the recipe example, Assert.assertEquals verifies that the MathAdder is correctly adding the two integers. While the scope of this class is trivial, it shows the bare minimum requirements to have a fully functional unit test.

If the Assert call succeeds, it gets reported in the unit test framework as a "Passed" test; if the Assert call fails, then the unit test framework will stop and display a message showing where the unit test failed. Most modern IDEs have the capability of running unit test classes by simply right-clicking its name and selecting Run/Debug (and that's the intended way of running Chapter_9_3_MathAdderTest recipe).

While it is true that IDEs can run unit tests while developing, they are created with the intention of being run automatically (usually triggered by a scheduled build or by a version control system's check-in), which is what the recipe 9-3 talks about.

9-3. Scripting Your Unit Tests

Problem

You need to automatically run your unit tests.

Solution

Use and configure JUnit + Ant. To do so, follow these steps:

1. Download Apache Ant (located at `http://ant.apache.org/`).

2. Uncompress Apache Ant into a folder (for example, `c:\ant` for Windows systems).

3. Make sure that Apache Ant can be executed from the command line. In Windows, this means adding the `apache-ant/bin` folder to the path as follows:

a. Go to Control Panel   System.

b. Click Advanced system settings.

c. Click Environment Variables.

d. In the System Variables list, double-click the variable name PATH.

e. At the end of the string, add ";C:\apache-ant-1.8.2\bin" (or the folder that you uncompressed Apache Ant into).

f. Click OK (on each of the popup boxes that were opened before) to accept the changes.

Make sure that the JAVA_HOME environment variable is defined. In Windows, this means adding a new environment variable called JAVA_HOME. For example:

1. Go to Control Panel   System.

2. Click Advanced system settings.

3. Click Environment Variables.

a. In the System Variables list, check to see whether there is variable named JAVA_HOME and that the value points to your JDK distribution,

b. If JAVA_HOME is not present, click New. Set the variable name to JAVA_HOME and set the variable value to C:\Program Files\Java\jdk1.7.0 or the root of your JDK 7 installation.

Test that you can reach Ant, and that Ant can find your JDK installation. To test that the changes took effect in Windows, do the following:

1. Open a command window

2. Type ANT.

a. If you receive the message "Ant is not recognized as an internal or external command", redo the first steps of setting up the PATH variable (the first set of instructions).

b. If you receive the message "unable to locate tools.jar" You need to create and/or update the JAVA_HOME path for your installation (the second set of instructions).

c. The message "Buildfile: build.xml does not exist!"means that your setup is ready to be built using Ant. Congratulations!

■ **Note** When changing environment variables in Microsoft Windows, it is necessary to close previous command line windows and reopen them because changes are only applied to new command windows. To open a command window in Microsoft Windows, click Start, type **CMD**, and press Enter.

Create build.xml at the root of your project, and put the following bare-bones Ant script as the contents of the build.xml file. This particular build.xml file contains information that Ant will use to compile and test this recipe.

```
<project default="test" name="Chapter9Project" basedir=".">
<property name="src" location="src"/>
<property name="build" location="build/"/>
<property name="src.tests" location="src/"/>
<property name="reports.tests" location="report/" />


<path id="build.path">
<fileset dir="dep">
<include name="**/*.jar" />
</fileset>
<pathelement path="build" />
</path>


<target name="build">
<mkdir dir="${build}" />
<javac srcdir="${src}" destdir="${build}">
<classpath refid="build.path" />
</javac>
</target>

<target name="test" depends="build">
<mkdir dir="${reports.tests}" />
<junit fork="yes" printsummary="yes" haltonfailure="yes">
<classpath refid="build.path" />
<formatter type="plain"/>

<batchtest fork="yes" todir="${reports.tests}">
<fileset dir="${src.tests}">
<include name="**/*Test*.java"/>
</fileset>
</batchtest>
</junit>
</target>
</project>
```

■ **Note** To execute this recipe, open a command line window, navigate to the Chapter 9 folder, type **ant**, and press Enter.

How It Works

Apache Ant (or simply Ant) is a program that allows you to script your project's build and unit testing. By configuring Ant, you can build, test, and deploy your application using the command line (In turn, it can then be scheduled to be run automatically by the operating system). Ant can have tasks to automatically run unit tests and give a report on the result of these tests. These results can then be analyzed after each run to pinpoint changes in behavior.

Although Ant might be difficult to understand, it allows for a lot of flexibility on how to compile, build, and weave code. By using Ant, you are allowing utmost configuration on how your project is built.

■ **Tip**   Visit `http://ant.apache.org/manual/tutorial-helloworldwithant.html` for a more in-depth tutorial of Ant.

The build.xmlfile contains instructions on how to compile your project, which classpath to use, and what unit tests to run. Each build.xml will have a `<project>` tag that contains the steps to build the project. Within each `<project>` there are targets, which are "steps" in the build process. A `<target>` can depend on other targets, allowing you to establish dependencies in your project (in this recipe's example, the target "test" depends on the target "build"; meaning that to run the test target, Ant will first run the build target).

Each target has tasks. These tasks are extensible, and there is a core set of tasks that you can use out of the box. The `<javac>`task will compile a set of Java files specified in the `src` attribute and write the output to the `dest` attribute. As part of the `<javac>` task, you can specify the classpath to use. In this example, the classpath is specified by referring to a previously defined path, called build.path. Ant provides ample support for creating classpaths. In this recipe, the classpath is defined as any file that has the `.jar` extension located in the `dep` folder.

The other task in the build target is the `<junit>` task. This task will find unit test specified in its task and run it. The unit tests are defined in the `<batchtest>` property. By using the `<fileset>` property, you tell JUnit to find any file that has the word `Test` in its name and ends with the `.java` extension. Once the JUnit runs each test, it will write out a summary to the console and write a report on the results of the unit tests to the `reports.tests` folder.

■ **Tip**   Even though they look strange, you can define variables in a build.xml file by using the `<property>` tag. Once a property is defined, it can be accessed as part of other task by using the `${propertyName}` syntax. This allows you to quickly change your build script in response to project changes (for example, switching target/source folders around).

9-4. Determining Code Coverage

Problem

You need to generate reports on how much of your project the unit tests cover.

Solution

Use the Emma code coverage tool to create code coverage reports. For example, the following is a new version of build.xml that adds Emma code coverage to our unit testing:

```
<project default="test" name="Chapter9Project" basedir=".">
<property name="src" location="src"/>
<property name="build" location="build/"/>
<property name="reports.tests" location="report/" />


<!-- Emma Code Coverage Info -->
<property name="emma.dir" value="dep/emma" />
<property name="emma.enabled" value="true" />
<path id="emma.lib" >
<pathelement location="${emma.dir}/emma.jar" />
<pathelement location="${emma.dir}/emma_ant.jar" />
</path>
<property name="coverage.dir" value="coverage" />
<taskdef resource="emma_ant.properties" classpathref="emma.lib" />


<path id="build.path">
<fileset dir="dep">
<include name="**/*.jar" />
</fileset>
<pathelement path="build" />
</path>

<target name="clean">
<delete dir="${build}" />
<delete dir="${reports.tests}" />
<delete dir="${coverage.dir}" />
<mkdir dir="${build}" />
<mkdir dir="${reports.tests}" />
<mkdir dir="${coverage.dir}" />
</target>

<target name="build">
<javac srcdir="${src}" destdir="${build}">
<classpath refid="build.path" />
</javac>
</target>
```

```
<target name="test" depends="clean,build">
<emma enabled="${emma.enabled}" >
<instr mode="overwrite" metadatafile="${coverage.dir}/metadata.emma" >
<instrpath>
<pathelement path="${build}" />
</instrpath>
<filter excludes="*Test*" />
</instr>
</emma>

<junit fork="yes" printsummary="yes" haltonfailure="yes">
<classpath refid="build.path" />
<formatter type="plain"/>

<batchtest fork="yes" todir="${reports.tests}">
<fileset dir="${build}">
<include name="**/*Test*.class"/>
</fileset>
</batchtest>
<jvmarg value="-XX:-UseSplitVerifier" />
<jvmarg value="-Demma.coverage.out.file=${coverage.dir}/coverage.emma" />
<jvmarg value="-Demma.coverage.out.merge=true" />
</junit>


<emma enabled="${emma.enabled}" >
<report sourcepath="${src}" >
<fileset dir="${coverage.dir}" >
<include name="*.emma" />
</fileset>

<txt outfile="${coverage.dir}/coverage.txt" />
<html outfile="${coverage.dir}/coverage.html" />
</report>
</emma>
</target>
</project>
```

To run this recipe, you will need to download and add the Emma code coverage .jar files. To do so, go to http://emma.sourceforge.net/ and download the latest Emma code coverage version. After downloading, uncompress the Emma download into a folder in your computer. Copy the /lib folder from the uncompressed Emma folder into dep/emma in your application. Make sure that dep/emma/emma.jar and dep/emma/emma_ant.jar are present.

■ **Note** To execute this recipe from Ant, open a command-line window, navigate to the Chapter 9 folder, type **ant f emmabuild.xml** and press Enter.

How It Works

An important feature of creating unit tests is measuring how much code they execute of the tested classes. The more project code the unit tests execute, the safer it is to assume that changes in expected behavior will be caught by the unit tests. *Code coverage* is defined as the percentage of lines of code that the unit tests have run versus the total lines of code the project has. By having a larger code coverage, most of the code base is being verified. (A typical code coverage goal is about 80 percent of the lines of code tested; more coverage than that and you might be testing trivial functionality such as getters and setters of a simple Java class.

By combining Emma, Ant, and JUnit you can get code coverage reporting for your application. Code coverage is a very important measure for a lot of programming disciplines. It offers a way of understanding how effectively the current codebase is covered, and how solid the unit tests are in terms of covering functionality.

In this build.xml file, there are new sections that describe how to measure code coverage. The first section of build.xml defines a new Emma task that can be used by Ant. The way Emma's code coverage works is by going through a process called *instrumentation*, which refers to a task that changes the compiled bytecode. In Emma's case, it's adding extra instructions that record coverage information. Using the recorded coverage information, Emma puts together a report that shows code coverage that was achieved when running the unit tests.

In the build.xml script, Emma instrumentation happens at the beginning of the <target name="test">. The first <Emma> task defines what files to instrument. For the recipe, the files to instrument are located in the /build folder. The Emma task also specifies how to instrument (overwrite). *Overwrite instrumentation* means that Emma takes the original class file, instruments it (changes the content to add the new instructions), and saves it with the same name. Within our instrumentation step, you also specify to exclude any file that has the Test name in it because it is a common practice not to include unit test lines of code as part of the code coverage.

The second part of the <target name="test"> involves running the unit tests. This is very similar to recipe 9-3; even so, there are a couple of differences. The first difference is that you specify the unit tests to run as .class files instead of .java files. The second difference is that there are new JVM arguments added for unit tests. JVM arguments are defined by the <jvmarg> properties. These properties tell the instrumented classes that information related to code coverage should be written to a file named coverage.emma, and that it should be done in aggregate (don't overwrite the file for each unit test being executed).

■ **Note** Due to the new Java 7 bytecode, you need to add the <jvmarg value="-XX:-UseSplitVerifier" /> property. This is due to an incompatibility between Emma and the new Java 7 bytecode, which the jvmarg property fixes.

After running the unit tests, the third part of the <target name="test"> involves generating a report of the collected code coverage statistics (Figure 9-1 shows an example of the coverage of our unit tests from recipe 9-2). This is done by adding a new <emma><report> task that specifies the location and formatting of the report. By using these three tools (Ant, JUnit, and Emma) you have created an automated build that runs unit tests and reports on code coverage exercised by unit tests.

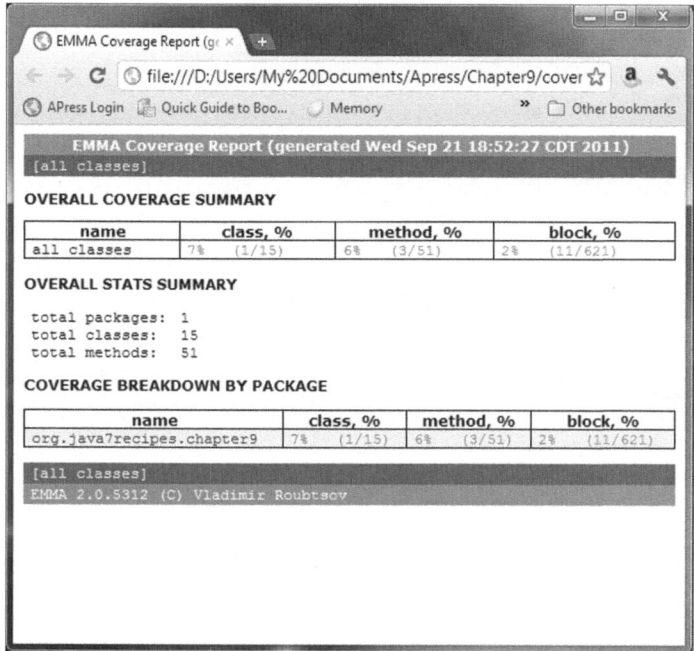

Figure 9-1. Emma code coverage report

9-5. Finding Bugs Early

Problem

You want to find the most number of bugs at design time.

Solution

Use FindBugs to scan your software for issues.

The following is our new build.xml file that adds FindBugs reporting:

```
<project default="test" name="Chapter9Project" basedir=".">

<property name="src" location="src"/>
<property name="build" location="build/"/>
<property name="reports.tests" location="report/" />
<property name="classpath" location="dep/" />


<!-- Emma Code Coverage Info -->
<property name="emma.dir" value="dep/emma" />
```

```xml
<property name="emma.enabled" value="true" />
<path id="emma.lib" >
<pathelement location="${emma.dir}/emma.jar" />
<pathelement location="${emma.dir}/emma_ant.jar" />
</path>
<property name="coverage.dir" value="coverage" />
<taskdef resource="emma_ant.properties" classpathref="emma.lib" />


<!-- Findbugs Static Analyzer Info -->
<property name="findbugs.dir" value="dep/findbugs" />
<property name="findbugs.report" value="findbugs" />

<path id="findbugs.lib" >
<fileset dir="${findbugs.dir}" includes="*.jar"/>
</path>
<taskdef name="findbugs" classpathref="findbugs.lib"
classname="edu.umd.cs.findbugs.anttask.FindBugsTask"/>


<path id="build.path">
<fileset dir="dep">
<include name="**/*.jar" />
</fileset>
</path>

<target name="clean">
<delete dir="${build}" />
<delete dir="${reports.tests}" />
<delete dir="${coverage.dir}" />
<delete dir="${instrumented}" />
<mkdir dir="${build}" />
<mkdir dir="${reports.tests}" />
<mkdir dir="${coverage.dir}" />

</target>

<target name="build">
<javac srcdir="${src}" destdir="${build}" debug="${debug}">
<classpath refid="build.path" />
</javac>
</target>

<target name="test" depends="clean,build">
<emma enabled="${emma.enabled}" >
<instr mode="overwrite" metadatafile="${coverage.dir}/metadata.emma" >
<instrpath>
<pathelement path="${build}" />
</instrpath>
<filter excludes="*Test*" />
</instr>
</emma>
```

```
<junit fork="yes" printsummary="yes" haltonfailure="yes">
<classpath refid="build.path" />
<formatter type="plain"/>

<batchtest fork="yes" todir="${reports.tests}">
<fileset dir="${build}">
<include name="**/*Test*.class"/>
</fileset>
</batchtest>
<jvmarg value="-XX:-UseSplitVerifier" />
<jvmarg value="-Demma.coverage.out.file=${coverage.dir}/coverage.emma" />
<jvmarg value="-Demma.coverage.out.merge=true" />
</junit>


<emma enabled="${emma.enabled}" >
<report sourcepath="${src}" >
<fileset dir="${coverage.dir}" >
<include name="*.emma" />
</fileset>

<txt outfile="${coverage.dir}/coverage.txt" />
<html outfile="${coverage.dir}/coverage.html" />
</report>
</emma>
</target>

<target name="findbugs" depends="clean">
<antcall target="build">
<param name="debug" value="true" />
</antcall>

<mkdir dir="${findbugs.report}" />
<findbugs home="${findbugs.dir}"
              output="html"
              outputFile="${findbugs.report}/index.html"
              reportLevel="low"
>
<class location="${build}/" />
<auxClasspath refid="build.path" />
<sourcePath path="${src}" />
</findbugs>
</target>
</project>
```

To run this recipe, download FindBugs (`http://findbugs.sourceforge.net/downloads.html`).
Uncompress into a folder in your computer; then copy the contents of the `./lib/` folder into your
project's `/dep/findbugs` folder (create the `/dep/findbugs` folder if necessary). Make sure that
/dep/findbugs/findbugs.jar and /dep/findbugs/findbugs-ant.jar are present.

How It Works

FindBugs is a *Static Code Analyzer (SCA)*. It will parse your program's compiled file and spot errors in coding (not syntax errors, but certain types of logic errors). As an example, one of the errors that FindBugs will spot is comparing two Strings using == instead of String.equals(). The analysis is then written as HTML (or text) that can be viewed with a browser. Catching errors from FindBugs is easy, and adding it as part of your continuous integration process is extremely beneficial.

At the beginning of build.xml, you define the FindBugs tasks. Much the same as you did for the Emma tasks (see *Recipe 9.4*), this section specifies where are the jar files that defines the new task (dep\findbugs), and also defines a property of where to put the report when done.

The build.xml also has a new target project called "findbugs." The findbugs target compiles the source files with debug information (having debug information helps on the FindBugs report as it will include the line# when reporting errors), and then proceeds to analyze the bytecode for errors. In the findbugs task, you specify the location of the compiled .class files (this is the <class> property), the location of the dependencies for your project (<auxClasspath> property), and the location of the source code (<sourcePath> property).

Within the findbugs target, there is a <antcall> task. The <antcall> task simply runs the target specified within the <antcall> task. Just before the <antcall> task, you assign the debug <property> to true. This, in turns gets passed to the <javac> task as debug="${debug}". When the debug <property> is set to true, the <javac>task will include debug information into the compilation of the Java source files. Having debug information in the compiled files will help generate a more readable FindBugs report as it will include line numbers for where issues are found. The trick of assigning properties from within an Ant target is used throughout build.xml files to selectively enable certain behavior when going through specific build targets. If you were to build the regular build target, the results of the build would not contain debug information. If instead, you were to build the findbugs target because the findbugs target replaces the debug <property> to true, the result of the build would have debug information.

■ **Tip**   To invoke Ant to run the default "target" (as specified in the build.xml), you just type **ant**. To specify another .xml file (instead of build.xml), you type **ant   f nameofotherfile.xml**. To change the default target to run, you type the name of the target at the end (for example, ant clean).To run this example, type **ant   f findbugsbuild.xml findbugs**. This will ask Ant to use findbugsbuild.xml file and to run the findbugs target.

9-6.Monitoring Garbage Collection in your Application

Problem

You notice that your application seems to be slowing down and suspect that there are garbage collections happening.

Solution 1

Add -Xloggc:gc.log-XX:+PrintGCDetails-XX:+PrintGCTimeStamps as parameters when starting your Java program. These parameters will allow you to log garbage collection information to the gc.log file, including the time garbage collections happen and the details (if it was a minor or major garbage collection and how long it took).

Ant target that executes Recipe 9_6 with garbage logging on.

```
<target name="Recipe9_6" depends="build">
<java classname="org.java7recipes.chapter9.Recipe9_6" fork="true">
        <classpath refid="build.path" />
        <jvmarg value="-Xloggc:gc.log" />
        <jvmarg value="-XX:+PrintGCDetails" />
        <jvmarg value="-XX:+PrintGCTimeStamps" />
</java>
</target>
```

In this build.xml file, the Java task is being used to add the arguments for garbage collection logging to the compiler before launching the application. To run this example throughout Ant, type **ant Recipe9_6**.

Solution 2

Analyze your program's memory consumption by using VisualVM (an external GNU Open Source Java profiler and visualization tool).To use and install VisualVM, go to http://visualvm.java.net/, download and follow the steps for installation (usually uncompressing in the folder of your choice and then clicking the provided executable). Figure 9-2 shows a screenshot of VisualVM profiling Recipe9_6.

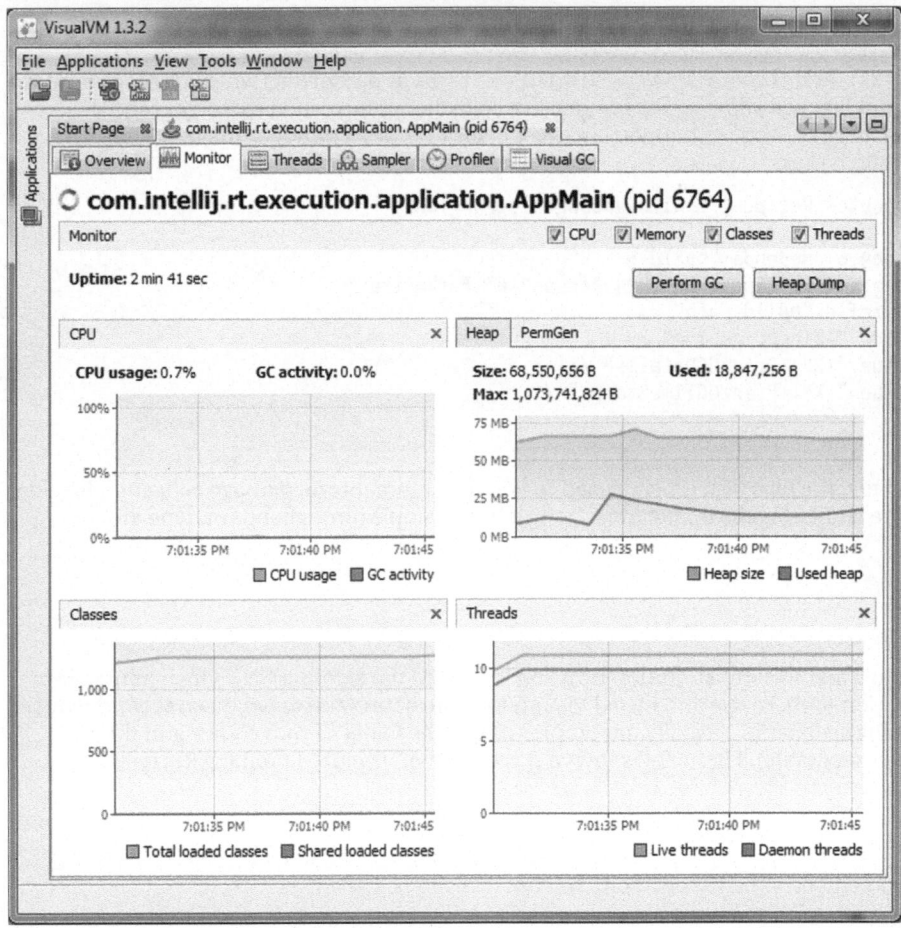

Figure 9-2. VisualVMprofiling Recipe9-6

How It Works

Adding the flag to log garbage collection in solution 1 will cause your Java application to write minor and major garbage collections information into a log file. This allows you to "reconstruct" in time what happened to the application and allows you to spot probable memory leaks (or at least other memory-related issues). This is the preferred troubleshooting method for production systems as it is usually lightweight and can be analyzed after the fact.

Solution 2 instead involves using an open-source tool called VisualVM. This tool allows you to profile code live. It is a great tool to understanding *in situ* what's happening inside your application, as you can see real-time monitoring of CPU consumption, garbage collections, threads created, and classes loaded. VisualVM has its own extensive list of features that should be visited and that every Java developer should have as part of his or her arsenal of tools.

For solution 2, while Recipe9_6 is running, start VisualVM. You will see that there is a list of running virtual machines on the left tree view (under Local). Double-click the Recipe9_6 virtual machine, and you should see the current Memory consumption under the Monitor tab.

■ **Tip**   While explaining all VisualVM options is beyond the scope of the book, it is a good idea to visit and view the different VisualVM plug-ins. One especially useful plug-in when debugging Memory issues is called Visual GC, which is accessible from the VisualVM interface by going to Tool   Plugins   Available Plugins, and selecting Visual GC. This plug-in will display even more information on Garbage Collections, including the different Memory spaces (Eden, Tenured, PermGen), and visually show how these spaces are growing/garbage collected.

9-7: Spotting Memory Leaks in Your Application

Problem

You notice that your application keeps consuming memory until it cannot continue working.

Solution

Use VisualVM to take and view the memory dump.

For this recipe, run the Recipe9_7 program in the example download. That program will launch a Swing frame. On this frame there is a button called Let's Create Windows that when clicked will create a new frame. The frame also has another button (Let's Close The Windows) that when clicked will close all the created frames. This program has a memory leak, and the memory leak is apparent when looking at the VisualVM memory graph.

Using VisualVM, you will see that there is an org.java7recipes.chapter9.Recipe9_7 Java process. Click it to connect. You should be able to see in the Monitor tab what the current memory consumption is. By clicking the Let's Create Windows button and the Let's Close The Windows button, you will see that the Memory consumption in the Monitor tab keeps going up. Look at Figure 9-3 for an example of what you should see.

After the memory size is up around 250Kb, click the button called Heap Dump, which will take a memory dump. The heap dump then will describe what is being held onto memory.

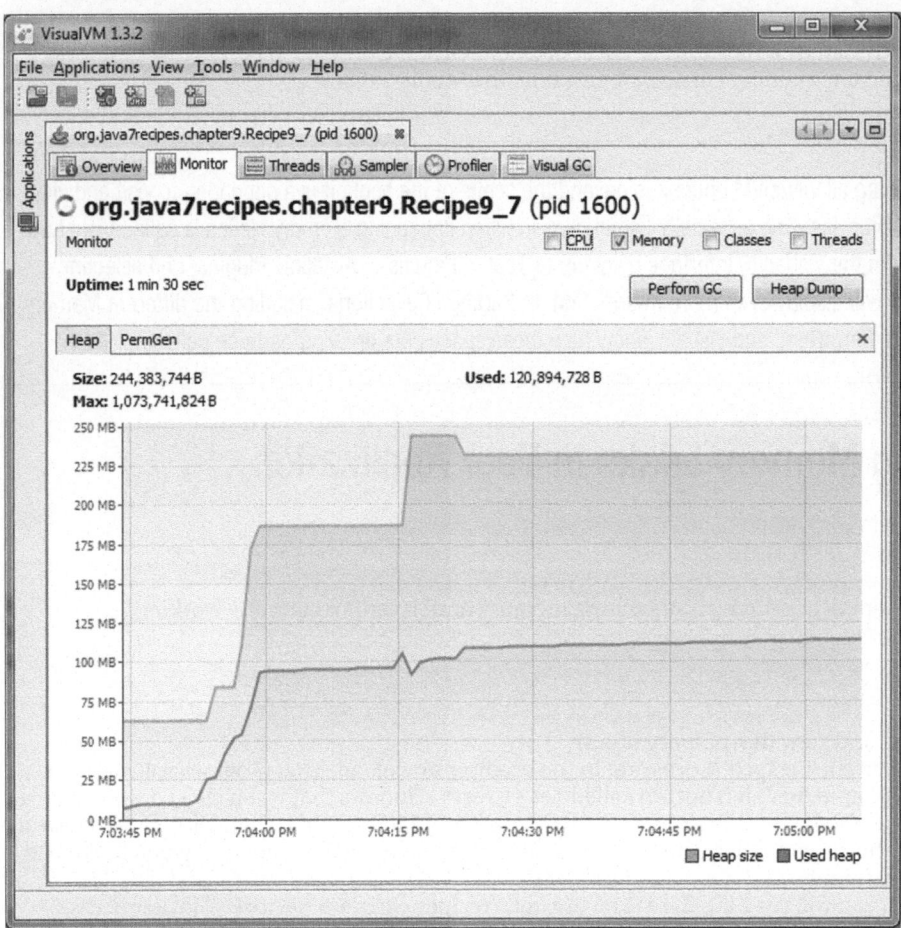

Figure 9-3. Memory image from Recipe9-7

How It Works

VisualVM allows you to take a snapshot on what is happening in the JVM. When hunting for memory leaks, you want to concentrate on what is the object that has the most memory allocation (the usual suspects are Maps). Once you find the objects that use the most memory, it is a matter to see who has the reference to it. By then removing the references to the object (for example, removing it from the map) you can gain control of memory and fix memory leaks.

■ **Note** VisualVM will satisfy most of the needs when it comes to troubleshooting memory issues, but there are JDK-provided tools as well. The most well-known is JMap, which will get a memory dump from the application specified by the process ID (PID). A typical usage is `JMap -dump:format=b <pid>`, which will create a heap dump with the default file name of heap_dump.out. Memory dumps collected using JMap can be viewed in VisualVM. The JDK also has an included viewer called JHat (`http://download.oracle.com/javase/7/docs/technotes/tools/share/jhat.html`).

When you take a heap dump (as described in this recipe), VisualVM will open up a new tab that shows the contents of the heap. Close to the top are Summary, Classes, Instances, and OQL Console buttons. For the purpose of this recipe, you will need to click the Classes button, which will give you a screen similar to Figure 9-4.

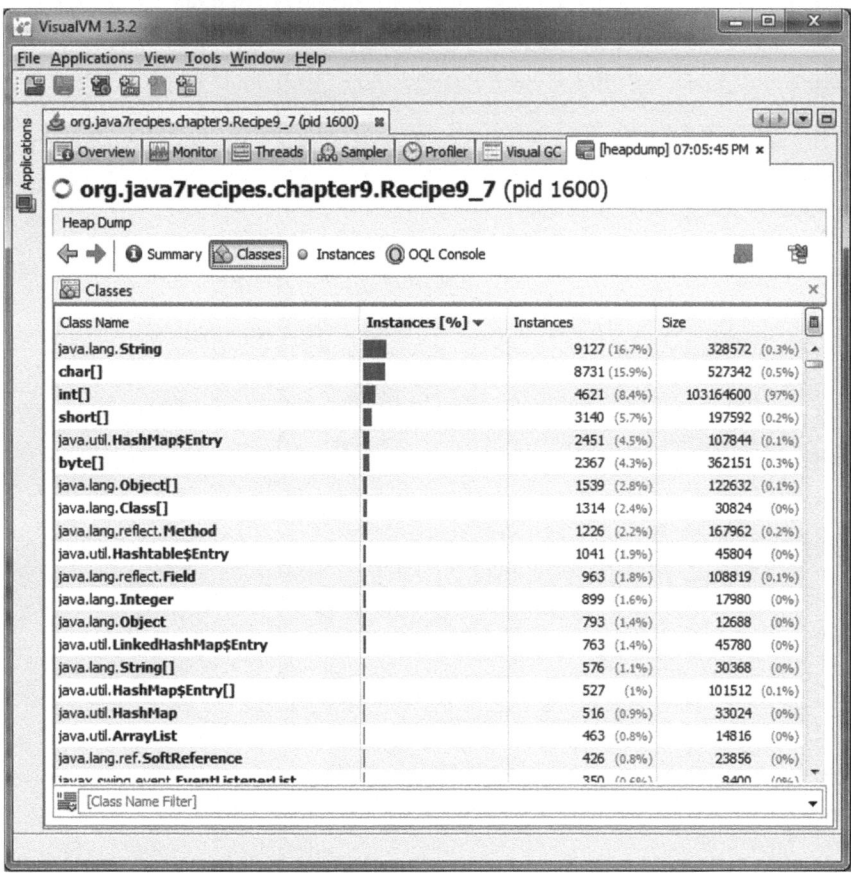

Figure 9-4. Class breakdown in VisualVM

On this view, if you sort by Size (by clicking the Size column), you will notice that object that uses the most memory is the int[] (an Int array). Even though the recipe's program doesn't have any Int arrays defined, the memory leak seems to be related to those Int arrays. To explore the int[], double-click the int[] at the beginning. It will take you to the Instances tab, and describe all the int[] instances that are currently defined in your application.

When debugging memory leaks, sometimes it is not obvious where is the leak coming from. This particular example shows int[] as the cause of the leak, even though when looking at the recipe's code there isn't any int[]. This happens because you have not defined int[], but instead have defined something that uses int[]. (You will find out at the end of the recipe what object was defining and causing the leak.)

In the left of the instance view, you can see each instance of int[] that is on the system, while on the right (under the section titled References),VisualVM displays who is using the int[]. For this exercise, click an int[] instance that has the size of 1800024, and look at the references. On the references, you can expand to "walk upwards" on who owns the int[]. After expanding the references, you will eventually see that they are being held by an Icon, which in turn is held by a JFrame. This presents the clue that JFrames are being held in memory and that the JFrames are not being disposed of. See Figure 9-5 for a screenshot on where to spot the JFrame (it's in the selected row of the bottom-right table).

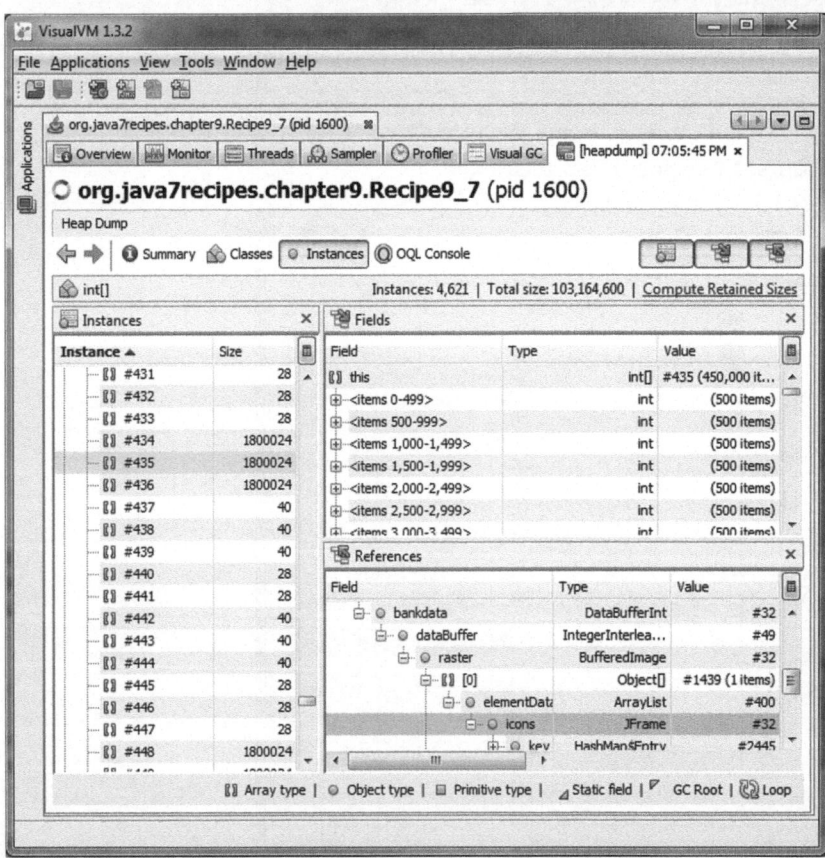

Figure 9-5. Int[] references pointing to icons on a JFrame

With this newfound knowledge that JFrames is what is being "held," you can then go back to the Classes tab and search for JFrame. You can see that there are 100+ JFrames still in memory, even though the recipe specifies them to be DISPOSE_ON_CLOSE. Clicking the JFrame will give you the list of instances of the JFrame and you can drill down on "who" is holding a reference to the JFrame.

After some digging through VisualVM (as shown in Figure 9-6), you find out that the reference to the JFrame is being held by the created Windows set. Upon closer inspection of the code, you can see that the created Windows set is populated with newly created JFrames, but never "emptied." So the JFrame, being "held" by the set, couldn't be garbage collected when closed. The fix for the leak can be found in Recipe9_7_Fixed for the curious at heart.

In short, finding memory leaks usually involves following strange paths. At the beginning of this recipe, the memory dump showed int[] as the culprit, but in the end, it was a Set that held a reference to the JFrames that was never cleared, which in turn held an Icon, which in turn held an int[].

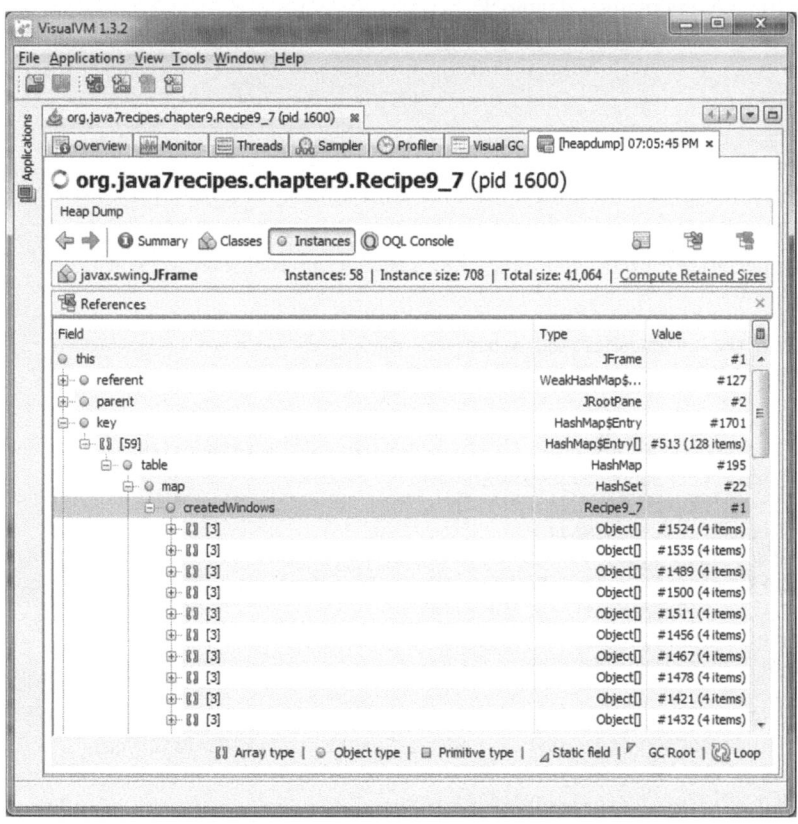

Figure 9-6. JFrame references being held in a createdWindows Set

9-8. Getting a Thread Dump

Problem

Your program seems to "hang" without doing anything, and you suspect that there might be a deadlock.

Solution

Use JStack to get a thread dump, and then analyze the thread dump for deadlocks. The following JStack is a thread dump from Recipe 9_8, which creates a deadlock:

C:>Jstack -l 9588

```
01  Found one Java-level deadlock:
02  =============================
03  Thread-0:
04    waiting for ownable synchronizer 0x00000000eab716b8, (a ReentrantLock$NonfairSync),
05    which is held by "main"
06  main:
07    waiting for ownable synchronizer 0x00000000eab716e8, (aReentrantLock$NonfairSync),
08    which is held by "Thread-0"
09
10  Java stack information for the threads listed above:
11  ===================================================
12  Thread-0:
13    at sun.misc.Unsafe.park(Native Method)
14    - parking to wait for  <0x00000000eab716b8> (a j.u.c.l.ReentrantLock$NonfairSync)
15    at j.u.c.l.LockSupport.park(LockSupport.java:186)
16    at j.u.c.l.aqs.parkAndCheckInterrupt(aqs.java:834)
17    at j.u.c.l.aqs.acquireQueued(aqs.java:867)
18    at j.u.c.l.aqs.acquire(aqs.java:1197)
19    at j.u.c.l.ReentrantLock$NonfairSync.lock(ReentrantLock.java:214)
20    at j.u.c.l.ReentrantLock.lock(ReentrantLock.java:290)
21    at org.java7recipes.chapter9.Recipe9_8$1.run(Recipe9_8.java:28)
22    at java.lang.Thread.run(Thread.java:722)
23  main:
24    at sun.misc.Unsafe.park(Native Method)
25    - parking to wait for  <0x00000000eab716e8> (a j.u.c.l.ReentrantLock$NonfairSync)
26    at j.u.c.l.LockSupport.park(LockSupport.java:186)
27    at j.u.c.l.aqs.parkAndCheckInterrupt(aqs.java:834)
28    at j.u.c.l.aqs.acquireQueued(aqs.java:867)
29    at j.u.c.l.aqs.acquire(aqs.java:1197)
30    at j.u.c.l.ReentrantLock$NonfairSync.lock(ReentrantLock.java:214)
31    at j.u.c.l.ReentrantLock.lock(ReentrantLock.java:290)
32    at org.java7recipes.chapter9.Recipe9_8.start(Recipe9_8.java:38)
33    at org.java7recipes.chapter9.Recipe9_8.main(Recipe9_8.java:20)
34
35  Found 1 deadlock.
```

For this recipe to work, you must have as part of your PATH environment variable the JDK's bin folder (For example C:\Program Files\java\jdk1.7.0\bin). If you have this path, you can run the tools such as JStack and JPS.

The JStack command uses as an argument –l (a dash and the letter *L*), which specifies a Long listing (it does extra work to get more information about the threads running). The JStack also needs to know the PID of the target VM. A quick way to list all running JVMs is to type **JPS** and press Enter. This will list the running VMs and their PIDs. Figure 9-7 shows a screenshot of a JStack finding a deadlock in Recipe 9-8.

■ **Note** For the purposes of this example, j.u.c.l represents java.util.concurrent.locks, and aqs represents AbstractQueuedSynchronizer.

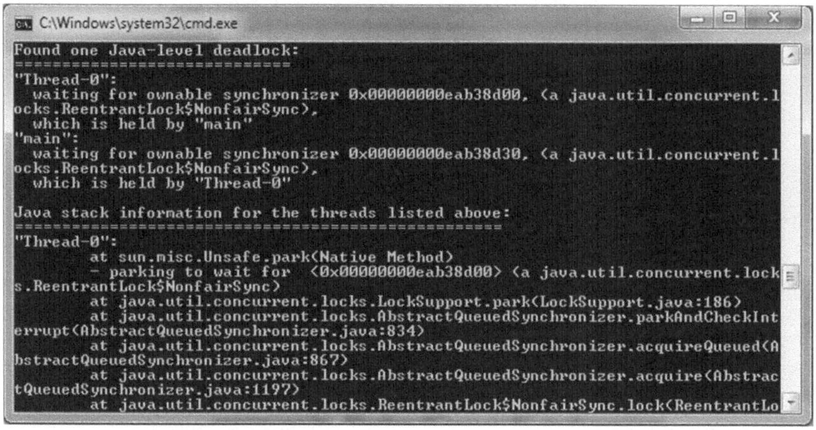

Figure 9-7. JStack results

How It Works

JStack allows you to see all the stack traces that the current running threads have. JStack will also try to find deadlocks (circular dependencies of locks) that might be stalling your system. JStack will not find other problems such as livelock(when a thread is always spinning, i.e. something like while(true)), or starvation (when a thread cannot execute because it is too low of a priority or there are too many threads competing for resources), but it will help you understand what each of the threads in your program is doing.

Deadlocks happen because one thread is waiting for a resource that another thread has, and the second thread is waiting for a resource that the first thread has. In this situation, neither thread can continue because both are waiting for each other to release the resource that each one owns. Deadlocks don't only happen between two threads, but can also involve a "string" of threads so that Thread A is waiting for Thread B is waiting for Thread C is waiting for Thread D is waiting for the original Thread A. It is important to understand the dump to find the culprit resource.

In this recipe's example, Thread-0 wants to acquire the lock named "0x00000000eab716b8"; it's described in the thread dump as "waiting for ownable synchronizer". Thread-0 cannot acquire the lock because it is held by the main thread. The main thread, on the other hand, wants to acquire the lock "0x00000000eab716e8" (notice that they are different; the first lock ends in b8, while the second ends in e8), which is held by Thread-0. This is a textbook definition of a deadlock on which each thread is forever waiting for each other to release the lock the other thread has.

Aside from deadlock, looking at thread dumps gives you an idea about what your program is doing in realtime. Especially in multithreaded systems, using thread dumps will help clarify where a thread is sleeping or what condition it is waiting for.

■ **Tip**   JStack is usually lightweight enough to be run in a live system, so if you need to troubleshoot live problems, you can safely use JStack.

CHAPTER 10

Unicode, Internationalization, and Currency Codes

The Java platform provides a rich set of internationalization features to help you create applications that can be used across the world. The platform provides the means to localize your applications, format dates and numbers in a variety of culturally-sensitive formats, and display characters used in dozens of writing systems.

This chapter describes only some of the most frequent and common tasks that programmers must perform when developing internationalized applications. Because Java 7 adds new features around its abstraction of languages and regions, this chapter describes some of the new ways you might use the Locale class.

■ **Note** The source code for this chapter's examples is available in the org.java7recipes.chapter10 package. Please see the introductory chapters for instructions on how to find and download sample source code.

10-1. Converting Unicode **Characters to Digits**

Problem

You want to convert a Unicode digit character to its respective integer value. For example, you have a string containing the Thai digit for the value 8 and you wish to generate an integer with that value.

Solution

The java.lang.Character class has several static methods to convert characters to integer digit values:

- public static intdigit(char ch, int radix)

- public static intdigit(intch, int radix)

The following code snippet iterates through the entire range of Unicode code points from 0x0000 through 0x10FFFF. For each code point that is also a digit, it displays the character and its digit value 0 through 9. You can find this example in the org.java7recipes.chapter10.DigitConversion class.

```
int x = 0;
for (int c=0; c <= 0x10FFFF; c++) {
    if (Character.isDigit(c)) {
        ++x;
        System.out.printf("Codepoint: 0x%04X\tCharacter: %c\tDigit: %d\tName: %s\n", c, c,
            Character.digit(c, 10), Character.getName(c));
    }
}
System.out.printf("Total digits: %d\n", x);
```

Some of the output follows:

```
Codepoint: 0x0030    Character: 0    Digit: 0    Name: DIGIT ZERO
Codepoint: 0x0031    Character: 1    Digit: 1    Name: DIGIT ONE
Codepoint: 0x0032    Character: 2    Digit: 2    Name: DIGIT TWO
Codepoint: 0x0033    Character: 3    Digit: 3    Name: DIGIT THREE
Codepoint: 0x0034    Character: 4    Digit: 4    Name: DIGIT FOUR
Codepoint: 0x0035    Character: 5    Digit: 5    Name: DIGIT FIVE
Codepoint: 0x0036    Character: 6    Digit: 6    Name: DIGIT SIX
Codepoint: 0x0037    Character: 7    Digit: 7    Name: DIGIT SEVEN
Codepoint: 0x0038    Character: 8    Digit: 8    Name: DIGIT EIGHT
Codepoint: 0x0039    Character: 9    Digit: 9    Name: DIGIT NINE
Codepoint: 0x0660    Character: ٠    Digit: 0    Name: ARABIC-INDIC DIGIT ZERO
Codepoint: 0x0661    Character: ١    Digit: 1    Name: ARABIC-INDIC DIGIT ONE
Codepoint: 0x0662    Character: ٢    Digit: 2    Name: ARABIC-INDIC DIGIT TWO
Codepoint: 0x0663    Character: ٣    Digit: 3    Name: ARABIC-INDIC DIGIT THREE
Codepoint: 0x0664    Character: ٤    Digit: 4    Name: ARABIC-INDIC DIGIT FOUR
Codepoint: 0x0665    Character: ٥    Digit: 5    Name: ARABIC-INDIC DIGIT FIVE
Codepoint: 0x0666    Character: ٦    Digit: 6    Name: ARABIC-INDIC DIGIT SIX
Codepoint: 0x0667    Character: ٧    Digit: 7    Name: ARABIC-INDIC DIGIT SEVEN
Codepoint: 0x0668    Character: ٨    Digit: 8    Name: ARABIC-INDIC DIGIT EIGHT
Codepoint: 0x0669    Character: ٩    Digit: 9    Name: ARABIC-INDIC DIGIT NINE
!
Codepoint: 0x0E50    Character: ๐    Digit: 0    Name: THAI DIGIT ZERO
Codepoint: 0x0E51    Character: ๑    Digit: 1    Name: THAI DIGIT ONE
Codepoint: 0x0E52    Character: ๒    Digit: 2    Name: THAI DIGIT TWO
Codepoint: 0x0E53    Character: ๓    Digit: 3    Name: THAI DIGIT THREE
Codepoint: 0x0E54    Character: ๔    Digit: 4    Name: THAI DIGIT FOUR
Codepoint: 0x0E55    Character: ๕    Digit: 5    Name: THAI DIGIT FIVE
Codepoint: 0x0E56    Character: ๖    Digit: 6    Name: THAI DIGIT SIX
```

```
Codepoint: 0x0E57     Character: ๗    Digit: 7    Name: THAI DIGIT SEVEN
Codepoint: 0x0E58     Character: ๘    Digit: 8    Name: THAI DIGIT EIGHT
Codepoint: 0x0E59     Character: ๙    Digit: 9    Name: THAI DIGIT NINE
!
Total digits: 420
```

■ **Note**   The sample code prints to the console. Your console may not print all the character glyphs shown in this example because of font or platform differences. However, the characters will be converted to integers correctly.

How It Works

The Unicode character set is large, containing more than a million unique code points with integer values ranging from 0x0000 through 0x10FFFF. Each character value has a set of properties. One of the properties is the isDigit property. If this property is true, the character represents a numeric digit from 0 through 9. For example, the characters with code point values 0x30 through 0x39 have the character glyphs 0, 1, 2, 3, 4, 5, 6, 7, 8, 9. If you simply convert these code values to their corresponding integer values, you would get the hexadecimal values 0x30 through 0x39. The corresponding decimal values are 48 through 57. However, these characters also represent numeric digits. When using them in calculations, we expect these characters to represent the values 0 through 9.

When a character has the digit property, use the Character.digit() static method to convert it to its corresponding integer digit value. Note that the digit() method is overloaded to accept either char or int arguments. Additionally, the method requires a radix. Common values for radix are 2, 10, and 16. Interestingly, although the characters a-f and A-F do not have the digit property, they can be used as digits using radix 16. For these characters, the digit() method returns the expected integer values 10 through 15.

A complete understanding of the Unicode character set and Java's implementation requires familiarity with several new terms: character, code point, char, encoding, serialization encoding, UTF-8, UTF-16. These terms are beyond the scope of this recipe, but you can learn more about these and other Unicode concepts from the Unicode web site at http://unicode.org or from the Character class Java API documentation.

10-2. Creating and Working with Locales

Problem

You want to display numbers, dates, and time in a user-friendly way that conforms to the language and cultural expectations of your customers.

Solution

The display format for numbers, dates, and time varies across the world and depends upon your user's language and cultural region. Additionally, text collation rules vary by language. The `java.util.Locale` class represents a specific language and region of the world. By determining and using your customer's locale, you can apply that locale to a variety of format classes that create user-visible data in expected forms. Classes that use `Locale` instances to modify their behavior for a particular language or region are called locale-sensitive classes. You can learn more about locale-sensitive classes in the "Numbers and Dates" chapter. That chapter shows you how to use `Locale` instances in the `NumberFormat` and `DateFormat` classes. In this recipe, however, you will learn options for creating these `Locale` instances.

Create a `Locale` instance in any of the following ways:

- Use the `Locale.Builder` class to configure and build a `Locale` object.

- Use the static `Locale.forLanguageTag()` method.

- Use the `Locale` constructors to create an object.

- Use preconfigured static `Locale` objects.

The Java 7 `Locale.Builder` class has setter methods that allow you to create locales that can be transformed into well-formed Best Common Practices (BCP) 47 language tags. The "How It Works" section will describe the BCP 47 standard in more detail. For now, you should simply understand that a `Builder` creates `Locale` instances that comply with that standard.

The following code snippet from the `org.java7recipes.chapter10.LocaleCreator` class demonstrates how to create `Builder` and `Locale` instances. You use the created locales in locale-sensitive classes to produce culturally correct display formats:

```
private static final long number = 123456789L;
private static final Date now = new Date();

private void createFromBuilder() {
    System.out.printf("Creating from Builder...\n\n");
    String[][] langRegions = {{"fr", "FR"}, {"ja", "JP"}, {"en", "US"}};
    Builder builder = new Builder();
    Locale l = null;
    NumberFormat nf = null;
    DateFormat df = null;
    for (String[] lr: langRegions) {
        builder.clear();
        builder.setLanguage(lr[0]).setRegion(lr[1]);
        l = builder.build();
        nf = NumberFormat.getInstance(l);
        df = DateFormat.getDateTimeInstance(DateFormat.LONG, DateFormat.LONG, l);
        System.out.printf("Locale: %s\nNumber: %s\nDate: %s\n\n",
```

```
        l.getDisplayName(),
        nf.format(number),
        df.format(now));
}
```

The previous code prints the following to the standard console:

```
Creating from Builder...

Locale: French (France)
Number: 123 456 789
Date: 14 septembre 2011 00:08:06 PDT

Locale: Japanese (Japan)
Number: 123,456,789
Date: 2011/09/14 0:08:06 PDT

Locale: English (United States)
Number: 123,456,789
Date: September 14, 2011 12:08:06 AM PDT
```

Another way to create locale instances is by using the static `Locale.forLanguageTag()` method. This method allows you to use BCP 47 language tag arguments.The following code uses the forLanguageTag() method to create three locales from their corresponding language tags:

```
!
System.out.printf("Creating from BCP 47 language tags...\n\n");
String[] bcp47LangTags= {"fr-FR", "ja-JP", "en-US"};
Locale l = null;
NumberFormat nf = null;
DateFormat df = null;
for (String langTag: bcp47LangTags) {
    l = Locale.forLanguageTag(langTag);
    nf = NumberFormat.getInstance(l);
    df = DateFormat.getDateTimeInstance(DateFormat.LONG, DateFormat.LONG, l);
    System.out.printf("Locale: %s\nNumber: %s\nDate: %s\n\n",
        l.getDisplayName(),
        nf.format(number),
        df.format(now));
}
!
```

The output is similar to the results created from the `Builder`-generated locale instance:

```
Creating from BCP 47 language tags...

Locale: French (France)
```

```
Number: 123 456 789
Date: 14 septembre 2011 01:07:22 PDT
!
```

You can also use constructors to create instances. The following code shows how to do this:

```
Locale l = new Locale("fr", "FR");
```

Other constructors allow you to pass fewer or more arguments. The argument parameters can include language, region, and optional variant codes.

Finally, the `Locale` class has many predefined static instances for some commonly used cases. Because the instances are predefined, your code needs to reference only the static instances. For example, the following example shows how to reference existing static instances representing `fr-FR`, `ja-JP`, and `en-US` locales:

```
Locale frenchInFrance = Locale.FRANCE;
Locale japaneseInJapan = Locale.JAPAN;
Locale englishInUS = Locale.US;
```

Refer to the `Locale` Java API documentation for examples of other static instances.

How It Works

The `Locale` class gives locale-sensitive classes the context they need to perform culture-sensitive data formatting and parsing. Some of the locale-sensitive classes include the following:

- `java.text.NumberFormat`

- `java.text.DateFormat`

- `java.util.Calendar`

A `Locale` instance identifies a specific language, and can be finely tuned to identify languages written in a particular script or spoken in a specific world region. `Locale` is an important and necessary element for creating anything thathas dependencies on language or regional influences.

The Java 7 `Locale` class introduces a few significant changes that give it support for modern BCP 47 language tags. BCP 47 defines Best Common Practices for using ISO standards for language, region, script, and variant identifiers. Although the existing `Locale` constructors continue to be compatible with prior versions of the Java platform, the constructors do not support the additional script tags. For example, only the new `Locale.Builder` class and `Locale.forLanguageTag()` method support the new functionality that identifies scripts. This new class and method were introduced in Java 7. Because the `Locale` constructors do not enforce strict BCP 47 compliance, you should avoid the constructors in any new code. Instead, developers should migrate their code to use the new `Builder` class and the `forLanguageTag()` method.

A `Locale.Builder` instance has a variety of setter methods that help you configure it to create a valid, BCP 47–compliant `Locale` instance:

- `public Locale.BuildersetLanguage(String language)`

- `public Locale.BuildersetRegion(String region)`

- `public Locale.BuildersetScript(String script)`

Each of these methods throws a `java.util.IllFormedLocaleException` if its argument is not a well-formed element of the BCP 47 standard. The language parameter must be a valid two or three-letter ISO 639 language identifier. The region parameter must be a valid two-letter ISO 3166 region code or a three-digit M.49 United Nations "area" code. Finally, the script parameter must be a valid four-letter ISO 15924 script code.

The `Builder` lets you configure it to create a specific BCP 47–compliant `Locale`. Once you set all the configurations, the `build()` method creates and returns a `Locale` instance. Notice that all the setters can be chained together for a single statement. The `Builder` pattern works by having each configuration method return a reference to the current instance, on which further configuration methods may be called.

```
Locale aLocale = new Builder().setLanguage("fr").setRegion("FR").build();
```

The BCP 47 document and the standards that comprise it can be found at the following locations:

- BCP 47 (language tags): `http://www.rfc-editor.org/rfc/bcp/bcp47.txt`

- ISO 639 (language identifiers): `http://www.loc.gov/standards/iso639-2/php/code_list.php`

- ISO 3166 (region identifiers): `http://www.iso.org/iso/country_codes/iso_3166_code_lists/country_names_and_code_elements.htm`

- ISO 15924 (script identifiers): `http://unicode.org/iso15924/`

- United Nations M.49 (Area identifiers): `http://unstats.un.org/unsd/methods/m49/m49.htm`

10-3. Setting the Default Locale

Problem

You want to set the default locale for all locale-sensitive classes.

Solution

Use the `Locale.setDefault()` method to set a `Locale` instance that all locale-sensitive classes will use by default. This method is overloaded with two forms:

- `Locale.setDefault(Locale aLocale)`

- `Locale.setDefault(Locale.Category c, Locale aLocale)`

This example code demonstrates how to set the default locale for all locale-sensitive classes:

```
Locale.setDefault(Locale.FRANCE);
```

You can also set the default for two additional locale categories, DISPLAY and FORMAT:

```
Locale.setDefault(Locale.Category.DISPLAY, Locale.US);
Locale.setDefault(Locale.Category.FORMAT, Locale.FR);
```

You can create code that uses these specific locale categories within your application to mix locale choices for different purposes. For example, you may choose to use the DISPLAY locale for ResourceBundle text while using the FORMAT locale for date and time formats. The example code from the `org.java7recipes.chapter10.DefaultLocale` class demonstrates this more complex usage:

```java
public class DefaultLocale {

    private static final Date NOW = new Date();

    public void run() {
        // Set ALL locales to fr-FR
        Locale.setDefault(Locale.FRANCE);
        demoDefaultLocaleSettings();

        // System default is still fr-FR
        // DISPLAY default is es-MX
        // FORMAT default is en-US
        Locale.setDefault(Locale.Category.DISPLAY, Locale.forLanguageTag("es-MX"));
        Locale.setDefault(Locale.Category.FORMAT, Locale.US);
        demoDefaultLocaleSettings();

        // System default is still fr-FR
        // DISPLAY default is en-US
        // FORMAT default is es-MX
        Locale.setDefault(Locale.Category.DISPLAY, Locale.US);
        Locale.setDefault(Locale.Category.FORMAT, Locale.forLanguageTag("es-MX"));
        demoDefaultLocaleSettings();
```

```
// Reset system, DISPLAY, and FORMAT locales to en-US.
        Locale.setDefault(Locale.US);
        demoDefaultLocaleSettings();
    }

    public void demoDefaultLocaleSettings() {
        DateFormat df = DateFormat.getDateTimeInstance(DateFormat.SHORT, DateFormat.SHORT);
            ResourceBundle resource =

            ResourceBundle.getBundle("org.java7recipes.chapter10.recipe10_1.resource.
        SimpleResources",
                Locale.getDefault(Locale.Category.DISPLAY));
        String greeting = resource.getString("GOOD_MORNING");
        String date = df.format(NOW);
        System.out.printf("DEFAULT LOCALE: %s\n", Locale.getDefault());
        System.out.printf("DISPLAY LOCALE: %s\n", Locale.getDefault(Locale.Category.DISPLAY));
        System.out.printf("FORMAT LOCALE:  %s\n", Locale.getDefault(Locale.Category.FORMAT));
        System.out.printf("%s, %s\n\n", greeting, date );
    }

    public static void main(String[] args) {
        DefaultLocale app = new DefaultLocale();
        app.run();
    }
}
```

This code produces the following output:

```
DEFAULT LOCALE: fr_FR
DISPLAY LOCALE: fr_FR
FORMAT LOCALE:  fr_FR
Bonjour!, 19/09/11 20:31

DEFAULT LOCALE: fr_FR
DISPLAY LOCALE: es_MX
FORMAT LOCALE:  en_US
¡Buenos días!, 9/19/11 8:31 PM

DEFAULT LOCALE: fr_FR
DISPLAY LOCALE: en_US
FORMAT LOCALE:  es_MX
Good morning!, 19/09/11 08:31 PM

DEFAULT LOCALE: en_US
DISPLAY LOCALE: en_US
```

```
FORMAT LOCALE:  en_US
Good morning!, 9/19/11 8:31 PM
```

How It Works

The Locale class allows you to set the default Locale for two different categories. The categories are represented by the Locale.Category enumeration:

- Locale.Category.DISPLAY

- Locale.Category.FORMAT

Use the DISPLAY category for your application's user interface. Setting the default DISPLAY locale means that the ResourceBundle class can load user interface resources for that particular locale independently from the FORMAT locale. Setting the FORMAT default locale affects how the various Format subclasses behave. For example, a default DateFormat instance will use the FORMATdefault locale to create a locale-sensitive output format. Again, these two categories are independent, so you can use different Locale instances for different needs.

In this recipe's sample code, the Locale.setDefault(Locale.FRANCE) method call sets the default system, DISPLAY, and FORMAT locales to fr-FR (French in France). This method always resets both DISPLAY and FORMAT locales to match the system locale. When creating a new resource bundle, the ResourceBundle class uses the system locale by default. However, by providing a locale instance argument, you tell the bundle to load resources for a specific locale. For example, even though the system locale is Locale.FRANCE, you can specify a DISPLAY default locale and use that DISPLAY locale in your ResourceBundle.getBundle() method call. For example, this code attempts to load a language bundle for es-MX even though the system locale is still Locale.FRANCE:

```
Locale.setDefault(Locale.Category.DISPLAY, Locale.forLanguageTag("es-MX"));
Locale.setDefault(Locale.Category.FORMAT, Locale.US);
DateFormat df = DateFormat.getDateTimeInstance(DateFormat.SHORT, DateFormat.SHORT);
ResourceBundle resource =
        ResourceBundle.getBundle("org.java7recipes.chapter10..resource.SimpleResources",
                Locale.getDefault(Locale.Category.DISPLAY));
String greeting = resource.getString("GOOD_MORNING");
```

In this case, it finds a GOOD_MORNING resource with the "¡Buenos días!" value because the DISPLAY default locale is an argument. The resource bundle is a file with translated property strings for various locales. The file named SimpleResources_en.properties (English) has a GOOD_MORNING property that is written "Good morning!" Note that translations of each property in the resource bundle must exist in the locale-specific resource files in order to be displayed. The Java code does not translate these strings. Instead, it just selects an appropriate translation of the desired property based on the selected locale.

■ **Note** Although `DateFormat` and `NumberFormat` classes will automatically use the default `FORMAT` locale if you do not provide a locale argument in their creation method, the `ResourceBundle.getBundle()` method always uses the system locale by default. To use the `DISPLAY` default locale in a `ResourceBundle()`, you must explicitly provide it as an argument.

10-4. Searching Unicode with Regular Expressions

Problem

You want to find or match Unicode characters in a `String`. You want to do that using regular expression syntax.

Solution 1

The easiest way to find or match characters is to use the `String` class itself. `String` instances store Unicode character sequences and provide relatively simple operations for finding, replacing, and tokenizing characters using regular expressions.

To determine whether a `String` matches a regular expression, use the `matches()` method. The `matches()` method returns `true` if the entire string exactly matches the regular expression.

The following code from the `org.java7recipes.chapter10.Regex` class uses two different expressions with two strings. The regular expression matches simply confirm that the strings match a particular pattern as defined in the variables enRegEx and jaRegEx.

```java
private String enText = "The fat cat sat on the mat with a brown rat.";
private String jaText = "Fight 文字化け!";

boolean found = false;
String enRegEx = "^The \\w+ cat.*";
String jaRegEx = ".*文字.*";
String jaRegExEscaped = ".*\u6587\u5B57.*";
found = enText.matches(enRegEx);
if (found) {
    System.out.printf("Matches %s.\n", enRegEx);
}
found = jaText.matches(jaRegEx);
if (found) {
    System.out.printf("Matches %s.\n", jaRegEx);
}
```

```
found = jaText.matches(jaRegExEscaped);
if (found) {
    System.out.printf("Matches %s.\n", jaRegExEscaped);
}
```

This code prints the following:

```
Matches ^The \w+ cat.*.
Matches .*文字.*.
Matches .*文字.*.
```

Use the `replaceFirst()` method to create a new `String` instance in which the first occurrence of the regular expression in the target text is replaced with the replacement text. The code demonstrates how to use this method:

```
String replaced = jaText.replaceFirst("文字化け", "mojibake");
System.out.printf("Replaced: %s\n", replaced);
```

The replacement text is shown in the output:

```
Replaced: Fight mojibake!
```

The `replaceAll()` method replaces all occurrences of the expression with the replacement text.

Finally, the `split()` method creates a `String[]` that contains text that is separated by the matched expression. In other words, it returns text that is delimited by the expression. Optionally, you can provide a `limit` argument that constrains the number of times the delimiter will be applied in the source text. The following code demonstrates the `split()` method splitting on space characters:

```
String[] matches = enText.split("\\s", 3);
for(String match: matches) {
    System.out.printf("Split: %s\n",match);
}
```

The code's output is as follows:

```
Split: The
Split: fat
Split: cat sat on the mat with a brown rat.
```

Solution 2

When the simple `String` methods aren't sufficient, you can use the more powerful `java.util.regex` package to work with regular expressions. Create a regular expression using the `Pattern` class. A `Matcher` works on a `String` instance using the pattern. All `Matcher` operations perform their functions using `Pattern` and `String` instances.

The following code demonstrates how to search for both ASCII and non-ASCII text in two separate strings. See the `org.java7recipes.chapter10.Regex` class for the complete source code. The `demoSimple()` method finds text with any character followed by ".at". The `demoComplex()` method finds two Japanese symbols in a string:

```java
public void demoSimple() {
Pattern p = Pattern.compile(".at");
    Matcher m = p.matcher(enText);
    while(m.find()) {
        System.out.printf("%s\n", m.group());
    }
}

public void demoComplex() {
    Pattern p = Pattern.compile("文字");
    Matcher m = p.matcher(jaText);
    if (m.find()) {
        System.out.println(m.group());
    }
}
```

Running these two methods on the previously defined English and Japanese text shows the following:

```
fat
cat
sat
mat
rat
文字
```

How It Works

The `String` methods that work with regular expressions are the following:

- `public boolean matches(String regex)`

- `public String replaceFirst(String regex, String replacement)`

- `public String replaceAll(String regex, String replacement)`

- `public String[] split(String regex, int limit)`

- `public String[] split(String regex)`

The `String` methods are limited and relatively simple wrappers around the more powerful functionality of the `java.util.regex` classes:

- `java.util.regex.Pattern`

- `java.util.regex.Matcher`

- `java.util.regex.PatternSyntaxException`

The Java regular expressions are similar to those used in the Perl language. Although there is a lot to learn about Java regular expressions, probably the most important points to understand from this recipe are these:

- Your regular expressions can definitely contain non-ASCII characters from the full range of Unicode characters.

- Because of a peculiarity of how the Java language compiler understands the backslash character, you will have to use two backslashes in your code instead of one for the predefined character class expressions.

The most convenient and readable way to use non-ASCII characters in regular expressions is to type them directly into your source files using your keyboard input methods. Operating systems and editors differ in how they allow you to enter complex text outside of ASCII. Regardless of operating system, you should save the file in the UTF-8 encoding if your editor allows. As an alternate but more difficult way to use non-ASCII regular expressions, you can encode characters using the \uXXXX notation. Using this notation, instead of directly typing the character using your keyboard, you enter "\u" or "\U", followed by the hexadecimal representation of the Unicode code point. This recipe's code sample uses the Japanese word "文字" (pronounced *mo-ji*). As the example shows, you can use the actual characters in the regular expression or you can look up the Unicode code point values instead. For this particular Japanese word, the encoding will be "\u6587\u5B57".

The Java language's regular expression support includes special character classes. For example, \d and \w are shortcut notations for the regular expressions [0-9] and [a-zA-Z_0-9], respectively. However, because of the Java compiler's special handling of the backslash character, you must use an extra backslash when using predefined character classes such as \d (digits), \w (word characters), and \s (space characters). To use them in source code, for example, you would enter "\\d", "\\w", and "\\s", respectively. The sample code used the double backslash in Solution 1 to represent the \w character class:

```
String enRegEx = "^The \\w+ cat.*";
```

10-5. Overriding the Default Currency

Problem

You want to display a number value using a currency that is not associated with the default locale.

Solution

Take control of what currency is printed with a formatted currency value by explicitly setting the currency used in a `NumberFormat` instance. The following example assumes that the default locale is `Locale.JAPAN`. It changes the currency by calling the `setCurrency(Currency c)` method of its `NumberFormat` instance. This example comes from the `org.java7recipes.chapter10.CurrencyOverride` class

```
BigDecimal value = new BigDecimal(12345);
System.out.printf("Default locale: %s\n", Locale.getDefault().getDisplayName());
NumberFormat nf = NumberFormat.getCurrencyInstance();
String formattedCurrency = nf.format(value);
System.out.printf("%s\n", formattedCurrency);
Currency c = Currency.getInstance(Locale.US);
nf.setCurrency(c);
formattedCurrency = nf.format(value);
System.out.printf("%s\n\n", formattedCurrency);
```

The previous code prints out the following:

```
Default locale: 日本語 (日本)
￥12,345
USD12,345
```

How It Works

You will use a `NumberFormat` instance to format currency values. You should explicitly call the `getCurrencyInstance()` method to create a formatter for currencies:

```
NumberFormat nf = NumberFormat.getCurrencyInstance();
```

The previous formatter will use your default locale's preferences for formatting numbers as currency values. Also, it will use a currency symbol that is associated with the locale's region. However, one very common use case involves formatting a value for a different region's currency.

Use the `setCurrency()` method to explicitly set the currency in the number formatter:

```
nf.setCurrency(aCurrencyInstance); // requires a Currency instance
```

Note that the `java.util.Currency` class is a factory. It allows you to create currency objects in two ways:

- `Currency.getInstance(Locale locale)`

- `Currency.getInstance(String currencyCode)`

The first `getInstance` call uses a `Locale` instance to retrieve a currency object. The Java platform associates a default currency with the locale's region. In this case, the default currency currently associated with the United States is the U.S. dollar:

```
Currency c1 = Currency.getInstance(Locale.US);
```

The second `getInstance` call uses a valid ISO 4217 currency code. The currency code for the U.S. dollar is USD:

```
Currency c2 = Currency.getInstance("USD");
```

Once you have a currency instance, you simply have to use that instance in your formatter:

```
nf.setCurrency(c2);
```

This formatter now is configured to use the default locale's number format symbols and patterns to format the number value, but it will display the targeted currency code as part of the displayable text. This allows you to mix the default number format patterns with other currency codes.

■ **Note**   Currencies have both symbols and codes. A currency code always refers to the three-letter ISO 4217 code. A currency symbol is often different from the code. For example, the U.S. dollar has the code USD and the symbol $. A currency formatter will typically use a symbol when formatting a number in the default locale using the currency of that locale's region. However, when you explicitly change the currency of a formatter, the formatter doesn't always have knowledge of a localized symbol for the target currency. In that case, the format instance will often use the currency code in the displayed text.

10-6. Converting Byte Arrays to and from Strings

Problem

You need to convert characters in a byte array from a legacy character set encoding to a Unicode String.

Solution

Convert legacy character encodings from a byte array to a Unicode String using the String class. The following code snippet from the org.java7recipes.CharacterEncodingConversion class demonstrates how to convert a legacy Shift-JIS encoded byte array to a String. Later in this same example, the code demonstrates how to convert from Unicode back into the Shift-JIS byte array.

```
byte[] legacySJIS = {(byte)0x82,(byte)0xB1,(byte)0x82,(byte)0xF1,
(byte)0x82,(byte)0xC9,(byte)0x82,(byte)0xBF,
(byte)0x82,(byte)0xCD,(byte)0x81,(byte)0x41,
(byte)0x90,(byte)0xA2,(byte)0x8A,(byte)0x45,
(byte)0x81,(byte)0x49};

// Convert a byte[] to a String
Charset cs =Charset.forName("SJIS");
String greeting = new String(legacySJIS, cs);
System.out.printf("Greeting: %s\n", greeting);
```

The previous code prints out the converted text, which is "Hello, world!" in Japanese:

```
Greeting: こんにちは、世界！
```

Use the getBytes() method to convert characters from a String to a byte array. Building upon the previous code, convert back to the original encoding with the following code, and compare the results:

```
// Convert a String to a byte[]
byte[] toSJIS = greeting.getBytes(cs);

// Confirm that the original array and newly converted array are same
Boolean same = false;
if (legacySJIS.length == toSJIS.length) {
    for (int x=0; x< legacySJIS.length; x++) {
        if(legacySJIS[x] != toSJIS[x]) break;
    }
    same = true;
}
System.out.printf("Same: %s\n", same.toString());
```

As expected, the output indicates that the round-trip conversion back to the legacy encoding was successful. The original byte array and the converted byte array contain the same bytes:

```
Same: true
```

How It Works

The Java platform provides conversion support for many legacy character set encodings. When you create a `String` instance from a `byte` array, you must provide a `Charset` argument to the `String` constructor so that the platform knows how to perform the mapping from the legacy encoding to Unicode. All Java `Strings` use Unicode as their native encoding.

The number of bytes in the original array does not usually equal the number of characters in the result string. In this recipe's example, the original array contains 18 bytes. The 18 bytes are needed by the Shift-JIS encoding to represent the Japanese text. However, after conversion, the result string contains nine characters. There is not a 1:1 relationship between bytes and characters. In this example, each character requires two bytes in the original Shift-JIS encoding.

There are literally hundreds of different charset encodings. The number of encodings is dependent upon your Java platform implementation. However, you are guaranteed support of several of the most common encodings, and your platform most likely contains many more than this minimal set:

- US-ASCII

- ISO-8859-1

- UTF-8

- UTF-16BE

- UTF-16LE

- UTF-16

When constructing a `Charset`, you should be prepared to handle the possible exceptions that can occur when the character set is not supported:

- `java.nio.charset.IllegalCharsetNameException`, thrown when the charset name is illegal

- `java.lang.IllegalArgumentException`, thrown if charset name is `null`

- `java.nio.charset.UnsupportedCharsetException`, thrown if your JVM doesn't support the targeted charset

10-7. Converting Character Streams and Buffers

Problem

You need to convert large blocks of Unicode character text to and from an arbitrary byte-oriented encoding. Large blocks of text may come from streams or files.

Solution 1

Use the `java.io.InputStreamReader` to decode a byte stream to Unicode characters. Use `java.io.OutputStreamWriter` to encode Unicode characters to a byte stream.

The following code uses an `InputStreamReader` to read and convert a potentially large block of text bytes from a file in the classpath. The `org.java7reciptes.chapter10.StreamConversion` class provides the complete code for this example:

```
public String readStream() throws IOException {
    InputStream is = getClass().getResourceAsStream("resource/helloworld.sjis.txt");
    InputStreamReader reader = null;
    StringBuilder sb = new StringBuilder();
    if (is != null){
        reader = new InputStreamReader(is, Charset.forName("SJIS"));
        int ch = reader.read();
        while(ch != -1) {
            sb.append((char)ch);
            ch = reader.read();
        }
        reader.close();
    }
    return sb.toString();
}
```

Similarly, you can use an `OutputStreamWriter` to write text to a byte stream. The following code writes a `String` to a UTF-8 encoded byte stream:

```
public void writeStream(String text) throws IOException {
    OutputStreamWriter writer = null;
    FileOutputStream fos = new FileOutputStream("helloworld.utf8.txt");
    writer = new OutputStreamWriter(fos, Charset.forName("UTF-8"));
    writer.write(text);
    writer.close();
}
```

Solution 2

Use a java.nio.charset.CharsetEncoder and java.nio.charset.CharsetDecoder to convert Unicode character buffers to and from byte buffers. Retrieve an encoder or decoder from a Charset instance with the newEncoder() or newDecoder() method. Then use the encoder's encode() method to create byte buffers. Use the decoder's decode() method to create character buffers. The following code from the org.java7recipes.BufferConversion class encodes and decodes character sets from buffers:

```
    public ByteBuffer encodeBuffer(String charsetName, CharBuffer charBuffer)
            throws CharacterCodingException {
        Charset charset = Charset.forName(charsetName);
CharsetEncoder encoder = charset.newEncoder();
        ByteBuffer targetBuffer = encoder.encode(charBuffer);
return targetBuffer;

    }
    public CharBuffer decodeBuffer(String charsetName, ByteBuffer srcBuffer)
            throws CharacterCodingException {
        Charset charset = Charset.forName(charsetName);
        CharsetDecoder decoder = charset.newDecoder();
        CharBuffer charBuffer = decoder.decode(srcBuffer);
        return charBuffer;
    }
```

How It Works

The java.io and java.nio.charset packages contain several classes that can help you perform encoding conversions on large text streams or buffers. Streams are convenient abstractions that can assist you in converting text using a variety of sources and targets. A stream can represent incoming or outgoing text in an HTTP connection or even a file.

If you use an InputStream to represent the underlying source text, you will wrap that stream in an InputStreamReader to perform conversions from a byte stream. The reader instance performs the conversion from bytes to Unicode characters.

Using an OutputStream instance to represent the target text, wrap the stream in an OutputStreamWriter. A writer will convert your Unicode text to a byte-oriented encoding in the target stream.

To effectively use either an OutputStreamWriter or an InputStreamReader, you must know the character encoding of your target or source text. When you use an OutputStreamWriter, the source text is always Unicode, and you must supply a Charset argument to tell the writer how to convert to the target byte-oriented text encoding. When you use an InputStreamReader, the target encoding is always Unicode. You must supply the source text encoding as an argument so that the reader understands how to convert the text.

■ **Note** The Java platform's String represents characters in the UTF-16 encoding of Unicode. Unicode can have several encodings, including UTF-16, UTF-8, and even UTF-32. Converting to Unicode in this discussion always means converting to UTF-16. Converting to a byte-oriented encoding usually means to a legacy non Unicode charset encoding. However, a common byte-oriented encoding is UTF-8, and it is entirely reasonable to convert Java's "native" UTF-16 Unicode characters to or from UTF-8 using the InputStreamReader or OutputStreamWriter classes.

Yet another way to perform encoding conversions is to use the CharsetEncoder and CharsetDecoder classes. A CharsetEncoder will encode your Unicode CharBuffer instances to ByteBuffer instances. A CharsetDecoder will decode ByteBuffer instances into CharBuffer instances. In either case, you must provide a Charset argument.

A Charset represents a character set encoding in defined in the IANA Charset Registry. When creating a Charset instance, you should use the canonical or alias names of the charset as defined by the registry. You can find the registry at http://www.iana.org/assignments/character-sets.

Remember that your Java implementation will not necessarily support all the IANA charset names. However, all implementations are required to support at least those shown in recipe 10-6 of this chapter.

CHAPTER 11

Working with Databases

Almost any nontrivial application contains a database of some sort. Some applications use in-memory databases, while others use traditional relational database management systems (RDBMSs). Whatever the case, it is essential that every Java developer have some skills working with databases. Over the years, the Java Database Connectivity (JDBC) API has evolved quite a bit, and with Java SE 7 there are a couple of major advancements.

This chapter will cover the basics of using JDBC for working with databases. You will learn how to perform all the standard database operations, as well as some advanced techniques for manipulating data. You'll also learn how you can help to create secure database applications and how to save some time on development using some of the latest advancements in the API. In the end, you will be able to develop Java applications that can work with traditional RDBMSs such as Oracle database and MySQL.

■ **Note** To follow along with the examples in this chapter, run the `create_user.sql` script to create a database user schema. Then, run the `create_database.sql` script within the database schema that you just created.

11-1. Connecting to a Database

Problem

You want to create a connection to a database from within a desktop Java application.

Solution 1

Use a JDBC `Connection` object to obtain the connection. Do this by creating a new connection object, and then load the driver that you need to use for your particular database vendor. Once the connection object is ready, call its `getConnection()` method. The following code demonstrates how to obtain a connection to an Oracle database.

```java
public Connection getConnection() throws SQLException {
    Connection conn = null;

    String jdbcUrl = "jdbc:oracle:thin:@" + this.hostname + ":" +
                    this.port  + ":" + this.database;
    conn = DriverManager.getConnection(jdbcUrl, username, password);
    System.out.println("Successfully connected");
    return conn;
}
```

The method portrayed in this example returns a `Connection` object that is ready to be used for database access.

Solution 2

Use a `DataSource` to create a connection pool. The `DataSource` object must have been properly implemented and deployed to an application server environment. After a `DataSource` object has been implemented and deployed, it can be used by an application to obtain a connection to a database. The following code shows code that one might use to obtain a database connection via a `DataSource` object:

```java
public Connection getDSConnection() {
    Connection conn = null;
    try {
        Context ctx = new InitialContext();
        DataSource ds = (DataSource)ctx.lookup("jdbc/myOracleDS");
        conn = ds.getConnection();

    } catch (NamingException | SQLException ex) {
        ex.printStackTrace();
    }
    return conn;
}
```

Notice that the only information required in the `DataSource` implementation is the name of a valid `DataSource` object. All the information that is required to obtain a connection with the database is managed within the application server.

How It Works

There are a couple of different ways to create a connection to a database within a Java application. How you do so depends on the type of application you are writing. JDBC is often used if an application will be stand-alone or if it is a desktop application. Web-based and intranet applications commonly rely on the application server to provide the connection for the application via a `DataSource` object.

Creating a JDBC connection involves a few steps. First, you need to determine which database driver you will need to use. After you've determined which driver you will need to use then download the

JAR file containing that driver and place it into your CLASSPATH. For this recipe, an Oracle database connection is made. Therefore, the `ojdbc6.jar` JAR file (or the most recently available JDBC driver) is downloaded and placed into the CLASSPATH. (However, other database vendors will provide different JDBC drivers packaged in JAR files that have different names; please consult the documentation for your particular database for more information.) Once you have the JAR file in your application CLASSPATH, you can use a JDBC `DriverManager` to obtain a connection to the database. As of JDBC version 4.0, drivers that are contained within the CLASSPATH are automatically loaded into the `DriverManager` object. If you are using a JDBC version prior to 4.0, the driver will have to be manually loaded.

To obtain a connection to your database using the `DriverManager`, you need to pass a String containing the JDBC URL to it. The JDBC URL consists of the database vendor name, along with the name of the server that hosts the database, the name of the database, the database port number, and a valid database username and password that has access to the schema that you want to work with. Many times, the values used to create the JDBC URL are obtained from a `Properties` file so that they can be easily changed if needed. To learn more about using a `Properties` file to store connection values, please see Recipe 11-5. The code that is used to create the JDBC URL for Solution #1 looks like the following:

```
String jdbcUrl = "jdbc:oracle:thin:@" + this.hostname + ":" +
                    this.port  + ":" + this.database;
```

Once all the variables have been substituted into the String, it will look something like the following:

```
jdbc:oracle:thin:@hostname:1521:database
```

Once the JDBC URL has been created, it can be passed to the `DriverManager.getConnection()` method to obtain a `java.sql.Connection` object. If incorrect information has been passed to the `getConnection()` method, a `java.sql.SQLException` will be thrown; otherwise, a valid `Connection` object will be returned.

The preferred way to obtain a database connection is to use a `DataSource` when running on an application server or to have access to a Java Naming and Directory Interface (JNDI) service. To work with a `DataSource` object, you need to have an application server to deploy it to. Any compliant Java application server such as Glassfish, Oracle Weblogic, or Jboss will work. Most of the application servers contain a web interface that can be used to easily deploy a `DataSource` object. However, you can manually deploy a `DataSource` object by using code that will look like the following:

```
org.java7recipes.chapter11.recipe11_01.FakeDataSourceDriver ds =
        new org.java7recipes.chapter11.recipe11_1.FakeDataSourceDriver();
ds.setServerName("my-server");
ds.setDatabaseName("JavaRecipes");
ds.setDescription("Database connection for Java 7 Recipes");
```

This code instantiates a new `DataSource` driver class and then it sets properties based upon the database that you want to register. `DataSource` code such as that demonstrated here is typically used when registering a `DataSource` in an application server or with access to a JNDI server. Application servers usually do this work behind the scenes if you are using a web-based administration tool to deploy a `DataSource`. Most database vendors will supply a `DataSource` driver along with their JDBC drivers, so if the correct JAR resides within the application or server CLASSPATH, it should be recognized and available for use. Once a `DataSource` has been instantiated and configured, the next step is to register the `DataSource` with a JNDI naming service.

The following code demonstrates the registration of a DataSource with JNDI:

```
try {
    Context ctx = new InitialContext();
    DataSource ds =
            (DataSource) ctx.bind("jdbc/java7recipesDB");
} catch (NamingException ex) {
    ex.printStackTrace();
}
```

Once the DataSource has been deployed, any application that has been deployed to the same application server will have access to it. The beauty of working with a DataSource object is that your application code doesn't need to know anything about the database; it only needs to know the name of the DataSource. Usually the name of the DataSource begins with a jdbc/ prefix, followed by an identifier. To look up the DataSource object, an InitialContext is used. The InitialContext looks at all the DataSources available within the application server and it returns a valid DataSource if it is found; otherwise, it will throw a java.naming.NamingException exception. In Solution #2, you can see that the InitialContext returns an object that must be casted as a DataSource.

```
Context ctx = new InitialContext();
DataSource ds = (DataSource)ctx.lookup("jdbc/myOracleDS");
```

If the DataSource is a connection pool cache, it will send one of the available connections within the pool when an application requests it. The following line of code returns a Connection object from the DataSource:

```
conn = ds.getConnection();
```

Of course, if no valid connection can be obtained, a java.sql.SQLException is thrown. The DataSource technique is preferred over the DriverManager because database connection information is only stored in one place: the application server. Once a valid DataSource is deployed, it can be used by many applications.

After a valid connection has been obtained by your application, it can be used to work with the database. To learn more about working with the database using a Connection object, please see Recipes 11-2 and 11-4.

11-2. Handling Connection and SQL Exceptions

Problem

A database activity in your application has thrown an exception. You need to handle that SQL exception so that your application does not crash.

Solution

Use a try-catch block in order to capture and handle any SQL exceptions that are thrown by your JDBC connection or SQL queries. The following code demonstrates how to implement a try-catch block in order to capture SQL exceptions:

```
try {
    // perform database tasks
} catch (java.sql.SQLException){
    // perform exception handling
}
```

How It Works

A standard `try-catch` block can be used to catch `java.sql.Connection` or `java.sql.SQLException` exceptions. Your code will not compile if these exceptions are not handled, and it is a good idea to handle them in order to prevent your application from crashing if one of these exceptions is thrown. Almost any work that is performed against a `java.sql.Connection` object will need to perform error handling to ensure that database exceptions are handled correctly. In fact, nested `try-catch` blocks are often required to handle all the possible exceptions. You need to ensure that connections are closed once work has been performed and the `Connection` object is no longer used. Similarly, it is a good idea to close `java.sql.Statement` objects for memory allocation cleanup as well.

Because `Statement` and `Connection` objects need to be closed, it is common to see `try-catch-finally` blocks used to ensure that all resources have been tended to as needed. It is not unlikely that you will see JDBC code that resembles the following style:

```
try {
    // perform database tasks
} catch (java.sql.SQLException ex) {
    // perform exception handling
} finally {
    try {
        // close Connection and Statement objects
    } catch (java.sql.SQLException ex){
        // perform exception handling
    }
}
```

As seen in the previous pseudo code, nested `try-catch` blocks are often required in order to clean up unused resources. Proper exception handling sometimes makes JDBC code rather laborious to write, but it will also ensure that an application requiring database access will not fail, causing data to be lost.

11-3. Querying a Database and Retrieving Results

Problem

A process in your application needs to query a database table for data.

Solution

Obtain a JDBC connection using one of the techniques as described in Recipe 11-1; then use the java.sql.Connection object to create a Statement object. A java.sql.Statement object has the executeQuery() method, which parses a String of text and uses it to query a database. Once you've executed the query, you can retrieve the results of the query into a ResultSet object. The following example queries a database table named RECIPES and prints results:

```
String qry = "select recipe_num, name, description from recipes";
Statement stmt = null;

try {
    stmt = conn.createStatement();
    ResultSet rs = stmt.executeQuery(qry);
    while (rs.next()) {
        String recipe = rs.getString("RECIPE_NUM");
        String name = rs.getString("NAME");
        String desc = rs.getString("DESCRIPTION");

        System.out.println(recipe + "\t" + name + "\t" + desc);
    }
} catch (SQLException e) {
    e.printStackTrace();
} finally {
    if (stmt != null) {
        try {
            stmt.close();
        } catch (SQLException ex) {
            ex.printStackTrace();
        }
    }
    if (conn != null) {
        try {
            conn.close();
        } catch (SQLException ex) {
            ex.printStackTrace();
        }
    }
}
```

If you execute this code using the database script that is included with Chapter 11, you will receive the following results:

11-1	Connecting to a Database	DriverManager and DataSource Implementations
11-2	Querying a Database and Retrieving Results	Obtaining and Using Data from a DBMS
11-3	Handling SQL Exceptions Using SQLException	

How It Works

One of the most commonly performed operations against a database is a query. Performing database queries using JDBC is quite easy, although there is a bit of boilerplate code that needs to be used each time a query is executed. First, you need to obtain a Connection object for the database and schema that you want to run the query against. You can do this by using one of the solutions found in Recipe 11-1. Next, you need to form a query and store it in String format. The Connection object is then used to create a Statement. Your query String will be passed to the Statement object's executeQuery() method in order to actually query the database.

```
String qry = "select recipe_num, name, description from recipes";
Statement stmt = null;

try {
    stmt = conn.createStatement();
    ResultSet rs = stmt.executeQuery(qry);
!
```

As you can see, the Statement object's executeQuery() method accepts a String and returns a ResultSet object. The ResultSet object makes it easy to work with the query results so that you can obtain the information you need in any order. If you take a look at the next line of code, a while-loop is created on the ResultSet object. This loop will continue to call the ResultSet object's next() method, obtaining the next row that is returned from the query with each iteration. In this case, the ResultSet object is named rs, so while rs.next() returns true, the loop will continue to be processed. Once all the returned rows have been processed, rs.next() will return a false to indicate that there are no more rows to be processed.

Within the while-loop, each returned row is processed. The ResultSet object is parsed to obtain the values of the given column names with each pass. Notice that if the column is expected to return a String, you must call the ResultSet getString() method, passing the column name in String format. Similarly, if the column is expected to return an int, you'd call the ResultSet getInt() method, passing the column name in String format. The same holds true for the other data types. These methods will return the corresponding column values. In the example in the solution to this recipe, those values are stored into local variables.

```
String recipe = rs.getString("RECIPE_NUM");
String name = rs.getString("NAME");
String desc = rs.getString("DESCRIPTION");
```

Once the column value has been obtained, you can do what you want to do with the values you have stored within local variables. In this case, they are printed out using the System.out() method.

```
System.out.println(recipe + "\t" + name + "\t" + desc);
```

Notice that there is a try-catch-finally block used in this example. A `java.sql.SQLException` could be thrown when attempting to query a database (for instance, if the `Connection` object has not been properly obtained or if the database tables that you are trying to query do not exist). You must provide exception handling to handle errors in these situations. Therefore, all database-processing code should be placed within a `try` block. The `catch` block then handles a `SQLException`, so if one is thrown the exception will be handled using the code within the `catch` block. Sounds easy enough, right? It is, but you must do it each time you perform a database query. Lots of boilerplate code. Inside the `finally` block, you will see that the `Statement` and `Connection` objects are closed if they are not equal to `null`. Performing these tasks also incurs the overhead of handling `java.sql.SQLException` when it is thrown. They might occur if an attempt is made to close a `null` object.

It is always a good idea to close statements and connections if they are open. This will help ensure that the system can reallocate resources as needed, and act respectfully on the database. It is important to close connections as soon as possible so that other processes can reuse them.

11-4. Performing CRUD Operations

Problem

You need to have the ability to perform standard database operations within your application. That is, you need the ability to create, retrieve, update, and delete (CRUD) database records.

Solution

Create a `Connection` object and obtain a database connection using one of the solutions provided in Recipe 11-1; then perform the CRUD operation using a `java.sql.Statement` object that is obtained from the `java.sql.Connection` object. The following code excerpts demonstrate how to perform each of the CRUD operations using JDBC:

```
import java.sql.Connection;
import java.sql.ResultSet;
import java.sql.SQLException;
import java.sql.Statement;
import org.java7recipes.chapter11.recipe11_01.CreateConnection;

public class CrudOperations {
    public static Connection conn = null;

    public static void main(String[] args) {
        try {
            CreateConnection createConn = new CreateConnection();
            conn = createConn.getConnection();
            performCreate();
            performRead();
            performUpdate();
```

```java
            performDelete();
            System.out.println("-- Final State --");
            performRead();
        } catch (java.sql.SQLException ex) {
            System.out.println(ex);
        } finally {
            if (conn != null) {
                try {
                    conn.close();
                } catch (SQLException ex) {
                    ex.printStackTrace();
                }
            }
        }
    }

}

private static void performCreate(){
    String sql = "INSERT INTO RECIPES VALUES(" +
                "RECIPES_SEQ.NEXTVAL, " +
                "'11-4', " +
                "'Performing CRUD Operations', " +
                "'How to perform create, read, update, delete functions', " +
                "'Recipe Text')";
    Statement stmt = null;

    try {
        stmt = conn.createStatement();
        // Returns row-count or 0 if not successful
        int result = stmt.executeUpdate(sql);
        if (result > 0){
            System.out.println("-- Record created --");
        } else {
            System.out.println("!! Record NOT Created !!");
        }
    } catch (SQLException e) {
        e.printStackTrace();
    } finally {
        if (stmt != null) {
            try {
                stmt.close();
            } catch (SQLException ex) {
                ex.printStackTrace();
            }
        }
```

```java
        }

    }

    private static void performRead(){
        String qry = "select recipe_num, name, description from recipes";
        Statement stmt = null;

        try {
            stmt = conn.createStatement();
            ResultSet rs = stmt.executeQuery(qry);
            while (rs.next()) {
                String recipe = rs.getString("RECIPE_NUM");
                String name = rs.getString("NAME");
                String desc = rs.getString("DESCRIPTION");

                System.out.println(recipe + "\t" + name + "\t" + desc);
            }
        } catch (SQLException e) {
            e.printStackTrace();
        } finally {
            if (stmt != null) {
                try {
                    stmt.close();
                } catch (SQLException ex) {
                    ex.printStackTrace();
                }
            }

        }

    }

    private static void performUpdate(){
        String sql = "UPDATE RECIPES " +
                     "SET RECIPE_NUM = '11-5' " +
                     "WHERE RECIPE_NUM = '11-4'";
        Statement stmt = null;

        try {
            stmt = conn.createStatement();
            int result = stmt.executeUpdate(sql);
            if (result > 0){
                System.out.println("-- Record Updated --");
```

```java
            } else {
                System.out.println("!! Record NOT Updated !!");
            }
        } catch (SQLException e) {
            e.printStackTrace();
        } finally {
            if (stmt != null) {
                try {
                    stmt.close();
                } catch (SQLException ex) {
                    ex.printStackTrace();
                }
            }
        }

    }

    private static void performDelete(){
        String sql = "DELETE FROM RECIPES WHERE RECIPE_NUM = '11-5'";
        Statement stmt = null;

        try {
            stmt = conn.createStatement();
            int result = stmt.executeUpdate(sql);
            if (result > 0){
                System.out.println("-- Record Deleted --");
            } else {
                System.out.println("!! Record NOT Deleted!!");
            }
        } catch (SQLException e) {
            e.printStackTrace();
        } finally {
            if (stmt != null) {
                try {
                    stmt.close();
                } catch (SQLException ex) {
                    ex.printStackTrace();
                }
            }
        }
    }

}
```

The result of running the code:

```
Successfully connected
-- Record created --
11-1    Connecting to a Database DriverManager and DataSource Implementations
11-2    Querying a Database and Retrieving Results    Obtaining and Using Data from a DBMS
11-3    Handling SQL Exceptions Using SQLException
11-4    Performing CRUD Operations    How to Perform Create, Read, Update, Delete Functions
-- Record Updated --
-- Record Deleted --
-- Final State --
11-1    Connecting to a Database    DriverManager and DataSource Implementations
11-2    Querying a Database and Retrieving Results    Obtaining and Using Data from a DBMS
11-3    Handling SQL Exceptions Using SQLException
```

How It Works

The same basic code format is used for performing just about every database task. The format is as follows:

1. Obtain a connection to the database.

2. Create a statement from the connection.

3. Perform a database task with the statement.

4. Do something with the results of the database task.

5. Close the statement (and database connection if finished using it).

The main difference between performing a query using JDBC and using data manipulation language (DML) is that you will call different methods on the Statement object, depending on which operation you want to perform. To perform a query, you need to call the Statement executeQuery() method. In order to perform DML tasks such as insert, update, and delete, call the executeUpdate() method.

The performCreate() method in the solution to this recipe demonstrates the operation of inserting a record into a database. To insert a record in the database, you will construct an SQL insert statement in String format. To perform the insert, pass the SQL string to the Statement object's executeUpdate() method. If the insert is performed, an int value will be returned that specifies the number or rows that have been inserted. If the insert operation is not performed successfully, either a zero will be returned or an SQLException will be thrown, indicating a problem with the statement or database connection.

The performRead() method in the solution to this recipe demonstrates the operation of querying the database. To execute a query, you will call the Statement object's executeQuery() method, passing an SQL statement in String format. The result will be a ResultSet object, which can then be used to work with the returned data. For more information on performing queries, please see Recipe 11-3.

The performUpdate() method in the solution to this recipe demonstrates the operation of updating record(s) within a database table. First, you will construct an SQL update statement in String format. Next, to perform the update operation you will pass the SQL string to the Statement object's executeUpdate() method. If the update is successfully performed, an int value will be returned, which specifies the number of records that were updated. If the update operation is not performed successfully, either a zero will be returned or an SQLException will be thrown, indicating a problem with the statement or database connection.

The last database operation that needs to be covered is the delete operation. The performDelete() method in the solution to this recipe demonstrates the operation of deleting record(s) from the database. First, you will construct an SQL delete statement in String format. Next, to execute the deletion, you will pass the SQL string to the Statement object's executeUpdate() method. If the deletion is successful, an int value specifying the number of rows deleted will be returned. Otherwise, if the deletion fails, a zero will be returned or an SQLException will be thrown, indicating a problem with the statement or database connection.

Almost every database application uses at least one of the CRUD operations at some point. This is foundational JDBC that needs to be known if you are working with databases within Java applications. Even if you will not work directly with the JDBC API, it is good to know these foundational basics.

11-5. Simplifying Connection Management

Problem

Your application requires the use of a database. In order to work with the database, you need to open a connection. Rather than code the logic to open a database connection every time you need to access the database, you'd like to use a single class to perform that task.

Solution

Write a class to handle all the connection management within your application. Doing so will allow you to call that class in order to obtain a connection, rather than setting up a new Connection object each time you need access to the database. Perform the following steps to set up a connection management environment for your JDBC application:

1. Create a class named CreateConnection.java that will encapsulate all the connection logic for your application.

2. Create a properties file to store your connection information. Place the file somewhere on your CLASSPATH so that the CreateConnection class can load it.

3. Use the CreateConnection class to obtain your database connections.

The following code is a listing of the CreateConnection class that can be used for centralized connection management:

```
import java.io.File;
import java.io.FileInputStream;
import java.io.FileNotFoundException;
import java.io.IOException;
```

```java
import java.io.InputStream;
import java.nio.file.FileSystems;
import java.nio.file.Files;
import java.sql.Connection;
import java.sql.DriverManager;
import java.sql.SQLException;
import java.util.Properties;
import javax.naming.Context;
import javax.naming.InitialContext;
import javax.naming.NamingException;
import javax.sql.DataSource;

public class CreateConnection {

    static Properties props = new Properties();


    String hostname = null;
    String port = null;
    String database = null;
    String username = null;
    String password = null;
    String jndi = null;

    public CreateConnection(){
        InputStream in = null;
        try {
            // Looks for properties file in the root of the src directory in Netbeans project
            in =
Files.newInputStream(FileSystems.getDefault().getPath(System.getProperty("user.dir") +
File.separator + "db_props.properties"));
            props.load(in);
            in.close();
        } catch (IOException ex) {
            ex.printStackTrace();

        } finally {
            try {
                in.close();
            } catch (IOException ex) {
                ex.printStackTrace();
            }
        }
        loadProperties();
```

```java
    }

    public void loadProperties(){
        hostname = props.getProperty("host_name");
        port = props.getProperty("port_number");
        database = props.getProperty("db_name");
        username = props.getProperty("username");
        password = props.getProperty("password");
        jndi = props.getProperty("jndi");

    }

    /**
     * Demonstrates obtaining a connection via DriverManager
     * @return
     * @throws SQLException
     */
    public Connection getConnection() throws SQLException {
        Connection conn = null;

        String jdbcUrl = "jdbc:oracle:thin:@" + this.hostname + ":" +
                         this.port + ":" + this.database;
        conn = DriverManager.getConnection(jdbcUrl, username, password);
        System.out.println("Successfully connected");
        return conn;
    }

    /**
     * Demonstrates obtaining a connection via a DataSource object
     * @return
     */
    public Connection getDSConnection() {
        Connection conn = null;
        try {
            Context ctx = new InitialContext();
            DataSource ds = (DataSource)ctx.lookup(this.jndi);
            conn = ds.getConnection();

        } catch (NamingException | SQLException ex) {
            ex.printStackTrace();
        }
        return conn;
    }
}
```

Next, the following lines of text are an example of what should be contained in the properties file that is used for obtaining a connection to the database. For this example, the properties file is named `db_props.properties`.

```
host_name=your_db_server_name
db_name=your_db_name
username=db_username
password=db_username_password
port_number=db_port_number
jndi=jndi_connection_string
```

Finally, use the `CreateConnection` class to obtain connections for your application. The following code demonstrates this concept:

```
try {
    CreateConnection createConn = new CreateConnection();
    conn = createConn.getConnection();
    performDbTask();
} catch (java.sql.SQLException ex) {
    System.out.println(ex);
} finally {
    if (conn != null) {
        try {
            conn.close();
        } catch (SQLException ex) {
            ex.printStackTrace();
        }
    }
}
```

How It Works

Obtaining a connection within a database application can be code intensive. Moreover, the process can be prone to error if you retype the code each time you need to obtain a connection. By encapsulating database connection logic within a single class, you can reuse the same connection code each time you require a connection to the database. This increases your productivity, reduces the chances of typing errors, and also enhances manageability because if you have to make a change, it can occur in one place rather than in several different locations.

Creating a strategic connection methodology is beneficial to you and others who might need to maintain your code in the future. Although data sources are the preferred technique for managing database connections when using an application server or JNDI, the solution to this recipe demonstrates the use standard JDBC `DriverManager` connections. One of the security implications of using the `DriverManager` is that you will need to store the database credentials somewhere for use by the application. It is not safe to store those credentials in plain text anywhere, and it is also not safe to embed them in application code, which might be decompiled at some point in the future. As seen in the solution, a properties file that on disk is used to store the database credentials. Assume that this properties file will be encrypted at some point before deployment to a server.

As seen in the solution, the code reads the database credentials, hostname, database name, and port number from the properties file. That information is then pieced together to form a JDBC URL that can be used by DriverManager to obtain a connection to the database. Once obtained, that connection can be used anywhere and then closed. Similarly, if using a DataSource that has been deployed to an application server, the properties file can be used to store the JNDI connection. That is the only piece of information that is needed to obtain a connection to the database using the DataSource. To the developer, the only difference between the two types of connections would be the method name that is called in order to obtain the Connection object.

One could develop a JDBC application so that the code that is used to obtain a connection needs to be hard-coded throughout. Instead, this solution enables all the code for obtaining a connection to be encapsulated by a single class so that the developer does not need to worry about it. Such a technique also allows the code to be more maintainable. For instance, if the application were originally deployed using the DriverManager, but then later had the ability to use a DataSource, very little code would need to be changed.

11-6. Guarding Against SQL Injection

Problem

Your application performs database tasks. To reduce the chances of an SQL injection attack, you need to ensure that no unfiltered Strings of text are being appended to SQL statements and executed against the database.

■ **Tip** Prepared statements are for more than just protecting against SQL injection. They also give you a way to centralize and better control the SQL used in an application. Instead of creating multiple, possibly different versions of the same query, for example, you can create the query once as a prepared statement and invoke it from many places in your code. Any change to the query logic need happen only at the point that you prepare the statement.

Solution

Use PreparedStatements for performing the database tasks. PreparedStatements send a precompiled SQL statement to the DBMS rather than a String. The following code demonstrates how to perform a database query and a database update using a java.sql.PreparedStatement object.

In the following code example, a PreparedStatement is used to query a database for a given record. Assume that the String recipeNumber is passed to this code as a variable.

```
String sql = "SELECT ID, RECIPE_NUM, NAME, DESCRIPTION " +
             "FROM RECIPES " +
             "WHERE RECIPE_NUM = ?";
PreparedStatement pstmt = null;
```

```
try {
    pstmt = conn.prepareStatement(sql);
    pstmt.setString(1, recipeNumber);
    ResultSet rs = pstmt.executeQuery();
    while(rs.next()){
        System.out.println(rs.getString(2) + ": " + rs.getString(3) +
                        " - " + rs.getString(4));
    }
} catch (SQLException ex) {
    ex.printStackTrace();
} finally {
    if (pstmt != null){
        try {
            pstmt.close();
        } catch (SQLException ex) {
            ex.printStackTrace();
        }
    }
}
```

The next example demonstrates the use of a PreparedStatement for inserting a record into the database. Assume that the Strings recipeNumber, title, description, and text are passed to this code as variables.

```
String sql = "INSERT INTO RECIPES VALUES(" +
            "RECIPES_SEQ.NEXTVAL, ?,?,?,?)";
PreparedStatement pstmt = null;
try{
    pstmt = conn.prepareStatement(sql);
    pstmt.setString(1, recipeNumber);
    pstmt.setString(2, title);
    pstmt.setString(3, description);
    pstmt.setString(4, text);
    pstmt.executeUpdate();
    System.out.println("Record successfully inserted.");
} catch (SQLException ex){
    ex.printStackTrace();
} finally {
    if (pstmt != null){
        try {
            pstmt.close();
        } catch (SQLException ex) {
            ex.printStackTrace();
        }
    }
}
```

In this last example, a `PreparedStatement` is used to delete a record from the database. Again, assume that the String `recipeNumber` is passed to this code as a variable.

```
String sql = "DELETE FROM RECIPES WHERE " +
             "RECIPE_NUM = ?";
PreparedStatement pstmt = null;
try{
    pstmt = conn.prepareStatement(sql);
    pstmt.setString(1, recipeNumber);
    pstmt.executeUpdate();
    System.out.println("Recipe " + recipeNumber + " successfully deleted.");
} catch (SQLException ex){
    ex.printStackTrace();
} finally {
    if (pstmt != null){
        try {
            pstmt.close();
        } catch (SQLException ex) {
            ex.printStackTrace();
        }
    }
}
```

As you can see, a `PreparedStatement` is very much the same as a standard JDBC Statement object, but instead it sends precompiled SQL to the DBMS rather than Strings of text.

How It Works

While standard JDBC statements will get the job done, the harsh reality is that they can sometimes be insecure and difficult to work with. For instance, bad things can occur if a dynamic SQL statement is used to query a database, and a user-accepted String is assigned to a variable and concatenated with the intended SQL String. In most ordinary cases, the user-accepted String would be concatenated, and the SQL String would be used to query the database as expected. However, an attacker could decide to place malicious code inside of the String (a.k.a. SQL Injection), which would then be inadvertently sent to the database using a standard `Statement` object. The use of `PreparedStatements` prevents such malicious Strings from being concatenated into a SQL string and passed to the DBMS because they use a different approach. `PreparedStatements` use substitution variables rather than concatenation to make SQL strings dynamic. They are also precompiled, which means that a valid SQL string is formed prior to the SQL being sent to the DBMS. Moreover, `PreparedStatements` can help your application perform better because if the same SQL has to be run more than one time, it has to be compiled only once. After that, the substitution variables are interchangeable, but the overall SQL can be executed by the `PreparedStatement` very quickly.

Let's take a look at how a `PreparedStatement` works in practice. If you look at the first example in the solution to this recipe, you can see that the database table `RECIPES` is being queried, passing a `RECIPE_NUM` and retrieving the results for the matching record. The SQL string looks like the following:

```
String sql = "SELECT ID, RECIPE_NUM, NAME, DESCRIPTION " +
             "FROM RECIPES " +
             "WHERE RECIPE_NUM = ?";
```

Everything looks standard with the SQL text except for the question mark (?) at the end of the string. Placing a question mark within a string of SQL signifies that a substitute variable will be used in-place of that question mark when the SQL is executed. The next step for using a `PreparedStatement` is to declare a variable of type `PreparedStatement`. This can be seen with the following line of code:

```
PreparedStatement pstmt = null;
```

Now that a `PreparedStatement` has been declared, it can be put to use. However, use of a `PreparedStatement` might or might not cause an exception to be thrown. Therefore, any use of a `PreparedStatement` should occur within a try-catch block so that any exceptions can be handled gracefully. For instance, exceptions can occur if the database connection is unavailable for some reason or if the SQL string is invalid. Rather than crashing an application due to such issues, it is best to handle the exceptions wisely within a `catch` block. The following try-catch block includes the code that is necessary to send the SQL string to the database and retrieve results:

```
try {
    pstmt = conn.prepareStatement(sql);
    pstmt.setString(1, recipeNumber);
    ResultSet rs = pstmt.executeQuery();
    while(rs.next()){
        System.out.println(rs.getString(2) + ": " + rs.getString(3) +
                          " - " + rs.getString(4));
    }
} catch (SQLException ex) {
    ex.printStackTrace();
}
```

First, you can see that the `Connection` object is used to instantiate a `PreparedStatement` object. The SQL string is passed to the `PreparedStatement` object's constructor upon creation. Next, the `PreparedStatement` object is used to set values for any substitution variables that have been placed into the SQL string. As you can see, the `PreparedStatement` `setString()` method is used in the example to set the substitution variable at position 1 equal to the contents of the `recipeNumber` variable. The positioning of the substitution variable is associated with the placement of the question mark (?) within the SQL string. The first question mark within the string is assigned to the first position, the second one is assigned to the second position, and so forth. If there were more than one substitution variable to be assigned, there would be more than one call against the `PreparedStatement`, assigning each of the variables until each one has been accounted for. `PreparedStatements` can accept substitution variables of many different data types. For instance, if an `int` value were being assigned to a substitution variable, a call to the `setInt(position, variable)` method would be in order. Please see online documentation or your IDE's code completion for a complete set of methods that can be used for assigning substitution variables using `PreparedStatement` objects.

Once all the variables have been assigned, the SQL string can be executed. The `PreparedStatement` object contains an `executeQuery()` method that is used to execute a SQL string that represents a query. The `executeQuery()` method returns a `ResultSet` object, which contains the results that have been fetched from the database for the particular SQL query. Next, the `ResultSet` can be traversed to obtain the values retrieved from the database. Again, positional assignments are used to retrieve the results by calling the `ResultSet` object's corresponding getter methods and passing the position of the column value that you want to obtain. The position is determined by the order in which the column names appear within the SQL string. In the example, the first position corresponds to the `RECIPE_NUM` column, the second corresponds to the `NAME` column, and so forth. If the `recipeNumber` String variable was equal to "11-1", the results of executing the query in the example would look something like the following:

11-1: Connecting to a Database - DriverManager and DataSource Implementations

Of course, if the substitution variable is not set correctly or if there is an issue with the SQL string, an exception will be thrown. This would cause the code that is contained within the `catch` block to be executed. You should also be sure to clean up after using `PreparedStatements` by closing the statement when you are finished using it. It is a good practice to put all the cleanup code within a `finally` block to be sure that it is executed even if an exception is thrown. In the example, the `finally` block looks like the following:

```
finally {
    if (pstmt != null){
        try {
            pstmt.close();
        } catch (SQLException ex) {
            ex.printStackTrace();
        }
    }
}
```

You can see that the `PreparedStatement` object that was instantiated, `pstmt`, is checked to see whether it is NULL. If not, it is closed by calling the `close()` method.

Working through the code in the solution to this recipe, you can see that similar code is used to process database insert, update, and delete statements. The only difference in those cases is that the `PreparedStatement` `executeUpdate()` method is called rather than the `executeQuery()` method. The `executeUpdate()` method will return an `int` value representing the number of rows affected by the SQL statement.

The use of `PreparedStatement` objects is preferred over JDBC `Statement` objects. This is due to the fact that they are more secure and perform better. They can also make your code easier to follow, and easier to maintain.

11-7. Performing Transactions

Problem

The way in which your application is structured requires a sequential processing of tasks. One task depends upon another, and each process performs a different database action. If one of the tasks along the way fails, the database processing that has already occurred needs to be reversed.

Solution

Set your Connection object auto-commit to false and then perform the transactions you want to complete. Once you've successfully performed each of the transactions, manually commit the Connection object; otherwise roll back each of the transactions that have taken place. In the following code example, you can see transaction management take place. If you look within the main() method of the TransactionExample class, you will see that the Connection object's autoCommit() preference has been set to false; then the database transactions are performed. If all the transactions are successful, the Connection object is manually committed by calling the commit() method; otherwise, all the transactions are rolled back by calling the rollback() method.

```java
import java.sql.Connection;
import java.sql.PreparedStatement;
import java.sql.ResultSet;
import java.sql.SQLException;
import org.java7recipes.chapter11.recipe11_01.CreateConnection;

public class TransactionExample {
    public static Connection conn = null;

    public static void main(String[] args) {
        boolean successFlag = false;
        try {
            CreateConnection createConn = new CreateConnection();
            conn = createConn.getConnection();
            conn.setAutoCommit(false);
            queryDbRecipes();
            successFlag = insertRecord(
                    "11-6",
                    "Simplifying and Adding Security with Prepared Statements",
                    "Working with Prepared Statements",
                    "Recipe Text");

            if (successFlag = true){
```

```
                    successFlag = insertRecord(
                            null,
                            "Simplifying and Adding Security with Prepared Statements",
                            "Working with Prepared Statements",
                            "Recipe Text");
            }

            // Commit Transactions
            if (successFlag == true)
                conn.commit();
            else
                conn.rollback();

            conn.setAutoCommit(true);
            queryDbRecipes();
        } catch (java.sql.SQLException ex) {
            System.out.println(ex);
        } finally {
            if (conn != null) {
                try {
                    conn.close();
                } catch (SQLException ex) {
                    ex.printStackTrace();
                }
            }
        }

    }

    private static void queryDbRecipes(){
        String sql = "SELECT ID, RECIPE_NUM, NAME, DESCRIPTION " +
                    "FROM RECIPES";
        PreparedStatement pstmt = null;
        try {
            pstmt = conn.prepareStatement(sql);
            ResultSet rs = pstmt.executeQuery();
            while(rs.next()){
                System.out.println(rs.getString(2) + ": " + rs.getString(3) +
                            " - " + rs.getString(4));
            }
        } catch (SQLException ex) {
            ex.printStackTrace();
        } finally {
            if (pstmt != null){
                try {
```

```java
                pstmt.close();
            } catch (SQLException ex) {
                ex.printStackTrace();
            }
        }
    }

}

private static boolean insertRecord(String recipeNumber,
                        String title,
                        String description,
                        String text){
    String sql = "INSERT INTO RECIPES VALUES(" +
                "RECIPES_SEQ.NEXTVAL, ?,?,?,?)";
    boolean success = false;
    PreparedStatement pstmt = null;
    try{
        pstmt = conn.prepareStatement(sql);
        pstmt.setString(1, recipeNumber);
        pstmt.setString(2, title);
        pstmt.setString(3, description);
        pstmt.setString(4, text);
        pstmt.executeUpdate();
        System.out.println("Record successfully inserted.");
        success = true;
    } catch (SQLException ex){
        success = false;
        ex.printStackTrace();
    } finally {
        if (pstmt != null){
            try {
                pstmt.close();
            } catch (SQLException ex) {
                ex.printStackTrace();
            }
        }
    }
    return success;

}

}
```

In the end, if any of the statements fails, all transactions will be rolled back. However, if all the statements execute properly, everything will be committed.

How It Works

Transaction management can play an important role in an application. This holds true especially for applications that perform different tasks that depend upon each other. In many cases, if one of the tasks that is performed within a transaction fails, it is preferable for the entire transaction to fail rather than having it only partially complete. For instance, imagine that you were adding database user records to your application database. Now let's say that adding a user for your application required a couple of different database tables to be modified, maybe a table for roles, and so on. What would happen if your first table was modified correctly, and the second table modification failed? You would be left with a partially complete application user addition, and your user would most likely not be able to access the application as expected. In such a situation, it would be nicer to roll back all the already-completed database modifications if one of the updates failed so that the database was left in a clean state and the transaction could be attempted once again.

By default, a Connection object is set up so that auto-commit is turned on. That means that each database insert, update, or delete statement is committed right away. Usually, this is the way that we would like for our applications to function. However, in circumstances where we might have many database statements that rely upon one another, it is important to turn off auto-commit so that all the statements can be committed at once. To do so, call the Connection object's setAutoCommit() method and pass a false value. As you can see in the solution to this recipe, the setAutoCommit() method is called passing a false value, the database statements are executed. Doing so will cause all the database statement changes to be temporary until the Connection object's commit() method is called. This provides you with the ability to ensure that all the statements execute properly before calling commit(). Take a look at this transaction management code that is contained within the main() method of the TransactionExample class within the solution to this recipe:

```
CreateConnection createConn = new CreateConnection();
conn = createConn.getConnection();
conn.setAutoCommit(false);
queryDbRecipes();
successFlag = insertRecord(
                  "11-6",
                  "Simplifying and Adding Security with Prepared Statements",
                  "Working with Prepared Statements",
                  "Recipe Text");

if (successFlag = true){

    successFlag = insertRecord(
        null,
        "Simplifying and Adding Security with Prepared Statements",
        "Working with Prepared Statements",
        "Recipe Text");
}
// Commit Transactions
```

```
if (successFlag == true)
    conn.commit();
else
    conn.rollback();

conn.setAutoCommit(true);
```

Note that the commit() method is only called if all transaction statements were processed successfully. If any of them fail, the successFlag is equal to false, which would cause the rollback() method to be called instead. In the solution to this recipe, the second call to insertRecord() attempts to insert a NULL value into the RECIPE.ID column, which is not allowed. Therefore, that insert fails and everything, including the previous insert, gets rolled back.

11-8. Creating a Scrollable ResultSet

Problem

You have queried the database and obtained some results. You want to store those results in an object that will allow you to traverse forward and backward through the results, updating values as needed.

Solution

Create a scrollable ResultSet object and then you will have the ability to read the next, first record, last, and previous record. Using a scrollable ResultSet allows the results of a query to be fetched in any direction so that the data can be retrieved as needed. The following example method demonstrates the creation of a scrollable ResultSet object:

```
private static void queryDbRecipes(){
        String sql = "SELECT ID, RECIPE_NUM, NAME, DESCRIPTION " +
                    "FROM RECIPES";
        PreparedStatement pstmt = null;
        try {
            pstmt = conn.prepareStatement(sql, ResultSet.TYPE_SCROLL_INSENSITIVE,
ResultSet.CONCUR_READ_ONLY);
            ResultSet rs = pstmt.executeQuery();
            rs.first();
            System.out.println(rs.getString(2) + ": " + rs.getString(3) +
                        " - " + rs.getString(4));
            rs.next();
            System.out.println(rs.getString(2) + ": " + rs.getString(3) +
                        " - " + rs.getString(4));
            rs.previous();
            System.out.println(rs.getString(2) + ": " + rs.getString(3) +
```

```
                              " - " + rs.getString(4));
        rs.last();
        System.out.println(rs.getString(2) + ": " + rs.getString(3) +
                              " - " + rs.getString(4));
    } catch (SQLException ex) {
        ex.printStackTrace();
    } finally {
        if (pstmt != null){
            try {
                pstmt.close();
            } catch (SQLException ex) {
                ex.printStackTrace();
            }
        }
    }

}
```

Executing this method will result in the following output using the data that was originally loaded for this chapter:

```
Successfully connected
11-1: Connecting to a Database - DriverManager and DataSource Implementations - More to Come
11-2: Querying a Database and Retrieving Results - Obtaining and Using Data from a DBMS
11-1: Connecting to a Database - DriverManager and DataSource Implementations - More to Come
11-3: Handling SQL Exceptions - Using SQLException
```

How It Works

Ordinary `ResultSet` objects allow results to be fetched in a forward direction. That is, an application can process a default `ResultSet` object from the first record retrieved forward to the last. Sometimes an application requires more functionality when it comes to traversing a `ResultSet`. For instance, let's say you want to write an application that allows for someone to display the first or last record that was retrieved, or perhaps page forward or backwards through results. You could not do this very easily using a standard ResultSet. However, by creating a scrollable `ResultSet`, you can easily move backwards and forwards through the results.

To create a scrollable `ResultSet`, you must first create an instance of a `Statement` or `PreparedStatement` that has the ability to create a scrollable `ResultSet`. That is, when creating the `Statement`, you must pass the `ResultSet` scroll type constant value to the Connection object's `createStatement()` method. Likewise, you must pass the scroll type constant value to the `Connection` object's `prepareStatement()` method when using a `PreparedStatement`. There are three different scroll type constants that can be used. Table 11-1 displays those three constants.

Table 11-1. ResultSet Scroll Type Constants

Constant	Description
ResultSet.TYPE_FORWARD_ONLY	Default type, allows forward movement only.
ResultSet.TYPE_SCROLL_INSENSITIVE	Allows forward and backward movement. Not sensitive to ResultSet updates.
ResultSet.TYPE_SCROLL_SENSITIVE	Allows forward and backward movement. Sensitive to ResultSet updates.

You must also pass a ResultSet concurrency constant to advise whether the ResultSet is intended to be updatable or not. The default is ResultSet.CONCUR_READ_ONLY, which means that the ResultSet is not updatable. The other concurrency type is ResultSet.CONCUR_UPDATABLE, which signifies an updatable ResultSet object.

In the solution to this recipe, a PreparedStatement object is used, and the code to create a PreparedStatement object that has the ability to generate a scrollable ResultSet looks like the following line:

```
pstmt = conn.prepareStatement(sql, ResultSet.TYPE_SCROLL_INSENSITIVE,
                                          ResultSet.CONCUR_READ_ONLY);
```

Once the PreparedStatement has been created as such, a scrollable ResultSet is returned. You can traverse in several different directions using a scrollable ResultSet by calling the ResultSet methods indicating the direction you want to move or the placement that you want to be. The following line of code will retrieve the first record within the ResultSet:

```
ResultSet rs = pstmt.executeQuery();
rs.first();
```

The solution to this recipe demonstrates a few different scroll directions. Specifically, you can see that the ResultSet first(), next(), last(), and previous() methods are called in order to move to different positions within the ResultSet. For a complete reference to the ResultSet object, please see the online documentation that can be found at http://download.oracle.com/javase/7/docs/api/java/sql/ResultSet.html.

Scrollable ResultSet objects have a niche in application development. They are one of those niceties that are there when you need them, but they are also something that you might not need very often.

11-9. Creating an Updatable ResultSet

Problem

An application task has queried the database and obtained results. You have stored those results into a ResultSet object, and you want to update some of those values in the ResultSet and commit them back to the database.

Solution

Make your ResultSet object updatable and then update the rows as needed while iterating through the results. The following example method demonstrates how to make ResultSet updatable and then how to update content within that ResultSet, eventually persisting it in the database:

```
private static void queryAndUpdateDbRecipes(String recipeNumber){
        String sql = "SELECT ID, RECIPE_NUM, NAME, DESCRIPTION " +
                        "FROM RECIPES " +
                        "WHERE RECIPE_NUM = ?";
        PreparedStatement pstmt = null;
        try {
            pstmt = conn.prepareStatement(sql, ResultSet.TYPE_SCROLL_SENSITIVE,
ResultSet.CONCUR_UPDATABLE);
            pstmt.setString(1, recipeNumber);
            ResultSet rs = pstmt.executeQuery();
            while(rs.next()){
                String desc = rs.getString(4);
                System.out.println("Updating row" + desc);

                rs.updateString(4, desc + " -- More to come");
                rs.updateRow();
            }

        } catch (SQLException ex) {
            ex.printStackTrace();
        } finally {
            if (pstmt != null){
                try {
                    pstmt.close();
                } catch (SQLException ex) {
                    ex.printStackTrace();
                }
            }
        }

    }
```

This method could be called passing a String value containing a recipe number. Suppose that the recipe number "11-1" was passed to this method; the following output would be the result:

```
Successfully connected
11-1: Connecting to a Database - DriverManager and DataSource Implementations
11-2: Querying a Database and Retrieving Results - Obtaining and Using Data from a DBMS
11-3: Handling SQL Exceptions - Using SQLException
Updating rowDriverManager and DataSource Implementations
```

11-1: Connecting to a Database - DriverManager and DataSource Implementations - More to come
11-2: Querying a Database and Retrieving Results - Obtaining and Using Data from a DBMS
11-3: Handling SQL Exceptions - Using SQLException

How It Works

Sometimes it makes sense to update data as you are parsing it. Usually this technique involves testing the values that are being returned from the database and updating them if they compare to some other value in one way or another. The easiest way to do this is to make the ResultSet object updatable by passing the ResultSet.CONCUR_UPDATABLE constant to the Connection object's createStatement() or prepareStatement() methods. Doing so will allow the Statement or PreparedStatement object that is returned as a result of calling those methods to produce an updatable ResultSet.

■ **Note**   Some database JDBC drivers do not support updatable ResultSets. Please see the documentation for your JDBC driver for more information. This code was run using Oracle's ojdbc6.jar JDBC driver on Oracle database 11.2 release.

The format for creating a Statement that will produce an updatable ResultSet is to pass the ResultSet type as the first argument and the ResultSet concurrency as the second argument. The scroll type must be TYPE_SCROLL_SENSITIVE to ensure that the ResultSet will be sensitive to any updates that are made. The following code demonstrates this technique by creating a Statement object that will produce a scrollable and updatable ResultSet object:

```
Statement stmt = conn.createStatement(ResultSet.TYPE_SCROLL_SENSITIVE,
ResultSet.CONCUR_UPDATABLE);
```

The format for creating a PreparedStatement that will produce an updatable ResultSet is to pass the SQL string as the first argument, the ResultSet type as the second argument, and the ResultSet concurrency as the third argument. The solution to this recipe demonstrates this technique using the following line of code:

```
pstmt = conn.prepareStatement(sql, ResultSet.TYPE_SCROLL_SENSITIVE,

ResultSet.CONCUR_UPDATABLE);
```

Both of the lines of code discussed in this section will produce scrollable and updatable ResultSet objects. Once you have obtained an updatable ResultSet, you can use it just like an ordinary ResultSet for fetching values that are retrieved from the database. In addition, you can call one of the ResultSet object's updateXXX() methods to update any value within the ResultSet. In the solution to this recipe, the updateString() method is called, passing the position of the value from the query as the first argument and the updated text as the second argument. In this case, the fourth element column listed in the SQL query will be updated.

```
rs.updateString(4, desc + " -- More to come");
```

Finally, to persist the values that you have changed, call the ResultSet updateRow() method, as seen in the solution to this recipe:

```
rs.updateRow();
```

Creating an updatable ResultSet is not something that you will need to do every day. In fact, you might never need to create an updatable ResultSet. However, for the cases in which such a strategy is needed, this technique can come in very handy.

11-10. Caching Data for Use When Disconnected

Problem

You want to work with data from a DBMS when you are in a disconnected state. That is, you are working on a device that is not connected to the database, and you still want to have the ability to work with a set of data as though you are connected. For instance, you are working with data on a small portable device, and you are away from the office without a connection. You want the ability to query, insert, update, and delete data, even though there is no connection available. Once a connection becomes available, you want to have your device synchronize any database changes that have been made while disconnected.

Solution

Use a CachedRowSet object to store the data that you want to work with while offline. This will afford your application the ability to work with data as though it were connected to a database. Once your connection is restored or you connect back to the database, synchronize the data that has been changed within the CachedRowSet with the database repository. The following example class demonstrates the usage of a CachedRowSet. In this scenario, the main() method executes the example. Suppose that there was no main() method, though, and that another application on a portable device were to invoke the methods of this class. Follow the code in the example and consider the possibility of working with the results that are stored within the CachedRowSet while not connected to the database. For instance, suppose that you began some work in the office while connected to the network and are now outside of the office, where the network is spotty and you cannot maintain a constant connection to the database:

```
package org.java7recipes.chapter11.recipe11_10;

import java.sql.Connection;
import java.sql.PreparedStatement;
import java.sql.ResultSet;
import java.sql.SQLException;
import javax.sql.rowset.CachedRowSet;
import javax.sql.rowset.RowSetFactory;
import javax.sql.rowset.RowSetProvider;
import javax.sql.rowset.spi.SyncProviderException;
import org.java7recipes.chapter11.recipe11_10.CreateConnection;
```

```java
public class CachedRowSetExample {

    public static Connection conn = null;
    public static CreateConnection createConn;
    public static CachedRowSet crs = null;

    public static void main(String[] args) {
        boolean successFlag = false;
        try {
            createConn = new CreateConnection();
            conn = createConn.getConnection();
            // Perform Scrollable Query
            queryWithRowSet();
            updateData();
            syncWithDatabase();
        } catch (java.sql.SQLException ex) {
            System.out.println(ex);
        } finally {

            if (conn != null) {
                try {
                    conn.close();
                } catch (SQLException ex) {
                    ex.printStackTrace();
                }
            }
        }

    }

    /**
     * Call this method to synchronize the data that has been used in the
     * CachedRowSet with the database
     */
    public static void syncWithDatabase() {
        try {
            crs.acceptChanges(conn);
        } catch (SyncProviderException ex) {
            // If there is a conflict while synchronizing, this exception
            // will be thrown.
            ex.printStackTrace();
        } finally {
            // Clean up resources by closing CachedRowSet
            if (crs != null) {
                try {
```

```
                    crs.close();
                } catch (SQLException ex) {
                    ex.printStackTrace();
                }
            }
        }
    }

    public static void queryWithRowSet() {
        RowSetFactory factory;

        try {
            // Create a new RowSetFactory
            factory = RowSetProvider.newFactory();

            // Create a CachedRowSet object using the factory
            crs = factory.createCachedRowSet();

            // Alternatively populate the CachedRowSet connection settings
            // crs.setUsername(createConn.getUsername());
            // crs.setPassword(createConn.getPassword());
            // crs.setUrl(createConn.getJdbcUrl());

            // Populate a query that will obtain the data that will be used
            crs.setCommand("select id, recipe_num, name, description from recipes");
// Set key columns
            int[] keys = {1};
            crs.setKeyColumns(keys);
            // Execute query
            crs.execute(conn);

            // You can now work with the object contents in a disconnected state
            while (crs.next()) {
                System.out.println(crs.getString(2) + ": " + crs.getString(3)
                        + " - " + crs.getString(4));
            }

        } catch (SQLException ex) {
            ex.printStackTrace();
        }
    }

    public static boolean updateData() {
        boolean returnValue = false;
        try {
```

```
            // Move to the position before the first row in the result set
            crs.beforeFirst();

            // traverse result set
            while (crs.next()) {
                // If the recipe_num equals 11-2 then update
                if (crs.getString("RECIPE_NUM").equals("11-2")) {
                    System.out.println("updating recipe 11-2");
                    crs.updateString("description", "Subject to change");
                    crs.updateRow();
                }

            }
        returnValue = true;

            // Move to the position before the first row in the result set
            crs.beforeFirst();

            // traverse result set to see changes
            while (crs.next()) {

                    System.out.println(crs.getString(2) + ": " + crs.getString(3)
                        + " - " + crs.getString(4));
            }

        } catch (SQLException ex) {
            returnValue = false;
            ex.printStackTrace();
        }
        return returnValue;
    }
}
```

Running this example code will display output that looks similar to the following code, although the text might vary depending upon the values in the database. Notice that the database record for Recipe 11-2 has a changed description after the update of the CachedRowSet.

```
Successfully connected
11-1: Connecting to a Database - DriverManager and DataSource Implementations - More to Come
11-2: Querying a Database and Retrieving Results - Subject to Change
11-3: Handling SQL Exceptions - Using SQLException
Updating Recipe 11-2
11-1: Connecting to a Database - DriverManager and DataSource Implementations - More to Come
11-2: Querying a Database and Retrieving Results - Obtaining and Using Data from a DBMS
11-3: Handling SQL Exceptions - Using SQLException
```

How It Works

It is not possible to remain connected to the Internet 100 percent of the time if you are working on a mobile device and traveling. Nowadays there are devices that allow us to perform substantial work while we are on the go, even when we are not connected directly to a database. In such cases, solutions like the CachedRowSet object can come into play. The CachedRowSet is the same as a regular ResultSet object, except it does not have to maintain a connection to a database in order to remain usable. You can query the database, obtain the results, and place them into a CachedRowSet object; and then work with them while not connected to the database. If changes are made to the data at any point, those changes can be synchronized with the database at a later time.

There are a couple of different ways to create a CachedRowSet. The solution to this recipe uses a RowSetFactory to instantiate a CachedRowSet because this is new to Java SE 7. However, you can also use the CachedRowSet default constructor to create a new instance. Doing so would look like the following line of code:

```
CachedRowSet crs = new CachedRowSetImpl();
```

Once instantiated, you need to set up a connection to the database. There are also a couple of ways to do this. Properties could be set for the connection that will be used, and the solution to this recipe demonstrates this technique within comments. The following excerpt from the solution sets the connection properties using the CachedRowSet object's setUsername(), setPassword(), and setUrl() methods. Each of them accepts a String value, and in the example that String is obtained from the CreateConnection class:

```
// Alternatively populate the CachedRowSet connection settings
// crs.setUsername(createConn.getUsername());
// crs.setPassword(createConn.getPassword());
// crs.setUrl(createConn.getJdbcUrl());
```

Another way to set up the connection is to wait until the query is executed and pass a Connection object to the executeQuery() method. This is the technique that is used in the solution to this recipe. But before we can execute the query, it must be set using the setCommand() method, which accepts a String value. In this case, the String is the SQL query that we need to execute:

```
crs.setCommand("select id, recipe_num, name, description from recipes");
```

Next, if a CachedRowSet will be used for updates, the primary key values should be noted using the setKeys() method. This method accepts an int array that includes the positional indices of the key columns. These keys are used to identify unique columns. In this case, the first column listed in the query, ID, is the primary key:

```
int[] keys = {1};
crs.setKeyColumns(keys);
```

Finally, execute the query and populate the CachedRowSet using the execute() method. As mentioned previously, the execute() method optionally accepts a Connection object, which allows the CachedRowSet to obtain a database connection.

```
crs.execute(conn);
```

Once the query has been executed and the `CachedRowSet` has been populated, it can be used just like any other `ResultSet`. You can use it to fetch records forward and backward, or by specifying the absolute position of the row you'd like to retrieve. The solution to this recipe only demonstrates a couple of these fetching methods, but the most-often-used ones are listed in Table 11-2.

Table 11-2. CachedRowSet Fetching Methods

Method	Description
`first()`	Moves to the first row in the set.
`beforeFirst()`	Moves to the position before the first row in the set.
`afterLast`	Moves to the position after the last row in the set.
`next()`	Moves to the next position in the set.
`last()`	Moves to the last position in the set.

It is possible to insert and update rows within a `CachedRowSet`. To insert rows, use the `moveToInsertRow()` method to move to a new row position. Then populate a row by using the various methods [`CachedRowSet`, `updateString()`, `updateInt()`, and so on] that correspond to the data type of the column you are populating within the row. Once you have populated each of the required columns within the row, call the `insertRow()` method, followed by the `moveToCurrentRow()` method. The following lines of code demonstrate inserting a record into the `RECIPES` table:

```
crs.moveToInsertRow();
crs.updateInt(1, sequenceValue); // obtain current sequence values with a prior query
crs.updateString(2, "11-x");
crs.updateString(3, "This is a new recipe title");
crs.insertRow();
crs.moveToCurrentRow();
```

Updating rows is similar to using an updatable `ResultSet`. Simply update the values using the `CachedRowSet` object's methods [`updateString()`, `updateInt()`, and so on] methods that correspond to the data type of the column that you are updating within the row. Once you have updated the column or columns within the row, call the `updateRow()` method. This technique is demonstrated in the solution to this recipe.

```
crs.updateString("description", "Subject to change");
crs.updateRow();
```

To make any updates or inserts propagate to the database, the `acceptChanges()` method must be called. This method can accept an optional Connection argument in order to connect to the database. Once called, all changes are flushed to the database. Unfortunately, because time might have elapsed since the data was last retrieved for the `CachedRowSet`, there could be conflicts. If such a conflict arises, a `SyncProviderException` will be thrown. You can catch these exceptions and handle the conflicts manually using a `SyncResolver` object. However, resolving conflicts is out of the scope of this recipe, so for more information, please see the online documentation that can be found at `http://download.oracle.com/javase/tutorial/jdbc/basics/cachedrowset.html`.

CachedRowSet objects provide great flexibility for working with data, especially when you are using a device that is not always connected to the database. However, they can also be overkill in situations where you can simply use a standard ResultSet or even a scrollable ResultSet.

11-11. Joining RowSet Objects When Not Connected to the Data Source

Problem

You want to join two or more RowSets while not connected to a database. Perhaps your application is loaded on a mobile device that is not connected to the database 100 percent of the time. In such a case, you are looking for a solution that will allow you to join the results of two or more queries.

Solution

Use a JoinRowSet to take data from two relational database tables and join them. The data from each table that will be joined should be fetched into a RowSet and then the JoinRowSet can be used to join each of those RowSet objects based upon related elements that are contained within them. For instance, suppose that there were two related tables contained within a database. One of the tables stores a list of authors, and the other table contains a list of chapters that are written by those authors. The two tables can be joined using SQL by the primary and foreign key relationship.

■ **Note** A *primary key* is a unique identifier within each record of a database table, and a foreign key is a referential constraint between two tables.

However, the application will not be connected to the database to make the JOIN query, so it must be done using a JoinRowSet. The following class listing demonstrates one strategy that can be used in this scenario:

```
package org.java7recipes.chapter11.recipe11_11;

import com.sun.rowset.JoinRowSetImpl;
import java.sql.Connection;
import java.sql.SQLException;
import javax.sql.rowset.CachedRowSet;
import javax.sql.rowset.JoinRowSet;
import javax.sql.rowset.RowSetFactory;
import javax.sql.rowset.RowSetProvider;
import org.java7recipes.chapter11.recipe11_10.CreateConnection;
```

```
public class JoinRowSetExample {

    public static Connection conn = null;
    public static CreateConnection createConn;
    public static CachedRowSet bookAuthors = null;
    public static CachedRowSet authorWork = null;
    public static JoinRowSet jrs = null;

    public static void main(String[] args) {
        boolean successFlag = false;
        try {
            createConn = new CreateConnection();
            conn = createConn.getConnection();
            // Perform Scrollable Query
            queryBookAuthor();
            queryAuthorWork();

            joinRowQuery();
        } catch (java.sql.SQLException ex) {
            System.out.println(ex);
        } finally {

            if (conn != null) {
                try {
                    conn.close();
                } catch (SQLException ex) {
                    ex.printStackTrace();
                }
            }
            if (bookAuthors != null) {
                try {
                    bookAuthors.close();
                } catch (SQLException ex) {
                    ex.printStackTrace();
                }
            }
            if (authorWork != null) {
                try {
                    authorWork.close();
                } catch (SQLException ex) {
                    ex.printStackTrace();
                }
            }
            if (jrs != null) {
```

```java
            try {
                jrs.close();
            } catch (SQLException ex) {
                ex.printStackTrace();
            }
        }
    }

}

public static void queryBookAuthor() {
    RowSetFactory factory;

    try {
        // Create a new RowSetFactory
        factory = RowSetProvider.newFactory();

        // Create a CachedRowSet object using the factory
        bookAuthors = factory.createCachedRowSet();

        // Alternatively opulate the CachedRowSet connection settings
        // crs.setUsername(createConn.getUsername());
        // crs.setPassword(createConn.getPassword());
        // crs.setUrl(createConn.getJdbcUrl());

        // Populate a query that will obtain the data that will be used
        bookAuthors.setCommand("SELECT ID, LAST, FIRST FROM BOOK_AUTHOR");

        bookAuthors.execute(conn);

        // You can now work with the object contents in a disconnected state
        while (bookAuthors.next()) {
            System.out.println(bookAuthors.getString(1) + ": " + bookAuthors.getString(2)
                    + ", " + bookAuthors.getString(3));
        }

    } catch (SQLException ex) {
        ex.printStackTrace();
    }
}

public static void queryAuthorWork() {
    RowSetFactory factory;

    try {
```

```java
            // Create a new RowSetFactory
            factory = RowSetProvider.newFactory();

            // Create a CachedRowSet object using the factory
            authorWork = factory.createCachedRowSet();

            // Alternatively opulate the CachedRowSet connection settings
            // crs.setUsername(createConn.getUsername());
            // crs.setPassword(createConn.getPassword());
            // crs.setUrl(createConn.getJdbcUrl());

            // Populate a query that will obtain the data that will be used
            authorWork.setCommand("SELECT ID, AUTHOR_ID, CHAPTER_NUMBER, " +
            "CHAPTER_TITLE FROM AUTHOR_WORK");

            authorWork.execute(conn);

            // You can now work with the object contents in a disconnected state
            while (authorWork.next()) {
                System.out.println(authorWork.getString(1) + ": " + authorWork.getInt(3)
                        + " - " + authorWork.getString(4));
            }

    } catch (SQLException ex) {
        ex.printStackTrace();
    }
}

public static void joinRowQuery() {
    try {
        // Create JoinRowSet
        jrs = new JoinRowSetImpl();

        // Add RowSet & Corresponding Keys
        jrs.addRowSet(bookAuthors, 1);
        jrs.addRowSet(authorWork, 2);

        // Traverse Results
        while(jrs.next()){
            System.out.println(jrs.getInt("CHAPTER_NUMBER") + ": " +
                                jrs.getString("CHAPTER_TITLE") + " - " +
                                jrs.getString("FIRST") + " " +
                                jrs.getString("LAST"));
        }
```

```
        } catch (SQLException ex) {
            ex.printStackTrace();
        }

    }
}
```

Running this class will result in output that resembles the following:

```
Successfully connected
2: JUNEAU, JOSH
3: DEA, CARL
4: BEATY, MARK
5: GUIME, FREDDY
2: 1 - Getting Started With Java 7
3: 2 - Strings
4: 4 - Data Structures, Conditionals, and Iteration
5: 5 - Input and Output
6: 6 - Exceptions, Logging, Debugging
7: 7 - Object Oriented Java
8: 8 - Concurrency
9: 9 - Debugging and Unit Testing
10: 11 - Working with Databases
11: 3 - Numbers and Dates
9: Debugging and Unit Testing - FREDDY GUIME
8: Concurrency - FREDDY GUIME
6: Exceptions, Logging, Debugging - FREDDY GUIME
5: Input and Output - FREDDY GUIME
4: Data Structures, Conditionals, and Iteration - MARK BEATY
3: Numbers and Dates - JOSH JUNEAU
11: Working with Databases - JOSH JUNEAU
7: Object Oriented Java - JOSH JUNEAU
2: Strings - JOSH JUNEAU
1: Getting Started With Java 7 - JOSH JUNEAU
```

How It Works

A JoinRowSet is a combination of two or more populated RowSet objects. It can be used to join two RowSet objects based upon key value relationships, just as if it were a SQL JOIN query. In order to create a JoinRowSet, you must first populate two or more RowSet objects with related data, and then they can each be added to the JoinRowSet to create the combined result.

In the solution to this recipe, the two tables that are queried are named BOOK_AUTHOR and AUTHOR_WORK. The BOOK_AUTHOR table contains a list of author names, while the AUTHOR_WORK table contains the list of chapters in a book along with the AUTHOR_ID for the author who wrote the chapter. Following along with the main() method, first the BOOK_AUTHOR table is queried, and its results are fetched into a

CachedRowSet using the queryBookAuthor() method. For more details regarding the use of CachedRowSet objects, please see Recipe 11-10.

Next, another CachedRowSet is populated with the results of querying the AUTHOR_WORK table, as the queryAuthorBook() method is called. At this point, there are two populated CacheRowSet objects, and they can now be combined using a JoinRowSet. In order to do so, each table must contain one or more columns that relate to the other table. In this case, the BOOK_AUTHOR.ID column relates to the AUTHOR_WORK.AUTHOR_ID column, so the RowSet objects must be joined on those column results.

The final method that is invoked within the main() is joinRowQuery(). This method is where all the JoinRowSet work takes place. First, a new JoinRowSet is created by instantiating a JoinRowSetImpl() object:

```
jrs = new JoinRowSetImpl();
```

■ **Note** You will receive a compile-time warning when using JoinRowSetImpl because it is an internal SUN proprietary API. However, the Oracle version is OracleJoinRowSet, which is not as versatile.

Next, the two CachedRowSet objects are added to the newly created JoinRowSet by calling its addRowSet() method. The addRowSet() method accepts a couple of arguments. The first is the name of the RowSet object that you want to add to the JoinRowSet, and the second is an int value indicating the position within the CachedRowSet, which contains the key value that will be used to implement the join. In the solution to this recipe, the first call to addRowSet() passes the bookAuthors CachedRowSet, along with the number 1 because the element in the first position of the bookAuthors CachedRowSet corresponds to the BOOK_AUTHOR.ID column. The second call to addRowSet() passes the authorWork CachedRowSet, along with number 2 because the element in the second position of the authorWork CachedRowSet corresponds to the AUTHOR_WORK.AUTHOR_ID column.

```
// Add RowSet & Corresponding Keys
jrs.addRowSet(bookAuthors, 1);
jrs.addRowSet(authorWork, 2);
```

The JoinRowSet can now be used to fetch the results of the join, just as if it were a normal RowSet. When calling the corresponding methods [getString(), getInt(), and so on] of the JoinRowSet, pass the name of the database column corresponding to the data you want to store:

```
while(jrs.next()){
System.out.println(jrs.getInt("CHAPTER_NUMBER") + ": " +
jrs.getString("CHAPTER_TITLE") + " - " +
jrs.getString("FIRST") + " " +
jrs.getString("LAST"));
}
```

Although a JoinRowSet is not needed every day, it can be handy when performing work against two related sets of data. This especially holds true if the application is not connected to a database all the time, or if you are trying to use as few Connection objects as possible.

11-12. Filtering Data in a RowSet

Problem

Your application queries the database and returns a large number of rows. The number of rows within the cached ResultSet is too large for the user to work with at one time. You would like to limit the number of rows that are made visible so that you can perform different activities with different sets of data that have been queried from the table.

Solution

Use a FilteredRowSet to query the database and store the contents. The FilteredRowSet can be configured to filter the results that are returned from the query so that the only contents visible are the rows that you want to see. In the following example, a filter class is created that will be used to filter the results that are returned from a database query. The filter in the example is used to limit the number of rows that are visible based upon author name. The following class contains the implementation of the filter:

```
package org.java7recipes.chapter11.recipe11_12;

import java.sql.SQLException;
import javax.sql.RowSet;
import javax.sql.rowset.Predicate;

public class AuthorFilter implements Predicate {

  private String[] authors;
  private String colName = null;
  private int colNumber = -1;

  public AuthorFilter(String[] authors, String colName) {
    this.authors = authors;
    this.colNumber = -1;
    this.colName = colName;
  }

  public AuthorFilter(String[] authors, int colNumber) {
    this.authors = authors;
    this.colNumber = colNumber;
    this.colName = null;
  }

  public boolean evaluate(Object value, String colName) {
```

```java
    if (colName.equalsIgnoreCase(this.colName)) {
      for (int i = 0; i < this.authors.length; i++) {
        if (this.authors[i].equalsIgnoreCase((String)value)) {
          return true;
        }
      }
    }
    return false;
  }

  public boolean evaluate(Object value, int colNumber) {

    if (colNumber == this.colNumber) {
      for (int i = 0; i < this.authors.length; i++) {
        if (this.authors[i].equalsIgnoreCase((String)value)) {
          return true;
        }
      }
    }
    return false;
  }


  public boolean evaluate(RowSet rs) {

    if (rs == null)
      return false;

    try {
      for (int i = 0; i < this.authors.length; i++) {

        String authorLast = null;

        if (this.colNumber > 0) {
          authorLast = (String)rs.getObject(this.colNumber);
        } else if (this.colName != null) {
          authorLast = (String)rs.getObject(this.colName);
        } else {
          return false;
        }

        if (authorLast.equalsIgnoreCase(authors[i])) {
          return true;
        }
```

```
      }
   } catch (SQLException e) {
     return false;
   }
   return false;
  }

}
```

The filter is used by a FilteredRowSet to limit the visible results from a query. The following class demonstrates how to implement a FilteredRowSet. The main() method calls a method that is appropriately named implementFilteredRowSet(), which contains the code that is used to filter the results of a query on the BOOK_AUTHOR and AUTHOR_WORK tables so that only results from the authors with the last name of "DEA" and "JUNEAU" are returned:

```java
package org.java7recipes.chapter11.recipe11_12;

import com.sun.rowset.FilteredRowSetImpl;
import com.sun.rowset.JoinRowSetImpl;
import java.sql.Connection;
import java.sql.SQLException;
import javax.sql.RowSet;
import javax.sql.rowset.CachedRowSet;
import javax.sql.rowset.FilteredRowSet;
import javax.sql.rowset.JoinRowSet;
import javax.sql.rowset.RowSetFactory;
import javax.sql.rowset.RowSetProvider;
import org.java7recipes.chapter11.recipe11_1.CreateConnection;

public class FilteredRowSetExample {

    public static Connection conn = null;
    public static CreateConnection createConn;
    public static FilteredRowSet frs = null;

    public static void main(String[] args) {
        boolean successFlag = false;
        try {
            createConn = new CreateConnection();
            conn = createConn.getConnection();
            // Perform Scrollable Query
            implementFilteredRowSet();
        } catch (java.sql.SQLException ex) {
            System.out.println(ex);
        } finally {
```

```
            if (conn != null) {
                try {
                    conn.close();
                } catch (SQLException ex) {
                    ex.printStackTrace();
                }
            }
            if (frs != null) {
                try {
                    frs.close();
                } catch (SQLException ex) {
                    ex.printStackTrace();
                }
            }
        }
    }
}

/**
 * Demonstrates the FilteredRowSet
 */
public static void implementFilteredRowSet() {

    String[] authorArray = {"DEA", "JUNEAU"};

    // Creates a filter using the array of authors
    AuthorFilter authorFilter = new AuthorFilter(authorArray, 3);

    try {
        // Instantiate a new FilteredRowSet
        frs = new FilteredRowSetImpl();

        // Set the query
        frs.setCommand("SELECT CHAPTER_NUMBER, CHAPTER_TITLE, LAST "
                + "FROM BOOK_AUTHOR BA, "
                + "     AUTHOR_WORK AW "
                + "WHERE AW.AUTHOR_ID = BA.ID");

        // Execute the query
        frs.execute(conn);

        // View the results
        System.out.println("Prior to adding filter:");
        viewRowSet(frs);
        System.out.println("Adding author filter:");
        frs.beforeFirst();
```

```
            frs.setFilter(authorFilter);
            viewRowSet(frs);
        } catch (SQLException e) {
            e.printStackTrace();
        }

    }

    /**
    •   Method used to display results of a RowSet
    */
    public static void viewRowSet(RowSet rs) {
        try {
            while (rs.next()) {
                System.out.println(rs.getString(1) + " " + rs.getString(2) + " - "
                        + rs.getString(3));
            }
        } catch (SQLException ex) {
            ex.printStackTrace();
        }
    }
}
```

The results of running this code would look similar to the following lines. Notice that only the rows of data corresponding to the authors listed in the filter are returned with the FilteredRowSet.

```
Successfully connected
Prior to adding filter:
1 Getting Started With Java 7 - JUNEAU
2 Strings - JUNEAU
4 Data Structures, Conditionals, and Iteration - BEATY
5 Input and Output - GUIME
6 Exceptions, Logging, Debugging - GUIME
7 Object Oriented Java - JUNEAU
8 Concurrency - GUIME
9 Debugging and Unit Testing - GUIME
11 Working with Databases - JUNEAU
3 Numbers and Dates - JUNEAU
12 Java 2D Graphics and Media - DEA
13 Java 3D - GUIME
14 Swing API - DEA
15 JavaFX Fundamentals - DEA
16 Graphics with JavaFX - DEA
17 Media with JavaFX - DEA
18 Working with Servlets and Applets - JUNEAU
19 Intro to Android - JUNEAU
```

```
20 JavaFX and the Web - DEA
21 Email - GUIME
22 XML and Web Services - JUNEAU
23 Networking - JUNEAU
10 Unicode, Internationalization, Currency - GUIME
Adding author filter:
1 Getting Started With Java 7 - JUNEAU
2 Strings - JUNEAU
7 Object Oriented Java - JUNEAU
11 Working with Databases - JUNEAU
3 Numbers and Dates - JUNEAU
12 Java 2D Graphics and Media - DEA
14 Swing API - DEA
15 JavaFX Fundamentals - DEA
16 Graphics with JavaFX - DEA
17 Media with JavaFX - DEA
18 Working with Servlets and Applets - JUNEAU
19 Intro to Android - JUNEAU
20 JavaFX and the Web - DEA
22 XML and Web Services - JUNEAU
23 Networking - JUNEAU
```

How It Works

Often, the results that are returned from a database query contain a large number of rows. As you probably know, too many rows can create issues when it comes to visually working with data. It usually helps to limit the number of rows that are returned from a query by using a WHERE clause on an SQL statement. However, if an application retrieves data into an in-memory RowSet and then needs to filter the data by various criteria without additional database requests, an approach other than a query needs to be used. A FilteredRowSet can be used to filter data that is displayed within a populated RowSet so that it can be more manageable to work with.

There are two parts to working with a FilteredRowSet. First, a filter needs to be created that will be used to specify how the data should be filtered. The filter class should implement the Predicate interface. There should be multiple constructors, each accepting a different set of arguments, and the filter should contain multiple evaluate() methods that each accept different arguments and contain different implementations. The constructors should accept an array of contents that can be used to filter the RowSet. They should also accept a second argument, either the column name that the filter should be used against or the position of the column that the filter should be used against. In the solution to this recipe, the filter class is named AuthorFilter, and it is used to filter data per an array of author names. Its constructors each accept an array containing the author names to filter, along with either the column name or position. Each of the evaluate() methods has the task of determining whether a given row of data matches the specified filter; in this case, the author names that have been passed in via an array. The first evaluate() method is called if a column name is passed to the filter rather than a position, and the second evaluate() method is called if a column position is passed. The final evaluate() method accepts the RowSet itself, and it does the work of going through it and returning a Boolean to indicate whether the corresponding column name/position values match the filter data.

The second part of the `FilteredRowSet` implementation is the work of the FilteredRowSet. This can be seen within the `implementFilteredRowSet()` method of the `FilteredRowSetExample` class. The `FilteredRowSet` will actually use the filter class that we've written to determine which rows to display. You can see that the array of values that will be passed to the filter class is the first declaration within the method. The second declaration is the instantiation of the filter class `AuthorFilter`. Of course, the array of filter values and the column position that corresponds to the filter values is passed into the filter constructor.

```
String[] authorArray = {"DEA", "JUNEAU"};

// Creates a filter using the array of authors
AuthorFilter authorFilter = new AuthorFilter(authorArray, 3);
```

To instantiate a `FilteredRowSet`, create a new instance of the `FilteredRowSetImpl` class. After it is instantiated, simply set the SQL query that will be used to obtain the results using the `setCommand()` method and then execute it by calling the `executeQuery()` method.

```
// Instantiate a new FilteredRowSet
frs = new FilteredRowSetImpl();
// Set the query
frs.setCommand("SELECT CHAPTER_NUMBER, CHAPTER_TITLE, LAST "
+ "FROM BOOK_AUTHOR BA, "
+ "     AUTHOR_WORK AW "
+ "WHERE AW.AUTHOR_ID = BA.ID");
// Execute the query
frs.execute(conn);
```

■ **Note** You will receive a compile-time warning when using `FilteredRowSetImpl` because it is an internal SUN proprietary API.

Notice that the filter has not yet been applied. Actually, at this point what we have is a scrollable RowSet that is populated with all the results from the query. The example displays those results before applying the filter. To apply the filter, use the `setFilter()` method, passing the filter as an argument. Once that has been done, the `FilteredResultSet` will display only those rows that match the criteria specified by the filter.

Again, the `FilteredRowSet` is a technique that has its place, especially when you are working with an application that might not always be connected to a database. It is a powerful tool to use for filtering data, working with it, and then applying different filters and working on the new results. It is like applying `WHERE` clauses to a query without querying the database.

11-13. Querying and Storing Large Objects

Problem

The application that you are developing requires the storage of Strings of text that can include an unlimited number of characters.

Solution

Because the size of the Strings that need to be stored is unlimited, it is best to use a character large object (CLOB) data type to store the data. The code in the following example demonstrates how to load a CLOB into the database and how to query it:

```
package org.java7recipes.chapter11.recipe11_13;

import java.io.File;
import java.io.FileInputStream;
import java.io.IOException;
import java.io.OutputStream;
import java.sql.Blob;

import java.sql.Clob;
import java.sql.Connection;
import java.sql.PreparedStatement;
import java.sql.ResultSet;
import java.sql.SQLException;
import org.java7recipes.chapter11.recipe11_01.CreateConnection;

public class LobExamples {
    public static Connection conn = null;
    public static CreateConnection createConn;

    public static void main(String[] args) {
        boolean successFlag = false;
        try {
            createConn = new CreateConnection();
            conn = createConn.getConnection();
            loadClob();
            readClob();
        } catch (java.sql.SQLException ex) {
            System.out.println(ex);
        } finally {
```

```java
            if (conn != null) {
                try {
                    conn.close();
                } catch (SQLException ex) {
                    ex.printStackTrace();
                }
            }
        }
    }

    public static void loadClob(){
        PreparedStatement pstmt = null;
        String sql = null;
        Clob textClob = null;
        try{
            textClob = conn.createClob();
            textClob.setString(1, "This will be the recipe text in clob format");
            sql = "INSERT INTO RECIPE_TEXT VALUES(" +
                    "?, " +
                    "(select id from recipes where recipe_num = '11-1'), " +
                    "?)";
            pstmt = conn.prepareStatement(sql);

            // don!t do this ! obtain the sequence number in real world
            pstmt.setInt(1, 1);
            // set the clob value
            pstmt.setClob(2, textClob);
            pstmt.executeUpdate();
        } catch (SQLException ex){
            ex.printStackTrace();
        } finally {
            if(pstmt != null){
                try {
                    pstmt.close();
                } catch (SQLException ex) {
                    ex.printStackTrace();
                }
            }
            if (textClob != null){
                try {
                    textClob.free();
                } catch (SQLException ex) {
                    ex.printStackTrace();
                }
            }
```

```
        }
    }
    public static void readClob(){
        PreparedStatement pstmt = null;
        String qry = null;
        Clob theClob = null;
        ResultSet rs = null;
        try {
            qry = "select text from recipe_text";
            pstmt = conn.prepareStatement(qry);
            rs = pstmt.executeQuery();

            while (rs.next()){
                theClob = rs.getClob(1);
                System.out.println("Clob length: " + theClob.length());
System.out.println(theClob.toString());
                java.io.InputStream in =
                    theClob.getAsciiStream();
                int i;
                while( (i = in.read()) > -1 ) {
                    System.out.print( (char)i );
                }
            }
        } catch (IOException ex){
            ex.printStackTrace();
        } catch (SQLException ex){
            ex.printStackTrace();
        } finally {
            if (pstmt != null){
                try {
                    pstmt.close();
                } catch (SQLException ex) {
                    ex.printStackTrace();
                }
            }
            if (rs != null){
                try {
                    rs.close();
                } catch (SQLException ex) {
                    ex.printStackTrace();
                }
            }
        }
    }
}
```

How It Works

If your application requires the storage of String values, you need to know how large those Strings might possibly become. Most databases have an upper boundary when it comes to the storage size of VARCHAR fields. For instance, the Oracle database has an upper boundary of 2000 characters and anything exceeding that length will be cut off. If you have large amounts of text that need to be stored, use a CLOB field in the database.

A CLOB is handled a bit differently from a String within Java code. In fact, it is actually a bit odd to work with the first couple of times you use it because you have to create a CLOB from a Connection.

▪ **Note** In reality, CLOBs and BLOBs (binary large objects) are not stored in the Oracle table where they are defined. Instead, a large object (LOB) locator is stored in the table column. Oracle might place the CLOB in a separate file on the database server. When Java creates the Clob object, it can be used to hold data for update to a specific LOB location in the database or to retrieve the data from a specific LOB location within the database.

Let's take a look at the loadClob() method that is contained in the solution to this recipe. As you can see, a Clob object is created using the Connection createClob() method. Once the Clob has been created, you set its contents using the setString() method by passing the position indicating where to place the String, and the String of text itself:

```
textClob = conn.createClob();
textClob.setString(1, "This will be the recipe text in clob format");
```

Once you have created and populated the Clob, you simply pass it to the database using the PreparedStatement setClob() method. In the case of this example, the PreparedStatement performs a database insert into the RECIPE_TEXT table by calling the executeUpdate() method as usual.

Querying a Clob is fairly straightforward as well. As you can see in the readClob() method that is contained within the solution to this recipe, a PreparedStatement query is set up an the results are retrieved into a ResultSet. The only difference between using a Clob and a String is that you must load the Clob into a Clob type. Calling the Clob getString() method will pass you a funny-looking String of text that denotes a Clob object. Therefore, calling the Clob object's getAsciiStream() method will return the actual data that is stored in the Clob. This technique is used in the solution to this recipe.

Although Clobs are fairly easy to use, they take a couple of extra steps to prepare. It is best to plan your applications accordingly and try to estimate whether the database fields you are using might need to be CLOBs due to size restrictions. Proper planning will prevent you from going back and changing standard String-based code to work with Clobs later.

11-14. Storing Array Values

Problem

The database you are working with includes some VARRAY columns that need to be populated by your application.

■ **Note**   This recipe solution is specific to the Oracle database, but other vendors have similar data structures that can be used in a similar manner.

Solution

Use a combination of Oracle database's `oracle.sql.ARRAY` and the `java.sql.Array` to convert values into a format that can be inserted into the database using JDBC. To create a VARRAY type within an Oracle database, you must first define a TYPE, which you would like to use for the VARRAY. The following SQL declares a TYPE of CHAP_LIST_TYPE, which will be used to create the VARRAY column. This SQL is executed within the database.

```
create type chap_list_type as varray(10) of number;
```

Now that an SQL TYPE has been created, it can be used to represent a VARRAY column in a database table. The following SQL can be used to create a table that contains a VARRAY column of the CHAP_LIST_TYPE type:

```
create table author_recipes (
id              number primary key,
author_id       number,
chapter_list    chap_list_type);
```

The following Java code uses a combination of `oracle.sql.ARRAY` and `java.sql.Array` to store an array of values into the VARRAY column of the AUTHOR_RECIPES database table:

```
package org.java7recipes.chapter11.recipe11_14;

import java.sql.Array;
import java.sql.Connection;
import java.sql.PreparedStatement;
import java.sql.SQLException;
import oracle.sql.ARRAY;
import oracle.sql.ArrayDescriptor;
import org.java7recipes.chapter11.recipe11_01.CreateConnection;
```

```java
public class ArrayExamples {
    public static Connection conn = null;
    public static CreateConnection createConn;

    public static void main(String[] args) {
        boolean successFlag = false;
        try {
            createConn = new CreateConnection();
            conn = createConn.getConnection();
            storeArray();
        } catch (java.sql.SQLException ex) {
            System.out.println(ex);
        } finally {

            if (conn != null) {
                try {
                    conn.close();
                } catch (SQLException ex) {
                    ex.printStackTrace();
                }
            }

        }
    }

    public static void storeArray() throws SQLException{
        PreparedStatement pstmt = null;
        String sql = null;
        Object [] chapters = {1,2,3};
        ARRAY chapterArray = null;
        try{
            ArrayDescriptor descriptor =
                    ArrayDescriptor.createDescriptor("CHAP_LIST_TYPE", conn);
            chapterArray = new ARRAY(descriptor, conn, chapters);
            sql = "INSERT INTO AUTHOR_RECIPES VALUES(" +
                "author_recipes_seq.nextval, " +
                "(select id from BOOK_AUTHOR where last = ?), " +
                "?)";
            pstmt = conn.prepareStatement(sql);
            pstmt.setString(1, "JUNEAU");
            pstmt.setArray(2, chapterArray);
            pstmt.executeUpdate();
        } catch (SQLException ex){
            ex.printStackTrace();
        } finally {
```

```
            if (pstmt != null){
                pstmt.close();
            }
        }
    }
}
```

Executing the class in this example will cause a record to be inserted into the AUTHOR_RECIPES table, including the array of content that lists the chapters that have been written by the corresponding author.

How It Works

Most databases contain a data type that can be mapped to a Java array. Such data types allow an array of data to be stored within a single column of a database table. Such is the case with the table that is used in the solution to this recipe: AUTHOR_RECIPES. This table contains a column that accepts an array of NUMBER values that correspond to the chapter numbers that were written by the author that is tied to the AUTHOR_ID. In an Oracle database, the data type for this column is known as a VARRAY, and there is a special Java class, oracle.sql.ARRAY, that can be used to populate the database column with a Java array of values.

There are a couple of steps that need to be taken on a standard Java array before it can be inserted into a database. If you take a look at the storeArray() method in the solution to this recipe, you can see that an Object[] has been declared that contains a set of numbers. These numbers correspond to the chapters that we want to populate into the database VARRAY column. A variable of type oracle.sql.ARRAY is also declared and will later be used to manipulate the Object[] so that it can be inserted into the database.

```
Object [] chapters = {1,2,3}; // Each int within the array is autoboxed as an Integer object
ARRAY chapterArray = null;
```

Next an ArrayDescriptor is created, which will identify the VARRAY type within the database. In this case, the type is CHAP_LIST_TYPE. Once the descriptor has been created, it can be used to generate a new oracle.sql.ARRAY object by passing it as an argument along with the Connection and Object[]:

```
ArrayDescriptor descriptor =
                    ArrayDescriptor.createDescriptor("CHAP_LIST_TYPE", conn);
chapterArray = new ARRAY(descriptor, conn, chapters);
```

The chapterArray is now in a format that can be inserted into the database. This is done by using the PreparedStatement setArray() method, passing the position of the parameter along with the ARRAY. Calling the executeUpdate() method will execute the insert.

```
pstmt = conn.prepareStatement(sql);
pstmt.setString(1, "JUNEAU");
pstmt.setArray(2, chapterArray);
pstmt.executeUpdate();
```

Different RDBMSs contain different implementations of the array data type. The Oracle database uses the VARRAY, and this solution will work for the purpose of inserting objects into that data type.

However, the same solution will work for inserting into other database array types. All you need to do is substitute the specific RDBMS data type that is used to convert the standard Java array. In this case, we used the `oracle.sql.ARRAY`; however, that class might be different with another RDBMS.

11-15. Retrieving Array Values

Problem

You have stored some objects into a database in **VARRAY** format and would like to retrieve them via your application.

■ **Note** This recipe solution is specific to the Oracle database, but other vendors have similar data structures that can be used in a similar manner.

Solution

Load the contents of a **VARRAY** or another database array type into a `java.sql.Array` object. Once they have been loaded into an `Array`, extract the contents into a standard array corresponding to the data type of the values that are contained within the array. The following class queries a database table that contains a **VARRAY** column. The **VARRAY** column is populated with data that corresponds to the database **NUMBER** data type.

```
PreparedStatement pstmt = null;
    String sql = null;
    ResultSet rset = null;
    Array chapters = null;
    try{

        sql = "SELECT AUTHOR_ID, CHAPTER_LIST, LAST " +
              "FROM AUTHOR_RECIPES AR, " +
              " BOOK_AUTHOR BA " +
              "WHERE AR.AUTHOR_ID = BA.ID";
        pstmt = conn.prepareStatement(sql);

        rset = pstmt.executeQuery(sql);
        while(rset.next()){
            chapters = rset.getArray(2);
            BigDecimal[] chapterNumbers = (BigDecimal[]) chapters.getArray();
            System.out.println(rset.getString(3) + " Chapters \n");
            for (BigDecimal idx:chapterNumbers){
                System.out.println(idx + "\n");
```

```
                }
            }
        } catch (SQLException ex){
            ex.printStackTrace();
        } finally {
            if (pstmt != null){
                try {
                    pstmt.close();
                } catch (SQLException ex) {
                    ex.printStackTrace();
                }
            }
            if (rset != null){
                try {
                    pstmt.close();
                } catch (SQLException ex) {
                    ex.printStackTrace();
                }
            }
        }
    }
}
```

The results of running this code will look something like the following, depending upon the data that is contained within your local database:

```
Successfully connected
JUNEAU Chapters

1

2

3

7

11

18

19

23

24
```

How It Works

In order to work with data that has been stored in an array format within a database table, you must convert the data into a standard Java array so that it can be parsed. In the solution to this recipe, an Oracle database table that contains a VARRAY column is queried and then the results of the VARRAY column are converted into a standard Java array. After the conversion has taken place, the results are printed out.

To retrieve the Oracle VARRAY data, create a java.sql.Array object and fetch the contents into it using the PreparedStatement getArray() method. In the solution to this recipe, a java.sql.Array object named chapters is used to hold the data from the database VARRAY column.

```
chapters = rset.getArray(2);
```

After the java.sql.Array has been populated with the data, it can be converted into a standard Java array by calling the getArray() method and casting it based upon the data type of the values contained within the array. Because the Oracle type was defined as an array of type NUMBER, the values are returned to Java as an array of type BigDecimal. Once the standard Java array object has been populated, the values can be used. In the solution to this recipe, the values are printed out.

```
BigDecimal[] chapterNumbers = (BigDecimal[]) chapters.getArray();
System.out.println(rset.getString(3) + " Chapters \n");
for (BigDecimal idx:chapterNumbers){
    System.out.println(idx + "\n");
}
```

Although this example was written against an Oracle database that contains a table with a VARRAY column, the same techniques could be used to extract the data from another RDBMS that contained a table with an array type column.

11-16. Invoking Stored Procedures

Problem

Some logic that is required for your application is written as a database stored procedure. You require the ability to invoke the stored procedure from within your application.

Solution

The following block of code shows the PL/SQL that is required to create the stored procedure that will be called by Java. The functionality of this stored procedure is very minor; it simply accepts a value and assigns that value to an OUT parameter so that the program can display it:

```
create or replace procedure dummy_proc (text IN VARCHAR2,
                                        msg OUT VARCHAR2) as

begin
```

```
    -- Do something, in this case the IN parameter value is assigned to the OUT parameter
    msg :=text;
end;
```

The `CallableStatement` in the following code executes this stored procedure that is contained within the database, passing the necessary parameters. The results of the `OUT` parameter are then displayed back to the user.

```
CallableStatement cs = null;
try {
    cs = conn.prepareCall("{call DUMMY_PROC(?,?)}");
    cs.setString(1, "This is a test");
    cs.registerOutParameter(2, Types.VARCHAR);
    cs.executeQuery();

    System.out.println(cs.getString(2));

} catch (SQLException ex){
    ex.printStackTrace();
}
```

Running the example class for this recipe will display the following output, which is the same as the input. This is because the `DUMMY_PROC` procedure simply assigns the contents if the IN parameter to the `OUT` parameter.

```
Successfully connected
This is a test
```

How It Works

It is not uncommon for an application to use database stored procedures for logic that can be executed directly within the database. In order to call a database stored procedure from Java, you must create a `CallableStatement` object, rather than using a `PreparedStatement`. In the solution to this recipe, a `CallableStatement` is used to invoke a stored procedure named `DUMMY_PROC`. The syntax for instantiating the `CallableStatement` is similar to that of using a `PreparedStatement`. Use the `Connection` object's prepareCall() method, passing the call to the stored procedure. The stored procedure call must be enclosed in curly braces {} or the application will throw an exception.

```
cs = conn.prepareCall("{call DUMMY_PROC(?,?)}");
```

Once the `CallableStatement` has been instantiated, it can be used just like a `PreparedStatement` for setting the values of parameters. However, if a parameter is registered within the database stored procedure as an `OUT` parameter, you must call a special method, `registerOutParameter()`, passing the parameter position and database type of the `OUT` parameter that you want to register. In the solution to this recipe, the `OUT` parameter is in the second position and it has a `VARCHAR` type.

```
cs.registerOutParameter(2, Types.VARCHAR);
```

To execute the stored procedure, call the executeQuery() method on the CallableStatement. Once this has been done, you can see the value of the OUT parameter by making a call to the CallableStatement getXXX() method that corresponds to the data type:

```
System.out.println(cs.getString(2));
```

A NOTE REGARDING STORED FUNCTIONS

Calling a stored database function is essentially the same as calling a stored procedure. However, the syntax to prepareCall() is slightly modified. To call a stored function, change the call within the curly braces to entail a returned value using a ? character. For instance, suppose that a function named DUMMY_FUNC accepted one parameter and returned a value. The following code would be used to make the call and return the value:

```
cs = conn.prepareCall("{? = call DUMMY_FUNC(?)}");
cs.registerOutParameter(1, Types.VARCHAR);
cs.setString(2, "This is a test");
cs.execute();
```

A call to cs.getString(1) would then retrieve the returned value.

11-17. Handling Resources Automatically

Problem

Rather than manually opening and closing resources with each database call, you would prefer to have the application handle such boilerplate code for you.

Solution

Use the try-with-resources syntax to automatically close the resources that you open. The following block of code uses this tactic to automatically close the Connection, Statement, and ResultSet resources when it is finished using them:

```
String qry = "select recipe_num, name, description from recipes";

try (Connection conn = createConn.getConnection();
        Statement stmt = conn.createStatement();
        ResultSet rs = stmt.executeQuery(qry);) {

    while (rs.next()) {
```

```
        String recipe = rs.getString("RECIPE_NUM");
        String name = rs.getString("NAME");
        String desc = rs.getString("DESCRIPTION");

        System.out.println(recipe + "\t" + name + "\t" + desc);
    }
} catch (SQLException e) {
    e.printStackTrace();
}
```

The resulting output from running this code should look similar to the following:

```
Successfully connected
11-1    Connecting to a Database        DriverManager and DataSource Implementations - More to
Come
11-2    Querying a Database and Retrieving Results      Subject to Change
11-3    Handling SQL Exceptions Using SQLException
```

How It Works

Handling JDBC resources has always been a pain in the neck. There is a lot of boilerplate code that is required for closing resources when they are no longer needed. This is no longer the case with the release of Java SE 7. This new release introduces automatic resource management using try-with-resources. Through the use of this technique, the developer no longer needs to close each resource manually, which is a change that can cut down on many lines of code.

In order to use this technique, you must instantiate all the resources for which you want to have automatic handling enabled within a set of parentheses after a `try` clause. In the solution to this recipe, the resources that are declared are `Connection`, `Statement`, and `ResultSet`.

```
try (Connection conn = createConn.getConnection();
        Statement stmt = conn.createStatement();
        ResultSet rs = stmt.executeQuery(qry);) {
```

Once those resources are out of scope, they are automatically closed. This means there is no longer a requirement to code a `finally` block to ensure that resources are closed. The solution to this recipe executes the same query as that of Recipe 11-3. Go back and compare the amount of code that is written in order to handle the resources manually with this code using the automatic resource handling; it can leave a developer wondering what they are going to do with all their newly found "free time"!

The automatic resource handling is not only available to database work, but to any resource that complies with the new `java.lang.Autocloseable` API. Other operations such as File I/O adhere to the new API as well. There is a single `close()` method within `java.lang.Autoclosable` that manages the closing of the resource. Classes that implement the `java.io.Closeable` interface can adhere to the API.

CHAPTER 12

Java 2D Graphics

To put things simply, Java 2D is an API to render two-dimensional graphics on surfaces such as computer screens, printers, and devices. This powerful API allows you to do things such as drawing geometric shapes, image processing, alpha compositing (combining images), text font rendering, antialiasing, clipping, creating transformations, stroking, filling, and printing.

Breaking news! When giving news I'm sure you've heard people say, "I've got good news and bad news". Well, in the case of Java 2D, it is good news and more good news. First, the Java 2D API has virtually been unchanged since its major release (Java 2), which is a testament to good design. Now for more good news, new to Java 7 is that the 2D API is getting a new graphics pipeline called XRender. XRender will have access to hardware accelerated features on systems with modern graphics processing units (GPUs). This is great news to many existing Java applications that use Java 2D already because they will gain excellent rendering performance without changing any code. Things can only get better as the major players get onboard with the Open JDK initiative.

Helper Class for This Chapter

This chapter will familiarize you with recipes pertaining to Java's 2D APIs. Regarding the 2D API, you will notice that most recipes will rely on a utility helper class to launch an application window to display the examples. Shown below is the utility helper class `SimpleAppLauncher.java` which will utilize a `javax.swing.JComponent` object as a drawing surface to be displayed in an application window (`javax.swing.JFrame`).

Note For more on the latest Java 7 features including XRender, see OpenJDK
`http://openjdk.java.net/projects/jdk7/features` (Oracle Corporation, 2011).

```
package org.java7recipes.chapter12;

import java.awt.BorderLayout;
import java.awt.Component;
import java.awt.Dimension;
import java.awt.Toolkit;
import java.awt.event.ComponentAdapter;
```

```java
import java.awt.event.ComponentEvent;
import javax.swing.JComponent;
import javax.swing.JFrame;
import javax.swing.SwingUtilities;

/**
 * SimpleAppLauncher will create a window and display a component and
 * abide by the event dispatch thread rules.
 *
 * @author cdea
 */
public class SimpleAppLauncher {
    /**
     * @param title the Chapter and recipe.
     * @param canvas the drawing surface.
     */
    protected static void displayGUI(final String title, final JComponent component) {

        // create window with title
        final JFrame frame = new JFrame(title);
        if (component instanceof AppSetup) {
            AppSetup ms = (AppSetup) component;
            ms.apply(frame);
        }

        // set window's close button to exit application
        frame.setDefaultCloseOperation(JFrame.EXIT_ON_CLOSE);

        component.addComponentListener(new ComponentAdapter() {
            // This method is called after the component's size changes
            public void componentResized(ComponentEvent evt) {
                Component c = (Component)evt.getSource();

                // Get new size
                Dimension newSize = c.getSize();
                System.out.println("component size w,h = " + newSize.getWidth() + ", " +
                    newSize.getHeight());
            }
        });

        // place component in the center using BorderLayout
        frame.getContentPane().add(component, BorderLayout.CENTER);

        // size window based on layout
        frame.pack();

        // center window
        Dimension scrnSize = Toolkit.getDefaultToolkit().getScreenSize();
        int scrnWidth = frame.getSize().width;
        int scrnHeight = frame.getSize().height;
        int x = (scrnSize.width - scrnWidth) / 2;
        int y = (scrnSize.height - scrnHeight) / 2;
```

```
        // Move the window
        frame.setLocation(x, y);

        // display
        frame.setVisible(true);
    }

    public static void launch(final String title, final JComponent component) {

        SwingUtilities.invokeLater(new Runnable() {
            public void run() {
                displayGUI(title, component);
            }
        });// invokeLater()
    }// launch()
} // SimpleAppLauncher
```

This helper class allows you to focus on the actual recipe solution without having to see the application's launching and displaying details. All recipes are individual Java applications with a main() method and most will call out to the helper class (SimpleAppLauncher) to display its graphics in a window (javax.swing.JFrame) while adhering to thread safety. Here is an example of launching a Chapter 12 recipe 2 within its main() method:

```
DrawLines c = new DrawLines();
c.setPreferredSize(new Dimension(272, 227));
SimpleAppLauncher.launch("Chapter 12-2 Draw Lines", c);
```

Most of the recipes in this chapter extend the JComponent class and also containing a main() method that calls out to the SimpleAppLauncher.launch() method. The launch() method will then call displayGUI() via Java Swing's SwingUtilities.invokeLater() method. This ensures that graphics rendering will happen on the event dispatching thread. This code will display your GUI in a threadsafe manner using Swing's invokeLater():

```
SwingUtilities.invokeLater(new Runnable() {
    public void run() {
        displayGUI(title, component);
    }
});
```

The SimpleAppLauncher class uses Java's Swing API, a lightweight windowing toolkit (see Chapter 14). Most recipes here will use many graphics primitives to draw on Swing's javax.swing.JComponent component. The javax.swing.JComponent class contains a method called paintComponent(Graphics graphics), which is where all the painting happens (actually where all the drawing happens). The method is triggered every time something obscures the drawing surface or when the window (javax.swing.JFrame) containing the component is resized.

The Graphics object (system generated) that is passed into the paintComponent() method is the heart of Java 2D API and Swing API. It is the workhorse responsible for rendering all the pixels that we see on the screen today. (To learn more about how to create GUIs or run Swing-based applications, please see recipes 14-1 and 14-2. To learn how to execute a Java program with passed-in arguments via the command line or terminal, please see recipe 1-4.)

Next, you will be looking at recipes that will help you understand the Java 2D API basics such as creating points, drawing lines, drawing shapes, and painting colors.

■ **Note** For more on painting using Java's Swing, see the web article *Painting in AWT and Swing*, by Amy Fowler at `http://java.sun.com/products/jfc/tsc/articles/painting` (Oracle Corporation, 1999)

12-1. Creating Points

Problem

You want to create points that are similar to points on a Cartesian coordinate system.

Solution

Use Java's `java.awt.geom.Point2D` class to represent an ordered pair *(x, y)*. The *x* denotes a positive or negative number on the x-axis and the *y* denotes a positive or negative number on the y-axis. In Java there are three subclasses that can represent points: `Point2D.Double`, `Point2D.Float`, and `java.awt.Point` classes. All three extend from the class `java.awt.geom.Point2D`. By using the correct constructor your points can maintain different number types with integer or decimal precision. Following is the source code that uses the three `Point2D` subclasses:

```
package org.java7recipes.chapter12.recipe12_01;

import java.awt.Point;
import java.awt.geom.Point2D;

public class CreatePoints {
    public static void main(String[] args) {
        Point2D pointA = new Point2D.Double(2.555555555555555, 3.7777777777777777);
        Point2D.Float pointB = new Point2D.Float(11.555555555555555555555555555f, 10.2f);
        Point pointC = new Point(100, 100);

        System.out.println("pointA = " + pointA.getX() + ", " + pointA.getY());
        System.out.println("pointB = " + pointB.x      + ", " + pointB.y);
        System.out.println("pointC = " + pointC.x      + ", " + pointC.y);
    }
}
```

Shown below is the output from the program above:
```
pointA = 2.555555555555555, 3.7777777777777777
pointB = 11.555555, 10.2
pointC = 100, 100
```

How It Works

When using any of the three `Point2D` subclasses, keep in mind that the methods `getX()` and `getY()` in all cases will return a double precision number. The derived class `Point2D.Float` will allow the user of the API to access public instance variables `x` and `y` that will hold values of type `float`; while the `java.awt.Point` class will also have public instance variables, but hold values of type `int`. When looking at `pointB`, you'll notice that its class is declared oddly (with a dot between two types), that's because `Point2D.Float` is an inner class owned by `Point2D`. Shown following are the three `Point2D` subclasses:

```
Point2D.Double(double x, double y)
Point2D.Float(double x, float y)
Point(int x, int y)
```

You may be wondering why the variable "pointC" (an instance of `java.awt.Point`) does not begin with `java.awt.geom.*`. Well, a long time ago before the 2D API, the class was part of the original Java 1.0 AWT API, which only stored values as integers. Keep in mind that the values can be positive or negative in order to represent points in a Cartesian coordinate system also called *user space*.

Now that you know what kind of values are able to be stored you will want to plot or use points to draw lines, shapes, and so on. It is important to know how to draw on a computer screen (also known as the device space). The *device space* is the physical surface in which drawing will take place. Figure 12-1 shows the device space and the output from this recipe's code.

You may be wondering how to plot things onto the surface using points similar to a Cartesian graph or user space. Because many devices vary in size, the 2D API is set up where the origin at coordinate (0, 0) is located at the far upper-left corner of the screen. The x-coordinate values on the x-axis are positive values that increase from zero to the width of the device (as in user space). However, the y-coordinate is different from a Cartesian system. The coordinate's values are also positive, but increase in a downward direction to the bottom of the screen (opposite of user space). In other words, all visible pixels on the device surface are positive values, including zero for *(x, y)* in device space. Your x and y values can be negative values, but those pixels won't be displayed on the screen. Shown in Figure 12-1 are shapes drawn on the device space.

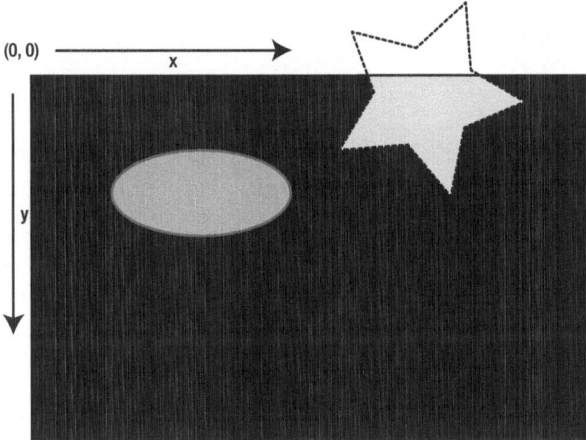

Figure 12-1. Device space

325

Since these objects represent points similar to Euclidean geometry, the 2D API also has other methods such as determining the distance between two points. See `java.awt.geom.Point2D` in the Javadoc for more details.

■ **Note** A point is not a pixel. Points represent x- and y-coordinates in user space. By definition, points do not have size nor color, so Java does not have a method such as `drawPoint()`. To draw a pixel, you can use the `java.awt.Graphics` class and its `drawLine(int x1, int y1, int x2, int y2)` method with a starting and ending point being the same coordinates; for example, `drawLine(10,15,10,15)`. See `DrawPixels.java`.

12-2. Drawing Lines

Problem

You want to draw lines on the computer screen.

Solution

Use the Java `java.awt.Graphics2D` class's `drawLine()` or `draw()` methods. Also use other graphic primitives such as stroke (`java.awt.BasicStroke`) and setting color (`java.awt.Color`) when drawing on the graphics surface. The code for recipe 12-2 is shown here:

```
package org.java7recipes.chapter12.recipe12_02;

import java.awt.BasicStroke;
import org.java7recipes.chapter12.SimpleAppLauncher;
import java.awt.Color;
import java.awt.Dimension;
import java.awt.Graphics;
import java.awt.Graphics2D;
import java.awt.RenderingHints;
import java.awt.Stroke;
import java.awt.geom.Line2D;
import java.awt.geom.Point2D;
import javax.swing.JComponent;

/**
 * Draws lines. Lines are colored Red, White and Blue.
 * @author cdea
 */
public class DrawLines extends JComponent {

    @Override
    protected void paintComponent(Graphics g) {
```

```
        super.paintComponent(g);

        Graphics2D g2d = (Graphics2D) g;
        g2d.setBackground(Color.LIGHT_GRAY);
        g2d.clearRect(0, 0, getParent().getWidth(), getParent().getHeight());

        // Red line
        g2d.setPaint(Color.RED);
        // 5 visible, 5 invisible
        final float dash[] = {5, 5};

        // 10 thick, end lines with no cap,
        // any joins make round, miter limit,
        // dash array, dash phase
        final BasicStroke dashed = new BasicStroke(10, BasicStroke.CAP_BUTT,
                BasicStroke.JOIN_ROUND, 0, dash, 0);

        g2d.setStroke(dashed);
        g2d.drawLine(100, 10, 10, 110);

        // White line
        g2d.setPaint(Color.WHITE);
        g2d.setStroke(new BasicStroke(10.0f));
        g2d.draw(new Line2D.Float(150, 10, 10, 160));

        // Blue line
        g2d.setPaint(Color.BLUE);
        Stroke solidStroke = new BasicStroke(10, BasicStroke.CAP_ROUND,
                BasicStroke.JOIN_ROUND);
        g2d.setStroke(solidStroke);
        g2d.draw(new Line2D.Float(new Point2D.Float(200, 10),
                new Point2D.Double(10, 210)));
    }

    public static void main(String[] args) {
        final DrawLines c = new DrawLines();
        c.setPreferredSize(new Dimension(272, 227));
        SimpleAppLauncher.launch("Chapter 12-2 Draw Lines", c);
    }
}
```

Figure 12-2 shows the output from this code example.

Figure 12-2. Drawing lines

How It Works

Although the code in the recipe solution looks simple, there is a lot of magic going on behind the scenes, and I would like to share with you some of the fundamentals. Once you get the fundamentals down, the rest of the recipes will be easier to digest and understand.

There are three basic steps when drawing lines or shapes: painting, stroking, and drawing. There are actually more steps, but for brevity I'll be using the 80/20 rule (Pareto principle), which means that 80 percent of the timelines or shapes will be drawn using those three steps, and 20 percent of the time you'll take additional steps.

I would like to explain the code block right before you get to the code that actually draws lines. The first method call is a call to `super.paintComponent(g)` and its job is to paint other components owned by the parent class. In this case, the call isn't necessary because our `DrawLine` class is directly extending from the `JComponent` class (which is the base class of all Java Swing components and therefore doesn't have any descendents to draw). Shown here is the `DrawLines` class that extends from the `JComponent` class and overrides the `paintComponent()` method:

```
public class DrawLines extends JComponent {

    @Override
    protected void paintComponent(Graphics g) {
        super.paintComponent(g);

        // drawing code below
        ...
    }

    // other methods
    ...
}
```

The call to `super.paintComponent(g)` does nothing for now, but when dealing with Swing components that have a UI delegate with descendents such as `JButton`, `JCheckBox`, `JPanel`, and so on, it will make the call to `super.paintComponent(g)` necessary. Moreover, it is a good habit, so keep the call to `super.paintComponent(g)` in your code because you will see more of it in Chapter 14 when you work with borders and panes. The call to `super.paintComponent(g)` will simply update the UI delegate's descendents to be rendered on the graphics surface; otherwise, certain things won't appear.

Next is `Graphics2D g2d = (Graphics2D) g;` where g is downcasted from a `java.awt.Graphics` object to a `java.awt.Graphics2D` object, which exposes methods to enable you to do more advanced graphics operations while still being able to access the methods on the `Graphics` class. Shown here is the `Graphics` object cast into a `Graphics2D`:

```
Graphics2D g2d = (Graphics2D) g;
```

Finally, you will be painting the background with a color of light gray. Here you will set the background color using the call to `g2d.setBackground(Color.LIGHT_GRAY)` and `g2d.clearRect(0, 0, getParent().getWidth(), getParent().getHeight())`, which will clear a rectangular area with the background color. The width and height are derived from the parent container (in this case, the `JFrame`). Because the `paintComponent()` method will be called during a resizing of the window, the `clearRect()` method will dynamically fill the background to gray as we resize the window. For example, this code is clearing the background based on the dimensions of the parent container (`JComponent`):

```
g2d.setBackground(Color.lightGray);
g2d.clearRect(0, 0, getParent().getWidth(), getParent().getHeight());
```

Now let's talk about drawing lines. The first step in drawing a line is setting the paint color. To draw a red line, you will set the `Graphics` object's paint color with a `java.awt.Color.RED` object via `setPaint(Color.RED)` before you begin to draw. The `Color` class has many predefined colors to choose from, but also there are many ways to construct a custom color (see recipe 12-4). Shown here is how to set the graphic context with the predefined color red:

```
g2d.setPaint(Color.RED)
```

On to the second step: stroking. Notice that the red line has a dashed pattern and is somewhat thick, That's because right before you are about to draw on the graphics surface you have an opportunity to set the stroke (`java.awt.Stroke`) using the method `setStroke()` on the `Graphics2D` object. (A stroke is synonymous with an artist's paintbrush or a pencil, except you are using virtual ink to draw shapes.) By creating `Stroke` objects you will be able to influence a shape's appearance such as its thickness, endpoint style, join point style, and dashed pattern. The only known concrete class implementing the interface `java.awt.Stroke` is the `java.awt.BasicStroke` class. I chose the `BasicStroke` constructor with the larger number of parameters in order for us to discuss all the ways you can create a stroke. First, you will create an array to represent a dashed pattern by simply using two values, 5.0f and 5.0f, which are the width of the stroke to display and the width of the stroke to not display, respectively. The dashed pattern represented an array of floats that is passed into the `BasicStroke`'s constructor. Here's an example of creating an instance of a `BasicStroke`:

```
public BasicStroke(float width, int cap, int join, float miterLimit,
                   float dash[], float dashPhase);
```

Table 12-1 shows the available parameters when using one of the `BasicStroke`'s constructors. This class is used to assist in drawing all shapes.

Table 12-1. BasicStroke Constructor Parameters

Parameter	Data Type	Example	Description
width	float	2.0f	Thickness of the stroke.
cap	int	CAP_BUTT, CAP_ROUND, CAP_SQUARE	End style. The kind of cap on the end of a line, curve, and open arc.
join	float	JOIN_BEVEL, JOIN_MITER, JOIN_ROUND	Join type style when two line segment ends join.
miterLimit	float	5	Limits the miter joint from getting too long and unwieldy when the thick line segment joins.
dash	float[]	{5.0f, 5.0f}	Dashed pattern alternating from visible to invisible based on a float value each representing the thickness.
dashPhase	float	3	An offset difference when starting the dashed pattern. For example, if the dashed pattern is {5,5} and dashPhase is 3 we determine the difference: 5.0f – 3 = 2.Translated as draw 2 pixels thick as visible (starting) then 5.0f invisible, next is 5.0f thick of visible and so on.

Shown here is a code snippet on how to set the Graphics2D stroke by using a java.awt.BasicStroke instance:

```
// 5 visible, 5 invisible
final float dash[] = {5, 5};

// 10 thick, end lines with no cap,
// any joins make round, miter limit,
// dash array, dash phase
final BasicStroke dashed = new BasicStroke(10, BasicStroke.CAP_BUTT,
    BasicStroke.JOIN_ROUND, 0, dash, 0);

g2d.setStroke(dashed);
```

Now that you understand how to set the stroke, the final step is to actually draw lines using the drawLine()method. Fundamentally, lines in a Cartesian system are created using a starting point and an ending point. In Java's drawLine() method, it also needs a starting point and an ending point. Looking at the source code for drawing the red line, you'll notice it uses the standard drawLine() method, but the white and blue lines are drawn using the draw() method. So, what is exactly the difference? The drawLine() method only draws lines using integer values for start- and endpoints, and the draw() method accepts any object of type java.awt.Shape. Since a Line2D is a shape, the draw() method will accept Line2D objects and, of course, other kinds of shapes. In the source code, the white line (center) is instantiated using the java.awt.Line2D.Double class, which is a subclass of java.awt.Shape. The Line2D.Double class allows you to specify (x, y) coordinates for the start- and endpoints of a line with values with precision of type Double. The 2D API also has a `java.awt.Line2D.Float` class that allows you to draw lines using values with a float precision.

Here are two code statement examples that can be used to draw lines. The `drawLine()` and `draw()` methods are shown here:

```
g2d.drawLine(100, 10, 10, 110);
g2d.draw(new Line2D.Double(150, 10, 10, 160));
```

Since Line2D objects represent lines similar to Euclidean geometry (the math of 2D and 3D shapes), the Line2D API has methods that determine distances and other relationships between points and lines. See `java.awt.geom.Line2D` in the Javadocs for more details.

■ **Note** The `BasicStroke` object has three types of join styles: `JOIN_BEVEL`, `JOIN_MITER`, and `JOIN_ROUND`. When shapes or lines join (or meet together), they can appear flat, pointed, or round, respectively. As a reminder when using the constructor that has the parameter for miter limit, it will be ignored if the join style is not using `JOIN_MITER`. Since you aren't using the `JOIN_MITER` in this example, the miter parameters are set to zero. See the Javadocs on `java.awt.BasicStroke` for details.

12-3. Drawing Shapes

Problem

You want to draw shapes on the computer screen.

Solution

Use Java's many common shape classes that implement the `java.awt.Shape` interface. Here are the most common subclasses that implement `java.awt.Shape`:

- Arc2D
- CubicCurve2D
- Ellipse2D
- Line2D
- Path2D
- QuadCurve2D
- Rectangle2D
- RoundRectangle2D

This code recipe will draw shapes using Arc2D, Ellipse2D, Rectangle2D, and RoundRectangle2D. All others (CubicCurve2D, Path2D, andQuadCurve2D) from the preceding list (excluding Line2D) will be discussed in recipe 12-7. (For more details on Line2D, refer to recipe 12-2.)

Shown next is an example of drawing simple shapes such as an arc, ellipse, rectangle, and rounded rectangle:

```java
package org.java7recipes.chapter12.recipe12_03;

import java.awt.BasicStroke;
import org.java7recipes.chapter12.SimpleAppLauncher;
import java.awt.Color;
import java.awt.Dimension;
import java.awt.Graphics;
import java.awt.Graphics2D;
import java.awt.RenderingHints;
import java.awt.geom.AffineTransform;
import java.awt.geom.Arc2D;
import java.awt.geom.Ellipse2D;
import java.awt.geom.Rectangle2D;
import java.awt.geom.RoundRectangle2D;
import javax.swing.JComponent;

/**
 * Draw a ellipse, rectangle, rounded rectangle.
 *
 * @author cdea
 */
public class DrawShapes extends JComponent {

    @Override
    protected void paintComponent(Graphics g) {
        super.paintComponent(g);

        Graphics2D g2d = (Graphics2D) g;
        g2d.setBackground(Color.WHITE);
        g2d.clearRect(0, 0, getParent().getWidth(), getParent().getHeight());
        // antialising
        g2d.setRenderingHint(RenderingHints.KEY_ANTIALIASING,
RenderingHints.VALUE_ANTIALIAS_ON);

        // save current transform
        AffineTransform origTransform = g2d.getTransform();

        // paint black
        g2d.setPaint(Color.BLACK);

        // 3 thickness
        g2d.setStroke(new BasicStroke(3));

        // Arc with open type
        Arc2D arc = new Arc2D.Float(50, // x coordinate
```

```
            50,                     // y coordinate
            100,                    // bounds width
            100,                    // bounds height
            45,                     // start angle in degrees
            270,                    // degrees plus start angle
            Arc2D.OPEN              // Open type arc
);
g2d.draw(arc);
//drawArc(int x, int y, int width, int height,
//         int startAngle, int arcAngle);

// Arc with chord type
Arc2D arc2 = new Arc2D.Float(50, // x coordinate
            50,                     // y coordinate
            100,                    // bounds width
            100,                    // bounds height
            45,                     // start angle in degrees
            270,                    // degrees plus start angle
            Arc2D.CHORD             // Chord type arc
);

g2d.translate(arc.getBounds().width + 10, 0);
g2d.draw(arc2);

// Arc with Pie type (PacMan)
Arc2D arc3 = new Arc2D.Float(50, // x coordinate
            50,                     // y coordinate
            100,                    // bounds width
            100,                    // bounds height
            45,                     // start angle in degrees
            270,                    // degrees plus start angle
            Arc2D.PIE               // pie type arc
);

g2d.translate(arc2.getBounds().width + 10, 0);
g2d.draw(arc3);


// reset transform
g2d.setTransform(origTransform);
g2d.translate(0, arc3.getHeight() + 10);


//Ellipse2D
Ellipse2D ellipse = new Ellipse2D.Float(50, 50, 100, 70);
g2d.draw(ellipse);
// g.drawOval(50, 50, 100, 70);

g2d.translate(0, ellipse.getBounds().getHeight() + 10);

//Rectangle2D
Rectangle2D rectangle = new Rectangle2D.Float(50, 50, 100, 70);
```

```
        g2d.draw(rectangle);
        // g.drawRect(50, 50, 100, 70);

        g2d.translate(0, rectangle.getBounds().getHeight() + 10);

        //RoundRectangle2D
        RoundRectangle2D roundRect = new RoundRectangle2D.Float(50, 50, 100, 70, 20, 20);
        g2d.draw(roundRect);
        // g.drawRoundRect(50, 50, 100, 70, 20, 20);

    }

    public static void main(String[] args) {
        final DrawShapes c = new DrawShapes();
        c.setPreferredSize(new Dimension(374, 415));
        SimpleAppLauncher.launch("Chapter 12-3 Draw Shapes", c);
    }
}
```

Figure 12-3 shows the output of the DrawShapes recipe that draws simple shapes such as arcs, rectangles, and an ellipse.

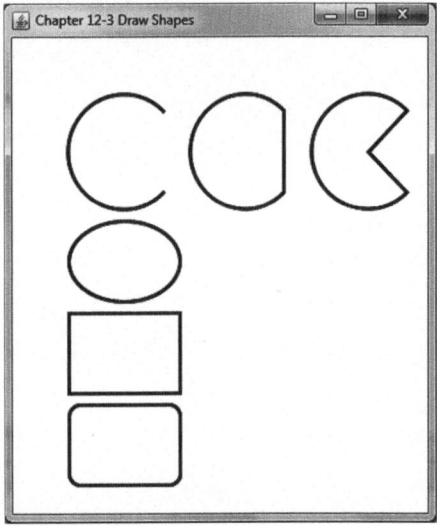

Figure 12-3. Drawing shapes

How It Works

The recipe starts by clearing the background to the color white (java.awt.Color.White) and turns antialiasing on. *Antialiasing* is an excellent technique to smooth out the jaggies or pixelation when shapes are drawn using the default rendering algorithms. In recipe 12-2, the lines didn't appear straight or smooth. The Graphics2D object's method setRenderingHints() is responsible for telling (hinting) the graphics engine to choose the appropriate algorithm for the right rendering job. This often depends on accuracy (quality) versus speed when rendering artifacts. To see more ways to give a hint to the graphics engine, look for java.awt.RenderingHints in the Javadoc. Set a rendering hint for antialiasing as follows:

```
g2d.setRenderingHint(RenderingHints.KEY_ANTIALIASING,
RenderingHints.VALUE_ANTIALIAS_ON);
```

The next step is obtaining the current transform to assist in placement of shapes on the drawing surface. Transforms will be discussed in recipe 12-6, but suffice it to say that transforms enable the developer to position (translate), scale, rotate, and shear shapes. Throughout the recipes you will use a common transform called translate to move the shape using its bounding box's upper-left (x, y) coordinate. For each shape you will set the upper-left location (translate) so that the shapes won't overlap one another when they are drawn. For example, the second arc will be positioned to the right of the previous arc by translating its x-coordinate. In the recipe code, the second arc is positioned 10 pixels to the right of the first arc. Later, you will reset the Graphics object's transform so that drawing can begin on the upper left with a coordinate of (0, 0). Shown here is the code snippet used to save the original transform for later reset:

```
// save current transform
AffineTransform origTransform = g2d.getTransform();
```

Before you draw shapes, you will first set the paint to the color black (java.awt.Color.Black) and the thickness of the stroke to 3.

```
g2d.setPaint(Color.BLACK);
g2d.setStroke(new BasicStroke(3));
```

At the top of the window there are three types of arcs shown consecutively. Each arc is drawn using the Arc2D.Float class. The Java 2D API also has an Arc2D.Double class and a standard drawArc() method to draw arcs. You should notice a common pattern emerging when creating shapes. There seems to be three ways to create the same kind of shape, and these types of shapes are based on using number values of type float, double, and int precision. When using theArc2D.Float and Arc2D.Double classes, you'll notice they are of decimal type precision for shapes and when using the method drawArc()'s parameters you will have int (integer) number type precision.

Table 12-2 shows one of theArc2D.Float constructors:

Table 12-2. An Arc2D.Float Constructor s Parameters

Parameter	Data Type	Example	Description
X	float	50	Bounding box x-coordinate
Y	float	50	Bounding box y-coordinate
Width	float	100	Bounding box width
Height	float	100	Bounding box height
Start	float	45	Start drawing at 45 degrees
Extent	float	270	When to stop drawing arc; stops drawing at (start angle + extent angle)
Type	int	Arc2D.OPEN, Arc2D.CHORD, Arc2D.PIE	Arc type

The following is an Arc2D constructor using a float precision:

```
Arc2D.Float(float x, float y, float w, float h, float start, float extent, int type)
```

When drawing an arc you will specify a bounding box similar to building a rectangle by specifying the upper-left corner using (x, y) coordinates, then the width and height of the rectangle. Once the bounding box is defined, you can think of it as an invisible ellipse inscribed in the bounding box. Next, is defining the starting angle that is where to start drawing or tracing the ellipse. After the start angle is specified, you will set the extent. The *extent* is the angle in degrees plus the start angle to indicate where the stroking or tracing of the ellipse stops. Finally, the arc type parameter is how the arc opening should connect. The arc can appear open, a straight line (chord), or a shape of a pie wedge. Figure 12-4 describes properties of a Java2D arc.

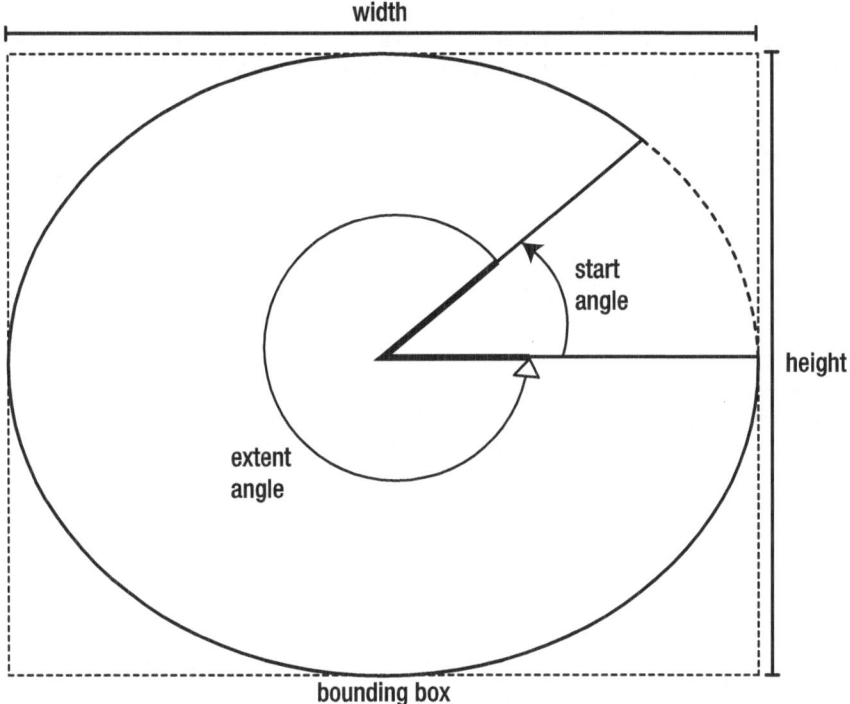

Figure 12-4. *Defining an Arc2D.Float instance*

Figure 12-5 shows the three types of arcs: open, chord, and pie.

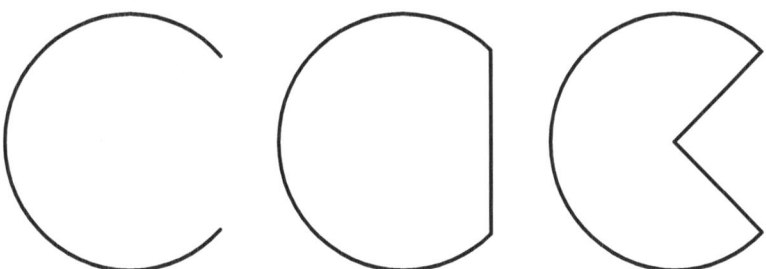

Figure 12-5. *Arc types: open, chord, and pie*

Later in this chapter, you will learn about transforms and how to use the `translate()` method, I will briefly explain how the shapes are drawn and positioned. First, the open arc is drawn onto the graphics surface, starting with its upper-left bounding box coordinate at (50, 50) with the width and height both set to 100. Next is drawing the chord type arc offset to the right of the previous open arc shape. Here you will position the chord arc to the right of the previous open arc by translating its x-coordinate based on the width of the open arc's bounding box plus 10 pixels for additional spacing. Finally, you will repeat the steps to draw the pie-shaped arc. Once the three types of arcs are drawn, you will reset the current transform to the saved transform in order to draw the ellipse shape underneath the first arc shape (open arc).

Next, is drawing an ellipse using the `Ellipse2D` class. Similar to the `Arc2D` shape, you will imagine drawing an invisible rectangle or a bounding box where the x, y coordinate is the upper-left corner and the width and height is specified to inscribe an ellipse by using the giving stroke. The following code statements are the three ways to create an ellipse:

```
Ellipse2D.Float(float x, float y, float w, float h)
Ellipse2D.Double(double x, double y, double w, double h)
Graphics.drawOval(int x, int y, int w, int h);
```

After drawing the ellipse, you will be drawing a rectangle using the `Rectangle2D` class. In the example, you will use the `Rectangle2D.Float` by first setting its x-coordinate to 50 and y-coordinate to 50. Second, you will set its width to 100 and height to 70. Next you will draw the shape on the graphics surface with the `Graphics2D` object's `draw()` method. Shown here is how to draw a rectangle:

```
Rectangle2D rectangle = new Rectangle2D.Float(50, 50, 100, 70);
g2d.draw(rectangle);
```

Finally, you will be drawing a round rectangle shape. As you can see the last shape in the figure 12-3 how similar it is with a `Rectangle2D` shape, except that its corners are nice and round. To make the corners rounded, you would specify the arc width and height. When dealing with the arc width or height when the value is zero, it is identical to a regular rectangle, but as the value increases the arc becomes more curved moving away from the corner. The following is the code to draw a rounded rectangle with 20 as its arc width and height:

```
RoundRectangle2D roundRect = new RoundRectangle2D.Float(50, 50, 100, 70, 20, 20);
g2d.draw(roundRect);
```

12-4.Filling Shapes

Problem

You want to fill shapes with color paints and display them on the computer screen.

Solution

After drawing shapes, you will want to call the `Graphics2D` `setPaint()` method by passing in a color (`java.awt.Color`) that you want to fill the shape with. Next, you will actual fill the shape with the paint color using the `fill()` method on the `Graphics` object and passing in the shape. The following code sets paint color and fills an ellipse shape:

```
g2d.setPaint(Color.RED);
g2d.fill(ellipse);
%
```

Shown here is the code recipe on filling shapes with colors:

```
package org.java7recipes.chapter12.recipe12_04;

import java.awt.*;
import java.awt.geom.*;
import javax.swing.JComponent;
import org.java7recipes.chapter12.SimpleAppLauncher;

/**
 * Draws lines. Lines are colored Red, White and Blue.
 * @author cdea
 */
public class FillColorShapes extends JComponent {

    @Override
    protected void paintComponent(Graphics g) {

        Graphics2D g2d = (Graphics2D) g;
        g2d.setBackground(Color.WHITE);
        g2d.clearRect(0, 0, getParent().getWidth(), getParent().getHeight());
        g2d.setRenderingHint(RenderingHints.KEY_ANTIALIASING,
RenderingHints.VALUE_ANTIALIAS_ON);

        g2d.setPaint(Color.BLACK);
        g2d.setStroke(new BasicStroke(3));

        //Ellipse2D
        Ellipse2D ellipse = new Ellipse2D.Float(50, 50, 100, 70);
        g2d.draw(ellipse);
        g2d.setPaint(Color.RED);
        g2d.fill(ellipse);

        g2d.translate(0, ellipse.getBounds().getHeight() + 10);

        Stroke defaultStroke = g2d.getStroke();
        // Draw black line
        Line2D blackLine = new Line2D.Float(170, 30, 20, 140);
        g2d.setPaint(Color.BLACK);
        g2d.setStroke(new BasicStroke(10.0f));
        g2d.draw(blackLine);
        // set stroke back to normal
        g2d.setStroke(defaultStroke);

        //Rectangle2D
        Rectangle2D rectangle = new Rectangle2D.Float(50, 50, 100, 70);
        g2d.setPaint(Color.BLACK);
        g2d.draw(rectangle);
        g2d.setPaint(new Color(255, 200, 0, 200));

        g2d.fill(rectangle);

        g2d.translate(0, rectangle.getBounds().getHeight() + 10);
```

```
        //RoundRectangle2D
        RoundRectangle2D roundRect = new RoundRectangle2D.Float(50, 50, 100, 70, 20, 20);
        g2d.setPaint(Color.BLACK);
        g2d.draw(roundRect);
        g2d.setPaint(Color.GREEN);
        g2d.fill(roundRect);
    }

    public static void main(String[] args) {
        final FillColorShapes c = new FillColorShapes();
        c.setPreferredSize(new Dimension(340, 320));
        SimpleAppLauncher.launch("Chapter 12-4 Filling Shapes with Colors", c);
    }
}
```

Figure 12-6 displays the various types of colorized fills that can be applied onto shapes. A solid black line (as depicted in Figure 12-6) also appears in the recipe to demonstrate the transparency of the shape's color.

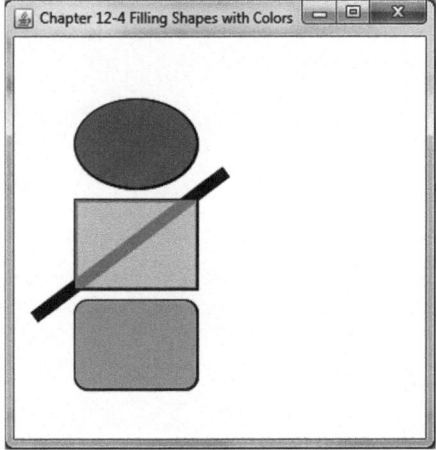

Figure 12-6. Filling shapes with color

How It Works

The recipe first clears the background to white and sets antialiasing on (smooth rendering). Next, it sets the stroke thickness and color (java.awt.Color.BLACK). The color black is used when drawing the ellipse outline.

After the ellipse is drawn, you will use the Graphics2D's method fill() to fill the interior of the ellipse with the color red. The order of drawing a shape prior to filling a shape can matter depending on the desired effect you are trying to achieve. In our current example you will draw an ellipse with a thickness of 3 and then fill it with the color red. Imagine if you will, an ellipse that is drawn with three pencils held together where the center pencil is the outline of the actual ellipse shape and some of the inner outline is considered inside (interior) of the ellipse, and the outer outline is the outside area surrounding the ellipse. Knowing this, you will see that the red paint fills the ellipse and therefore overwrites the inner part of the ellipse including some of the inner outline. This will leave the outer part of the outline black. Figure 12-7 shown below depicts a shapes's stroke:

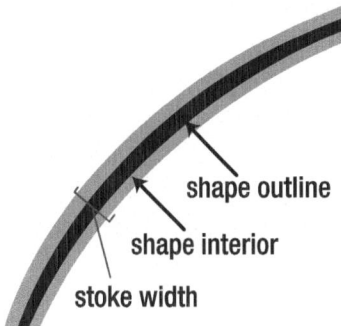

Figure 12-7. Shape s stroke width

Let's talk more about color. In Java there are common primary colors that are predefined to be used easily when filling shapes such as `java.awt.Color.BLUE`, `java.awt.Color.RED`, and so on.

Colors can be defined with four components: red, green, blue, and alpha channel. Although there are many ways to create colors, a common method is representing each component as an integer value range of 0–255. The red, green, and blue (RGB) components will mix colors based a web standard color model. When all three color components are zeroes (0, 0, 0), they will yield the color black. When all the color components have the value 255, they will yield the color white (255, 255, 255). A fourth component is the alpha channel, which controls the opacity level from 0 (fully transparent) to 255 (fully opaque). See the Javadocs on `java.awt.Color` for more details. Shown following is a `Color` constructor using alpha channel:

```
Color(int r, int g, int b, int a)
```

■ **Note** For more on color standards, see *A Standard Default Color Space for the Internet sRGB* (`http://www.w3.org/Graphics/Color/sRGB.html` by Michael Stokes (Hewlett-Packard), Matthew Anderson (Microsoft), Srinivasan Chandrasekar (Microsoft), Ricardo Motta (Hewlett-Packard), Version 1.10, November 5, 1996.

Next is filling the rectangle shape with the color orange and having the alpha channel set to be partially transparent. Shown here is filling a rectangle with paint:

```
g2d.setPaint(new Color(255, 200, 0, 200));
g2d.fill(rectangle);
```

Finally, you will use the predefined color green to fill the round rectangle shown here:

```
g2d.setPaint(Color.GREEN);
g2d.fill(roundRect);
```

12-5. Gradients

Problem

You want to fill shapes by using color gradients to be displayed on the computer screen.

Solution

Use the following classes when applying gradient paint:

- `java.awt.GradientPaint`

- `java.awt.LinearGradientPaint`

- `java.awt.RadialGradientPaint`

To use gradient paint, you will be setting the `Graphics2D` `setPaint()` method by passing in a gradient paint (`java.awt.GradientPaint`) object. Next, you will actually fill the shape with the paint color using the `fill()` method on the `Graphics` object and passing in the shape. This code creates a gradient paint and fills the shape:

```
GradientPaint gradient = new GradientPaint(100, 50, Color.RED, 100, 150, Color.BLACK);
g2d.setPaint(gradient);
g2d.fill(myShape);
...
```

The following code uses the preceding classes to add radial and linear gradient colors as well as transparent (alpha channel level) colors to the shapes. You will be using an ellipse, rectangle, and rounded rectangle in this recipe. A solid black line (as depicted in Figure 12-8) also appears in the recipe to demonstrate the transparency of the shape's color.

```
package org.java7recipes.chapter12.recipe12_05;

import java.awt.*;
import org.java7recipes.chapter12.SimpleAppLauncher;
import java.awt.geom.*;
import javax.swing.JComponent;

/**
 * Draw a ellipse, rectangle, rounded rectangle.
 *
```

```
 * @author cdea
 */
public class Gradients extends JComponent {

    @Override
    protected void paintComponent(Graphics g) {
        super.paintComponent(g);

        Graphics2D g2d = (Graphics2D) g;
        g2d.setBackground(new Color(255, 255, 255, 200));
        g2d.clearRect(0, 0, getParent().getWidth(), getParent().getHeight());
        g2d.setRenderingHint(RenderingHints.KEY_ANTIALIASING,
RenderingHints.VALUE_ANTIALIAS_ON);

        //Ellipse2D
        Ellipse2D ellipse = new Ellipse2D.Float(50, 50, 100, 70);

        float[] dists = { .3f, 1.0f};
        Color[] colors = {Color.RED, Color.BLACK};
        RadialGradientPaint gradient1 = new RadialGradientPaint(50, 50, 100, dists, colors);
        g2d.setPaint(gradient1);
        g2d.fill(ellipse);

        g2d.translate(0, ellipse.getBounds().getHeight() + 10);

        Stroke defaultStroke = g2d.getStroke();
        // Draw black line
        Line2D blackLine = new Line2D.Float(170, 30, 20, 140);
        g2d.setPaint(Color.BLACK);
        g2d.setStroke(new BasicStroke(10.0f));
        g2d.draw(blackLine);
        // set stroke back to normal
        g2d.setStroke(defaultStroke);

        //Rectangle2D
        Rectangle2D rectangle = new Rectangle2D.Float(50, 50, 100, 70);
        float[] dists2 = { .1f, 1.0f};
        Color[] colors2 = {new Color(255, 200, 0, 200), new Color(0, 0, 0, 200)};
        LinearGradientPaint gradient2 = new LinearGradientPaint(100, 50, 100, 150, dists2,
colors2);

        g2d.setPaint(gradient2);
        g2d.fill(rectangle);

        g2d.translate(0, rectangle.getBounds().getHeight() + 10);

        //RoundRectangle2D
        RoundRectangle2D roundRect = new RoundRectangle2D.Float(50, 50, 100, 70, 20, 20);
        GradientPaint gradient3 = new GradientPaint(50, 50, Color.GREEN, 70,70, Color.BLACK,
true);
        g2d.setPaint(gradient3);
        g2d.fill(roundRect);
```

```
    }

    public static void main(String[] args) {
        final Gradients c = new Gradients();
        c.setPreferredSize(new Dimension(287, 320));
        SimpleAppLauncher.launch("Chapter 12-5 Gradients", c);
    }
}
```

Figure 12-8 displays the various types of gradient fills that can be applied onto shapes.

Figure 12-8. Adding gradient paints to shapes

How It Works

Similar to past recipes, you will clear the background and set antialiasing on before you begin to draw onto the graphics surface. This recipe is the same as recipe 12-4, but instead of using simple solid colors to fill shapes, you will be using gradient paint. Gradients provide a way to fill shapes by interpolating between two or more colors. For example, when using a starting color of white and an end color as black, the gradient color will gradually go from light to dark with varying shades of gray in between. The pattern is a smooth transition from one color to another in a linear fashion.

Running the example code, you will see three main shapes filled with a gradient color. The first shape is an ellipse using a radial gradient from red to black. You'll notice the ellipse looks almost 3D as if there were a light source coming from the upper left. Shown here is a constructor for a RadialGradientPaint class:

```
    public RadialGradientPaint(float cx,
                               float cy,
```

```
                    float radius,
                    float[] fractions,
                    Color[] colors)
```

To create a `RadialGradientPaint` you can imagine a tiny circle positioned on a shape that expands with a circular gradient. To define the center of the gradient, you pass in the `cx` and `cy` parameters. The center of the gradient can be positioned anywhere within the ellipse, allowing you to give the illusion of changing the light source angle onto the shape. The `radius` parameter specifies the end of the gradient. The `fractions` array (floats) denotes the distribution of colors when moving from the center out to the perimeter. An array of colors specifies the start and end colors used when painting the gradient. The following code paints a radial gradient onto an ellipse shape (Red Ellipse):

```
float[] dists = { .3f, 1.0f};
Color[] colors = {Color.RED, Color.BLACK};
RadialGradientPaint gradient1 = new RadialGradientPaint(50, 50, 100, dists, colors);
g2d.setPaint(gradient1);
g2d.fill(ellipse);
```

The second shape is a rectangle filled with a transparent linear gradient using yellow and black with a transparency alpha value of 200.The following is a constructor for theLinearGradientPaint class:

```
LinearGradientPaint(float startX, float startY, float endX, float endY, float[]
fractions, Color[] colors)
```

To create a linear gradient paint, you will specify `startX`, `startY`, `endX`, and `endY` for the start- and endpoints. The start- and endpoint coordinates denote where the gradient pattern begins and stops. The `fractions` array is the amount of distribution as it interpolates over a color. Again, similar to the `RadialGradientPaint`, the `colors` array specifies the different colors to be used in the gradient. This code instantiates a yellow, semitransparent, linear gradient paint object that fills a rectangle:

```
float[] dists2 = { .1f, 1.0f};
Color[] colors2 = {new Color(255, 200, 0, 200), new Color(0, 0, 0, 200)};
LinearGradientPaint gradient2 = new LinearGradientPaint(100, 50, 100, 150, dists2,
colors2);
g2d.setPaint(gradient2);
```

Notice a rounded rectangle with a repeating pattern of a gradient using green and black in a diagonal direction. This is a simple gradient paint that is the same as the `LinearGradientPaint`, except it allows only two colors, and `startX`, `startY`, `endX`, and `endY` are set in a diagonal line position. The `cycle` parameter is set to `true`, which will cause the gradient pattern to repeat or cycle between the colors giving the illusion of glowing bars or pipes.

This code draws a `RoundRectangle2Dobject` with a cyclic pattern:

```
RoundRectangle2D roundRect = new RoundRectangle2D.Float(50, 50, 100, 70, 20, 20);
GradientPaint gradient3 = new GradientPaint(50, 50, Color.GREEN, 70,70, Color.BLACK, true);
g2d.setPaint(gradient3);
g2d.fill(roundRect);
```

12-6. Transforming Shapes

Problem

You want to shear, rotate, scale, and translate shapes on the screen.

Solution

Use the `java.awt.geom.AffineTransform` class to transform shapes. Shown here is the recipe that will transform a square by shearing, rotating, scaling, and translating:

```java
package org.java7recipes.chapter12.recipe12_06;

import java.awt.*;
import java.awt.geom.*;
import javax.swing.JComponent;
import org.java7recipes.chapter12.SimpleAppLauncher;

/**
 * Transforming shapes.
 *
 * @author cdea
 */
public class TransformingShapes extends JComponent {


    @Override
    protected void paintComponent(Graphics g) {
super.paintComponent(g);

        Graphics2D g2d = (Graphics2D) g;
        // clear background
        g2d.setBackground(Color.WHITE);
        g2d.clearRect(0, 0, getParent().getWidth(), getParent().getHeight());

        // turn on antialiasing
        g2d.setRenderingHint(RenderingHints.KEY_ANTIALIASING,
RenderingHints.VALUE_ANTIALIAS_ON);

        // save transform
        AffineTransform origTransform = g2d.getTransform();

        g2d.setPaint(Color.BLACK);
        g2d.setStroke(new BasicStroke(3f));

        //Rectangle2D (original)
        Rectangle2D rectangle = new Rectangle2D.Float(50, 50, 50, 50);
        g2d.draw(rectangle);
```

```
    // Shearing
    AffineTransform shear = new AffineTransform();

    // move to upper right
    shear.translate(rectangle.getX() + rectangle.getWidth() + 50, 0);

    shear.shear(-.5, 0);

    g2d.transform(shear);
    g2d.draw(rectangle);

    g2d.setTransform(origTransform);

    // rotate
    AffineTransform rotate = new AffineTransform();

    // move to bottom left
    rotate.translate(0, rectangle.getY() + rectangle.getHeight());

    rotate.rotate(Math.PI/4, rectangle.getCenterX() , rectangle.getCenterY());

    g2d.transform(rotate);
    g2d.draw(rectangle);

    g2d.setTransform(origTransform);

    // scale
    AffineTransform scale = new AffineTransform();

    // move to bottom right
    scale.translate(rectangle.getX() + 30, rectangle.getY());

    // scale
    scale.scale(1.5, 1.5);

    g2d.transform(scale);
    g2d.draw(rectangle);

}

public static void main(String[] args) {
    final TransformingShapes c = new TransformingShapes();
    c.setPreferredSize(new Dimension(317, 246));
    SimpleAppLauncher.launch("Chapter 12-6 Transforming Shapes", c);
}
}
```

Figure 12-9 shows four squares that demonstrate the different transforms. The top-left square is the original that has no transforms applied to it and serves as our reference shape.

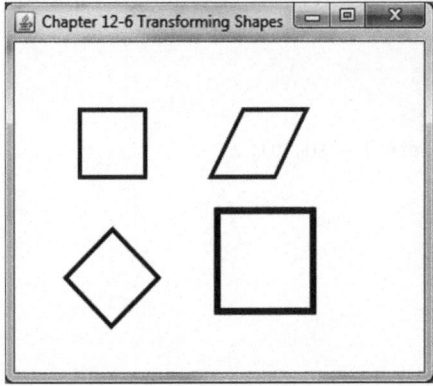

Figure 12-9. Transform shapes

How It Works

Pictured in the output are four squares (rectangles) transformed. Starting from left to right and top to bottom, you will have a square, rhombus, diamond, and a larger square. The square is considered the original object without any transforms applied. The following are transforms used in this recipe:

- Shear
- Rotate
- Scale

You'll notice an initial `translate` operation right before the desired transform. The `translate` transform will move and position the shape (relative to the preceding shape) on the graphics surface, making it appear as if it occupies one of four quadrants. An `AffineTransform` allows you to perform compound transform operations. An example of the `translate` operation before the desired transform follows:

```
// Shearing
AffineTransform shear = new AffineTransform();
// move to upper right
shear.translate(rectangle.getX() + rectangle.getWidth() + 50, 0);
// desired transform
shear.shear(-.5, 0);
```

You will begin by clearing the background with white and setting antialiasing on. Next, you will save the current transform. This allows you to save the original state of the `Graphics2D` object before you begin moving or transforming shapes. Before you start drawing, you will set the paint to `black` and the stroke thickness to `3f` (`float`) using the `java.awt.BasicStroke` class. (To see more on stroking, refer to recipe 12-2.)

The first shape drawn is a 50-by-50 square using the `Rectangle2D` class. This shape will be called the original with its position starting at (x, y) coordinate at (50, 50). This shape is reused to transform the other three shapes described earlier. That is, you will draw the shape four times, transforming it each time, and translating (placing) it relative to the preceding shape. The following code draws the original square (rectangle) shape:

```
//Rectangle2D (original)
Rectangle2D rectangle = new Rectangle2D.Float(50, 50, 50, 50);
g2d.draw(rectangle);
```

Next, you will shear the shape by instantiating an AffineTransform and invoking the shear() method. Here's an example of shearing using AffineTransform:

```
AffineTransform shear = new AffineTransform();
shear.shear(-.5, 0);
```

Compared to the original square shape, you will notice the shape forms as a parallelogram or a rhombus. The (x, y) coordinates are transformed using these equivalent equations:

```
x = x + (shearX * y)
y = y + (shearY * x)
```

After drawing the rhombus, you will draw a rectangle using the original shape to then position it beneath the original and rotating it (diamond shape). By using the rotate() method, you pass in a radian angle and a point on the shape to rotate around. This code moves and rotates the square displayed below the original square:

```
AffineTransform rotate = new AffineTransform();
rotate.translate(0, rectangle.getY() + rectangle.getHeight());
rotate.rotate(Math.PI/4, rectangle.getCenterX() , rectangle.getCenterY());
```

Finally, you will scale the original rectangle by a scaling by a factor of 1.5 along the x-axis and y-axis direction. The stroke thickness is even sized by the factor given. A neat is to use negative values that will flip the shape along the x- and y-axis. The following code snippet scales a rectangle shape by increasing its size:

```
AffineTransform scale = new AffineTransform();
scale.scale(1.5, 1.5);
```

■ **Note** For more on AffineTransforms go to the Javadoc at

http://download.oracle.com/javase/7/docs/api/index.html?java/awt/geom/AffineTransform.html.

12-7. Making Complex Shapes

Problem

You want to draw complex shapes on the screen.

Solution

Use Java 2D's CubicCurve2D, Path2D, and QuadCurve2D classes. You can also build new shapes by using constructive area geometry via the java.awt.geom.Area class.

The following code draws various complex shapes. The first complex shape involves a cubic curve drawn in the shape of a sine wave. The next shape, which I call the *ice cream cone*, uses the Path2D class. The third shape is a quadratic Bézier curve (QuadCurve2D) forming a smile. The final shape is a scrumptious donut. You will create this donut shape by subtracting two ellipses (one smaller and one larger):

```
package org.java7recipes.chapter12.recipe12_07;

import java.awt.*;
import java.awt.geom.*;
import javax.swing.JComponent;
import org.java7recipes.chapter12.SimpleAppLauncher;

/**
 * Draws Complex shapes.
 * @author cdea
 */
public class DrawComplexShapes extends JComponent {

    @Override
    protected void paintComponent(Graphics g) {
        super.paintComponent(g);

        Graphics2D g2d = (Graphics2D) g;
        g2d.setBackground(Color.WHITE);
        g2d.clearRect(0, 0, getParent().getWidth(), getParent().getHeight());
        g2d.setRenderingHint(RenderingHints.KEY_ANTIALIASING,
RenderingHints.VALUE_ANTIALIAS_ON);

        // set color and thickness of stroke
        g2d.setPaint(Color.BLACK);
        g2d.setStroke(new BasicStroke(3));

        //CubicCurve2D
        CubicCurve2D cubicCurve = new CubicCurve2D.Float(
                50, 75,             // start pt (x1,y1)
                50+30, 75-100,      // control pt1
                50+60, 75+100,      // control pt2
                50+90, 75           // end pt (x2,y2)
        );

        g2d.draw(cubicCurve);

        // move below previous shape
        g2d.translate(0, cubicCurve.getBounds().y + 50);

        //Path2D (IceCream shape)
```

```java
    Path2D path = new Path2D.Float();
    path.moveTo(50, 150);
    path.quadTo(100, 50, 150, 150);
    path.lineTo(50, 150);
    path.lineTo(100, 150 + 125);
    path.lineTo(150, 150);
    path.closePath();

    g2d.draw(path);

    // move below previous shape
    g2d.translate(0, path.getBounds().height + 50);

    //QuadCurve2D
    QuadCurve2D quadCurve = new QuadCurve2D.Float(50, 50,
            125, 150,
            150, 50
    );

    g2d.draw(quadCurve);

    // move below previous shape
    g2d.translate(0, quadCurve.getBounds().y + 50);

    // donut
    g2d.setStroke(new BasicStroke(1));
    Ellipse2D bigCircle = new Ellipse2D.Float(50, 50, 100, 75);
    Ellipse2D smallCircle = new Ellipse2D.Float(80, 75, 35, 25);
    Area donut = new Area(bigCircle);
    Area donutHole = new Area(smallCircle);
    donut.subtract(donutHole);

    // drop shadow
    GradientPaint gradient2 = new GradientPaint(150 +1, 50+75 +1,
            new Color(255, 255, 255, 200),
            55, 55,
            new Color(0, 0, 0, 200)
    );
    // gradient fill
    g2d.setPaint(gradient2);
    g2d.fill(donut);
    g2d.draw(donut);

    // draw orange donut
    g2d.translate(-3, -3);
    g2d.setPaint(Color.ORANGE);
    g2d.fill(donut);

    // outline the donut
    g2d.setPaint(Color.BLACK);
    g2d.draw(donut);
}
```

```
    public static void main(String[] args) {
        final DrawComplexShapes c = new DrawComplexShapes();
        c.setPreferredSize(new Dimension(409, 726));
        SimpleAppLauncher.launch("Chapter 12-7 Draw Complex Shapes", c);
    }
}
```

Figure 12-10 displays the sine wave, ice cream cone, smile, and donut shapes that we have created using Java2D.

Figure 12-10. Draw complex shapes

How It Works

If you have gotten this far, you will notice we have done the same thing as before in previous recipes; you will clear the graphics surface and turn antialiasing on. Displayed in the output window are four shapes: sine wave (CubicCurve2D), ice cream cone (Path2D), smile (QuadCurve2D), and a donut (Area). Before you begin, you'll notice code statements that employ the translate() method, which repositions shapes. Most recipes often use the translate operation, via the AffineTransform class, to move shapes, so I will not go into great detail about the translate operation (refer to recipe 12-6 to see more). Let's dive into the shapes and see how they are drawn.

First, you will create a CubicCurve2D object by instantiating a CubicCurve2D.Float. Shown here is a CubicCurve2D.Float constructor:

```
CubicCurve2D.Float(float x1, float y1, float ctrlx1, float ctrly1, float ctrlx2, float
ctrly2, float x2, float y2)
```

The x1, y1, x2, y2 parameters are the starting point and ending point of a curve. The ctrlx1, ctrly1, ctrlx2, ctrly2 are control point 1 and control point 2. A *control point* is a point that pulls the curve toward it. In this example, you will simply have a control point 1 above to pull the curve upward to form a hill and control point 2 below to pull the curve downward to form a valley. Figure 12-11 depicts a cubic curve with two control points positioned above and below the start point and end point, respectively.

Figure 12-11. Cubic curve

Next, you will create a complex shape such as an ice cream cone using the java.awt.geom.Path2D class. When using the Path2D class, you will be using it like a pencil on a piece of graph paper moving from point to point. Between any points you can decide to draw the following: line, quadratic curve or cubic curve. Once you have finished the drawing, the last point can close the path forming a shape using the closePath() method. The following code creates the path shape forming an ice cream cone:

```
//Path2D (IceCream shape)
Path2D path = new Path2D.Float();
path.moveTo(50, 150);
path.quadTo(100, 50, 150, 150);
path.lineTo(50, 150);
path.lineTo(100, 150 + 125);
path.lineTo(150, 150);
path.closePath();

g2d.draw(path);
```

Third, you will be drawing a quadratic parametric curve using the (QuadCurve2D) class. Shown here is a QuadCurve2D constructor used in this example to form a smile:

QuadCurve2D.Float(float x1, float y1, float ctrlx, float ctrly, float x2, float y2)

This is similar to the cubic curve example, but instead of two control points you have only one control point. Figure 12-12 shows a QuadCurve2D with a control point below its starting and ending points:

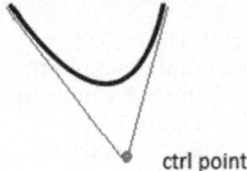

Figure 12-12. *Quadratic curve*

Last, you have a created a shape that looks like a tasty donut. This shape was created with constructive area geometry using Java's `java.awt.geom.Area` class. This class provides many ways to combine shapes. Here are the operations to combine shape areas:

- `Add (union)`

- `Subtract`

- `Intersect`

- `Exclusive Or`

We aren't going into all the operations, which are beyond the scope this book. To see more, refer to the Javadoc API on `java.awt.geom.Area`. For now, we will be discussing the subtract operation. In this example, you will simply create a big ellipse representing the whole donut and a smaller ellipse representing the hole of the donut to subtract. This code creates a donut shape by using the area's `subtract()` method:

```
Ellipse2D bigCircle = new Ellipse2D.Float(50, 50, 100, 75);
Ellipse2D smallCircle = new Ellipse2D.Float(80, 75, 35, 25);
Area donut = new Area(bigCircle);
Area donutHole = new Area(smallCircle);
donut.subtract(donutHole);
```

You can finish the donut area like any other shape, such as filling it in with a color. You will create a gradient fill to make a drop shadow effect. Then reuse the shape by shifting it diagonally to the upper left by three pixels and fill it with a solid orange color. You can then outline the donut to give it a cartoonish look.

12-8. Creating Interactive Shapes

Problem

You want to interact with a shape by manipulating its points with the mouse pointer.

Solution

Implement a `MouseListener` and a `MouseMotionListener` interface, and use an `AffineTransform` class to size and move the shape. The major classes or interfaces used in this recipe are these:

```
java.awt.event.MouseListener
java.awt.event.MouseMotionListener
java.awt.geom.AffineTransform
```

The shape you will be interacting with is a `java.awt.geom.QuadCurve2D` object using a mouse pointer. (To know more about how to draw a `QuadCurve2D` shape, refer to recipe 12-7.) Interacting with the shape via the mouse pointer will dynamically change or move the shape about the screen, thus transforming it. For the sake of brevity, I will not be discussing transforms in detail. (For more about how to use transforms, refer to recipe 12-6).

Shown here is the recipe that creates an application to allow the user to manipulate a cubic curve shape by using the mouse pointer to move positioning handles:

```java
package org.java7recipes.chapter12.recipe12_08;

import java.awt.*;
import java.awt.event.*;
import java.awt.geom.*;
import javax.swing.JComponent;
import org.java7recipes.chapter12.SimpleAppLauncher;

/**
 * Interactive shapes.
 * @author cdea
 */
public class InteractiveShapes extends JComponent implements MouseListener,
        MouseMotionListener {

    private boolean selectedShape;
    private boolean hoveredShape;
    private QuadCurve2D s;
    private Point2D translatePt;
    private Point2D anchorPt;
    private AffineTransform moveTranslate = new AffineTransform();
    private int moveType = -1;
    public static final int START_PT = 1;
    public static final int CNTRL_PT = 2;
    public static final int END_PT = 3;
    public static final int MOVE_RECT = 4;

    public InteractiveShapes() {
        s = new QuadCurve2D.Float(50, 50,
                125, 150,
                150, 50);
    }

    @Override
    protected void paintComponent(Graphics g) {
        super.paintComponent(g);

        Graphics2D g2d = (Graphics2D) g;
```

```
g2d.setBackground(Color.WHITE);
g2d.clearRect(0, 0, getParent().getWidth(), getParent().getHeight());
g2d.setRenderingHint(RenderingHints.KEY_ANTIALIASING,
        RenderingHints.VALUE_ANTIALIAS_ON);

g2d.drawString("Bounded Rectangle " + s.getBounds2D().getX() + ", " +
        s.getBounds2D().getY(), 10, 10);
AffineTransform origTransform = g2d.getTransform();

// selected and move shape
if (selectedShape && translatePt != null && moveType == MOVE_RECT) {

    // move the shape
    moveTranslate.setToTranslation(translatePt.getX() - anchorPt.getX(),
            translatePt.getY() - anchorPt.getY());
    g2d.setTransform(moveTranslate);

}

// set color and thickness of stroke
g2d.setPaint(Color.BLACK);
g2d.setStroke(new BasicStroke(3));

// Draw the quad curve shape
g2d.draw(s);

// hovering over shape (gray dotted box)
if (hoveredShape) {
    g2d.setColor(Color.LIGHT_GRAY);
    final float dash[] = {2, 2};
    g2d.setStroke(new BasicStroke(2, BasicStroke.CAP_BUTT,
            BasicStroke.JOIN_BEVEL, 0, dash, 0));
    g2d.draw(s.getBounds2D());

}

// selected shape
if (selectedShape) {

    // draw red dotted box
    g2d.setColor(Color.RED);
    final float dash[] = {2, 2};
    g2d.setStroke(new BasicStroke(2, BasicStroke.CAP_BUTT,
            BasicStroke.JOIN_BEVEL, 0, dash, 2));
    g2d.draw(s.getBounds2D());

    // draw ctrl point rect
    g2d.setPaint(Color.BLACK);
    g2d.setStroke(new BasicStroke(1));
    Rectangle2D ctrl1Rect = new Rectangle2D.Double(
            s.getCtrlPt().getX() - 2, s.getCtrlY() - 2, 5, 5);
    g2d.draw(ctrl1Rect);
```

```java
            // draw starting point rect
            Rectangle2D startPtRect = new Rectangle2D.Double(
                    s.getX1() - 2, s.getY1() - 2, 5, 5);
            g2d.setPaint(Color.WHITE);
            g2d.fill(startPtRect);
            g2d.setPaint(Color.BLACK);
            g2d.draw(startPtRect);

            // draw end point rect
            Rectangle2D endPtRect = new Rectangle2D.Double(
                    s.getX2() - 2, s.getY2() - 2, 5, 5);
            g2d.setPaint(Color.WHITE);
            g2d.fill(endPtRect);
            g2d.setPaint(Color.BLACK);
            g2d.draw(endPtRect);

        }

        // reset
        g2d.setTransform(origTransform);

    }

    public static void main(String[] args) {
        final InteractiveShapes c = new InteractiveShapes();
        c.addMouseListener(c);
        c.addMouseMotionListener(c);
        c.setPreferredSize(new Dimension(409, 726));
        SimpleAppLauncher.launch("Chapter 12-8 Interactive Shapes", c);
    }

    @Override
    public void mouseClicked(MouseEvent e) {
    }

    @Override
    public void mousePressed(MouseEvent e) {

        boolean anySelected = false;

        if (selectedShape) {
            // is control point position handle selected?
            Rectangle2D ctrl1Rect = new Rectangle2D.Double(
                    s.getCtrlX() - 2, s.getCtrlY() - 2, 5, 5);
            if (ctrl1Rect.contains(e.getPoint())) {
                moveType = CNTRL_PT;
                repaint();
                return;
            }

            // is start point position handle selected?
```

```
            Rectangle2D startRect = new Rectangle2D.Double(
                    s.getX1() - 2, s.getY1() - 2, 5, 5);
            if (startRect.contains(e.getPoint())) {
                moveType = START_PT;
                repaint();
                return;
            }

            // is end point position handle selected?
            Rectangle2D endRect = new Rectangle2D.Double(
                    s.getX2() - 2,
                    s.getY2() - 2, 5, 5);
            if (endRect.contains(e.getPoint())) {
                moveType = END_PT;
                repaint();
                return;
            }

            // is mouse inside shape
            if (s.contains(e.getPoint())) {
                moveType = MOVE_RECT;
                anchorPt = (Point2D) e.getPoint().clone();
                repaint();
                return;
            }
        }

        // select shape
        if (s.contains(e.getPoint()) && !selectedShape) {
            selectedShape = true;
            anySelected = true;
        }

        if (!anySelected) {
            selectedShape = false;
        }

        repaint();
    }

    @Override
    public void mouseReleased(final MouseEvent e) {
        moveType = -1;
        if (anchorPt != null) {
            double dx = e.getPoint().getX() - anchorPt.getX();
            double dy = e.getPoint().getY() - anchorPt.getY();

            // update all points in shape
            s.setCurve(s.getX1() + dx,
                    s.getY1() + dy,
                    s.getCtrlX() + dx,
                    s.getCtrlY() + dy,
```

```
                        s.getX2() + dx,
                        s.getY2() + dy);

            // reset for subsequent drag operation
            anchorPt = null;
            translatePt = null;
        }
        repaint();
}

@Override
public void mouseEntered(MouseEvent e) {
}

@Override
public void mouseExited(MouseEvent e) {
}

@Override
public void mouseDragged(MouseEvent e) {
    if (selectedShape) {
        switch (moveType) {
            case START_PT:
                s.setCurve(e.getPoint(), s.getCtrlPt(), s.getP2());
                break;
            case CNTRL_PT:
                s.setCurve(s.getP1(), e.getPoint(), s.getP2());
                break;
            case END_PT:
                s.setCurve(s.getP1(), s.getCtrlPt(), e.getPoint());
                break;
            case MOVE_RECT:
                translatePt = e.getPoint();
                break;
        }
    }

    repaint();
}

@Override
public void mouseMoved(MouseEvent e) {
    // move over shape
    if (s.contains(e.getPoint()) && !hoveredShape) {
        hoveredShape = true;
    }

    // move away from shape
    if (!s.contains(e.getPoint()) && hoveredShape) {
        hoveredShape = false;
    }
    repaint();
```

```
        }
}
```

Figure 12-13 depicts the application interacting with a cubic curve shape.

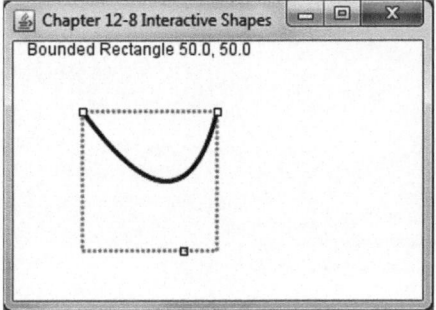

Figure 12-13. Interactive shape

How It Works

This recipe involves using your mouse pointer to interact with a shape on the graphics surface. Let's start with some instructions on how to interact with the shape being displayed. Before explaining the commands of the application, I'll give a quick description of the positioning handles for the QuadCurve2D shown in Figure 12-14.

Positioning Handles

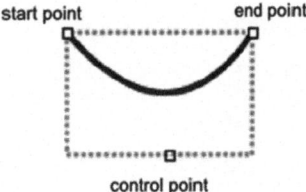

Figure 12-14. Positioning handles

Here are the commands to interact with a quadratic curve shape:

- **Hover:** Move the mouse pointer over the shape to create a gray dotted bounding box region around the shape

- **Select shape:** Click the mouse button to select the shape. This creates a red dotted bounding box region around the shape with positioning handles on the starting, ending, and control points (QuadCurve2D attributes).

- **Move shape:** Press the mouse button inside the shape's region while dragging the shape across the screen.

- **Change starting point:** While the shape is selected with a mouse press, hold and drag the positioning handle (situated at the start of the curve) to stretch or squeeze the curve's length.

- **Change ending point:** While the shape is selected with a mouse press, hold and drag the positioning handle (situated at the end of the curve) to stretch or squeeze the curve's length.

- **Change control point:** While the shape is selected with a mouse press, hold and drag the positioning handle (control point) of a quadratic curve (bottom center).

Our class begins by implementing both the MouseListener and MouseMotionListener interfaces. The MouseListener interface contains methods that are responsible for mouse events such as pressing, releasing, clicking, entering, and exiting a component. In our case, the whole graphics surface is a component (JComponent), and you are only focusing on the mousePressed() and mouseReleased() methods. The rest of the methods are empty or no-op. You also are implementing the MouseMotionListener interface, in which methods are responsible for catching mouse events such as dragging and moving. The mouseDragged() and mouseMoved() methods are implemented, respectively.

The mousePressed() method basically determines when the shape is selected and what positioning handle was selected before a drag operation is performed. The mouseReleased() method is responsible for when the user releases the mouse after a drag operation. Also, it will reset the transform on the shape for subsequent mouse events.

Next, when implementing the MouseMotionListener interface, the mouseDragged() method is responsible for moving the whole shape or repositioning the positioning handles. The mouseMoved() method is basically responsible for bringing focus to the shape by creating a gray dotted bounding box region. When moving away from the shape, the gray box disappears.

In the class InteractiveShapes there are instance variables that maintain the state of the user's actions and the shape's information while being modified. Table 12-3 lists the instance variables used in this recipe to maintain the state of the shape to be manipulated:

Table 12-3. Instance Variables

Variable	Data Type	Example	Description
selectedShape	boolean	true, false	True means a shape is selected, otherwise false.
hoveredShape	boolean	True, false	True denotes that a user is hovering over a shape.
s	QuadCurve2D		The actual shape.
translatePt	Point2D		The (x, y) coordinate of the translate transform of the shape when being moved by the mouse.
anchorPt	Point2D		The (x, y) coordinate of mouse press before a mouse drag operation.
moveTranslate	AffineTransform		The actual transform to be applied

			before rendering the shape.
moveType	int	START_PT, CNTRL_PT, END_PT, MOVE_RECT	Keeps track of the dragging action the user is currently performing. Are they dragging the start point, control point, or end point; or moving the bounding rectangle?

The key to this recipe is to understand the order or workflow of events occurring before the shape is actually rendered. When a user uses the mouse, the various methods are being invoked by listening to mouse events. The methods that handle these mouse events will update state information (instance variables) and call the component's repaint() method. This will call the paintComponent() method to render the shape on the graphics surface.

12-9. Changing Text Font

Problem

You want to change the default text font to be used to draw on the graphics surface.

Solution

Before drawing text, set the graphics context to a new font style by using the java.awt.Font class and the Graphics object's setFont() method.

The code recipe here prints the book's title in four different font styles, including a drop shadow effect:

```
package org.java7recipes.chapter12.recipe12_09;

import java.awt.*;
import javax.swing.JComponent;
import org.java7recipes.chapter12.SimpleAppLauncher;

/**
 * Changing the text font.
 *
 * @author cdea
 */
public class ChangeTextFont extends JComponent {

    @Override
    protected void paintComponent(Graphics g) {
        super.paintComponent(g);

        Graphics2D g2d = (Graphics2D) g;
        g2d.setBackground(Color.WHITE);
        g2d.clearRect(0, 0, getParent().getWidth(), getParent().getHeight());
        // antialising
```

```
        g2d.setRenderingHint(RenderingHints.KEY_ANTIALIASING,
RenderingHints.VALUE_ANTIALIAS_ON);


        // Serif with drop shadow
        Font serif = new Font("Serif", Font.PLAIN, 30);
        g2d.setFont(serif);
        g2d.setPaint(new Color(50,50,50,150));
        g2d.drawString("Java 7 Recipes", 52, 52);
        // paint red
        g2d.setPaint(Color.RED);
        g2d.drawString("Java 7 Recipes", 50, 50);


        // SanSerif
        g2d.setPaint(Color.BLUE);
        Font sanSerif = new Font("SanSerif", Font.PLAIN, 30);
        g2d.setFont(sanSerif);
        g2d.drawString("Java 7 Recipes", 50, 100);

        // Dialog
        g2d.setPaint(Color.GREEN);
        Font dialog = new Font("Dialog", Font.PLAIN, 30);
        g2d.setFont(dialog);
        g2d.drawString("Java 7 Recipes", 50, 150);

        // Monospaced
        g2d.setPaint(Color.BLACK);
        Font monospaced = new Font("Monospaced", Font.PLAIN, 30);
        g2d.setFont(monospaced);
        g2d.drawString("Java 7 Recipes", 50, 200);

    }

    public static void main(String[] args) {
        final ChangeTextFont c = new ChangeTextFont();
        c.setPreferredSize(new Dimension(330, 217));
        SimpleAppLauncher.launch("Chapter 12-9 Changing Text Font", c);
    }
}
```

Figure 12-15 displays the book title in four font styles with varying colors.

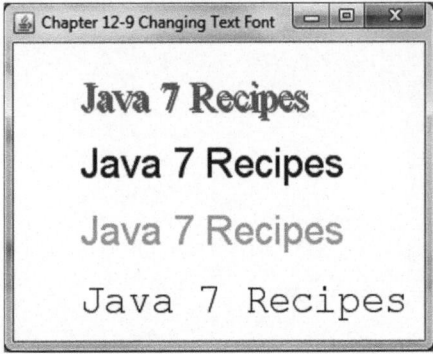

Figure 12-15. Changing text font

How It Works

The recipe begins by clearing the background to white and turning antialiasing on. The first text string rendered is the title of the book, Java 7 Recipes, in red with a drop shadow. Actually, this is a trick. What's really happening are two calls to the `drawstring()` method, which first draws the text lettering in gray and then applies the red lettering on top. When drawing the drop shadow, you will create a gray, semitransparent, 30-point, plain serif font. Next, you will use the same font style in the color red and invoke the `drawstring()` method. Positioning the text string just 2 pixels diagonally to the upper left gives the appearance of a drop shadow adding depth to the text. Shown here is how you will set the font with a Serif font:

```
// Serif with drop shadow
Font serif = new Font("Serif", Font.PLAIN, 30);
g2d.setFont(serif);
```

The rest of the text font renderings are the same as the previous code snippet. I trust you get the idea!

12-10. Adding Attributes to Text

Problem

You want to add different attributes to text. For example, you want to set the color on an individual or a range of characters. Some of the types of attributes are color, bold, italic, strikethrough, and font style.

Solution

Combining the `java.text.AttributedString` and `java.awt.font.TextAttribute` classes enables you to set attributes on text. Following is a code example to specify various attributes onto your text to be displayed on the graphics surface:

```java
package org.java7recipes.chapter12.recipe12_10;

import java.awt.*;
import java.awt.font.*;
import java.text.AttributedString;
import javax.swing.JComponent;
import org.java7recipes.chapter12.SimpleAppLauncher;

/**
 * Adding Attributes to Text.
 *
 * @author cdea
 */
public class AddingAttributesToText extends JComponent {


    @Override
    protected void paintComponent(Graphics g) {
        super.paintComponent(g);

        Graphics2D g2d = (Graphics2D) g;
        g2d.setBackground(Color.WHITE);
        g2d.clearRect(0, 0, getParent().getWidth(), getParent().getHeight());
        // antialising
        g2d.setRenderingHint(RenderingHints.KEY_ANTIALIASING,
RenderingHints.VALUE_ANTIALIAS_ON);

        AttributedString attrStr = new AttributedString("Java7Recipes");

        // Serif, plain 'Java'
        Font serif = new Font(Font.SERIF, Font.PLAIN, 50);
        attrStr.addAttribute(TextAttribute.FONT, serif, 0, 4);

        // Underline 'Java'
        attrStr.addAttribute(TextAttribute.UNDERLINE, TextAttribute.UNDERLINE_ON, 0, 4);

        // Background black for 'Java'
        attrStr.addAttribute(TextAttribute.BACKGROUND, Color.BLACK, 0, 4);

        // SanSerif, Bold, Italic '7' - !|! or will make font bold and italic
        Font sanSerif = new Font(Font.SANS_SERIF, Font.BOLD | Font.ITALIC, 50);
        attrStr.addAttribute(TextAttribute.FONT, sanSerif, 4, 5);

        // Make a rainbow colors on 'Java7Re'
        // Roy G. Biv (red, orange, yellow, green, blue, indigo, violet)
        Paint[] rainbow = new Color[] {Color.RED, Color.ORANGE, Color.YELLOW,
            Color.GREEN,
            Color.BLUE, new Color(75, 0, 130), new Color(127, 0, 255)
        };

        for (int i=0; i<rainbow.length; i++) {
```

365

```
                attrStr.addAttribute(TextAttribute.FOREGROUND, rainbow[i], i, i+1);
        }

        // MonoSpaced, Bold 'Recipes'
        Font monoSpaced = new Font(Font.MONOSPACED, Font.BOLD, 50);
        attrStr.addAttribute(TextAttribute.FONT, monoSpaced, 5, 12);

        // Strike through 'Recipes'
        attrStr.addAttribute(TextAttribute.STRIKETHROUGH, Boolean.TRUE, 5, 12);
        g2d.drawString(attrStr.getIterator(), 50, 100);

    }

    public static void main(String[] args) {
        final AddingAttributesToText c = new AddingAttributesToText();
        c.setPreferredSize(new Dimension(410, 148));
        SimpleAppLauncher.launch("Chapter 12-10 Adding Attributes To Text", c);
    }
}
```

Figure 12-16 shows various attribute types applied to the text.

Figure 12-16. Adding attributes to text

How It Works

I was trying to be creative by adding different attributes to different parts of the title of the book "Java 7 Recipes." Here is a rundown of the requirements:

- 'Java' should be a 50-point, plain, serif font.

- 'Java' should be underlined.

- 'Java' background should be black.

- '7' should be a 50-point, italic, sans serif font.

- 'Java7Re' should be a rainbow.

- 'Recipes' should be a 50-point, bold, monospace font.

- • 'Recipes' should be strikethrough (crossed out).

The first thing you do is to instantiate an instance of the `AttributedString` with the text you want to add attributes to. `AttributedString` instance:

```
AttributedString attrStr = new AttributedString("Java7Recipes");
```

Second, start adding attributes using the `addAttribute()` method:

```
addAttribute(AttributedCharacterIterator.Attribute attribute, Object value, int
beginIndex, int endIndex)
```

The attribute parameter is an instance of an `AttributedCharacterIterator.Attribute`, and in our example you are using `TextAttribute` instances, which are subclasses of `AttributedCharacterIterator.Attribute` class. `TextAttribute` has many attribute types that can be applied to text. To see all the available options and values, refer to the Javadoc on `java.awt.font.TextAttribute`. Shown here is an example of adding strikethough to the text string 'Recipes' with a start index of 5 and an end index of 12:

```
// Strike through 'Recipes'
attrStr.addAttribute(TextAttribute.STRIKETHROUGH, Boolean.TRUE, 5, 12);
g2d.drawString(attrStr.getIterator(), 50, 100);
```

12-11. Measuring Text

Problem

You want to align text to display left-, center-, or right-justified on the display area like a word processor would shift a sentence.

Solution

Create an application that will demonstrate text drawn to be positioned left-, center-, or right-justified. Also allow the user to select menu options to justify the lines of text. You will be using the `java.awt.FontMetrics` and `java.awt.font.FontRenderContext` classes to determine the width and height of text to dynamically display it on the canvas.

Shown here is the code recipe that creates an application that will allow the user to choose left, center, or right justification of the current text on the graphics surface. Currently, there are two lines of text being displayed that contain the phrases "The quick brown fox jumped" and "over the lazy dog." When the user has selected the menu option "left," the two phrases will be aligned to the left margin of the display area. When selecting the "right" menu option, the two phrases will be aligned to the right margin. The center menu option when selected will align the text phrases between the left and right margins.

```
package org.java7recipes.chapter12.recipe12_11;

import java.awt.*;
```

```java
import java.awt.event.ActionEvent;
import java.awt.font.FontRenderContext;
import java.awt.geom.Rectangle2D;
import javax.swing.*;
import org.java7recipes.chapter12.AppSetup;
import org.java7recipes.chapter12.SimpleAppLauncher;

/**
 * Measuring Text.
 *
 * @author cdea
 */
public class MeasuringText extends JComponent implements AppSetup {
    public static final String LEFT = "left";
    public static final String CENTER = "center";
    public static final String RIGHT = "right";

    private String justifyText = "left";

    public String getJustification() {
        return justifyText;
    }

    public void setJustification(String justify) {
        justifyText = justify.toLowerCase();
    }

    @Override
    protected void paintComponent(Graphics g) {
        super.paintComponent(g);

        Graphics2D g2d = (Graphics2D) g;
        g2d.setBackground(Color.WHITE);
        g2d.clearRect(0, 0, getParent().getWidth(), getParent().getHeight());
        // antialising
        g2d.setRenderingHint(RenderingHints.KEY_ANTIALIASING,
                RenderingHints.VALUE_ANTIALIAS_ON);


        // SanSerif
        g2d.setPaint(Color.BLUE);
        Font serif = new Font(Font.SERIF, Font.PLAIN, 30);
        g2d.setFont(serif);

        String sentence1 = "The quick brown fox jumped";
        String sentence2 = "over the lazy dog.";

        FontRenderContext fontRenderCtx = g2d.getFontRenderContext();
        Rectangle2D bounds1 = serif.getStringBounds(sentence1, fontRenderCtx);
        Rectangle2D bounds2 = serif.getStringBounds(sentence2, fontRenderCtx);

        int y = 50;
```

```java
        int x = 0;
        FontMetrics fm = g2d.getFontMetrics();
        int spaceRow = fm.getDescent() + fm.getLeading() + fm.getAscent();

        String justify = getJustification();
        switch(justify) {
            case CENTER:
                x = (getParent().getWidth() - (int)bounds1.getWidth())/2;
                g2d.drawString(sentence1, x, y);
                x = (getParent().getWidth() - (int)bounds2.getWidth())/2;
                g2d.drawString(sentence2, x, y + spaceRow);
                break;
            case RIGHT:
                x = (getParent().getWidth() - (int) bounds1.getWidth());
                g2d.drawString(sentence1, x, y);
                x = (getParent().getWidth() - (int) bounds2.getWidth());
                g2d.drawString(sentence2, x, y + spaceRow);
                break;
            case LEFT:
            default:
                g2d.drawString(sentence1, x, y);
                g2d.drawString(sentence2, x, y + spaceRow);
                break;
        }
    }

    @Override
    public void apply(JFrame frame) {

        JMenuBar menuBar = new JMenuBar();
        JMenu menu = new JMenu("Justification");
        menuBar.add(menu);

        JMenuItem leftMenuItem = new JMenuItem("Left");
        menu.add(leftMenuItem);
        leftMenuItem.addActionListener(
                new JustificationAction(leftMenuItem.getText(), this));

        JMenuItem centerMenuItem = new JMenuItem("Center");
        menu.add(centerMenuItem);
        centerMenuItem.addActionListener(
                new JustificationAction(centerMenuItem.getText(), this));

        JMenuItem rightMenuItem = new JMenuItem("Right");
        menu.add(rightMenuItem);
        rightMenuItem.addActionListener(
                new JustificationAction(rightMenuItem.getText(), this));

        frame.setJMenuBar(menuBar);
    }

    public static void main(String[] args) {
```

```
            final MeasuringText c = new MeasuringText();
            c.setPreferredSize(new Dimension(391, 114));
            SimpleAppLauncher.launch("Chapter 12-11 Measuring Text", c);
        }
    }

/**
 * Action to set the justification.
 */
class JustificationAction extends AbstractAction {
    private MeasuringText component;

    public JustificationAction(String command, MeasuringText component) {
        super(command);
        this.component = component;
    }

    @Override
    public void actionPerformed(ActionEvent e) {
        String command = e.getActionCommand().toLowerCase();
        component.setJustification(command);
        component.repaint();
    }
}
```

Figure 12-17 shows the application displaying the text phrases with a center justification.

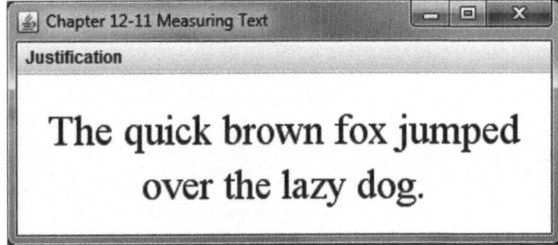

Figure 12-17. Measuring text

How It Works

Before going about creating this recipe example, you will notice the MeasuringText class that implements the AppSetup interface. This interface is co-located with the SimpleAppLauncher class from the very first recipe. The AppSetup interface has only one method: the apply() method. This method is a way for the SimpleAppLauncher class to invoke the apply() method. This allows SimpleAppLauncher to apply changes to the UI. As you saw in the first recipe example in this chapter, the SimpleAppLauncher class is responsible for creating the main application window or, in this case, a new JFrame. In this recipe, you will implement the apply() method to add menus to the main JFrame window. This provides a simple facility to allow (you) the developer to wire up menus and allow the application launcher to launch the window in a threadsafe way. Shown here is the code section used in the `SimpleAppLauncher`'s `displayGUI()` method that calls the `apply()` method:

```
protected static void displayGUI(final String title, final JComponent component) {

    // create window with title
    final JFrame frame = new JFrame(title);
    if (component instanceof AppSetup) {
        AppSetup ms = (AppSetup) component;
        ms.apply(frame);
    }
    ...// the rest of displayGUI
} // end of displayGUI
```

Did you ever wonder how to justify text similar to word processors? Here is an example in which you can left-, center-, and right-justify text on the graphics surface. Before you begin to determine the size or bounding box of text, you must obtain the font that will be used in the rendering of text. Once you have a font instance, you can obtain the `Graphics2D`'s font render context (`java.awt.font.FontRenderContext`). To obtain the font render context:

```
FontRenderContext fontRenderCtx = g2d.getFontRenderContext();
```

Next, with the desired font you will invoke `getStringBounds()`. Here you will pass in the string that will be rendered and `FontRenderContext`, which will return an instance of a `Rectangle2D` representing the bounding box containing the width and height of the text. To obtain the bounding box:

```
Rectangle2D bounds1 = serif.getStringBounds(sentence1, fontRenderCtx);
```

Finally, you can use `FontMetrics` to determine the low-level parts of the font such as ascent, descent, and leading. These parts make up the height measurements of a text font character. The first thing to know about font metrics is where the baseline is located. The *baseline* is an invisible line that the characters will sit on top of (similar to primary school handwriting paper). When using the `drawString()` method, you will specify the x and y, which is where the baseline will begin. The ascent is the distance from the top of the character to the baseline. The descent is the distance of how far parts of a character font will extend below the baseline, such as the lowercase letters *g* or *j*. Last is the leading that is used when characters are positioned beneath another character to provide proper spacing so they won't appear to be touching. The code snippet here determines the space needed for the second row of text:

```
FontMetrics fm = g2d.getFontMetrics();

int spaceRow = fm.getDescent() + fm.getLeading() + fm.getAscent();
```

When the user chooses the justification through the menu selection option, I used the Java 7 nifty string switch statement. Another nice feature from Project Coin, which is new to Java 7. Here, I use simple math to move the x coordinates to position the sentences based on the width of the `JComponent`. The code here uses the `bounds` width to calculate the center justification of text (center justify):

```
x = (getParent().getWidth() - (int)bounds1.getWidth())/2;
g2d.drawString(sentence1, x, y);
x = (getParent().getWidth() - (int)bounds2.getWidth())/2;
g2d.drawString(sentence2, x, y + spaceRow);
```

Next up is how to display large text passages having multiple lines that will word wrap text as the user resizes the window area.

12-12. Display Multiple Lines of Text

Problem

You want to fit large passages of text into your window area. In other words, you want to word wrap the text when the sentence runs beyond the right edge of the window area.

Solution

Create an application that allows the user to view text with the ability to word wrap when the user resizes the window. The main classes used in this recipe are these:

- `AttributedString`

- `AttributedCharacterIterator`

- `LineBreakMeasurer`

Shown here is the code recipe to display a large text passage having the ability to word wrap based on the window's width:

```
package org.java7recipes.chapter12.recipe12_12;

import java.awt.*;
import java.awt.font.*;
import java.text.*;
import javax.swing.JComponent;
import org.java7recipes.chapter12.SimpleAppLauncher;

/**
 * Changing the text font.
 *
 * @author cdea
 */
public class MultipleLinesOfText extends JComponent {

    @Override
    protected void paintComponent(Graphics g) {
        super.paintComponent(g);

        Graphics2D g2d = (Graphics2D) g;
        g2d.setBackground(Color.BLACK);
        g2d.clearRect(0, 0, getParent().getWidth(), getParent().getHeight());
        // antialising
```

```
            g2d.setRenderingHint(RenderingHints.KEY_ANTIALIASING,
                    RenderingHints.VALUE_ANTIALIAS_ON);

            // Serif bold
            Font serif = new Font("Serif", Font.BOLD, 22);
            g2d.setFont(serif);
            g2d.setPaint(Color.WHITE);
String latinText = "parvulus enim natus est nobis filius datus est "
                    + "nobis et factus est principatus super umerum eius et "
                    + "vocabitur nomen eius Admirabilis consiliarius Deus "
                    + "fortis Pater futuri saeculi Princeps pacis";

            AttributedString attrStr = new AttributedString(latinText);
            attrStr.addAttribute(TextAttribute.FONT, serif);
            AttributedCharacterIterator attrCharIter = attrStr.getIterator();
            FontRenderContext fontRenderCtx = g2d.getFontRenderContext();
            LineBreakMeasurer lineBreakMeasurer =
new LineBreakMeasurer(attrCharIter, fontRenderCtx);
            float wrapWidth = getParent().getWidth();
            float x = 0;
            float y = 0;
            while (lineBreakMeasurer.getPosition() < attrCharIter.getEndIndex()) {
                TextLayout textLayout = lineBreakMeasurer.nextLayout(wrapWidth);
                y += textLayout.getAscent();
                textLayout.draw(g2d, x, y);
                y += textLayout.getDescent() + textLayout.getLeading();
            }
        }
    }

    public static void main(String[] args) {
        final MultipleLinesOfText c = new MultipleLinesOfText();
        c.setPreferredSize(new Dimension(330, 217));
        SimpleAppLauncher.launch("Chapter 12-12 Multiple Lines of Text", c);
    }
}
```

Figure 12-18 depicts an application containing a large text passage wrapping words based on the width of the window.

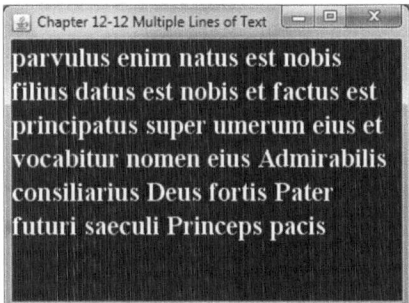

Figure 12-18. Multiple lines of text

How It Works

Most word processors and even simple editors have a word wrap feature. Long text strings go beyond the width of the window and move to the next line as if someone were hitting the carriage return key. To perform this behavior, you will first obtain the font to be added as an attribute to the text by using the `AttributedString` class. The following code snippet adds the serif font style as an attribute on the attributed text (`AttributedString`):

```
Font serif = new Font("Serif", Font.BOLD, 22);
AttributedString attrStr = new AttributedString(latinText);
attrStr.addAttribute(TextAttribute.FONT, serif);
```

Next, you will see the magic of the `LineBreakerMeasurer` class, in which it determines each character's position and text layout. From an `AttributedString` you will obtain an iterator (`AttributedCharacterIterator`) to be passed in along with the `FontRenderContext` object in order for you to create an instance of a `LineBreakMeasurer` object. An instance of a `LineBreakMeasurer`:

```
AttributedCharacterIterator attrCharIter = attrStr.getIterator();
FontRenderContext fontRenderCtx = g2d.getFontRenderContext();
LineBreakMeasurer lineBreakMeasurer = new LineBreakMeasurer(attrCharIter,
fontRenderCtx);
```

By determining the width of the `JComponent` or visible graphics surface area, you can then use that width to help determine where to perform a line break. In this case, it is a matter of moving the text down the y-axis according to the ascent and leading height. The following code iterates through each text layout, based on a wrap width and height calculation to determine its y-coordinate to position words to the next line:

```
while (lineBreakMeasurer.getPosition() < attrCharIter.getEndIndex()) {
    TextLayout textLayout = lineBreakMeasurer.nextLayout(wrapWidth);
    y += textLayout.getAscent();
    textLayout.draw(g2d, x, y);
    y += textLayout.getDescent() + textLayout.getLeading();
}
```

For more on measuring text, refer to recipe 12-11.

12-13. Adding Shadows to Drawings

Problem

You want to create a drop shadow effect when drawing shapes on the graphics surface.

Solution

Use a simple technique by drawing two congruent shapes on top of one another except one shape is slightly offset relative to the other, and the bottom shape is filled with a dark color that appears as a drop shadow.

The following code recipe is an application that will display a donut shape appearing with a drop shadow effect.

```java
package org.java7recipes.chapter12.recipe12_13;

import java.awt.*;
import java.awt.geom.*;
import java.awt.image.*;
import javax.swing.JComponent;
import org.java7recipes.chapter12.SimpleAppLauncher;

/**
 * Adding Shadows on Shapes
 * @author cdea
 */
public class AddingShadows extends JComponent {

    private void createDropShadow(Graphics g, Shape s) {

        int margin = 10;
        int padding = 5;
        int width = s.getBounds().width + padding + margin;
        int height = s.getBounds().height + padding + margin;
        Graphics2D g2d = (Graphics2D) g;
        GraphicsConfiguration gc = g2d.getDeviceConfiguration();
        BufferedImage srcImg = gc.createCompatibleImage(width, height,
Transparency.TRANSLUCENT);
        BufferedImage destImg = gc.createCompatibleImage(width, height,
Transparency.TRANSLUCENT);
        Graphics2D g2 = srcImg.createGraphics();

        g2.setComposite(AlphaComposite.Clear);
        g2.fillRect(0, 0, width, height);

        g2.setComposite(AlphaComposite.Src);
        g2.setRenderingHint(RenderingHints.KEY_ANTIALIASING,
RenderingHints.VALUE_ANTIALIAS_ON);
        g2.setStroke(new BasicStroke(3.0f));
        g2.setPaint(Color.BLACK);
        g2.translate(-s.getBounds().x, -s.getBounds().y);
        int centerX = (width - s.getBounds().width ) / 2;
        int centerY = (height - s.getBounds().height ) / 2;
        g2.translate(centerX, centerY);

        g2.draw(s);
        float blurValue = 1.0f / 49.0f;
```

```
        float data[] = new float[49];
        for (int i=0; i<49; i++) {
            data[i] = blurValue;
        }

        Kernel kernel = new Kernel(7, 7, data);
        ConvolveOp convolve = new ConvolveOp(kernel, ConvolveOp.EDGE_ZERO_FILL,
null);

        convolve.filter(srcImg, destImg);

        g2.dispose();

        g2d.drawImage(destImg, s.getBounds().y -padding, s.getBounds().x -padding, null);

    }


    @Override
    protected void paintComponent(Graphics g) {
        super.paintComponent(g);

        Graphics2D g2d = (Graphics2D) g;
        g2d.setBackground(Color.WHITE);
        g2d.clearRect(0, 0, getParent().getWidth(), getParent().getHeight());
        g2d.setRenderingHint(RenderingHints.KEY_ANTIALIASING,
RenderingHints.VALUE_ANTIALIAS_ON);

        // set color and thickness of stroke
        g2d.setPaint(Color.BLACK);
        g2d.setStroke(new BasicStroke(2));

        // donut
        //g2d.setStroke(new BasicStroke(2));
        Ellipse2D bigCircle = new Ellipse2D.Float(50, 50, 100, 75);
        Ellipse2D smallCircle = new Ellipse2D.Float(80, 75, 35, 25);
        Area donut = new Area(bigCircle);
        Area donutHole = new Area(smallCircle);
        donut.subtract(donutHole);

        // draw drop shadow
        createDropShadow(g2d, donut);

        // draw orange donut
        g2d.setPaint(Color.ORANGE);
        g2d.fill(donut);

        // outline the donut
        g2d.setPaint(Color.BLACK);
        g2d.draw(donut);
    }
```

```
public static void main(String[] args) {
    final AddingShadows c = new AddingShadows();
    c.setPreferredSize(new Dimension(334, 174));
    SimpleAppLauncher.launch("Chapter 12-13 Adding Shadows", c);
}
}
```

Figure 12-19 displays a donut shape with an applied drop shadow effect.

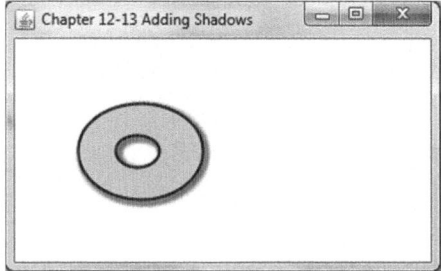

Figure 12-19. Adding shadows

How It Works

Amazingly, there are numerous ways to produce the drop shadow effect on shapes and images when rendering things on the canvas. To simply create a drop shadow effect, draw the shape a little offset with the color black. Then draw the shape again with a different color over the top of the previous shape (black shadow). Repeating the last strategy using gradient paint instead of black provides another simple way to produce a shadow. (The gradient drop shadow technique was used in recipe 12-7.) Of course, you'll notice that this tasty donut looks vaguely familiar because it's the same shape also used in recipe 12-7. Interestingly enough, I went the extra mile and decided to use yet another strategy to produce a cool-looking drop shadow effect. You will be using the ConvolveOp class to blur pixels, which gives the shadow a misty appearance.

When using the ConvolveOp class, you will need to create a source and a resultant (destination) image. You can think of the ConvolveOp as a filter that takes the source image as input and converts the pixels onto the resultant image. The following code creates a source and destination image for you to perform the convolve operation:

```
Graphics2D g2d = (Graphics2D) g;
GraphicsConfiguration gc = g2d.getDeviceConfiguration();
BufferedImage srcImg = gc.createCompatibleImage(width, height,
Transparency.TRANSLUCENT);
BufferedImage destImg = gc.createCompatibleImage(width, height,
Transparency.TRANSLUCENT);
```

To blur an image using the Java2D API, you will need to use a Kernel class, which represents a matrix consisting of values that are used to affect a destination pixel color value. You will first create a 7x7 matrix with each value set to 1/49. For less blur, use a smaller matrix. The total matrix value will determine the destination pixel value. When adding all values of this matrix together, the total matrix value equals 1. In order to blur an image, the total matrix value must equal 1. Shown here is the code used to create a 7x7 matrix or kernel to blur an image:

```
    float blurValue = 1.0f / 49.0f;
    float data[] = new float[49];
    for (int i=0; i<49; i++) {
        data[i] = blurValue;
    }
Kernel kernel = new Kernel(7, 7, data);
```

Once you create an instance of a ConvolveOp, you can perform the filter() method that makes the mysterious shadowy donut. The following code creates an instance of a ConvolveOp used to apply a blur filter:

```
ConvolveOp convolve = new ConvolveOp(kernel, ConvolveOp.EDGE_ZERO_FILL,null);
convolve.filter(srcImg, destImg);
```

To know many more filter operations, see the Javadoc on ConvolveOp.

12-14. Printing Documents

Problem

You want to print the graphics surface onto a printer.

Solution

Create an application allowing the user to print the graphic surface using the following classes:

- java.awt.print.PrinterJob
- java.awt.print.Printable

The code recipe here generates an application similar to recipe 12-9 that displays the book title with varied font styles. Although it is quite similar, this recipe will allow the user to print the graphics surface.

```
package org.java7recipes.chapter12.recipe12_14;

import java.awt.*;
import java.awt.event.*;
import java.awt.print.*;
import javax.swing.*;
import org.java7recipes.chapter12.AppSetup;
import org.java7recipes.chapter12.SimpleAppLauncher;

/**
 * Printing Documents.
 *
```

```java
 * @author cdea
 */
public class PrintingDocuments extends JComponent implements AppSetup, Printable {

    @Override
    protected void paintComponent(Graphics g) {
        super.paintComponent(g);
        draw(g);
}
}

    private void draw(Graphics g) {
        Graphics2D g2d = (Graphics2D) g;
        g2d.setBackground(Color.WHITE);
        g2d.clearRect(0, 0, getParent().getWidth(), getParent().getHeight());

        // antialising
        g2d.setRenderingHint(RenderingHints.KEY_ANTIALIASING,
RenderingHints.VALUE_ANTIALIAS_ON);

        // Serif with drop shadow
        Font serif = new Font("Serif", Font.PLAIN, 30);
        g2d.setFont(serif);
        g2d.setPaint(new Color(50, 50, 50, 150));
        g2d.drawString("Java 7 Recipes", 52, 52);
        // paint red
        g2d.setPaint(Color.RED);
        g2d.drawString("Java 7 Recipes", 50, 50);


        // SanSerif
        g2d.setPaint(Color.BLUE);
        Font sanSerif = new Font("SanSerif", Font.PLAIN, 30);
        g2d.setFont(sanSerif);
        g2d.drawString("Java 7 Recipes", 50, 100);

        // Dialog
        g2d.setPaint(Color.GREEN);
        Font dialog = new Font("Dialog", Font.PLAIN, 30);
        g2d.setFont(dialog);
        g2d.drawString("Java 7 Recipes", 50, 150);

        // Monospaced
        g2d.setPaint(Color.BLACK);
        Font monospaced = new Font("Monospaced", Font.PLAIN, 30);
        g2d.setFont(monospaced);
        g2d.drawString("Java 7 Recipes", 50, 200);
    }

    @Override
    public int print(Graphics g, PageFormat pgFormat, int page) throws
            PrinterException {
```

```java
        if (page > 0) {
            return Printable.NO_SUCH_PAGE;
        }

        Graphics2D g2d = (Graphics2D) g;

        g2d.translate(pgFormat.getImageableX(), pgFormat.getImageableY());

        draw(g2d);

        return Printable.PAGE_EXISTS;
    }

    public void apply(JFrame frame) {
        JMenuBar menuBar = new JMenuBar();
        JMenu menu = new JMenu("File");
        JMenuItem printMenuItem = new JMenuItem("Print...");
        final Printable printSurface = this;
        printMenuItem.addActionListener(new ActionListener() {
            @Override
            public void actionPerformed(ActionEvent e) {
                PrinterJob job = PrinterJob.getPrinterJob();
                job.setPrintable(printSurface);
                boolean ok = job.printDialog();
                if (ok) {
                 try {
                      job.print();
                 } catch (PrinterException ex) {
                     ex.printStackTrace();
                 }
                }
            }
        });
        menu.add(printMenuItem);
        menuBar.add(menu);
        frame.setJMenuBar(menuBar);
    }
    public static void main(String[] args) {
        final PrintingDocuments c = new PrintingDocuments();
        c.setPreferredSize(new Dimension(330, 217));
        SimpleAppLauncher.launch("Chapter 12-10 Printing Documents", c);
    }
}
```

Figure 12-20 shows the Print dialog box that is launched after the user selects Print.

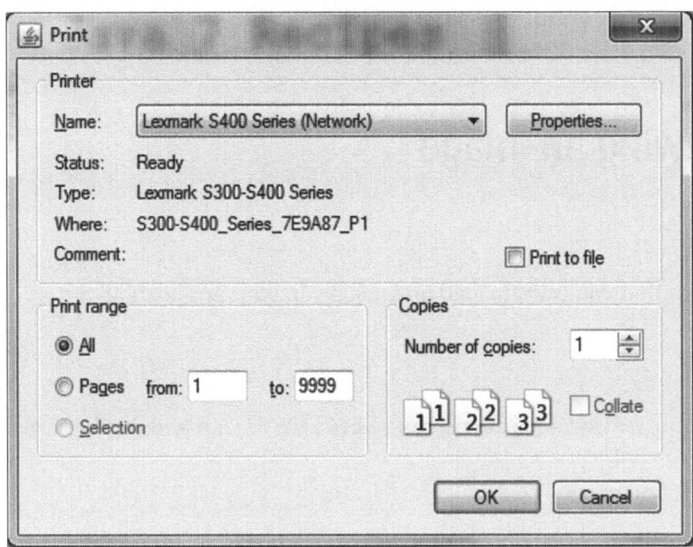

Figure 12-20. Print dialog box

How It Works

While this chapter goes into great detail about drawing onto the 2D surface, wouldn't it be nice to actually send your drawings to the printer? In the Java 2D API (as discussed in recipe 12-1), the device surface is a screen. However, in this recipe, the device space will be your printer.

Let's begin with the main application class that implements the (Printable) interface. The (Printable) interface has a method called print(), which is the code that interacts with the PrinterJob object (aka "the printer"). The following code statement is the print() method on the (Printable) interface:

```
public int print(Graphics g, PageFormat pgFormat, int page) throws PrinterException
```

This recipe is a refactored version of recipe 12-9. If you remember, it displays the book title Java 7 Recipes in various font styles. So, what actually got refactored? Well, I moved all the drawing code from the paintComponent() method into another method called draw(). By doing this, the paintComponent()and print() methods can call the draw() method. This allows us to see and print the graphics surface at the same time.

This recipe is assembled using Java Swing API to create menu options for the user to select and print the display. You will notice the apply() method creates a JMenuItem instance with an inner class definition containing an actionPerformed() method. The actionPerformed() method is responsible for presenting the Print dialog box to the user. Shown here is the code snippet to launch the Print dialog box :

```
PrinterJob job = PrinterJob.getPrinterJob();
job.setPrintable(printSurface);
boolean ok = job.printDialog();
```

Once the user clicks OK, the `print()` method is invoked on the `PrinterJob` object. Next, the `Printable` object's `print()` method is called. Finally, walk over to the printer and% voilà!

12-15. Loading and Drawing an Image

Problem

You have digital images on the file system that you want to load and display in your application.

Solution

Create an application that will allow you to provide a file chooser to select a file to load and display. The following are the main classes used in this recipe:

- `javax.swing.SwingWorker`
- `javax.imageio.ImageIO`

The following code listing is an application that loads and displays image from the file system:

```
package org.java7recipes.chapter12.recipe12_15;

import java.awt.*;
import java.awt.event.*;
import java.awt.image.*;
import java.io.*;
import javax.imageio.*;
import javax.swing.*;
import org.java7recipes.chapter12.AppSetup;
import org.java7recipes.chapter12.SimpleAppLauncher;

/**
 * Load and draw image.
 *
 * @author cdea
 */
public class LoadingAnImage extends JComponent implements AppSetup {

    private static BufferedImage image = null;

    @Override
    protected void paintComponent(Graphics g) {
        super.paintComponent(g);

        Graphics2D g2d = (Graphics2D) g;
```

```
            g2d.setBackground(Color.WHITE);
            g2d.clearRect(0, 0, getParent().getWidth(), getParent().getHeight());
            if (image != null) {
                g2d.drawImage(image, 0, 0, image.getWidth(), image.getHeight(), null);
            }
        }

    @Override
    public void apply(JFrame frame) {
        JMenuBar menuBar = new JMenuBar();
        JMenu menu = new JMenu("File");
        JMenuItem printMenuItem = new JMenuItem("Load Image...");

        printMenuItem.addActionListener(new ActionListener() {
            @Override
            public void actionPerformed(ActionEvent e) {
                final FileDialog loadImageDlg = new FileDialog((JFrame) null);
                loadImageDlg.setVisible(true);
                if (loadImageDlg.getFile() != null) {
                    SwingWorker<BufferedImage, Void> worker = new SwingWorker<>() {
                        @Override
                        protected BufferedImage doInBackground() throws Exception {
                            try {
                                File imageFile = new File(loadImageDlg.getDirectory() +
File.separator + loadImageDlg.getFile());
                                image = ImageIO.read(imageFile);
                            } catch (IOException e1) {
                                e1.printStackTrace();
                            }
                            return image;
                        }

                        @Override
                        protected void done() {
                            try {
                                image = get();
                            } catch (Exception ex) {
                                ex.printStackTrace();
                            }
                            repaint();
                        }
                    };
                    worker.execute();
                }
            }
        });
        menu.add(printMenuItem);
        menuBar.add(menu);
        frame.setJMenuBar(menuBar);
    }
```

```
    public static void main(String[] args) {
        final LoadingAnImage c = new LoadingAnImage();
        c.setPreferredSize(new Dimension(374, 415));
        SimpleAppLauncher.launch("Chapter 12-15 Loading Image", c);
    }
}
```

Figure 12-21 depicts an open dialog box to load an image file.

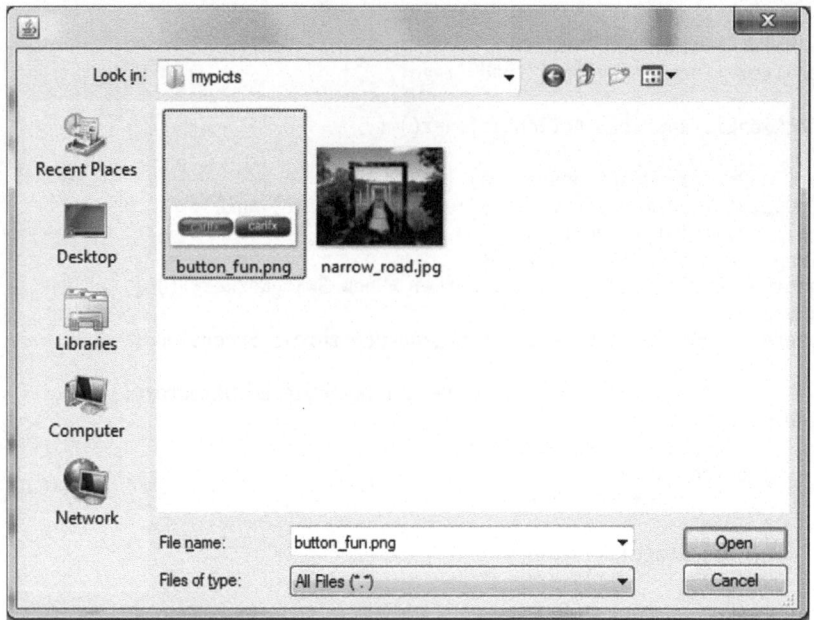

Figure 12-21. Open dialog box

Figure 12-22 displays the image after it was loaded.

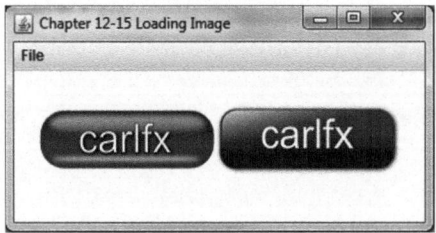

Figure 12-22. Loading image

How It Works

Every time you see an advertisement on a new camera being sold you seem to immediately pay attention to the number of megapixels or the other cool features. Of course, you know that the higher the megapixels the better the image quality. With the increase in the number of megapixels, viewing and loading images can often make applications appear quite sluggish. When developing Swing GUI applications, it is imperative to understand how to effectively interact with its event dispatching thread (EDT). The EDT is responsible for rendering graphics. Things such as disk I/O should not be included in the same transaction (method call). The key is to delegate work to another thread (worker thread). Because the EDT is single threaded, it is important to offload work onto a separate thread so it doesn't block. When blocking occurs, the application will freeze the GUI window, and users will become upset. Because of this common scenario, the guys and gals on the Java client/UI team have included a SwingWorker class in Java 6 that provides the callback behavior that you are looking for. The following code lines are two ways to instantiate the SwingWorker class:

```
SwingWorker<T, V> worker = new SwingWorker<>()

SwingWorker<BufferedImage, Void>imageLoadWorker = new SwingWorker<>();
```

The SwingWorker class uses generics to enable the user of the API to specify types of result objects returned during and after the worker thread task is completed. When instantiating an instance of a SwingWorker, the T (Type) is the result object after the doInBackground() method has been called. Once the doInBackground() method is complete, it returns the image object and hands off the control to the done() method (on the EDT). While inside the done() method you will encounter the get() method that returns the image object from the doInBackground() method (non-EDT).

The SwingWorker's V (Value) is an intermediate object that is updated and used by publish() and process() methods. The V is used often when displaying progress indicators. In our example, you only care about the loaded image, and V is declared Void. You'll also notice a shortcut notation whenever you are instantiating objects with generics by using the less-than and greater-than symbol: <>. To cut down on verbosity, new to Java 7 is what is known as the *diamond operator*. It isn't really an operator; it's a type inference notation for constructors. Either way you look at it, on the productivity side of things there is less to type and your code is a lot easier to read. Another thing to note is when using the diamond notation make sure your IDE has its Source/Binary format set to JDK 7, or else your code won't compile. Shown here is the before and after using the diamond operator notation:

```
SwingWorker<BufferedImage, Void> imageLoadWorker = new SwingWorker<BufferedImage,
Void >();
```

Shown here is applying the diamond operator notation:

```
SwingWorker<BufferedImage, Void> imageLoadWorker = new SwingWorker<>();
```

■ **Note** An excellent article on using the SwingWorker class is "Improve Application Performance with SwingWorker in Java SE 6" by John O'Conner, January 2007:

http://java.sun.com/developer/technicalArticles/javase/swingworker

---

Loading an image is pretty simple: you basically invoke the `ImageIO.read()` method by passing in a `File` object representing the image file on the file system. You can also load an image via a URL by using the following code snippet:

```
URL url = new URL(getCodeBase(), "myFamily.png");
BufferedImage image = ImageIO.read(url);
```

Java can currently load `.jpg`, `.gif`, and `.png` image formats. In this example, I used a `FileDialog` class to allow the user to find a picture to load.

Last but not least, drawing an image is very much like drawing a rectangular shape using an (x, y), width, and height. There are many overloaded `drawImage()` methods on the `Graphics` object used to draw images. Here, I've only provided the most common method signature to render an image on the graphics surface. One of the many overloaded `drawImage()` methods you can use is shown here:

```
public abstract boolean drawImage(Image img,
                int x,
                int y,
                int width,
                int height,
                ImageObserver observer)
```

Keep in mind that the underlying `Graphics` object is a `Graphics2D` class that contains even more overloaded `drawImage()` methods. You might want to explore the interesting effects that can be applied to images. To learn more about `Graphics2D`'s `drawImage()` methods, please see the Javadoc for details. Because you aren't monitoring the process of the image loading, I passed in a `null` into the parameter `observer`. When drawing on the graphics surface, you will use the `drawImage()` method as shown here:

```
Graphics2D g2d = (Graphics2D) g;
g2d.drawImage(image, 50, 50, image.getWidth(), image.getHeight(), null);
```

12-16. Altering an Image

Problem

After loading an image, you want to simulate a special effect similar to night vision goggles.

Solution

Alter the image's underlying pixel information by removing the red and blue component of each pixel in the image. When altering an image, you will be using `java.awt.image.BufferedImage`'s methods `getRGB()` and `setRGB()`:

```
package org.java7recipes.chapter12.recipe12_16;

import java.awt.*;
import java.awt.event.*;
import java.awt.image.BufferedImage;
```

```java
import java.io.*;
import javax.imageio.ImageIO;
import javax.swing.*;
import org.java7recipes.chapter12.AppSetup;
import org.java7recipes.chapter12.SimpleAppLauncher;

/**
 * Altering an Image.
 * requires sdk 7
 * @author cdea
 */
public class AlteringAnImage extends JComponent implements AppSetup {
    private static BufferedImage image = null;

    @Override
    protected void paintComponent(Graphics g) {
        super.paintComponent(g);

        Graphics2D g2d = (Graphics2D) g;
        g2d.setBackground(Color.WHITE);
        g2d.clearRect(0, 0, getParent().getWidth(), getParent().getHeight());
        if (image != null) {
            g2d.drawImage(image, 0, 0, image.getWidth(), image.getHeight(), null);
        } // end of if
    } // end of paintComponent()

    public void alterImage(BufferedImage image) {
        int width = image.getWidth(null);
        int height = image.getHeight(null);

        int[] argbData; // Array holding the ARGB data

        // Prepare the ARGB array
        argbData = new int[width * height];

        // Grab the ARGB data
        image.getRGB(0, 0, width, height, argbData, 0, width);


        // Loop through each pixel in the array
        for (int i = 0 ; i < argbData.length ; i++) {
            argbData[i] = (argbData[i] & 0xFF00FF00);
        }

        //  Set the return Bitmap to use this altered ARGB array
        image.setRGB(0, 0, width, height, argbData, 0, width);
    }

    @Override
    public void apply(JFrame frame) {
        JMenuBar menuBar = new JMenuBar();
        JMenu menu = new JMenu("File");
```

```
                JMenuItem loadMenuItem = new JMenuItem("Load Image...");

            loadMenuItem.addActionListener(new ActionListener() {
                @Override
                public void actionPerformed(ActionEvent e) {
                    final FileDialog loadImageDlg = new FileDialog((JFrame) null);
                    loadImageDlg.setVisible(true);
                    if (loadImageDlg.getFile() != null) {
                        SwingWorker<BufferedImage, Void> worker = new SwingWorker<>() {
                            @Override
                            protected BufferedImage doInBackground() throws Exception {
                                try {
                                    File imageFile = new File(loadImageDlg.getDirectory() +
File.separator + loadImageDlg.getFile());
                                    image = ImageIO.read(imageFile);
                                } catch (IOException e1) {
                                    e1.printStackTrace();
                                }
                                alterImage(image);
                                return image;
                            } // end of doInBackground()

                            @Override
                            protected void done() {
                                try {
                                    image = get();
                                } catch (Exception ex) {
                                    ex.printStackTrace();
                                }
                                repaint();
                            } // end of done()
                        }; // end of SwingWorker

                        worker.execute();

                    } // end of if
                } // end of actionPerformed()
            }); // end of addActionListener()
            menu.add(loadMenuItem);
            menuBar.add(menu);
            frame.setJMenuBar(menuBar);

    }
    public static void main(String[] args) {
        final AlteringAnImage c = new AlteringAnImage();
        c.setPreferredSize(new Dimension(374, 415));
        SimpleAppLauncher.launch("Chapter 12-16 Altering an Image", c);
    }
}
```

Figure 12-23 displays a picture altered by removing the red and blue components of image data.

Figure 12-23. Altering an image

How It Works

To make things a little more interesting, I wanted to simulate night vision goggles similar to the ones used by Navy Seal teams. I thought it would be easy to just remove the red and blue components from each colored pixel from the image and leave the green and alpha components alone.

When manipulating an image (`BufferedImage`), you have the opportunity to get color information detailing each pixel. The default `getRGB()` method returns an `int` (integer) value representing the four components(alpha, red, green, and blue) of a pixel. Of course, in Java the data type `int` (integer)is composed of 4 bytes, and in the RGB color space each byte represents a color component making each value with an 8-bit precision. Although the default is an 8-bit precision, you may want to dig deeper into the image data by exploring the Javadoc on details relating to the `java.awt.image.ColorModel` and `java.awt.image.Raster` API.

If you understand the RGB color space, you will be moving right along. (However, if you do not understand it, refer to recipe 12-4.) The first step is to obtain pixel data for examination and to invoke the `setRGB()`method that updates the pixel information, thus altering the image.

Instead of returning a single pixel at a time by using the `getRGB(x, y)` method, I used the overloaded `getRGB()` method that returns an array of `int` (integer) values. The code here shows the `BufferedImage`'s `getRGB()` method that returns an array of `int`s:

```
public int[] getRGB(int startX, int startY, int w, int h, int[] rgbArray, int offset, int
scansize)
```

When calling the getRGB() method to return an array of ints, you can do one of two things. Either you can construct an integer array to be populated or you can pass in a null into the rgbArray parameter. In our example, I created an array of ints to be populated:

```
int[] argbData;
// Prepare the ARGB array
argbData = new int[width * height];

// Grab the ARGB data
image.getRGB(0, 0, width, height, argbData, 0, width);
```

Finally, the pixel data will be manipulated by using the setRGB() method. In a simple for loop, I simply mask each int in the array by making the red and blue components to zero. In other words when you perform a bitwise AND any byte and F Hex (bitwise one) is itself; any byte and 0 (bitwise 0) is 0. Here is the code to create a loop to alter an image's pixel data:

```
// Loop through each pixel in the array
for (int i = 0 ; i < argbData.length ; i++) {
    argbData[i] = (argbData[i] & 0xFF00FF00);
}

//  Set the return Bitmap to use this altered ARGB array
image.setRGB(0, 0, width, height, argbData, 0, width);
```

12-17. Storing an Image

Problem

You want to load an image and save it to your file system as another file name.

Solution

Create an application that will load your image into memory to be later saved as another file name onto your file system. You will use the java.awt.image.BufferedImage class and javax.imageio.ImageIO.write() method to write an image from memory onto the file system.

The code listed here creates an image loader application that has the ability to save an image file to the file system:

```
package org.java7recipes.chapter12.recipe12_17;

import org.java7recipes.chapter12.AppSetup;
import org.java7recipes.chapter12.SimpleAppLauncher;
import java.awt.*;
import java.awt.event.*;
import java.awt.image.BufferedImage;
```

```java
import java.io.*;
import javax.imageio.ImageIO;
import javax.swing.*;

/**
 * Saving an Image.
 *
 * @author cdea
 */
public class SavingAnImage extends JComponent implements AppSetup {

    private static BufferedImage image = null;

    @Override
    protected void paintComponent(Graphics g) {
        super.paintComponent(g);

        Graphics2D g2d = (Graphics2D) g;
        g2d.setBackground(Color.WHITE);
        g2d.clearRect(0, 0, getParent().getWidth(), getParent().getHeight());
        if (image != null) {
            g2d.drawImage(image, 0, 0, image.getWidth(), image.getHeight(), null);
        }
    }

    @Override
    public void apply(final JFrame frame) {
        JMenuBar menuBar = new JMenuBar();
        JMenu menu = new JMenu("File");
        menuBar.add(menu);

        JMenuItem loadMenuItem = new JMenuItem("Load Image...");

        loadMenuItem.addActionListener(new ActionListener() {

            @Override
            public void actionPerformed(ActionEvent e) {
                final FileDialog loadImageDlg = new FileDialog((JFrame) null);
                loadImageDlg.setVisible(true);
                if (loadImageDlg.getFile() != null) {
                    SwingWorker<BufferedImage, Void> worker = new SwingWorker<>() {

                        @Override
                        protected BufferedImage doInBackground() throws Exception {
                            try {
                                File imageFile = new File(loadImageDlg.getDirectory() +
File.separator + loadImageDlg.getFile());
                                image = ImageIO.read(imageFile);
                            } catch (IOException e1) {
                                e1.printStackTrace();
                            }
                            return image;
```

```
                              }

                              @Override
                              protected void done() {
                                  try {
                                      image = get();
                                  } catch (Exception ex) {
                                      ex.printStackTrace();
                                  }
                                  repaint();
                              }
                          };
                          worker.execute();
                      }
                  }
              });
          menu.add(loadMenuItem);

          JMenuItem saveAsMenuItem = new JMenuItem("Save Image As...");
          saveAsMenuItem.addActionListener(new ActionListener() {

              @Override
              public void actionPerformed(ActionEvent e) {
                  final JFileChooser saveImageDlg = new JFileChooser(new
      File(System.getProperty("user.home")));
                  int response = saveImageDlg.showSaveDialog(frame);

                  if (response == JFileChooser.APPROVE_OPTION) {
                      File fileToSaveAs = saveImageDlg.getSelectedFile();
                      String fileName = fileToSaveAs.getName();
                      String fileType = null;
                      if (fileName.indexOf(".") > 0) {
                          fileType =
      fileName.substring(fileName.lastIndexOf(".")).toLowerCase();
                      }
                      if (fileType != null && fileType.length() == 4 && image != null) {
                          try {
                              BufferedImage bi = image; // retrieve image
                              switch(fileType){
                                  case ".jpg":
                                  case ".png":
                                  case ".gif":
                                      ImageIO.write(bi, fileType.substring(1), fileToSaveAs);
                                      break;
                              }
                          } catch (IOException e2) {
                              e2.printStackTrace();
                          }
                      } else {
                          // error
                          JOptionPane.showMessageDialog(frame, "Sorry couldn't save. \nTry
      loading an image and saving with a file name using extension as: .gif .jpg or .png");
```

```
                }
            }
        }
    });
    menu.add(saveAsMenuItem);
    frame.setJMenuBar(menuBar);
}

public static void main(String[] args) {
    final SavingAnImage c = new SavingAnImage();
    c.setPreferredSize(new Dimension(374, 415));
    SimpleAppLauncher.launch("Chapter 12-17 Saving an Image", c);
}
}
```

Figure 12-24 shows the image loader application with an image loaded and displayed onto the screen:

Figure 12-24. Saving an image

Figure 12-25 depicts the Save dialog box that allows the user to save the image to the file system with a specified file name. Notice the file extension is .png, which is one of the supported image file formats.

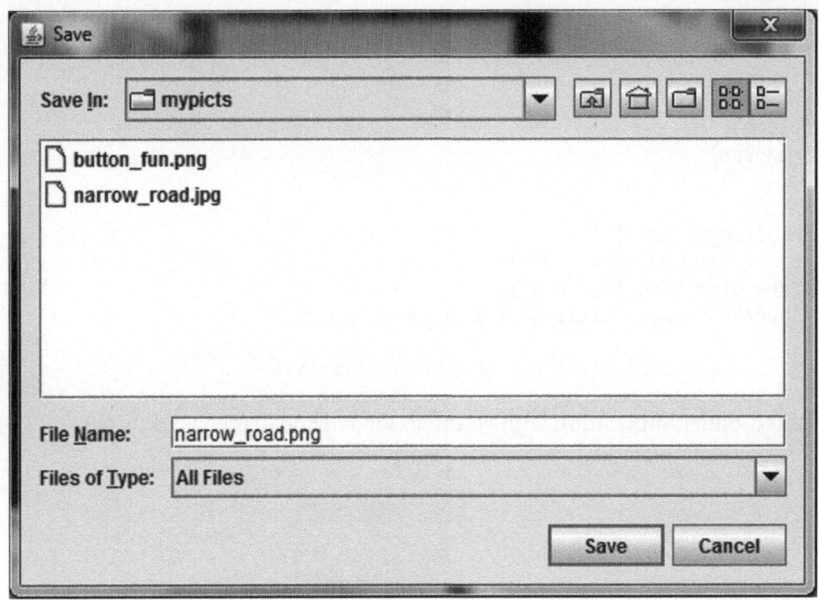

Figure 12-25. Save As dialog box

How It Works

Before we discuss saving an image, I want to remind you that the recipe application requires the user to load an image first. Because loading and drawing an image onto the graphics surface is discussed in earlier recipes, I need not go into those details any further. Once an image is loaded and displayed in the application, the user can select the menu option Save Image As to save the image as a file onto the file system.

The Save dialog box application expects the user to select or type in a file name with a valid graphic format file extension. The valid graphics format file extensions are `.jpg`, `.gif` and `.png`. In this example I am saving the file as a `.png` image file format. The user will receive an alert dialog box if the file name is not valid. Figure 12-26 shows a warning dialog message letting the user know that the file has an invalid file extension:

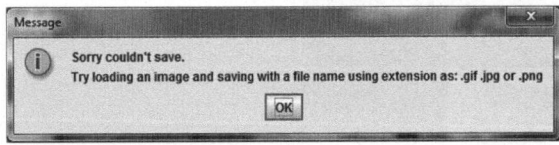

Figure 12-26. Warning message

Assuming that the user has entered a valid file name and clicked the Save button in the Save dialog box, the application will convert and save the image into a valid graphics file format. The

ImageIO.write() method needs to know the type of graphics format to save the image file as. Here is the code used to save a BufferedImage image:

```
BufferedImage bi = !
ImageIO.write(bi, "png", "/home/cdea/myimages/coolpict.png");
```

Notice that the Save Image As dialog code is rather bare where the code performs the ImageIO.write() statement. Why is this such a bad thing? Well, saving an image could take longer than 250 milliseconds making your GUI application appear frozen (while the user clenches his jaw). To fix this problem, surround the code with a SwingWorker class. In order to do this, place the call ImageIO.write() inside of the doBackground() method, thus deferring work off of the EDT. (To see more on SwingWorker, see recipes 12-15 and 14-7.)

CHAPTER 13

Java3D

Writing 3D applications used to be hard because a developer needed to know math, have intimate hardware knowledge, and it that hardware knowledge usually didn't transfer very well across platforms. A typical application would have to be programmed for a specific video card. As time progressed, there were new abstractions that within a platform allowed the use of a common API. This common API then either used the capabilities of the video card or implemented them in software, but it was still OS-dependent (Direct3D for Windows, OpenGL for Windows, and other OSs). Finally with Java3D, you get platform-independence and the choice of rendering technology (works with DirectX or OpenGL). While 3D programming still requires (some) math, at the very least there aren't drivers to worry about. It's more about what you want to create than the hardware details of how to create it.

■**Tip** The source code for this chapter contains an actual game that puts all the chapter's recipes together. If you would like to see the different interactions between recipes, you should take a look at the source of SpaceGame.java.

13-1. Installing Java3D

Problem

You need to install Java3D for use by your application.

Solution

Download Java3D from java.net's web site and install it locally. Java3D currently lives at http://java3d.java.net/. Make sure to choose the right version of Java3D for your target OS because there are Windows, Linux, and Mac distributions, and each has 32- or 64-bit variants. Once installed, add a dependency to your application of the <installed Java3d Path>/lib/ package. Your application should have then access to the Java3D classes and methods.

How it works

After installing the Java3D package, you will have access to the accelerated graphics environment provided by the computer's video card. Java3D uses OpenGL/Directx (depending on the operating system running), and has native libraries for the major operating systems. This is why you need to specify the target operating system when downloading Java3D.

13-2. Creating a Simple 3D Object

Problem

You want to create a Java3D object and display it on the screen.

Solution

Using the Java3D's `Canvas3D` and creating a Scene graph, you can instantiate and display a 3D object onscreen. The following example creates a color cube object, which is a cube with different colors on each side, and displays it onscreen at the default view location (which is looking straight at the cube):

```
private void start() {
    JFrame frame = new JFrame("Space Game");
    GraphicsConfiguration configuration = SimpleUniverse.getPreferredConfiguration();
    final Canvas3D canvas = new Canvas3D(configuration);
    JPanel contentPane = new JPanel(new BorderLayout());
    contentPane.add (canvas);
    frame.setContentPane(contentPane);
    // Set universe Viewing Plate where we want it..
    SimpleUniverse universe = new SimpleUniverse(canvas);
    universe.getViewingPlatform().setNominalViewingTransform();
    View view = canvas.getView();
    view.setBackClipDistance(300f);

    // Our Scene
    BranchGroup scene = createScene();
    universe.addBranchGraph(scene);
    frame.setDefaultCloseOperation(JFrame.EXIT_ON_CLOSE);
    frame.setSize(800,600);
    frame.setVisible(true);
}

private BranchGroup createScene() {
    BranchGroup branchGroup = new BranchGroup();
    branchGroup.addChild(new ColorCube(.3f));
    branchGroup.compile();
    return branchGroup;
}
```

The Canvas3D instance takes care of rendering the application. This is the component that gets added to the JPanel (or other components) and will be a "Window" to the 3D universe created in Java3D.

The SimpleUniverse offers a way of creating a simplified 3D universe; the difference is that it makes certain assumptions like not needing different canvases, and gets sensible defaults for the viewing platform.

The viewing platform is the "eye" positioned within the universe. Only objects that are "in front" and "visible" through the eye are rendered in the canvas. The universe can be very big, and the position (where it is within the universe) and direction (where is it pointing at) determines what do we see in the canvas.

In the example, the viewing platform is located at the origin of the universe (0,0,0), and points toward the depth (-z) space (default). The result is the image in Figure 13-1.

Figure 13-1. Rendering a cube in Java3D

How It Works

Java3D works with trees and nodes. The root node is where a scene starts, and it will include different nodes that represent the objects to be rendered. Each root node will have children nodes that describe transformations on an object. The leaf nodes of the tree will contain actual 3D objects to be rendered. To render an object you add the 3D object to a node and then add the node to the universe. Figure 13-2 illustrates this concept.

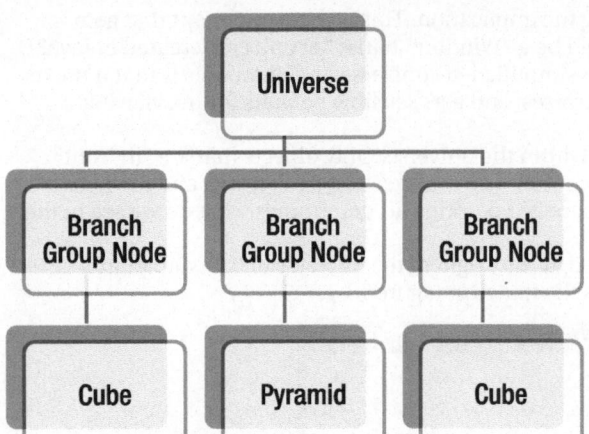

Figure 13-2. Java3D basic universe hierarchy

Within a tree, there are two main types of nodes: branch group nodes and transformation nodes. Transformation nodes are nodes that specify a change for their children. The change can be rotation, translation, and/or scaling. A transformation node can have as children other branch group nodes, other transformation nodes, or the actual 3D objects. Any children of the transformation node will have the transformation (rotation, translation, scaling) applied to all its children as a whole.

Branch group nodes, on the other hand, allow grouping of children nodes and/or 3D objects as a single unit. By adding children to branch group nodes, a branch group node can be manipulated as a single unit. An example would be having a chair composed of different individual 3D objects (six boxes). Each box will be added to a transform group (where the position of each box is specified). After the transform nodes are created, you can add them to a single group node that represents a single "chair." This group node can be rotated as a unit by attaching it to a transformation node. An example of such a hierarchy is presented in Figure 13-3.

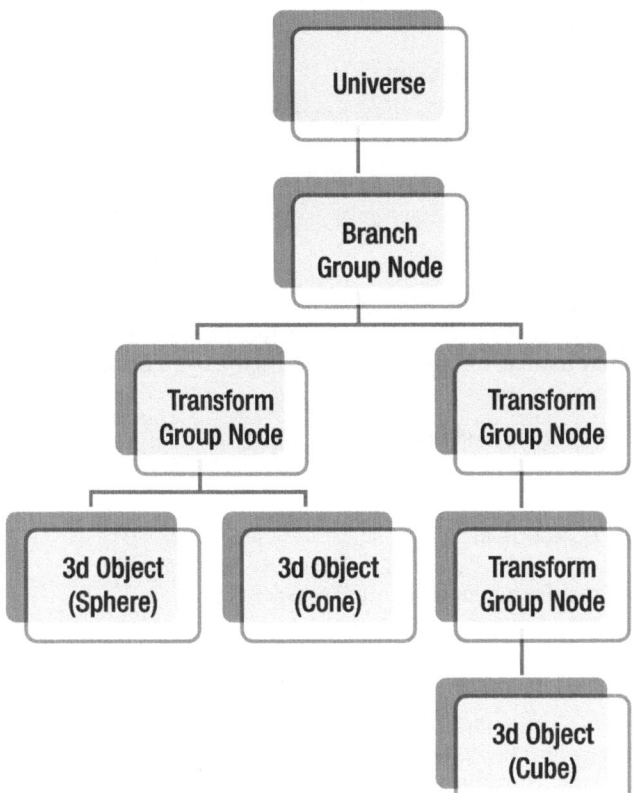

Figure 13-3. Java3D typical universe hierarchy

The easiest way to think of Java3D object is by starting on the "leaves" of the tree (or the actual object that you want to position); then working the way up by making this object a part of a branch group and then adding "transformations" to it. The first one usually will be rotation (which, by default, rotates at the center of the world). Then you make another parent node that does translation; then you add another parent node that makes it part of another group (say part of a chair), and finally you add it to the "top" of the universe. This way you have a complete set of changes you want for each object added to the universe.

■ **Note** Java3D's universe uses a Cartesian coordinate system. Most of the measures are done in meters; even so the universe supports any arbitrary distance unit convention. As long as your objects (and your viewing platform) within the universe agree on their relative scale, the universe will render correctly.

13-3. Transforming Objects

Problem

Now that you have an object rendered in the canvas, you want to place it in a specific place on a specific rotation.

Solution

By creating a TransformGroup object and specifying transformations, you can define how an object looks in the canvas. The following example builds on our red cube from the previous recipe by rotating it so that you view two sides at once:

```
private TransformGroup createAsteroid( double x, double z) {
    // Leaf, the Cube
    ColorCube child = new ColorCube(0.3f);

    Transform3D rotationTransform = new Transform3D();
    rotationTransform.rotY(Math.PI/8);              // pi/8 radians == 22.5 degrees
    TransformGroup rotationGroup = new TransformGroup(rotationTransform);
    rotationGroup.addChild(child);


    // 2nd Transform Group, translates.
    Transform3D locationTransform = new Transform3D();
    locationTransform.setTranslation(new Vector3d(x, 0d, z));
    TransformGroup translateGroup = new TransformGroup(locationTransform);
    translateGroup.setTransform(locationTransform);
    translateGroup.addChild(rotationGroup);


    return translateGroup;
}
```

In this code, the colorCube is created, and then added to a rotationTransform. In the rotationTransform you specify (by creating a Transform3D object) to rotate the cube by 22.5 degrees (pi/8 in radians). Following the first transform group, another transform group is created that translates (moves) the object to the x,z coordinates specified in the function. Note that the location transform adds the rotationTransform as a child. The translation transform is then added to the universe (not shown). Figure 13-4 shows the solution's result.

Figure 13-4. Rendering a rotated and translated cube in Java3D.

How It Works

The transform group node is a node in the universe tree that specifies the transformations that are going to be applied to any children of it. A `TransformGroup` object can have a leaf as a child (like a `colorCube` or a pyramid) or it can have other transform groups/branch groups as children. The transform group changes the object's rotation, scaling, and/or location.

In this recipe's example, you start with the cube (which is a cube that has each face rendered with a different color) and then add it to a transform group that rotates the cube 22.5 degrees (expressed in radians, this translates to pi/8). After rotating, you add another transform group that translates the location of the rotated group. This is a common process when creating and adding objects to a scene. Chaining up transform groups (with branch groups and all) allows for expressing complex behavior with simple building blocks.

Each transform group needs a transform3D object to specify the changes to the children of the transform group. Within 3D development, there is the concept of transformation matrices. These matrices (double-dimensional arrays of numbers) allow you to specify how an object is rotated, translated, and scaled, all at the same time. The transform3D contains a transformation matrix method (on which rotation, translation, and scaling can all be changed at once), but it also contains helper methods for rotating, translating, and scaling (among other 3D operations) that don't require you to specify a transformation matrix.

13-4. Animating a 3D object

Problem

Now that you have the object looking as you wished, you want to animate it by moving it or rotating it.

Solution

By specifying interpolators, you can change a transform group on a timed interval. For example, the following code creates a spinning cube:

```
private TransformGroup createAsteroid( double x, double z) {
    // Leaf, the Cube
    ColorCube child = new ColorCube(0.3f);
    //Wrap around a branchgroup
    BranchGroup asteroidGroup = new BranchGroup();
    asteroidGroup.addChild(child);

    // 1st transform group, rotates
    TransformGroup rotateGroup = new TransformGroup();
    rotateGroup.setCapability(TransformGroup.ALLOW_TRANSFORM_READ);
    rotateGroup.setCapability(TransformGroup.ALLOW_TRANSFORM_WRITE);
    rotateGroup.addChild(asteroidGroup);

    Alpha scaleAlpha = new Alpha(-1,random.nextInt(16000));
    RotationInterpolator rotationInterpolator = new RotationInterpolator(scaleAlpha,
rotateGroup);
    rotationInterpolator.setSchedulingBounds(new BoundingSphere(new Point3d(),1000f));
// rotate when we're 1000f
    rotationInterpolator.setTransformAxis(new Transform3D());
    rotateGroup.addChild(rotationInterpolator);

    // 2nd Transform Group, translates.
    TransformGroup translateGroup = new TransformGroup();
    Transform3D locationTransform = new Transform3D();
    locationTransform.setTranslation(new Vector3d(x,0d,z));
    translateGroup.setTransform(locationTransform);
    translateGroup.addChild(rotateGroup);
    translateGroup.setCapability(BranchGroup.ALLOW_DETACH);

    return translateGroup;
}
```

In this example, you create an interpolator (which is the class responsible for animating and changing the transform group). The interpolator requires an **Alpha** object, which describes the timeline on which the transformation happens (**Alpha** will produce a number between 0 and 1 that indicates how much to rotate). The alpha is specified to go from 0 to 1 in a random number (up to 16,000) of milliseconds, and is specified to repeat this task infinitely (the first argument in the **Alpha** constructor). Figure 13-5 shows a frame of the resulting spinning cubes.

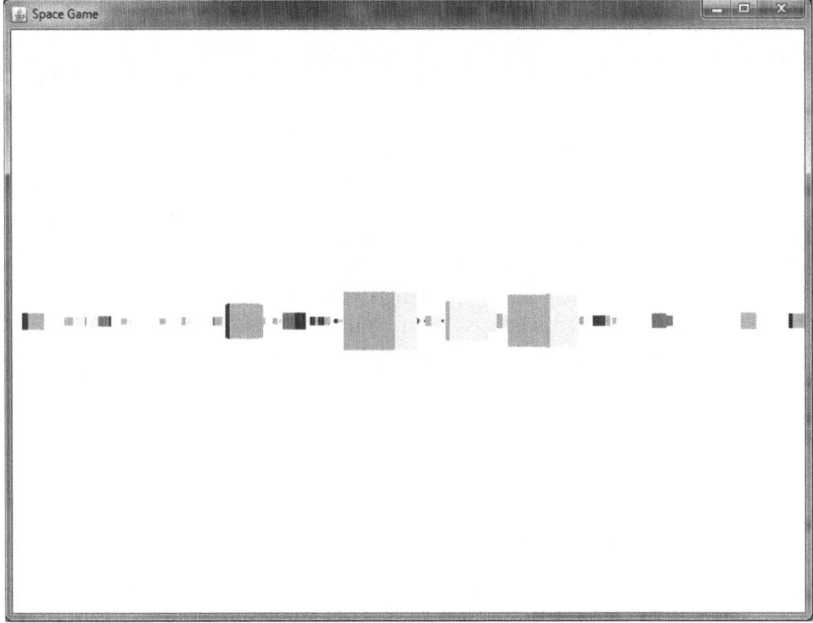

Figure 13-5. Animating many cubes in Java3D

How It Works

There are three main concepts that you have to understand to achieve animation. The first is the `Alpha` class, which specifies the timing and repeatability of an animation. It produces a value between 0 and 1, and the value produced depends on time and its initial parameters. You can specify the following in the `Alpha` class:

- How the Alpha class transforms from 0 to 1 and back again. You can choose between a linear and an exponential approach.

- How many times to repeat the transformation. Do you wish to animate once or cyclically?

- When to start (the `starttime` attribute).

The second concept is of interpolators. Each subclass of interpolators changes a specific property of a transform group. The recipe example uses `rotationInterpolator` to change the rotation of the object. By combining an interpolator with an `Alpha`, you can get smooth animation that is platform-independent because the `Alpha` object specifies the time to take. In very fast systems, you might see 30 frames per second, whereas in slow systems you might see 15 frames per second. But even so, the rotation will take the same number of seconds to finish. When you create an interpolator, you add it as a child of the transform group you want animated.

Finally, the animation occurs only when the viewer is within certain bounds. If the viewer is outside of those bounds, the Canvas3D will not animate the object. To do so, you specify the setTransformBounds property on each transformGroup. This is done for performance reasons. If an object is very far away, it might not be necessary or useful to animate it. Specifying the transform bounds allows you to lower the amount of CPU that is devoted to transformations because it will only animate when the view is within those bounds. The bounds are specified by an implementer of the Bounds class. The boundingSphere is the simplest implementation because it just involves a sphere centered where the transform group is, with a specified sphere ratio.

So far, before the current recipe, there were only "static" scenes, on which things have been added at the beginning and then rendered without any animation. As you move into changing objects by time (or by responding to things such as key presses), you must make each branch group/transform group aware that you are going to change their state after you add them to their universe. In the case of the recipe's rotation animation, you need to specify the transform group capabilities of ALLOW_TRANSFORM_READ, ALLOW_TRANSFORM_WRITE. This signals the universe that you might go and revisit this transform group and change its transformation parameters by using the rotation interpolator.

13-5. Navigating the Created 3D Universe

Problem

You are creating the 3D universe by adding transform/branch groups and want to navigate it.

Solution

Using KeyNavigatorBehavior and MouseRotate, you can create a navigable universe. The following example creates a cluster of cubes, on which you can navigate by using the keyboard or the mouse. Figure 13-6 shows a screenshot of what the example looks like.

```
        KeyNavigatorBehavior keyNavigatorBehavior = new
KeyNavigatorBehavior(universe.getViewingPlatform().getViewPlatformTransform());
        keyNavigatorBehavior.setSchedulingBounds(new BoundingSphere(new Point3d(), 1000.0));
        branchGroup.addChild(keyNavigatorBehavior);

        TransformGroup transformGroup = new TransformGroup();
        transformGroup.addChild(branchGroup);
        transformGroup.setCapability(TransformGroup.ALLOW_TRANSFORM_WRITE);
        transformGroup.setCapability(TransformGroup.ALLOW_TRANSFORM_READ);
        MouseRotate mouseRotate = new MouseRotate();
        mouseRotate.setTransformGroup(transformGroup);
        mouseRotate.setSchedulingBounds(new BoundingSphere(new Point3d(),1000f));
        BranchGroup topGroup = new BranchGroup();
        topGroup.addChild(transformGroup);
        topGroup.addChild(mouseRotate);
        topGroup.compile();
```

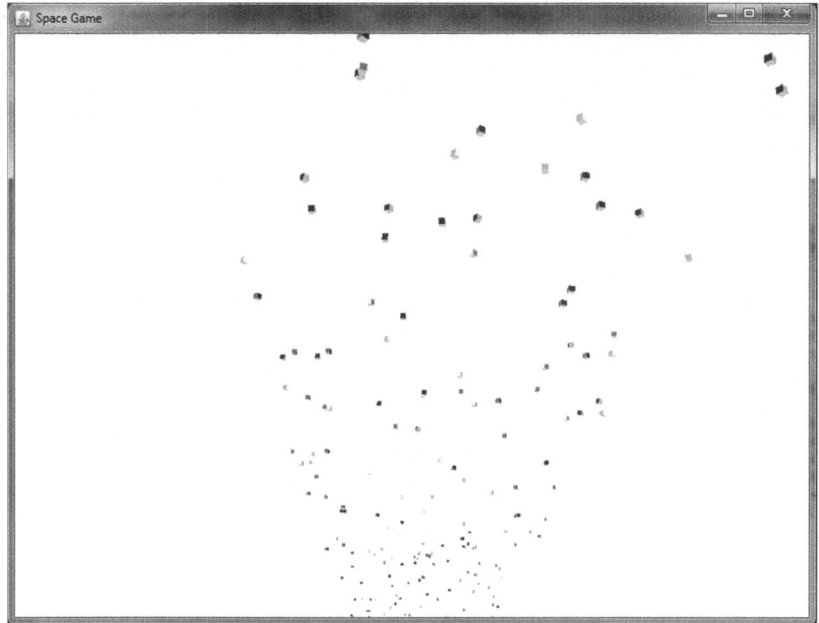

Figure 13-6. Navigating the universe in Java3D

How It Works

KeyNavigatorBehavior sets up a default keyboard mapping that allows you change the viewing platform. Pressing the keyboard's navigation keys moves the viewing platform around the universe. KeyNavigatorBehavior (like all other objects that change or interact with the universe) requires a scheduling bound. The scheduling bound allows Java3D to figure out whether we are close enough to check for the iteration and move the transform group. The use of SchedulingBounds is common in all objects that cause an interaction with the universe; it should be the first thing to debug when the universe doesn't respond to the intended stimuli.

KeyNavigatorBehavior is added then to the ViewPlatform's transform group. ViewPlatform is another "leaf" of the universe. To position the view, you change the transform group that contains the ViewPlatform, which is available by calling the ViewPlatform's getViewPlatformTransform(), which in turn changes how we see the universe. Table 13-1 describes the navigation keys at your disposal.

The mouseRotate behavior allows you to use the mouse to rotate a transform group's children. By creating a transform group that contains the whole scene in the universe, you can use mouseRotate to rotate the universe. mouseRotate needs to be added to the TransformGroup that will be rotated, and also needs the SchedulingBounds property set. Because mouseRotate is changing the TransformGroup after it was created, the TransformGroup needs to have the ALLOW_TRANSFORM_READ and ALLOW_TRANSFORM_WRITE capabilities set.

Table 13-1. Key Navigation Behavior Keys

Keyboard Key	Effect
Left key	Rotate left
Right key	Rotate right
Up key	Move forward
Down key	Move backward
Pg Up key	Rotate up
Pg Down key	Rotate down
=	Return to the origin
-	Reduce rendering distance
+	Reset rendering distance and return to origin

■ **Caution** Having these utility classes will interfere with any other viewer positioning and/or behavior that you later add in your program. If you intend to introduce different navigation by keyboard, you should remove the keyboard/mouse navigators in this recipe.

13-6. Responding to Keyboard Events

Problem

You need to change the universe when someone presses a key.

Solution

Use behaviors to capture keyboard events, and change transform groups in response to the behaviors. The following recipe solution moves our spaceship left or right depending on the key pressed.

```
/// createSpaceShip
        TransformGroup userTransformGroup = new TransformGroup();
        userTransformGroup.addChild(positionGroup);
        userTransformGroup.setCapability(TransformGroup.ALLOW_TRANSFORM_READ);
        userTransformGroup.setCapability(TransformGroup.ALLOW_TRANSFORM_WRITE);

        KeyboardMoveBehavior keyboardMoveBehavior
```

```
                = new KeyboardMoveBehavior(userMovementGroup, transformGroup);
        keyboardMoveBehavior.setSchedulingBounds(new BoundingSphere(new Point3d(), 1000f));
        userTransformGroup.addChild(keyboardMoveBehavior);
        transformGroup.addChild(userTransformGroup);



/// Class definition
    class KeyboardMoveBehavior extends Behavior {

        @Override
        public void initialize() {
            this.wakeupOn(new WakeupOnAWTEvent(KeyEvent.KEY_PRESSED));
            currentAxis = 0f;
        }

        @Override
        public void processStimulus(Enumeration criteria) {
            while (criteria.hasMoreElements()) {
                Object element = criteria.nextElement();
                if (element instanceof WakeupOnAWTEvent) {
                    WakeupOnAWTEvent event = (WakeupOnAWTEvent) element;
                    for (AWTEvent awtEvent : event.getAWTEvent()) {
                        if (awtEvent instanceof KeyEvent) {
                            KeyEvent keyEvent = (KeyEvent) awtEvent;
                            if (keyEvent.getKeyCode() == KeyEvent.VK_LEFT) {
                                moveLeft();
                            } else if (keyEvent.getKeyCode() == KeyEvent.VK_RIGHT) {
                                moveRight();
                            } else if (keyEvent.getKeyCode() == KeyEvent.VK_UP) {
                                moveForward();
                            } else if (keyEvent.getKeyCode() == KeyEvent.VK_DOWN) {
                                moveBackwards();
                            }
                        }
                    }
                }
            }
            this.wakeupOn(new WakeupOnAWTEvent(KeyEvent.KEY_PRESSED));
        }
    }
```

The KeyboardBehavior extends the Behavior class and implements the initialize() and processStimulus() methods. The initialize() method registers the stimuli that the behavior class will respond to. This recipe calls upon wakeupOn(new WakeupOnAWTEvent(KeyEvent.KEY_PRESSED)) to register an interest in any key that is pressed.

How It Works

Behavior classes allow you to register callbacks on certain conditions called stimuli (like a key press or an object collision). When the stimulus happens, the behavior then calls its `processStimulus` method with information about the stimulus (for example, what key was pressed). Within the `processStimulus`, you can then make changes to a transform group (or add/remove children groups) to update the universe. The behavior class can be used to register for many types of stimuli, allowing for an efficient event dispatching. Behavior classes are registered into transform groups.

Like any other Java3D that receives information at runtime, the behavior classes have a scheduling bound on which they will listen for the stimuli to happen. Also, if the behavior class changes a transform group, the transform group will need to have the capabilities set for the changes being made (for example, `ALLOW_TRANSFORM_READ, ALLOW_TRANSFORM_WRITE`).

■ **Note** When a behavior processes a stimulus, it is necessary to reregister the stimuli that we want the behavior to listen to. This is done by making a call to the `wakeupOn()` method at the end of the `processStimulus()` method. This gives you the choice of keeping listening to the stimulus (by reregistering it) or listening to another set of stimuli altogether.

13-7: Changing an Object's Lighting

Problem

You want your object to look illuminated by a light source.

Solution

Using the `Appearance` class, you can set the rendered object's attribute such as color, material, and shade model. For example, the following solution creates random planets that hang below the asteroids (we're suspending belief for a minute and assume that planets can just be randomly thrown together for the sake of visual effects!): Figure 13-7 shows an example of a rendered planet in the game.

```
        Appearance appearance = new Appearance();
        Material material = new Material();
        appearance.setMaterial(material);
        appearance.setColoringAttributes(new ColoringAttributes(new Color3f(Color.yellow),
ColoringAttributes.SHADE_GOURAUD));
        Sphere sun = new Sphere(size, Sphere.GENERATE_NORMALS, appearance);
        sunGroup.addChild(sun);

        DirectionalLight directionalLight = new DirectionalLight();
        directionalLight.setDirection(0,1,-1);
        directionalLight.setColor(new Color3f(new Color(random.nextInt())));
        directionalLight.setInfluencingBounds(new BoundingSphere(new Point3d(),50f));
        sunGroup.addChild(directionalLight);
```

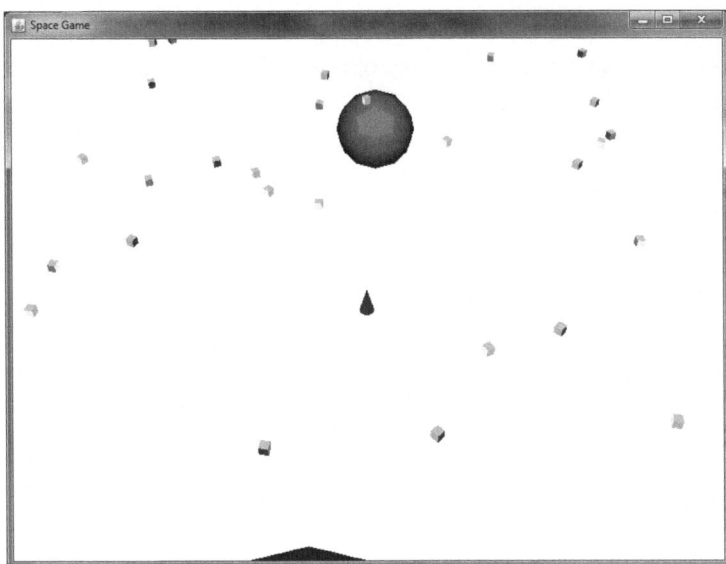

Figure 13-7. Shading objects in Java3D

How It Works

You can set the appearance of each leaf (primitive) object. The `Appearance` class describes information on the color of the object, the material (different materials will render differently under a light source), and the shade model. The shade model describes the detail on which the Java3D renders the color of the model. All objects (even smooth ones like spheres) are composed of geometric primitives (like triangles and squares). When painting the surface of an object, it is quicker to paint each primitive on a solid color (`FLAT_SHADING`), but it's not very realistic-looking. In contrast, `GOURAUD_SHADING` paints each primitive by interpolating the colors of the primitive with its neighbors. It creates a very smooth surface, but requires more CPU processing.

Aside from the appearance, you need a light source. There are four light sources that you can choose for Java3D. These are described in Table 13-2.

Table 13-2. Light Sources for Java3D

Class Name	Effect
Ambient light	A light that shines everywhere (everything gets shaded by its color)
Directional light	A light that has a source (that is infinitively large), so that its light always comes at the same angle for all objects
Point light	A light source that attenuates exponentially
Spot light	A point light for a specific direction only

■ **Note** For a light to work, you need to define an object's appearance (including material), a light source, and the influencing bounds of the light source (Up to what distance can it affect other objects). If any one of these is missing, objects will not render with a light source.

A light gets added to a group (usually a transform group). Depending on the type of light, it either affects objects uniformly (ambient, directional) or affects them proportionally from the location of the light. Lights have another set of bounds called influencing bounds. By specifying influencing bounds, you are telling the light to affect every object that is within the bounds of the light. Lights influence any object in the scene graph that is in its influencing bounds. It is not limited to the group that the light is a child of.

Figure 13-8 shows a screenshot of the completed space game. The object of the game is to avoid (or destroy) the asteroids that are in your path. To do so, you use the left and right keys to move your spaceship and then use the spacebar to fire your laser gun. If an asteroid collides with you, it's game over!

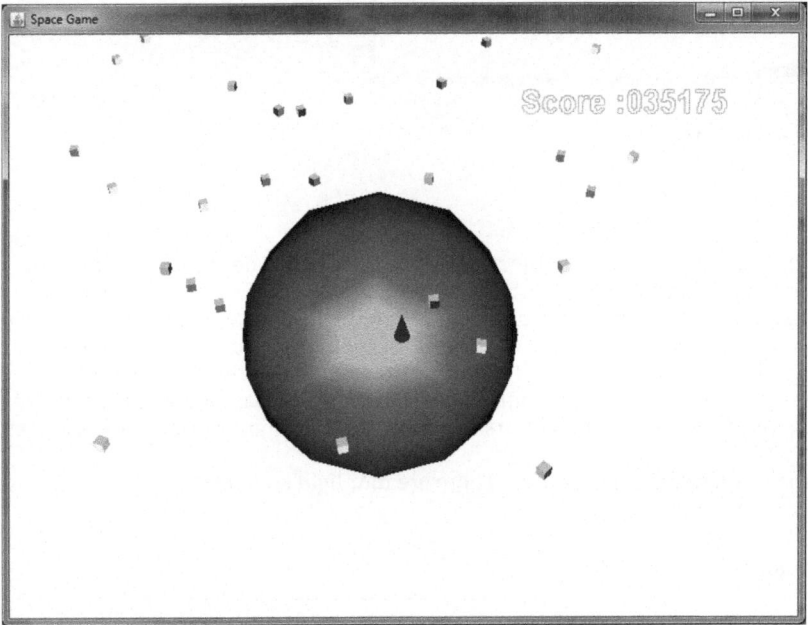

Figure 13-8. Space game

## CHAPTER 14

Swing API

The Java Swing API is a GUI toolkit for developers to build client-side, cross-platform desktop applications. Swing is based on the Model View Controller (MVC) architectural framework pattern.

Long before the Swing API, the Abstract Window Toolkit (AWT) alone provided an abstraction layer over the native platform to enable standard windowing functionality. With the creation of Swing, a new dimension was added that allows greater cross-platform capabilities. Some of these capabilities include pluggable look and feel, advanced components (not found in AWT), and keyboard event bindings. Swing goes beyond AWT's abilities by rendering lightweight components that are platform independent. Swing and its foundational toolkit AWT are still heavily used.

Swing is a mature GUI toolkit that has been used in the enterprise for over a decade and still remains to be a viable desktop development solution today. As we move into the future, some user interfaces can become dated or lacking in cultural appeal. Swing was designed from the ground up to keep up with many modern look and feels by allowing many third parties to develop different themes (skins). Later in this chapter, you will learn how to set the look and feel of our applications.

Although there is a vast array of books about Swing, I will touch on the fundamentals and key concepts that will allow you to hit the ground running. In this chapter you will learn how the Swing API allows developers to create windows, custom layouts, buttons, menus, dialog boxes, animation, validation icon feedback, saving data to a database, and much more. So, let's get started on building GUI applications.

14-1. Creating a GUI

Problem

You want to create a simple GUI application.

Solution

Use Java's Swing API to create a simple GUI application. The following classes are the main classes used in this recipe:

- `javax.swing.JFrame`
- `javax.swing.JComponent`

- `javax.swing.SwingUtilities`

The following code will create a simple GUI application using Java's Swing API. When the GUI application is launched, you will see a blank window with a title bar with the standard minimize, maximize, and close buttons.

```java
package org.java7recipes.chapter14.recipe14_01;

import java.awt.BorderLayout;
import java.awt.Dimension;
import java.awt.Toolkit;
import javax.swing.JComponent;
import javax.swing.JFrame;
import javax.swing.SwingUtilities;

/**
 * Creating a GUI.
 * @author cdea
 */
public class CreatingAGui extends JComponent {

    /**
     * @param title the Chapter and recipe.
     * @param canvas the drawing surface.
     */
    protected static void displayGUI(final String title, final JComponent component) {

        // create window with title
        final JFrame frame = new JFrame(title);

        // set window's close button to exit application
        frame.setDefaultCloseOperation(JFrame.EXIT_ON_CLOSE);

        // place component in the center using BorderLayout
        frame.getContentPane().add(component, BorderLayout.CENTER);

        // size window based on layout
        frame.pack();

        // center window
        Dimension scrnSize = Toolkit.getDefaultToolkit().getScreenSize();
        int scrnWidth = frame.getSize().width;
        int scrnHeight = frame.getSize().height;
        int x = (scrnSize.width - scrnWidth) / 2;
        int y = (scrnSize.height - scrnHeight) / 2;

        // Move the window
        frame.setLocation(x, y);

        // display
        frame.setVisible(true);
    }
```

```
public static void main(String[] args) {
    final CreatingAGui c = new CreatingAGui();
    c.setPreferredSize(new Dimension(290, 227));

    // Queueing GUI work to be run using the EDT.
    SwingUtilities.invokeLater(new Runnable() {
        public void run() {
            displayGUI("Chapter 14-1 Creating a GUI", c);
        }
    });
}
}
```

Figure 14-1 shows the output from executing the preceding code. Shown here is a basic Swing GUI application with a title and standard window buttons.

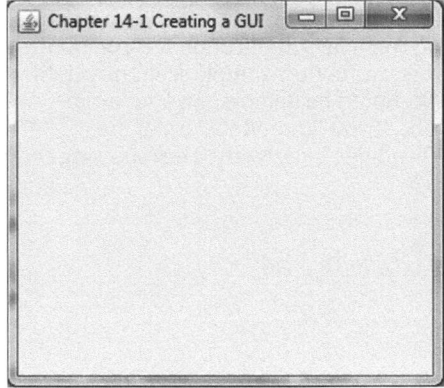

Figure 14-1. Basic GUI application

How It Works

This recipe is pretty straightforward and is the way most Java Swing GUI applications are started and run. They are similar to Java command-line applications, in which they use the main() method as an entry point when executing programs. However, Swing applications will additionally launch a separate thread responsible for displaying the application's UI and graphics. Knowing this fact, it is important to know the appropriate way to manage resources between the main and GUI thread. Before going into the steps of this recipe that assembles and displays the application window frame (javax.swing.JFrame), let's talk about a very important topic called thread safety. What is thread safety and how does it affect your applications?

Thread safety sounds quite scary at first, but it means that concurrent threads that operate on a single resource (data object) can cause any number of issues such as data corruption, race conditions, and even dead locks. However, more often when we talk about it in the GUI world, thread safety is mainly about blocking the GUI thread. In layman's (caveman) terms, your GUI application is frozen (GUI bad). Like most GUI toolkits, Swing uses a single-threaded model in which any GUI renderings are delegated (dispatched) to the GUI thread. In Swing, the GUI thread is called the EDT. The EDT expects events to be queued and ready to be invoked.

So what is the big deal with the EDT? Well, let's say you are periodically retrieving data and updating your GUI screen. The retrieval of the data can be pretty expensive, which can spend approximately one to five seconds (a lifetime IMO). If the retrieval code is called from the EDT, many controls such as buttons, graphics, and animations will typically appear frozen for long periods of time. It is important to defer non-GUI–related work on a separate thread so that blocking doesn't occur. When it's time to render Swing GUI components, you should allow the EDT to execute the code, but most often it's hard to distinguish a thread's context. The Swing API has a convenient way to ensure GUI code gets run on the EDT. This convenience method is the `SwingUtilities.invokeLater()`, which will asynchronously queue up GUI work to be run on the EDT. Shown here is the method call to queue GUI work onto the EDT:

```
SwingUtilities.invokeLater()
```

So let's get down to business. In the `main()` method, you will call `SwingUtilities.invokeLater()` by passing in an anonymous inner class of type `Runnable` where its `run()` method will invoke the method `displayGUI()` on the EDT. This may not be obvious, but when you run a Java application it is run on the main thread and not the EDT. This is an important concept because, as in the example scenario relating to the periodic retrieval of data (non-GUI–related work), the work should be deferred on a separate thread; likewise non-GUI threads should not call GUI-related work. If you ignored the use of the `invokeLater()` method, your application would likely render GUI widgets incorrectly. The following code snippet shows how to dispatch GUI work onto the EDT:

```
%
final CreatingAGui c = new CreatingAGui();
c.setPreferredSize(new Dimension(290, 227));

// Queueing GUI work to be run using the EDT.
SwingUtilities.invokeLater(new Runnable() {
    public void run() {
            displayGUI("Chapter 14-1 Creating a GUI", c);
    }
});
```

Having said all those rules relating to the EDT, you're probably wondering why the two code lines above `invokeLater()` are not being invoked on the EDT and appearing to violate the rules mentioned earlier. Well, I have to tell you about an exception to the rule. Let me restate one of the rules mentioning threading responsibilities: *non-GUI threads should not call GUI-related work*. The exception to the rule is that it is okay if the GUI has not been *realized*. Being realized means the components are about to be shown or are currently being shown.

Now that you know how to safely display a GUI, let's look at the method `displayGUI()`. It is responsible for the actual creation of the GUI application. It first creates an instance of `JFrame` with a title. The `JFrame` is a native window frame that will house your Swing application along with GUI components. Next, you will set the default behavior when the user clicks the close button on the window. You will then take the component passed in to be placed in the content pane using the `JFrame`'s default layout called the `BorderLayout`. Later, in recipe 14-4 you'll see how to align and position components using layouts. Once components are placed in the content pane along with the layout, you will invoke the `JFrame`'s `pack()` method. The `pack()` method is responsible for taking preferred width, window dimension, and other sizing information to properly calculate GUI components that eventually is shown. Following the `pack()` method you will do a little math to center the window frame on the monitor display. Lastly, you will call the `JFrame`'s `setVisible()` to `true` to display to display the GUI application window. When the pack() and setVisible() methods are called to show the components in the window frame, the displayed components are now considered to be *realized*.

14-2. Running a Swing Application

Problem

You want to run a Java Swing application.

Solution 1: Execute a Java App

On the command prompt, type the following and then press Enter:
java com.myproject.App

Solution 2: Execute a .jar Executable

Double click a .jar executable or on the command prompt type the following and then press Enter:
java -jar myapp.jar

Solution 3: Invoke from a Web Page

Click the Launch button on a web page containing a Java Web Start link. Figure 14-2 shows an example of the sort of button you might see.

Figure 14-2. Java Web Start

How It Works

There are three main ways to launch Java Swing applications. The first two solutions are run on the command line, and the last is via a link on a web page or an icon on your desktop.

Solution 1 is used when your class files are available in your classpath (compiled). This solution is as easy as running any Java application on the command line. To learn how to execute Java applications and pass arguments via the command line or terminal, please see recipe 1-4.

Solution 2 is used when the Java Swing application is packaged in a file called a .jar file (better known as a Java archive). Java archives that are run as a Swing application are specially built to contain metadata on details such as what class file contains a main() method as its entry point. To see more on how to create .jar file executables, see recipe 14-22.

Solution 3 is used when a user clicks a special hyperlink on a web page that launches the Swing application that will be pushed (installed) onto the local workstation. This technology is called Java Web Start. Underneath the covers, Java Web Start provides a network launching protocol called JNLP. Similar to solution 2, in which a .jar file contains a meta file (manifest), solution 3 uses a file with a extension of

.jnlp. This file is hosted on the web server along with the .jar file ready to be served up. When a Swing application is launched, you will be presented with a dialog box relating to security (certificates and trusted authorities) and asking the option to put an icon on your desktop. For more details on deploying Swing, see recipe 14-22.

14-3. Adding Components to a GUI

Problem

Your boss has trouble remembering names of people and needs a way to capture a person's contact information.

Solution

Create a simple GUI application with some of Swing's standard UI components representing labels and input fields to allow a user to enter a person's name. I want to remind you that this recipe does not save any information. The following Swing-based UI components used in this recipe example are listed here:

- javax.swing.JPanel

- javax.swing.JButton

- javax.swing.JLabel

- javax.swing.JTextField

In this recipe you will be creating a simple form type application that allows you to type in a person's first and last name. The application screen will contain labels beside the text fields to describe the input field. The form also has a save button to simulate the ability to save the information to a data store. Later in this chapter, you will learn how to save data into an embedded database. The following code listing is a simple form-type application containing some of Swing's standard UI components:

```
package org.java7recipes.chapter14.recipe14_03;

import javax.swing.JButton;
import javax.swing.JLabel;
import javax.swing.JPanel;
import javax.swing.JTextField;
import org.java7recipes.chapter14.SimpleAppLauncher;

/**
 * Adding Component to GUI.
 * @author cdea
 */
public class AddingComponent2Gui extends JPanel {

    public AddingComponent2Gui(){
        // first name
        add(new JLabel("First Name"));
```

```
        add(new JTextField("Fred"));

        // last name
        add(new JLabel("Last Name"));
        add(new JTextField("Sanford"));

        // save button
        add(new JButton("Save"));
    }

    public static void main(String[] args) {
        final JPanel c = new AddingComponent2Gui();
        // Queueing GUI work to be run using the EDT.
        SimpleAppLauncher.launch("Chapter 14-3 Adding Components to GUI", c);
    }
}
```

The following code listing is the helper class SimpleAppLauncher.java that assists in launching Swing applications by displaying the GUI in a thread safe way:

```
import java.awt.BorderLayout;
import java.awt.Component;
import java.awt.Dimension;
import java.awt.Toolkit;
import java.awt.event.ComponentAdapter;
import java.awt.event.ComponentEvent;
import javax.swing.JComponent;
import javax.swing.JFrame;
import javax.swing.SwingUtilities;

/**
 * SimpleAppLauncher will create a window and display a component and
 * abide by the event dispatch thread rules.
 *
 * @author cdea
 */
public class SimpleAppLauncher {
    /**
     * @param title the Chapter and recipe.
     * @param canvas the drawing surface.
     */
    protected static void displayGUI(final String title, final JComponent component) {

        // create window with title
        final JFrame frame = new JFrame(title);
        if (component instanceof AppSetup) {
            AppSetup ms = (AppSetup) component;
            ms.apply(frame);
        }

        // set window's close button to exit application
```

```
            frame.setDefaultCloseOperation(JFrame.EXIT_ON_CLOSE);

        component.addComponentListener(new ComponentAdapter() {
            // This method is called after the component's size changes
            @Override
            public void componentResized(ComponentEvent evt) {
                Component c = (Component)evt.getSource();

                // Get new size
                Dimension newSize = c.getSize();
                System.out.println("component size w,h = " + newSize.getWidth() + ", " +
newSize.getHeight());
            }
        });

        // place component in the center using BorderLayout
        frame.getContentPane().add(component, BorderLayout.CENTER);
        frame.setMinimumSize(component.getMinimumSize());

        // size window based on layout
        frame.pack();

        // center window
        Dimension scrnSize = Toolkit.getDefaultToolkit().getScreenSize();
        int scrnWidth = frame.getSize().width;
        int scrnHeight = frame.getSize().height;
        int x = (scrnSize.width - scrnWidth) / 2;
        int y = (scrnSize.height - scrnHeight) / 2;

        // Move the window
        frame.setLocation(x, y);

        // display
        frame.setVisible(true);
    }

    public static void launch(final String title, final JComponent component) {

        SwingUtilities.invokeLater(new Runnable() {
            public void run() {
                displayGUI(title, component);
            }
        });// invokeLater()
    }// launch()
} // SimpleAppLauncher
```

Shown here is the AppSetup interface (AppSetup.java) used in later chapters to allow the SimpleAppLauncher class to apply UI components to the main application window. This is primarily used to add menu options to the main application window (JFrame). (It is not used in this recipe, but is mentioned in future recipes.)

```
public interface AppSetup {
    void apply(JFrame frame);
}
```

Figure 14-3 displays a simple form containing some of Swing's standard UI components used to allow a user to enter a person's first and last name.

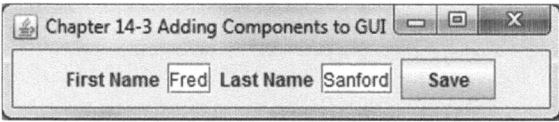

Figure 14-3. Adding components to a GUI

How It Works

When adding components to a GUI application, the first thing you will need is a container to hold components to eventually be displayed. In Swing, a common container that is often used is the JPanel class, which is not only a container but also a component (JComponent). It is just like other components it contains. In the inheritance hierarchy, all Swing components such as the JLabel, JTextField and JPanel classes extend from the JComponent class. So containers can contain other containers, and so on. By default, the JPanel uses a FlowLayout layout to position and size components according to certain layout constraints. In short, the flow layout will lay out the components horizontally and move them to the next line if the component reaches beyond the edge of the panel. Later, we will discuss layouts, but for now let's add some components onto the GUI.

In our default constructor, you will use JPanel's add() method to put components into the container. You will first add a JLabel component that represents a read-only label denoting the first name beside the input field. Next is an input field using Swing's JTextField component, allowing the user to enter and edit text. After the first name components are added, the last name components are added using the same steps as before. Finally, you will add a JButton component onto the JPanel. The following code line adds a save button onto the JPanel panel:

```
add(new JButton("Save"));
```

I know the UI form doesn't look very attractive, and the button doesn't do much of anything, you'll see in later recipes how to remedy these things. If you must know, go ahead and jump to layouts (recipe 14-4). To handle button events see recipe 14-5.

Before moving forward, I want to bring your attention to the main() method in this recipe, in which you will call out to the SimpleAppLauncher.launch() method to launch the GUI application window. This convenient method simply displays content in a JFrame window while honoring thread safety (EDT). The SimpleAppLauncher helper class is actually a refactoring of recipe 14-1, which abstracts away common GUI application code. Creating this helper class will enable us to focus on key concepts without being bogged down with application details. The rest of the recipes in Chapter 14 will be using SimpleAppLauncher.launch(), so you won't be scratching your head not knowing where the JFrame code resides.

One last thing to address is the AppSetup interface that I also created in support of SimpleAppLauncher; it is co-located with the org.java7recipes.chapter14.SimpleAppLauncher class. The AppSetup interface contains a single method called apply() that provides an opportunity for the developer to apply settings or menu components onto the parent application window (JFrame)

421

independent of the launching code. The following code is the apply() method from the AppSetup interface:

```
void apply(JFrame frame);
```

When implementing the interface AppSetup, the SimpleAppLauncher.displayGUI() method will see whether the component is an instance of an AppSetup before executing the apply() method. Shown here is the SimpleAppLauncher.displayGUI() method:

```
protected static void displayGUI(final String title, final JComponent component) {

    // create window with title
    final JFrame frame = new JFrame(title);
    if (component instanceof AppSetup) {
        AppSetup ms = (AppSetup) component;
        ms.apply(frame);
    }
    ...
    // rest of displayGUI() method
```

Continuing with the rest of the displayGUI() method, I will detail the code line steps to launch and display the application window. After the conditional statement checks to see whether the component is an instance of an AppSetup class, you will be setting the application window close operation by calling the method setDefaultCloseOperation() on the JFrame object with the value JFrame.EXIT_ON_CLOSE. Shown here is the code line to set the application window frame's default close operation when the user clicks the close button:

```
// set window's close button to exit application
frame.setDefaultCloseOperation(JFrame.EXIT_ON_CLOSE);
```

Most of the recipe code examples in this chapter will call the displayGUI() method by passing in the GUI content or component (JPanel container). When component is passed in, you may want to know the dimensions of the panel while the window is being resized. To know the dimensions of the panel, you will need to add a component listener (ComponentAdapter), allowing you to print out the width and height to the console. Shown here is the code snippet to add a component listener to output the component's dimension when the window is resized:

```
component.addComponentListener(new ComponentAdapter() {
    // This method is called after the component's size changes
    @Override
    public void componentResized(ComponentEvent evt) {
        Component c = (Component)evt.getSource();

        // Get new size
        Dimension newSize = c.getSize();
        System.out.println("component size w,h = " + newSize.getWidth() + ", " +
newSize.getHeight());
    }
});
```

Next, you will want to set the component panel as the content pane and set the minimum size of the window frame based on the panel. You'll notice when adding the component panel to the content pane you will be able to specify the BorderLayout.CENTER constraint. Later, we will discuss layouts, but for now the main content pane by default uses a border layout (BorderLayout) that has a center content area. The center area will take up all the available space when other content areas (North, South, East, and West) don't contain any content. The following code sets the content pane (with a `BorderLayout.Center`) and sets the minimum size of the application window frame:

```
// place component in the center using BorderLayout
frame.getContentPane().add(component, BorderLayout.CENTER);
frame.setMinimumSize(component.getMinimumSize());
```

Once the frame's content pane and dimension is set, you will need to invoke the `pack()` method on the window frame to notify the Swing toolkit to perform a layout on the UI components and apply constraints on the parent window. Shown here is the `pack()` method to notify the Swing toolkit to perform a layout:

```
// size window based on layout
frame.pack();
```

Then you will want to center the application window frame. By using the `Toolkit` utility class, you can obtain the screen's physical screen size by calling the `Toolkit.getDefaultToolkit().getScreenSize()` method. Next, you will calculate the window frame's upper-left coordinate in order to center the screen. Once calculated, you will set the location and display the application window to the user. Shown here is the code to center the application window (`JFrame`) and display to the user:

```
// center window
Dimension scrnSize = Toolkit.getDefaultToolkit().getScreenSize();
int scrnWidth = frame.getSize().width;
int scrnHeight = frame.getSize().height;
int x = (scrnSize.width - scrnWidth) / 2;
int y = (scrnSize.height - scrnHeight) / 2;

// Move the window
frame.setLocation(x, y);

// display
frame.setVisible(true);
```

With all the necessary code to launch Swing-based GUIs, it's nice to think of `SimpleAppLauncher` as a mini utility or application framework to launch applications easily while adhering to thread safety so you can focus on making your GUIs look amazing!

14-4. Laying Out GUI Components

Problem

Your boss complains about how ugly the UI looks and asks to have components laid out similar to a grid.

Solution

Create a custom layout to position your UI components in a grid-like display. You will create a simple input form like the recipe before that allows a user (your absent-minded boss) to enter a person's first and last name. The following are the main classes used and discussed in this recipe:

- `java.awt.BorderLayout`

- `java.awt.FlowLayout`

- `java.awt.GridBagLayout`

- `java.awt.LayoutManager2`

In the previous recipe, you created a GUI form application that allows the user to enter a person's first and last name where the components were not laid out nicely. In this recipe, you will be able to lay out the same UI components in a grid-like form by creating a custom layout. The custom layout will allow you to add components similar to a table in HTML or Swing's `GridBagLayout`, except it will be a lot simpler to use. To add components to the layout, you will be able to programmatically specify in which column and row (cell) it will reside. You will also be able to align components using a constraint object within its respective cell based on the column and row. Shown here are three code listings: `LayingOutComponentsOnGui.java`, `MyCustomGridLayout.java`, and `MyCellConstraint.java`. The `LayingOutComponentsOnGui` class is the main application to be run. The `MyCustomGridLayout` class is the custom layout that will be used to display UI controls in a grid-like display. The `MyCellConstraint` class is used to set constraints to align UI controls within a cell.

Shown here is the code listing for `LayingOutComponentsOnGui.java` file. This is the main application for this recipe:

```
package org.java7recipes.chapter14.recipe14_04;

import java.awt.Component;
import java.awt.Dimension;
import javax.swing.JButton;
import javax.swing.JLabel;
import javax.swing.JPanel;
import javax.swing.JTextField;
import static org.java7recipes.chapter14.recipe14_04.MyCellConstraint.LEFT;
import static org.java7recipes.chapter14.recipe14_04.MyCellConstraint.RIGHT;
import org.java7recipes.chapter14.SimpleAppLauncher;

/**
 * <pre>
 *
 * +----------------------+
 * | [label ] [  field  ] |
 * | [label ] [  field  ] |
 * |          [ button ] |
 * +----------------------+
 * </pre>
 * Laying GUI Components.
 * @author cdea
 */
```

```java
public class LayingOutComponentsOnGui extends JPanel {

    public LayingOutComponentsOnGui(){
        super();
        JLabel fNameLbl = new JLabel("First Name");
        JTextField fNameFld = new JTextField(15);
        JLabel lNameLbl = new JLabel("Last Name");
        JTextField lNameFld = new JTextField(15);
        JButton saveButt = new JButton("Save");

        // Create a 2x3 grid with 5 horizontal and vertical gaps
        // between components.
        MyCustomGridLayout cglayout = new MyCustomGridLayout(5, 5, 2, 3);

        setLayout(cglayout);

        // First name label
        addToPanel(fNameLbl, 0, 0, RIGHT);

        // Last name label
        addToPanel(lNameLbl, 0, 1, RIGHT);

        // First name field
        addToPanel(fNameFld, 1, 0, LEFT);

        // Last name field
        addToPanel(lNameFld, 1, 1, LEFT);

        // Save button
        addToPanel(saveButt, 1, 2, RIGHT);
    }

    private void addToPanel(Component comp, int colNum, int rowNum, int align) {
        MyCellConstraint constr = new MyCellConstraint()
                .setColNum(colNum)
                .setRowNum(rowNum)
                .setAlign(align);
        add(comp, constr);
    }

    public static void main(String[] args) {
        final JPanel c = new LayingOutComponentsOnGui();
        c.setPreferredSize(new Dimension(380, 118));
        // Queueing GUI work to be run using the EDT.
        SimpleAppLauncher.launch("Chapter 14-4 Laying GUI Components", c);
    }
}
```

The code listing shown here is a custom layout called the MyCustomGridLayout class. This layout is responsible for managing components by calculating the available space, width, height, and UI component alignments:
package org.java7recipes.chapter14.recipe14_04;

```java
import java.awt.Component;
import java.awt.Container;
import java.awt.Dimension;
import java.awt.Insets;
import java.awt.LayoutManager2;

/**
 * My Custom Grid Layout.
 * @author cdea
 */
public class MyCustomGridLayout implements LayoutManager2 {

    private int vgap;
    private int hgap;
    private int rows = 2;
    private int cols = 2;
    private int minWidth;
    private int minHeight;
    private int preferredWidth;
    private int preferredHeight;
    private boolean sizeUnknown = true;
    private Component[][] components;
    private MyCellConstraint[][] constraints;

    public MyCustomGridLayout(int hgap, int vgap, int cols, int rows) {
        this.hgap = hgap;
        this.vgap = vgap;
        this.rows = rows;
        this.cols = cols;
        components = new Component[rows][cols];
        constraints = new MyCellConstraint[rows][cols];
    }

    public void addLayoutComponent(String name, Component comp) {
    }

    public void removeLayoutComponent(Component comp) {
    }

    private void setSizes(Container parent) {
        preferredWidth = 0;
        preferredHeight = 0;
        minWidth = 0;
        minHeight = 0;

        // calculate the largest width of all columns
        int maxColWidth[] = new int[cols];
        int maxColHeight[] = new int[rows];
        updateMaxColWidthAndHeight(maxColWidth, maxColHeight);

        // update preferred width
        for (int colIndx = 0; colIndx < maxColWidth.length; colIndx++) {
            preferredWidth += maxColWidth[colIndx];
            preferredWidth += hgap;
```

```
    }
    preferredWidth += hgap;
    for (int rowIndx = 0; rowIndx < maxColHeight.length; rowIndx++) {
        preferredHeight += maxColHeight[rowIndx];
        preferredHeight += vgap;
    }
    preferredHeight += vgap;
}

public Dimension preferredLayoutSize(Container parent) {
    Dimension dim = new Dimension(0, 0);

    setSizes(parent);

    //Add the container's insets
    Insets insets = parent.getInsets();
    dim.width = preferredWidth + insets.left + insets.right;
    dim.height = preferredHeight + insets.top + insets.bottom;

    sizeUnknown = false;

    return dim;
}

public Dimension minimumLayoutSize(Container parent) {
    Dimension dim = new Dimension(0, 0);

    //Add the container's insets
    Insets insets = parent.getInsets();
    dim.width = minWidth + insets.left + insets.right;
    dim.height = minHeight + insets.top + insets.bottom;

    sizeUnknown = false;

    return dim;
}

public void layoutContainer(Container parent) {
    Insets insets = parent.getInsets();
    int availableWidth = parent.getWidth() - (insets.left + insets.right);
    int availableHeight = parent.getHeight() - (insets.top + insets.bottom);

    int x = 0, y = insets.top;

    if (sizeUnknown) {
        setSizes(parent);
    }

    // calculate the largest width of all columns
    int maxColWidth[] = new int[cols];

    // calculate the largest height of all columns
```

```java
        int maxColHeight[] = new int[rows];
        updateMaxColWidthAndHeight(maxColWidth, maxColHeight);


        int previousWidth = 0, previousHeight = 0;

        for (int rowNum = 0; rowNum < components.length; rowNum++) {
            y += previousHeight + vgap;
            x = 0;
            previousWidth = 0;
            for (int colNum = 0; colNum < components[rowNum].length; colNum++) {
                Component curComp = components[rowNum][colNum];
                Dimension cDim = null;
                if (curComp == null) {
                    cDim = new Dimension(maxColWidth[colNum], maxColHeight[rowNum]);
                } else {
                    cDim = curComp.getPreferredSize();
                }

                x += previousWidth + hgap;

                MyCellConstraint cConstr = constraints[rowNum][colNum];

                if (cConstr != null) {
                    switch (cConstr.getAlign()) {
                        case MyCellConstraint.RIGHT:
                            x += maxColWidth[colNum] - cDim.width;
                            break;
                        case MyCellConstraint.CENTER:
                            x += (maxColWidth[colNum] - cDim.width) / 2;
                            break;
                    }
                }

                if (curComp != null) {
                    // Set the component's size and position.
                    curComp.setBounds(x, y, cDim.width, cDim.height);
                }
                previousWidth = cDim.width;

            }

            previousHeight = maxColHeight[rowNum];

        }
        previousWidth += hgap;
        previousHeight += vgap;
    }

    @Override
    public void addLayoutComponent(Component comp, Object constraint) {
        MyCellConstraint targetC = (MyCellConstraint) constraint;
```

```
            if (targetC != null) {
                components[targetC.getRowNum()][targetC.getColNum()] = comp;
                constraints[targetC.getRowNum()][targetC.getColNum()] = targetC;
            }
        }

        @Override
        public float getLayoutAlignmentX(Container target) {
            return 1f; // center
        }

        @Override
        public float getLayoutAlignmentY(Container target) {
            return 0f; // leading
        }

        @Override
        public void invalidateLayout(Container target) {
        }

        @Override
        public Dimension maximumLayoutSize(Container target) {
            return preferredLayoutSize(target);
        }

        private void updateMaxColWidthAndHeight(int[] maxColWidth, int[] maxColHeight) {
            for (int rowNum = 0; rowNum < components.length; rowNum++) {
                for (int colNum = 0; colNum < components[rowNum].length; colNum++) {
                    Component curComp = components[rowNum][colNum];
                    if (curComp == null) {
                        continue;
                    }
                    Dimension cDim = curComp.getPreferredSize();
                    maxColWidth[colNum] = Math.max(maxColWidth[colNum], cDim.width);
                    maxColHeight[rowNum] = Math.max(maxColHeight[rowNum], cDim.height);
                }
            }
        }
    }
```

Shown here is the source code listing of the file MyCellConstraint.java. This class is responsible for allowing the developer to specify a cell constraint for a UI component within a cell (as long as there is a UI control within that cell):

```
/**
 * Cell Constraints. Aligns components on the custom grid layout.
 * @author cdea
 */
public class MyCellConstraint {
    private int rowNum=0;
    private int colNum=0;
```

```
        public final static int LEFT = -1;
        public final static int CENTER = 0;
        public final static int RIGHT = 1;
        private int align = LEFT; // left

        public int getAlign() {
            return align;
        }

        public MyCellConstraint setAlign(int align) {
            this.align = align;
            return this;
        }

        public int getColNum() {
            return colNum;
        }

        public MyCellConstraint setColNum(int colNum) {
            this.colNum = colNum;
            return this;
        }

        public int getRowNum() {
            return rowNum;
        }

        public MyCellConstraint setRowNum(int rowNum) {
            this.rowNum = rowNum;
            return this;
        }
    }
}
```

Figure 14-4 displays a form-type application using a custom layout, allowing a user to enter a person's first and last name.

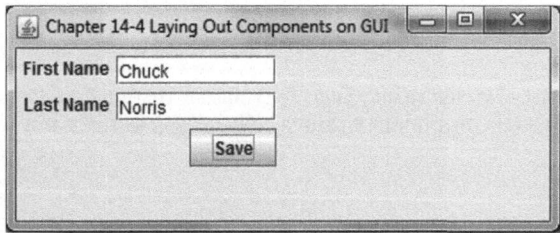

Figure 14-4. Custom layout

How It Works

When developing GUI applications, it is ideal for an application to allow the user to move and adjust the size of their viewable area while maintaining a pleasant user experience. The Java Swing API provides many layouts to choose from straight out of the box. The most common layouts used are BorderLayout, FlowLayout, and GridBagLayout.

■ **Note** I will discuss the common layouts very briefly and will not go into detail. My reasoning is that there are numerous sources detailing the common layouts and don't often see many examples of real world layouts that behave well. In other words, in this recipe you will be creating a custom layout in which you will have more control of components. It also gives you a chance to see how things work under the hood. Before you get into the code, I will briefly explain the commonly used layouts.

When using the JPanel component without a layout manager, it defaults to Swing's FlowLayout manager. The FlowLayout manager simply lays out components horizontally on a row. The FlowLayout manager will honor a component's preferred size; however, a component's position can move depending on the available space width-wise. Similar to a word processor or text editor having word wrap on, whenever a window is resized smaller than the width of the row components, the FlowLayout manager will reposition the component to the next row. Like all Layout managers, the FlowLayout manager has constraints or settings which allow you to control the alignment of components. To see more, refer to the Javadoc for details. The following code statement sets a JPanel component with a FlowLayout manager with a center constraint:

```
setLayout(new FlowLayout(FlowLayout.CENTER);
```

The most commonly used layout is the BorderLayout manager. This is probably the case because it is similar to web pages in a browser. Web pages often have navigation at the top, bottom, left, or right side of the display area and a main content region in the center. The BorderLayout class calls these areas surrounding the center content region NORTH, SOUTH, EAST, and WEST. Of course, the center content region is called CENTER. When adding components to the surrounding regions, it is similar to the FlowLayout where the preferred size is used and positioning occurs based on the width of the region. When adding a component to the center region, the layout manager will give the component as much of the available space as possible. Shown here is the code that sets a JPanel container with a BorderLayout and adds a component in the center content region:

```
setLayout(new BorderLayout());
add(saveButton, BorderLayout.CENTER);
```

Another popular (or unpopular) layout is called the GridBagLayout. This layout is used to have finer-grain control over the placement and constraints of components. To set constraints for each component, you would use the GridBagConstraints class. Typically, this layout is used to present a table-like structure. By using the GridBagConstraints class, you can let the layout manager know how to treat components' sizes in each cell in the grid table. Often, constraints can often be so complicated and unwieldy that you have to start all over from scratch. Shown here is setting a JPanel container component with a GridBagLayout layout and adding the JLabel UI component to the cell at column 0 and row 0:

```
setLayout(new GridBagLayout());
GridBagConstraints c = new GridBagConstraints();
c.fill = GridBagConstraints.HORIZONTAL;
c.gridx = 0;
c.gridy = 0;
add(firstNameLbl, c);
```

Let's get to the code, shall we? For starters, when developing or designing user interfaces you will need to have requirements. Most applications in the business world are data entry type interfaces or better known as forms. Form interfaces are often symmetrical and similar to a grid-type layout. You are probably thinking about the GridBagLayout, but in our custom layout the API is simpler to use and has expected (predictable) behavior.

Pretend your boss is requesting a form interface to enter contact information. You'll begin with a simple form mockup that has labels, fields, and a button. Shown here is a mockup of our interface:

```
+------------------------+

| [label ] [   field   ] |
| [label ] [   field   ] |
|           [ button ]   |
+------------------------+
```

Before getting into the guts of our custom layout implementation, it is better to explain how to use the layout's API first. Does this sound like the chicken-or-the-egg scenario? Well, when developing/designing APIs, it's always important to design interfaces before creating concrete implementations (Design by Contract). A similar scenario is pretending the layout manager has already been created, and the developer is using the API. The requirements for the custom layout are these:

- Specify the horizontal gap in (pixels) between components.

- Specify the vertical gap (pixels) between components.

- Specify the number of columns in the grid.

- Specify the number of rows in the grid.

- Align components left, right, or center within a cell width default (left).

- Use the components' preferred height and width.

When using the already created layout (custom layout), you can specify the horizontal gap, vertical gap, number of columns, and number of rows through its constructor. Shown here is setting up the JPanel with the MyCustomGridLayout layout:

```
// Create a 2x3 grid with 5 horizontal and vertical gaps
// between components.
MyCustomGridLayout cglayout = new MyCustomGridLayout(5, 5, 2, 3);
setLayout(cglayout);
```

Next, you will set constraints in order to let the custom layout decide where to position and size components within a cell. I created a constraint object called MyCellConstraint which is a plain old Java object (POJO) used when calling the add(JComponent comp, Object constraint) method of a JPanel component. The MyCellConstraint class allows the user of the API to specify which cell in the grid to place the component and an alignment within the cell. The three alignments are left, right, or center where left is the default. In this code recipe, I used the `Builder` pattern, so specifying cell constraints will resemble a more declarative feel and not be as verbose as using the `GridBagConstraints` object. When you set the `JPanel` component's layout, the `add()` method will delegate to the custom layout's `layoutContainer()` method to position and size components.

This code adds a `JTextField` component to a `JPanel` container with constraints by placing the component in column 1 and row 0 centered within the cell horizontally. You'll also notice it here when specifying properties of the `MyCellConstraint` object:

```
JTextField fNameFld = new JTextField(15);
MyCellConstraint constr = new MyCellConstraint()
    .setColNum(1)
    .setRowNum(0)
    .setAlign(MyCellConstraint.CENTER);
add(fNameFld, constr);
```

Now that you know how to use the custom layout, we can discuss how it was implemented. Before you get to each of the layout manager methods, take a look at Table 14-1 below which describes the instance variables of the `MyCustomGridLayout` class.

Table 14-1. MyCustomGridLayout s instance variables

Variable	Data Type	Example	Description
vgap	int	10	Vertical gaps between components
hgap	int	10	Horizontal gaps between components
cols	int	3	Number of columns
rows	int	3	Number of rows
minWidth	int	200	Minimum width
MinHeight	int	150	Minimum height
preferredWidth	int	200	Preferred width
preferredHeight	int	150	Preferred width
sizeUnknown	boolean	false	Flag to detect whether component's size has been determined
components	Component[][]	-	Array containing components mapped to each cell in the grid
constraints	MyCellConstraint[][]	-	Array containing constraints mapped to each cell in the grid

The `MyCustomGridLayout` class begins by implementing the Swing's `LayoutManager2` interface. In `MyCustomGridLayout`'s constructor you will simply set up the horizontal gap, vertical gap, number of rows, and number of columns for the custom grid layout. For brevity, you will only implement the following methods:

```
public void addLayoutComponent(Component comp, Object constraint);
public Dimension preferredLayoutSize(Container parent);
public Dimension minimumLayoutSize(Container parent);
public Dimension maximumLayoutSize(Container target);
public void layoutContainer(Container parent);
```

Table 14-2 provides the descriptions of the methods you will implement from the LayoutManager2 interface. This is in support for the MyCustomGridLayout custom layout class.

Table 14-2. LayoutManager2 Methods

Method	Description
addLayoutComponent()	Stores the component and its constraint.
preferredLayoutSize()	Calculates the preferred size. Invoked when the Container class's getPreferredSize() method is called.
minimumLayoutSize()	Calculates the minimum size of the layout.
maximumLayoutSize()	Calculates the maximum size of the layout. To make things simple, this calls the preferredLayoutSize().
layoutContainer()	Is responsible for positioning and sizing components. When calculating a component's bounds, it takes into account the horizontal gap, vertical gap, parent's insets, component's preferred width/height, and cell constraint.

When a layout occurs (invalidation), the layoutContainer() will be called to reposition components. This method first obtains the parent's insets to calculate the available width and height you can use to resize components within each cell. Although these variables (availableWidth, availableHeight) aren't used, I implemented them and left them for you as an exercise if you want to make this layout more robust. You may want to create thresholds for components to expand and contract. Next, you will iterate through all the columns to determine the widest component in each column. You will also iterate through all rows to determine the largest height for each row that makes things spaced like a grid. The cell sizes are being determined by obtaining the UI component's preferred size and horizontal and vertical gaps. Each component's upper-left bounding box (x, y) coordinate is updated to be positioned within the cell. With a parallel array containing each cell constraint the (x, y) coordinate gets updated based on the cell constraint's alignment (RIGHT, CENTER, and LEFT).

Many of the recipe examples will reuse a copy of this custom layout called CustomGridLayout along with its CellConstraint class co-located in the package namespace org.java7recipes.chapter14.

Layout management can be quite challenging at times, but understanding the fundamentals will help you decide the best approach when building aesthetically pleasing applications. When developing small applications you should use the stock layouts. But for larger-scale applications you might want to explore more powerful solutions. Shown here are layouts that I highly recommend when creating professional looking applications:

- MigLayout by Mikael Grev: http://www.miglayout.com

- DesignGridLayout by Jean-Francois Poilpret: http://designgridlayout.java.net

- GroupLayout: NetBeans IDE's WYSIWYG editor Swing GUI Builder (formerly Project Matisse): http://netbeans.org/features/java/swing.html

- JGoodies Forms by Karsten Lentzsch: http://www.jgoodies.com

14-5. Generating Events with Buttons

Problem

As a hard worker you often get stressed out and are in search of an easy button.

Solution

Create and application with an easy button that will offer calming advice. The main classes you will be using in this recipe are the following:

- java.awt.event.ActionListener

- javax.swing.JButton

The following code listing creates an application that will display a button that when pressed will display text. This code recipe will demonstrate button actions:

```java
package org.java7recipes.chapter14.recipe14_05;

import java.awt.*;
import java.awt.event.*;
import javax.swing.*;
import org.java7recipes.chapter14.SimpleAppLauncher;

/**
 * Generating Event with Buttons.
 * @author cdea
 */
public class GeneratingEventWithButtons extends JPanel {

    public GeneratingEventWithButtons(){
        final JLabel status = new JLabel("Press the easy button to solve all your
problems.");
        add(status);

        // save button
        JButton saveMe = new JButton("Easy");
        saveMe.addActionListener(new ActionListener() {

            @Override
            public void actionPerformed(ActionEvent e) {
                status.setText("You will recieve two tickets to the petting zoo...");
            }
        });
        add(saveMe);
```

```
    }

    public static void main(String[] args) {
        final JPanel c = new GeneratingEventWithButtons();
        c.setPreferredSize(new Dimension(384, 45));
        // Queueing GUI work to be run using the EDT.
        SimpleAppLauncher.launch("Chapter 14-5 Generating Events With Buttons", c);
    }
}
```

Figure 14-5 depicts the initial window that displays when the application is launched.

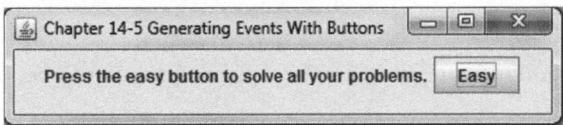

Figure 14-5. Generating events with buttons

How It Works

You want your button to do something when you press it. In Swing, the JButton component has a method called addActionListener() to add code to respond when the button has been clicked or pressed. You'll also notice the method begins with the word *add* and not *set*, meaning you can add many actions to the button. Whenever a button is pressed, all ActionListener instances will be notified, so they can carry out their action. Here you will create an anonymous inner instance of an ActionListener that sets the JLabel's text when the user presses the button. The following code adds an ActionListener instance:

```
JButton saveMe = new JButton("Easy");
saveMe.addActionListener(new ActionListener() {
        @Override
        public void actionPerformed(ActionEvent e) {
                status.setText("You will recieve two tickets to the petting zoo...");
        }
});
```

In some scenarios, you may want to associate keyboard shortcuts to buttons. To do this, you use the AbstractAction class, which is also an ActionListener instance but can do much more (toolbar, property change support, and so on). See the Javadoc for details.

14-6. Refreshing a User Interface

Problem

When copying many files, you want to display the status and percentage being completed in a GUI that is updated periodically.

Solution

Create an application to simulate files being copied or transferred. This application will contain a start button, cancel button, progress bar, and text area displaying the amount of time in milliseconds each file is being transferred. The primary class you will be focusing on is Java's `SwingWorker` class, which will be used to update the GUI periodically.

Shown here is the code to create an application that simulates a file transfer:

```
package org.java7recipes.chapter14.recipe14_06;

import java.awt.*;
import java.awt.event.*;
import java.util.*;
import java.util.concurrent.ExecutionException;
import javax.swing.*;
import org.java7recipes.chapter14.SimpleAppLauncher;

/**
 * Refreshing a GUI.
 * requires jdk7
 * @author cdea
 */
public class RefreshingGUI extends JPanel {

    static SwingWorker<Boolean, String> copyWorker;
    final int numFiles = 30;

    public RefreshingGUI() {

        setLayout(new BorderLayout());

        JPanel topArea = new JPanel();

        // progress bar
        final JLabel label = new JLabel("Files Transfer:", JLabel.CENTER);
        topArea.add(label);

        // progress bar
        final JProgressBar progressBar = new JProgressBar();
        progressBar.setIndeterminate(false);
        progressBar.setStringPainted(true);
        progressBar.setMinimum(0);
        progressBar.setMaximum(numFiles);


        topArea.add(progressBar);

        // create the top area
        add(topArea, BorderLayout.NORTH);

        // build buttons start and cancel
```

```java
        JPanel buttonsArea = new JPanel(new FlowLayout(FlowLayout.RIGHT));
        final JButton startButton = new JButton("Start");
        final JButton cancelButton = new JButton("Cancel");
        cancelButton.setEnabled(false);
        buttonsArea.add(startButton);
        buttonsArea.add(cancelButton);

        // build status area
        final JTextArea textArea = new JTextArea(5, 15);
        textArea.setEditable(false);
        JScrollPane statusScroll = new JScrollPane(textArea);
        buttonsArea.add(statusScroll);

        // create the buttons area
        add(buttonsArea, BorderLayout.SOUTH);


        // spawn a worker thread
        startButton.addActionListener(new ActionListener() {
            @Override
            public void actionPerformed(ActionEvent e) {
                startButton.setEnabled(false);
                progressBar.setValue(0);
                textArea.setText("");
                cancelButton.setEnabled(true);
                copyWorker = createWorker(numFiles,
                                          startButton,
                                          cancelButton,
                                          textArea,
                                          progressBar);
                copyWorker.execute();
            } // end of actionPerformed()
        }); // end of addActionListener()

        // cancel button will kill worker and reset.
        cancelButton.addActionListener(new ActionListener() {
            @Override
            public void actionPerformed(ActionEvent e) {
                startButton.setEnabled(true);
                cancelButton.setEnabled(false);
                copyWorker.cancel(true);
                progressBar.setValue(0);

            }
        });

    }

    public SwingWorker<Boolean, String> createWorker(final int numFiles,
            final JButton startButton,
            final JButton cancelButton,
            final JTextArea status,
```

```java
final JProgressBar pBar){

return new SwingWorker<>() {

/**
 * Not on the EDT
 */
@Override
protected Boolean doInBackground() throws Exception {
    for (int i = 0; i < numFiles; i++) {
        long elapsedTime = System.currentTimeMillis();
        copyFile("some file", "some dest file");
        elapsedTime = System.currentTimeMillis() - elapsedTime;
        String status = elapsedTime + " milliseconds";
        // queue up status
        publish(status);
    }
    return true;
}

/**
 * On the EDT
 */
@Override
protected void process(List<String> chunks) {
    super.process(chunks);
    // with each update gui
    for (String chunk : chunks) {
        status.append(chunk + "\n");
        pBar.setValue(pBar.getValue() + 1);
    }
}

/**
 * On the EDT
 */
@Override
protected void done() {
    try {
        if (isCancelled()) {
            status.append("File transfer was cancelled.\n");
            return;
        }
        Boolean ack = get();
        if (Boolean.TRUE.equals(ack)) {
            status.append("All files were transferred successfully.\n");
        }
        startButton.setEnabled(true);
        cancelButton.setEnabled(false);
    } catch (InterruptedException ex) {
        status.append("File transfer was interupted.\n");
    } catch (ExecutionException ex) {
```

```
                    ex.printStackTrace();
                }
            }
        };
    }

    public void copyFile(String src, String dest) throws InterruptedException {
        // simulate a long time
        Random rnd = new Random(System.currentTimeMillis());
        long millis = rnd.nextInt(1000);
        Thread.sleep(millis);
    }

    public static void main(String[] args) {
        final JPanel c = new RefreshingGUI();
        c.setPreferredSize(new Dimension(386, 160));
        c.setMinimumSize(new Dimension(386, 160));

        // Queueing GUI work to be run using the EDT.
        SimpleAppLauncher.launch("Chapter 14-6 Refreshing the GUI", c);
    }
}
```

Figure 14-6 depicts an application that simulates files being copied or transferred.

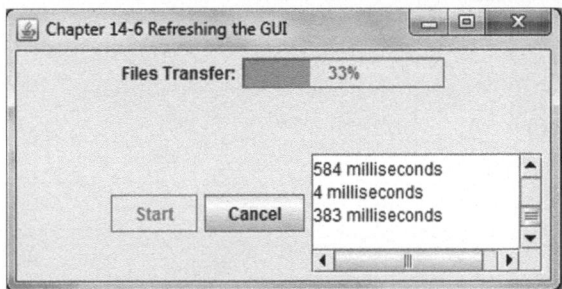

Figure 14-6. Refreshing the GUI

How It Works

In recipe 14-1 we discussed the importance of thread safety and using the EDT. The goal of this recipe is to create a responsive GUI which operates while expensive work is being done in the background, and still allow the user to interact with the application. Because this is a common behavior in GUI development, the amazing client-side Java engineers created a convenience class called the SwingWorker class. The SwingWorker class will properly handle non-GUI work and direct GUI events onto the EDT, thus abiding the thread safety rules in Swing. In this recipe, you will simulate files being transferred and concurrently displaying status to inform the user the percentage of files being transferred. As files are being transferred, the worker thread will update the text area with the amount of time in milliseconds each took to transfer. Before I discuss the details of the SwingWorker class, however, let's set up a GUI window with components.

First, you will add components onto the JPanel using a BorderLayout. On the north region, you will add a JProgressBar instance to let the user know the percentage of files transferred. Because you know how many files you are actually transferring, you will set the progress bar's indeterminate flag to false by calling the setIndeterminate(false) method. Next, you want the percentage string to be displayed while the progress bar is being updated by calling the setStringPainted() method with a value of true. The progress bar's minimum and maximum values are then set. In this scenario, there are 30 files to be transferred, so the maximum value is set to 30. The following code instantiates a new progress bar component (JProgressBar):

```
final JProgressBar progressBar = new JProgressBar();
progressBar.setIndeterminate(false);
progressBar.setStringPainted(true);
progressBar.setMinimum(0);
progressBar.setMaximum(numFiles);
```

You will add components to the south area of the BorderLayout manager consisting of buttons and a JTextArea component that will display the elapsed times in milliseconds when individual files are transferred. The buttons allow the user to start and stop the file transfer process.

The application doesn't actually transfer files, but simulates the process by generating random sleep times to block the thread as if it were doing work. The start button's action listener will generate an instance of a SwingWorker class to begin execution while the cancel button's action listener will have a reference to the same worker thread to cancel the operation.

■ **Note** Remember that all actionPerformed() methods are called via the EDT, so expensive calls are frowned upon. That is where the SwingWorker class will come to the rescue!

Now, let's talk about the SwingWorker class. You will create a method called createWorker() to return new instances of swing workers and execute them when the user presses the start button. When creating an instance of a SwingWorker class, you'll notice two generic types declared (SwingWorker<T,V>).The first thing to do is define the data type returned when the entire worker is finished. In this case, T will be a Boolean type that I chose to denote a successful transfer of all files. Second, you will want to define the type for the intermediate result values. In this case, V will be a String type. Intermediate result values are strings representing the time in milliseconds that will be displayed in the text area component. Here are the methods that you will implement from the SwingWorker class:

```
protected Boolean doInBackground();
protected void process(List<String> chunks);
protected void done();
```

The following methods describe the life cycle of a SwingWorker class:

- doInBackground(): The doInBackground() method is called from the SwingWorker.execute() method. This method is a background thread processing work. The doInBackground() method can call the publish() method to queue data for the process() method.

- `publish()`: The `publish()` method will be called from a `SwingWorker.doInBackground()` method. This method will call `process()`.

- `process()`: The `process()` method will be called from a `SwingWorker.publish()` invocation indirectly. A list of objects will be queued up for this method to process. The method is using the EDT thread to update the GUI based on a list of data elements.

- `done()`: The `done()` method can be called after the `SwingWorker.doInBackground()` and `SwingWorker.cancel()` methods are completed. The method is using the EDT thread to update the GUI with a final result to the caller.

14-7. Submitting Form Values to a Database

Problem

After creating a GUI form–type application to capture a person's name, you want to store that information locally onto your computer.

Solution

Use an embedded database such as the Derby database. When using relational databases, you will be using the Java Database Connectivity (JDBC) API.

The following code recipe is an application that allows a user to enter a person's first and last name to be saved into a database:

```
package org.java7recipes.chapter14.recipe14_07;

import java.awt.*;
import java.awt.event.*;
import java.util.concurrent.ExecutionException;
import javax.swing.*;
import org.java7recipes.chapter14.CellConstraint;
import org.java7recipes.chapter14.CustomGridLayout;
import org.java7recipes.chapter14.SimpleAppLauncher;

/**
 * <p>
 * +------------------------+
 * | [label ] [   field   ] |
 * | [label ] [   field   ] |
 * |              [ button ] |
 * +------------------------+
 * </p>
 *
 * Submitting Form Values to Database.
 * @author cdea
 */
```

```java
public class SubmittingFormValuestoDatabase extends JPanel {

    public SubmittingFormValuestoDatabase(){
        JLabel fNameLbl = new JLabel("First Name");
        final JTextField fNameFld = new JTextField(20);
        JLabel lNameLbl = new JLabel("Last Name");
        final JTextField lNameFld = new JTextField(20);
        final JButton saveButt = new JButton("Save");

        // Call Swing Worker to save to database.
        saveButt.addActionListener(new ActionListener() {

            @Override
            public void actionPerformed(ActionEvent e) {
                saveButt.setEnabled(false);
                SwingWorker<Integer, Void> worker = new SwingWorker<Integer, Void>() {

                    @Override
                    protected Integer doInBackground() throws Exception {
                        int pk = DBUtils.saveContact(fNameFld.getText(),
lNameFld.getText());
                        return pk;
                    }

                    @Override
                    protected void done() {
                        try {
                            System.out.println("Primary key = " + get());
                        } catch(InterruptedException | ExecutionException e) {
                            e.printStackTrace();
                        }
                        saveButt.setEnabled(true);
                    }
                };
                worker.execute();
            }
        });


        // create a layout 2 columns and 3 rows
        // horizontal and vertical gaps between components are 5 pixels
        CustomGridLayout cglayout = new CustomGridLayout(5, 5, 2, 3);

        setLayout(cglayout);

        // add first name label cell 0,0
        addToPanel(fNameLbl, 0, 0);

        // add last name label cell 0,1
        addToPanel(lNameLbl, 0, 1);

        // add first name field cell 1,0
```

443

```
        addToPanel(fNameFld, 1, 0);

        // add last name field cell 1,1
        addToPanel(lNameFld, 1, 1);

        // add save button and shift to the right
        CellConstraint saveButtConstr = new CellConstraint()
                .setColNum(1)
                .setRowNum(2)
                .setAlign(CellConstraint.RIGHT);
        add(saveButt, saveButtConstr);

    }

    private void addToPanel(Component comp, int colNum, int rowNum) {
        CellConstraint constr = new CellConstraint()
                .setColNum(colNum)
                .setRowNum(rowNum);
        add(comp, constr);
    }
    public static void main(String[] args) {
        final JPanel c = new SubmittingFormValuestoDatabase();
        c.setPreferredSize(new Dimension(402, 118));
        // Queueing GUI work to be run using the EDT.
        SimpleAppLauncher.launch("Chapter 14-7 Submitting Form Values to Database.", c);
    }
}
```

This recipe will be using an embedded database called Derby from the Apache group at http://www.apache.org. As a requirement, you will need to download the Derby software. To download the software, visit http://db.apache.org/derby/derby_downloads.html to download the latest version containing the libraries. Once it is downloaded, you can unzip or untar into a directory. To compile and run this recipe, you will need to update the classpath in your IDE or environment variable to point to Derby libraries (derby.jar and derbytools.jar). Shown here is the code listing of our database utility class DBUtils.java, which is capable of performing database transactions:

```
package org.java7recipes.chapter14.recipe14_07;

import java.sql.Connection;
import java.sql.DriverManager;
import java.sql.PreparedStatement;
import java.sql.ResultSet;
import java.sql.SQLException;
import java.sql.Statement;
import java.util.ArrayList;
import java.util.Properties;

/**
 * DBUtils class is responsible for saving contact information
 * into a database.
 * requires jdk7
```

```
    * @author cdea
    */
public class DBUtils {

    private static String framework = "embedded";
    private static String driver = "org.apache.derby.jdbc.EmbeddedDriver";
    private static String protocol = "jdbc:derby:";

    public static int saveContact(String fName, String lName) {
        int pk = (fName + lName).hashCode();

        loadDriver();

        Connection conn = null;
        ArrayList statements = new ArrayList();
        PreparedStatement psInsert = null;
        Statement s = null;
        ResultSet rs = null;
        try {
            // connection properties
            Properties props = new Properties();
            props.put("user", "scott");
            props.put("password", "tiger");

            // database name
            String dbName = "demoDB";

            conn = DriverManager.getConnection(protocol + dbName
                    + ";create=true", props);

            System.out.println("Creating database " + dbName);

            // handle transaction
            conn.setAutoCommit(false);

            s = conn.createStatement();
            statements.add(s);

//            s.execute("drop table contact");

            // Create a contact table...
            s.execute("create table contact(id int, fName varchar(40), lName varchar(40))");
            System.out.println("Created table contact");


            psInsert = conn.prepareStatement("insert into contact values (?, ?, ?)");
            statements.add(psInsert);
            psInsert.setInt(1, pk);
            psInsert.setString(2, fName);
            psInsert.setString(3, lName);
            psInsert.executeUpdate();
            conn.commit();
```

```
            System.out.println("Inserted " + fName + " " + lName);

            // delete the table for demo
            s.execute("drop table contact");
            System.out.println("Dropped table contact");

            conn.commit();
            System.out.println("Committed the transaction");

            // standard checking code when shutting down database.
            // code from http://db.apache.org/derby/
            if (framework.equals("embedded")) {
                try {
                    // shuts down Derby
                    DriverManager.getConnection("jdbc:derby:;shutdown=true");

                } catch (SQLException se) {
                    if (((se.getErrorCode() == 50000)
 && ("XJ015".equals(se.getSQLState())))) {
                        System.out.println("Derby shut down normally");
                    } else {
                        System.err.println("Derby did not shut down normally");
                        se.printStackTrace();
                    }
                }
            }
        } catch (SQLException sqle) {
            sqle.printStackTrace();
        } finally {
            close(rs);

            int i = 0;
            while (!statements.isEmpty()) {
                Statement st = (Statement) statements.remove(i);
                close(st);
            }

            close(conn);

        }

        return pk;
    }

    private static void close(AutoCloseable closable) {
        try {
            if (closable != null) {
                closable.close();
                closable = null;
            }
        } catch (Exception sqle) {
            sqle.printStackTrace();
```

```
        }
    }

    private static void loadDriver() {

            try {
                Class.forName(driver).newInstance();
                System.out.println("Loaded driver");

            } catch (Exception e) {
                e.printStackTrace();
            }

    }
}
```

Figure 14-7 depicts the form application allowing a user to save a person's name information into a local database.

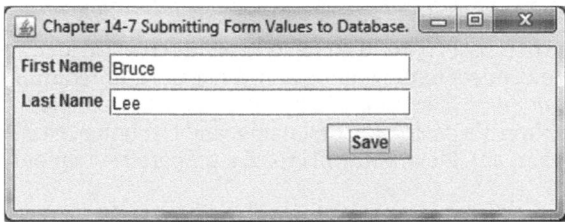

Figure 14-7. Submitting form values to a database

How It Works

When creating form interfaces, there will be a point in time when you have to write the data somewhere. I've been fortunate to work on projects in the past where data is stored locally in an embedded database. In this recipe, I chose the popular embedded database called Derby. Just as a heads-up on being able to run this recipe, you must include the derby.jar and derbytools.jar libraries into your classpath.

When working with form-based applications, you should separate your GUI code from your action code. I created two separate class files: the SubmittingFormValuestoDatabase class and the DBUtils class.

The SubmittingFormValuestoDatabase class is our form and is essentially identical to recipe 14-4, so I won't go into the layout of the components, but focus on the save button. The save button's action listener contains a SwingWorker that will invoke the DBUtils.saveContact() method that will save the form data. You will notice in the doInBackground() method's call to saveContact(), which will return a primary key (on a non-event dispatch thread). The doInBackground() method is not performing the work on the EDT (hence the name) and could take awhile to save the data. Once the doInBackground() method is completed and has returned the primary key the object will be available when the done() method calls the get() method. When inside the done() method, you are now on the EDT where you have an opportunity to update the GUI. Shown here is the done() method calling the get() method that contains the primary key:

```
@Override
protected void done() {
    try {
        System.out.println("Primary key = " + get());
    } catch(InterruptedException | ExecutionException e) {
        e.printStackTrace();
    }
    saveButt.setEnabled(true);
}
```

In the code recipe you will simply send the primary key to standard out. To invoke the get() method, you will need to surround it with exception handling. In the preceding code the catch exception code has a pipe symbol between two exception classes (InterruptedException and ExecutionException). This is because new to Java 7 is the "Handling More Than One Type of Exception" feature. This allows you to make your exception blocks smaller.

Next, the DBUtils class is responsible for persisting form data. To simplify things for this example I coded things to create the database and contact table in the beginning and later drop the table when done. So, feel free to take out these lines when creating a real application.

Here is a quick rundown of what is going on in the saveContact() method. First, it receives the contact information from the caller and derives a primary key using a hash of the first name and last name as a relatively unique identifier for a row in the database. Next, the call to loadDriver() will load the JDBC Derby driver. Then it prepares properties to connect to the database and sets the auto-commit to false. After setting the transactions to auto-commit mode false, you will create a table that will hold our contact information. The contact table contains three fields, the ID, first name, and last name. Id is a data type of int, and the name fields are of type varchar(40). Next, you will create a prepared statement that binds our data elements.

Once the prepared statement is executed via executeUpdate() method, it will indicate to the database a transaction is ready to be committed. Last, you will perform the commit() on the connection to flush changes to the database. The rest of the code basically drops the table and closes all resources. For more details on JDBC, see Chapter 11.

14-8. Making a Multi-Window Program

Problem

You want to create an application that generates random quotes displayed in individual windows inside the application (similar to a mini-desktop).

Solution

Create a multi-window application with display content using the JDesktopPane and JInternalFrame classes.

The following code recipe creates an application that allows a user to pop up internal windows with random quotes:

```
package org.java7recipes.chapter14.recipe14_08;
```

```java
import java.awt.*;
import java.awt.event.*;
import java.beans.PropertyVetoException;
import java.util.Random;
import javax.swing.*;
import org.java7recipes.chapter14.AppSetup;
import org.java7recipes.chapter14.SimpleAppLauncher;

/**
 * Making a Multi-Window Program.
 * @author cdea
 */
public class MultiWindowGUI extends JDesktopPane implements AppSetup {

    public MultiWindowGUI() {
        setDragMode(JDesktopPane.LIVE_DRAG_MODE);
        //setDragMode(JDesktopPane.OUTLINE_DRAG_MODE);
    }

    public void apply(final JFrame frame) {
        JMenuBar menuBar = new JMenuBar();
        JMenu menu = new JMenu("File");
        JMenuItem newWindowMenuItem = new JMenuItem("New Internal Frame");
        newWindowMenuItem.setMnemonic(KeyEvent.VK_N);
        newWindowMenuItem.setAccelerator(KeyStroke.getKeyStroke(
                KeyEvent.VK_N, ActionEvent.CTRL_MASK));
        final JDesktopPane desktop = this;
        newWindowMenuItem.addActionListener(new ActionListener() {

            @Override
            public void actionPerformed(ActionEvent e) {
                JInternalFrame frame = new InternalFrame();
                frame.setVisible(true);
                desktop.add(frame);
                try {
                    frame.setSelected(true);
                } catch (PropertyVetoException pve) {
                }
            }
        });
        menu.add(newWindowMenuItem);
        menuBar.add(menu);
        frame.setJMenuBar(menuBar);
    }

    public static void main(String[] args) {
        final JDesktopPane c = new MultiWindowGUI();
        c.setPreferredSize(new Dimension(433, 312));
        // Queueing GUI work to be run using the EDT.
        SimpleAppLauncher.launch("Chapter 14-8 Making a Multi-Window Program", c);
    }
}
```

```
class InternalFrame extends JInternalFrame {

    static int count = 0;
    static final int xOffset = 35;
    static final int yOffset = 35;
    final static String[] rndQuotes = {
        "Even in laughter the heart is sorrowful",
        "For what does it profit a man to gain the whole world, and forfeit his soul?",
        "The light of the body is the eye; if then your eye is true, all your body will be
full of light.",
        "For many are called, but few are chosen.",
        "A word fitly spoken is like apples of gold in pictures of silver.",
        "Iron sharpeneth iron; so a man sharpeneth the countenance of his friend."
    };

    public InternalFrame() {
        super("Window #" + (count++),
                true, //resizable
                true, //closable
                true, //maximizable
                true);//iconifiable
        Random rand = new Random();
        int q = rand.nextInt(rndQuotes.length);

        setLayout(new BorderLayout());
        JTextArea ta = new JTextArea(rndQuotes[q]);
        JScrollPane sp = new JScrollPane(ta);
        ta.setLineWrap(true);
        ta.setWrapStyleWord(true);
        add(sp, BorderLayout.CENTER);
        setSize(200, 100);

        // Stagger windows
        setLocation(xOffset * count, yOffset * count);
    }
}
```

Figure 14-8 shows the application displaying multiple internal windows, each containing a random quote.

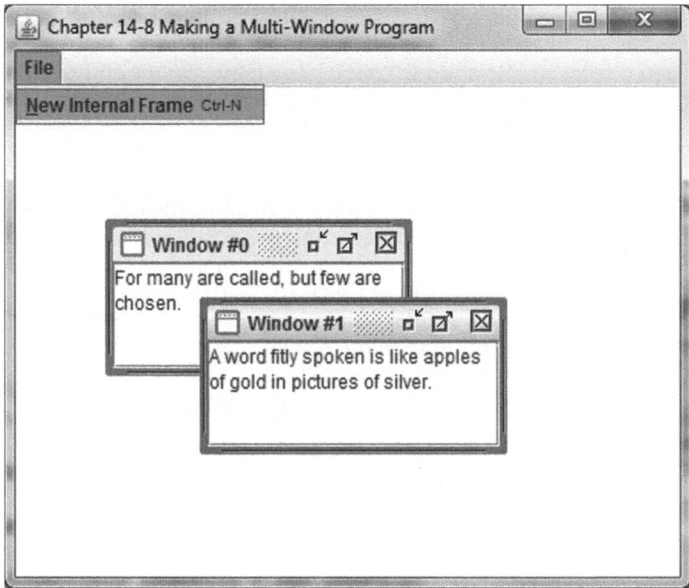

Figure 14-8. Making a multiwindow program

How It Works

Java Swing's JDesktopPane is a container component similar to a JPanel except that it manages mini internal frames (JInternalFrame) similar to a virtualized desktop. These internal frames act very similar to JFrames on your host desktop. Just like JFrames, you may add menu items and any swing components into internal frames.

To create a multi-window application, you will first extend from the JDesktopPane class with a default constructor. Notice that the MultiWindowGUI class extends from JDesktopPane class and therefore it is a JDesktopPane instance. The MultiWindowGUI instance will be passed into the SimpleAppLauncher.launch() method to be then placed onto the application window's content region. Shown here is the code to launch and display the application window (JFrame) having a desktop pane (JDesktopPane):

```
final JDesktopPane c = new MultiWindowGUI();
c.setPreferredSize(new Dimension(433, 312));
// Queueing GUI work to be run using the EDT.
SimpleAppLauncher.launch("Chapter 14-8 Making a Multi-Window Program", c);
```

When you place the JDesktopPane instance in the main JFrame window, it is placed in the center content region using the BorderLayout. Placing the JDesktopPane into the center will allow the virtualized desktop to take up all the available space. In the constructor, the call to setDragMode() sets the effect when you drag the internal windows across the desktop. With certain environments that have high latency or lower bandwidths, rendering internal frames across the network can be too expensive (for example, remoting using a VPN). If this is a concern, you will want to set your JDesktopPane's drag mode to outline drag mode (JDesktopPane.OUTLINE_DRAG_MODE). Because we are local and things are fast, you

451

will be setting your drag mode to `LIVE_DRAG_MODE` to mimic real desktops. In our example, I also implement the `AppSetup` to add menu options enabling the user to create new internal frames (`JInternalFrame`) with random quotes when displayed. (Recipe 14-9 discusses menu options and submenus.) You might also notice that the menu has the keyboard shortcut Ctrl+n. (Implementing keyboard shortcuts for menus are discussed in recipe 14-16.) In this recipe, you will want to focus your attention on the `newWindowMenu` variable, in which you will add an `ActionListener`. This is where an internal frame is instantiated and placed onto the desktop area.

You will create a class that extends from `JInternalFrame`. Your objective is to allow the user to select the menu option to create internal frames that will be staggered similarly on most windowed desktops. Each internal frame created will have a title denoting the sequence number or count of the frame when instantiated. You'll notice the call to `super()` where you will pass in `Booleans` to the super class to set the `JInternalFrame` object to be resizable, closable, maximizable, and iconifiable. Next, you will pick a random quote from the static `String` array `rndQuotes`. The random quote is placed in a scrollable (`JScrollPane`) text area (`JTextArea`) with text wrapping set to `true`. Once the internal window is sized `setSize(200, 100)`, you will stagger each window according to the count and the offset.

14-9. Adding a Menu to an Application

Problem

You are asked to create a UI for a building security application to allow a user to select items to control.

Solution

Create standard menu options to be added to your application. You will also want to add menus and menu items in your application using the Swing `JMenu`, `JMenuItem`, `JCheckBoxMenuItem`, and `JRadioButtonMenuItem` classes.

Shown here is the code recipe to create a menu-driven UI that simulates a building security application:

```
package org.java7recipes.chapter14.recipe14_09;

import java.awt.*;
import java.awt.event.*;
import javax.swing.*;
import org.java7recipes.chapter14.AppSetup;
import org.java7recipes.chapter14.SimpleAppLauncher;

/**
 * Adding Menus to an application.
 * @author cdea
 */
public class AddingMenus extends JPanel implements AppSetup{

    public AddingMenus(){

    }
```

```java
    public void apply(final JFrame frame) {
        JMenuBar menuBar = new JMenuBar();

        JMenu menu = new JMenu("File");
        JMenuItem newItem = new JMenuItem("New", null);
        menu.add(newItem);

        JMenuItem saveItem = new JMenuItem("Save", null);
        saveItem.setEnabled(false);
        menu.add(saveItem);

        menu.addSeparator();

        JMenuItem exitItem = new JMenuItem("Exit", null);
        menu.add(exitItem);

        menuBar.add(menu);

        JMenu tools = new JMenu("Cameras");
        JCheckBoxMenuItem showCamera1= new JCheckBoxMenuItem("Show Camera 1", null);
        showCamera1.setSelected(true);
        tools.add(showCamera1);

        JCheckBoxMenuItem showCamera2= new JCheckBoxMenuItem("Show Camera 2", null);
        tools.add(showCamera2);
        menuBar.add(tools);

        JMenu alarm = new JMenu("Alarm");
        ButtonGroup alarmGroup = new ButtonGroup();
        JRadioButtonMenuItem alertItem = new JRadioButtonMenuItem("Sound Alarm");
        alarm.add(alertItem);
        alarmGroup.add(alertItem);

        JRadioButtonMenuItem stopItem = new JRadioButtonMenuItem("Alarm Off", null);
        stopItem.setSelected(true);
        alarm.add(stopItem);
        alarmGroup.add(stopItem);

        JMenu contingencyPlans = new JMenu("Contingent Plans");
        JCheckBoxMenuItem selfDestruct = new JCheckBoxMenuItem("Self Destruct in T minus
50");
        contingencyPlans.add(selfDestruct);

        JCheckBoxMenuItem turnOffCoffee = new JCheckBoxMenuItem("Turn off the coffee machine
");
        contingencyPlans.add(turnOffCoffee);

        JCheckBoxMenuItem runOption= new JCheckBoxMenuItem("Run for your lives! ");
        contingencyPlans.add(runOption);
```

```
        alarm.add(contingencyPlans);

        menuBar.add(alarm);

        frame.setJMenuBar(menuBar);
    }

    public static void main(String[] args) {
        final JPanel c = new AddingMenus();
        c.setPreferredSize(new Dimension(433, 312));
        // Queueing GUI work to be run using the EDT.
        SimpleAppLauncher.launch("Chapter 14-9 Adding Menus to an Application", c);
    }
}
```

Figure 14-9 shows an application with menus, submenus, radio button menu items, and check box menu items.

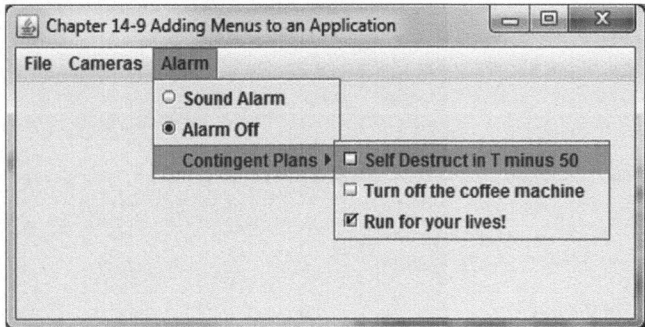

Figure 14-9. Adding menus to an application

How It Works

Menus are standard ways on windowed platform applications to allow users to select options. Menus should also have the functionality of hotkeys or accelerators or mnemonics. Often users will want to use the keyboard instead of the mouse to navigate the menu. When creating menus, you can only add them to the Swing `JFrame` or `JInternalFrame` container classes.

First, you will implement the `AppSetup` interface to allow the developer an opportunity to add components into the main window frame (`JFrame`). There you will create an instance of a `JMenuBar` that will contain one-to-many menu (`JMenu`) objects. The following code line creates a menu bar:

```
JMenuBar menuBar = new JMenuBar();
```

Second, you will create menu (`JMenu`) objects that contain one-to-many menu item (`JMenuItem`) objects and other `JMenu` object making submenus. The code statement here creates a file menu:

```
JMenu menu = new JMenu("File");
```

Third, you will create menu items to be added to JMenu objects such as JMenuItem, JCheckBoxMenuItem, and JRadioButtonMenuItem. A thing to note is that menu item can have icons in them. I don't showcase this in the recipe, but I encourage you to explore the various constructors for all JMenuItems. When creating a JRadioButtonMenuItem, you should be aware of the ButtonGroup class. The ButtonGroup class is also used on regular JRadioButtons to allow one selected option only. The following code creates JRadioButtonMenuItem items to be added to a JMenu object:

```
JMenu alarm = new JMenu("Alarm");
ButtonGroup alarmGroup = new ButtonGroup();
JRadioButtonMenuItem alertItem = new JRadioButtonMenuItem("Sound Alarm");
alarmGroup.add(alertItem);
alarm.add(alertItem);

JRadioButtonMenuItem stopItem = new JRadioButtonMenuItem("Alarm Off", null);
stopItem.setSelected(true);
alarmGroup.add(stopItem);
alarm.add(stopItem);
```

At times you may want some menu items separated by using visual line separators. To create a visual separator, call the addSeparator() method on the menu item. Other JMenuItems used are the JCheckBoxMenuItem and the JRadioButtonMenuItem classes where they are similar to their counterpart Swing components. Please refer to the Javadoc to see more on JMenuItems.

14-10. Adding Tabs to a Form

Problem

You want to add tabs in your application.

Solution

Create an application with tabs using the Swing container JTabbedPane class.

The code here builds and presents an application with tabs that can be arranged in different orientations. The application will consist of a menu option that allows the user to choose a left, right, top, and bottom orientation.

```
package org.java7recipes.chapter14.recipe14_10;

import java.awt.*;
import java.awt.event.*;
import javax.swing.*;
import org.java7recipes.chapter14.AppSetup;
import org.java7recipes.chapter14.SimpleAppLauncher;

/**
 * Adding tabs to an application.
 * Requires jdk7
```

```
 * @author cdea
 */
public class AddingTabbedPane extends JTabbedPane implements AppSetup{

    public AddingTabbedPane(){


        for (int i=0; i<10; i++) {
            JPanel tabPane = new JPanel();
            tabPane.add(new JLabel("Tab" + i));
            addTab("Tab " + i, null, tabPane, "Tab" + i);
        }
        setTabLayoutPolicy(JTabbedPane.SCROLL_TAB_LAYOUT);
    }

    public void apply(final JFrame frame) {
        JMenuBar menuBar = new JMenuBar();

        JMenu menu = new JMenu("Tabbed Panels");
        JMenuItem left = new JMenuItem("Left", null);
        left.addActionListener(new TabPlacementAction(this, "left"));
        menu.add(left);

        JMenuItem right = new JMenuItem("Right", null);
        right.addActionListener(new TabPlacementAction(this, "right"));
        menu.add(right);

        JMenuItem top = new JMenuItem("Top", null);
        top.addActionListener(new TabPlacementAction(this, "top"));
        menu.add(top);

        JMenuItem bottom = new JMenuItem("Bottom", null);
        bottom.addActionListener(new TabPlacementAction(this, "bottom"));
        menu.add(bottom);

        menuBar.add(menu);

        frame.setJMenuBar(menuBar);
    }

    public static void main(String[] args) {
        final JComponent c = new AddingTabbedPane();
        c.setPreferredSize(new Dimension(433, 312));
        // Queueing GUI work to be run using the EDT.
        SimpleAppLauncher.launch("Chapter 14-10 Adding Tabs to Forms ", c);
    }
}

class TabPlacementAction implements ActionListener {
    private String action;
    private JTabbedPane tabbedPane;
    public TabPlacementAction (JTabbedPane tabbedPane, String action) {
```

```
        this.action = action;
        this.tabbedPane = tabbedPane;
    }
    @Override
    public void actionPerformed(ActionEvent e) {
        if ("left".equalsIgnoreCase(action)) {
            tabbedPane.setTabPlacement(JTabbedPane.LEFT);
        } else if ("right".equalsIgnoreCase(action)) {
            tabbedPane.setTabPlacement(JTabbedPane.RIGHT);
        }   else if ("top".equalsIgnoreCase(action)) {
            tabbedPane.setTabPlacement(JTabbedPane.TOP);
        } else if ("bottom".equalsIgnoreCase(action)) {
            tabbedPane.setTabPlacement(JTabbedPane.BOTTOM);
        }
    }
}
```

Figure 14-10 depicts an application with a menu selection used to choose different tab orientations.

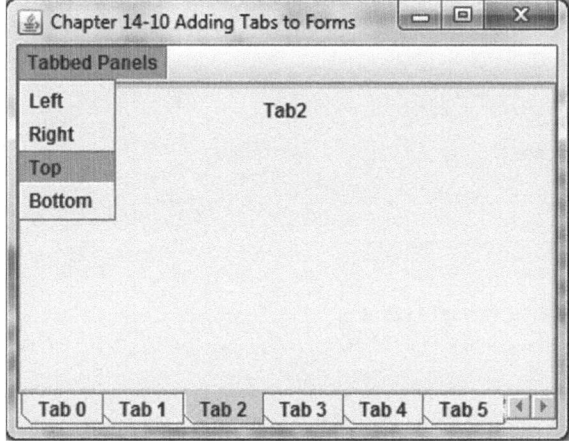

Figure 14-10. Adding tabs to forms

How It Works

Adding tabs to your GUI application is quite simple. You first will create a JTabbedPane contain class that will hold one-to-many JPanels. Each JPanel object added to the container becomes a tab.

In the constructor, I created 10 tabs with a JLabel containing the numbered tab (zero relative). Once the individual tabs were created, I set the tab layout policy to SCROLL_TAB_LAYOUT. Setting the layout policy will create button-like controls to paginate when too many tabs are being displayed at once. Figure 14-10 shows the left and right buttons to the right of Tab 5.

To make things interesting, I created menu options to allow the user to view the tab placement to showcase them displayed on the left, right, top, or bottom. Each menu option will add an instance of a TabPlacementAction that is responsible for calling the tabbed pane's setTabPlacement() method.

14-11. Drawing on a Canvas

Problem

You came across a great idea while at work and you must write it down before you forget. Sadly, your company has just cut its office supply budget, leaving you without pencil or paper.

Solution

Create a doodle application using the Java Swing `JPanel`, `MouseListener`, `MouseMotionListener`, and `Graphics2D` classes.

The following code recipe creates a doodle application allowing you to use your mouse pointer to draw on a canvas:

```java
package org.java7recipes.chapter14.recipe14_11;

import java.awt.*;
import java.awt.event.*;
import java.awt.geom.*;
import java.util.*;
import javax.swing.*;
import org.java7recipes.chapter14.SimpleAppLauncher;

/**
 * Drawing on a Canvas.
 * @author cdea
 */
public class DrawOnCanvas extends JPanel implements MouseListener,
        MouseMotionListener {

    Path2D oneDrawing = new Path2D.Double();
    List<Path2D> drawings = new ArrayList<>();
    private Point2D anchorPt;

    public DrawOnCanvas() {
        add(new JLabel("Java 7"));
        JTextField field = new JTextField(10);
        add(field);
    }

    @Override
    protected void paintComponent(Graphics g) {
        super.paintComponent(g);

        Graphics2D g2d = (Graphics2D) g;
        g2d.setBackground(Color.WHITE);
        g2d.clearRect(0, 0, getParent().getWidth(), getParent().getHeight());
        g2d.setRenderingHint(RenderingHints.KEY_ANTIALIASING,
```

```
                RenderingHints.VALUE_ANTIALIAS_ON);

        g2d.setPaint(Color.BLACK);
        if (oneDrawing != null) {
            g2d.draw(oneDrawing);
        }
        for (Path2D gp : drawings) {
            g2d.draw(gp);
        }

    }

    public static void main(String[] args) {
        final DrawOnCanvas c = new DrawOnCanvas();
        c.addMouseListener(c);
        c.addMouseMotionListener(c);
        c.setPreferredSize(new Dimension(409, 726));
        SimpleAppLauncher.launch("Chapter 14-11 Drawing on a Canvas", c);
    }

    @Override
    public void mouseClicked(MouseEvent e) {
    }

    @Override
public void mousePressed(MouseEvent e) {
        anchorPt = (Point2D) e.getPoint().clone();
        oneDrawing = new GeneralPath();
        oneDrawing.moveTo(anchorPt.getX(), anchorPt.getY());
        repaint();
    }

    @Override
public void mouseReleased(final MouseEvent e) {
        if (anchorPt != null) {
            drawings.add(oneDrawing);
            oneDrawing = null;
        }
        repaint();
    }

    @Override
    public void mouseEntered(MouseEvent e) {
    }

    @Override
    public void mouseExited(MouseEvent e) {
    }

    @Override
public void mouseDragged(MouseEvent e) {
        oneDrawing.lineTo(e.getX(), e.getY());
```

```
        repaint();
    }

    @Override
    public void mouseMoved(MouseEvent e) {
    }
}
```

Figure 14-11 depicts a doodle application with a text label, text field, and a drawing surface.

Figure 14-11. Drawing on canvas

How It Works

When you want to draw on a surface in Swing, you simply override the `paintComponent()` method of a `JComponent` class. In this recipe, I wanted to draw and have text components on the same surface; so, instead of extending from the `JComponent` class, I extended the `JPanel` container class. Once the `paintComponent()` method is overridden, you will be able to use the `Graphics2D` object to draw on the surface. To learn more on the `Graphics2D` object in Java 2D, see Chapter 12.

Before getting into the implementation, I want to point out the instance variables at the top of the class. The following are the application's instance variable descriptions:

- `oneDrawing`: A single instance of a `Path2D` variable that holds points of the current drawing when the mouse is pressed.

- `drawings`: A list of `Path2D` instances that contain the many paths or drawings. Once a mouse releases, the current path instance is added to this list.

- anchorPt: This is the point on the surface which starts the path to be drawn. When an initial mouse press occurs, the anchor point is assigned before a mouse drag event occurs.

To listen for mouse events in this recipe, you will implement the MouseListener and MouseMotionListener interfaces. You will implement three methods: mousePress(), mouseReleased(), and mouseDragged(). The following are the mouse method functions:

- mousePress(): Is responsible for creating the initial starting point and an instance of a Path2D.

- mouseDragged(): Will add points to be connected in the path instance using the lineTo().

- mouseRelease(): Is called when the user releases the mouse button after a drag operation. Also adds the current path instance into the list of Path2D objects.

You'll notice in the code that each method has a repaint() method. The repaint() method notifies the graphics context to repaint the surface via the paintComponent() method.

In the paintComponent() method, you will set the background to white, set anti-aliasing on, and set the color of the stroke to be black. You will draw the current path instance and then loop through the list of previously stored paths (drawings) to be drawn. There you have it a simple doodler!

14-12. Generating and Laying Out Icons

Problem

You want to load icons and position text on buttons and labels.

Solution

Use the ImageIcon, JButton, and JLabel classes.

The following code recipe creates an application to demonstrate loading icons and label as well as positioning text:

```
package org.java7recipes.chapter14.recipe14_12;

import java.awt.*;
import javax.swing.*;
import org.java7recipes.chapter14.CellConstraint;
import org.java7recipes.chapter14.CustomGridLayout;
import org.java7recipes.chapter14.SimpleAppLauncher;

/**
 * <p>
 * +------------------------+
 * | [label ] [ button ]    |
 * | [label ] [ button ]    |
 * | [label ] [ button ]    |
```

```
 * +------------------------+
 * </p>
 *
 * Generating and Laying Out Icons.
 * @author cdea
 */
public final class GeneratingAndLayingIcons extends JPanel {

    public GeneratingAndLayingIcons() {
        JLabel label1 = new JLabel("Gold Spiral", createImageIcon("goldspiral.png"),
JLabel.LEFT);
        label1.setHorizontalTextPosition(SwingConstants.RIGHT);
        JLabel label2 = new JLabel("Gold Circle", createImageIcon("goldcircle.png"),
JLabel.LEFT);
        label2.setHorizontalTextPosition(SwingConstants.CENTER);
        JLabel label3 = new JLabel("Gold Star", createImageIcon("goldstar.png"),
JLabel.LEFT);
        label3.setHorizontalTextPosition(SwingConstants.LEFT);

        JButton button1 = new JButton("Spiral", createImageIcon("spiral.png"));
        JButton button2 = new JButton("Cube", createImageIcon("cube.png"));
        button2.setHorizontalTextPosition(SwingConstants.CENTER);
        JButton button3 = new JButton("Pentagon", createImageIcon("pentagon.png"));
        button3.setHorizontalTextPosition(SwingConstants.LEFT);

        // create a layout 3x3 cell grid.
        // horizontal and vertical gaps between components are 5 pixels
        CustomGridLayout cglayout = new CustomGridLayout(10, 10, 3, 3);

        setLayout(cglayout);

        // add label1 cell 0,0
        addToPanel(label1, 0, 0, CellConstraint.RIGHT);

        // add label2 cell 1,0
        addToPanel(label2, 0,1, CellConstraint.RIGHT);

        // add label3 cell 2,0
        addToPanel(label3, 0,2, CellConstraint.RIGHT);

        // add button1 cell 0,1
        addToPanel(button1, 1, 0, CellConstraint.RIGHT);

        // add button2 cell 1,1
        addToPanel(button2, 1, 1, CellConstraint.RIGHT);

        // add button2 cell 2,1
        addToPanel(button3, 1, 2, CellConstraint.RIGHT);

    }

    protected ImageIcon createImageIcon(String path) {
        java.net.URL imageURL = getClass().getResource(path);
        if (imageURL != null) {
            return new ImageIcon(imageURL);
```

```
        } else {
            throw new RuntimeException("Unable to load " + path);
        }
    }

    private void addToPanel(Component comp, int colNum, int rowNum, int align) {
        CellConstraint constr = new CellConstraint()
                .setColNum(colNum)
                .setRowNum(rowNum)
                .setAlign(align);
        add(comp, constr);
    }

    public static void main(String[] args) {
        final JPanel c = new GeneratingAndLayingIcons();
        c.setPreferredSize(new Dimension(388, 194));
        // Queueing GUI work to be run using the EDT.
        SimpleAppLauncher.launch("Chapter 14-12 Generating and Laying Out Icons.", c);
    }
}
```

Figure 14-12 shows the application displaying labels and buttons with positioned text and icons.

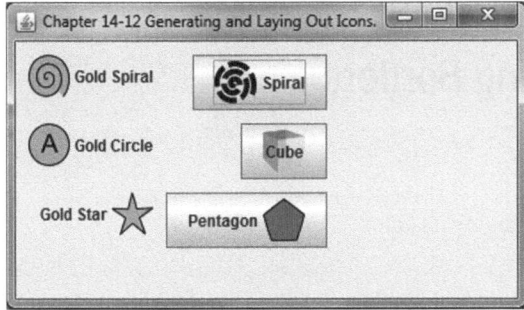

Figure 14-12. Generating and laying out icons

How It Works

Before we discuss the code details, I would like to mention layout. For this recipe you will be using the
CustomGridLayout manager to position the UI components in a grid-like table display. For brevity, I will
not go into great detail, but will refer you to recipe 14-4, in which the custom grid layout is discussed
more in depth. So, let's begin by creating icons, labels, and buttons!

When using JLabels and JButtons, you can easily add icons along with the text when displayed.
Another nice functionality of the JLabel and JButton components is to set the text position relative to the
icon image. In the recipe code, I created a convenience method called createImageIcon() to load and
return an ImageIcon object. The code here is the createImageIcon() method that creates and returns an
icon (ImageIcon) loaded from a URL:

```
public ImageIcon createImageIcon(String path) {
        java.net.URL imageURL = getClass().getResource(path);
        if (imageURL != null) {
            return new ImageIcon(imageURL);
        } else {
            throw new RuntimeException("Unable to load " + path);
        }
    }
}
```

■ **Note**   To run this recipe using the NetBeans IDE, you may have to perform a clean and build of the project to ensure the images get copied properly to reside on the classpath. This allows the getClass().getResource() method to load and create ImageIcon instances.

The image icons are loaded using the getClass().getResource() method, which returns a URL object representing the location of an image file. After instantiating the ImageIcon class, the method returns to the caller a newly loaded instance of an ImageIcon object.

When creating new instances of a JLabel, I chose the constructor that receives three parameters: the text, icon, and horizontal alignment.

14-13. Designing and Manipulating Borders

Problem

You want to preview different types of borders while changing its color.

Solution

Create an application with sample borders and color selections to allow the user to design a border. Use the Swing BorderFactory API.

The following code recipe creates an application with sample borders and color selections to allow the user to design a border:

```
package org.java7recipes.chapter14.recipe14_13;

import java.awt.*;
import java.awt.event.*;
import java.util.*;
import javax.swing.*;
import javax.swing.border.*;
import org.java7recipes.chapter14.CellConstraint;
import org.java7recipes.chapter14.CustomGridLayout;
import org.java7recipes.chapter14.SimpleAppLauncher;
```

```
/**
 * Border Designer.
 * @author cdea
 */
public final class BorderDesigner extends JTabbedPane {
    final static Map<String, Color> COLOR_MAP = new TreeMap<>();
    static {
        COLOR_MAP.put("Black", Color.BLACK);
        COLOR_MAP.put("Blue", Color.BLUE);
        COLOR_MAP.put("Green", Color.GREEN);
        COLOR_MAP.put("Red", Color.RED);
        COLOR_MAP.put("Gray", Color.GRAY);
        COLOR_MAP.put("Yellow", Color.YELLOW);
        COLOR_MAP.put("White", Color.WHITE);
    }
    final static Border[] BORDERS = new Border[8];
    static {
        BORDERS[0] = BorderFactory.createLineBorder(Color.BLACK);
        BORDERS[1] = BorderFactory.createLoweredBevelBorder();
        BORDERS[2] = BorderFactory.createRaisedBevelBorder();
        BORDERS[3] = BorderFactory.createEtchedBorder(EtchedBorder.LOWERED);
        BORDERS[4] = BorderFactory.createEtchedBorder(EtchedBorder.RAISED);
        BORDERS[5] = BorderFactory.createDashedBorder(Color.BLACK, 4, 4);
        BORDERS[6] = BorderFactory.createStrokeBorder(new BasicStroke(3));
        BORDERS[7] = BorderFactory.createTitledBorder(BORDERS[0], "Titled Border",
TitledBorder.LEFT, TitledBorder.DEFAULT_JUSTIFICATION);

    }
    final static String[] BORDER_TYPES = {"Line Border",
            "Lowered Bevel Border",
            "Raised Bevel Border",
            "Lowered Etched Border",
            "Raised Etched Border",
            "Dashed Border",
            "Stroke Border",
            "Titled Border"};

    public BorderDesigner() {


        JPanel borderTab = new JPanel();
        borderTab.setLayout(new CustomGridLayout(10, 20, 2, 2));

        // Border area
        final JPanel borderArea = new JPanel();
        borderArea.add(new JLabel("Java 7 Recipes"));
        borderArea.setPreferredSize(new Dimension(200, 100));
        borderArea.setBorder(BORDERS[0]);
        addToPanel(borderTab, borderArea, 1, 0, CellConstraint.CENTER);

        // ComboBox changing the individual borders
        final JComboBox<String> borderComboBox = new JComboBox<>(BORDER_TYPES);
```

```
            // Set border when selection changes
            final List<String> borderTypeList = Arrays.asList(BORDER_TYPES);

            borderComboBox.addActionListener(new ActionListener() {
                @Override
                public void actionPerformed(ActionEvent e) {
                    String selected = (String) borderComboBox.getSelectedItem();
                    int index = borderTypeList.indexOf(selected);
                    borderArea.setBorder(BORDERS[index]);
                }
            });

            // ComboBox to change the color on certain borders
            JComboBox<String> colorComboBox = createColorComboBox(BORDERS, borderArea);

            // Place both combo boxes on North and South of Border layout
            JPanel controlsArea = new JPanel(new BorderLayout(5, 5));
            controlsArea.add(borderComboBox, BorderLayout.NORTH);
            controlsArea.add(colorComboBox, BorderLayout.SOUTH);

            // Place controls area in grid cell 0,0(Left of the border area)
            addToPanel(borderTab, controlsArea, 0, 0, CellConstraint.RIGHT);

            // place borders tab in tabbed pane
            addTab("Borders", null, borderTab, "Simple Borders");

    }

    private JComboBox<String> createColorComboBox(final Border[] borders, final JPanel
borderArea) {

        final JComboBox<String> colorComboBox = new JComboBox<>();
        final DefaultComboBoxModel comboBoxModel = new
DefaultComboBoxModel(COLOR_MAP.keySet().toArray());
        colorComboBox.setModel(comboBoxModel);
        colorComboBox.addActionListener(new ActionListener() {

            @Override
            public void actionPerformed(ActionEvent e) {
                Color selected = COLOR_MAP.get(colorComboBox.getSelectedItem().toString());
                Border newColoredBorder = BorderFactory.createLineBorder(selected);
                borders[0] = newColoredBorder;

                newColoredBorder = BorderFactory.createDashedBorder(selected, 4, 4);
                borders[5] = newColoredBorder;

                newColoredBorder = BorderFactory.createStrokeBorder(new BasicStroke(3),
selected);
                borders[6] = newColoredBorder;
```

```
                newColoredBorder = BorderFactory.createTitledBorder(borders[0], "Titled
Border");

                borders[7] = newColoredBorder;

                Border currentBorder = borderArea.getBorder();

                if (currentBorder instanceof LineBorder) {
                    borderArea.setBorder(borders[0]);
                } else if (currentBorder instanceof StrokeBorder) {
                    StrokeBorder sborder = (StrokeBorder) borderArea.getBorder();
                    if (sborder.getStroke().getDashArray() != null) {
                        borderArea.setBorder(borders[5]);
                    } else {
                        borderArea.setBorder(borders[6]);
                    }
                } else if (currentBorder instanceof TitledBorder) {
                    borderArea.setBorder(borders[7]);
                }
            }
        });
        return colorComboBox;
    }

    private void addToPanel(Container container, Component comp, int colNum, int rowNum, int
align) {
        CellConstraint constr = new CellConstraint()
                .setColNum(colNum)
                .setRowNum(rowNum)
                .setAlign(align);
        container.add(comp, constr);
    }

    public static void main(String[] args) {
        final JTabbedPane c = new BorderDesigner();
        c.setPreferredSize(new Dimension(409, 204));
        // Queueing GUI work to be run using the EDT.
        SimpleAppLauncher.launch("Chapter 14-13 Designing Borders", c);
    }
}

int index = borderTypeList.indexOf(selected);
                borderArea.setBorder(BORDERS[index]);
```

Figure 14-13 depicts the border designer application with drop-down menus, allowing the user to select border styles and color.

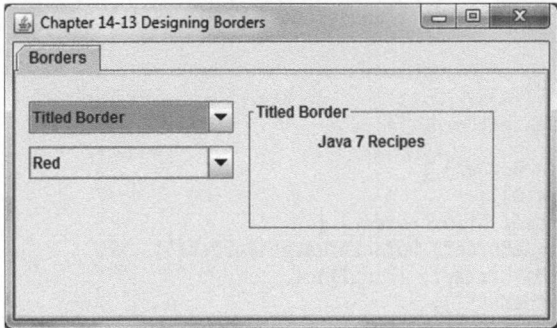

Figure 14-13. Designing borders

How It Works

Borders are simply a way to decorate a component's bordering edges. Throughout most of the recipes in this chapter, Swing components extend from the JComponent class. Knowing this fact means you can set the border on any Swing component using the JComponent's setBorder() method. In this recipe you will present to the user choices of different border styles and color options. The options to set color are only for the lined type borders such as the DashedBorder, StrokeBorder, and TitledBorder classes.

Before I discuss the methods that dynamically change the borders, I want to describe the constant (static final) variables that contain the various border types and colors to choose from. You'll notice that in the static initializer block below the BORDERS array declaration are eight instances of type Border created using the BorderFactory's many create methods. Table 14-3 lists the descriptions of the static final collection and arrays.

Table 14-3. Static map and array variables containing border type information

Variable	Data Type	Table Head
COLOR_MAP	Map<String, Color>	Predefined colors to choose from. Used for lined type borders only. Used in borders of type DashedBorder, StrokeBorder, and TitledBorder.
BORDERS	Border[]	An array of eight border types with instances of Border.
BORDER_TYPES	String[]	An array of eight strings denoting the border type.

In the BorderDesigner class's constructor is where the components are laid out. You will first create a panel with a custom grid layout. (To see more on layouts, please see recipe 14-4). Then you will create a component using an instance of a JPanel with a default border and a dimension of 200x100. Next you will create a combo box component with the types using the array of strings to allow the user to choose the type of border to display. Added to the combo box is an ActionListener that swaps out the currently displayed border component to the user. Last, you will create a combo box that will apply a chosen color from the user to the appropriate lined type border. You'll notice the method createColorComboBox() that creates the combo box responsible for changing the colors. Actually, it calls the BorderFactory create methods to generate a brand new border with the color applied.

14-14. Creating Text Components

Problem

Your million dollar idea (see recipe 14-11) must be protected from prying eyes.

Solution

Create a login screen having username and password text fields and a login button.

The main classes used in this recipe are JTextField, JPasswordField, and JTextArea classes. When using JTextArea, you should also use a JScrollPane to create scrollbars for larger text content.

The following code creates a login screen application:

```java
package org.java7recipes.chapter14.recipe14_14;

import java.awt.*;
import java.awt.event.ActionEvent;
import java.util.*;
import javax.swing.*;
import javax.swing.UIManager.LookAndFeelInfo;
import javax.swing.UnsupportedLookAndFeelException;
import org.java7recipes.chapter14.CellConstraint;
import org.java7recipes.chapter14.CustomGridLayout;
import org.java7recipes.chapter14.SimpleAppLauncher;


/**
 * Creating Text Components.
 * @author cdea
 */
public class CreatingTextComponents extends JPanel {

    public CreatingTextComponents() {

        CustomGridLayout cglayout = new CustomGridLayout(5, 5, 2, 5);

        setLayout(cglayout);

        JLabel mainLabel = new JLabel("Enter User Name & Password");
        addToPanel(mainLabel, 1, 0, CellConstraint.CENTER);

        JLabel userNameLbl = new JLabel("User Name: ");
        addToPanel(userNameLbl, 0, 1, CellConstraint.RIGHT);

        JLabel passwordLbl = new JLabel("Password: ");
        addToPanel(passwordLbl, 0, 2, CellConstraint.RIGHT);
```

```java
        JLabel statusLbl = new JLabel("Status: ");
        addToPanel(statusLbl, 0, 4, CellConstraint.RIGHT);

        // username text field
        final JTextField userNameFld = new JTextField("Admin", 20);
        addToPanel(userNameFld, 1, 1);

        // password field
        final JPasswordField passwordFld = new JPasswordField("drowssap", 20);
        addToPanel(passwordFld, 1, 2);

        JButton login = new JButton("Login");
        addToPanel(login, 1, 3, CellConstraint.RIGHT);

        // status text area
        final JTextArea taFld = new JTextArea(10, 20);
        JScrollPane statusScroll = new JScrollPane(taFld);
        taFld.setEditable(false);
        addToPanel(statusScroll, 1, 4);

        login.setAction(new AbstractAction("login") {

            @Override
            public void actionPerformed(ActionEvent e) {
                if ("Admin".equalsIgnoreCase(userNameFld.getText()) &&
                        Arrays.equals("drowssap".toCharArray(), passwordFld.getPassword()))
{

                    taFld.append("Login successful\n");
                } else {
                    taFld.append("Login failed\n");
                }
            }
        });

    }

    private void addToPanel(Component comp, int colNum, int rowNum) {
        CellConstraint constr = new CellConstraint()
                .setColNum(colNum)
                .setRowNum(rowNum);
        add(comp, constr);
    }
    private void addToPanel(Component comp, int colNum, int rowNum, int alignment) {
        CellConstraint constr = new CellConstraint()
                .setColNum(colNum)
                .setRowNum(rowNum)
                .setAlign(alignment);
        add(comp, constr);
    }

    public static void main(String[] args) {
        try {
```

```
            String lnf = null;
            for (LookAndFeelInfo info : UIManager.getInstalledLookAndFeels()) {
                if ("Nimbus".equalsIgnoreCase(info.getName())) {
                    lnf = info.getClassName();
                    UIManager.setLookAndFeel(lnf);
                    break;
                }
            }
            if (lnf == null) {
                UIManager.setLookAndFeel(UIManager.getSystemLookAndFeelClassName());
            }
        } catch (UnsupportedLookAndFeelException e) {
            // handle exception
        } catch (ClassNotFoundException e) {
            // handle exception
        } catch (InstantiationException e) {
            // handle exception
        } catch (IllegalAccessException e) {
            // handle exception
        }

        final JPanel c = new CreatingTextComponents();
        c.setPreferredSize(new Dimension(378, 359));
        // Queueing GUI work to be run using the EDT.
        SimpleAppLauncher.launch("Chapter 14-14 Creating Text Components", c);
    }
}
```

Figure 14-14 shows the login application complete with a text field, password field, text area, and login button.

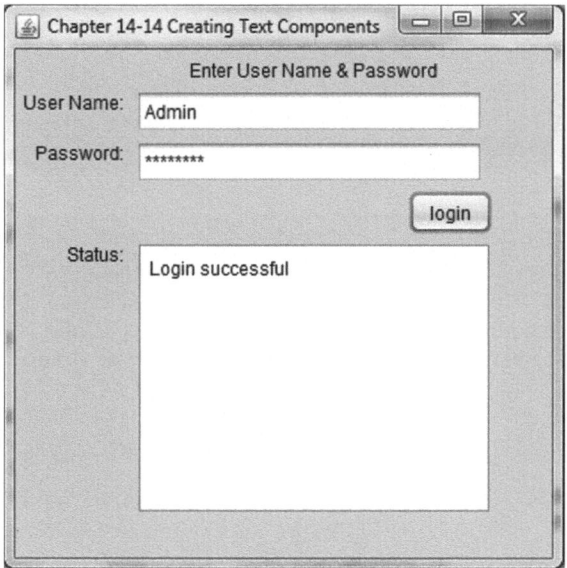

Figure 14-14. Generating events with buttons

How It Works

Have you ever seen a login screen? I'm sure you have. All login screens look the same where the display contains a username, password and login button. In this recipe I will be discussing common text components that are used in form interfaces. Advanced text components such as a JTextPane will be discussed in recipe 14-17. Here we will talk about components of type JTextField, JPasswordField, and JTextArea.

Talking about the same old same old, in this recipe I was a little tired of looking at the old default Look 'n' Feel, so I decided to set it to Java 7's new Nimbus Look 'n' Feel. For more on how to set your Look 'n' Feel, see recipe 14-21. So, on to login screens!

You will begin by using the custom layout to place labels and input fields. (If you don't understand custom layouts, please refer to recipe 14-4.) Moving onto UI controls, you will want to add the JLabel's object into the first column (column zero). Next is adding the JTextField into the second column (column 1) for the username. Then you will create a JPasswordField for the password input field. Added next is a JButton for the simulated login button. Last, you will create a JTextArea for the status in which messages are output when the user presses the login button to confirm. Instead of using an action listener I used an AbstractAction class with a command string as "login" that is set in the constructor. You'll see later in recipe 14-16 the difference between the AbstractAction and ActionListener classes. The last thing to point out is the actionPerformed() method, which checks the username and password. The JPasswordField UI component has a getPassword() method that returns an array of characters instead of a string. When systems use encryption, byte arrays are normally used not strings.

Of course, you'll never see this kind of code in production, but to not make things obvious I've obfuscated the admin password.

14-15. Associating Action Objects with Editing Commands

Problem

You want to create a simple editor with editing actions such as undo and redo.

Solution

Use the StyledDocument class to create a simple text editor and the UndoManager class to handle undo and redo actions.

The following code recipe constructs a simple text editor that demonstrates the ability to handle undo and redo actions. The keyboard shortcut used to perform undo and redo operations is Ctrl+z and Ctrl+y, respectively.

```
package org.java7recipes.chapter14.recipe14_15;

import java.awt.*;
import java.awt.event.*;
import javax.swing.*;
import javax.swing.event.UndoableEditEvent;
```

```java
import javax.swing.event.UndoableEditListener;
import javax.swing.text.AbstractDocument;
import javax.swing.undo.CannotRedoException;
import javax.swing.undo.CannotUndoException;
import javax.swing.undo.UndoManager;
import org.java7recipes.chapter14.AppSetup;
import org.java7recipes.chapter14.SimpleAppLauncher;

/**
 * Action with edit commands.
 * @author cdea
 */
public final class ActionWithEditCommand extends JPanel implements AppSetup {

AbstractDocument doc;
    protected UndoManager undo = new UndoManager();
    protected UndoAction undoAction;
    protected RedoAction redoAction;

    public ActionWithEditCommand() {
        setLayout(new BorderLayout(3, 3));

        JTextArea textArea = new JTextArea();
        JScrollPane sp = new JScrollPane(textArea);
        doc = (AbstractDocument) textArea.getDocument();
        undoAction = new UndoAction(undo);
        redoAction = new RedoAction(undo);

        // connect both
        redoAction.setUndoAction(undoAction);
        undoAction.setRedoAction(redoAction);
        doc.addUndoableEditListener(new MyUndoableEditListener());
        add(sp, BorderLayout.CENTER);

    }

    public void apply(final JFrame frame) {
        JMenuBar menuBar = new JMenuBar();

        JMenu editMenu = new JMenu("Edit");

        JMenuItem undoItem = new JMenuItem("Undo", null);
        undoItem.setMnemonic(KeyEvent.VK_Z);
        undoItem.setAccelerator(KeyStroke.getKeyStroke(KeyEvent.VK_Z,
ActionEvent.CTRL_MASK));
        undoItem.setAction(undoAction);
        editMenu.add(undoItem);

        JMenuItem redoItem = new JMenuItem("Redo", null);
redoItem.setMnemonic(KeyEvent.VK_Y);
        redoItem.setAccelerator(KeyStroke.getKeyStroke(KeyEvent.VK_Y,
ActionEvent.CTRL_MASK));
```

```
        redoItem.setAction(redoAction);
        editMenu.add(redoItem);
        menuBar.add(editMenu);

        frame.setJMenuBar(menuBar);
    }

    protected class MyUndoableEditListener implements UndoableEditListener {

        public void undoableEditHappened(UndoableEditEvent e) {
            undo.addEdit(e.getEdit());
            undoAction.updateState();
            redoAction.updateState();
        }
    }

    public static void main(String[] args) {
        final JPanel c = new ActionWithEditCommand();
        c.setPreferredSize(new Dimension(433, 312));
        // Queueing GUI work to be run using the EDT.
        SimpleAppLauncher.launch("Chapter 14-15 Action with edit commands", c);
    }
}

class UndoAction extends AbstractAction {

    private UndoManager undo = null;
    private RedoAction redoAction = null;

    public UndoAction(UndoManager undo) {
        super("Undo");
        putValue(ACCELERATOR_KEY, KeyStroke.getKeyStroke(KeyEvent.VK_Z,
ActionEvent.CTRL_MASK));
        putValue(MNEMONIC_KEY, KeyEvent.VK_Z);

        setEnabled(false);
        this.undo = undo;
    }

    public void setRedoAction(RedoAction redoAction) {
        this.redoAction = redoAction;
    }

    public void actionPerformed(ActionEvent e) {
        try {
            undo.undo();
        } catch (CannotUndoException ex) {
            ex.printStackTrace();
        }
        updateState();
        redoAction.updateState();
    }
```

```java
    protected void updateState() {
        if (undo.canUndo()) {
            setEnabled(true);
            putValue(Action.NAME, undo.getUndoPresentationName());
        } else {
            setEnabled(false);
            putValue(Action.NAME, "Undo");
        }
    }
}

class RedoAction extends AbstractAction {

    private UndoManager undo = null;
    private UndoAction undoAction = null;

    public RedoAction(UndoManager undo) {
        super("Redo");
        putValue(ACCELERATOR_KEY, KeyStroke.getKeyStroke(KeyEvent.VK_Y,
ActionEvent.CTRL_MASK));
        putValue(MNEMONIC_KEY, KeyEvent.VK_Y);

        setEnabled(false);
        this.undo = undo;
    }

    public void setUndoAction(UndoAction undoAction) {
        this.undoAction = undoAction;
    }

    public void actionPerformed(ActionEvent e) {
        try {
            undo.redo();
        } catch (CannotRedoException ex) {
            ex.printStackTrace();
        }
        updateState();
        undoAction.updateState();
    }

    protected void updateState() {
        if (undo.canRedo()) {
            setEnabled(true);
            putValue(Action.NAME, undo.getRedoPresentationName());
        } else {
            setEnabled(false);
            putValue(Action.NAME, "Redo");
        }
    }
}
```

Figure 14-15 depicts a simple text editor about to perform an undo operation.

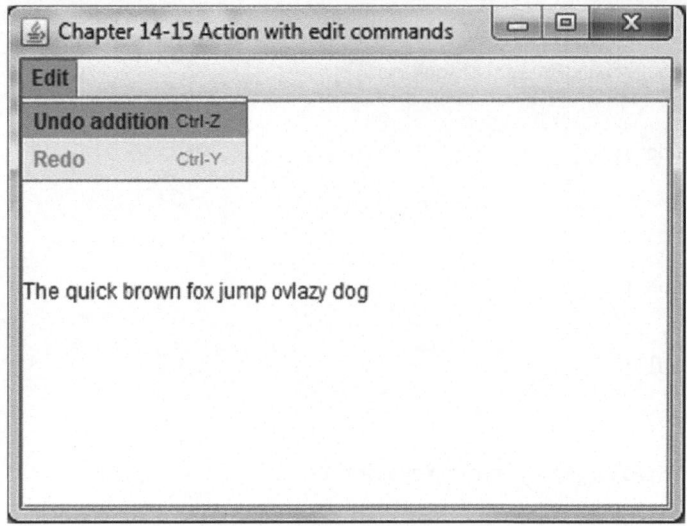

Figure 14-15. Action with edit commands

How It Works

Every editor that I've experienced has an undo or redo feature (vi does, too) when users edit text. A really nice feature in Swing is the UndoManager class. It manages keystrokes, text, and font changes as the user is editing text in a text component. In this recipe, you will be using the text component JTextArea. All text components contain a Document object that is the back end for many GUI text components. In other words, all the text content is maintained in a Document object. To step through this recipe, you will walk though things in the order they appear in the source code, starting with the constructor of the ActionWithEditCommand class for each of the AbstractAction instances.

In this section, you will be looking at the ActionWithEditCommand constructor. You will begin by creating a JTextArea with a JScrollPane for the user to type text into. Next, you will call the JTextArea's getDocument() method to obtain the Document object. Then it gets cast to an AbstractDocument to be referenced later on. This code line obtains the Document object from a text component:

```
AbstractDocument doc = (AbstractDocument) textArea.getDocument();
```

Next is the creation of UndoAction and RedoAction instances by passing in an UndoManager object (undo). The UndoManager will maintain an ordered list of all edit actions in the Document object. For instance when the last edit was a word being deleted, the UndoManager can restore the word and its attributes. The following code shows UndoAction and RedoAction created with a reference to the UndoManager:

```
undoAction = new UndoAction(undo);
redoAction = new RedoAction(undo);
```

Because UndoAction and RedoAction are closely connected, I created methods to allow them to reference each other. The following code lines set the RedoAction and UndoAction objects to reference each other:

```
// connect both
redoAction.setUndoAction(undoAction);
undoAction.setRedoAction(redoAction);
```

Once UndoAction and RedoAction have been set and associated, you will need to set the Document object with a MyUndoableEditListener instance. The MyUndoableEditListener listener is responsible for listening for UndoableEditEvent objects. The listener will add UndoableEdit objects every time an edit occurs in the document. After adding a UndoableEdit object to the UndoManager the UndoAction and RedoAction updateState() method is called to update its enabled state so that menu buttons could be grayed-out. Any time there are undo or redo events, the UndoManager will record the change such as a user pressing Backspace to delete a character. When a group of changes occur such as a word being bolded, an undo being performed will revert the whole word and its attributes. The following code is a class that implements an undoableEditHappened() method from the MyUndoableEditListener class:

```
protected class MyUndoableEditListener implements UndoableEditListener {
    public void undoableEditHappened(UndoableEditEvent e) {
        undo.addEdit(e.getEdit());
        undoAction.updateState();
        redoAction.updateState();
    }
}
```

To implement the UndoAction and RedoAction classes, you will need to extend the AbstractAction class. Each action will invoke the putValue() method to set up the keyboard shortcuts to allow the user to use the keystrokes Ctrl+z and Ctrl+y to undo and redo an edit, respectively. When the action is triggered via a keyboard shortcut, the actionPerformed() method will be invoked. To implement the actionPerformed() method, you will call the UndoManager to perform an undo or redo of the edit and call the updateState() to update the action's enabled state that actually will update the menu options' enabled state and its text. The following code snippet is the UndoAction's actionPerformed() method:

```
public void actionPerformed(ActionEvent e) {
    try {
        undo.undo();
    } catch (CannotUndoException ex) {
        ex.printStackTrace();
    }
    updateState();
    redoAction.updateState();
}
```

14-16. Creating Keyboard Shortcuts

Problem

You want to create keyboard shortcuts or hot keys to quickly select menu options without having to use the mouse.

Solution

Use the KeyEvent, KeyStroke, and AbstractAction classes.

The following code recipe is an application with menu options assigned keyboard shortcuts. A "New" button is also displayed that is assigned a keyboard shortcut. The available keyboard shortcuts are Alt+n, Ctrl+s, and Alt+x. Alt+n will invoke the action to pop up a dialog box alerting the user of the new option being selected. This action is also bound to the "New" button, as mentioned before. When the user presses the Ctrl+s key combination a popup will display a "saved% " message dialog box. Finally, the Alt+x keyboard shortcut will exit the application.

```java
package org.java7recipes.chapter14.recipe14_16;

import java.awt.BorderLayout;
import java.awt.Dimension;
import java.awt.event.ActionEvent;
import java.awt.event.ActionListener;
import java.awt.event.KeyEvent;
import javax.swing.*;
import org.java7recipes.chapter14.AppSetup;
import org.java7recipes.chapter14.SimpleAppLauncher;

/**
 * Adding Component to GUI.
 * @author cdea
 */
public class KeyboardShortcuts extends JPanel implements AppSetup{

    public KeyboardShortcuts(){

    }

    public void apply(final JFrame frame) {
        JMenuBar menuBar = new JMenuBar();

        JMenu menu = new JMenu("File");
        menu.setMnemonic(KeyEvent.VK_F);
        JMenuItem newItem = new JMenuItem("New", null);
        newItem.setMnemonic(KeyEvent.VK_N);

        AbstractAction newAction = new AbstractAction("New") {
            public void actionPerformed(ActionEvent e) {
```

```
                JOptionPane.showMessageDialog(frame, "New option selected");
            }
        };
        newAction.putValue(AbstractAction.MNEMONIC_KEY, new Integer(KeyEvent.VK_N));
        newItem.addActionListener(newAction);
        menu.add(newItem);

        JButton button = new JButton(newAction);
        frame.getContentPane().add(button, BorderLayout.NORTH);

        JMenuItem saveItem = new JMenuItem("Save", null);
        saveItem.setMnemonic(KeyEvent.VK_S);
        saveItem.setAccelerator(KeyStroke.getKeyStroke(KeyEvent.VK_S,
ActionEvent.CTRL_MASK));
        saveItem.addActionListener(new ActionListener() {

            @Override
            public void actionPerformed(ActionEvent e) {
                JOptionPane.showMessageDialog(frame, "Saved..");
            }
        });
        menu.add(saveItem);

        menu.addSeparator();

        JMenuItem exitItem = new JMenuItem("Exit", null);
        exitItem.setMnemonic(KeyEvent.VK_X);
        exitItem.setAccelerator(KeyStroke.getKeyStroke(KeyEvent.VK_X,
ActionEvent.ALT_MASK));
        exitItem.addActionListener(new ActionListener() {

            @Override
            public void actionPerformed(ActionEvent e) {
                System.exit(0);
            }
        });
        menu.add(exitItem);

        menuBar.add(menu);

        frame.setJMenuBar(menuBar);
    }

    public static void main(String[] args) {
        final JPanel c = new KeyboardShortcuts();
        c.setPreferredSize(new Dimension(433, 312));
        // Queueing GUI work to be run using the EDT.
        SimpleAppLauncher.launch("Chapter 14-16 Creating Keyboard Shortcuts", c);
    }
}
```

In the application there are three menu options with designated keyboard shortcuts along with a "New" button, as shown in Figure 14-16.

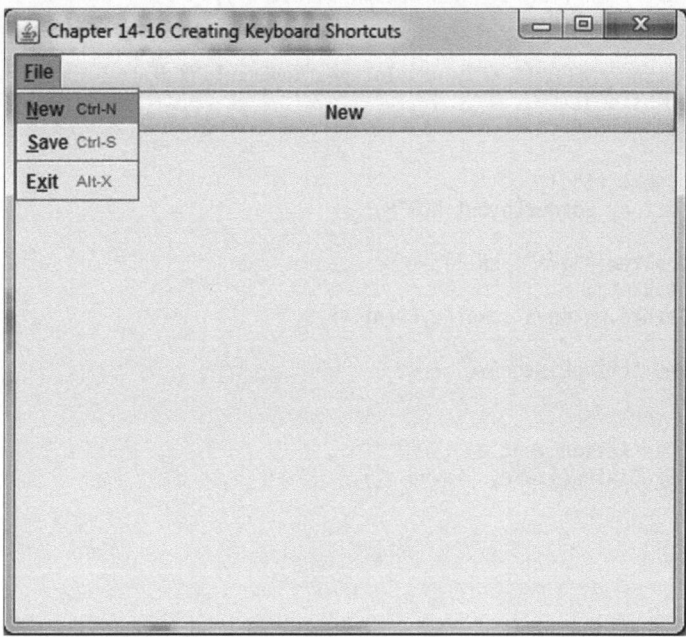

Figure 14-16. *Creating keyboard shortcuts*

How It Works

When creating menu items, you can set a mnemonic (Alt key) that associates a key on the keyboard to allow the user to select the menu item when the parent menu is visible. For example, when pressing Alt+f, the "File" menu is displayed, which is the parent menu of the menu item for the "New" option (Alt+n). Here you can press Alt+n (or n) to invoke the action to pop up the message dialog box. The same action attached to the "New" menu option is also attached to the "New" button, to also be invoked immediately with a hot key (Alt+n). Menu items can also be set to associate with key combinations that are called *key accelerators* (for example, Ctrl+S in Windows). An example is when a user wants to save a file using a key combination (shortcut) instead of using the mouse to navigate through menus. The following code sets the "Save" menu item's key mnemonic and key accelerator with the letter *s*. The s or Alt+s (mnemonic) can be used if the "File" menu is visible. If the Ctrl+s (accelerator) is pressed, the dialog box is immediately shown.

```
saveItem.setMnemonic(KeyEvent.VK_S);
saveItem.setAccelerator(KeyStroke.getKeyStroke(KeyEvent.VK_S, ActionEvent.CTRL_MASK));
```

Once the user performs a keyboard shortcut, the `ActionListener` object will receive the action event and perform the action (display dialog box). In this recipe code listing, actions (`AbstractActions`) can also contain keyboard shortcuts via the `putValue()` method. Because an `AbstractAction` object can contain keyboard shortcuts and because it is an `ActionListener`, you can not only set them in menu items but also set them in `JButtons`. Shown here is an `AbstractAction` instance bound to a menu item and a button:

```
        AbstractAction newAction = new AbstractAction("New") {
            public void actionPerformed(ActionEvent e) {
                JOptionPane.showMessageDialog(frame, "New option selected");
            }
        };
        newAction.putValue(AbstractAction.MNEMONIC_KEY, new Integer(KeyEvent.VK_N));
        newItem.addActionListener(newAction);
        menu.add(newItem);

        JButton button = new JButton(newAction);
```

This is also convenient because you can have one action that can control two or more components at the same time. This can allow the developer to disable a menu item and button simultaneously.

14-17. Creating a Document

Problem

You need to write an important business letter. The problem is that you are too cheap to buy Microsoft Word, and your broadband connection has been severed in the middle of your Open Office download.

Solution

Create a simple word processor that can change the font, size, and style of the text. You will be using Java Swing's TextPane and StyledDocument API.

The following code recipe creates a simple word processor application that allows you to select font, size, and style of your text:

```
package org.java7recipes.chapter14.recipe14_17;

import java.awt.*;
import javax.swing.*;
import javax.swing.text.AbstractDocument;
import javax.swing.text.StyledDocument;
import javax.swing.text.StyledEditorKit;
import org.java7recipes.chapter14.AppSetup;
import org.java7recipes.chapter14.SimpleAppLauncher;

/**
 * Creating A Document.
 * @author cdea
 */
public class CreatingDocument extends JPanel implements AppSetup{

    JTextPane textPane = null;
    public CreatingDocument(){
        setLayout(new BorderLayout(3,3));
        textPane = new JTextPane();
```

```java
        textPane.setCaretPosition(0);
        textPane.setMargin(new Insets(5,5,5,5));

        add(textPane, BorderLayout.CENTER);

    }

    public void apply(final JFrame frame) {
        JMenuBar menuBar = new JMenuBar();

        JMenu fontsMenu = new JMenu("Fonts");

        ButtonGroup fontGroup = new ButtonGroup();
        JRadioButtonMenuItem serifItem = new JRadioButtonMenuItem("Serif");
        serifItem.setAction(new StyledEditorKit.FontFamilyAction(Font.SERIF, Font.SERIF));
        fontsMenu.add(serifItem);
        fontGroup.add(serifItem);

        JRadioButtonMenuItem sansSerifItem = new JRadioButtonMenuItem("SansSerif", null);
        sansSerifItem.setSelected(true);
        sansSerifItem.setAction(new StyledEditorKit.FontFamilyAction(Font.SANS_SERIF,
    Font.SANS_SERIF));
        fontsMenu.add(sansSerifItem);
        fontGroup.add(sansSerifItem);

        JRadioButtonMenuItem monoItem = new JRadioButtonMenuItem("MONO SPACED", null);
        monoItem.setAction(new StyledEditorKit.FontFamilyAction(Font.MONOSPACED,
    Font.MONOSPACED));
        fontsMenu.add(monoItem);
        fontGroup.add(monoItem);

        menuBar.add(fontsMenu);


        JMenu sizeMenu = new JMenu("Size");

        ButtonGroup sizeGroup = new ButtonGroup();
        JRadioButtonMenuItem size12Item = new JRadioButtonMenuItem("12");
        size12Item.setSelected(true);
        size12Item.setAction(new StyledEditorKit.FontSizeAction("12", 12));
        sizeMenu.add(size12Item);
        sizeGroup.add(size12Item);

        JRadioButtonMenuItem size14Item = new JRadioButtonMenuItem("14");
        size14Item.setAction(new StyledEditorKit.FontSizeAction("14", 14));
        sizeMenu.add(size14Item);
        sizeGroup.add(size14Item);

        JRadioButtonMenuItem size16Item = new JRadioButtonMenuItem("16");
        size16Item.setAction(new StyledEditorKit.FontSizeAction("16", 16));
        sizeMenu.add(size16Item);
        sizeGroup.add(size16Item);
```

```
        JRadioButtonMenuItem size18Item = new JRadioButtonMenuItem("18");
        size18Item.setAction(new StyledEditorKit.FontSizeAction("18", 18));
        sizeMenu.add(size18Item);
        sizeGroup.add(size18Item);


        menuBar.add(sizeMenu);


        JMenu styleMenu = new JMenu("Style");

        JCheckBoxMenuItem boldItem = new JCheckBoxMenuItem("Bold", null);
        styleMenu.add(boldItem);
        boldItem.setAction(new StyledEditorKit.BoldAction());

        JCheckBoxMenuItem italicItem = new JCheckBoxMenuItem("Italic", null);
        italicItem.setAction(new StyledEditorKit.ItalicAction());
        styleMenu.add(italicItem);

        menuBar.add(styleMenu);

        frame.setJMenuBar(menuBar);
    }

    public static void main(String[] args) {
        final JPanel c = new CreatingDocument();
        c.setPreferredSize(new Dimension(433, 312));
        // Queueing GUI work to be run using the EDT.
        SimpleAppLauncher.launch("Chapter 14-17 Creating A Document", c);
    }
}
```

Figure 14-17 depicts the simple word processor that allows you to change the font, size, and style of the text.

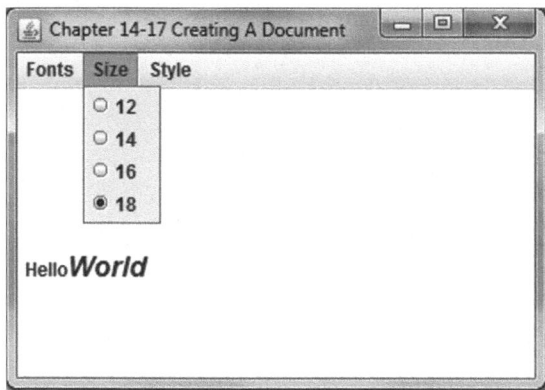

Figure 14-17. Creating keyboard shortcuts

How It Works

Most desktop operating systems often provide simple editor applications that allow users to type stylized text. In the Microsoft world there is an application called WordPad that is similar to Notepad, but allows the user to create documents with stylized text and even allows images to be embedded. In this recipe, you will be creating a WordPad-like application. The application will allow the user to change a font's type (family), size, and style (attribute).

You will start off in the constructor, in which you will create a `JTextPane` component in a `BorderLayout`'s center content region. This will allow the text editing area to take up the available space when the window is resized. Next, you will learn how to set up menu options to change the fonts when the user types into the text pane area.

Interestingly, `JTextPane` components can have different types of editor kits. Editor kits are implementations of *editors* for different document content types. When talking about stylized text, there are currently three editor kit types in Java: `HTMLEditorKit`, `RTFEditorKit`, and the default `StyledEditorKit`. Fortunately, a `JTextPane` component contains the default `StyledEditorKit` object. Editor kits have many actions defined to allow the developer to change font styles and even cut and paste actions. An editor kit is just that, a mini editor connected to your `JTextPane` component. So, let's look at the `apply()` method where all the actions are attached to menu items.

First menu section is the "Fonts" menu where the user is able to change the font family. Because a `JTextPane`'s default editor kit is a `StyledEditorKit`, you will create an instance of a `FontFamilyAction` and set it into the menu option. When the menu option is selected, the font style will be applied to the selected text. This code sets a `FontFamilyAction` instance on a `JRadioButtonMenuItem` object:

```
JRadioButtonMenuItem serifItem = new JRadioButtonMenuItem("Serif");
serifItem.setAction(new StyledEditorKit.FontFamilyAction(Font.SERIF, Font.SERIF));
```

The second menu section is the "Size" menu, in which the user can change the font's size. Again, you will use the available actions in the `StyledEditorKit`. In this case, it is the `FontSizeAction` class. Here is the code used to set a `FontSizeAction` instance on a `JRadioButtonMenuItem` menu item:

```
JRadioButtonMenuItem size14Item = new JRadioButtonMenuItem("14");
size14Item.setAction(new StyledEditorKit.FontSizeAction("14", 14));
```

Last is our "Style" menu section, in which the user can change the font's attributes such as bold, underline, and italic. Shown here is the code used to set an `ItalicAction` instance on a `JCheckBoxMenuItem` menu item:

```
JCheckBoxMenuItem italicItem = new JCheckBoxMenuItem("Italic", null);
italicItem.setAction(new StyledEditorKit.ItalicAction());
```

14-18. Developing a Dialog Box

Problem

When creating an application, you want to prompt a user with a window popup to simulate changing a password. You want to present to the user a modal or non-modal dialog box.

Solution

Create an application with a menu option to prompt the user with a dialog box (JDialog). Also, you will create menu option with the ability to change the dialog box's modality.

The following code creates an application with a menu option to allow a user to change their password. It will also demonstrate the ability to change the popup dialog box's modal state:

```java
package org.java7recipes.chapter14.recipe14_18;

import java.awt.*;
import java.awt.event.*;
import javax.swing.*;
import org.java7recipes.chapter14.AppSetup;
import org.java7recipes.chapter14.CellConstraint;
import org.java7recipes.chapter14.CustomGridLayout;
import org.java7recipes.chapter14.SimpleAppLauncher;

/**
 * Developing A Dialog
 * @author cdea
 */
public class DevelopingADialog extends JPanel implements AppSetup {

    static JDialog LOGIN_DIALOG;

    public void apply(final JFrame frame) {

        if (LOGIN_DIALOG == null) {
            LOGIN_DIALOG = new MyDialog(frame);
        }

        JMenuBar menuBar = new JMenuBar();

        JMenu menu = new JMenu("Home");
        JMenuItem newItem = new JMenuItem("Change Password", null);
        newItem.addActionListener(new ActionListener() {

            @Override
            public void actionPerformed(ActionEvent e) {
                LOGIN_DIALOG.pack();

                // center dialog
                Dimension scrnSize = Toolkit.getDefaultToolkit().getScreenSize();
                int scrnWidth = LOGIN_DIALOG.getSize().width;
                int scrnHeight = LOGIN_DIALOG.getSize().height;
                int x = (scrnSize.width - scrnWidth) / 2;
                int y = (scrnSize.height - scrnHeight) / 2;

                // Move the window
                LOGIN_DIALOG.setLocation(x, y);
                LOGIN_DIALOG.setResizable(false);
```

```java
                LOGIN_DIALOG.setVisible(true);
            }
        });

        menu.add(newItem);

        menu.addSeparator();

        JRadioButtonMenuItem nonModalItem = new JRadioButtonMenuItem("Non Modal", null);

        nonModalItem.addActionListener(new ActionListener() {

            @Override
            public void actionPerformed(ActionEvent e) {
                LOGIN_DIALOG.setModal(false);
            }
        });
        menu.add(nonModalItem);
        ButtonGroup modalGroup = new ButtonGroup();
        modalGroup.add(nonModalItem);

        JRadioButtonMenuItem modalItem = new JRadioButtonMenuItem("Modal", null);
        modalItem.setSelected(true);
        modalItem.addActionListener(new ActionListener() {

            @Override
            public void actionPerformed(ActionEvent e) {
                LOGIN_DIALOG.setModal(true);
            }
        });
        menu.add(modalItem);
        modalGroup.add(modalItem);

        menu.addSeparator();
        JMenuItem exitItem = new JMenuItem("Exit", null);
        exitItem.setMnemonic(KeyEvent.VK_X);
        exitItem.setAccelerator(KeyStroke.getKeyStroke(KeyEvent.VK_X,
ActionEvent.ALT_MASK));
        exitItem.addActionListener(new ActionListener() {

            @Override
            public void actionPerformed(ActionEvent e) {
                System.exit(0);
            }
        });
        menu.add(exitItem);

        menuBar.add(menu);

        frame.setJMenuBar(menuBar);
    }
```

```java
    public static void main(String[] args) {
        final JPanel c = new DevelopingADialog();
        c.setPreferredSize(new Dimension(433, 312));
        // Queueing GUI work to be run using the EDT.
        SimpleAppLauncher.launch("Chapter 14-18 Developing a Dialog", c);
    }
}

class MyDialog extends JDialog {

    public MyDialog(Frame owner) {
        super(owner, true);
        CustomGridLayout cglayout = new CustomGridLayout(20, 20, 2, 4);

        setLayout(cglayout);
        JLabel mainLabel = new JLabel("Enter User Name & Password");
        addToPanel(mainLabel, 1, 0, CellConstraint.CENTER);

        JLabel userNameLbl = new JLabel("User Name: ");
        addToPanel(userNameLbl, 0, 1, CellConstraint.RIGHT);

        JLabel passwordLbl = new JLabel("Password: ");
        addToPanel(passwordLbl, 0, 2, CellConstraint.RIGHT);

        // username text field
        final JTextField userNameFld = new JTextField("Admin", 20);
        addToPanel(userNameFld, 1, 1, CellConstraint.LEFT);

        // password field
        final JPasswordField passwordFld = new JPasswordField("drowssap", 20);
        addToPanel(passwordFld, 1, 2, CellConstraint.LEFT);

        JButton login = new JButton("Change");
        addToPanel(login, 1, 3, CellConstraint.RIGHT);

        final JDialog dialog = this;
        login.addActionListener(new ActionListener() {

            @Override
            public void actionPerformed(ActionEvent e) {
                dialog.setVisible(false);
                dialog.dispose();
            }
        });


    }

    private void addToPanel(Component comp, int colNum, int rowNum, int alignment) {
        CellConstraint constr = new CellConstraint()
                .setColNum(colNum)
```

```
                    .setRowNum(rowNum)
                    .setAlign(alignment);
            add(comp, constr);
        }
    }
}
```

The output is shown in Figure 14-18.

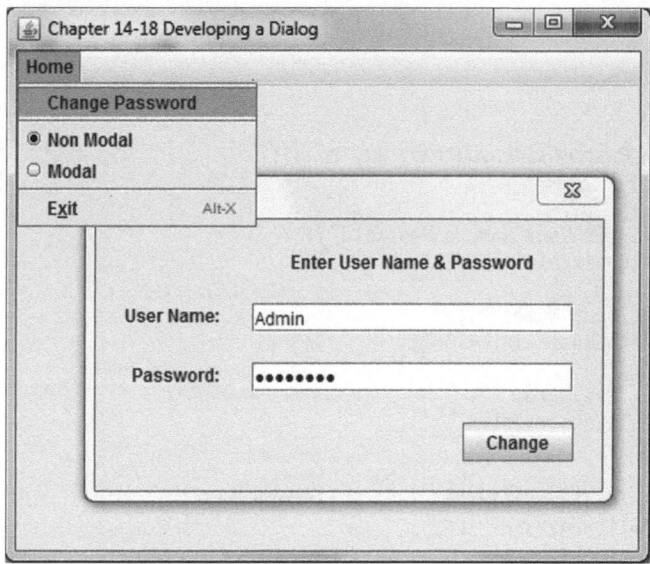

Figure 14-18. Developing a dialog box

How It Works

Oh, brother is this recipe about another login form? Well, this time it's about changing your password with a similar login form. Of course, I don't have a second password field to confirm that it's the same as the first, but I digress. Actually, this recipe is about the JDialog box and setting modality.

Before discussing the apply() method in which the menu items are created to manage the dialog box, we will talk about the JDialog container class. I hope you'll believe me when I tell you how simple it is to create a JDialog. It is as simple as extending the JDialog and adding components onto its content pane. It's just like any other container class except it is a real window similar to the JFrame class. In the MyDialog class, you will extend from JDialog class; however, there is a minor detail, to point out in our constructor. In our constructor you should specify the owner or parent window that the dialog box is called from (JFrame). When calling super() and passing in the owner, this will enable the window toolkit to display the dialog box based on its modal state in relation to the parent window. For instance, if a dialog box's modality is set to non-modal or false, the user will be able to click items in the parent window. When set to modal or true, the user will not be able to click items in the parent and must respond to the dialog such as a login screen. Back to our constructor, you will simply add the components on the content area like other examples. Finally, you will add an ActionListener to the change password button (JButton). The change password button will dismiss the dialog box that simulates a password change. Here is how to close a JDialog:

```
login.addActionListener(new ActionListener() {
    @Override
    public void actionPerformed(ActionEvent e) {
        dialog.setVisible(false);
        dialog.dispose();
    }
});
```

Like many recipes that have menus you will simply implement the apply() method from the Chapter 14 interface org.java7recipes.chapter14.AppSetup. In the apply() method, you will begin by instantiating an instance of the MyDialog class, as mentioned previously. Next, you create a "Home" menu with menu items to show the dialog and menu items that set the dialog's modal state. In the "change password" menu item, the ActionListener will show the dialog box just as you would with a JFrame. To show the dialog box, you will call the pack() method. You will then center the window and call the setVisible() method to display the dialog box. Finally, to set the dialog box's modal state, you will call the JDialog's setModal() method with a Boolean value before displaying the dialog box again. Shown in this code is the menu item's action that sets the dialog box's modal state to false.

```
nonModalItem.addActionListener(new ActionListener() {

    @Override
    public void actionPerformed(ActionEvent e) {
        LOGIN_DIALOG.setModal(false);
    }
});
```

14-19. Associating Listeners with a Document

Problem

You are tired of looking up words in the dictionary that you don't know how to spell.

Solution

Create a dictionary application with a simple auto-completion component. You will use Java Swing's DocumentListener and Document API.

The following code recipe creates a dictionary application with an auto-completion component narrowing a search as the user types the beginning of the word to search:

```
package org.java7recipes.chapter14.recipe14_19;

import java.awt.BorderLayout;
import java.awt.Dimension;
import javax.swing.DefaultListModel;
import javax.swing.JList;
```

```java
import javax.swing.JPanel;
import javax.swing.JTextField;
import javax.swing.event.DocumentEvent;
import javax.swing.event.DocumentListener;
import javax.swing.text.BadLocationException;
import javax.swing.text.Document;
import org.java7recipes.chapter14.SimpleAppLauncher;

/**
 * Adding a Listener to Document.
 * @author cdea
 */
public class AddingListenerToDocument extends JPanel {

    public AddingListenerToDocument() {
        setLayout(new BorderLayout());

        DefaultListModel<String> listModel = new DefaultListModel<>();
        JList people = new JList(listModel);
        add(people, BorderLayout.CENTER);

        JTextField searchFld = new JTextField();
        searchFld.getDocument().addDocumentListener(new MyDocumentListener(people));
        add(searchFld, BorderLayout.NORTH);

    }

    public static void main(String[] args) {
        final JPanel c = new AddingListenerToDocument();
        c.setPreferredSize(new Dimension(379, 200));
        // Queueing GUI work to be run using the EDT.
        SimpleAppLauncher.launch("Chapter 14-19 Adding Listener to Document", c);
    }
}

class MyDocumentListener implements DocumentListener {

    private static String[] dictionary = {"apress",
        "caitlin", "car", "carl", "cat", "cathode",
        "bat", "batter", "barney",
        "fred", "fredrick",
        "gillian", "goose",
        "java", "javafx",
        "swan", "swing"};
    private JList listBox;

    MyDocumentListener(JList listBox) {
        this.listBox = listBox;
    }
    String newline = "\n";

    public void insertUpdate(DocumentEvent e) {
        searchDictionary(e);
```

```
    }

    public void removeUpdate(DocumentEvent e) {
        searchDictionary(e);
    }

    public void changedUpdate(DocumentEvent e) {
        System.out.println("change: " + e);
    }

    public void searchDictionary(DocumentEvent e) {
        try {
            Document doc = (Document) e.getDocument();
            String text = doc.getText(0, doc.getLength());
            DefaultListModel dlm = (DefaultListModel) listBox.getModel();
            dlm.removeAllElements();
            if (text != null && text.length() > 0) {
                for (String word : dictionary) {
                    if (word.startsWith(text)) {
                        dlm.addElement(word);
                    }
                }
            }
        } catch (BadLocationException ex) {
            ex.printStackTrace();
        }

    }
}
```

Figure 14-19 depicts the dictionary application narrowing a search as the user types a word.

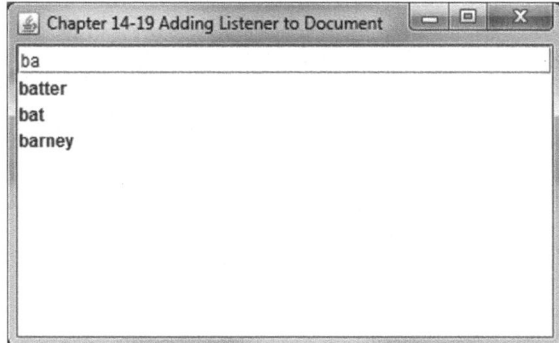

Figure 14-19. Associating listeners with a document

How It Works

Did you ever notice when you begin to type the name of a contact in an e-mail application or a phone number on your smartphone, the application begins to search and display similar names? Well, this can easily be done with Swing's `DocumentListener` interface. In the recipe example, you will create an input area and a list box below to show the similar items as the user types letters. In Swing, all text components contain a `Document` object. The `Document` object allows the developer to add listeners to monitor document events that correspond to the user's interactions with the text component (`JTextField`).

You will first create a class that implements the `DocumentListener` interface. Shown here are three methods that you will be implementing in order to listen to document events:

```
public void insertUpdate(DocumentEvent e);
public void removeUpdate(DocumentEvent e);
public void changedUpdate(DocumentEvent e);
```

You will only really have to implement the `insertUpdate()` and `removeUpdate()` methods to monitor user inserts or remove text as they type into the input field. In the constructor you'll notice it takes a reference to a `JListBox`; this is where to display the words as the user is typing characters. The methods `insertUpdate()` and `removeUpdate()` simply call the `searchDictionary()` method to compare the beginnings of the words that match and place them into the `JList` component's `ListModel` model.

Now that you have a reusable class such as the `MyDocumentListener` class, you can now create a simple auto-completion application. To create an application using a `MyDocumentListener,` you will first create a `JList` view component with an instance of a `DefaultListModel` class. Second, you will need to create an instance of a `DefaultListModel` class because (remember the code detailing the `searchDictionary()` method) it obtains the list model and expects it to be a `DefaultListModel` object through a cast. The reason for creating a `DefaultListModel` object is because a `JList`'s default list model is read-only and you wouldn't be able to remove items in the list box via the `removeAllElements()` method. The following two lines of code will create a `JList` and `DefaultListModel`:

```
DefaultListModel<String> listModel = new DefaultListModel<>();
JList people = new JList(listModel);
```

Finally, the `JTextField` is created by adding the document listener (`MyDocumentListener`). Shown here is the creation of a custom search text field component:

```
JTextField searchFld = new JTextField();
searchFld.getDocument().addDocumentListener(new MyDocumentListener(people));
```

14-20. Formatting GUI Applications with HTML

Problem

You want to format text in Swing's label and button components with basic HTML.

Solution

Create a simple demonstration application with labels and button. Use basic HTML to apply styling when setting the text for the components.

The following code recipe will create three labels in a column to the left and three buttons also in a column to the right. All labels and buttons with HTML applied will have varying text font, size, and style attributes.

```java
package org.java7recipes.chapter14.recipe14_20;

import java.awt.*;
import javax.swing.*;
import org.java7recipes.chapter14.CellConstraint;
import org.java7recipes.chapter14.CustomGridLayout;
import org.java7recipes.chapter14.SimpleAppLauncher;

/**
 * <p>
 * +-----------------------+
 * | [label ] [ button ]   |
 * | [label ] [ button ]   |
 * | [label ] [ button ]   |
 * +-----------------------+
 * </p>
 *
 * Formatting components with HTML.
 * @author cdea
 */
public class FormattingGuiWithHtml extends JPanel {

    public FormattingGuiWithHtml() {
        JLabel label1 = new JLabel("<html><center><b>Label 1</b><br>"
                + "<font color=#7f7fdd>Bold</font>");
        JLabel label2 = new JLabel("<html><center><i>Label 2</i><br>"
                + "<font color=#7f7fdd>Italic</font>");
        JLabel label3 = new JLabel("<html><center><font size=+4>Label 3</font><br>"
                + "<font color=#7f7fdd>Larger</font>");

        JButton button1 = new JButton("<html><center><b><u>Button 1</u></b><br>"
                + "<font color=#7f7fdd>underline</font>");

        JButton button2 = new JButton("<html><font color=blue>Button 2</font><br>"
                + "<font color=#7f7fdd>Blue Left</font>");

        JButton button3 = new JButton("<html>Bu<sub>tt</sub>on 3<br>"
                + "<font color=#7f7fdd>Subscript</font>");

        // create a layout 3x3 cell grid.
        // horizontal and vertical gaps between components are 5 pixels
        CustomGridLayout cglayout = new CustomGridLayout(10, 10, 3, 3);

        setLayout(cglayout);

        // add label1 cell 0,0
        addToPanel(label1, 0, 0, CellConstraint.RIGHT);

        // add label2 cell 0,1
```

```java
        addToPanel(label2, 0, 1, CellConstraint.RIGHT);

        // add label3 cell 0,2
        addToPanel(label3, 0, 2, CellConstraint.RIGHT);

        // add button1 cell 1,0
        addToPanel(button1, 1, 0, CellConstraint.CENTER);

        // add button2 cell 1,1
        addToPanel(button2, 1, 1, CellConstraint.CENTER);

        // add button2 cell 1,2
        addToPanel(button3, 1, 2, CellConstraint.CENTER);

    }
    private void addToPanel(Component comp, int colNum, int rowNum, int align) {
        CellConstraint constr = new CellConstraint()
                .setColNum(colNum)
                .setRowNum(rowNum)
                .setAlign(align);
        add(comp, constr);
    }
    public static void main(String[] args) {
        final JPanel c = new FormattingGuiWithHtml();
        c.setPreferredSize(new Dimension(377, 194));
        // Queueing GUI work to be run using the EDT.
        SimpleAppLauncher.launch("Chapter 14-20 Formatting GUI with Html.", c);
    }
}
```

Figure 14-20 shows the various labels and buttons styled with HTML:

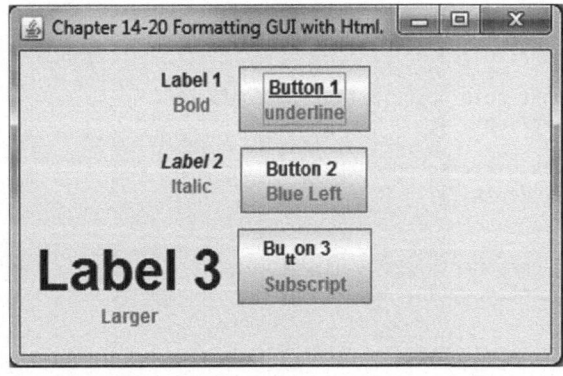

Figure 14-20. Formatting GUI applications with HTML

How It Works

Well, isn't that just dandy? That's a phrase used a long time ago to describe something or someone as having good quality of appearance. In this recipe, you will be able to change the appearance of labels and buttons with simple HTML. That's right HTML. Recipe 14-17 shows that it involves a tad more work to change a text's attributes. Amazingly, the JLabel and JButton components have HTML formatting baked into it. It's as simple as specifying a string containing HTML markup. Shown here is the code to format a JLabel component's text with HTML:

```
JLabel label1 = new JLabel("<html><center><b>Label 1</b><br><font
color=#7f7fdd>Bold</font>");
```

The HTML code makes the text Label 1 centered and bold. It then breaks to a new line with the text Bold set as the color #7f7fdd.

14-21. Changing the Look and Feel of a GUI

Problem

You want to change your application's UI look and feel or theme.

Solution

Create an application with some standard UI components and set the UI to Java 7's new Look 'n' Feel called Nimbus. To do this, you will be using Swing's UIManager.setLookAndFeel() method.

The following code listing builds an application showcasing many of Swing's standard components with the new Nimbus Look 'n' Feel:

```java
package org.java7recipes.chapter14.recipe14_21;

import java.awt.*;
import javax.swing.*;
import javax.swing.UIManager;
import javax.swing.UIManager.LookAndFeelInfo;
import javax.swing.UnsupportedLookAndFeelException;
import org.java7recipes.chapter14.CellConstraint;
import org.java7recipes.chapter14.CustomGridLayout;
import org.java7recipes.chapter14.SimpleAppLauncher;


/**
 * Adding a Listener to Document.
 * @author cdea
 */
public class ChangingLookNFeel extends JPanel {

    public ChangingLookNFeel() {
```

```java
        CustomGridLayout cglayout = new CustomGridLayout(5, 5, 1, 7);

        setLayout(cglayout);

        JLabel mainLabel = new JLabel("Setting Look N Feel : " +
UIManager.getLookAndFeel().getName());
        addToPanel(mainLabel, 0, 0);

        JTextField textField = new JTextField(10);
        addToPanel(textField, 0, 1);

        JButton button = new JButton("Button");
        addToPanel(button, 0, 2);

        JList list = new JList(new String[] {"Carl", "Jonathan", "Joshua", "Mark", "John",
"Paul", "Ringo", "George"} );
        JScrollPane listScrollPane = new JScrollPane(list);
        listScrollPane.setPreferredSize(new Dimension(200, 100));
        addToPanel(listScrollPane, 0, 3);

        JCheckBox checkBox = new JCheckBox("Check box control");
        addToPanel(checkBox, 0, 4);

        String[][] data = {{"", "", "8", "8", "8", "9", "7"},
            {"", "", "9", "7", "8", "8", "8"},
            {"", "", "8", "8", "8", "9", "6"},
            {"", "", "8", "8.5", "8", "9", "8"},
            {"", "", "8.5", "8.5", "8", "9", "8"},
            {"", "", "8.5", "8.5", "8", "9", "8"},
            {"", "", "8.5", "8.5", "8", "9", "8"},
            {"", "", "8.5", "8.5", "8", "9", "8"}
        };
        String[] colHeaders = {"Sat", "Sun", "Mon", "Tue", "Wed", "Thu", "Fri"};
        JTable table = new JTable(data, colHeaders);
        JScrollPane tableScrollPane = new JScrollPane(table);
        tableScrollPane.setPreferredSize(new Dimension(300, 150));

        addToPanel(tableScrollPane, 0, 5);

        JTree tree = new JTree();
        JScrollPane tScrollPane = new JScrollPane(tree);
        tScrollPane.setPreferredSize(new Dimension(200, 150));
        addToPanel(tScrollPane, 0, 6);

    }

    private void addToPanel(Component comp, int colNum, int rowNum) {
        CellConstraint constr = new CellConstraint()
                .setColNum(colNum)
                .setRowNum(rowNum);
        add(comp, constr);
    }

    public static void main(String[] args) {
        try {
```

```
        String lnf = null;
        for (LookAndFeelInfo info : UIManager.getInstalledLookAndFeels()) {
            if ("Nimbus".equalsIgnoreCase(info.getName())) {
                lnf = info.getClassName();
                UIManager.setLookAndFeel(lnf);
                break;
            }
        }
        if (lnf == null) {
            UIManager.setLookAndFeel(UIManager.getSystemLookAndFeelClassName());
        }
    } catch (UnsupportedLookAndFeelException e) {
        // handle exception
    } catch (ClassNotFoundException e) {
        // handle exception
    } catch (InstantiationException e) {
        // handle exception
    } catch (IllegalAccessException e) {
        // handle exception
    }

    final JPanel c = new ChangingLookNFeel();
    c.setPreferredSize(new Dimension(446, 505));
    // Queueing GUI work to be run using the EDT.
    SimpleAppLauncher.launch("Chapter 14-21 Changing Look n Feel", c);
    }
}
```

Figure 14-21 depicts the demo application showcasing a sleek text box, button, list, check box, table, and tree component with the Nimbus Look 'n' Feel:

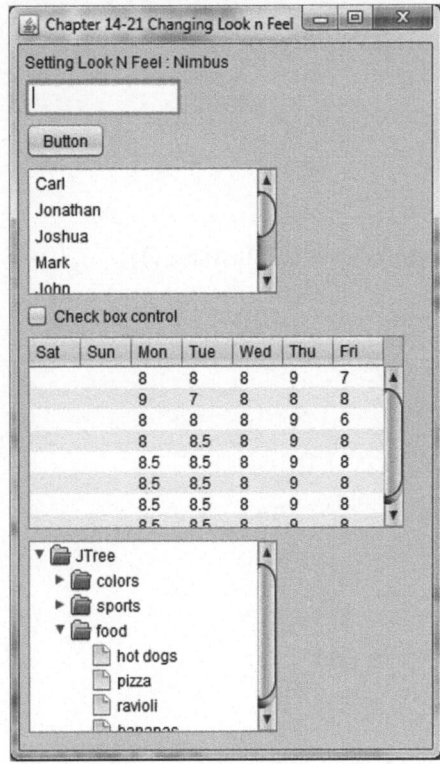

Figure 14-21. Nimbus Look n Feel

How It Works

One of the most impressive things about Swing is the Look 'n' Feel API. The API allows developers to create themes or skins for Swing components. A pluggable Look 'n' Feel can virtually transform the appearance and behavior of all components. Although it is beyond the scope of this book to dig into those APIs, I'll show you how to set the Look 'n' Feel of choice.

New to Java 7 is the Nimbus Look 'n' Feel that provides a clean and professional look to applications. So I decided to just present a handful of common Swing components in the Nimbus Look 'n' Feel. In the `main()` method before launching the GUI, we loop through all the available Look 'n' Feels using the `UIManager.getInstalledLookAndFeels()` method. Each element (`LookAndFeelInfo`) in the list is compared using its name to locate the Nimbus Look 'n' Feel. Once determined, the Look 'n' Feel is set on the `UIManager`. The following code sets the Look 'n' Feel using a string with the class's fully qualified name:

```
UIManager.setLookAndFeel("some.fully.qualified.Looknfeel");
```

If the Nimbus Look 'n' Feel is not found, the system Look 'n' Feel will be chosen. The following code sets the application to use the system Look 'n' Feel:

```
UIManager.setLookAndFeel(UIManager.getSystemLookAndFeelClassName());
```

14-22. Distributing a Swing Application

Problem

You want to distribute a Swing application.

Solution 1: Create an Executable Jar File

Here are the steps to create an executable jar file to run a Java Swing application:

Step 1: Create a text file called `manifest.mf` with the following contents:

```
Main-Class: package_name.MyGuiApp
```

■ **Note**   The last line of the file must be an end of line or carriage return.

Step 2: Jar up your application along with the manifest file by typing the following:

```
jarcfm myapp.jarmanifest.mfpackage_name/*.class
```

Step 3: Run `myapp.jar`:

```
java -jar myapp.jar
```

Solution 2: Create a Web Start Application

Here are the steps to create a Java Web Start application:

Step 1: Create a `.jar` file by completing solution 1.

Step 2: Create a `.jnlp` file named "`myapp.jnlp`" as an XML file with the contents shown below.

The following XML file myapp.jnlp file specifies deployment information contained in a `.jnlp` file:

```
<?xml version="1.0" encoding="UTF-8"?>
<jnlp spec="1.0+" codebase="http://www.yourhost.com" href="myapp.jnlp">
<information>
<title>My GUI App</title>
<vendor>Java 7 Recipes</vendor>
</information>
```

```
<resources>
<!-- Application Resources -->
<j2se version="1.6+" href="http://java.sun.com/products/autodl/j2se"/>
<jar href="myapp.jar" main="true" />
</resources>
<application-desc
        name="My Simple Gui Application"
        main-class="CreatingAGui"
        width="200"
        height="200">
</application-desc>
<update check="background"/>
</jnlp>
```

Step 3: Create an HTML file named "myapp.html" which will contain the contents shown below.

Shown here is the code to create an HTML file (myapp.html) that will launch as a Java Web Start application:

```
<html lang="en-US">
<head>
<title>My Gui App</title>
</head>
<body>
<h1>My Gui App</h1>
<script src="http://www.java.com/js/deployJava.js"></script>
<script>
        var url = "http://www.yourhost.com/myapp.jnlp";
        deployJava.createWebStartLaunchButton(url, '1.6.0');
</script>
<noscript>JavaScript is required for this page.</noscript>

</body>
</html>
```

How It Works

Once you have created your awesome Swing GUI application, you will want to distribute or deploy your application. I've provided basically two solutions. Solution 1 is about creating a single jar file as an executable so a user can launch it by double-clicking or running it on the command-line prompt. Solution 2 is a more modern approach: it pushes changes onto the workstation, essentially installing the application locally. Next I will be pointing out things to look out for in each step of solution 1 and solution 2.

Solution 1 assumes that your files are in a directory relative to your class files. You will begin by creating a manifest.mf file in order to reference the entry point or the class containing a main() method. Be sure to read the important note. In Step 2, you will only be jarring up class files, not other resources. To jar other items, please refer to the documentation on the Ant jar task. That's it for solution 1. The downside is getting the jar file to your user's workstation. Solution 2 will resolve the issue of installation.

Solution 2 is almost the same with the first step, except it needs two addition files. Keep in mind that these three files will be deployed on a web server to be served up. So in order to launch the application, they will be clicking a button or link represented in a `.jnlp` file. In Step 2, you will create a `.jnlp` file that the user will click to launch the application. The `.jnlp` element's attribute `codebase` will contain your web server URL. If you are using Apache or Tomcat it would probably be something like `codebase="http://localhost:8080"`.The `href` attribute would be the name of the `jnlp` file. The `codebase` and `href` are optional in Java 6 and above. You'll also notice the `application-desc` element's attribute `main-class` containing the class that has the `main()` method. Also, when specifying the main class attribute, be sure to specify the fully qualified name such as "`com.acme.myapp.Main`". Last but not least, you will create the HTML file that represents the web page in the user's browser to be able to launch the application. In this HTML file, you'll notice the script element containing a JavaScript library (`deployJava.js`) to generate the commonly recognized orange Java Web Start button along with your `.jnlp` URL. The following code line creates the Java Web Start button:

```
deployJava.createWebStartLaunchButton(url, '1.6.0');
```

With solution 2's files all created and ready to go, you will need to copy them over to a web server. Any web server will do, but it is very important to ensure the mime types are set up properly. If not, the user will just see the `.jnlp` document as an XML text. If you are using Apache Tomcat you can set the mime type in the `web.xml` file using the following elements:

```
<mime-mapping>
<extension>jnlp</extension>
<mime-type>application/x-java-jnlp-file</mime-type>
</mime-mapping>
```

Following are some useful references that you can use when implementing the technique shown in this recipe:

- Help on setting an application's entry point:
  http://download.oracle.com/javase/tutorial/deployment/jar/appman.html

- Help deploying a Java Web Start application:
  http://download.oracle.com/javase/tutorial/deployment/webstart/deploying.html

- Help with Apache Tomcat: http://tomcat.apache.org/

14-23. Creating an Animation

Problem

You want to create a glow effect on a button.

Solution

Use a Java Swing timer (`javax.swing.Timer`).
  The following code creates an application that demonstrates a glowing animation effect when the user's mouse pointer hovers over the button:

```java
package org.java7recipes.chapter14.recipe14_23;

import java.awt.*;
import java.awt.event.*;
import javax.swing.*;
import org.java7recipes.chapter14.SimpleAppLauncher;

/**
 * Creating an Animation.
 * @author cdea
 */
public class CreatingAnAnimation extends JPanel {

    public CreatingAnAnimation() {

        // glow button
        final JButton animButton = new JButton("<html><font size=+2>Press Me!</font>");
        animButton.addMouseListener(new MouseAdapter() {

            Color startColor = Color.BLACK;
            Color endColor = Color.RED;
            Color currentColor = startColor;
            int animDuration = 250;
            long startTime;
            Timer timer = new Timer(30, new ActionListener() {

                @Override
                public void actionPerformed(ActionEvent e) {
                    long currentTime = System.nanoTime() / 1000000;
                    long totalTime = currentTime - startTime;
                    if (totalTime > animDuration) {
                        startTime = currentTime;
                        timer.stop();
                        return;
                    }

                    // interpolate
                    float fraction = (float) totalTime / animDuration;
                    int red = (int) ((1 - fraction) * startColor.getRed() + fraction *
endColor.getRed());
                    int green = (int) ((1 - fraction) * startColor.getGreen() + fraction *
endColor.getGreen());
                    int blue = (int) ((1 - fraction) * startColor.getBlue() + fraction *
endColor.getBlue());
                    currentColor = new Color(red, green, blue);
                    animButton.setForeground(currentColor);

                    repaint();
                }
            });

            @Override
```

```
        public void mouseEntered(MouseEvent e) {
            currentColor = startColor;
            startTime = System.nanoTime() / 1000000;
            timer.start();
        }

        @Override
        public void mouseExited(MouseEvent e) {
            currentColor = startColor;
            animButton.setForeground(currentColor);
            repaint();
            timer.stop();
        }
    });

    add(animButton);
}

public static void main(String[] args) {
    final JPanel c = new CreatingAnAnimation();
    c.setPreferredSize(new Dimension(384, 100));
    // Queueing GUI work to be run using the EDT.
    SimpleAppLauncher.launch("Chapter 14-23 Creating an Animation.", c);
}
}
```

Figure 14-22 shows the application with its glowing animated button effect.

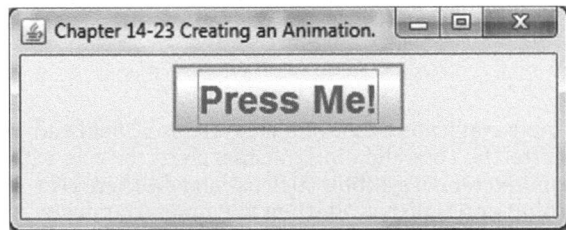

Figure 14-22. Creating an animation

How It Works

When you run this example, you may be wondering where is the animation I speak of? Well, just because it doesn't move around the screen doesn't mean it's not being animated. In this example, the button starts off with its text Press Me! colored black, then as the user begins to hover over the button using the mouse pointer, the text gradually turns red, appearing as if it is pulsing or glowing. Fundamentally, animation is an illusion of things changing over time. Quite similar to a cartoon flip book, each page represents a frame or picture that will be displayed on the timeline for a period of time.

To mimic an animation timeline you will be using Swing's Timer API. Relating to the analogy of a flip book in which each frame can be shown for a certain amount of time; however, in our simple example each frame will be the same amount of time (30 milliseconds, to be precise). Here you will create a linear interpolation that changes the foreground color gradually as it approaches the allotted time. To create timed cycles in support of animating our button, I used the Swing Timer object. Shown here is the code used to create a Swing Timer that invokes its action performed method every 30 milliseconds:

```
Timer timer = new Timer(30, new ActionListener() {
    @Override
    public void actionPerformed(ActionEvent e) {
        // every 30 milliseconds run code here...
    }
});
```

The duration of the entire animation is 250 milliseconds using the variable animDuration. When animDuration has run out, the timer's stop() method is invoked. Also, when the user moves the mouse cursor away from the button, the timer's stop() method is invoked to stop the animation. In the actionPerformed() method that is responsible for interpolating the color of the foreground of the button, the repaint() method is called to refresh the GUI.

14-24. Working with the JLayer Component

Problem

You want to validate a field on a form by warning the user with an icon to indicate the problem.

Solution

Use Java 7's new JLayer component.

Shown here is the code recipe used to build a simple application that validates an e-mail field and displays icon indicators when the e-mail is typed incorrectly. The validation rule that alerts the user with an error icon is when the user has not entered the required e-mail symbols such as . and @ .There also must be at least one character for the domain. A warning icon is displayed when the domain contains more than three characters.

```
package org.java7recipes.chapter14.recipe14_24;

import java.awt.*;
import java.io.IOException;
import javax.imageio.*;
import javax.swing.*;
import javax.swing.plaf.LayerUI;
import org.java7recipes.chapter14.SimpleAppLauncher;

/**
 * <p>
 * +-----------------------+
 * | [label ] [   field   ] |
```

```
 *  |              [ button ] |
 *  +------------------------+
 *  </p>
 *
 *  Using JLayer.
 *  @author cdea
 */
public class UsingJXLayer extends JPanel {

    public UsingJXLayer() {

        setLayout(new BorderLayout(10, 20));

        // create input area
        JPanel inputArea = new JPanel();

        JLabel emailLbl = new JLabel("Email");

        // target email field
        final JTextField emailFld = new JTextField(20);

        Image error = null;
        Image warning= null;
        try {
            error = ImageIO.read(this.getClass().getResource("error.png"));
            warning = ImageIO.read(this.getClass().getResource("warning.png"));
        } catch (IOException ex) {
            ex.printStackTrace();
        }

        // email LayerUI
        LayerUI<JTextField> layerUI = new EmailValidationLayerUI(error, warning);

        // JLayer applying layerUI to email field
        JLayer<JTextField> layeredEmail = new JLayer<>(emailFld, layerUI);

        inputArea.add(emailLbl);
        inputArea.add(layeredEmail);

        add(inputArea, BorderLayout.NORTH);

        JComponent buttonArea = new JPanel(new FlowLayout(FlowLayout.RIGHT));
        final JButton saveButt = new JButton("Save");

        buttonArea.add(saveButt);

        add(buttonArea, BorderLayout.SOUTH);

    }

    public static void main(String[] args) {
        final JPanel c = new UsingJXLayer();
```

```
            c.setPreferredSize(new Dimension(402, 118));
            // Queueing GUI work to be run using the EDT.
            SimpleAppLauncher.launch("Chapter 14-24 Using JLayer.", c);
        }
    }

class EmailValidationLayerUI extends LayerUI<JTextField> {

    Image errorImg;
    Image warningImg;

    public EmailValidationLayerUI(Image error, Image warning) {
        this.errorImg = error;
        this.warningImg = warning;
    }
    @Override
    public void paint(Graphics g, JComponent comp) {
        super.paint(g, comp);

        JLayer jlayer = (JLayer) comp;
        JTextField emailFld = (JTextField) jlayer.getView();
        String text = emailFld.getText();
        String regEx = ".+@.+\\.[A-Za-z]+";

        int x = comp.getWidth() - 12;
        int y = (comp.getHeight() - 8) / 2;

        if (text.length() > 0 && !(text.matches(regEx))) {
            Graphics2D g2 = (Graphics2D) g.create();
g2.drawImage(errorImg, x, y, comp);
g2.dispose();
        } else if (text.length() > 0 && text.substring(text.lastIndexOf("."),
text.length()).length() > 4) {
            Graphics2D g2 = (Graphics2D) g.create();
            g2.drawImage(warningImg, x, y, comp);
            g2.dispose();
        }
    }

}
```

Figure 14-23 depicts the application validating an invalid e-mail address:

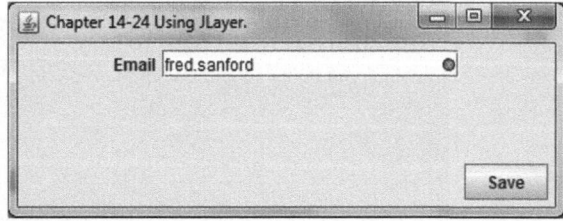

Figure 14-23. Error: e-mail format is required

Figure 14-24 shows the application displaying a warning icon when the user has typed in a root domain with more than three characters.

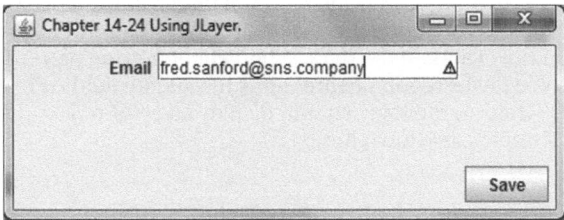

Figure 14-24. Warning: root domain is greater than three characters

How It Works

Hopefully you have gone through most of the recipes in this chapter to give you an idea of how to build a GUI application. Most of the recipes try to touch on all the aspects of building form-type applications from entering data to submitting form information to a database. An important piece missing from the puzzle is validation. Validation can be applied on all layers of a multitier system. I believe it's imperative to have server-side validation, but for better usability, client-side validation can add that extra polish your application needs. In this recipe, you will not only validate a field but also present to the user an error or warning indicator on top of the components. I created a simple form with one input field to allow the user to enter an e-mail address. If the user enters an invalid e-mail address, an error icon is displayed. Now, if an e-mail is valid, but its root domain is more than three characters, a warning icon is displayed. For example: `fred.g.sanford@sanfordandson.company` will show a warning icon.

In our `UsingJXLayer` class constructor, you will lay components down on the panel as usual, except you will want to associate a `JLayer` to the e-mail field (`JTextField`) for validation with an icon feedback. We first load the error and warning icons using `ImageIO.read()` from the classpath to be passed into an `EmailValidationLayerUI` constructor. We'll talk about `EmailValidationLayerUI` class later when we finish assembling the `JLayer`.

When instantiating a `JLayer`, it expects two parameters: the e-mail field (`JTextField`) and the `LayerUI<JTextField>` instance (`EmailValidationLayerUI`).The following code assembles a `JLayer` component:

```
// target email field
final JTextField emailFld = new JTextField(20);

// ... image loading code for error and warning icons

// email LayerUI
LayerUI<JTextField> layerUI = new EmailValidationLayerUI(error, warning);

// JLayer applying layerUI to email field
JLayer<JTextField> layeredEmail = new JLayer<>(emailFld, layerUI);
```

To create a validation layer on top of an ordinary component, extend from the LayerUI generic class. You can think of the LayerUI class as a piece of glass over the top of a component (JTextField). Any time a change occurs in the text field, the paint() method is notified. The paint() method is where the developer will have an opportunity to draw on the imaginary glass layer. In this scenario, you will be drawing an error or warning icon overlaid to the right side of the component. You'll notice in the paint() method how you would obtain the JLayer and the text field by calling the JLayer.getView() method. After obtaining the text from the e-mail field, you can now validate the data. When encountering pattern matches such as an e-mail address, you will want to use Java's regular expressions to validate fields. At last, you will implement the conditionals that decide whether the layer should display an error or a warning icon by drawing an image onto the Graphics object, as shown here:

```
String text = emailFld.getText();
String regEx = ".+@.+\\.[A-Za-z]+";
// not empty and doesn!t match regex pattern
if (text.length() > 0 && !(text.matches(regEx))) {
    // draw error icon
    Graphics2D g2 = (Graphics2D) g.create();
    g2.drawImage(errorImg, x, y, comp);
    g2.dispose();
}
```

To see more details on drawing images, refer to recipe 12-16. For more on regular expressions, refer to recipe 10-4.

14-25. Adding Printing Support to Swing Components

Problem

You want to print items that are contained in a table component similar to a spreadsheet.

Solution

Use Swing's JTable print() method.
The code recipe here constructs a simple timesheet application containing the days of the week with hours worked. As the timesheet is displaying the hours worked, you can click the Print button to send the timesheet to the printer.

```
package org.java7recipes.chapter14.recipe14_25;

import java.awt.*;
import java.awt.event.*;
import java.awt.print.PrinterException;
import javax.swing.*;
import org.java7recipes.chapter14.SimpleAppLauncher;

/**
```

```
 * Printable components.
 * @author cdea
 */
public class PrintableComponents extends JPanel {

    public PrintableComponents(){
        setLayout(new BorderLayout(5, 5));
        String[][] data = {
            {"", "", "8", "8", "8", "9", "7"},
            {"", "", "9", "7", "8", "8", "8"},
            {"", "", "8", "8", "8", "9", "6"},
            {"", "", "8", "8.5", "8", "9", "8"},
            {"", "", "8.5", "8.5", "8", "9", "8"}
        };
        String[] colHeaders = {"Sat", "Sun", "Mon", "Tue", "Wed", "Thu", "Fri"};
        final JTable timeSheet = new JTable(data, colHeaders);

        JScrollPane sp = new JScrollPane(timeSheet);

        add(sp, BorderLayout.CENTER);

        JButton printButton = new JButton("Print");
        add(printButton, BorderLayout.SOUTH);
        printButton.addActionListener(new ActionListener() {

            @Override
            public void actionPerformed(ActionEvent e) {
                try {
                    timeSheet.print();
                } catch (PrinterException ex) {
                    ex.printStackTrace();
                }
            }
        });
    }

    public static void main(String[] args) {
        final JPanel c = new PrintableComponents();
        c.setPreferredSize(new Dimension(384, 45));
        c.setMinimumSize(new Dimension(384, 277));
        // Queueing GUI work to be run using the EDT.
        SimpleAppLauncher.launch("Chapter 14-25 Printable Components", c);
    }
}
```

Figure 14-25 shows the timesheet application displaying hours worked.

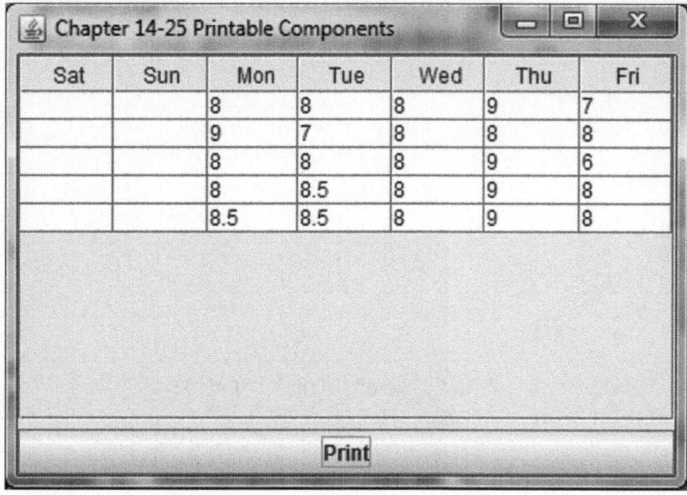

Figure 14-25. Printable components application

Figure 14-26 depicts the Print dialog box after the user has clicked the Print button.

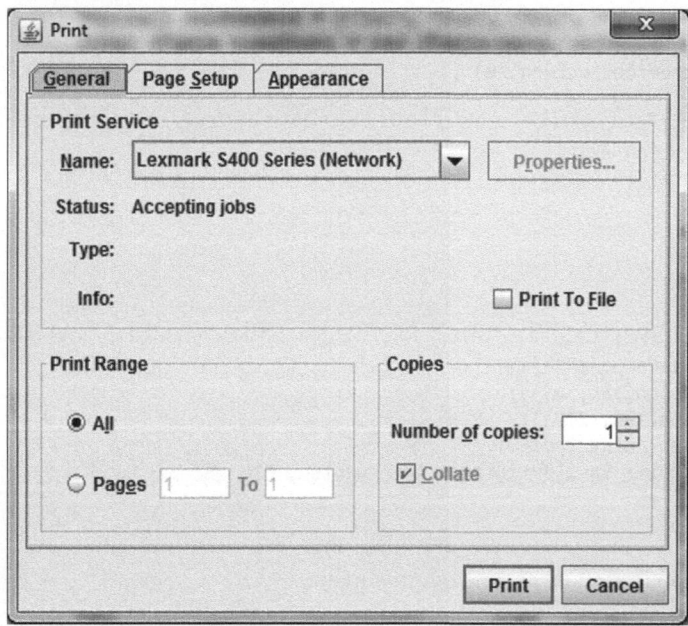

Figure 14-26. Print dialog box

How It Works

On the surface, Java's Swing API may look just like an ordinary GUI toolkit, but this powerful API has a lot of built-in features that you would never expect to see. For instance, recipe 14-20 discussed how JLabels and JButtons contain the ability to format text using HTML. And in recipe 14-17, you learned that a Document object has editor kits that can handle many content types. Well, did you know that some components have the ability to print to the printer all from a single print() method? Normally, when printing documents it involves using the java.awt.print.PrinterJob and java.awt.print.Printable APIs. But some components just have printing baked into it, and you don't have to mess with those APIs. The component I used in this recipe is a JTable that contains this built-in print() method.

In this recipe, the GUI application simulates a weekly timesheet with days and hours, table cells similar to spreadsheet applications (MS Excel). To print your timesheet, just press the Print button, and you'll see a print dialog box. It can't get any simpler than that! Shown here is the Print button's actionPerformed() method that will launch the Print dialog box:

```java
public void actionPerformed(ActionEvent e) {
    try {
        timeSheet.print();
    } catch (PrinterException ex) {
        ex.printStackTrace();
    }
}
```

CHAPTER 15

JavaFX Fundamentals

The JavaFX 2.0 API is Java's next generation GUI toolkit for developers to build rich cross-platform applications. JavaFX 2.0 is based on a scene graph paradigm (retained mode) as opposed to the traditional immediate mode style rendering. JavaFX's scene graph is a tree-like data structure that maintains vector-based graphic nodes. The goal of JavaFX is to be used across many types of devices such as mobile devices, smartphones, TVs, tablet computers, and desktops.

Before the creation of JavaFX, the development of rich Internet applications (RIAs) involved the gathering of many separate libraries and APIs to achieve highly functional applications. These separate libraries include Media, UI controls, Web, 3D, and 2D APIs. Because integrating these APIs together can be rather difficult, the talented engineers at Sun Microsystems (now Oracle) created a new set of JavaFX libraries that roll up all the same capabilities under one roof. JavaFX is the Swiss Army Knife of GUIs (see Figure 15-1). JavaFX 2.0 is a pure Java (language) API that allows developers to leverage existing Java libraries and tools.

Figure 15-1. JavaFX

Depending on who you talk to, you will likely encounter different definitions of "user experience" (or in the UI world, UX). But one fact still remains; the users will always demand better content and increased usability from GUI applications. In light of this fact, developers and designers often work together to craft applications to fulfill this demand. JavaFX provides a toolkit that helps both the developer and designer (in some cases, they happen to be the same person) to create functional yet esthetically pleasing applications. Another thing to acknowledge is that if you are developing a game, media player, or the usual enterprise application, JavaFX will not only assist in developing richer UIs but you'll also find that the APIs are extremely well designed to greatly improve developer productivity (I'm all about the user of the API's perspective).

Again, I want to remind you that there are entire books written on JavaFX, and it would be impossible for us to cover all the capabilities of the toolkit. Hopefully, these recipes can lead you in the right direction by providing practical and real-world examples. So I encourage you to explore other resources to gain further insight into JavaFX. I highly recommend the book Pro JavaFX Platform (Apress, 2009) and the soon to released Pro JavaFX 2.0 Platform (Apress, 2012), which is an invaluable resource. This book goes in depth to help you create professional grade applications.

In this chapter you will learn the fundamentals of JavaFX to rapidly develop RIAs. Before we begin I want to give you a heads up relating to the recipes in this chapter and how much they resemble prior chapters. I will often parallel recipes from Chapter 12 and Chapter 14 in order for the reader to compare existing APIs against the newer JavaFX 2.0 APIs.

So without further ado, let's get started, shall we?

15-1. Installing Required Software

Problem

You want to start developing JavaFX applications, but you don't know what software is required to be installed.

Solution

You'll need to install the following software in order to get started with JavaFX:

- Java 7 JDK or greater
- JavaFX 2.0 SDK
- NetBeans IDE 7.1 or greater

■ **Note** As of this writing, things are subject to change. To see additional requirements, refer to

`http://download.oracle.com/javafx/2.0/system_requirements/jfxpub-system_requirements.htm`.

As of this writing, things are subject to change. By the time you read this; you will likely find JavaFX able to run on your favorite OS. For this recipe, I assume that Java 7 is already installed so I won't detail those installation steps. (If Java 7 is not installed, refer to recipe 1-1 in Chapter 1.) Following are steps to install all other required software components:

1. Download JavaFX 2.0 and NetBeans IDE 7.1.x from the following locations:

- JavaFX 2.0 SDK:
  `http://www.oracle.com/technetwork/java/javafx/downloads/index.html`

- NetBeans 7.1 beta SDK: http://netbeans.org

2.   Install JavaFX 2.0 SDK. The screen in Figure 15-2 will appear once you've launched the JavaFX SDK Setup executable.

Once you have launched the JavaFX SDK setup executable you will see the start of the wizard in Figure 15-2.

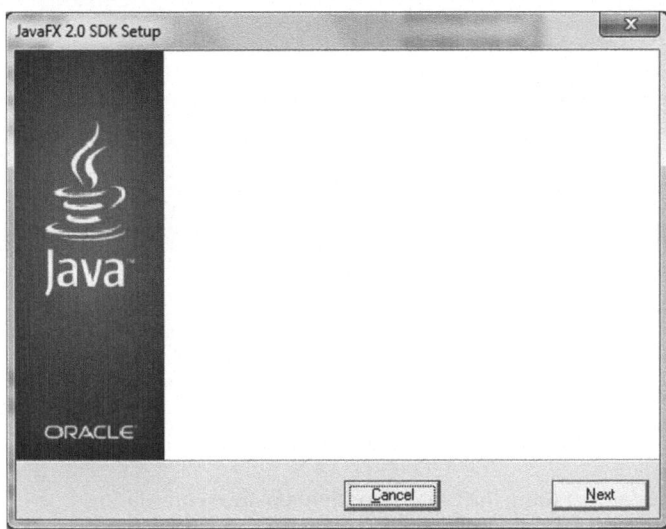

Figure 15-2. JavaFX 2.0 SDK Setup Wizard

3.   Next, you can specify the home directory of the JavaFX SDK by clicking the Browse button. Figure 15-3 shows the default location for the JavaFX SDK's home directory. You might want to jot this location down in order to configure your CLASSPATH in Step 6.

Figure 15-3 displays Setup Options, which allow you to specify the JavaFX 2.0 SDK's home directory.

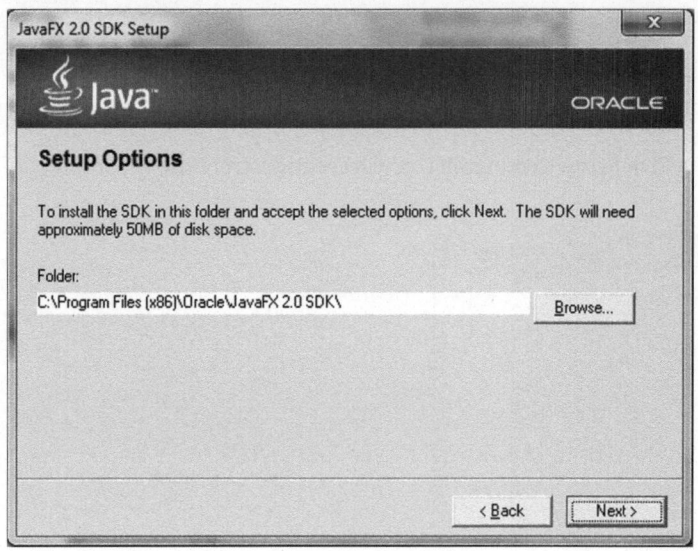

Figure 15-3. JavaFX SDK home directory

4.   After you click Next, the components will install and the screen shown in Figure 15-4 will appear.

Figure 15-4 displays the progress indicator installing the last components before completing.

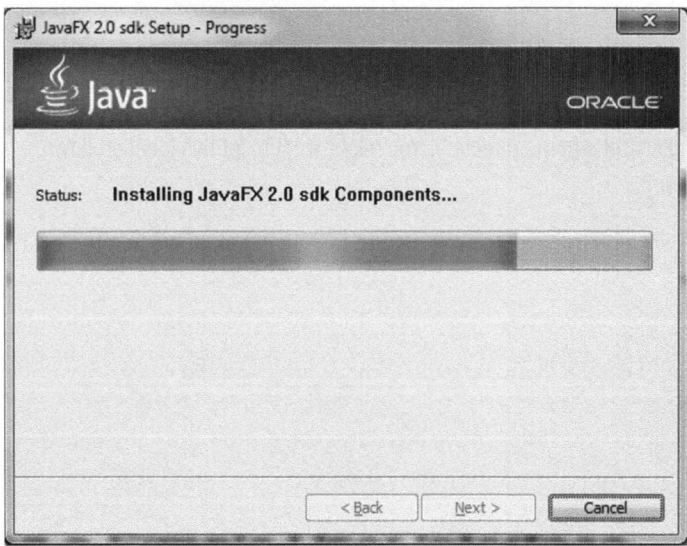

Figure 15-4. Completing the install

5. Install the NetBeans IDE, which includes the JavaFX 2.0 plug-in.

When installing, you will follow the default wizard screens. For additional instructions, you may refer to `http://netbeans.org/community/releases/71/install.html`.

6. Configuring your environment variable CLASSPATH to include the JavaFX runtime library. The name and location of the runtime library is at `<JavaFX SDK Home directory>\rt\lib\jfxrt.jar`. (Linux uses the forward slash: /).

How It Works

This recipe shows how to install Java FX 2.0 and the NetBeans IDE onto the Windows platform. You may need to modify your steps slightly when installing JavaFX 2.0 on other operating systems as they become available. Although the steps described here are for NetBeans, you can also develop using other IDEs such as Eclipse, IntelliJ, or vi. While most of the example recipes were created using the NetBeans IDE, you can also compile and run JavaFX applications using the command-line prompt.

To compile and run JavaFX applications using the command-line prompt you will need to configure your CLASSPATH. After you have followed the wizards to install the prerequisite software you will need to set your environment's CLASSPATH variable to include the JavaFX runtime library `<JavaFX SDK Home directory>/rt/lib/jfxrt.jar` (Step 6). Setting this library will later assist in compiling and running JavaFX-based applications on the command-line. The following code configures your CLASSPATH environment variable based on your platform:

Setting CLASSPATH on Windows Platforms

```
set JAVAFX_HOME=C:\Program Files (x86)\Oracle\JavaFX 2.0 SDK
set JAVA_HOME=C:\Program Files (x86)\Java\jdk1.7.0
set CLASSPATH=%JAVAFX_HOME%\rt\lib\jfxrt.jar;.
```

Setting CLASSPATH on UNIX/Linux/Mac OS platforms

```
# bash environments
export JAVAFX_HOME=<JavaFX SDK Home>
export CLASSPATH=$CLASSPATH:$JAVAFX_HOME/rt/lib/jfxrt.jar

#csh environments
setenv JAVAFX_HOME <JavaFX SDK Home>
setenv CLASSPATH ${CLASSPATH}:${JAVAFX_HOME}/rt/lib/jfxrt.jar
```

In recipe 15-2 you will learn how to create a simple Hello World application. Once your Hello World application is created, you will be able to compile and run a JavaFX-based application.

15-2. Creating a Simple User Interface

Problem

You want to create, code, compile, and run a simple JavaFX Hello World application.

Solution 1

Develop a JavaFX HelloWorld application using the JavaFX project creation wizard in the NetBeans IDE.

Creating a JavaFX Hello World Application in NetBeans

To quickly get started with creating, coding, compiling, and running a simple JavaFX HelloWorld application using the NetBeans IDE, follow these steps:

1) Launch NetBeans IDE.

2) On the File menu, select New Project.

3) Under Choose Project and Categories, select the JavaFX folder.

4) Under Projects, select Java FX Application, and click Next.

5) Specify **HelloWorldMain** for your project name.

6) Change or accept the defaults for the Project Location and Project Folder fields.

7) Make sure the Create Application Class check box option is selected. Click Finish.

8) In the NetBeans IDE on the Projects tab, select the newly created project. Open the Project Properties dialog box to verify that the Source/Binary format settings are JDK 7. Click Sources under Categories.

9) While still in the Project Properties dialog box, under Categories, select Libraries to verify that the Java 7 and JavaFX platform are configured properly. Click the Manage Platforms button. Make sure a tab showing JavaFX libraries appears. Figure 15-5 depicts the JavaFX tab detailing its SDK home, Runtime, and Javadoc directory locations. Once verified, click the Close button.

Figure 15-5 shows the Java Platform Manager window containing JavaFX as a managed platform included with JDK 7.

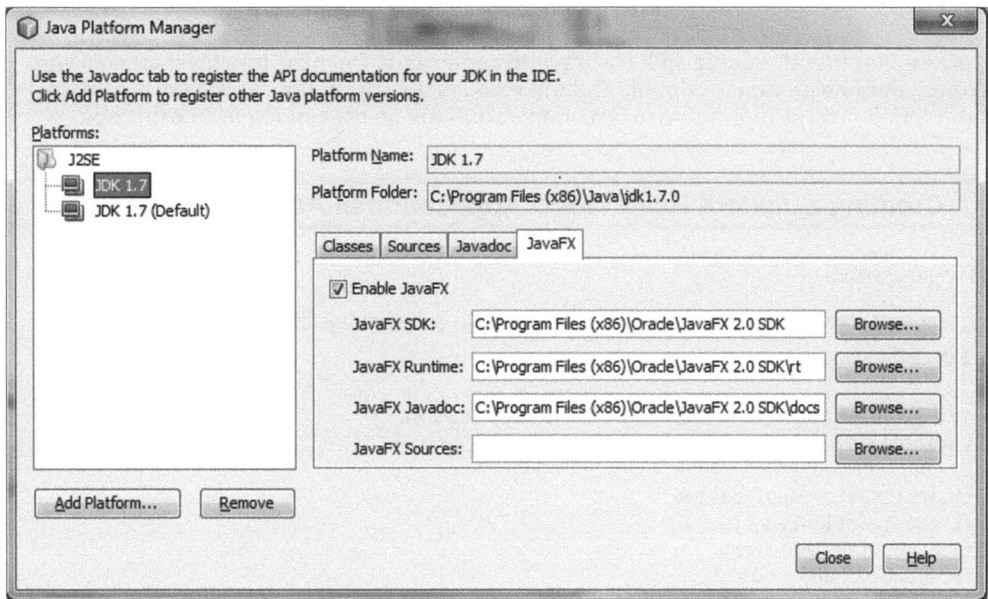

Figure 15-5. Java Platform Manager

10) After closing the Java Platform Manager window, click OK to close the Project Properties window.

11) To run and test your JavaFX Hello World application, access the Run menu, and select Run Main Project or hit the F6 key.

Shown in Figure 15-6 is a simple JavaFX Hello World application launched from the NetBeans IDE.

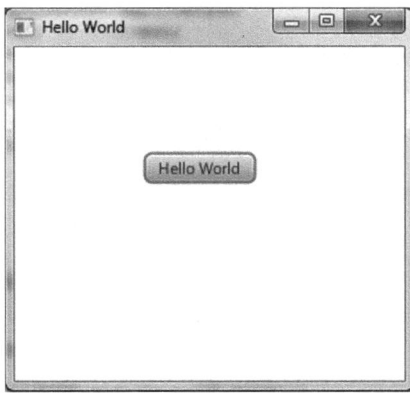

Figure 15-6. *JavaFX Hello World launched from the NetBeans IDE*

Solution 2

Use your favorite editor to code your JavaFX Hello World application. Once the Java file is created you will use the command-line prompt to compile and run your JavaFX application. Following are the steps to create a JavaFX Hello World application to be compiled and run on the command-line prompt.

Creating a JavaFX Hello World Application in Another IDE

To quickly get started:

1.   Copy and paste the following code into your favorite editor and save the file as
HelloWorldMain.java.

The following source code is a JavaFX Hello World application:

```java
package helloworldmain;

import javafx.application.Application;
import javafx.event.ActionEvent;
import javafx.event.EventHandler;
import javafx.scene.Group;
import javafx.scene.Scene;
import javafx.scene.control.Button;
import javafx.stage.Stage;

/**
 *
 * @author cdea
 */
public class HelloWorldMain extends Application {

    /**
     * @param args the command line arguments
     */
    public static void main(String[] args) {
        Application.launch(args);
    }

    @Override
    public void start(Stage primaryStage) {
        primaryStage.setTitle("Hello World");
        Group root = new Group();
        Scene scene = new Scene(root, 300, 250);
        Button btn = new Button();
        btn.setLayoutX(100);
        btn.setLayoutY(80);
        btn.setText("Hello World");
        btn.setOnAction(new EventHandler<ActionEvent>() {

            public void handle(ActionEvent event) {
```

```
            System.out.println("Hello World");
        }
    });
    root.getChildren().add(btn);
    primaryStage.setScene(scene);
    primaryStage.show();
    }
}
```

2.   After saving the file named `HelloWorldMain.java`, on the command-line prompt you will navigate to the directory location of the file.

3.   Compile the source code file `HelloWorldMain.java` using the Java compiler `javac`:

```
javac -d . HelloWorldMain.java
```

4.   Run and test your JavaFX Hello World application. Assuming you are located in the same directory as the `HelloWorldMain.java` file, type the following command to run your JavaFX Hello World application from the command-line prompt:

```
java helloworldmain.HelloWorldMain
```

Shown in Figure 15-7 is a simple JavaFX Hello World application launched from the command-line prompt.

Figure 15-7. JavaFX Hello World launched from the command-line prompt

How It Works

Following are descriptions of the two solutions. Both solutions require prerequisite software. (I cover how to install required software in recipe 15-1.) In Solution #1 you will be creating a JavaFX application using the NetBeans IDE. Solution #2 allows you to choose your favorite editor and use the command-line prompt to compile and execute JavaFX programs.

Solution 1

To create a simple JavaFX Hello World application, using the NetBeans you will use the JavaFX project creation wizard as specified in Steps 1 through 7. In Steps 8 through 10, you will verify two settings to ensure that the project is configured to compile and run JavaFX 2.0 applications properly. Finally, in Step 11 you will run the JavaFX Hello World application by selecting the Run Main Project menu option.

You shouldn't encounter any difficulty when following Steps 1 through 7. However, Steps 8 through 10 address a minor NetBeans bug that has to do with setting your project source/binary format to JDK 7 and making sure that the managed platform includes the JavaFX runtime libraries. If you are not experiencing this issue, the NetBeans team may have already corrected the problem. To be on the safe side, it wouldn't hurt to follow Steps 8 through 10 to verify your configurations before you begin.

Solution 2

To create a simple JavaFX Hello World application using your favorite IDE, follow Steps 1 and 2. To compile and run your Hello World program on the command line, follow Steps 3 and 4.

Once the source code is entered into your favorite editor and the source file has been saved, you will want to compile and run your JavaFX program. Open the command-line prompt window and navigate to the directory location of the Java file named `HelloWorldMain.java`.

Here I would like to point out the way you compile the file using the command `javac -d . HelloWorldMain.java`. You will notice the `-d .` before the file name. This lets the Java compiler know where to put class files based on their package name. In this scenario, the `HelloWorldMain` package statement is `helloworldmain`, which will create a subdirectory under the current directory. When finished compiling, your directory structure should resemble the following:

```
|projects
       |helloworld
              |HelloWorldMain.java
              | helloworldmain
                     |HelloWorldMain.class
```

With the preceding directory structure in mind, the following commands will compile and run our JavaFX Hello World application:

```
cd /projects/helloworld

javac -d . HelloWorldMain.java

java helloworldmain.HelloWorldMain
```

■ **Note** There are many ways to package and deploy JavaFX applications. To learn more, please see "Learning how to deploy and package JavaFX applications" at
http://blogs.oracle.com/thejavatutorials/entry/javafx_2_0_beta_packager. For in-depth JavaFX deployment strategies, see Oracle's "Deploying JavaFX Applications" at
http://download.oracle.com/javafx/2.0/deployment/deployment_toolkit.htm.

In both solutions you'll notice in the source code that JavaFX applications extend the `javafx.application.Application` class. The `Application` class provides application life cycle functions such as launching and stopping during runtime. This also provides a mechanism for Java applications to launch JavaFX GUI components in a threadsafe manner. Keep in mind that synonymous to Java Swing's event dispatch thread, JavaFX will have its own JavaFX application thread. To learn more about thread safety refer to Chapter 14 Swing API.

In our `main()` method's entry point we launch the JavaFX application by simply passing in the command line arguments to the `Application.launch()` method. Once the application is in a ready state, the framework internals will invoke the `start()` method to begin. When the `start()` method is invoked, a JavaFX `javafx.stage.Stage` object is available for the developer to use and manipulate.

You'll notice that some objects are oddly named, such as `Stage` or `Scene`. The designers of the API have modeled things similar to a theater or a play in which actors perform in front of an audience. With this same analogy, in order to show a play, there are basically one-to-many scenes that actors perform in. And, of course, all scenes are performed on a stage. In JavaFX the `Stage` is equivalent to an application window similar to Java Swing API `JFrame` or `JDialog`. You may think of a `Scene` object as a content pane capable of holding zero-to-many `Node` objects. A `Node` is a fundamental base class for all scene graph nodes to be rendered. Commonly used nodes are UI controls and `Shape` objects. Similar to a tree data structure, a scene graph will contain children nodes by using a container class `Group`. We'll learn more about the `Group` class later when we look at the `ObservableList`, but for now we can think of them as Java `Lists` or `Collections` that are capable of holding `Nodes`.

Once the child nodes have been added, we set the `primaryStage`'s (`Stage`) scene and call the `show()` method on the `Stage` object to show the JavaFX window.

One last thing: in this chapter most of the example applications will be structured the same as this example in which recipe code solutions will reside inside the `start()` method. Having said this, most of the recipes in this chapter will follow the same pattern. In other words, for the sake of brevity, much of the boiler plate code will not be shown. To see the full source listings of all the recipes, please download the source code from the book's web site.

15-3: Drawing Text

Problem

You want to draw text onto the JavaFX scene graph.

Solution

Create `Text` nodes to be placed on the JavaFX scene graph by utilizing the `javafx.scene.text.Text` class. As `Text` nodes are to be placed on the scene graph, you decide you want to create randomly positioned `Text` nodes rotated around their (x, y) positions scattered about the scene area.

The following code implements a JavaFX application that displays `Text` nodes scattered about the scene graph with random positions and colors:

```
primaryStage.setTitle("Chapter 15-3 Drawing Text");
Group root = new Group();
Scene scene = new Scene(root, 300, 250, Color.WHITE);
Random rand = new Random(System.currentTimeMillis());
for (int i = 0; i < 100; i++) {
    int x = rand.nextInt((int) scene.getWidth());
```

```
        int y = rand.nextInt((int) scene.getHeight());
        int red = rand.nextInt(255);
        int green = rand.nextInt(255);
        int blue = rand.nextInt(255);

        Text text = new Text(x, y, "Java 7 Recipes");

        int rot = rand.nextInt(360);
        text.setFill(Color.rgb(red, green, blue, .99));
        text.setRotate(rot);
        root.getChildren().add(text);
    }

    primaryStage.setScene(scene);
    primaryStage.show();
```

Figure 15-8 shows random Text nodes scattered about the JavaFX scene graph.

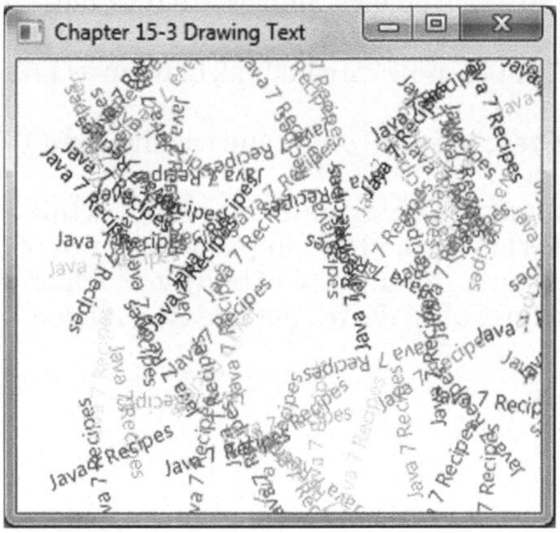

Figure 15-8. Drawing text

How It Works

To draw text in JavaFX you will be creating a `javafx.scene.text.Text` node to be placed on the scene graph (`javafx.scene.Scene`). In this example you'll notice text objects with random colors and positions scattered about the Scene area.

First, we create a loop to generate random (x,y) coordinates to position Text nodes. Second, we create random color components between (0–255 rgb) to be applied to the Text nodes. Third, the rotation angle (in degrees) is a randomly generated value between (0–360 degrees) to cause the text to be slanted. The following code creates random values that will be assigned to a Text node's position, color, and rotation:

```
int x = rand.nextInt((int) scene.getWidth());
int y = rand.nextInt((int) scene.getHeight());
int red = rand.nextInt(255);
```

```
int green = rand.nextInt(255);
int blue = rand.nextInt(255);
int rot = rand.nextInt(360);
```

Once the random values are generated, they will be applied to the Text nodes, which will be drawn onto the scene graph. The following code snippet applies position (x, y), color (rgb), and rotation (angle in degrees) onto the Text node:

```
Text text = new Text(x, y, "Java 7 Recipes");
text.setFill(Color.rgb(red, green, blue, .99));
text.setRotate(rot);

root.getChildren().add(text);
```

You will begin to see the power of the scene graph API by its ease of use. Text nodes can be easily manipulated as if they were Shapes. Well, actually they really are Shapes. Defined in the inheritance hierarchy, Text nodes extend from the javafx.scene.shape.Shape class and are therefore capable of doing interesting things such as being filled with colors or rotated about an angle. Although the text is colorized, they still tend to be somewhat boring. However, in the next recipe we will demonstrate how to change a text's font.

15-4: Changing Text Fonts

Problem

You want to change text fonts and add special effect to Text nodes.

Solution

Create a JavaFX application that uses the following classes to set the text font and apply effects on Text nodes:

- javafx.scene.text.Font
- javafx.scene.effect.DropShadow
- javafx.scene.effect.Reflection

The code that follows sets the font and applies effects to Text nodes. We will be using the Serif, SanSerif, Dialog, and Monospaced fonts along with the drop shadow and reflection effects:

```
// Serif with drop shadow
      Text java7Recipes2 = new Text(50, 50,  "Java 7 Recipes");
Font serif = Font.font("Serif", 30);
      java7Recipes2.setFont(serif);
      java7Recipes2.setFill(Color.RED);

      DropShadow dropShadow = new DropShadow();
      dropShadow.setOffsetX(2.0f);
```

```
        dropShadow.setOffsetY(2.0f);
dropShadow.setColor(Color.rgb(50, 50, 50, .588));
        java7Recipes2.setEffect(dropShadow);
        root.getChildren().add(java7Recipes2);

        // SanSerif
        Text java7Recipes3 = new Text(50, 100,  "Java 7 Recipes");
Font sanSerif = Font.font("SanSerif", 30);
        java7Recipes3.setFont(sanSerif);
        java7Recipes3.setFill(Color.BLUE);
        root.getChildren().add(java7Recipes3);

        // Dialog
        Text java7Recipes4 = new Text(50, 150,  "Java 7 Recipes");
        Font dialogFont = Font.font("Dialog", 30);
        java7Recipes4.setFont(dialogFont);
        java7Recipes4.setFill(Color.rgb(0, 255, 0));
root.getChildren().add(java7Recipes4);

        // Monospaced
        Text java7Recipes5 = new Text(50, 200,  "Java 7 Recipes");
Font monoFont = Font.font("Monospaced", 30);
        java7Recipes5.setFont(monoFont);
        java7Recipes5.setFill(Color.BLACK);
        root.getChildren().add(java7Recipes5);

Reflection refl = new Reflection();
        refl.setFraction(0.8f);
        java7Recipes5.setEffect(refl);
```

Figure 15-9 shows the JavaFX application setting various font styles and applying effects (drop shadow and reflection) to the Text nodes.

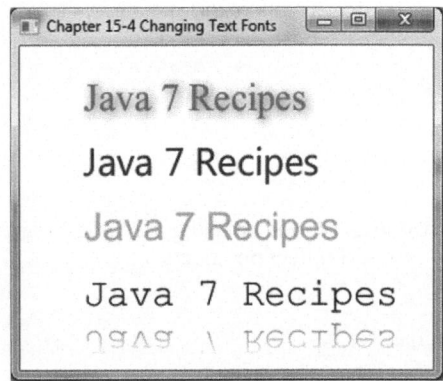

Figure 15-9. Changing text fonts

How It Works

Is this déjà vu? Well, not exactly; I simply mimicked recipe 12-9 (shown in Figure 12-15) to help us compare the difference between the Java2D and JavaFX APIs. The major difference is that in Chapter 12 I used the Java 2D API's Graphics object to draw (a pixel at a time), and here I basically used JavaFX's scene graph to display Text nodes. The difference between Java 2D and JavaFX is that Java 2D is based on an immediate mode-rendering strategy in which drawing shapes are pixel-based. Being pixel-based, it is often difficult to apply effects onto shapes easily (without a lot of math). JavaFX takes the retained mode approach, in which nodes use vector-based graphics. Vector-based graphics allow you to scale shapes and apply effects without issues of pixilation (jaggies). In each Text node you can create and set the font to be rendered onto the scene graph. Here is the code to create and set the font on a Text node:

```
Text java7Recipes2 = new Text(50, 50, "Java 7 Recipes");
Font serif = Font.font("Serif", 30);
java7Recipes2.setFont(serif);
```

Hopefully you read recipe 12-9, in which I created a drop shadow effect by creating two separate text drawings. In this recipe the drop shadow is a real effect (DropShadow) object and actually applied to a single Text node instance. The DropShadow object is set to be positioned based on an x and y offset in relation to the Text node. Also we can set the color of the shadow; here we set it to gray with a .588 opacity. Following is an example of setting a Text node's effect property with a drop shadow effect (DropShadow):

```
DropShadow dropShadow = new DropShadow();
dropShadow.setOffsetX(2.0f);
dropShadow.setOffsetY(2.0f);
dropShadow.setColor(Color.rgb(50, 50, 50, .588));
java7Recipes2.setEffect(dropShadow);
```

Although this is about setting text fonts, we applied effects to Text nodes. I've added yet another effect (just kicking it up a notch). While creating the last Text node using the monospaced font, I applied the popular reflection effect. Here it is, set so that .8 or 80 percent of the reflection will be shown. The reflection values range from zero (0%) to one (100%). The following code snippet implements a reflection of 80% with a float value of 0.8f:

```
Reflection refl = new Reflection();
refl.setFraction(0.8f);

java7Recipes5.setEffect(refl);
```

15-5. Creating Shapes

Problem

You want to create shapes to be placed on the scene graph.

Solution

Use JavaFX's Arc, Circle, CubicCurve, Ellipse, Line, Path, Polygon, Polyline, QuadCurve, Rectangle, SVGPath, Text class in the javafx.scene.shape.* package. You may also use builder classes associated with each shape in the javafx.builders.* package.

   The following code draws various complex shapes. The first complex shape involves a cubic curve drawn in the shape of a sine wave. The next shape, which I would like to call the *ice cream cone*, uses the path class that contains path elements (javafx.scene.shape.PathElement). The third shape is a Quadratic Bézier curve (QuadCurve) forming a smile. Our final shape is a delectable donut. We create this donut shape by subtracting two ellipses (one smaller and one larger):

```
// CubicCurve
CubicCurve cubicCurve = CubicCurveBuilder.create()
        .startX(50).startY(75)             // start pt (x1,y1)
        .controlX1(80).controlY1(-25)      // control pt1
        .controlX2(110).controlY2(175)     // control pt2
        .endX(140).endY(75)                // end pt (x2,y2)
        .strokeType(StrokeType.CENTERED).strokeWidth(1)
        .stroke(Color.BLACK)
        .strokeWidth(3)
        .fill(Color.WHITE)
        .build();
root.getChildren().add(cubicCurve);

// Ice cream
Path path = new Path();

MoveTo moveTo = new MoveTo();
moveTo.setX(50);
moveTo.setY(150);

QuadCurveTo quadCurveTo = new QuadCurveTo();
quadCurveTo.setX(150);
quadCurveTo.setY(150);
quadCurveTo.setControlX(100);
quadCurveTo.setControlY(50);

LineTo lineTo1 = new LineTo();
lineTo1.setX(50);
lineTo1.setY(150);

LineTo lineTo2 = new LineTo();
lineTo2.setX(100);
lineTo2.setY(275);

LineTo lineTo3 = new LineTo();
lineTo3.setX(150);
lineTo3.setY(150);
path.getElements().add(moveTo);
path.getElements().add(quadCurveTo);
path.getElements().add(lineTo1);
```

```
path.getElements().add(lineTo2);
path.getElements().add(lineTo3);
path.setTranslateY(30);
path.setStrokeWidth(3);
path.setStroke(Color.BLACK);

root.getChildren().add(path);

// QuadCurve create a smile
QuadCurve quad =QuadCurveBuilder.create()
        .startX(50)
        .startY(50)
        .endX(150)
        .endY(50)
        .controlX(125)
        .controlY(150)
        .translateY(path.getBoundsInParent().getMaxY())
        .strokeWidth(3)
        .stroke(Color.BLACK)
        .fill(Color.WHITE)
        .build();

root.getChildren().add(quad);

// outer donut
Ellipse bigCircle = EllipseBuilder.create()
        .centerX(100)
        .centerY(100)
        .radiusX(50)
        .radiusY(75/2)
        .translateY(quad.getBoundsInParent().getMaxY())
        .strokeWidth(3)
        .stroke(Color.BLACK)
        .fill(Color.WHITE)
        .build();

// donut hole
Ellipse smallCircle = EllipseBuilder.create()
        .centerX(100)
        .centerY(100)
        .radiusX(35/2)
        .radiusY(25/2)

        .build();

// make a donut
Shape donut = Path.subtract(bigCircle, smallCircle);
// orange glaze
donut.setFill(Color.rgb(255, 200, 0));

// add drop shadow
DropShadow dropShadow = new DropShadow();
```

```
        dropShadow.setOffsetX(2.0f);
        dropShadow.setOffsetY(2.0f);
        dropShadow.setColor(Color.rgb(50, 50, 50, .588));
        donut.setEffect(dropShadow);

        // move slightly down
        donut.setTranslateY(quad.getBoundsInParent().getMinY() + 30);

        root.getChildren().add(donut);
```

Figure 15-10 displays the sine wave, ice cream cone, smile, and donut shapes that we have created using JavaFX:

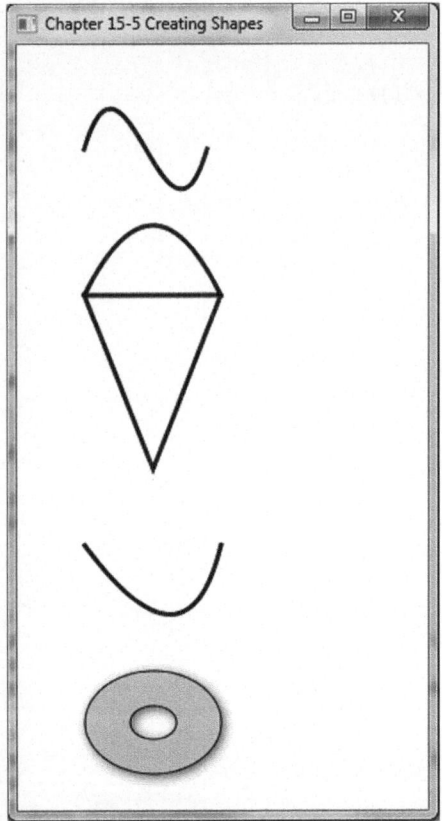

Figure 15-10. Creating shapes

How It Works

This is a blast from the past if you remember Figure 12-10 from recipe 12-7. Here, we simply used the same coordinates, stroke, and color values to render the same kind of shapes. In JavaFX there are equivalent shapes and drawing primitives. For brevity I will not go into details relating to stroking, color, transforms, paths, and curve control points (they are all mentioned in Chapter 12). But I will go over the JavaFX conventions, concepts, and APIs to render shapes.

Instead of re-creating a JavaFX version of recipe 12-3 (simple shapes), I decided to re-create recipe 12-7 to really put JavaFX to the test. My intent was to see how easy it would be to migrate from existing Java 2D code to the new JavaFX 2.0 APIs.

The first shape is a `javafx.scene.shape.CubicCurve` class using the same information as recipe 12-7. To create a cubic curve, you simply look for the appropriate constructor to be instantiated. The following code snippet is used to create a `javafx.scene.shape.CubicCurve` instance:

```
CubicCurve cubicCurve = new CubicCurve();
cubicCurve.setStartX(0.0f);
```

But, right off the bat in the source code listing in the solution section, you'll notice that I didn't use the usual `new CubicCurve()` constructor like the previous snippet, but instead I use a class having a suffix of `Builder` on the end of it. `Builder` classes are convenience classes that follow a design pattern called the Builder pattern. `Builder` classes provide a way to method chain invocations by enabling the developer to specify attributes in an ad hoc way (declarative). This makes code more readable and less verbose, thus increasing developer productivity. When using this facility while developing graphics applications, you may also find that coding tends to be more expressive and reminiscent of the JavaFX 1.x script language when using declarative syntax to construct UI objects.

Back to `CubicCurveBuilder`; we begin with the `create()` method that will instantiate a `Builder` class. Next is specifying a cubic curve's attributes in any order. Similar to mutators or setter methods, you simply pass a single value to the method. The convention is that the `set` prefixed on the method is removed, and the method returns the `this` pointer of the builder object instance. By returning itself it allows you to continue to use the dot notation to specify parameters, thus the method chaining behavior. Once finished with specifying values on the `Builder` class, a call to the `build()` method will return an instance of the desired class (in this case, the `CubicCurve` class).

The ice cream cone shape is created using the `javafx.scene.shape.Path` class and is pretty much identical to recipe 12-7. Here, instead of using the builder convenience classes, I resorted to the verbose Java code style. As each path element is created and added to the `Path` object, each element is *not* considered a graph node (`javafx.scene.Node`). This means they do not extend from the `javafx.scene.shape.Shape` class and cannot be a child node in a scene graph to be displayed. When looking at the Javadoc, you will notice that a `Path` class extends from the `Shape` class that extends from the (`javafx.scene.Node`) class, and therefore a `Path` is a graph node, but path elements do not extend from the `Shape` class. Path elements actually extend from the `javafx.scene.shape.PathElement` class, which is only used in the context of a `Path` object. So you won't be able to instantiate a `LineTo` class to be put in the scene graph. Just remember that the classes with `To` as a suffix is a path element, not a real `Shape` node. For example, the `MoveTo` and `LineTo` object instances are `Path` elements added to a `Path` object, not shapes that can be added to the scene. Shown following are `Path` elements added to a `Path` object to draw an ice cream cone:

```
// Ice cream
Path path = new Path();

MoveTo moveTo = new MoveTo();
moveTo.setX(50);
moveTo.setY(150);
```

```
.../// Additional Path Elements created.
LineTo lineTo1 = new LineTo();
lineTo1.setX(50);
lineTo1.setY(150);

.../// Additional Path Elements created.

path.getElements().add(moveTo);
path.getElements().add(quadCurveTo);
path.getElements().add(lineTo1);
```

Rendering the QuadCurve (smile) object I used the QuadCurveBuilder similar to the CubicCurveBuilder class, and you'll notice the simplicity of creating such a shape. Once your builder class is complete you will finish things off by invoking the build() method.

Last is our tasty donut shape with a drop shadow effect. When creating the donut, we begin by creating two circular ellipses. By subtracting the smaller ellipse (donut hole) from the larger ellipse area, a newly derived shape is created and returned using the Path.subtract() method. Following is the code snippet that creates the donut shape using the Path.subtract() method:

```
// outer donut
Ellipse bigCircle = ...//Outer shape area

// donut hole
Ellipse smallCircle = ...// Inner shape area

// make a donut
Shape donut = Path.subtract(bigCircle, smallCircle);
```

Next, is applying a drop shadow effect onto our donut. This time instead of drawing the shape twice, similar to a prior recipe we draw it once and use the setEffect() method to apply a DropShadow object instance. Similar to our prior technique, we can set the offset of the shadow by calling setOffsetX() and setOffsetY().

15-6. Assigning Colors to Objects

Problem

You want to fill your shapes with simple colors and gradient colors.

Solution

In JavaFX, all shapes can be filled with simple colors and gradient colors. The following are the main classes used to fill shape nodes:

- `javafx.scene.paint.Color`

- `javafx.scene.paint.LinearGradient`

- `javafx.scene.paint.Stop`

- `javafx.scene.paint.RadialGradient`

The following code uses the preceding classes to add radial and linear gradient colors as well as transparent (alpha channel level) colors to our shapes. We will be using an ellipse, rectangle, and rounded rectangle in our recipe. A solid black line (as depicted in Figure 15-11) also appears in our recipe to demonstrate the transparency of our shape's color.

```
primaryStage.setTitle("Chapter 15-6 Assigning Colors To Objects");
        Group root = new Group();
        Scene scene = new Scene(root, 350, 300, Color.WHITE);

        Ellipse ellipse = new Ellipse(100, 50 + 70/2, 50, 70/2);
        RadialGradient gradient1 = RadialGradientBuilder.create()
                .focusAngle(0)
                .focusDistance(.1)
                .centerX(80)
                .centerY(45)
                .radius(120)
                .proportional(false)
                .cycleMethod(CycleMethod.NO_CYCLE)
                .stops(new Stop(0, Color.RED), new Stop(1, Color.BLACK))
                .build();

        ellipse.setFill(gradient1);
        root.getChildren().add(ellipse);

        Line blackLine = LineBuilder.create()
                .startX(170)
                .startY(30)
                .endX(20)
                .endY(140)
                .fill(Color.BLACK)
                .strokeWidth(10.0f)
                .translateY(ellipse.prefHeight(-1) + ellipse.getLayoutY() + 10)
                .build();

        root.getChildren().add(blackLine);

        Rectangle rectangle = RectangleBuilder.create()
                .x(50)
                .y(50)
                .width(100)
                .height(70)
```

```
            .translateY(ellipse.prefHeight(-1) + ellipse.getLayoutY() + 10)
            .build();

    LinearGradient linearGrad = LinearGradientBuilder.create()
            .startX(50)
            .startY(50)
            .endX(50)
            .endY(50 + rectangle.prefHeight(-1) + 25)
            .proportional(false)
            .cycleMethod(CycleMethod.NO_CYCLE)
            .stops( new Stop(0.1f, Color.rgb(255, 200, 0, .784)),
                    new Stop(1.0f, Color.rgb(0, 0, 0, .784)))
            .build();

    rectangle.setFill(linearGrad);
    root.getChildren().add(rectangle);

    Rectangle roundRect = RectangleBuilder.create()
            .x(50)
            .y(50)
            .width(100)
            .height(70)
            .arcWidth(20)
            .arcHeight(20)
            .translateY(ellipse.prefHeight(-1) +
                        ellipse.getLayoutY() +
                        10 +
                        rectangle.prefHeight(-1) +
                        rectangle.getLayoutY() + 10)
            .build();

    LinearGradient cycleGrad = LinearGradientBuilder.create()
            .startX(50)
            .startY(50)
            .endX(70)
            .endY(70)
            .proportional(false)
            .cycleMethod(CycleMethod.REFLECT)
            .stops(new Stop(0f, Color.rgb(0, 255, 0, .784)),
                    new Stop(1.0f, Color.rgb(0, 0, 0, .784)))
            .build();

    roundRect.setFill(cycleGrad);
    root.getChildren().add(roundRect);

    primaryStage.setScene(scene);
    primaryStage.show();
```

Figure15-11 displays the various types of colorized fills that can be applied onto shapes.

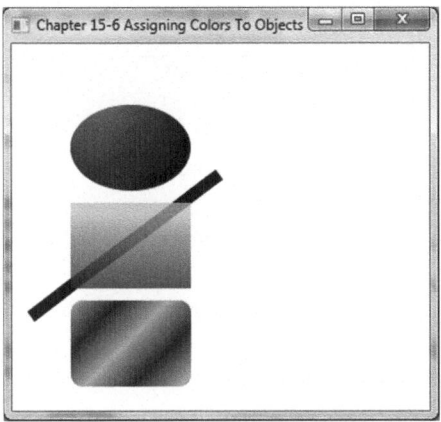

Figure 15-11. Color shapes

How It Works

Figure 15-11 shows shapes displayed from top to bottom starting with an ellipse, rectangle, and a rounded rectangle having colored gradient fills. When drawing the eclipse shape you will be using a radial gradient that appears as if it were a 3D spherical object. Next, you will be creating a rectangle filled with a yellow semitransparent linear gradient. A thick black line shape was drawn behind the yellow rectangle to demonstrate the rectangle's semitransparent color. Last, you will implement a rounded rectangle filled with a green-and-black reflective linear gradient resembling 3D tubes in a diagonal direction.

The amazing thing about colors with gradients is that they can often make shapes appear three-dimensional. Gradient paint allows you to interpolate between two or more colors, which gives depth to the shape. JavaFX provides two types of gradients: a radial (`RadialGradient`) and a linear (`LinearGradient`) gradient. For our ellipse shape you will be using a radial gradient (`RadialGradient`).

I created Table 15-1 from the JavaFX 2.0 Javadoc definitions found for the `RadialGradient` class (`http://download.oracle.com/javafx/2.0/api/javafx/scene/paint/RadialGradient.html`).

Table 15-1. RadialGradient Properties

Property	Data Type	Description
focusAngle	double	Angle in degrees from the center of the gradient to the focus point to which the first color is mapped
focusDistance	double	Distance from the center of the gradient to the focus point to which the first color is mapped
centerX	double	X coordinate of the center point of the gradient's circle
centerY	double	Y coordinate of the center point of the gradient's circle
radius	double	Radius of the circle defining the extents of the color gradient
proportional	boolean	Coordinates and sizes are proportional to the shape which this gradient fills
cycleMethod	CycleMethod	Cycle method applied to the gradient
stops	List<Stop>	Gradient's color specification

In our recipe the focus angle is set to zero, distance is set to .1, center X and Y is set to (80,45), radius is set to 120 pixels, proportional is set to false, cycle method is set to the no cycle (CycleMethod.NO_CYCLE), and two color stop values set to red (Color.RED) and black (Color.BLACK). These settings give a radial gradient to our ellipse by starting with the color red with a center position of (80, 45) (upper left of the ellipse) that interpolates to the color black with a distance of 120 pixels (radius).

Next, you will be creating a rectangle having a yellow semitransparent linear gradient. For our yellow rectangle you will be using linear gradient (LinearGradient) paint.

I created Table 15-2 from the JavaFX 2.0 Javadoc definitions found for the LinearGradient class (http://download.oracle.com/javafx/2.0/api/javafx/scene/paint/LinearGradient.html).

Table 15-2. LinearGradient Properties

Property	Data Type	Description
startX	double	X coordinate of the gradient axis start point
startY	double	Y coordinate of the gradient axis start point
endX	double	X coordinate of the gradient axis end point
endY	double	Y coordinate of the gradient axis end point
proportional	boolean	Whether the coordinates are proportional to the shape which this gradient fills
cycleMethod	CycleMethod	Cycle method applied to the gradient
stops	List<Stop>	Gradient's color specification

To create a linear gradient paint you will specify the startX, startY, endX, and endY for the start and end points. The start and end point coordinates denote where the gradient pattern begins and stops.

To create the second shape (yellow rectangle) you will set the start X and Y to (50, 50), end X and Y to (50, 75), proportional to false, cycle method to no cycle (CycleMethod.NO_CYCLE), and two color stop values to yellow (Color.YELLOW) and black (Color.BLACK) with an alpha transparency of .784.These settings give a linear gradient to our rectangle from top to bottom with a starting point of (50, 50) (top left of rectangle) that interpolates to the color black (bottom left of rectangle).

Finally, you'll notice a rounded rectangle with a repeating pattern of a gradient using green and black in a diagonal direction. This is a simple linear gradient paint that is the same as the linear gradient paint (LinearGradient) except that the start X, Y and the end X, Y are set in a diagonal position, and the cycle method is set to reflect (CycleMethod.REFLECT). When specifying the cycle method to reflect (CycleMethod.REFLECT), the gradient pattern will repeat or cycle between the colors. The following code snippet implements the rounded rectangle having a cycle method of reflect (CycleMethod.REFLECT):

```
LinearGradient cycleGrad = LinearGradientBuilder.create()
        .startX(50)
        .startY(50)
        .endX(70)
        .endY(70)
        .proportional(false)
        .cycleMethod(CycleMethod.REFLECT)
        .stops(new Stop(0f, Color.rgb(0, 255, 0, .784)),
               new Stop(1.0f, Color.rgb(0, 0, 0, .784)))
        .build();
```

15-7. Creating Menus

Problem

You want to create standard menus in your JavaFX applications.

Solution

Employ JavaFX's menu controls to provide standardized menuing capabilities such as check box menus, radio menus, submenus, and separators. The following are the main classes used to create menus.

- `javafx.scene.control.MenuBar`

- `javafx.scene.control.Menu`

- `javafx.scene.control.MenuItem`

The following code calls into play all the menuing capabilities listed previously. The example code will simulate a building security application containing menu options to turn on cameras, sound an alarm, and select contingency plans.

```
primaryStage.setTitle("Chapter 15-7 Creating Menus");
Group root = new Group();
Scene scene = new Scene(root, 300, 250, Color.WHITE);

MenuBar menuBar = new MenuBar();

// File menu - new, save, exit
Menu menu = new Menu("File");
menu.getItems().add(new MenuItem("New"));
menu.getItems().add(new MenuItem("Save"));
menu.getItems().add(new SeparatorMenuItem());
menu.getItems().add(new MenuItem("Exit"));

menuBar.getMenus().add(menu);

// Cameras menu - camera 1, camera 2
Menu tools = new Menu("Cameras");
tools.getItems().add(CheckMenuItemBuilder.create()
        .text("Show Camera 1")
        .selected(true)
        .build());

tools.getItems().add(CheckMenuItemBuilder.create()
        .text("Show Camera 2")
        .selected(true)
        .build());
menuBar.getMenus().add(tools);


// Alarm
Menu alarm = new Menu("Alarm");
ToggleGroup tGroup = new ToggleGroup();
RadioMenuItem soundAlarmItem = RadioMenuItemBuilder.create()
        .toggleGroup(tGroup)
        .text("Sound Alarm")
        .build();
RadioMenuItem stopAlarmItem = RadioMenuItemBuilder.create()
        .toggleGroup(tGroup)
```

```
                    .text("Alarm Off")
                    .selected(true)
                    .build();

            alarm.getItems().add(soundAlarmItem);
            alarm.getItems().add(stopAlarmItem);

            Menu contingencyPlans = new Menu("Contingent Plans");
            contingencyPlans.getItems().add(new CheckMenuItem("Self Destruct in T minus 50"));
            contingencyPlans.getItems().add(new CheckMenuItem("Turn off the coffee machine "));
            contingencyPlans.getItems().add(new CheckMenuItem("Run for your lives! "));

            alarm.getItems().add(contingencyPlans);
            menuBar.getMenus().add(alarm);


            menuBar.prefWidthProperty().bind(primaryStage.widthProperty());

            root.getChildren().add(menuBar);
            primaryStage.setScene(scene);
            primaryStage.show();
```

Figure 15-12 shows a simulated building security application containing radio, checked, and submenu items.

Figure 15-12. Creating menus

How It Works

Menus are standard ways on windowed platform applications to allow users to select options. Menus should also have the functionality of hot keys or keyboard equivalents. Often users will want to use the keyboard instead of the mouse to navigate the menu. Because this recipe parallels recipe 14-9, you'll notice lots of similarities.

First, we create an instance of a `MenuBar` that will contain one to many menu (`MenuItem`) objects. Creating a menu bar:

```
MenuBar menuBar = new MenuBar();
```

Secondly, we create menu (`Menu`) objects that contain one-to-many menu item (`MenuItem`) objects and other `Menu` objects making submenus. To create a menu:

```
Menu menu = new Menu("File");
```

Third, we create menu items to be added to `Menu` objects, such as menu (`MenuItem`), check (`CheckMenuItem`), and radio menu items (`RadioMenuItem`). Menu items can have icons in them. I don't showcase this in the recipe, but I encourage you to explore the various constructors for all menu items (`MenuItem`). When creating a radio menu item (`RadioMenuItem`), you should be aware of the `ToggleGroup` class. The `ToggleGroup` class is also used on regular radio buttons (`RadioButtons`) to allow one selected option only. The following code creates radio menu items (`RadioMenuItems`) to be added to a `Menu` object:

```
// Alarm
Menu alarm = new Menu("Alarm");
ToggleGroup tGroup = new ToggleGroup();
RadioMenuItem soundAlarmItem = RadioMenuItemBuilder.create()
    .toggleGroup(tGroup)
    .text("Sound Alarm")
    .build();
RadioMenuItem stopAlarmItem = RadioMenuItemBuilder.create()
    .toggleGroup(tGroup)
    .text("Alarm Off")
    .selected(true)
    .build();

alarm.getItems().add(soundAlarmItem);
alarm.getItems().add(stopAlarmItem);
```

At times you may want some menu items separated with a visual line separator. To create a visual separator, create an instance of a `SeparatorMenuItem` class to be added to a menu via the `getItems()` method. The method `getItems()` returns an observable list of `MenuItem` objects (`ObservableList<MenuItem>`). As you will see later in recipe 15-11, you will learn about the ability to be notified when items in a collection are altered. The following code line adds a visual line separator (`SeparatorMenuItem`) to the menu:

```
menu.getItems().add(new SeparatorMenuItem());
```

Other menu items used are the check menu item (`CheckMenuItem`) and the radio menu item (`RadioMenuItem`), which are similar to their counterparts in JavaFX UI controls check box (`CheckBox`) and radio button (`RadioButton`), respectively.

Prior to our adding the menu bar to the scene, you will notice the bound property between the preferred width of the menu bar and the width of the `Stage` object via the `bind()` method. When binding these properties you will see the menu bar's width stretch when the user resizes the screen. Later you will see how binding works in recipe 15-10, "Binding Expressions." This code snippet shows the binding between the menu bar's `width` property and the stage's `width` property.

```
menuBar.prefWidthProperty().bind(primaryStage.widthProperty());

root.getChildren().add(menuBar);
```

15-8. Adding Components to a Layout

Problem

You want to add UI components to a layout similar to a grid type layout.

Solution

Use JavaFX's `javafx.scene.layout.GridPane` class. This source code implements a simple UI form containing a first and last name field controls using the grid pane layout node (`javafx.scene.layout.GridPane`):

```
GridPane gridpane = new GridPane();
gridpane.setPadding(new Insets(5));
gridpane.setHgap(5);
gridpane.setVgap(5);

Label fNameLbl = new Label("First Name");
TextField fNameFld = new TextField();
Label lNameLbl = new Label("First Name");
TextField lNameFld = new TextField();
Button saveButt = new Button("Save");

// First name label
GridPane.setHalignment(fNameLbl, HPos.RIGHT);
gridpane.add(fNameLbl, 0, 0);


// Last name label
GridPane.setHalignment(lNameLbl, HPos.RIGHT);
gridpane.add(lNameLbl, 0, 1);

// First name field
GridPane.setHalignment(fNameFld, HPos.LEFT);
gridpane.add(fNameFld, 1, 0);

// Last name field
GridPane.setHalignment(lNameFld, HPos.LEFT);
gridpane.add(lNameFld, 1, 1);

// Save button
GridPane.setHalignment(saveButt, HPos.RIGHT);
gridpane.add(saveButt, 1, 2);

root.getChildren().add(gridpane);
```

Figure 15-3 depicts a small form containing UI controls laid out using a grid pane layout node.

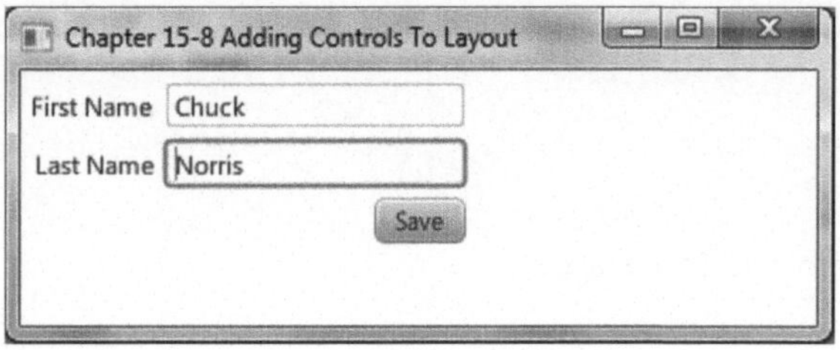

Figure 15-13. *Adding controls to a layout*

How It Works

One of the greatest challenges in building user interfaces is the laying out of controls onto the display area. When developing GUI applications it is ideal for an application to allow the user to move and adjust the size of their viewable area while maintaining a pleasant user experience. Similar to Java Swing, JavaFX layout has stock layouts that provide the most common ways to display UI controls on the scene graph. This recipe demonstrates the GridPane class.

You may recall recipe 14-4, in which we implemented a custom layout to display components in a grid-like manner. You may notice similarities, but I left a lot of implementation features out such as adjusting min/max sizes, padding, and vertical alignments. Amazingly, the JavaFX team has created a robust grid-like layout called the GridPane.

First we create an instance of a GridPane. Next, we set the padding by using an instance of an Inset object. After setting the padding, we simply set the horizontal and vertical gap. The following code snippet instantiates a grid pane (GridPane) with padding, horizontal, and vertical gaps set to 5 (pixels):

```
GridPane gridpane = new GridPane();
gridpane.setPadding(new Insets(5));
gridpane.setHgap(5);
gridpane.setVgap(5);
```

The padding is the top, right, bottom, and left spacing around the region's content in pixels. When obtaining the preferred size, the padding will be included in the calculation. Setting the horizontal and vertical gaps relate to the spacing between UI controls within the cells.

Next is simply putting each UI control into its respective cell location. All cells are zero relative. Following is a code snippet that adds a save button UI control into a grid pane layout node (GridPane) at cell (1, 2):

```
gridpane.add(saveButt, 1, 2);
```

The layout also allows you to horizontally or vertically align controls within the cell. The following code statement right-aligns the save button:

```
GridPane.setHalignment(saveButt, HPos.RIGHT);
```

15-9. Generating Borders

Problem

You want to create and customize borders around an image.

Solution

Create an application to dynamically customized border regions using JavaFX's CSS styling API.

The following code creates an application that has a CSS editor text area and a border view region surrounding an image. By default the editor's text area will contain JavaFX styling selectors that create a dashed-blue line surrounding the image. You will have the opportunity to modify styling selector values in the CSS Editor by clicking the Bling! button to apply border settings.

```
primaryStage.setTitle("Chapter 15-9 Generating Borders");
Group root = new Group();
Scene scene = new Scene(root, 600, 330, Color.WHITE);

// create a grid pane
GridPane gridpane = new GridPane();
gridpane.setPadding(new Insets(5));
gridpane.setHgap(10);
gridpane.setVgap(10);

// label CSS Editor
Label cssEditorLbl = new Label("CSS Editor");
GridPane.setHalignment(cssEditorLbl, HPos.CENTER);
gridpane.add(cssEditorLbl, 0, 0);

// label Border View
Label borderLbl = new Label("Border View");
GridPane.setHalignment(borderLbl, HPos.CENTER);
gridpane.add(borderLbl, 1, 0);

// Text area for CSS editor
final TextArea cssEditorFld = new TextArea();
cssEditorFld.setPrefRowCount(10);
cssEditorFld.setPrefColumnCount(100);
cssEditorFld.setWrapText(true);
cssEditorFld.setPrefWidth(150);
GridPane.setHalignment(cssEditorFld, HPos.CENTER);
gridpane.add(cssEditorFld, 0, 1);

String cssDefault = "-fx-border-color: blue;\n"
        + "-fx-border-insets: 5;\n"
        + "-fx-border-width: 3;\n"
        + "-fx-border-style: dashed;\n";
```

```
cssEditorFld.setText(cssDefault);

// Border decorate the picture
final ImageView imv = new ImageView();
final Image image2 = new
Image(GeneratingBorders.class.getResourceAsStream("smoke_glass_buttons1.png"));
imv.setImage(image2);


final HBox pictureRegion = new HBox();
pictureRegion.setStyle(cssDefault);
pictureRegion.getChildren().add(imv);
gridpane.add(pictureRegion, 1, 1);


Button apply = new Button("Bling!");
GridPane.setHalignment(apply, HPos.RIGHT);
gridpane.add(apply, 0, 2);

apply.setOnAction(new EventHandler<ActionEvent>() {
    public void handle(ActionEvent event) {
        pictureRegion.setStyle(cssEditorFld.getText());
    }
});

root.getChildren().add(gridpane);
primaryStage.setScene(scene);
primaryStage.show();
```

Figure 15-14 illustrates the border customizer application.

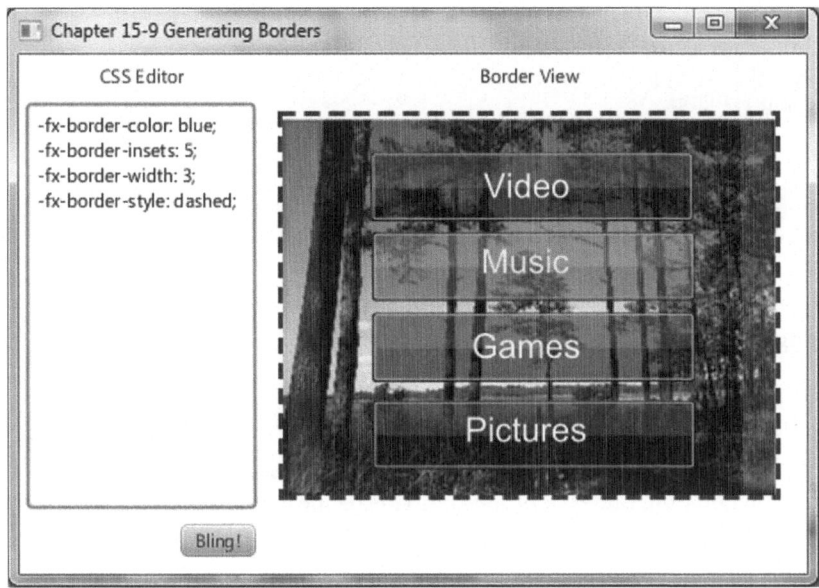

Figure 15-14. Generating borders

How It Works

JavaFX is capable of styling JavaFX nodes similar to Cascading Style Sheets (CSS) in the world of web development. This powerful API can alter a node's background color, font, border, and many other attributes essentially allowing a developer or designer to skin GUI controls using CSS.

This recipe allows a user to enter JavaFX CSS styles in the left text area and, by clicking the Bling! button below, to apply the style around the image shown to the right. Based on the type of node there are limitations to what styles you can set. To see a full listing of all style selectors refer to the JavaFX CSS Reference Guide:

http://download.oracle.com/docs/cd/E17802_01/javafx/javafx/1.3/docs/api/javafx.scene/doc-files/cssref.html.

In the first step of applying JavaFX CSS styles, you must determine what type of node you want to style. When setting attributes on various node types, you will discover that certain nodes have limitations. In our recipe the intent is to put a border around the ImageView object. Because ImageView is not extending from Region it doesn't have border style properties. So, to resolve this I simply create an HBox layout to contain the imageView and apply the JavaFX CSS against the HBox. Shown here is code to apply JavaFX CSS border styles to a horizontal box region (HBox) using the setStyle() method:

```
String cssDefault = "-fx-border-color: blue;\n"
  + "-fx-border-insets: 5;\n"
  + "-fx-border-width: 3;\n"
  + "-fx-border-style: dashed;\n";
final ImageView imv = new ImageView();
```

545

```
.../ /
final HBox pictureRegion = new HBox();
pictureRegion.setStyle(cssDefault);
pictureRegion.getChildren().add(imv);
```

15-10. Binding Expressions

Problem

You want to synchronize changes between two values.

Solution

Use `javafx.beans.binding.*` and `javafx.beans.property.*` packages to bind variables. There is more than one scenario to consider when binding values or properties. This recipe demonstrates the following three binding strategies:

- Bidirectional binding on a Java Bean

- High-level binding using the Fluent API

- Low-level binding using `javafx.beans.binding.*` Binding objects

The following code is a console application implementing these three strategies. The console application will output property values based on various binding scenarios. The first scenario is a bidirectional binding between a String property variable and a String property owned by a domain object (`Contact`) such as the `firstName` property. The next scenario is a high-level binding using a fluent interface API to calculate the area of rectangle. The last scenario is using a low-level binding strategy to calculate the volume of a sphere. The difference between the high-and low-level binding is that the high level uses methods such as `multiply()`, `subtract()` instead of the operators * and -. When using low-level binding, you would use a derived `NumberBinding` class such as a `DoubleBinding` class. With a `DoubleBinding` class you will override its `computeValue()` method so that you can use the familiar operators such as * and - to formulate complex math equations:

```
package org.java7recipes.chapter15.recipe15_10;

import javafx.beans.binding.DoubleBinding;
import javafx.beans.binding.NumberBinding;
import javafx.beans.property.DoubleProperty;
import javafx.beans.property.IntegerProperty;
import javafx.beans.property.SimpleDoubleProperty;
import javafx.beans.property.SimpleIntegerProperty;
import javafx.beans.property.SimpleStringProperty;
import javafx.beans.property.StringProperty;

/**
 * Binding Expressions
 * @author cdea
 */
```

```java
public class BindingExpressions {

    /**
     * @param args the command line arguments
     */
    public static void main(String[] args) {
        System.out.println("Chapter 15-10 Binding Expressions\n");

        System.out.println("Binding a Contact bean [Bi-directional binding]");
        Contact contact = new Contact("John", "Doe");
        StringProperty fname = new SimpleStringProperty();
        fname.bindBidirectional(contact.firstNameProperty());
        StringProperty lname = new SimpleStringProperty();
        lname.bindBidirectional(contact.lastNameProperty());

        System.out.println("Current - StringProperty values   : " + fname.getValue() + " " +
lname.getValue());
        System.out.println("Current - Contact values          : " + contact.getFirstName() +
" " + contact.getLastName());

        System.out.println("Modifying StringProperty values");
        fname.setValue("Jane");
        lname.setValue("Deer");

        System.out.println("After - StringProperty values   : " + fname.getValue() + " " +
lname.getValue());
        System.out.println("After - Contact values          : " + contact.getFirstName() + "
" + contact.getLastName());

        System.out.println();
        System.out.println("A Area of a Rectangle [High level Fluent API]");

        // Area = width * height
        final IntegerProperty width = new SimpleIntegerProperty(10);
        final IntegerProperty height = new SimpleIntegerProperty(10);

        NumberBinding area = width.multiply(height);

        System.out.println("Current - Width and Height     : " + width.get() + " " +
height.get());
        System.out.println("Current - Area of the Rectangle: " + area.getValue());
        System.out.println("Modifying width and height");

        width.set(100);
        height.set(700);

        System.out.println("After - Width and Height     : " + width.get() + " " +
height.get());
        System.out.println("After - Area of the Rectangle: " + area.getValue());

        System.out.println();
        System.out.println("A Volume of a Sphere [low level API]");
```

```
        // volume = 4/3 * pi r^3
        final DoubleProperty radius = new SimpleDoubleProperty(2);

        DoubleBinding volumeOfSphere = new DoubleBinding() {
            {
                super.bind(radius);
            }

            @Override
            protected double computeValue() {
                return (4 / 3 * Math.PI * Math.pow(radius.get(), 3));
            }
        };

        System.out.println("Current - radius for Sphere: " + radius.get());
        System.out.println("Current - volume for Sphere: " + volumeOfSphere.get());
        System.out.println("Modifying DoubleProperty radius");

        radius.set(50);
        System.out.println("After - radius for Sphere: " + radius.get());
        System.out.println("After - volume for Sphere: " + volumeOfSphere.get());

    }
}

class Contact {

    private SimpleStringProperty firstName = new SimpleStringProperty();
    private SimpleStringProperty lastName = new SimpleStringProperty();

    public Contact(String fn, String ln) {
        firstName.setValue(fn);
        lastName.setValue(ln);
    }

    public final String getFirstName() {
        return firstName.getValue();
    }

    public StringProperty firstNameProperty() {
        return firstName;
    }

    public final void setFirstName(String firstName) {
        this.firstName.setValue(firstName);
    }

    public final String getLastName() {
        return lastName.getValue();
    }
```

```
    public StringProperty lastNameProperty() {
        return lastName;
    }

    public final void setLastName(String lastName) {
        this.lastName.setValue(lastName);
    }
}
```

The following output demonstrates the three binding scenarios:

```
Binding a Contact bean [Bi-directional binding]
Current - StringProperty values   : John Doe
Current - Contact values          : John Doe
Modifying StringProperty values
After - StringProperty values  : Jane Deer
After - Contact values         : Jane Deer

A Area of a Rectangle [High level Fluent API]
Current - Width and Height      : 10 10
Current - Area of the Rectangle: 100
Modifying width and height
After - Width and Height      : 100 700
After - Area of the Rectangle: 70000

A Volume of a Sphere [low level API]
Current - radius for Sphere: 2.0
Current - volume for Sphere: 25.132741228718345
Modifying DoubleProperty radius
After - radius for Sphere: 50.0
After - volume for Sphere: 392699.0816987241
```

How It Works

Binding has the idea of at least two values being synchronized. This means when a dependent variable changes the other variable changes. JavaFX provides many binding options that enable the developer to synchronize properties in domain objects and GUI controls. This recipe will demonstrate the three common binding scenarios.

One of the easiest ways to bind variables is a *bidirectional bind*. This scenario is often used when domain objects contain data that will be bound to a GUI form. In our recipe we create a simple contact (Contact) object containing a first name and last name. Notice the instance variables using the SimpleStringProperty class. Many of these classes, which end in Property, are javafx.beans.Observable classes that all have the ability to be bound. In order for these properties to be bound, they must be the same data type. In the preceding example we create first name and last name variables of type SimpleStringProperty outside the created Contact domain object. Once they have been created we bind them bidirectionally to allow changes to update on either end. So if you change the domain object, the other bound properties get updated. And when the outside variables are modified, the domain object's properties get updated. The following demonstrates bidirectional binding against string properties on a domain object (Contact):

```
Contact contact = new Contact("John", "Doe");
StringProperty fname = new SimpleStringProperty();
fname.bindBidirectional(contact.firstNameProperty());
StringProperty lname = new SimpleStringProperty();
lname.bindBidirectional(contact.lastNameProperty());
```

Next up is how to bind numbers. Binding numbers is simple when using the new Fluent API. This high-level mechanism allows a developer to bind variables to compute values using simple arithmetic. Basically, a formula is "bound" to change its result based on changes to the variables it is bound to. Please look at the Javadoc for details on all the available methods and number types. In this example we simply create a formula for an area of a rectangle. The area (NumberBinding) is the binding, and its dependencies are the width and height (IntegerProperty) properties. When binding using the fluent interface API, you'll notice the multiply() method. According to the Javadoc, all property classes inherit from the NumberExpressionBase class, which contains the number-based fluent interface APIs. The following code snippet uses the fluent interface API:

```
// Area = width * height
final IntegerProperty width = new SimpleIntegerProperty(10);
final IntegerProperty height = new SimpleIntegerProperty(10);
NumberBinding area = width.multiply(height);
```

The last scenario on binding numbers is considered more of a low-level approach. This allows the developer to use primitives and more-complex math operations. Here we use a DoubleBinding class to solve the volume of a sphere given the radius. We begin by implementing the computeValue() method to perform our calculation of the volume. Shown is the low-level binding scenario to compute the volume of a sphere by overriding the computeValue() method:

```
final DoubleProperty radius = new SimpleDoubleProperty(2);

DoubleBinding volumeOfSphere = new DoubleBinding() {
    {
        super.bind(radius);
    }

    @Override
    protected double computeValue() {
        return (4 / 3 * Math.PI * Math.pow(radius.get(), 3));
    }
};
```

15-11. Creating and Working with Observable Lists

Problem

You want to create a GUI application containing two list view controls allowing the user pass items between the two lists.

Solution

Take advantage of JavaFX's `javafx.collections.ObservableList` and `javafx.scene.control.ListView` classes to provide a model-view-controller (MVC) mechanism that updates the UI's list view control whenever the back-end list is manipulated.

The following code creates a GUI application containing two lists that allow the user to send items contained in one list to be sent to the other. Here you will create a contrived application to pick candidates to be considered heroes. The user will pick potential candidates from the list on the left to be moved into the list on the right to be considered heroes. This demonstrates UI list controls' (`ListView`) ability to be synchronized with back-end store lists (`ObservableList`).

```
primaryStage.setTitle("Chapter 15-11 Creating and Working with ObservableLists");
Group root = new Group();
Scene scene = new Scene(root, 400, 250, Color.WHITE);

// create a grid pane
GridPane gridpane = new GridPane();
gridpane.setPadding(new Insets(5));
gridpane.setHgap(10);
gridpane.setVgap(10);

// candidates label
Label candidatesLbl = new Label("Candidates");
GridPane.setHalignment(candidatesLbl, HPos.CENTER);
gridpane.add(candidatesLbl, 0, 0);

Label heroesLbl = new Label("Heroes");
gridpane.add(heroesLbl, 2, 0);
GridPane.setHalignment(heroesLbl, HPos.CENTER);

// candidates
final ObservableList<String> candidates = FXCollections.observableArrayList("Super
man",
            "Spider man",
            "Wolverine",
            "Police",
            "Fire Rescue",
            "Solders",
            "Dad & Mom",
            "Doctor",
            "Politician",
            "Pastor",
            "Teacher");
final ListView<String> candidatesListView = new ListView<String>(candidates);
candidatesListView.setPrefWidth(150);
candidatesListView.setPrefHeight(150);

gridpane.add(candidatesListView, 0, 1);

// heros
final ObservableList<String> heroes = FXCollections.observableArrayList();
final ListView<String> heroListView = new ListView<String>(heroes);
heroListView.setPrefWidth(150);
```

```
heroListView.setPrefHeight(150);

gridpane.add(heroListView, 2, 1);

// select heroes
Button sendRightButton = new Button(">");
sendRightButton.setOnAction(new EventHandler<ActionEvent>() {

    public void handle(ActionEvent event) {
        String potential = candidatesListView.getSelectionModel().getSelectedItem();
        if (potential != null) {
            candidatesListView.getSelectionModel().clearSelection();
            candidates.remove(potential);
            heroes.add(potential);
        }
    }
});

// deselect heroes
Button sendLeftButton = new Button("<");
sendLeftButton.setOnAction(new EventHandler<ActionEvent>() {

    public void handle(ActionEvent event) {
        String notHero = heroListView.getSelectionModel().getSelectedItem();
        if (notHero != null) {
            heroListView.getSelectionModel().clearSelection();
            heroes.remove(notHero);
            candidates.add(notHero);
        }
    }
});

VBox vbox = new VBox(5);
vbox.getChildren().addAll(sendRightButton,sendLeftButton);

gridpane.add(vbox, 1, 1);
GridPane.setConstraints(vbox, 1, 1, 1, 2,HPos.CENTER, VPos.CENTER);

root.getChildren().add(gridpane);
primaryStage.setScene(scene);
primaryStage.show();
```

Figure 15-15 depicts our hero selection application.

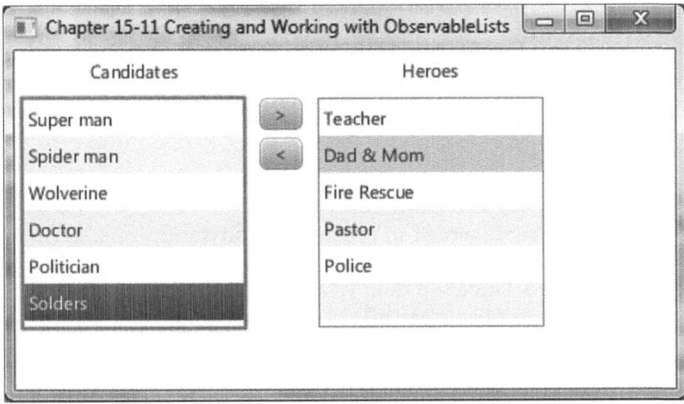

Figure 15-15. ListViews and ObservableLists

How It Works

When dealing with Java collections you'll notice there are so many useful container classes that represent all kinds of data structures. One commonly used collection is the java.util.ArrayList class. When building applications with domain objects that contain an ArrayList, a developer can easily manipulate objects inside the collection. But, in the past (back in the day), when using Java Swing components combined with collections can often be a challenge, especially updating the GUI to reflect changes in the domain object. How do we resolve this issue? Well, JavaFX's ObservableList to the rescue!

Speaking of rescue, I've created a GUI application to allow users to choose their favorite heroes. This is quite similar to application screens that manage user roles by adding or removing items from list box components. In JavaFX we will be using a ListView control to hold String objects. Before we create an instance of a ListView we create an ObservableList containing our candidates. Here you'll notice the use of a factory class called FXCollections, in which you can pass in common collection types to be wrapped and returned to the caller as an ObservableList. In the recipe I passed in an array of Strings instead of an ArrayList, so hopefully you get the idea about how to use the FXCollections class. I trust you will use it wisely: "With great power, there must also come great responsibility". This code line calls the FXCollections class to return an observable list (ObservableList):

```
ObservableList<String> candidates = FXCollections.observableArrayList(...);
```

After creating an ObservableList, a ListView class is instantiated using a constructor that receives the observable list. Shown here is code to create and populate a ListView object:

```
ListView<String> candidatesListView = new ListView<String>(candidates);
```

In the last item of business, our code will manipulate the ObservableLists as if they were java.util.ArrayLists. Once manipulated, the ListView will be notified and automatically updated to reflect the changes of the ObservableList. The following code snippet implements the event handler and action event when the user presses the send right button:

```
// select heroes
Button sendRightButton = new Button(">");
sendRightButton.setOnAction(new EventHandler<ActionEvent>() {

    public void handle(ActionEvent event) {
        String potential = candidatesListView.getSelectionModel().getSelectedItem();
```

```
        if (potential != null) {
            candidatesListView.getSelectionModel().clearSelection();
            candidates.remove(potential);
            heroes.add(potential);
        }
    }
});
```

When setting an action we use the generic class `EventHandler` to create an anonymous inner class with the `handle()` method to listen for a button press event. When a button press event arrives, the code will determine which item in the `ListView` was selected. Once the item was determined, we clear the selection, remove the item, and add the item to the hero's `ObserverableList`.

15-12. Generating a Background Process

Problem

You want to create a GUI application that simulates the copying of files using background processing while displaying the progress to the user.

Solution

Create an application typical of a dialog box showing progress indicators while copying files in the background. The following are the main classes used in this recipe:

- `javafx.scene.control.ProgressBar`

- `javafx.scene.control.ProgressIndicator`

- `javafx.concurrent.Task` classes

The following source code is an application that simulates a file copy dialog box displaying progress indicators and performing background processes:

```
package org.java7recipes.chapter15.recipe15_12;

import java.util.Random;
import javafx.application.Application;
import javafx.beans.value.ChangeListener;
import javafx.beans.value.ObservableValue;
import javafx.concurrent.Task;
import javafx.event.ActionEvent;
import javafx.event.EventHandler;
import javafx.geometry.Pos;
import javafx.scene.Group;
import javafx.scene.Scene;
import javafx.scene.control.Button;
import javafx.scene.control.Label;
import javafx.scene.control.ProgressBar;
```

```java
import javafx.scene.control.ProgressIndicator;
import javafx.scene.control.TextArea;
import javafx.scene.layout.BorderPane;
import javafx.scene.layout.HBox;
import javafx.scene.paint.Color;
import javafx.stage.Stage;

/**
 * Background Processes
 * @author cdea
 */
public class BackgroundProcesses extends Application {

    static Task copyWorker;
    final int numFiles = 30;

    /**
     * @param args the command line arguments
     */
    public static void main(String[] args) {
        Application.launch(args);
    }

    @Override
    public void start(Stage primaryStage) {
        primaryStage.setTitle("Chapter 15-12 Background Processes");
        Group root = new Group();
        Scene scene = new Scene(root, 330, 120, Color.WHITE);

        BorderPane mainPane = new BorderPane();

mainPane.layoutXProperty().bind(scene.widthProperty().subtract(mainPane.widthProperty()).div
ide(2));
        root.getChildren().add(mainPane);

        final Label label = new Label("Files Transfer:");
        final ProgressBar progressBar = new ProgressBar(0);
        final ProgressIndicator progressIndicator = new ProgressIndicator(0);

        final HBox hb = new HBox();
        hb.setSpacing(5);
        hb.setAlignment(Pos.CENTER);
        hb.getChildren().addAll(label, progressBar, progressIndicator);
        mainPane.setTop(hb);


        final Button startButton = new Button("Start");
        final Button cancelButton = new Button("Cancel");
        final TextArea textArea = new TextArea();
        textArea.setEditable(false);
        textArea.setPrefSize(200, 70);
        final HBox hb2 = new HBox();
```

```java
            hb2.setSpacing(5);
            hb2.setAlignment(Pos.CENTER);
            hb2.getChildren().addAll(startButton, cancelButton, textArea);
            mainPane.setBottom(hb2);

            // wire up start button
            startButton.setOnAction(new EventHandler<ActionEvent>() {

                public void handle(ActionEvent event) {
                    startButton.setDisable(true);
                    progressBar.setProgress(0);
                    progressIndicator.setProgress(0);
                    textArea.setText("");
                    cancelButton.setDisable(false);
                    copyWorker = createWorker(numFiles);

                    // wire up progress bar
                    progressBar.progressProperty().unbind();
                    progressBar.progressProperty().bind(copyWorker.progressProperty());
                    progressIndicator.progressProperty().unbind();
                    progressIndicator.progressProperty().bind(copyWorker.progressProperty());

                    // append to text area box
                    copyWorker.messageProperty().addListener(new ChangeListener<String>() {

                        public void changed(ObservableValue<? extends String> observable, String
oldValue, String newValue) {
                            textArea.appendText(newValue + "\n");
                        }
                    });

                    new Thread(copyWorker).start();
                }
            });

            // cancel button will kill worker and reset.
            cancelButton.setOnAction(new EventHandler<ActionEvent>() {

                public void handle(ActionEvent event) {
                    startButton.setDisable(false);
                    cancelButton.setDisable(true);
                    copyWorker.cancel(true);

                    // reset
                    progressBar.progressProperty().unbind();
                    progressBar.setProgress(0);
                    progressIndicator.progressProperty().unbind();
                    progressIndicator.setProgress(0);
                    textArea.appendText("File transfer was cancelled.");
                }
            });
```

```
        primaryStage.setScene(scene);
        primaryStage.show();
    }

    public Task createWorker(final int numFiles) {
        return new Task() {

            @Override
            protected Object call() throws Exception {
                for (int i = 0; i < numFiles; i++) {
                    long elapsedTime = System.currentTimeMillis();
                    copyFile("some file", "some dest file");
                    elapsedTime = System.currentTimeMillis() - elapsedTime;
                    String status = elapsedTime + " milliseconds";

                    // queue up status
                    updateMessage(status);
                    updateProgress(i + 1, numFiles);
                }
                return true;
            }
        };
    }

    public void copyFile(String src, String dest) throws InterruptedException {
        // simulate a long time
        Random rnd = new Random(System.currentTimeMillis());
        long millis = rnd.nextInt(1000);
        Thread.sleep(millis);
    }
}
```

Figure 15-16 shows our Background Processes application simulating a file copy window.

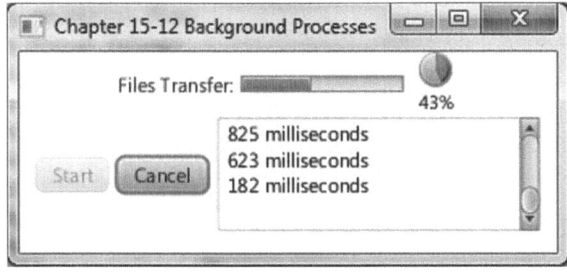

Figure 15-16. Background processes

How It Works

One of the main pitfalls of GUI development is knowing when and how to delegate work (Threads). We are constantly reminded of thread safety, especially when it comes to blocking the GUI thread. As in recipe 14-6, we discuss and implement the SwingWorker object to defer non-GUI work off of the event dispatch thread (EDT). Similar patterns and principles still apply in the world of JavaFX. Again, this recipe will be a JavaFX version of recipe 14-6.

We begin by creating not one but two progress controls to show off to the user the work being done. One is a progress bar, and the other is a progress indicator. The progress indicator shows a percentage below the indicator icon. The following code snippet shows the initial creation of progress controls:

```
final ProgressBar progressBar = new ProgressBar(0);
final ProgressIndicator progressIndicator = new ProgressIndicator(0);
```

Next, we create a worker thread via our createWorker() method. The createWorker() convenience method will instantiate and return a javafx.concurrent.Task object, which is similar to the Java Swing's SwingWorker class. Unlike the SwingWorker class, the Task object is greatly simplified and easier to use. If you've compared the last recipe you will notice that none of the GUI controls is passed into the Task. The clever JavaFX team has created observable properties that allow us to bind to. This fosters a more event-driven approach to handling work (tasks). When creating an instance of a Task object you will implement the call() method to do work in the background. During the work being done, you may want to queue up intermediate results such as progress or text info, you can call the updateProgress() and updateMessage() methods. These methods will update information in a threadsafe way so that the observer of the progress properties will be able to update the GUI safely without blocking the GUI thread. The following code snippet demonstrates the ability to queue up messages and progress:

```
// queue up status
updateMessage(status);
updateProgress(i + 1, numFiles);
```

After creating a worker Task we unbind any old tasks bound to the progress controls. Once the progress controls are unbound, we then bind the progress controls to our newly created Task object copyWorker. Shown here is the code used to rebind a new Task object to the progress UI controls:

```
// wire up progress bar
progressBar.progressProperty().unbind();
progressBar.progressProperty().bind(copyWorker.progressProperty());
progressIndicator.progressProperty().unbind();
progressIndicator.progressProperty().bind(copyWorker.progressProperty());
```

Next, we implement a ChangeListener to append the queued results into the TextArea control. Another remarkable thing about JavaFX Properties is that you can attach many listeners similar to Java Swing components. Finally our worker and controls are all wired up to spawn a thread to go off in the background. The following code line shows the launching of a Task worker object:

```
new Thread(copyWorker).start();
```

Finally, we discuss the cancel button. The cancel button will simply call the Task object's cancel() method to kill the process. Once the task is cancelled the progress controls are reset. Once a worker Task is cancelled it cannot be reused. That is why the start button re-creates a new Task. If you want a more-robust solution, you should look at the `javafx.concurrent.Service` class. The following code line will cancel a `Task` worker object:

```
copyWorker.cancel(true);
```

15-13. Associating Keyboard Sequences to Applications

Problem

You want to create keyboard shortcuts for menu options.

Solution

Create an application that will use JavaFX's key combination APIs. The main classes you will be using are shown here:

- `javafx.scene.input.KeyCode`

- `javafx.scene.input.KeyCodeCombination`

- `javafx.scene.input.KeyCombination`

The following source code listing is an application that displays the available keyboard shortcuts that are bound to menu items. When the user performs a keyboard shortcut the application will display the key combination on the screen:

```
primaryStage.setTitle("Chapter 15-13 Associating Keyboard Sequences");
Group root = new Group();
Scene scene = new Scene(root, 530, 300, Color.WHITE);

final StringProperty statusProperty = new SimpleStringProperty();

InnerShadow iShadow = InnerShadowBuilder.create()
        .offsetX(3.5f)
        .offsetY(3.5f)
        .build();
final Text status = TextBuilder.create()
    .effect(iShadow)
    .x(100)
    .y(50)
    .fill(Color.LIME)
    .font(Font.font(null, FontWeight.BOLD, 35))
    .translateY(50)
    .build();
status.textProperty().bind(statusProperty);
statusProperty.set("Keyboard Shortcuts \nCtrl-N, \nCtrl-S, \nCtrl-X");
root.getChildren().add(status);

MenuBar menuBar = new MenuBar();
```

```
        menuBar.prefWidthProperty().bind(primaryStage.widthProperty());
        root.getChildren().add(menuBar);

        Menu menu = new Menu("File");
        menuBar.getMenus().add(menu);

        MenuItem newItem = MenuItemBuilder.create()
                .text("New")
                .accelerator(new KeyCodeCombination(KeyCode.N, KeyCombination.CONTROL_DOWN))
                .onAction(new EventHandler<ActionEvent>() {
                        public void handle(ActionEvent event) {
                            statusProperty.set("Ctrl-N");
                        }
                    })
                .build();
        menu.getItems().add(newItem);


        MenuItem saveItem = MenuItemBuilder.create()
                .text("Save")
                .accelerator(new KeyCodeCombination(KeyCode.S, KeyCombination.CONTROL_DOWN))
                .onAction(new EventHandler<ActionEvent>() {
                        public void handle(ActionEvent event) {
                            statusProperty.set("Ctrl-S");
                        }
                    })
                .build();
        menu.getItems().add(saveItem);

        menu.getItems().add(new SeparatorMenuItem());

        MenuItem exitItem = MenuItemBuilder.create()
                .text("Exit")
                .accelerator(new KeyCodeCombination(KeyCode.X, KeyCombination.CONTROL_DOWN))
                .onAction(new EventHandler<ActionEvent>() {
                        public void handle(ActionEvent event) {
                            statusProperty.set("Ctrl-X");
                        }
                    })
                .build();
        menu.getItems().add(exitItem);

        primaryStage.setScene(scene);
        primaryStage.show();
```

Figure 15-17 displays an application that demonstrates keyboard sequences or keyboard shortcuts.

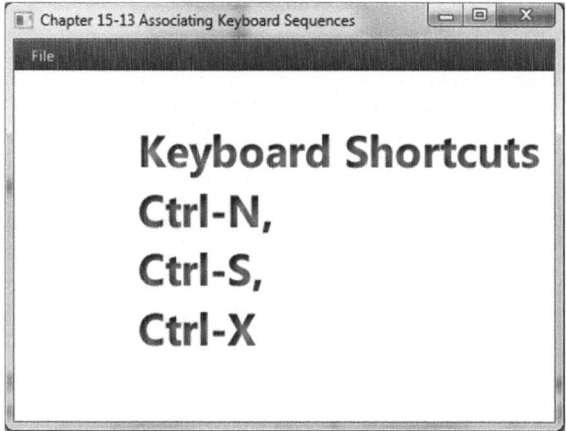

Figure 15-17. *Keyboard sequences*

How It Works

Similar to recipe 14-16, we will be creating key combination or keyboard shortcuts using the new
`javafx.scene.input.KeyCodeCombination` and `javafx.scene.input.KeyCombination` classes.

Seeing that the previous recipe was a tad boring, I decided to make things a little more interesting.
This recipe will display Text nodes onto the scene graph when the user performs the key combinations.
When displaying the Text nodes I applied an inner shadow effect. The following code snippet creates a
Text node with an inner shadow effect:

```
InnerShadow iShadow = InnerShadowBuilder.create()
        .offsetX(3.5f)
        .offsetY(3.5f)
        .build();
final Text status = TextBuilder.create()
    .effect(iShadow)
    .x(100)
    .y(50)
    .fill(Color.LIME)
    .build();
```

So to create a keyboard shortcut you simply call a menu or button control's `setAccelerator()`
method. In this recipe we use a `Builder` class and set the key combination using the `accelerator()`
method. The following code line specifies the key combinations for a control N:

```
MenuItem newItem = MenuItemBuilder.create()
        .text("New")
        .accelerator(new KeyCodeCombination(KeyCode.N, KeyCombination.CONTROL_DOWN))
        .build():
```

15-14. Creating and Working with Tables

Problem

You want to display items in a UI table control similar to Java Swing's JTable component.

Solution

Create an application using JavaFX's `javafx.scene.control.TableView` class. The `TableView` control provides the equivalent functionality similar to Swing's `JTable` component.

To exercise the `TableView` control you will be creating an application that will display bosses and employees. On the left you will implement a `ListView` control containing bosses, and employees (subordinates) will be displayed in a `TableView` control on the right.

Shown here is the source code of a simple domain (`Person`) class to represent a boss or an employee to be displayed in a `ListView` or `TableView` control:

```
package org.java7recipes.chapter15.recipe15_14;

import javafx.beans.property.SimpleStringProperty;
import javafx.beans.property.StringProperty;
import javafx.collections.FXCollections;
import javafx.collections.ObservableList;

/**
 *
 * @author cdea
 */
public class Person {

    private StringProperty aliasName;
    private StringProperty firstName;
    private StringProperty lastName;
    private ObservableList<Person> employees = FXCollections.observableArrayList();

    public final void setAliasName(String value) {
        aliasNameProperty().set(value);
    }

    public final String getAliasName() {
        return aliasNameProperty().get();
    }

    public StringProperty aliasNameProperty() {
        if (aliasName == null) {
            aliasName = new SimpleStringProperty();
        }
        return aliasName;
    }
```

```java
    public final void setFirstName(String value) {
        firstNameProperty().set(value);
    }

    public final String getFirstName() {
        return firstNameProperty().get();
    }

    public StringProperty firstNameProperty() {
        if (firstName == null) {
            firstName = new SimpleStringProperty();
        }
        return firstName;
    }

    public final void setLastName(String value) {
        lastNameProperty().set(value);
    }

    public final String getLastName() {
        return lastNameProperty().get();
    }

    public StringProperty lastNameProperty() {
        if (lastName == null) {
            lastName = new SimpleStringProperty();
        }
        return lastName;
    }

    public ObservableList<Person> employeesProperty() {
        return employees;
    }

    public Person(String alias, String firstName, String lastName) {
        setAliasName(alias);
        setFirstName(firstName);
        setLastName(lastName);
    }

}
```

The following is our main application code that displays a list view component on the left containing bosses and a table view control on the right containing employees:

```java
        primaryStage.setTitle("Chapter 15-14 Working with Tables");
        Group root = new Group();
        Scene scene = new Scene(root, 500, 250, Color.WHITE);

        // create a grid pane
        GridPane gridpane = new GridPane();
        gridpane.setPadding(new Insets(5));
```

```
gridpane.setHgap(10);
gridpane.setVgap(10);

// candidates label
Label candidatesLbl = new Label("Boss");
GridPane.setHalignment(candidatesLbl, HPos.CENTER);
gridpane.add(candidatesLbl, 0, 0);

// List of leaders
ObservableList<Person> leaders = getPeople();
final ListView<Person> leaderListView = new ListView<>(leaders);
leaderListView.setPrefWidth(150);
leaderListView.setPrefHeight(150);

// display first and last name with tooltip using alias
leaderListView.setCellFactory(new Callback<ListView<Person>, ListCell<Person>>() {

    public ListCell<Person> call(ListView<Person> param) {
        final Label leadLbl = new Label();
        final Tooltip tooltip = new Tooltip();
            final ListCell<Person> cell = new ListCell<Person>() {
                @Override
                public void updateItem(Person item, boolean empty) {
                        super.updateItem(item, empty);
                        if (item != null) {
                            leadLbl.setText(item.getAliasName());
                            setText(item.getFirstName() + " " + item.getLastName());
                            tooltip.setText(item.getAliasName());
                            setTooltip(tooltip);
                        }
                }
            }; // ListCell
            return cell;

    }
}); // setCellFactory

gridpane.add(leaderListView, 0, 1);

Label emplLbl = new Label("Employees");
gridpane.add(emplLbl, 2, 0);
GridPane.setHalignment(emplLbl, HPos.CENTER);

final TableView<Person> employeeTableView = new TableView<>();
employeeTableView.setPrefWidth(300);

final ObservableList<Person> teamMembers = FXCollections.observableArrayList();
employeeTableView.setItems(teamMembers);

TableColumn<Person, String> aliasNameCol = new TableColumn<>("Alias");
aliasNameCol.setEditable(true);
aliasNameCol.setCellValueFactory(new PropertyValueFactory("aliasName"));
```

```
        aliasNameCol.setPrefWidth(employeeTableView.getPrefWidth() / 3);

        TableColumn<Person, String> firstNameCol = new TableColumn<>("First Name");
        firstNameCol.setCellValueFactory(new PropertyValueFactory("firstName"));
        firstNameCol.setPrefWidth(employeeTableView.getPrefWidth() / 3);

        TableColumn<Person, String> lastNameCol = new TableColumn<>("Last Name");
        lastNameCol.setCellValueFactory(new PropertyValueFactory("lastName"));
        lastNameCol.setPrefWidth(employeeTableView.getPrefWidth() / 3);

        employeeTableView.getColumns().setAll(aliasNameCol, firstNameCol, lastNameCol);
        gridpane.add(employeeTableView, 2, 1);

        // selection listening
        leaderListView.getSelectionModel().selectedItemProperty().addListener(new
ChangeListener<Person>() {
            public void changed(ObservableValue<? extends Person> observable, Person
oldValue, Person newValue) {
                if (observable != null && observable.getValue() != null) {
                    teamMembers.clear();
                    teamMembers.addAll(observable.getValue().employeesProperty());
                }
            }
        });

        root.getChildren().add(gridpane);

        primaryStage.setScene(scene);
        primaryStage.show();
```

The following code is the getPeople() method contained in the WorkingWithTables main application class. This method helps to populate the UI TableView control shown previously:

```
    private ObservableList<Person> getPeople() {
        ObservableList<Person> people = FXCollections.<Person>observableArrayList();
        Person docX = new Person("Professor X", "Charles", "Xavier");
        docX.employeesProperty().add(new Person("Wolverine", "James", "Howlett"));
        docX.employeesProperty().add(new Person("Cyclops", "Scott", "Summers"));
        docX.employeesProperty().add(new Person("Storm", "Ororo", "Munroe"));

        Person magneto = new Person("Magneto", "Max", "Eisenhardt");
        magneto.employeesProperty().add(new Person("Juggernaut", "Cain", "Marko"));
        magneto.employeesProperty().add(new Person("Mystique", "Raven", "Darkhölme"));
        magneto.employeesProperty().add(new Person("Sabretooth", "Victor", "Creed"));

        Person biker = new Person("Mountain Biker", "Jonathan", "Gennick");
        biker.employeesProperty().add(new Person("Josh", "Joshua", "Juneau"));
        biker.employeesProperty().add(new Person("Freddy", "Freddy", "Guime"));
        biker.employeesProperty().add(new Person("Mark", "Mark", "Beaty"));
        biker.employeesProperty().add(new Person("John", "John", "O'Conner"));
```

```
        biker.employeesProperty().add(new Person("D-Man", "Carl", "Dea"));

        people.add(docX);
        people.add(magneto);
        people.add(biker);

        return people;
    }
```

Figure 15-18 displays our application that demonstrates JavaFX's `TableView` control.

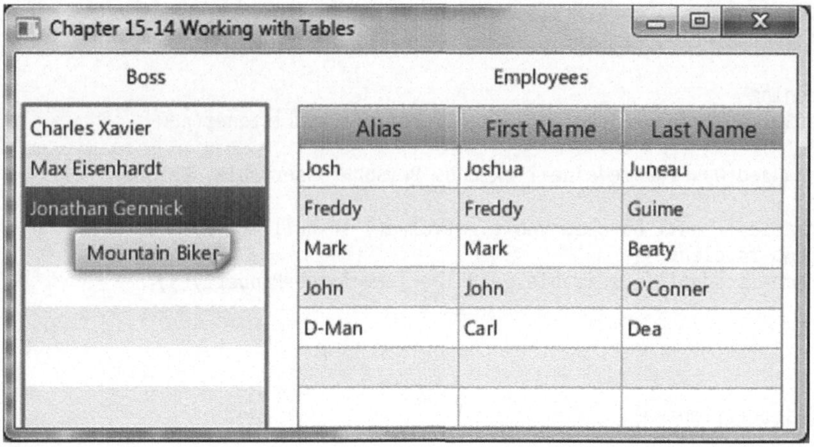

Figure 15-18. Working with tables

How It Works

Just for fun I created a simple GUI to display employees and their bosses. You notice in Figure 15-18 on the left is a list of people (Boss). When users click and select a boss, their employees will be shown to in the `TableView` area to the right. You'll also notice the tooltip when you hover over the selected boss.

Before we begin to discuss the `TableView` control I want to explain about the `ListView` that is responsible for updating the `TableView`. In model view fashion we first create an `ObservableList` containing all the bosses for the `ListView` control's constructor. In my code I was politically correct by calling bosses *leaders*. The following code creates a `ListView` control:

```
// List of leaders
ObservableList<Person> leaders = getPeople();
final ListView<Person> leaderListView = new ListView<Person>(leaders);
```

Next, we create a cell factory to properly display the person's name in the `ListView` control. Because each item is a `Person` object, the `ListView` does not know how to render each row in the `ListView` control. We simply create a `javafx.util.Callback` generic type object by specifying the `ListView<Person>` and a `ListCell<Person>` data types. With your trusty NetBeans IDE, it will pregenerate things such as the implementing method `call()`. Next is the variable cell of type `ListCell<Person>` (within the `call()`

method), in which we create an anonymous inner class. The inner class must implement an `updateItem()` method. To implement the `updateItem()` method you will obtain the person information and update the `Label` control (`leadLbl`). Hopefully, you're still with me. The last thing is our tooltip, which is set.

Finally, we get to create a `TableView` control to display the employee base on the selected boss from the `ListView`. When creating a `TableView` we first create the column headers. Use this to create a table column:

```
TableColumn<String> firstNameCol = new TableColumn<String>("First Name");
firstNameCol.setProperty("firstName");
```

Once you have created a column, you'll notice the `setProperty()` method, which is responsible for calling the Person bean's property. So when the list of employees is put into the `TableView`, it will know how to pull the properties to be placed in each cell in the table.

Last is the implementation of the selection listener on the `ListViewer` in JavaFX called a selection item property (`selectionItemProperty()`). We simply create and add a `ChangeListener` to listen to selection events. When a user selects a boss, the `TableView` is cleared and populated with the boss' employees. Actually it is the magic of the `ObservableList` that notifies the `TableView` of changes. To populate the `TableView` via the `teamMembers` (ObservableList) variable:

```
teamMembers.clear();
teamMembers.addAll(observable.getValue().employeesProperty());
```

15-15. Organizing UI with Split Views

Problem

You want to split up a GUI screen by using split divider controls.

Solution

Use JavaFX's split pane control. The `javafx.scene.control.SplitPane` class is a UI control that enables you to divide a screen into frame-like regions. The split control allows the user to use the mouse to move the divider between any two split regions.

Shown here is the code to create the GUI application that utilizes the `javafx.scene.control.SplitPane` class to divide the screen into three windowed regions. The three windowed regions are a lefthand column, an upper-right region, and a lower-right region. In addition, you will be adding `Text` nodes into the three regions.

```
// Left and right split pane
SplitPane splitPane = new SplitPane();
splitPane.prefWidthProperty().bind(scene.widthProperty());
splitPane.prefHeightProperty().bind(scene.heightProperty());

VBox leftArea = new VBox(10);

for (int i = 0; i < 5; i++) {
```

```
    HBox rowBox = new HBox(20);
    final Text leftText = TextBuilder.create()
        .text("Left " + i)
        .translateX(20)
        .fill(Color.BLUE)
.font(Font.font(null, FontWeight.BOLD, 20))
.build();

    rowBox.getChildren().add(leftText);
    leftArea.getChildren().add(rowBox);
}
leftArea.setAlignment(Pos.CENTER);

// Upper and lower split pane
SplitPane splitPane2 = new SplitPane();
splitPane2.setOrientation(Orientation.VERTICAL);
splitPane2.prefWidthProperty().bind(scene.widthProperty());
splitPane2.prefHeightProperty().bind(scene.heightProperty());

HBox centerArea = new HBox();

InnerShadow iShadow = InnerShadowBuilder.create()
    .offsetX(3.5f)
    .offsetY(3.5f)
    .build();
final Text upperRight = TextBuilder.create()
    .text("Upper Right")
    .x(100)
    .y(50)
    .effect(iShadow)
    .fill(Color.LIME)
.font(Font.font(null, FontWeight.BOLD, 35))
.translateY(50)
    .build();
centerArea.getChildren().add(upperRight);

HBox rightArea = new HBox();

final Text lowerRight = TextBuilder.create()
    .text("Lower Right")
    .x(100)
    .y(50)
    .effect(iShadow)
    .fill(Color.RED)
.font(Font.font(null, FontWeight.BOLD, 35))
.translateY(50)
    .build();
rightArea.getChildren().add(lowerRight);

splitPane2.getItems().add(centerArea);
splitPane2.getItems().add(rightArea);
```

```
// add left area
splitPane.getItems().add(leftArea);

// add right area
splitPane.getItems().add(splitPane2);

// evenly position divider
ObservableList<SplitPane.Divider> dividers = splitPane.getDividers();
for (int i = 0; i < dividers.size(); i++) {
    dividers.get(i).setPosition((i + 1.0) / 3);
}

HBox hbox = new HBox();
hbox.getChildren().add(splitPane);
root.getChildren().add(hbox);
```

Figure 15-19 depicts the application using split pane controls.

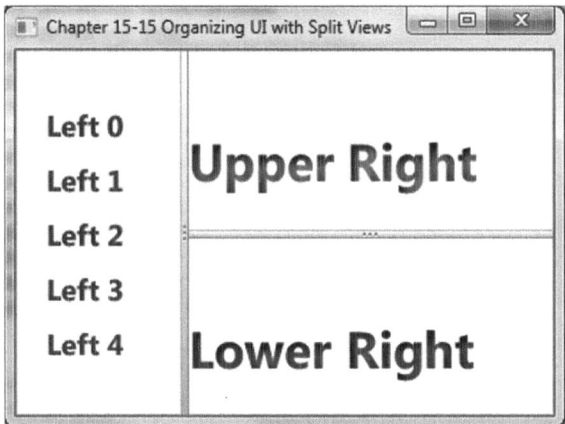

Figure 15-19. Split views

How It Works

If you've ever seen a simple RSS reader or the Javadocs, you'll notice that the screen is divided into sections with dividers that allow the user to adjust. In this recipe, three areas are on the left, upper right, and lower right.

I begin by creating a SplitPane that divides the left from the right area of the scene. Then I bind its width and height properties to the scene so the areas will take up the available space as the user resizes the Stage. Next I create a VBox layout control representing the left area. In the VBox (leftArea), I loop to generate a bunch of Text nodes. Next is creating the right side of the split pane. The following code snippet allows the split pane control (SplitPane) to divide horizontally:

```
SplitPane splitPane = new SplitPane();
splitPane.prefWidthProperty().bind(scene.widthProperty());
```

```
splitPane.prefHeightProperty().bind(scene.heightProperty());
```

Now we create the SplitPane to divide the area vertically forming the upper-right and lower-right region. Shown here is the code used to split a window region vertically:

```
// Upper and lower split pane
SplitPane splitPane2 = new SplitPane();
splitPane2.setOrientation(Orientation.VERTICAL);
```

At last we assemble the split panes and adjust the dividers to be positioned so that the screen real estate is divided evenly. The following code assembles the split panes and iterates through the list of dividers to update their positions:

```
splitPane.getItems().add(splitPane2);

// evenly position divider
ObservableList<SplitPane.Divider> dividers = splitPane.getDividers();
for (int i = 0; i < dividers.size(); i++) {
    dividers.get(i).setPosition((i + 1.0) / 3);
}

HBox hbox = new HBox();
hbox.getChildren().add(splitPane);
root.getChildren().add(hbox);
```

15-16. Adding Tabs to the UI

Problem

You want to create a GUI application with tabs.

Solution

Use JavaFX's tab and tab pane control. The tab (javafx.scene.control.Tab) and tab pane control (javafx.scene.control.TabPane) classes allow you to place graph nodes in individual tabs.

The following code example creates a simple application having menu options that allow the user to choose a tab orientation. The available tab orientations are top, bottom, left, and right.

```
@Override
public void start(Stage primaryStage) {
    primaryStage.setTitle("Chapter 15-16 Adding Tabs to a UI");
    Group root = new Group();
    Scene scene = new Scene(root, 400, 250, Color.WHITE);

    TabPane tabPane = new TabPane();

    MenuBar menuBar = new MenuBar();

    EventHandler<ActionEvent> action = changeTabPlacement(tabPane);

    Menu menu = new Menu("Tab Side");
```

```
        MenuItem left = new MenuItem("Left");

        left.setOnAction(action);
        menu.getItems().add(left);

        MenuItem right = new MenuItem("Right");
        right.setOnAction(action);
        menu.getItems().add(right);

        MenuItem top = new MenuItem("Top");
        top.setOnAction(action);
        menu.getItems().add(top);

        MenuItem bottom = new MenuItem("Bottom");
        bottom.setOnAction(action);
        menu.getItems().add(bottom);

        menuBar.getMenus().add(menu);

        BorderPane borderPane = new BorderPane();

        // generate 10 tabs
        for (int i = 0; i < 10; i++) {
            Tab tab = new Tab();
            tab.setText("Tab" + i);
            HBox hbox = new HBox();
            hbox.getChildren().add(new Label("Tab" + i));
            hbox.setAlignment(Pos.CENTER);
            tab.setContent(hbox);
            tabPane.getTabs().add(tab);
        }

        // add tab pane
        borderPane.setCenter(tabPane);

        // bind to take available space
        borderPane.prefHeightProperty().bind(scene.heightProperty());
        borderPane.prefWidthProperty().bind(scene.widthProperty());

        // added menu bar
        borderPane.setTop(menuBar);

        // add border Pane
        root.getChildren().add(borderPane);

        primaryStage.setScene(scene);
        primaryStage.show();
    }

    private EventHandler<ActionEvent> changeTabPlacement(final TabPane tabPane) {
        return new EventHandler<ActionEvent>() {
```

```
        public void handle(ActionEvent event) {
            MenuItem mItem = (MenuItem) event.getSource();
            String side = mItem.getText();
            if ("left".equalsIgnoreCase(side)) {
                tabPane.setSide(Side.LEFT);
            } else if ("right".equalsIgnoreCase(side)) {
                tabPane.setSide(Side.RIGHT);
            } else if ("top".equalsIgnoreCase(side)) {
                tabPane.setSide(Side.TOP);
            } else if ("bottom".equalsIgnoreCase(side)) {
                tabPane.setSide(Side.BOTTOM);
            }
        }
    };
}
```

Figure 15-20 displays the tabs application, which allows a user to change the tab orientation.

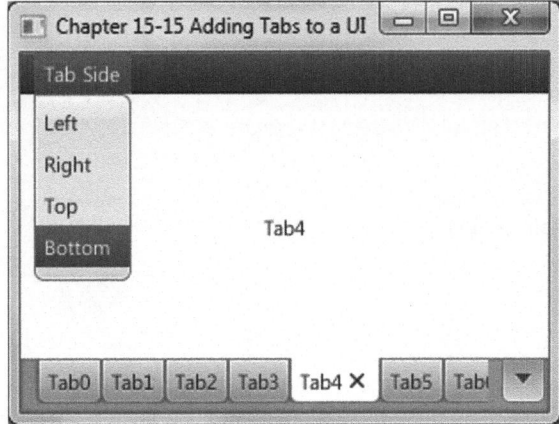

Figure 15-20. TabPane

How It Works

When you use the TabPane control, you might already know the orientation in which you want your tabs to appear. This application allows you to set the orientation by the menu options for Left, Right, Top, and Bottom.

To use the TabPane you will immediately notice how similar it is to Java Swing's JTabbedPanel. (To compare, refer to recipe 14-10.) Instead of adding JPanels, you simply add **javafx.scene.control.Tab** instances. The following code snippet adds Tab controls into a tab pane control:

```
TabPane tabPane = new TabPane();
Tab tab = new Tab();
tab.setText("Tab" + i);
tabPane.getTabs().add(tab);
```

When changing the orientation the TabPane control, use the setSide() method. The following code line sets the orientation of the tab pane control:

```
tabPane.setSide(Side.BOTTOM);
```

15-17. Developing a Dialog Box

Problem

You want to create an application that simulates a change password dialog box.

Solution

Use JavaFX's stage (javafx.stage.Stage) and scene (javafx.scene.Scene) APIs to create a dialog box.

The following source code listing is an application that simulates a change password dialog box. The application contains menu options to pop up the dialog box. In addition to the menu options, the user will have the ability to set the dialog box's modal state (modality).

```
/**
 * Developing A Dialog
 * @author cdea
 */
public class DevelopingADialog extends Application {

    static Stage LOGIN_DIALOG;
    static int dx = 1;
    static int dy = 1;

    /**
     * @param args the command line arguments
     */
    public static void main(String[] args) {
        Application.launch(args);
    }

    private static Stage createLoginDialog(Stage parent, boolean modal) {
        if (LOGIN_DIALOG != null) {
            LOGIN_DIALOG.close();
        }
        return new MyDialog(parent, modal, "Welcome to JavaFX!");
    }

    @Override
    public void start(final Stage primaryStage) {
        primaryStage.setTitle("Chapter 15-17 Developing a Dialog");
        Group root = new Group();
        Scene scene = new Scene(root, 433, 312, Color.WHITE);
```

```java
MenuBar menuBar = new MenuBar();
menuBar.prefWidthProperty().bind(primaryStage.widthProperty());

Menu menu = new Menu("Home");

// add change password menu itme
MenuItem newItem = new MenuItem("Change Password", null);
newItem.setOnAction(new EventHandler<ActionEvent>() {

    public void handle(ActionEvent event) {
        if (LOGIN_DIALOG == null) {
            LOGIN_DIALOG = createLoginDialog(primaryStage, true);
        }
        LOGIN_DIALOG.sizeToScene();
        LOGIN_DIALOG.show();
    }
});

menu.getItems().add(newItem);

// add separator
menu.getItems().add(new SeparatorMenuItem());

// add non modal menu item
ToggleGroup modalGroup = new ToggleGroup();
RadioMenuItem nonModalItem = RadioMenuItemBuilder.create()
        .toggleGroup(modalGroup)
        .text("Non Modal")
        .selected(true)
        .build();
nonModalItem.setOnAction(new EventHandler<ActionEvent>() {

    public void handle(ActionEvent event) {
        LOGIN_DIALOG = createLoginDialog(primaryStage, false);
    }
});

menu.getItems().add(nonModalItem);

// add modal selection
RadioMenuItem modalItem = RadioMenuItemBuilder.create()
        .toggleGroup(modalGroup)
        .text("Modal")
        .selected(true)
        .build();
modalItem.setOnAction(new EventHandler<ActionEvent>() {

    public void handle(ActionEvent event) {
        LOGIN_DIALOG = createLoginDialog(primaryStage, true);
    }
});
```

```java
        menu.getItems().add(modalItem);

        // add separator
        menu.getItems().add(new SeparatorMenuItem());

        // add exit
        MenuItem exitItem = new MenuItem("Exit", null);
        exitItem.setMnemonicParsing(true);
        exitItem.setAccelerator(new KeyCodeCombination(KeyCode.X,
KeyCombination.CONTROL_DOWN));
        exitItem.setOnAction(new EventHandler<ActionEvent>() {
            public void handle(ActionEvent event) {
                Platform.exit();
            }
        });
        menu.getItems().add(exitItem);

        // add menu
        menuBar.getMenus().add(menu);

        // menu bar to window
        root.getChildren().add(menuBar);

        primaryStage.setScene(scene);
        primaryStage.show();

        addBouncyBall(scene);
    }

    private void addBouncyBall(final Scene scene) {

        final Circle ball = new Circle(100, 100, 20);
        RadialGradient gradient1 = new RadialGradient(0,
                .1,
                100,
                100,
                20,
                false,
                CycleMethod.NO_CYCLE,
                new Stop(0, Color.RED),
                new Stop(1, Color.BLACK));

        ball.setFill(gradient1);

        final Group root = (Group) scene.getRoot();
        root.getChildren().add(ball);

        Timeline tl = new Timeline();
        tl.setCycleCount(Animation.INDEFINITE);
        KeyFrame moveBall = new KeyFrame(Duration.seconds(.0200),
                new EventHandler<ActionEvent>() {
```

```java
                public void handle(ActionEvent event) {

                        double xMin = ball.getBoundsInParent().getMinX();
                        double yMin = ball.getBoundsInParent().getMinY();
                        double xMax = ball.getBoundsInParent().getMaxX();
                        double yMax = ball.getBoundsInParent().getMaxY();

                        // Collision - boundaries
                        if (xMin < 0 || xMax > scene.getWidth()) {
                            dx = dx * -1;
                        }
                        if (yMin < 0 || yMax > scene.getHeight()) {
                            dy = dy * -1;
                        }

                        ball.setTranslateX(ball.getTranslateX() + dx);
                        ball.setTranslateY(ball.getTranslateY() + dy);

                    }
                });

        tl.getKeyFrames().add(moveBall);
        tl.play();
    }
}

class MyDialog extends Stage {

    public MyDialog(Stage owner, boolean modality, String title) {
        super();
        initOwner(owner);
        Modality m = modality ? Modality.APPLICATION_MODAL : Modality.NONE;
        initModality(m);
        setOpacity(.90);
        setTitle(title);
        Group root = new Group();
        Scene scene = new Scene(root, 250, 150, Color.WHITE);
        setScene(scene);

        GridPane gridpane = new GridPane();
        gridpane.setPadding(new Insets(5));
        gridpane.setHgap(5);
        gridpane.setVgap(5);

        Label mainLabel = new Label("Enter User Name & Password");
        gridpane.add(mainLabel, 1, 0, 2, 1);


        Label userNameLbl = new Label("User Name: ");
        gridpane.add(userNameLbl, 0, 1);

        Label passwordLbl = new Label("Password: ");
```

```
        gridpane.add(passwordLbl, 0, 2);


        // username text field
        final TextField userNameFld = new TextField("Admin");
        gridpane.add(userNameFld, 1, 1);

        // password field
        final PasswordField passwordFld = new PasswordField();
        passwordFld.setText("drowssap");
        gridpane.add(passwordFld, 1, 2);


        Button login = new Button("Change");
        login.setOnAction(new EventHandler<ActionEvent>() {

            public void handle(ActionEvent event) {
                close();
            }
        });
        gridpane.add(login, 1, 3);
        GridPane.setHalignment(login, HPos.RIGHT);
        root.getChildren().add(gridpane);
    }
}
```

Figure 15-21 depicts our change password dialog box application with the Non Modal option enabled.

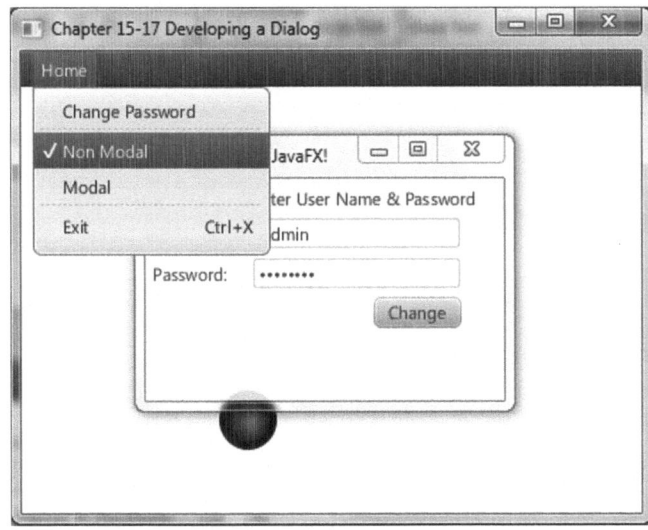

Figure 15-21. Developing a dialog box

How It Works

Here we go again% Not another recipe with a login screen! Well, this time it's rewritten in JavaFX so it's got to be better. Recipe 14-18 discussed modality and how JDialog is similar to JFrame. In this recipe we will primarily focus our attention on the javafx.stage.Stage class.

Remember recipe 14-18, in which I stated how simple it is to create a JDialog window? It is even simpler in JavaFX. Instead of two kinds of native window containers, JavaFX uses another instance of a javafx.stage.Stage class to be shown to the user. Similar to extending from a JDialog class, you simply extend from a Stage class. You have the opportunity (as in Swing) to pass in the owning window in the constructor, which then calls the initOwner() method. Next is setting the modal state of the dialog box using the initModality() method. Following is a class that extends from the Stage class having a constructor initializing the owning stage and modal state:

```
class MyDialog extends Stage {

    public MyDialog(Stage owner, boolean modality, String title) {
        super();
        initOwner(owner);
        Modality m = modality ? Modality.APPLICATION_MODAL : Modality.NONE;
initModality(m);

        ...// The rest of the class
```

The rest of the code creates a scene (Scene) similar to the main application's start() method. Because login forms are pretty boring, I decided to create an animation of a bouncing ball while the user is busy changing the password in the dialog box. (You will see more about creating animation in recipe 16-2.)

## CHAPTER 16

Graphics with JavaFX

Have you ever heard someone say, "When two worlds collide"? This expression is used when a person from a different background or culture is put in a situation where they are at odds and must face very hard decisions. When we build a GUI application needing animations, we are often in a collision course between business and gaming worlds.

In the ever-changing world of RIAs, you probably have noticed an increase of animations such as pulsing buttons, transitions, moving backgrounds, and so on. When GUI applications use animations, they can provide visual cues to the user to let them know what to do next. With JavaFX, you will be able to have the best of both worlds.

Figure 16-1 illustrates a simple drawing coming alive.

Figure 16-1. Graphics with JavaFX

In this chapter you will create images, animations, and Look 'N' Feels. Fasten your seatbelts; you'll discover solutions to integrate cool game-like interfaces into our everyday applications.

■ **Note** Refer to Chapter 15 if you are new to JavaFX. Among other things, it will help you get an environment created in which you can be productive in using JavaFX.

16-1. Creating Images

Problem

There are photos in your file directory that you would like to quickly browse through and showcase.

Solution

Create a simple JavaFX image viewer application. The main Java classes used in this recipe are:

- `javafx.scene.image.Image`

- `javafx.scene.image.ImageView`

- `EventHandler<DragEvent>` classes

The following source code is an implementation of an image viewer application:

```
package org.java7recipes.chapter16.recipe16_01;

import java.io.File;
import java.util.ArrayList;
import java.util.List;
import javafx.application.Application;
import javafx.event.EventHandler;
import javafx.scene.Group;
import javafx.scene.Scene;
import javafx.scene.image.Image;
import javafx.scene.image.ImageView;
import javafx.scene.input.DragEvent;
import javafx.scene.input.Dragboard;
import javafx.scene.input.MouseEvent;
import javafx.scene.input.TransferMode;
import javafx.scene.layout.HBox;
import javafx.scene.paint.Color;
import javafx.scene.shape.Arc;
import javafx.scene.shape.ArcBuilder;
import javafx.scene.shape.ArcType;
import javafx.scene.shape.Rectangle;
import javafx.scene.shape.RectangleBuilder;
import javafx.stage.Stage;

/**
 * Creating Images
 * @author cdea
 */
public class CreatingImages extends Application {
    private List<String> imageFiles = new ArrayList<>();
    private int currentIndex = -1;
    public enum ButtonMove {NEXT, PREV};
```

```
/**
 * @param args the command line arguments
 */
public static void main(String[] args) {
    Application.launch(args);
}

@Override
public void start(Stage primaryStage) {
    primaryStage.setTitle("Chapter 16-1 Creating a Image");
    Group root = new Group();
    Scene scene = new Scene(root, 551, 400, Color.BLACK);


    // image view
    final ImageView currentImageView = new ImageView();

    // maintain aspect ratio
    currentImageView.setPreserveRatio(true);

    // resize based on the scene
    currentImageView.fitWidthProperty().bind(scene.widthProperty());

    final HBox pictureRegion = new HBox();
    pictureRegion.getChildren().add(currentImageView);
    root.getChildren().add(pictureRegion);

    // Dragging over surface
    scene.setOnDragOver(new EventHandler<DragEvent>() {
        @Override
        public void handle(DragEvent event) {
            Dragboard db = event.getDragboard();
            if (db.hasFiles()) {
                event.acceptTransferModes(TransferMode.COPY);
            } else {
                event.consume();
            }
        }
    });

    // Dropping over surface
    scene.setOnDragDropped(new EventHandler<DragEvent>() {

        @Override
        public void handle(DragEvent event) {
            Dragboard db = event.getDragboard();
            boolean success = false;
            if (db.hasFiles()) {
                success = true;
                String filePath = null;
                for (File file:db.getFiles()) {
                    filePath = file.getAbsolutePath();
```

```
                    currentIndex +=1;
                    imageFiles.add(currentIndex, filePath);

                    // absolute file name
                    System.out.println("file: " + file);
                    // the index in the list of file names
                    System.out.println("currentImageFileIndex = " + currentIndex);
                }

                // set new image as the image to show.
                Image imageimage = new Image(filePath);
                currentImageView.setImage(imageimage);

            }
            event.setDropCompleted(success);
            event.consume();
        }
    });


    // create slide controls
    Group buttonGroup = new Group();

    // rounded rect
    Rectangle buttonArea = RectangleBuilder.create()
            .arcWidth(15)
            .arcHeight(20)
            .fill(new Color(0, 0, 0, .55))
            .x(0)
            .y(0)
            .width(60)
            .height(30)
            .stroke(Color.rgb(255, 255, 255, .70))
            .build();

    buttonGroup.getChildren().add(buttonArea);
    // left control
    Arc leftButton = ArcBuilder.create()
            .type(ArcType.ROUND)
            .centerX(12)
            .centerY(16)
            .radiusX(15)
            .radiusY(15)
            .startAngle(-30)
            .length(60)
            .fill(new Color(1,1,1, .90))
            .build();

    leftButton.addEventHandler(MouseEvent.MOUSE_PRESSED, new EventHandler<MouseEvent>()
{
        public void handle(MouseEvent me) {
```

```
                int indx = gotoImageIndex(ButtonMove.PREV);
                if (indx > -1) {
                    String namePict = imageFiles.get(indx);
                    final Image image = new Image(new File(namePict).getAbsolutePath());
                    currentImageView.setImage(image);
                }
            }
        });
        buttonGroup.getChildren().add(leftButton);

        // right control
        Arc rightButton = ArcBuilder.create()
                .type(ArcType.ROUND)
                .centerX(12)
                .centerY(16)
                .radiusX(15)
                .radiusY(15)
                .startAngle(180-30)
                .length(60)
                .fill(new Color(1,1,1, .90))
                .translateX(40)
                .build();
        buttonGroup.getChildren().add(rightButton);

        rightButton.addEventHandler(MouseEvent.MOUSE_PRESSED, new EventHandler<MouseEvent>()
{

            public void handle(MouseEvent me) {
                int indx = gotoImageIndex(ButtonMove.NEXT);
                if (indx > -1) {
                    String namePict = imageFiles.get(indx);
                    final Image image = new Image(new File(namePict).getAbsolutePath());
                    currentImageView.setImage(image);
                }
            }
        });

        // move button group when scene is resized
        buttonGroup.translateXProperty().bind(scene.widthProperty().subtract(buttonArea.getW
        idth() + 6));

        buttonGroup.translateYProperty().bind(scene.heightProperty().subtract(buttonArea.get
        Height() + 6));
        root.getChildren().add(buttonGroup);

        primaryStage.setScene(scene);
        primaryStage.show();
    }

    /**
     * Returns the next index in the list of files to go to next.
     *
     * @param direction PREV and NEXT to move backward or forward in the list of
```

```
 * pictures.
 * @return int the index to the previous or next picture to be shown.
 */
public int gotoImageIndex(ButtonMove direction) {
    int size = imageFiles.size();
    if (size == 0) {
        currentIndex = -1;
    } else if (direction == ButtonMove.NEXT && size > 1 && currentIndex < size - 1) {
        currentIndex += 1;
    } else if (direction == ButtonMove.PREV && size > 1 && currentIndex > 0) {
        currentIndex -= 1;
    }

    return currentIndex;
}

}
```

Figure 16-2 depicts the drag-and-drop operation that gives the user visual feedback with a thumbnail-sized image over the surface. In the figure, I'm dragging the image onto the application window.

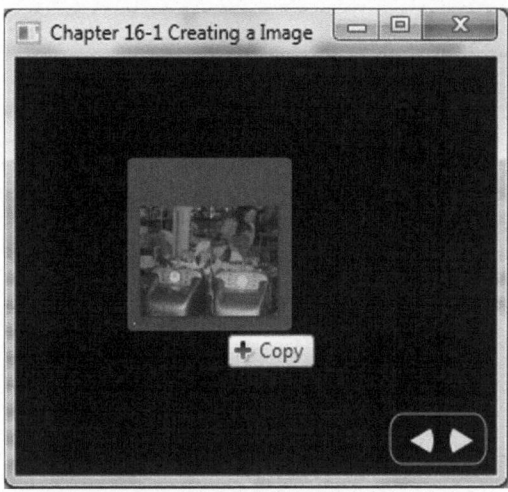

Figure 16-2. Drag and drop in progress

Figure 16-3 shows that the drop operation has succesfully loaded the image.

Figure 16-3. Drop operation completed

How It Works

This recipe is a simple application that allows you to view images having file formats such as .jpg, .png, and .gif. Loading an image requires using the mouse to drag and drop a file into the window area. The application also allows resizing of the window, which automatically causes scaling of the image's size while maintaining its aspect ratio. After a few images are successfully loaded, you will be able to page through each image conveniently by clicking the left and right button controls, as shown in Figure 16-3.

Before the code walk-through, let's discuss the application's variables. Table 16-1 describes instance variables for our sleek image viewer application.

Table 16-1. The CreatingImages Instance Variables

Variable	Data Type	Example	Description
imageFiles	List<String>	/home/cdea/fun .jpg	A list of Strings, each containing an image's absolute file path
currentIndex	int	0	A zero relative index number into the imageFiles list; negative 1 means no images to view
NEXT	enum	-	User clicks the right arrow button
PREV	enum	-	User clicks the left arrow button

When dragging an image into the application, the imageFiles variable will cache the absolute file path as a String instead of the actual image file in order to save space in memory. If a user drags the same image file into the display area, the list will contain duplicate strings representing the image file. As an image is being displayed, the `currentIndex` variable contains the index into the `imageFiles` list. That `imageFiles` list points to the String representing the current image file. As the user clicks the buttons to display the previous and next image, the `currentIndex` will decrement or increment, respectively. Next, you will walk through the code detailing the steps on how to load and display an image. Later I will discuss the steps on paging through each image with the next and previous buttons.

You will begin by instantiating an instance of a `javafx.scene.image.ImageView` class. The ImageView class is a graph node (`Node`) used to display an already loaded `javafx.scene.image.Image` object. Using the `ImageView` node will enable you to create special effects on the image to be displayed without manipulating the physical Image. To avoid performance degradation when rendering many effects, you can use numerous `ImageView` objects that reference a single Image object. Many types of effects include blurring, fading, and transforming an image.

One of the requirements is preserving the displayed image's aspect ratio as the user resizes the window. Here, you will simply call the `setPreserveRatio()` method with a value of `true` to preserve the image's aspect ratio. Remember that because the user resizes the window, you want to bind the width of the `ImageView` to the `Scene`'s width to allow the scaling of the image to take effect. After setting up the ImageView, you will want to pass it to an `HBox` instance (`pictureRegion`) to be put into the scene. The following code creates the `ImageView` instance, preserves the aspect ratio, and scales the image:

```
// image view
final ImageView currentImageView = new ImageView();

// maintain aspect ratio
currentImageView.setPreserveRatio(true);

// resize based on the scene
currentImageView.fitWidthProperty().bind(scene.widthProperty());
```

Next, I want to introduce JavaFX's new native drag-and-drop support, which offers many scenarios a user can perform, such as dragging visual objects from an application to be dropped into another application. In this scenario, the user will be dragging an image file from the host windowing operating system to your image viewer application. When performing this scenario, you must create `EventHandler` objects to listen to `DragEvents`. To fulfill this requirement, you only need to set-up a Scene's drag-over and drag-dropped event handler methods.

To setup the drag-over attribute, you will be calling the Scene's `setOnDragOver()` method with the appropriate generics `EventHandler<DragEvent>` type. Here you will implement the `handle()` method to listen to the drag-over event (`DragEvent`). In the `handle()` method notice the event (`DragEvent`) object's invocation to the `getDragboard()` method. The call to `getDragboard()` will return the drag source (`Dragboard`), better known as the *clipboard*. When you obtain the `Dragboard` object, you can determine and validate what is being dragged over the surface. In this scenario, you are trying to determine whether the `Dragboard` object contains any files. If so, call the event object's `acceptTransferModes()` by passing in the constant `TransferMode.COPY` to provide visual feedback to the user of the application (refer to Figure 16-2). Otherwise it should consume the event by calling the `event.consume()` method. The following code demonstrates setting up a Scene's `OnDragOver` attribute by instantiating an inner class of type `EventHandler` with a formal type parameter `<DragEvent>` and overriding its handle() method:

```
// Dragging over surface
scene.setOnDragOver(new EventHandler<DragEvent>() {
    @Override
    public void handle(DragEvent event) {
        Dragboard db = event.getDragboard();
        if (db.hasFiles()) {
```

```
                event.acceptTransferModes(TransferMode.COPY);
            } else {
                event.consume();
            }
        }
    }
});
```

Once the drag-over event handler attribute is set, you must create a drag-dropped event handler attribute in order that it may finalize the operation. Listening to a drag-dropped event is similar to listening to a drag-over event in which you will implement the handle() method. Once again you obtain the Dragboard object from the event to determine whether the clipboard contains any files. If so, you will iterate over the list of files and their names to be added to the imageFiles list. This demonstrates setting up a Scene's OnDragDropped attribute by instantiating an inner class of type EventHandler with a formal type parameter <DragEvent> and overriding its handle() method:

```
// Dropping over surface
scene.setOnDragDropped(new EventHandler<DragEvent>() {

    @Override
    public void handle(DragEvent event) {
        Dragboard db = event.getDragboard();
        boolean success = false;
        if (db.hasFiles()) {
            success = true;
            String filePath = null;
            for (File file:db.getFiles()) {
                filePath = file.getAbsolutePath();

                currentIndex +=1;
                imageFiles.add(currentIndex, filePath);
            }

            // set new image as the image to show.
            Image imageimage = new Image(filePath);
            currentImageView.setImage(imageimage);

        }
        event.setDropCompleted(success);
        event.consume();
    }
});
```

As the last file is determined, the current image is displayed. The following code demonstrates loading an image to be displayed:

```
// set new image as the image to show.
Image imageimage = new Image(filePath);
currentImageView.setImage(imageimage);
```

For the last requirements relating to the image viewer application, you will be creating simple controls that allow the user to view the next or previous image. I emphasize "simple" controls because

JavaFX contains two other methods for creating custom controls. One way (CSS Styling) is discussed later in recipe 16-5. To explore the other alternative, please refer to the Javadoc on the Skin and Skinnable APIs.

To create simple buttons I used Java FX's `javafx.scene.shape.Arc` to build the left and right arrows on top of a small transparent rounded rectangle `javafx.scene.shape.Rectangle`. Next is adding an `EventHandler` that listens to mouse-pressed events that will load and display the appropriate image based on enums `ButtonMove.PREV` and `ButtonMove.NEXT`. You will find the `EventHandler` indispensible and useful in so many ways. When instantiating a generics class with a type variable between the `<` and `>` symbols, the same type variable will be defined in the `handle()`'s signature. When implementing the `handle()` method I determine which button was pressed; it then returns the index into the `imageFiles` list of the next image to display. When loading an image using the Image class you can load images from the file system or a URL, but in this recipe I am using a `File` object. The following code instantiates an `EventHandler<MouseEvent>` with a `handle()` method to display the previous image in the `imageFiles` list:

```
Arc leftButton = //... create an Arc
leftButton.addEventHandler(MouseEvent.MOUSE_PRESSED, new EventHandler<MouseEvent>() {
    public void handle(MouseEvent me) {
        int indx = gotoImageIndex(ButtonMove.PREV);
        if (indx > -1) {
            String namePict = imageFiles.get(indx);
            final Image image = new Image(new File(namePict).getAbsolutePath());
            currentImageView.setImage(image);
        }
    }
});
```

The right button's (`rightButton`) event handler is identical, so I trust you get the idea. The only thing different is determining whether the previous button or the next button was pressed via the `ButtonMove` enum. This is passed to the `gotoImageIndex()` method to determine whether an image is available in that direction.

To finish the image viewer application, you have to bind the rectangular buttons control to the Scene's width and height, which repositions the control as the user resizes the window. Here, I bind the `translateXProperty()`to the Scene's width property by subtracting the `buttonArea!s` width (Fluent API). I also bind the `translateYProperty()` based on the Scene's height property. Once your buttons control is bound, your user will experience user interface goodness. The following code uses the Fluent API to bind the button control's properties to the Scene's properties:

```
// move button group when scene is resized
buttonGroup.translateXProperty().bind(scene.widthProperty().subtract(buttonArea.getW
idth() + 6));

buttonGroup.translateYProperty().bind(scene.heightProperty().subtract(buttonArea.get
Height() + 6));
root.getChildren().add(buttonGroup);
```

16-2. Generating an Animation

Problem

You want to generate an animation. For example, you want to create a news ticker and photo viewer application with the following requirements:

- It will have a news ticker control that scrolls to the left.

- It will fade out the current picture and fade in the next picture as the user clicks the button controls.

- It will fade in and out button controls when the cursor moves in and out of the scene area, respectively.

Solution

Create animated effects by accessing JavaFX's animation APIs (`javafx.animation.*`).To create a news ticker, you need the following classes:

- `javafx.animation.TranslateTransition`

- `javafx.util.Duration`

- `javafx.event.EventHandler<ActionEvent>`

- `javafx.scene.shape.Rectangle`

To fade out the current picture and fade in next picture, you need the following classes:

- `javafx.animation.SequentialTransition`

- `javafx.animation.FadeTransition`

- `javafx.event.EventHandler<ActionEvent>`

- `javafx.scene.image.Image`

- `javafx.scene.image.ImageView`

- `javafx.util.Duration`

To fade in and out button controls when the cursor moves into and out of the scene area, respectively, the following classes are needed:

- `javafx.animation.FadeTransition`

- `javafx.util.Duration`

Shown here is the code used to create a news ticker control:

```
// create ticker area
final Group tickerArea = new Group();
final Rectangle tickerRect = RectangleBuilder.create()
```

```
                    .arcWidth(15)
                    .arcHeight(20)
                    .fill(new Color(0, 0, 0, .55))
                    .x(0)
                    .y(0)
                    .width(scene.getWidth() - 6)
                    .height(30)
                    .stroke(Color.rgb(255, 255, 255, .70))
                    .build();

        Rectangle clipRegion = RectangleBuilder.create()
                    .arcWidth(15)
                    .arcHeight(20)
                    .x(0)
                    .y(0)
                    .width(scene.getWidth() - 6)
                    .height(30)
                    .stroke(Color.rgb(255, 255, 255, .70))
                    .build();

        tickerArea.setClip(clipRegion);

        // Resize the ticker area when the window is resized
        tickerArea.setTranslateX(6);
        tickerArea.translateYProperty().bind(scene.heightProperty().subtract(tickerRect.getHeigh
        t() + 6));
        tickerRect.widthProperty().bind(scene.widthProperty().subtract(buttonRect.getWidth() +
        16));
        clipRegion.widthProperty().bind(scene.widthProperty().subtract(buttonRect.getWidth() +
        16));
        tickerArea.getChildren().add(tickerRect);


        root.getChildren().add(tickerArea);


        // add news text
        Text news = TextBuilder.create()
                    .text("JavaFX 2.0 News! | 85 and sunny | :)")
                    .translateY(18)
                    .fill(Color.WHITE)
                    .build();
        tickerArea.getChildren().add(news);

        final TranslateTransition ticker = TranslateTransitionBuilder.create()
                    .node(news)
                    .duration(Duration.millis((scene.getWidth()/300) * 15000))
                    .fromX(scene.widthProperty().doubleValue())
                    .toX(-scene.widthProperty().doubleValue())
                    .fromY(19)
                    .interpolator(Interpolator.LINEAR)
                    .cycleCount(1)
```

```
        .build();
// when ticker has finished reset and replay ticker animation
ticker.setOnFinished(new EventHandler<ActionEvent>() {
    public void handle(ActionEvent ae){
        ticker.stop();
        ticker.setFromX(scene.getWidth());
        ticker.setDuration(new Duration((scene.getWidth()/300) * 15000));
        ticker.playFromStart();
    }
});

ticker.play();
```

Here is the code used to fade out the current picture and fade in next picture:

```
// previous button
Arc prevButton = // create arc ...

prevButton.addEventHandler(MouseEvent.MOUSE_PRESSED, new EventHandler<MouseEvent>() {

    public void handle(MouseEvent me) {
        int indx = gotoImageIndex(PREV);
        if (indx > -1) {
            String namePict = imagesFiles.get(indx);
            final Image nextImage = new Image(new File(namePict).getAbsolutePath());
            SequentialTransition seqTransition = transitionByFading(nextImage,
currentImageView);
            seqTransition.play();
        }
    }
});

buttonGroup.getChildren().add(prevButton);

// next button
Arc nextButton = //... create arc

buttonGroup.getChildren().add(nextButton);

nextButton.addEventHandler(MouseEvent.MOUSE_PRESSED, new EventHandler<MouseEvent>() {

    public void handle(MouseEvent me) {
        int indx = gotoImageIndex(NEXT);
        if (indx > -1) {
            String namePict = imagesFiles.get(indx);
            final Image nextImage = new Image(new File(namePict).getAbsolutePath());
            SequentialTransition seqTransition = transitionByFading(nextImage,
currentImageView);
            seqTransition.play();
        }
    }
```

```
        });

//... the rest of the start(Stage primaryStage) method


public int gotoImageIndex(int direction) {
    int size = imagesFiles.size();
    if (size == 0) {
        currentIndexImageFile = -1;
    } else if (direction == NEXT && size > 1 && currentIndexImageFile < size - 1) {
        currentIndexImageFile += 1;
    } else if (direction == PREV && size > 1 && currentIndexImageFile > 0) {
        currentIndexImageFile -= 1;
    }

    return currentIndexImageFile;
}

public SequentialTransition transitionByFading(final Image nextImage, final ImageView
imageView) {
    FadeTransition fadeOut = new FadeTransition(Duration.millis(500), imageView);
    fadeOut.setFromValue(1.0);
    fadeOut.setToValue(0.0);
    fadeOut.setOnFinished(new EventHandler<ActionEvent>() {
        public void handle(ActionEvent ae) {
            imageView.setImage(nextImage);
        }
    });
    FadeTransition fadeIn = new FadeTransition(Duration.millis(500), imageView);
    fadeIn.setFromValue(0.0);
    fadeIn.setToValue(1.0);
    SequentialTransition seqTransition = SequentialTransitionBuilder.create()
        .children(fadeOut, fadeIn)
        .build();
    return seqTransition;
}
```

The following code is used to fade in and out the button controls when the cursor moves into and out of the scene area, respectively:

```
// Fade in button controls
scene.setOnMouseEntered(new EventHandler<MouseEvent>() {
    public void handle(MouseEvent me) {
        FadeTransition fadeButtons = new FadeTransition(Duration.millis(500),
buttonGroup);
        fadeButtons.setFromValue(0.0);
        fadeButtons.setToValue(1.0);
        fadeButtons.play();
    }
});

// Fade out button controls
```

```
scene.setOnMouseExited(new EventHandler<MouseEvent>() {
    public void handle(MouseEvent me) {
        FadeTransition fadeButtons = new FadeTransition(Duration.millis(500),
buttonGroup);
        fadeButtons.setFromValue(1);
        fadeButtons.setToValue(0);
        fadeButtons.play();
    }
});
```

Figure 16-4 shows the photo viewer application with a ticker control at the bottom region of the screen.

Figure 16-4. Photo viewer with a news ticker

How It Works

In the photo viewer application I decided to incorporate animation effects. The main animation effects I focus on are translating and fading. First, you will create a news ticker control that scrolls Text nodes to the left by using a translation transition (`javafx.animation.TranslateTransition`). Next, you will apply another fading effect when the user clicks the previous and next buttons to transition from the current image to the next. To perform this effect, you will use a compound transition (`javafx.animation.SequentialTransition`) consisting of multiple animations. Finally, to create the effect of the button controls fading in and out based on where the mouse is located, you will need a fade transition (`javafx.animation.FadeTransition`).

Before I begin to discuss the steps to fulfill the requirements, I want to mention the basics of JavaFX animation. The JavaFX animation API allows you to assemble timed events that can interpolate over a node's attribute values to produce animated effects. Each timed event is called a keyframe (`KeyFrame`), which is responsible for interpolating over a Node's property over a period of time (javafx.util.Duration). Knowing that a keyframe's job is to operate on a Node's property value, you will have to create an instance of a KeyValue class that will reference the desired Node property. The idea of interpolation is simply the distributing of values between a start and end value. An example is to move a rectangle by its current x position (zero) to 100 pixels in 1000 milliseconds; in other words, move the rectangle 100 pixels to the right, spanning one second. Shown here is a keyframe and key value to interpolate a rectangle's x property for 1000 milliseconds:

```
final Rectangle rectangle = new Rectangle(0, 0, 50, 50);
KeyValue keyValue = new KeyValue(rectangle.xProperty(), 100);
KeyFrame keyFrame = new KeyFrame(Duration.millis(1000), keyValue);
```

When creating many keyframes that are assembled consecutively, you need to create a TimeLine. Because TimeLine is a subclass of javafx.animation.Animation, there are standard attributes such as its cycle count and auto-reverse that can be set. The *cycle count* is the number of times you want the timeline to play the animation. If you want the cycle count to play the animation indefinitely, use the value Timeline.INDEFINITE. The auto-reverse is the capability for the animation to play the timeline backward. By default, the cycle count is set to 1, and the auto-reverse is set to false. When adding keyframes you will simply add them using the getKeyFrames().add() method on the TimeLine object. The following code snippet demonstrates a timeline playing indefinitely and auto-reverse set to true:

```
Timeline timeline = new Timeline();
timeline.setCycleCount(Timeline.INDEFINITE);
timeline.setAutoReverse(true);
timeline.getKeyFrames().add(keyFrame);
timeline.play();
```

With this knowledge of timelines you can animate any graph node in JavaFX. Although you have the ability to create timelines in a low-level way, it can become very cumbersome. You are probably wondering whether there are easier ways to express common animations. Good news! JavaFX has transitions (Transition), which are convenience classes to perform common animated effects. Some of the common animation effects classes are these:

- javafx.animation.FadeTransition

- javafx.animation.PathTransition

- javafx.animation.ScaleTransition

- javafx.animation.TranslateTransition

To see more transitions, see javafx.animation in the Javadoc. Because Transition objects are also subclasses of the javafx.animation.Animation class, you will have the opportunity to set the cycle count and auto-reverse attributes. In this recipe you will be focusing on two transition effects: translate transition (TranslateTransition) and fade transition (FadeTransition).

The first requirement in our problem statement is to create a news ticker. When creating a news ticker control, Text nodes will scroll from right to left inside a rectangular region. When the text scrolls to the left edge of the rectangular region you will want the text to be clipped to create a view port that only shows pixels inside of the rectangle. Here, I first create a Group to hold all the components that comprise a ticker control. Next is the creation of a rectangle using the RectangleBuilder to build a white rounded rectangle filled with 55 percent opacity. After creating the visual region I create a similar rectangle that represents the clipped region using the setClip(someRectangle) method on the Group object. Figure 16-5 shows a rounded rectangular area as a clip region:

Figure 16-5. Setting the clip region on the Group object

Once the ticker control is created, you will bind the translate Y based on the Scene's height property minus the ticker control's height. You will also bind the ticker control's width property based on the width of scene minus the button control's width. By binding these properties, the ticker control can change its size and position whenever a user resizes the application window. This makes the ticker control appear to float at the bottom of the window. The following code binds the ticker control's translate Y, width, and clip region's width property:

```
tickerArea.translateYProperty().bind(scene.heightProperty().subtract(tickerRect.getHeight()
+ 6));
tickerRect.widthProperty().bind(scene.widthProperty().subtract(buttonRect.getWidth() + 16));
clipRegion.widthProperty().bind(scene.widthProperty().subtract(buttonRect.getWidth() + 16));
tickerArea.getChildren().add(tickerRect);
```

Now that you have finished creating a ticker control, you will need to create news to feed into it. You will create a Text node with text that represents a news feed. To add a newly created Text node to the ticker control, call its getChildren().add() method. The following code adds a Text node to the ticker control:

```
final Group tickerArea = new Group();
final Rectangle tickerRect = //...
Text news = TextBuilder.create()
    .text("JavaFX 2.0 News! | 85 and sunny | :)")
    // ... more properties defined
    .build();
// add news to ticker control
tickerArea.getChildren().add(news);
```

Next is scrolling the Text node from right to left using JavaFX's TranslateTransition API. Like many JavaFX classes, in which there are builder classes to easily create objects, you will be using the TranslateTransition class' associated builder class called TranslateTransitionBuilder. The first step is to set the target node to perform the TranslateTransition. Then you will set the duration, which is the total amount of time the TranslateTransition will spend when animating. A TranslateTransition simplifies the creation of an animation by exposing convenience methods that operate on a Node's translate X and Y properties. The convenience methods are prepended with from and to. For instance, in the scenario in which you use translate X on a Text node, there are methods fromX() and toX(). The fromX() is the starting value and the toX() is the end value that will be interpolated. Next, you will set the TranslateTransition to a linear transition (Interpolator.LINEAR) to interpolate evenly between the start and end values. To see more interpolator types or to see how to create custom interpolators, see the Javadoc on javafx.animation.Interpolators. Finally, I set the cycle count to 1, which will animate the ticker once based on the specified duration. The following code snippet details creating a TranslateTransition that animates a Text node from right to left:

```
final TranslateTransition ticker = TranslateTransitionBuilder.create()
        .node(news)
        .duration(Duration.millis((scene.getWidth()/300) * 15000))
        .fromX(scene.widthProperty().doubleValue())
        .toX(-scene.widthProperty().doubleValue())
        .fromY(19)
        .interpolator(Interpolator.LINEAR)
        .cycleCount(1)
        .build();
```

When the ticker's news has scrolled completely off of the ticker area to the far left of the Scene, you will want to stop and replay the news feed from the start (the far right). To do this you will create an instance of an EventHandler<ActionEvent> object to be set on the ticker (TranslateTransition) object using the setOnFinished() method. Shown here is how to replay the TranslateTransition animation:

```
// when window resizes width wise the ticker will know how far to move
ticker.setOnFinished(new EventHandler<ActionEvent>() {
    public void handle(ActionEvent ae){
        ticker.stop();
        ticker.setFromX(scene.getWidth());
        ticker.setDuration(new Duration((scene.getWidth()/300) * 15000));
        ticker.playFromStart();
    }
});
```

Once the animation is defined, you simply invoke the play() method to get it started. The following code snippet shows how to play a TranslateTransition:

```
ticker.play();
```

Now that you have a better understanding of animated transitions, what about a transition that can trigger any number of transitions? JavaFX has two transitions that provide this behavior. The two transitions can invoke individual dependent transitions sequentially or in parallel. In this recipe I use a sequential transition (SequentialTransition) to contain two FadeTransitions in order to fade out the current image displayed and to fade-in the next image into view. When creating the previous and next button's event handlers, you first determine the next image to be displayed by calling the gotoImageIndex() method. Once the next image to be displayed is determined, you will call the transitionByFading() method, which returns an instance of a SequentialTransition. When calling the transitionByFading() method, you'll notice the creation of two FadeTransitions. The first transition will change the opacity level from 1.0 to 0.0 to fade out the current image, and the second transition will interpolate the opacity level from 0.0 to 1.0, fading in the next image that then becomes the current image. At last the two FadeTransitions are added to the SequentialTransition and returned to the caller. The following code creates two FadeTransitions and adds them to a SequentialTransition:

```
FadeTransition fadeOut = new FadeTransition(Duration.millis(500), imageView);
fadeOut.setFromValue(1.0);
fadeOut.setToValue(0.0);
fadeOut.setOnFinished(new EventHandler<ActionEvent>() {
    public void handle(ActionEvent ae) {
        imageView.setImage(nextImage);
    }
```

```
});

FadeTransition fadeIn = new FadeTransition(Duration.millis(500), imageView);
fadeIn.setFromValue(0.0);
fadeIn.setToValue(1.0);

SequentialTransition seqTransition = SequentialTransitionBuilder.create()
        .children(fadeOut, fadeIn)
        .build();
```

For the last requirements relating to fading in and out, you use the button controls. You will yet again use the FadeTransition to create a ghostly animated effect. For starters, just like any event you are interested in you will be creating an EventHandler (more specifically, an EventHandler<MouseEvent>). It is easy peasy to add mouse events to the Scene; all you have to do is override the handle() method where the inbound parameter is a MouseEvent type (the same as its formal type parameter). Inside of the handle() method, you will create an instance of a FadeTransition object by using the constructor that takes the duration and node as parameters. Next, you'll notice the setFromValue() and setToValue() methods that are called to interpolate values between 1.0 and 0.0 for the opacity level, causing the fade-in effect to occur. The following code adds an EventHandler to create the fade-in effect when the mouse cursor is positioned inside of the Scene:

```
// Fade in button controls
scene.setOnMouseEntered(new EventHandler<MouseEvent>() {
    public void handle(MouseEvent me) {
        FadeTransition fadeButtons = new FadeTransition(Duration.millis(500),
buttonGroup);
        fadeButtons.setFromValue(0.0);
        fadeButtons.setToValue(1.0);
        fadeButtons.play();
    }
});
```

Last but not least, the fade-out EventHandler is basically the same as the fade-in, except that the opacity From and To values are from 1.0 to 0.0, which make the buttons vanish mysteriously when the mouse pointer moves off the Scene area.

16-3. Animating Shapes Along a Path

Problem

You want to create a way to animate shapes along a path.

Solution

Create an application that allows a user to draw the path for a shape to follow. The main Java classes used in this recipe are these:

- javafx.animation.PathTransition

- javafx.animation.PathTransitionBuilder

- javafx.scene.input.MouseEvent

- javafx.event.EventHandler

- javafx.geometry.Point2D

- javafx.scene.shape.LineTo

- javafx.scene.shape.MoveTo

- javafx.scene.shape.Path

The following code demonstrates drawing a path for a shape to follow:

```java
/**
 * Working with the Scene Graph
 * @author cdea
 */
public class WorkingWithTheSceneGraph extends Application {

    Path onePath = new Path();
    Point2D anchorPt;
    /**
     * @param args the command line arguments
     */
    public static void main(String[] args) {
        Application.launch(args);
    }

    @Override
    public void start(Stage primaryStage) {
        primaryStage.setTitle("Chapter 16-3 Working with the Scene Graph");

        final Group root = new Group();

        // add path
        root.getChildren().add(onePath);

        final Scene scene = SceneBuilder.create()
                .root(root)
                .width(300)
                .height(250)
                .fill(Color.WHITE)
                .build();

        RadialGradient gradient1 = new RadialGradient(0,
                .1,
                100,
                100,
                20,
                false,
```

```
            CycleMethod.NO_CYCLE,
            new Stop(0, Color.RED),
            new Stop(1, Color.BLACK));

// create a sphere
final Circle sphere = CircleBuilder.create()
        .centerX(100)
        .centerY(100)
        .radius(20)
        .fill(gradient1)
        .build();

// add sphere
root.getChildren().addAll(sphere);

// animate sphere by following the path.
final PathTransition pathTransition = PathTransitionBuilder.create()
    .duration(Duration.millis(4000))
    .cycleCount(1)
    .node(sphere)
    .path(onePath)
    .orientation(PathTransition.OrientationType.ORTHOGONAL_TO_TANGENT)
    .build();

// once finished clear path
pathTransition.onFinishedProperty().set(new EventHandler<ActionEvent>() {
    public void handle(ActionEvent event){
        onePath.getElements().clear();
    }
});

// starting initial path
scene.onMousePressedProperty().set(new EventHandler<MouseEvent>() {
    public void handle(MouseEvent event){
        // clear path
        onePath.getElements().clear();
        // start point in path
        anchorPt = new Point2D(event.getX(), event.getY());
        onePath.setStrokeWidth(3);
        onePath.setStroke(Color.BLACK);
        onePath.getElements().add(new MoveTo(anchorPt.getX(), anchorPt.getY()));
    }
});

// dragging creates lineTos added to the path
scene.onMouseDraggedProperty().set(new EventHandler<MouseEvent>() {
    public void handle(MouseEvent event){
        onePath.getElements().add(new LineTo(event.getX(), event.getY()));
    }
});

// end the path when mouse released event
```

```
scene.onMouseReleasedProperty().set(new EventHandler<MouseEvent>() {
    public void handle(MouseEvent event){
        onePath.setStrokeWidth(0);
        if (onePath.getElements().size() > 1) {
            pathTransition.stop();
            pathTransition.playFromStart();
        }
    }
});

primaryStage.setScene(scene);
primaryStage.show();
    }
}
```

Figure 16-6 shows the drawn path the circle will follow. When the user performs a mouse release, the drawn path will disappear, and the red ball will follow the path drawn earlier.

Figure 16-6. Path transition

How It Works

In this recipe you'll be creating a simple application enabling you to animate objects by following a drawn path on the Scene graph. To make things simple you will be using one shape (Circle) that will perform a path transition (javafx.animation.PathTransition). You will allow the user to draw a path on the scene surface by pressing the mouse button like a drawing program. Once you are satisfied with the path drawn, you will release the mouse press that triggers the red ball to follow the path similar to objects moving through pipes inside a building.

You will create two instance variables to maintain the coordinates that make up the path. To hold the path being drawn, you will create an instance of a javafx.scene.shape.Path object. You also should know that the path instance should be added to the Scene graph before the start of the application. Shown here is adding the instance variable onePath onto the Scene graph:

```
// add path
root.getChildren().add(onePath);
```

Next, you will create an instance variable anchorPt (javafx.geometry.Point2D) that will hold the path's starting point. Later, you will see how these variables will be updated based on mouse events. Shown here are the instance variables that maintain the currently drawn path:

```
Path onePath = new Path();
Point2D anchorPt;
```

First, let's create a shape that will be animated. In this scenario, you will be creating a cool-looking red ball. To create a spherical-looking ball you will create a gradient color RadialGradient that will be used to paint or fill a circle shape. (Refer to recipe 15-6 for how to fill shapes with gradient paint.) Once you have created the red spherical ball you need to create PathTransition object to perform the path following animation. By using the convenient PathTransitionBuilder class you simply set the duration to four seconds and the cycle count to one. The cycle count is the number of times the animation cycle will occur. Next, you will set the node to reference the red ball (sphere). Then, you will set the path() method to the instance variable onePath, which contains all the coordinates and lines that make up a drawn path. After setting the path for the sphere to animate, you should specify how the shape will follow the path such as perpendicular to a tangent point on the path. The following code creates an instance of a path transition:

```
// animate sphere by following the path.
final PathTransition pathTransition = PathTransitionBuilder.create()
    .duration(Duration.millis(4000))
    .cycleCount(1)
    .node(sphere)
    .path(onePath)
    .orientation(PathTransition.OrientationType.ORTHOGONAL_TO_TANGENT)
    .build();
```

After the creation of your path transition you will want it to clean up when the animation is completed. To reset or clean up the path variable when the animation is finished, you will create and add an event handler to listen to the onFinished property event on the path transition object.

The following code snippet adds an event handler to clear the current path information:

```
// once finished clear path
pathTransition.onFinishedProperty().set(new EventHandler<ActionEvent>() {
    public void handle(ActionEvent event){
        onePath.getElements().clear();
    }
});
```

With the shape and transition all set up, you will next respond to mouse events that will update the instance variable mentioned earlier. You will be listening to mouse events occurring on the Scene object. Here, you will once again rely on creating event handlers to be set on the Scene's onMouseXXXProperty methods where the XXX denotes the actual mouse event name such as pressed, dragged, and released.

When a user draws a path, he or she will perform a mouse press event to begin the start of the path. To listen to a mouse-pressed event, you will create an event handler with a formal type parameter of `MouseEvent`. Here you will override the `handle()` method. As a mouse-pressed event occurs, you want to clear the instance variable `onePath` of any prior drawn path information. Next, you will simply set the stroke width and color of the path so the user can see the path being drawn. Finally, you will add the starting point to the path using an instance of a `MoveTo` object. Shown here is the handler code to respond when the user performs a mouse press:

```
// starting initial path
scene.onMousePressedProperty().set(new EventHandler<MouseEvent>() {
    public void handle(MouseEvent event){
        // clear path
        onePath.getElements().clear();
        // start point in path
        anchorPt = new Point2D(event.getX(), event.getY());
        onePath.setStrokeWidth(3);
        onePath.setStroke(Color.BLACK);
        onePath.getElements().add(new MoveTo(anchorPt.getX(), anchorPt.getY()));
    }
});
```

Once the mouse-pressed event handler is in place, you will be creating another handler for mouse-dragged events. Again, you will look for the Scene's `onMouseXXXProperty()` methods that correspond to the proper mouse event that you care about. In this case, it will be the `onMouseDraggedProperty()` that you want to set. Inside the overridden `handle()` method you will be taking mouse coordinates that will be converted to `LineTo` objects to be added to the path (Path). These `LineTo` objects are instances of path element (`javafx.scene.shape.PathElement`) as discussed in recipe 15-5. The following code is an event handler responsible for mouse-dragged events:

```
// dragging creates lineTos added to the path
scene.onMouseDraggedProperty().set(new EventHandler<MouseEvent>() {
    public void handle(MouseEvent event){
        onePath.getElements().add(new LineTo(event.getX(), event.getY()));
    }
});
```

Finally, you will be creating an event handler to listen to a mouse-released event. When a user releases the mouse, the path's stroke is set to zero to appear as if it were removed. Then you will reset the path transition by stopping it and playing it from the start. The following code is an event handler responsible for mouse-released event:

```
// end the path when mouse released event
scene.onMouseReleasedProperty().set(new EventHandler<MouseEvent>() {
    public void handle(MouseEvent event){
        onePath.setStrokeWidth(0);
        if (onePath.getElements().size() > 1) {
            pathTransition.stop();
            pathTransition.playFromStart();
        }
    }
});
```

16-4. Manipulating Layout via Grids

Problem

You want to create a nice-looking form type user interface using grid type layout.

Solution

Create a simple form designer application to manipulate the user interface dynamically using the JavaFX's `javafx.scene.layout.GridPane`. The form designer application will have the following features:

- It will toggle the display of the Grid layout's grid lines for debugging.

- It will adjust the top padding of the `GridPane`.

- It will adjust the left padding of the `GridPane`.

- It will adjust the horizontal gap between cells in the `GridPane`.

- It will adjust the vertical gap between cells in the `GridPane`.

- It will align controls within cells horizontally.

- It will align controls within cells vertically.

The following code is the main launching point for the form designer application:

```
/**
 * Manipulating Layout Via Grids
 * @author cdea
 */
public class ManipulatingLayoutViaGrids extends Application {

    /**
     * @param args the command line arguments
     */
    public static void main(String[] args) {
        Application.launch(args);
    }

    @Override
    public void start(Stage primaryStage) {
        primaryStage.setTitle("Chapter 16-4 Manipulating Layout via Grids ");
        Group root = new Group();
        Scene scene = new Scene(root, 640, 480, Color.WHITE);

        // Left and right split pane
        SplitPane splitPane = new SplitPane();
        splitPane.prefWidthProperty().bind(scene.widthProperty());
        splitPane.prefHeightProperty().bind(scene.heightProperty());
```

```java
        // Form on the right
        GridPane rightGridPane = new MyForm();

        GridPane leftGridPane = new GridPaneControlPanel(rightGridPane);

        VBox leftArea = new VBox(10);
        leftArea.getChildren().add(leftGridPane);
        HBox hbox = new HBox();
        hbox.getChildren().add(splitPane);
        root.getChildren().add(hbox);
        splitPane.getItems().addAll(leftArea, rightGridPane);

        primaryStage.setScene(scene);

        primaryStage.show();
    }

}
```

When the form designer application is launched, the target form to be manipulated will be shown to the right side of the window's split pane. Shown following is the code of a simple grid-like form class that extends from GridPane that will be manipulated by the form designer application:

```java
/**
 * MyForm is a form to be manipulated by the user.
 * @author cdea
 */
public class MyForm extends GridPane{
    public MyForm() {

        setPadding(new Insets(5));
        setHgap(5);
        setVgap(5);

        Label fNameLbl = new Label("First Name");
        TextField fNameFld = new TextField();
        Label lNameLbl = new Label("Last Name");
        TextField lNameFld = new TextField();
        Label ageLbl = new Label("Age");
        TextField ageFld = new TextField();

        Button saveButt = new Button("Save");

        // First name label
        GridPane.setHalignment(fNameLbl, HPos.RIGHT);
        add(fNameLbl, 0, 0);

        // Last name label
        GridPane.setHalignment(lNameLbl, HPos.RIGHT);
        add(lNameLbl, 0, 1);
```

```
        // Age label
        GridPane.setHalignment(ageLbl, HPos.RIGHT);
        add(ageLbl, 0, 2);

        // First name field
        GridPane.setHalignment(fNameFld, HPos.LEFT);
        add(fNameFld, 1, 0);

        // Last name field
        GridPane.setHalignment(lNameFld, HPos.LEFT);
        add(lNameFld, 1, 1);

        // Age Field
        GridPane.setHalignment(ageFld, HPos.RIGHT);
        add(ageFld, 1, 2);

        // Save button
        GridPane.setHalignment(saveButt, HPos.RIGHT);
        add(saveButt, 1, 3);

    }
}
```

When the form designer application is launched, the grid property control panel will be shown to the left side of the window's split pane. The property control panel will allow a user to manipulate the target form's grid pane attributes dynamically. The following code represents the grid property control panel that will manipulate a target grid pane's properties:

```
/** GridPaneControlPanel represents the left area of the split pane
 * allowing the user to manipulate the GridPane on the right.
 *
 * Manipulating Layout Via Grids
 * @author cdea
 */
public class GridPaneControlPanel extends GridPane{
    public GridPaneControlPanel(final GridPane targetGridPane) {
        super();

        setPadding(new Insets(5));
        setHgap(5);
        setVgap(5);

        // Setting Grid lines
        Label gridLinesLbl = new Label("Grid Lines");
        final ToggleButton gridLinesToggle = new ToggleButton("Off");
        gridLinesToggle.selectedProperty().addListener(new ChangeListener<Boolean>(){
            public void changed(ObservableValue<? extends Boolean> ov, Boolean oldValue,
Boolean newVal) {
                targetGridPane.setGridLinesVisible(newVal);
                gridLinesToggle.setText(newVal ? "On" : "Off");
            }
```

```
        });

        // toggle grid lines label
        GridPane.setHalignment(gridLinesLbl, HPos.RIGHT);
        add(gridLinesLbl, 0, 0);

        // toggle grid lines
        GridPane.setHalignment(gridLinesToggle, HPos.LEFT);
        add(gridLinesToggle, 1, 0);

        // Setting padding [top]
        Label gridPaddingLbl = new Label("Top Padding");

        final Slider gridPaddingSlider = SliderBuilder.create()
                .min(0)
                .max(100)
                .value(5)
                .showTickLabels(true)
                .showTickMarks(true)
                .minorTickCount(1)
                .blockIncrement(5)
                .build();
        gridPaddingSlider.valueProperty().addListener(new ChangeListener<Number>() {
            public void changed(ObservableValue<? extends Number> ov, Number oldVal, Number
newVal) {
                double top = targetGridPane.getInsets().getTop();
                double right = targetGridPane.getInsets().getRight();
                double bottom = targetGridPane.getInsets().getBottom();
                double left = targetGridPane.getInsets().getLeft();

                Insets newInsets = new Insets((double) newVal, right, bottom, left);

                targetGridPane.setPadding(newInsets);
            }
        });


        // padding adjustment label
        GridPane.setHalignment(gridPaddingLbl, HPos.RIGHT);
        add(gridPaddingLbl, 0, 1);

        // padding adjustment slider
        GridPane.setHalignment(gridPaddingSlider, HPos.LEFT);
        add(gridPaddingSlider, 1, 1);

        // Setting padding [top]
        Label gridPaddingLeftLbl = new Label("Left Padding");

        final Slider gridPaddingLeftSlider = SliderBuilder.create()
                .min(0)
                .max(100)
                .value(5)
```

```
                .showTickLabels(true)
                .showTickMarks(true)
                .minorTickCount(1)
                .blockIncrement(5)
                .build();
        gridPaddingLeftSlider.valueProperty().addListener(new ChangeListener<Number>() {
            public void changed(ObservableValue<? extends Number> ov, Number oldVal, Number
newVal) {
                double top = targetGridPane.getInsets().getTop();
                double right = targetGridPane.getInsets().getRight();
                double bottom = targetGridPane.getInsets().getBottom();
                double left = targetGridPane.getInsets().getLeft();

                Insets newInsets = new Insets(top, right, bottom, (double) newVal);

                targetGridPane.setPadding(newInsets);
            }
        });


        // padding adjustment label
        GridPane.setHalignment(gridPaddingLeftLbl, HPos.RIGHT);
        add(gridPaddingLeftLbl, 0, 2);

        // padding adjustment slider
        GridPane.setHalignment(gridPaddingLeftSlider, HPos.LEFT);
        add(gridPaddingLeftSlider, 1, 2);

        // Horizontal gap
        Label gridHGapLbl = new Label("Horizontal Gap");

        final Slider gridHGapSlider = SliderBuilder.create()
                .min(0)
                .max(100)
                .value(5)
                .showTickLabels(true)
                .showTickMarks(true)
                .minorTickCount(1)
                .blockIncrement(5)
                .build();
        gridHGapSlider.valueProperty().addListener(new ChangeListener<Number>() {
            public void changed(ObservableValue<? extends Number> ov, Number oldVal, Number
newVal) {
                targetGridPane.setHgap((double) newVal);
            }
        });


        // hgap label
        GridPane.setHalignment(gridHGapLbl, HPos.RIGHT);
        add(gridHGapLbl, 0, 3);
```

607

```java
        // hgap slider
        GridPane.setHalignment(gridHGapSlider, HPos.LEFT);
        add(gridHGapSlider, 1, 3);

         // Vertical gap
         Label gridVGapLbl = new Label("Vertical Gap");

         final Slider gridVGapSlider = SliderBuilder.create()
                 .min(0)
                 .max(100)
                 .value(5)
                 .showTickLabels(true)
                 .showTickMarks(true)
                 .minorTickCount(1)
                 .blockIncrement(5)
                 .build();
        gridVGapSlider.valueProperty().addListener(new ChangeListener<Number>() {
            public void changed(ObservableValue<? extends Number> ov, Number oldVal, Number
newVal) {
                targetGridPane.setVgap((double) newVal);
            }
        });


        // vgap label
        GridPane.setHalignment(gridVGapLbl, HPos.RIGHT);
        add(gridVGapLbl, 0, 4);

        // vgap slider
        GridPane.setHalignment(gridVGapSlider, HPos.LEFT);
        add(gridVGapSlider, 1, 4);

        // Cell Column
        Label cellCol = new Label("Cell Column");
        final TextField cellColFld = new TextField("0");

        // cell Column label
        GridPane.setHalignment(cellCol, HPos.RIGHT);
        add(cellCol, 0, 5);

        // cell Column field
        GridPane.setHalignment(cellColFld, HPos.LEFT);
        add(cellColFld, 1, 5);

        // Cell Row
        Label cellRowLbl = new Label("Cell Row");
        final TextField cellRowFld = new TextField("0");

        // cell Row label
        GridPane.setHalignment(cellRowLbl, HPos.RIGHT);
        add(cellRowLbl, 0, 6);
```

```java
// cell Row field
GridPane.setHalignment(cellRowFld, HPos.LEFT);
add(cellRowFld, 1, 6);

// Horizontal Alignment
Label hAlignLbl = new Label("Horiz. Align");
final ChoiceBox hAlignFld = new ChoiceBox(FXCollections.observableArrayList(
    "CENTER", "LEFT", "RIGHT")
);
hAlignFld.getSelectionModel().select("LEFT");

// cell Row label
GridPane.setHalignment(hAlignLbl, HPos.RIGHT);
add(hAlignLbl, 0, 7);

// cell Row field
GridPane.setHalignment(hAlignFld, HPos.LEFT);
add(hAlignFld, 1, 7);

// Vertical Alignment
Label vAlignLbl = new Label("Vert. Align");
final ChoiceBox vAlignFld = new ChoiceBox(FXCollections.observableArrayList(
    "BASELINE", "BOTTOM", "CENTER", "TOP")
);
vAlignFld.getSelectionModel().select("TOP");
// cell Row label
GridPane.setHalignment(vAlignLbl, HPos.RIGHT);
add(vAlignLbl, 0, 8);

// cell Row field
GridPane.setHalignment(vAlignFld, HPos.LEFT);
add(vAlignFld, 1, 8);

// Vertical Alignment
Label cellApplyLbl = new Label("Cell Constraint");
final Button cellApplyButton = new Button("Apply");
cellApplyButton.setOnAction(new EventHandler<ActionEvent>() {

    public void handle(ActionEvent event) {

        for (Node child:targetGridPane.getChildren()) {

            int targetColIndx = 0;
            int targetRowIndx = 0;
            try {
                targetColIndx = Integer.parseInt(cellColFld.getText());
                targetRowIndx = Integer.parseInt(cellRowFld.getText());
            } catch (Exception e) {

            }
            System.out.println("child = " + child.getClass().getSimpleName());
            int col = GridPane.getColumnIndex(child);
```

```
                    int row = GridPane.getRowIndex(child);
                    if (col == targetColIndx && row == targetRowIndx) {
                        GridPane.setHalignment(child,
HPos.valueOf(hAlignFld.getSelectionModel().getSelectedItem().toString()));
                        GridPane.setValignment(child,
VPos.valueOf(vAlignFld.getSelectionModel().getSelectedItem().toString()));
                    }
                }
            }
        });

        // cell Row label
        GridPane.setHalignment(cellApplyLbl, HPos.RIGHT);
        add(cellApplyLbl, 0, 9);

        // cell Row field
        GridPane.setHalignment(cellApplyButton, HPos.LEFT);
        add(cellApplyButton, 1, 9);

    }
}
```

Figure 16-7 shows a form designer application with the `GridPane` property control panel on the left and the target form on the right.

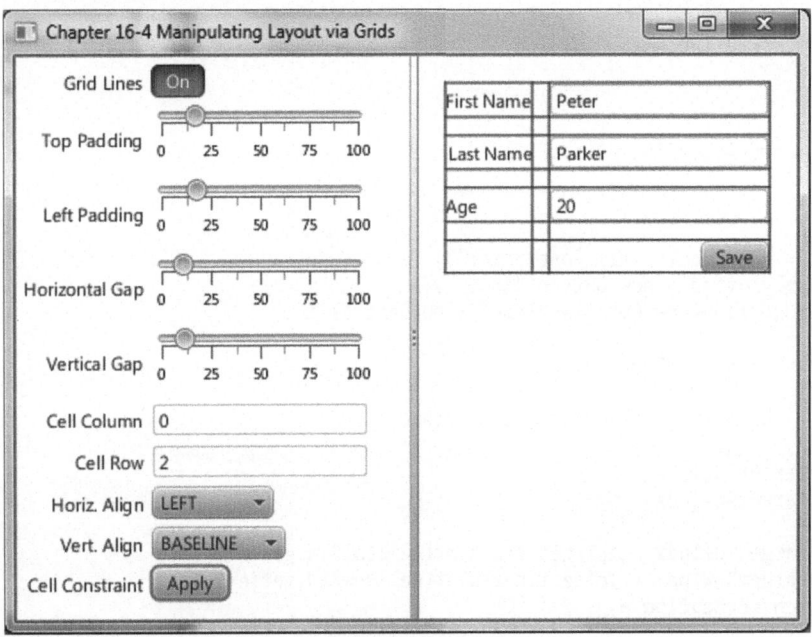

Figure 16-7. Manipulating layout via grids

How It Works

The form designer application will allow the user to adjust properties dynamically using the GridPane property control panel to the left. While adjusting properties from the left control panel the target form on the right side will be manipulated dynamically. When creating a simple form designer application you will be binding controls to various properties onto the target form (GridPane). This designer application is basically broken out into three classes: ManipulatingLayoutViaGrids, MyForm, and GridPaneControlPanel. First the ManipulatingLayoutViaGrids class is the main application to be launched. Second, MyForm is the target form that will be manipulated. Last, GridPaneControlPanel is the grid property control panel that has UI controls bound to the targets form's grid pane properties.

You begin by creating the main launching point for the application (ManipulatingLayoutViaGrids). This class is responsible for creating a split pane (SplitPane) that sets up the target form to the right and instantiates a GridPaneControlPanel to be displayed to the left. To instantiate a GridPaneControlPanel you must pass in the target form you want to manipulate into the constructor. I will discuss this further, but suffice it to say that the GridPaneControlPanel constructor will wire up its controls to properties on the target form.

Next, you will simply create a dummy form that I've called MyForm. This form will be your target form that the property control panel will be manipulating. Here, you will notice the MyForm extends GridPane. In the MyForm's constructor you will create and add controls to be put into the form (GridPane).

To learn more about the GridPane refer to recipe 15-8. The following code is a target form to be manipulated by the form designer application:

```java
/**
 * MyForm is a form to be manipulated by the user.
 * @author cdea
 */
public class MyForm extends GridPane{
    public MyForm() {

        setPadding(new Insets(5));
        setHgap(5);
        setVgap(5);

        Label fNameLbl = new Label("First Name");
        TextField fNameFld = new TextField();
        Label lNameLbl = new Label("Last Name");
        TextField lNameFld = new TextField();
        Label ageLbl = new Label("Age");
        TextField ageFld = new TextField();

        Button saveButt = new Button("Save");

        // First name label
        GridPane.setHalignment(fNameLbl, HPos.RIGHT);
        add(fNameLbl, 0, 0);
    //! The rest of the form code
```

To manipulate the target form you will need to create a grid property control panel (`GridPaneControlPanel`). This class is responsible for binding the target form's grid pane properties to UI controls that allow the user to adjust values using the keyboard and mouse. As you learned earlier in recipe 15-10, you can bind values with JavaFX Properties. But instead of binding values directly, you can also be notified when a property has changed.

Another feature that you can apply to properties is that you can add change listeners. JavaFX`javafx.beans.value.ChangeListeners` is similar to Java Swing's property change support (`java.beans.PropertyChangeListener`). Similarly, when a bean's property value has changed you will want to be notified of that change. Change listeners are designed to intercept the change by making the old and new value available to the developer. You will start by creating a `JavaFXchange` listener for the toggle button to turn gridlines on or off. When a user interacts with the toggle button, the change listener will simply update the target's grid pane's `gridlinesVisible` property. Because a toggle button's (`ToggleButton`) selected property is a `Boolean` value, you will instantiate a `ChangeListener` class with its formal type parameter as `Boolean`. You'll also notice the overridden method `changed()` where its inbound parameters will match the generics formal type parameter specified when instantiating a `ChangeListener<Boolean>`. When a property change event occurs, the change listener will invoke `setGridLinesVisible()` on the target grid pane with the new value and update the toggle button's text. The following code snippet shows a `ChangeListener<Boolean>` added to a `ToggleButton`:

```
gridLinesToggle.selectedProperty().addListener(
new ChangeListener<Boolean>(){
        public void changed(ObservableValue<? extends Boolean> ov, Boolean oldValue, Boolean
newVal) {
targetGridPane.setGridLinesVisible(newVal);
gridLinesToggle.setText(newVal ? "On" : "Off");
        }
});
```

Next, you will be applying a change listener to a slider control that allows the user to adjust the target grid pane's top padding. To create a change listener for a slider you will be instantiating a `ChangeListener<Number>`. Again, you will be overriding the `changed()` method with a signature the same as its formal type parameter `Number`. When a change occurs, the slider's value will be used to create an `Insets` object that becomes the new padding for the target grid pane. Shown here is the change listener for the top padding and slider control:

```
gridPaddingSlider.valueProperty().addListener(new ChangeListener<Number>() {
    public void changed(ObservableValue<? extends Number> ov, Number oldVal, Number
newVal) {
        double top = targetGridPane.getInsets().getTop();
        double right = targetGridPane.getInsets().getRight();
        double bottom = targetGridPane.getInsets().getBottom();
        double left = targetGridPane.getInsets().getLeft();

        Insets newInsets = new Insets((double) newVal, right, bottom, left);

        targetGridPane.setPadding(newInsets);
    }
});
```

Because the implementation of the other slider controls that handle left padding, horizontal gap, and vertical gap are virtually identical to the top padding slider control mentioned previously, you can fast forward to cell constraints controls.

The last bits of grid control panel properties that you want to manipulate are the target grid pane's cell constraints. For brevity I only allow the user to set a component's alignment inside of a cell of a GridPane. To see more properties to modify, refer to the Javadoc on javafx.scene.layout.GridPane. Figure 16-8 depicts the cell constraint settings for individual cells. An example is to left-justify the label Age on the target grid pane. Because cells are zero relative, you will enter 0 in the Cell Column field and two into the Cell Row field. Next, you will select the drop-down box Horiz. Align to LEFT. Once satisfied with the settings, click Apply. Figure 16-9 shows the Age label control left-aligned horizontally. To implement this, you will create an EventHandler<ActionEvent> for the apply button's onAction attribute by calling its setOnAction() method. Again when creating EventHandlers you will be overriding the handle() method. Inside of the handle() method you will basically iterate over all node children owned by the target grid pane to determine whether it is the specified cell. Once the specified cell and child node is determined the alignment will be applied. The following code is an EventHandler to apply cell constraint when the apply button is pressed:

```
final Button cellApplyButton = new Button("Apply");
cellApplyButton.setOnAction(new EventHandler<ActionEvent>() {

    public void handle(ActionEvent event) {

        for (Node child:targetGridPane.getChildren()) {

            int targetColIndx = 0;
            int targetRowIndx = 0;
            try {
                targetColIndx = Integer.parseInt(cellColFld.getText());
                targetRowIndx = Integer.parseInt(cellRowFld.getText());
            } catch (Exception e) {

            }
            System.out.println("child = " + child.getClass().getSimpleName());
            int col = GridPane.getColumnIndex(child);
            int row = GridPane.getRowIndex(child);
            if (col == targetColIndx && row == targetRowIndx) {
                GridPane.setHalignment(child,
HPos.valueOf(hAlignFld.getSelectionModel().getSelectedItem().toString()));
                GridPane.setValignment(child,
VPos.valueOf(vAlignFld.getSelectionModel().getSelectedItem().toString()));
            }
        }

    }
});
```

Figure 16-8 depicts the cell constraint grid control panel section that left-aligns the control at cell column zero and cell row 2.

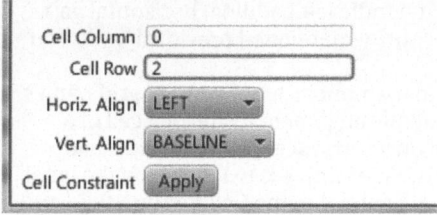

Figure 16-8. *Cell constraints*

Figure 16-9 depicts the target grid pane with the grid lines turned on along with the Age label left-aligned horizontally at cell column 0 and cell row 2.

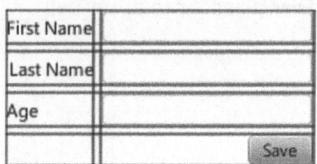

Figure 16-9. *Target grid pane*

16-5. Enhancing with CSS

Problem

You want to change the Look 'N' Feel of the GUI interface.

Solution

Use JavaFX's CSS styling to be applied on graph nodes. The following code demonstrates using CSS styling on graph nodes. The code creates four themes: Caspian, Control Style 1, Control Style 2, and Sky. Each theme is defined using CSS and affects the Look 'N' Feel of a dialog box. Following the code, you can see the two different renditions of the dialog box:

```
package org.java7recipes.chapter16.recipe16_05;

import javafx.application.Application;
import javafx.collections.FXCollections;
import javafx.collections.ObservableList;
import javafx.event.ActionEvent;
import javafx.event.EventHandler;
import javafx.scene.Group;
import javafx.scene.Scene;
import javafx.scene.control.Menu;
```

```java
import javafx.scene.control.MenuBar;
import javafx.scene.control.MenuItem;
import javafx.scene.control.SplitPane;
import javafx.scene.layout.GridPane;
import javafx.scene.layout.HBox;
import javafx.scene.layout.VBox;
import javafx.scene.paint.Color;
import javafx.stage.Stage;

/**
 * Enhancing with CSS
 * @author cdea
 */
public class EnhancingWithCss extends Application {

    /**
     * @param args the command line arguments
     */
    public static void main(String[] args) {
        Application.launch(args);
    }

    @Override
    public void start(Stage primaryStage) {

            primaryStage.setTitle("Chapter 16-5 Enhancing with CSS ");
            Group root = new Group();
            final Scene scene = new Scene(root, 640, 480, Color.BLACK);

            MenuBar menuBar = new MenuBar();
            Menu menu = new Menu("Look 'N' Feel");

            // default caspian look n feel
            ObservableList<String> caspian = FXCollections.observableArrayList();
            caspian.addAll(scene.getStylesheets());
            MenuItem caspianLnf = new MenuItem("Caspian");
            caspianLnf.setOnAction(skinForm(caspian, scene));
            menu.getItems().add(caspianLnf);

            menu.getItems().add(createMenuItem("Control Style 1", "controlStyle1.css",
scene));
            menu.getItems().add(createMenuItem("Control Style 2", "controlStyle2.css",
scene));
            menu.getItems().add(createMenuItem("Sky", "sky.css", scene));

            menuBar.getMenus().add(menu);
            // stretch menu
            menuBar.prefWidthProperty().bind(primaryStage.widthProperty());

            // Left and right split pane
            SplitPane splitPane = new SplitPane();
            splitPane.prefWidthProperty().bind(scene.widthProperty());
```

615

```java
        splitPane.prefHeightProperty().bind(scene.heightProperty());

        // Form on the right
        GridPane rightGridPane = new MyForm();

        GridPane leftGridPane = new GridPaneControlPanel(rightGridPane);
        VBox leftArea = new VBox(10);
        leftArea.getChildren().add(leftGridPane);


        HBox hbox = new HBox();
        hbox.getChildren().add(splitPane);
        VBox vbox = new VBox();
        vbox.getChildren().add(menuBar);
        vbox.getChildren().add(hbox);
        root.getChildren().add(vbox);
        splitPane.getItems().addAll(leftArea, rightGridPane);

        primaryStage.setScene(scene);

        primaryStage.show();

    }

    protected final MenuItem createMenuItem(String label, String css, final Scene scene){
        MenuItem menuItem = new MenuItem(label);
        ObservableList<String> cssStyle = loadSkin(css);
        menuItem.setOnAction(skinForm(cssStyle, scene));
        return menuItem;
    }

    protected final ObservableList<String> loadSkin(String cssFileName) {
        ObservableList<String> cssStyle = FXCollections.observableArrayList();
        cssStyle.addAll(getClass().getResource(cssFileName).toExternalForm());
        return cssStyle;
    }

    protected final EventHandler<ActionEvent> skinForm(final ObservableList<String>
cssStyle, final Scene scene) {
        return new EventHandler<ActionEvent>(){
            public void handle(ActionEvent event) {
                scene.getStylesheets().clear();
                scene.getStylesheets().addAll(cssStyle);
            }
        };
    }

}
```

Figure 16-10 depicts the standard JavaFX Caspian Look 'n' Feel (theme).

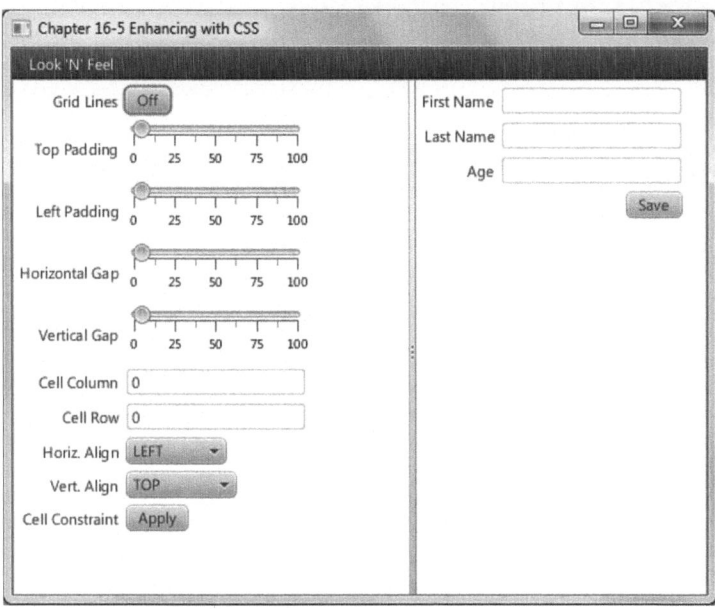

Figure 16-10. Caspian Look N Feel

Figure 16-11 depicts the Sky Look 'N' Feel (theme).

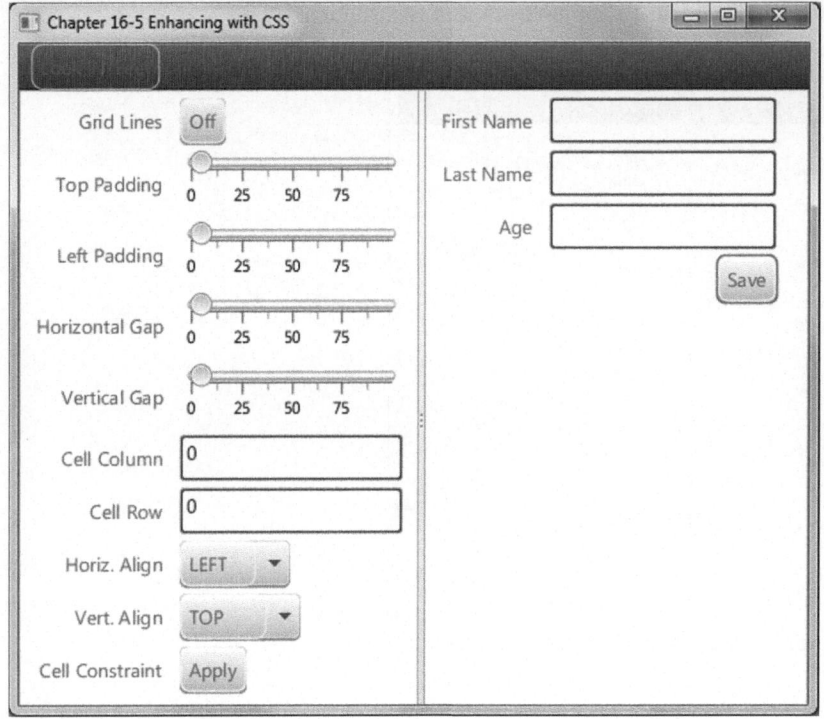

Figure 16-11. Sky Look N Feel

How It Works

JavaFX has the capability to apply CSS styles onto the Scene graph and its nodes very much like browsers applying CSS styles onto elements in an HTML document object model (DOM). In this recipe you will be skinning a user interface using JavaFX styling attributes. I basically used the recipe's UI to apply the various Look 'n' Feels. To showcase the available skins, a menu selection allows the user to choose the Look 'N' Feel to apply to the UI.

Before discussing CSS styling properties, I want to show you how to load the CSS styles to be applied to a JavaFX application. You will first need to create menu items to allow the user to choose the preferred Look 'N' Feel. When creating a menu item you will create a convenience method to build a menu item that would load the specified CSS and an `EventHandler` action to apply the chosen CSS style onto the current UI. To add the Caspian theme as a menu item you will notice that no resources are needed to be loaded because it is JavaFX's current Look 'n' Feel. Shown here is adding a menu item containing the Caspian Look 'N' Feel CSS style that can be applied to the current UI:

```
MenuItem caspianLnf = new MenuItem("Caspian");
caspianLnf.setOnAction(skinForm(caspian, scene));
```

Shown here is adding a menu item containing the sky Look 'N' Feel CSS style ready to be applied to the current UI:

```
MenuBar menuBar = new MenuBar();
Menu menu = new Menu("Look 'N' Feel");
menu.getItems().add(createMenuItem("Sky", "sky.css", scene));
```

Calling the createMenuItem() method will also call another convenience method to load the CSS file called loadSkin(). It will also set the menu items onAction attribute with an appropriate EventHandler by calling the skinForm() method. To recap, the loadSkin is responsible for loading the CSS file, and the skinForm() method's job is to apply the skin onto the UI application. Shown here are the convenience methods to build menu items that apply CSS styles onto a UI application:

```
protected final MenuItem createMenuItem(String label, String css, final Scene scene){
    MenuItem menuItem = new MenuItem(label);
    ObservableList<String> cssStyle = loadSkin(css);
    menuItem.setOnAction(skinForm(cssStyle, scene));
    return menuItem;
}

protected final ObservableList<String> loadSkin(String cssFileName) {
    ObservableList<String> cssStyle = FXCollections.observableArrayList();
    cssStyle.addAll(getClass().getResource(cssFileName).toExternalForm());
    return cssStyle;
}

protected final EventHandler<ActionEvent> skinForm(final ObservableList<String>
cssStyle, final Scene scene) {
    return new EventHandler<ActionEvent>(){
        public void handle(ActionEvent event) {
            scene.getStylesheets().clear();
            scene.getStylesheets().addAll(cssStyle);
        }
    };
}
```

■ **Note** To run this recipe example, make sure the CSS files are located in the compiled classes area. Resource files can be loaded easily when placed in the same directory (package) as the compiled class file that is loading them. The CSS files are co-located with this code example file. In NetBeans, you can select Clean and build project or you can copy files to your classes build area.

Now, that you know how to load CSS styles, let's talk about the JavaFX CSS selectors and styling properties. Like CSS style sheets, there are selectors or style classes associated with Node objects in the Scene graph. All Scene graph nodes have a method called setStyle() to apply styling properties that could potentially change the node's background color, border, stroke, and so on. Because all graph nodes extend from the Node class, derived classes will be able to inherit the same styling properties.

Knowing the inheritance hierarchy of node types is very important because the type of node will determine the types of styling properties you can affect. For instance a Rectangle extends from Shape, which extends from Node. The inheritance does not include -fx-border-style, which is the part of nodes that extends from Region. Based on the type of node there are limitations to what styles you are able to set. To see a full listing of all style selectors refer to the JavaFX CSS Reference Guide:

http://download.oracle.com/docs/cd/E17802_01/javafx/javafx/1.3/docs/api/javafx.scene.doc-files/cssref.html.

All JavaFX styling properties will be prefixed with -fx-. For example, all Nodes have the styling property to affect its opacity the attribute used is -fx-opacity. Following are selectors to style JavaFX javafx.scene.control.Labels and javafx.scene.control.Buttons:

```
.label {
    -fx-text-fill: rgba(17, 145, 213);
    -fx-border-color: rgba(255, 255, 255, .80);
    -fx-border-radius: 8;
    -fx-padding: 6 6 6 6;
    -fx-font: bold italic 20pt "LucidaBrightDemiBold";

}
.button{
    -fx-text-fill: rgba(17, 145, 213);
    -fx-border-color: rgba(255, 255, 255, .80);
    -fx-border-radius: 8;
    -fx-padding: 6 6 6 6;
    -fx-font: bold italic 20pt "LucidaBrightDemiBold";

}
```

CHAPTER 17

Media with JavaFX

JavaFX provides a media-rich API capable of playing audio and video. The Media API allows developers to incorporate audio and video into their RIAs. One of the main benefits of the Media API is its cross-platform abilities when distributing media content via the Web. With a range of devices (tablet, music player, TV, and so on) that need to play multimedia content, the need for a cross-platform API is essential.

Imagine a not-so-distant future where your TV or wall is capable of interacting with you in ways that you've never dreamed possible. For instance, while viewing a movie you could select items or clothing used in the movie to be immediately purchased, all from the comfort of your home. With this future in mind, developers seek to enhance the interactive qualities of their media-based applications.

In this chapter you will learn how to play audio and video in an interactive way. Find your seats for Act III of JavaFX as audio and video take center stage as depicted in Figure 17-1.

Figure 17-1. Audio and video

17-1. Playing Audio

Problem

You want to listen to music and become entertained with a graphical visualization.

Solution

Create an MP3 player by utilizing the following classes:

- `javafx.scene.media.Media`

- `javafx.scene.media.MediaPlayer`

- `javafx.scene.media.AudioSpectrumListener`

The following source code is an implementation a of simple MP3 player:

```
package java7recipeschap17.org.java7recipes.chapter17.recipe17_01;

import java.io.File;
import java.util.Random;
import javafx.application.*;
import javafx.event.EventHandler;
import javafx.geometry.Point2D;
import javafx.scene.*;
import javafx.scene.input.*;
import javafx.scene.media.*;
import javafx.scene.paint.Color;
import javafx.scene.shape.*;
import javafx.scene.text.Text;
import javafx.stage.*;

/**
 * Playing Audio
 * @author cdea
 */
public class PlayingAudio extends Application {
    private MediaPlayer mediaPlayer;
    private Point2D anchorPt;
    private Point2D previousLocation;

    /**
     * @param args the command line arguments
     */
    public static void main(String[] args) {
        Application.launch(args);
    }
```

```java
    @Override
    public void start(final Stage primaryStage) {
        primaryStage.setTitle("Chapter 17-1 Playing Audio");
        primaryStage.centerOnScreen();
        primaryStage.initStyle(StageStyle.TRANSPARENT);

        Group root = new Group();
        Scene scene = new Scene(root, 551, 270, Color.rgb(0, 0, 0, 0));

        // application area
        Rectangle applicationArea = RectangleBuilder.create()
                .arcWidth(20)
                .arcHeight(20)
                .fill(Color.rgb(0, 0, 0, .80))
                .x(0)
                .y(0)
                .strokeWidth(2)
                .stroke(Color.rgb(255, 255, 255, .70))
                .build();
        root.getChildren().add(applicationArea);
        applicationArea.widthProperty().bind(scene.widthProperty());
        applicationArea.heightProperty().bind(scene.heightProperty());

        final Group phaseNodes = new Group();
        root.getChildren().add(phaseNodes);


        // starting initial anchor point
        scene.setOnMousePressed(new EventHandler<MouseEvent>() {
            public void handle(MouseEvent event){
                anchorPt = new Point2D(event.getScreenX(), event.getScreenY());
            }
        });

        // dragging the entire stage
        scene.setOnMouseDragged(new EventHandler<MouseEvent>() {
            public void handle(MouseEvent event){
                if (anchorPt != null && previousLocation != null) {
                    primaryStage.setX(previousLocation.getX() + event.getScreenX() -
anchorPt.getX());
                    primaryStage.setY(previousLocation.getY() + event.getScreenY() -
anchorPt.getY());
                }
            }
        });

        // set the current location
        scene.setOnMouseReleased(new EventHandler<MouseEvent>() {
            public void handle(MouseEvent event){
                previousLocation = new Point2D(primaryStage.getX(), primaryStage.getY());
            }
        });
```

```java
        // Dragging over surface
        scene.setOnDragOver(new EventHandler<DragEvent>() {
            @Override
            public void handle(DragEvent event) {
                Dragboard db = event.getDragboard();
                if (db.hasFiles()) {
                    event.acceptTransferModes(TransferMode.COPY);
                } else {
                    event.consume();
                }
            }
        });


        // Dropping over surface
        scene.setOnDragDropped(new EventHandler<DragEvent>() {

            @Override
            public void handle(DragEvent event) {
                Dragboard db = event.getDragboard();
                boolean success = false;
                if (db.hasFiles()) {
                    success = true;
                    String filePath = null;
                    for (File file:db.getFiles()) {
                        filePath = file.getAbsolutePath();
                        System.out.println(filePath);
                    }
                    // play file
                    Media media = new Media(new File(filePath).toURI().toString());

                    if (mediaPlayer != null) {
                        mediaPlayer.stop();
                    }

                    mediaPlayer = MediaPlayerBuilder.create()
                            .media(media)
                            .audioSpectrumListener(new AudioSpectrumListener() {
                        @Override
                        public void spectrumDataUpdate(double timestamp, double duration,
    float[] magnitudes, float[] phases) {
                            phaseNodes.getChildren().clear();
                            int i = 0;
                            int x = 10;
                            int y = 150;
                            final Random rand = new Random(System.currentTimeMillis());
                            for(float phase:phases) {
                                int red = rand.nextInt(255);
                                int green = rand.nextInt(255);
```

```
                        int blue = rand.nextInt(255);

                        Circle circle = new Circle(10);
                        circle.setCenterX(x + i);
                        circle.setCenterY(y + (phase * 100));
                        circle.setFill(Color.rgb(red, green, blue, .70));
                        phaseNodes.getChildren().add(circle);
                        i+=5;
                    }
                }
            })
            .build();

        mediaPlayer.setOnReady(new Runnable() {
            @Override
            public void run() {
                mediaPlayer.play();
            }
        });
    }

    event.setDropCompleted(success);
    event.consume();
  }
}); // end of setOnDragDropped


// create slide controls
final Group buttonGroup = new Group();

// rounded rect
Rectangle buttonArea = RectangleBuilder.create()
        .arcWidth(15)
        .arcHeight(20)
        .fill(new Color(0, 0, 0, .55))
        .x(0)
        .y(0)
        .width(60)
        .height(30)
        .stroke(Color.rgb(255, 255, 255, .70))
        .build();

buttonGroup.getChildren().add(buttonArea);
// stop audio control
Node stopButton = RectangleBuilder.create()
        .arcWidth(5)
        .arcHeight(5)
        .fill(Color.rgb(255, 255, 255, .80))
        .x(0)
        .y(0)
        .width(10)
        .height(10)
```

```
            .translateX(15)
            .translateY(10)
            .stroke(Color.rgb(255, 255, 255, .70))
            .build();

    stopButton.setOnMousePressed(new EventHandler<MouseEvent>() {
        public void handle(MouseEvent me) {
            if (mediaPlayer!= null) {
             mediaPlayer.stop();
            }
        }
    });
    buttonGroup.getChildren().add(stopButton);

    // play control
    final Node playButton = ArcBuilder.create()
            .type(ArcType.ROUND)
            .centerX(12)
            .centerY(16)
            .radiusX(15)
            .radiusY(15)
            .startAngle(180-30)
            .length(60)
            .fill(new Color(1,1,1, .90))
            .translateX(40)
            .build();
    playButton.setOnMousePressed(new EventHandler<MouseEvent>() {
        public void handle(MouseEvent me) {
            mediaPlayer.play();
        }
    });


    // pause control
    final Group pause = new Group();
    final Node pauseButton = CircleBuilder.create()
            .centerX(12)
            .centerY(16)
            .radius(10)
            .stroke(new Color(1,1,1, .90))
            .translateX(30)
            .build();
    final Node firstLine = LineBuilder.create()
            .startX(6)
            .startY(16 - 10)
            .endX(6)
            .endY(16 - 2)
            .strokeWidth(3)
            .translateX(34)
            .translateY(6)
            .stroke(new Color(1,1,1, .90))
            .build();
```

```
        final Node secondLine = LineBuilder.create()
                .startX(6)
                .startY(16 - 10)
                .endX(6)
                .endY(16 - 2)
                .strokeWidth(3)
                .translateX(38)
                .translateY(6)
                .stroke(new Color(1,1,1, .90))
                .build();
        pause.getChildren().addAll(pauseButton, firstLine, secondLine);

        pause.setOnMousePressed(new EventHandler<MouseEvent>() {
            public void handle(MouseEvent me) {
                if (mediaPlayer!=null) {
                    buttonGroup.getChildren().remove(pause);
                    buttonGroup.getChildren().add(playButton);
                    mediaPlayer.pause();
                }
            }
        });

        playButton.setOnMousePressed(new EventHandler<MouseEvent>() {
            public void handle(MouseEvent me) {
                if (mediaPlayer != null) {
                    buttonGroup.getChildren().remove(playButton);
                    buttonGroup.getChildren().add(pause);
                    mediaPlayer.play();
                }
            }
        });

        buttonGroup.getChildren().add(pause);
        // move button group when scene is resized

buttonGroup.translateXProperty().bind(scene.widthProperty().subtract(buttonArea.getWidth() +
6));

buttonGroup.translateYProperty().bind(scene.heightProperty().subtract(buttonArea.getHeight()
+ 6));
        root.getChildren().add(buttonGroup);

        // close button
        final Group closeApp = new Group();
        Node closeButton = CircleBuilder.create()
                .centerX(5)
                .centerY(0)
                .radius(7)
                .fill(Color.rgb(255, 255, 255, .80))
                .build();
        Node closeXmark = new Text(2, 4, "X");
```

```
closeApp.translateXProperty().bind(scene.widthProperty().subtract(15));
closeApp.setTranslateY(10);
closeApp.getChildren().addAll(closeButton, closeXmark);
closeApp.setOnMouseClicked(new EventHandler<MouseEvent>() {
    @Override
    public void handle(MouseEvent event) {
        Platform.exit();
    }
});

root.getChildren().add(closeApp);

primaryStage.setScene(scene);
primaryStage.show();
previousLocation = new Point2D(primaryStage.getX(), primaryStage.getY());

    }
}
```

Figure 17-2 shows a JavaFX MP3 player with visualizations.

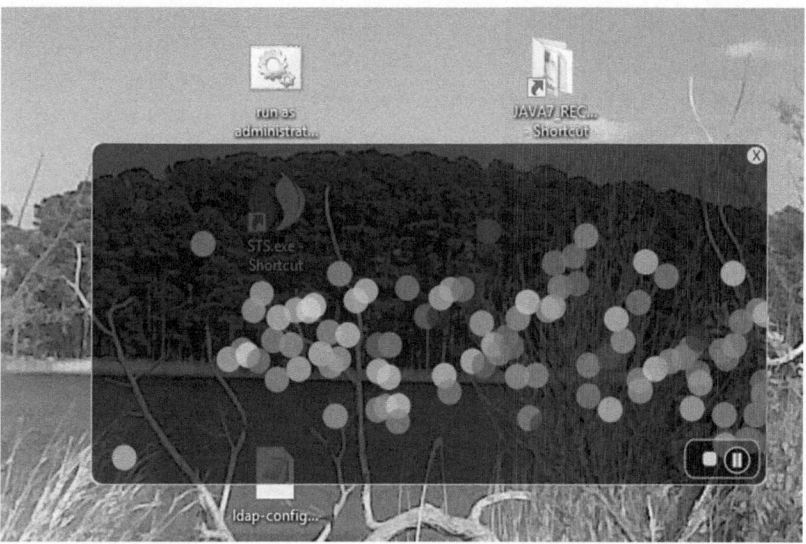

Figure 17-2. JavaFX MP3 player

How It Works

Before we get started, let's discuss the instructions on how to operate our MP3 player. A user will be able to drag and drop an audio file into the application area to be subsequently played. Located on the lower right of the application are buttons to stop, pause, and resume play of audio media. (The button controls are shown in Figure 17-2.) As the music is playing, the user will also notice randomly colored balls bouncing around to the music. Once the user is done with listening to music, he/she can quit the application by clicking the white rounded close button located in the upper-right corner.

It is similar to recipe 16-1, in which you learned how to use the drag-and-drop desktop metaphor to load files into a JavaFX application. Instead of image files, however, the user will be using audio files. To load audio files JavaFX currently supports the following file formats: .mp3, .wav, and .aiff.

Following the same look and feel, you will use the same style as recipe 16-1. In this recipe, I modified the button controls to resemble buttons, similar to many media player applications. When the pause button is pressed, it will pause the audio media from playing and toggle to the play button control, thus allowing the user to resume. As an added bonus, the MP3 player will appear as an irregular shaped, semitransparent window without borders that can also be dragged around the desktop using the mouse. Now that you know how to operate the music player, let's walk through the code.

First, you will create instance variables that will maintain state information for the lifetime of the application. Table 17-1 describes all instance variables used in our music player application. The first variable is a reference to a media player (MediaPlayer) object that will be created in conjunction with a Media object containing an audio file. Next, you will create an anchorPt variable used to save the starting coordinate of a mouse press when the user begins to drag the window across the screen. When calculating the upper-left bounds of the application window during a mouse-dragged operation, the previousLocation variable will contain the previous window's screen X and Y coordinates.

Table 17-1 lists the MP3 player application's instance variables:

Table 17-1. MP3 Player Application Instance Variables

Variable	Data Type	Example	Description
mediaPlayer	MediaPlayer	n/a	A media player control that plays audio and video
anchorPt	Point2D	100,100	A coordinate where the user begins to drag the window
previousLocation	Point2D	0,0	The upper-left corner of the stage's previous coordinate; assists in dragging the window

In previous chapters relating to GUIs, you saw that GUI applications normally contain a title bar and windowed borders surrounding the Scene. Here, I wanted to raise the bar a little by showing you how to create irregularly shaped semitransparent windows, thus making things look more hip or modern. As you begin to create the media player, you'll notice in the start() method that we prepare the Stage object by initializing the style using StageStyle.TRANSPARENT. After we initialize the style to StageStyle.TRANSPARENT, the window will be undecorated, with the entire window area opaque set to zero (invisible). The following code shows how to create a transparent window without a title bar or windowed borders:

```
primaryStage.initStyle(StageStyle.TRANSPARENT);
```

With the invisible stage you will create a rounded rectangular region that will be the applications surface, or main content area. Next, you will notice the width and height of the rectangle bound to the scene object in case the window is resized. Because the window isn't going to be resized, the bind isn't necessary (it will be needed, however in recipe 17-2, when you get a chance to enlarge your video screen to take on a full screen mode).

After creating a black, semitransparent, rounded, rectangular area (applicationArea), you'll be creating a simple Group object to hold all the randomly colored Circle nodes that will show off graphical visualizations while the audio is being played. Later, you will see how the phaseNodes (Group) variable is updated based on sound information using an AudioSpectrumListener.

Next, you will be adding EventHandler<MouseEvent> instances to the Scene object to monitor mouse events as the user drags the window around the screen. The first event in this scenario is a mouse press, which will save the cursor's current (X, Y) coordinates to the variable anchorPt. The following code is adding an EventHandler to the mouse pressed property of the Scene:

```
// starting initial anchor point
scene.setOnMousePressed(new EventHandler<MouseEvent>() {
    public void handle(MouseEvent event){
        anchorPt = new Point2D(event.getScreenX(), event.getScreenY());
    }
});
```

After implementing the mouse press event handler, you can create an EventHandler to the Scene's mouse-dragged property. The mouse–dragged event handler will update and position the application window (Stage) dynamically, based on the previous window's location (upper-left corner) along with the anchorPt variable. Shown here is an event handler responsible for the mouse-dragged event on the Scene object:

```
// dragging the entire stage
scene.setOnMouseDragged(new EventHandler<MouseEvent>() {
    public void handle(MouseEvent event){
        if (anchorPt != null && previousLocation != null) {
            primaryStage.setX(previousLocation.getX() + event.getScreenX() -
anchorPt.getX());
            primaryStage.setY(previousLocation.getY() + event.getScreenY() -
anchorPt.getY());
        }
    }
});
```

You will want to handle the mouse-released event. Once the mouse is released, the event handler will update the previousLocation variable for subsequent mouse-dragged events to move the application window about the screen. The following code snippet updates the previousLocation variable:

```
// set the current location
scene.setOnMouseReleased(new EventHandler<MouseEvent>() {
    public void handle(MouseEvent event){
        previousLocation = new Point2D(primaryStage.getX(), primaryStage.getY());
    }
});
```

Next, you will be implementing the drag-and-drop scenario to load the audio file from the file system (File manager). When handling a drag-and-drop scenario, it is similar to recipe 16-1, in which you created an EventHandler to handle DragEvents. Instead of loading image files we will be loading audio files from the host file system. For brevity, I will simply mention the code lines of the drag-and-dropped event handler. Once the audio file is available, you will create a Media object by passing in the file as a URI. The following code snippet is how to create a Media object:

Media media = new Media(new File(filePath).toURI().toString());

Once you have created a Media object you will have to create an instance of a MediaPlayer in order to play the sound file. Both the Media and MediaPlayer objects are immutable, which is why new instances of each will be created every time the user drags a file into the application. Next, you will check the instance variable `mediaPlayer` for a previous instance to make sure it is stopped before creating a new `MediaPlayer` instance. The following code checks for a prior media player to be stopped:

```
if (mediaPlayer != null) {
  mediaPlayer.stop();
}
```

So, here is where we create a `MediaPlayer` instance. For ease of coding you will be turning to the `MediaPlayer`'s builder class `MediaPlayerBuilder`. A `MediaPlayer` object is responsible for controlling the playing of media objects. Notice that a `MediaPlayer` will treat sound or video media the same in terms of playing, pausing, and stopping media. When creating a media player using the `MediaPlayerBuilder` class, you will be specifying the `media` and `audioSpectrumListener` attribute methods. Setting the autoPlay attribute to true will play the audio media immediately after it has been loaded. The last thing to specify on the `MediaPlayer` instance is an `AudioSpectrumListener`. So, what exactly is this type of listener, you say? Well, according to the Javadocs, it states that it is an observer receiving periodic updates of the audio spectrum. In layman's terms, it is the audio media's sound data such as volume and tempo, and so on. To create an instance of an `AudioSpectrumListener` you will create an inner class overriding the method `spectrumDataUpdate()`. Table 17-2 lists all inbound parameters for the audio spectrum listener's method. For more details refer to the Javadocs at `http://download.oracle.com/javafx/2.0/api/javafx/scene/media/AudioSpectrumListener.html`.

Table 17-2. The AudioSpectrumListener s Method spectrumDataUpdate() Inbound Parameters

Variable	Data Type	Example	Description
timestamp	double	2.4261	When the event occurred, in seconds
duration	Double	0.1	The duration of time (in seconds) the spectrum was computed
magnitudes	float[]	-50.474335	An array of float values representing each band's spectrum magnitude in decibels (nonpositive float value)
phases	float[]	1.2217305	An array of float values representing each band's phase

Here, you will be creating randomly colored circle nodes to be positioned and placed on the scene based on the variable phases (array of floats). To draw each colored circle, you will be incrementing the circle's center X by 5 pixels and adding the circle's center Y with each phase value multiplied by 100. Shown here is the code snippet that plots each randomly colored circle:

```
        circle.setCenterX(x + i);
        circle.setCenterY(y + (phase * 100));
        ... // setting the circle
        i+=5;
```

Here is an inner class implementation of an `AudioSpectrumListener`:

```
        new AudioSpectrumListener() {
            @Override
            public void spectrumDataUpdate(double timestamp, double duration, float[]
magnitudes, float[] phases) {

                phaseNodes.getChildren().clear();
```

```
                    int i = 0;
                    int x = 10;
                    int y = 150;
                    final Random rand = new Random(System.currentTimeMillis());
                    for(float phase:phases) {
                      int red = rand.nextInt(255);
                      int green = rand.nextInt(255);
                      int blue = rand.nextInt(255);

                      Circle circle = new Circle(10);
                      circle.setCenterX(x + i);
                      circle.setCenterY(y + (phase * 100));
                      circle.setFill(Color.rgb(red, green, blue, .70));
                      phaseNodes.getChildren().add(circle);
                      i+=5;
                    }

                  }
                };
```

Once the media player is created, you will create a `java.lang.Runnable` to be set into the `onReady` attribute to be invoked when the media is in a ready state. Once the ready event is realized the `run()` method will call the media player object's `play()` method to begin the audio. With the dragged-drop sequence completed, we appropriately notify the drag-and-drop system by invoking the event's `setDropCompleted()` method with a value of true. The following code snippet implements a `Runnable` to begin the media player as soon as the media player is in a ready state:

```
mediaPlayer.setOnReady(new Runnable() {
    @Override
    public void run() {
        mediaPlayer.play();
    }
});
```

Finally you will be creating buttons with JavaFX shapes to represent the stop, play, pause, and close buttons. When creating shapes or custom nodes, you can add event handlers to nodes in order to respond to mouse clicks. Although there are advanced ways to build custom controls in JavaFX, I chose to build my own button icons from simple rectangles, arcs, circles and lines. To see more-advanced ways to create custom controls, refer to the Javadocs on the `Skinnable` API or recipe 16-5. To attach event handlers for a mouse press, simply call the `setOnMousePress()` method by passing in an `EventHandler<MouseEvent>` instance. The following code demonstrates adding an `EventHandler` to respond to mouse press on the `stopButton` node:

```
        stopButton.setOnMousePressed(new EventHandler<MouseEvent>() {
            public void handle(MouseEvent me) {
                if (mediaPlayer!= null) {
                    mediaPlayer.stop();
                }
            }
        });
```

Because all the buttons use the same preceding code snippet, I will only list the method calls that each button will perform on the media player. The last button, Close, isn't related to the media player, but it is how to exit the MP3 player application. The following actions are responsible for stopping, pausing, playing, and exiting the MP3 player application:

```
Stop - mediaPlayer.stop();
Pause - mediaPlayer.pause();
Play - mediaPlayer.play();
Close - Platform.exit();
```

17-2. Playing Video

Problem

You want to view a video file complete with controls to play, pause, stop, and seek.

Solution

Create a video media player by utilizing the following classes:

- `javafx.scene.media.Media`

- `javafx.scene.media.MediaPlayer`

- `javafx.scene.media.MediaView`

The following code is an implementation of a JavaFX basic video player:

```
public void start(final Stage primaryStage) {
    primaryStage.setTitle("Chapter 17-2 Playing Video");
    ... setting up the stage

    // rounded rectangle with slightly transparent
    Node applicationArea = createBackground(scene);
    root.getChildren().add(applicationArea);

    // allow the user to drag window on the desktop
    attachMouseEvents(scene, primaryStage);

    // allows the user to see the progress of the video playing
    progressSlider = createSlider(scene);
    root.getChildren().add(progressSlider);

    // Dragging over surface
    scene.setOnDragOver(! Drag Over code );

    // update slider as video is progressing (later removal)
    progressListener = new ChangeListener<Duration>() {
```

```
            public void changed(ObservableValue<? extends Duration> observable, Duration
    oldValue, Duration newValue) {
            progressSlider.setValue(newValue.toSeconds());
        }
    };


    // Dropping over surface
    scene.setOnDragDropped(new EventHandler<DragEvent>() {

        @Override
        public void handle(DragEvent event) {
            Dragboard db = event.getDragboard();
            boolean success = false;
            URI resourceUrlOrFile = null;

            ! // detect and obtain media file

            // load media
            Media media = new Media(resourceUrlOrFile.toString());

            // stop previous media player and clean up
            if (mediaPlayer != null) {
                mediaPlayer.stop();
                mediaPlayer.currentTimeProperty().removeListener(progressListener);
                mediaPlayer.setOnPaused(null);
                mediaPlayer.setOnPlaying(null);
                mediaPlayer.setOnReady(null);
            }

            // create a new media player
            mediaPlayer = MediaPlayerBuilder.create()
                    .media(media)
                    .build();

            // as the media is playing move the slider for progress
            mediaPlayer.currentTimeProperty().addListener(progressListener);


            // play video when ready status
            mediaPlayer.setOnReady(new Runnable() {
                @Override
                public void run() {
                    progressSlider.setValue(1);

progressSlider.setMax(mediaPlayer.getMedia().getDuration().toMillis()/1000);
                    mediaPlayer.play();
                }
            });

            // Lazy init media viewer
            if (mediaView == null) {
```

634

```
                mediaView = MediaViewBuilder.create()
                        .mediaPlayer(mediaPlayer)
                        .x(4)
                        .y(4)
                        .preserveRatio(true)
                        .opacity(.85)
                        .smooth(true)
                        .build();

mediaView.fitWidthProperty().bind(scene.widthProperty().subtract(220));

mediaView.fitHeightProperty().bind(scene.heightProperty().subtract(30));

                // make media view as the second node on the scene.
                root.getChildren().add(1, mediaView);
            }

            // sometimes loading errors occur
            mediaView.setOnError(new EventHandler<MediaErrorEvent>() {
                public void handle(MediaErrorEvent event) {
                    event.getMediaError().printStackTrace();
                }
            });

            mediaView.setMediaPlayer(mediaPlayer);

            event.setDropCompleted(success);
            event.consume();
        }
    });

    // rectangular area holding buttons
    final Group buttonArea = createButtonArea(scene);

    // stop button will stop and rewind the media
    Node stopButton = createStopControl();

    // play button can resume or start a media
    final Node playButton = createPlayControl();

    // pauses media play
    final Node pauseButton = createPauseControl();

    stopButton.setOnMousePressed(new EventHandler<MouseEvent>() {
        public void handle(MouseEvent me) {
            if (mediaPlayer!= null) {
                buttonArea.getChildren().removeAll(pauseButton, playButton);
                buttonArea.getChildren().add(playButton);
                mediaPlayer.stop();
            }
        }
    });
```

```java
        // pause media and swap button with play button
        pauseButton.setOnMousePressed(new EventHandler<MouseEvent>() {
            public void handle(MouseEvent me) {
                if (mediaPlayer!=null) {
                    buttonArea.getChildren().removeAll(pauseButton, playButton);
                    buttonArea.getChildren().add(playButton);
                    mediaPlayer.pause();
                    paused = true;
                }
            }
        });

        // play media and swap button with pause button
        playButton.setOnMousePressed(new EventHandler<MouseEvent>() {
            public void handle(MouseEvent me) {
                if (mediaPlayer != null) {
                    buttonArea.getChildren().removeAll(pauseButton, playButton);
                    buttonArea.getChildren().add(pauseButton);
                    paused = false;
                    mediaPlayer.play();
                }
            }
        });

        // add stop button to button area
        buttonArea.getChildren().add(stopButton);

        // set pause button as default
        buttonArea.getChildren().add(pauseButton);

        // add buttons
        root.getChildren().add(buttonArea);

        // create a close button
        Node closeButton= createCloseButton(scene);
        root.getChildren().add(closeButton);

        primaryStage.setOnShown(new EventHandler<WindowEvent>() {
            public void handle(WindowEvent we) {
                previousLocation = new Point2D(primaryStage.getX(),
primaryStage.getY());
            }
        });

        primaryStage.setScene(scene);
        primaryStage.show();

    }
```

Following is our `attachMouseEvents()` method that adds an `EventHandler` to the `Scene` to provide the ability to make the video player go into full screen mode.

```
private void attachMouseEvents(Scene scene, final Stage primaryStage) {

    // Full screen toggle
    scene.setOnMouseClicked(new EventHandler<MouseEvent>() {
        public void handle(MouseEvent event){
            if (event.getClickCount() == 2) {
                primaryStage.setFullScreen(!primaryStage.isFullScreen());
            }
        }
    });
    ... // the rest of the EventHandlers
}
```

The following code is a method that creates a slider control with a `ChangeListener` to enable the user to seek backward and forward through the video:

```
private Slider createSlider(Scene scene) {
    Slider slider = SliderBuilder.create()
            .min(0)
            .max(100)
            .value(1)
            .showTickLabels(true)
            .showTickMarks(true)
            .build();

    slider.valueProperty().addListener(new ChangeListener<Number>() {
        public void changed(ObservableValue<? extends Number> observable, Number
oldValue, Number newValue) {
            if (paused) {
                long dur = newValue.intValue() * 1000;
                mediaPlayer.seek(new Duration(dur));
            }
        }
    });
    slider.translateYProperty().bind(scene.heightProperty().subtract(30));
    return slider;
}
```

Figure 17-3 depicts a JavaFX basic video player with a slider control.

Figure 17-3. JavaFX basic video player

How It Works

To create a video player you will model the application similar to recipe 17-1 by reusing the same application features such as drag-and-drop files, media button controls, and so on. For the sake of clarity, I took the previous recipe and moved much of the UI code into convenience functions so you will be able to focus on the Media APIs without getting lost in the UI code. The rest of the recipes in this chapter consist of adding simple features to the JavaFX basic media player created in this recipe. This being said, the code snippets in the following recipes will be brief, consisting of the necessary code needed for each new desired feature.

Before we begin, I want to talk about media formats. As of the writing of this book. JavaFX 2.0 supports a cross-platform video format called VP6 with a file extension of .flv (which stands for the popular Adobe Flash Video format). The actual encoder and decoder (Codec) to create VP6 and .flv files are licensed through a company called On2. In 2009, On2 was acquired by Google to build VP7 and VP8 to be open and free to advance HTML5. I don't want to confuse you with the drama, but it is difficult to see how things will unfold as media formats become favored or considered obsolete. Because JavaFX's goal is to be cross-platform, it would seem logical to use the most popular codec on the Net, but you will be forced to obtain a license to encode your videos into the VP6 .flv file format. So the bottom line is that JavaFX currently can only play video files that are encoded in VP6. (I try to keep in mind that this is the state of media formats today, so don't channel any frustrations toward the JavaFX SDK.) Please refer to the Javadoc API for more details on the formats to be used. A word to the wise: beware of web sites claiming to be able to convert videos for free. As of this writing, the only encoders capable of encoding video to VP6 legally are the commercial converters from Adobe and Wildform (http://www.wildform.com).

Now, that you know what is the acceptable file format you are probably wondering how to obtain such a file of this type if you don't have encoding software. If you don't have an .flv file lying around, you can obtain one from one of my favorite sites called the Media College (http://www.mediacollege.com). From photography to movies, Media College provides forums, tutorials, and resources that help guide you into the world of media. There you will obtain a particular media file to be used in the remaining recipes in this chapter. To obtain the .flv file you will navigate to the following URL: http://www.mediacollege.com/adobe/flash/video/tutorial/example-flv.html.

Next, you will locate the link entitled `Windy 50s Mobility Scooter Race` that points to our `.flv` media file (`20051210-w50s.flv`). In order to download a link consisting of a file, right-click to select "Save target as" or "Save link as". Once you have saved the file locally on your file system, you can drag the file into the media player application to begin the demo.

■ **Note** As of the writing of this book, the JavaFX media player API currently supports the video format VP6 using an `.flv` container.

Just like the audio player created in the last recipe, our JavaFX basic video player has the same basic media controls, including stop, pause, and play. In addition to these simple controls we have added new capabilities such as seeking and full screen mode.

When playing a video you'll need a view area (`javafx.scene.media.MediaView`) to show the video. You will also be creating a slider control to monitor the progress of the video, which is located at the lower left of the application shown in Figure 17-3. The slider control allows the user to seek backward and forward through the video. The ability to seek will work only if the video is paused. One last bonus feature is making the video become full screen by double-clicking the application window. To restore the window, repeat the double click or press Escape.

To quickly get started, let's jump into the code. After setting up the stage in the `start()` method, you will create a black semitransparent background by calling the `createBackground()` method (`applicationArea`). Next, you will be invoking the `attachMouseEvents()` method to wire up all the `EventHandlers` into the scene that will enable the user to drag the application window about the desktop. Another `EventHandler` to be attached to the `Scene` will allow the user to switch to full screen mode. To make a window turn into full screen mode, you will create a conditional to check for the double click of the application window. Once the double-click is performed you will call the `Stage`'s method `setFullScreen()` with a Boolean value opposite of the currently set value. Shown here is how to make a window go to full screen mode:

```
// Full screen toggle
scene.setOnMouseClicked(new EventHandler<MouseEvent>() {
    public void handle(MouseEvent event){
        if (event.getClickCount() == 2) {
            primaryStage.setFullScreen(!primaryStage.isFullScreen());
        }
    }
});
```

As we continue our steps inside the `start()` method, you will create a slider control by calling the convenience method `createSlider()`. The `createSlider()` method will instantiate a `Slider` control and add a `ChangeListener` to move the slider as the video is playing. The `ChangeListener`'s `changed()` method is invoked any time the slider's value changes. Once the `changed()` method is invoked you will have an opportunity to see the old value and the new value. The following code creates a `ChangeListener` to update the slider as the video is being played:

```
// update slider as video is progressing (later removal)
progressListener = new ChangeListener<Duration>() {
```

```
            public void changed(ObservableValue<? extends Duration> observable, Duration
    oldValue, Duration newValue) {
                progressSlider.setValue(newValue.toSeconds());
            }
        };
```

After creating the progress listener (progressListener), you will be creating the dragged-dropped EventHandler on the Scene.

The goal is to determine whether the pause button was pressed before the user can move the slider. Once a paused flag is determined, you will obtain the new value to be converted to milliseconds. The dur variable is used to move the mediaPlayer to seek the position into the video as the user slides the control left or right. The ChangeListener's changed() method is invoked any time the slider's value changes. The following code is responsible for moving the seek position into the video based on the user moving the slider.

```
slider.valueProperty().addListener(new ChangeListener<Number>() {
    public void changed(ObservableValue<? extends Number> observable, Number oldValue, Number
newValue) {
            if (paused) {
                long dur = newValue.intValue() * 1000;
                mediaPlayer.seek(new Duration(dur));
            }
        }
    });
```

Moving right along, you will be implementing a drag-dropped EventHandler to handle the .flv media file being dropped into the application window area. Here you'll first check to see whether there was a previous mediaPlayer. If so, you will stop the previous mediaPlayer object and do some cleanup:

```
        // stop previous media player and clean up
        if (mediaPlayer != null) {
            mediaPlayer.stop();
            mediaPlayer.currentTimeProperty().removeListener(progressListener);
            mediaPlayer.setOnPaused(null);
            mediaPlayer.setOnPlaying(null);
            mediaPlayer.setOnReady(null);
        }


        // play video when ready status
        mediaPlayer.setOnReady(new Runnable() {
            @Override
            public void run() {
                progressSlider.setValue(1);

        progressSlider.setMax(mediaPlayer.getMedia().getDuration().toMillis()/1000);
            mediaPlayer.play();
            }
    }); // setOnReady()
```

As with the audio player, we create a `Runnable` instance to be run when the media player is in a ready state. You'll notice also that the `progressSlider` control being set up to use values in seconds.

Once the media player object is in a ready state you will be creating a `MediaView` instance to display the media. Shown following is the creation of a `MediaView` object to be put into the scene graph to display video content:

```
// Lazy init media viewer
if (mediaView == null) {
    mediaView = MediaViewBuilder.create()
            .mediaPlayer(mediaPlayer)
            .x(4)
            .y(4)
            .preserveRatio(true)
            .opacity(.85)
            .build();


    mediaView.fitWidthProperty().bind(scene.widthProperty().subtract(220));

    mediaView.fitHeightProperty().bind(scene.heightProperty().subtract(30));

        // make media view as the second node on the scene.
        root.getChildren().add(1, mediaView);
    }

    // sometimes loading errors occur
    mediaView.setOnError(new EventHandler<MediaErrorEvent>() {
        public void handle(MediaErrorEvent event) {
            event.getMediaError().printStackTrace();
        }
    });

    mediaView.setMediaPlayer(mediaPlayer);
    event.setDropCompleted(success);
    event.consume();
    }
});
```

Whew! We are finally finished with our drag-dropped `EventHandler` for our Scene. Up next is pretty much the rest of the media button controls similar to the end of recipe 17-1. The only thing different is a single instance variable named `paused` of type `boolean` that denotes whether the video was paused. This `paused` flag when set to true will allow the slider control to seek forward or backward through the video; otherwise false. Following is the `pauseButton` and `playButton` controlling the `mediaPlayer` object and setting the `paused` flag accordingly:

```
// pause media and swap button with play button
pauseButton.setOnMousePressed(new EventHandler<MouseEvent>() {
    public void handle(MouseEvent me) {
        if (mediaPlayer!=null) {
            buttonArea.getChildren().removeAll(pauseButton, playButton);
            buttonArea.getChildren().add(playButton);
```

```
                    mediaPlayer.pause();
                    paused = true;
                }
            }
        });

        // play media and swap button with pause button
        playButton.setOnMousePressed(new EventHandler<MouseEvent>() {
            public void handle(MouseEvent me) {
                if (mediaPlayer != null) {
                    buttonArea.getChildren().removeAll(pauseButton, playButton);
                    buttonArea.getChildren().add(pauseButton);
                    paused = false;
                    mediaPlayer.play();
                }
            }
        });
```

So that is how to create a video media player. In the next recipe, you will be able to listen to media events and invoke actions.

17-3. Controlling Media Actions and Events

Problem

You want the media player to provide feedback in response to certain events. An example is displaying the text "Paused" on the screen when the media player's paused event is triggered.

Solution

You can use many media event handler methods. Shown in Table 17-3 are all the possible media events that are raised to allow the developer to attach EventHandlers or Runnables.

Table 17-3. Media Events

Class	Set On Method	On Method Property Method	Description
Media	setOnError()	onErrorProperty()	When an error occurs
MediaPlayer	setOnEndOfMedia()	onEndOfMediaProperty()	Reached the end of the media play
MediaPlayer	setOnError()	onErrorProperty()	Error occurred
MediaPlayer	setOnHalted()	onHaltedProperty()	Media status changes to HALTED
MediaPlayer	setOnMarker()	onMarkerProperty()	Marker event triggered
MediaPlayer	setOnPaused()	onPausedProperty()	Paused event occurred

MediaPlayer	setOnPlaying()	onPlayingProperty()	The media is currently playing
MediaPlayer	setOnReady()	onReadyProperty()	Media player is in Ready state
MediaPlayer	setOnRepeat()	onRepeatProperty()	Repeat property is set
MediaPlayer	setOnStalled()	onStalledProperty()	Media player is stalled
MediaPlayer	setOnStopped()	onStoppedProperty()	Media player has stopped
MediaView	setOnError()	onErrorProperty()	Error occurred in Media View

The following code will present to the user a text "Paused" with "Duration" with a decimal of milliseconds which is overlaid on top of the video when the user clicks the pause button (see Figure 17-4):

```
// when paused event display pause message
mediaPlayer.setOnPaused(new Runnable() {
    @Override
    public void run() {
        pauseMessage.setText("Paused \nDuration: " +
mediaPlayer.currentTimeProperty().getValue().toMillis());
        pauseMessage.setOpacity(.90);

    }
});
```

Figure 17-4. Paused event

How It Works

An event driven architecture (EDA) is a prominent architectural pattern used to model loosely coupled components and services that pass messages asynchronously. The JavaFX team has designed the Media API to be event driven. This recipe will demonstrate how to implement in response to media events.

With event-based programming in mind, you will discover nonblocking or callback behaviors when invoking functions. In this recipe you will implement the display of text in response to an onPaused event instead of placing your code into the pause button. Instead of tying code directly to a button via an EventHandler, you will be implementing code that will respond to the media player's onPaused event being triggered. When responding to media events, you will be implementing java.lang.Runnables.

You'll be happy to know that you've been using event properties and implementing Runnables all along. Hopefully you noticed this in all the recipes in this chapter. When the media player is in a ready state, the Runnable code will be invoked. Why is this correct? Well, when the media player is finished loading the media, the onReady property will be notified. That way you can be sure you can invoke the MediaPlayer's play() method. I trust that you will get used to event style programming. The following code snippet demonstrates the setting of a Runnable instance into a media player object's OnReady property:

```
mediaPlayer.setOnReady(new Runnable() {
    @Override
    public void run() {
        mediaPlayer.play();
    }
});
```

You will be taking steps similar to the onReady property. Once a Paused event has been triggered, the run() method will be invoked to present to the user a message containing a Text node with the word Paused and a duration showing the time in milliseconds into the video. Once displayed, you might want to write down the duration as markers (as you'll learn recipe 17-4). The following code snippet shows an attached Runnable instance, which is responsible for displaying a paused message and duration in milliseconds at the point in which it was paused in the video:

```
// when paused event display pause message
mediaPlayer.setOnPaused(new Runnable() {
    @Override
    public void run() {
        pauseMessage.setText("Paused \nDuration: " +
mediaPlayer.currentTimeProperty().getValue().toMillis());
        pauseMessage.setOpacity(.90);

    }
});
```

17-4. Marking a Position in a Video

Problem

You want to provide closed caption text while playing a video in the media player.

Solution

Begin by applying recipe 17-3. By obtaining the marked durations (in milliseconds) from the previous recipe you will create media marker events at points into the video. With each media marker you will associate text that will be displayed as closed captions. When a marker comes to pass, a text will be shown to the upper-right side.

The following code snippet demonstrates media marker events being handled in the onDragDropped event property of the Scene object:

```
... // inside the start() method

final VBox messageArea = createClosedCaptionArea(scene);
root.getChildren().add(messageArea);

// Dropping over surface
scene.setOnDragDropped(new EventHandler<DragEvent>() {

    @Override
    public void handle(DragEvent event) {
        Dragboard db = event.getDragboard();

        ... // drag dropped code goes here


        // load media
        Media media = new Media(resourceUrlOrFile.toString());

        ... // clean up media player

        // create a new media player
        mediaPlayer = MediaPlayerBuilder.create()
                .media(media)
                .build();

        ...// Set media !onXXX! event properties

        mediaView.setMediaPlayer(mediaPlayer);

        media.getMarkers().put("Starting race", Duration.millis(1959.183673));
        media.getMarkers().put("He is begining \nto get ahead",
Duration.millis(3395.918367));
        media.getMarkers().put("They are turning \nthe corner",
Duration.millis(6060.408163));
        media.getMarkers().put("The crowds cheer", Duration.millis(9064.489795));
        media.getMarkers().put("He makes the \nfinish line", Duration.millis(11546.122448));

        // display closed captions
        mediaPlayer.setOnMarker(new EventHandler<MediaMarkerEvent> (){
            public void handle(MediaMarkerEvent event){
                closedCaption.setText(event.getMarker().getKey());
```

```
            }
        });

        event.setDropCompleted(success);
        event.consume();
    }
}); // end of setOnDragDropped()
```

Shown following is a factory method that returns an area that will contain the closed caption to be displayed to the right of the video:

```
private VBox createClosedCaptionArea(final Scene scene) {
    // create message area
    final VBox messageArea = new VBox(3);
    messageArea.setTranslateY(30);
    messageArea.translateXProperty().bind(scene.widthProperty().subtract(152) );
    messageArea.setTranslateY(20);
    closedCaption = TextBuilder.create()
        .stroke(Color.WHITE)
        .fill(Color.YELLOW)
        .font(new Font(15))
        .build();
    messageArea.getChildren().add(closedCaption);
    return messageArea;
}
```

Figure 17-5 depicts the video media player displaying closed caption text.

Figure 17-5. Closed caption text

How It Works

The Media API has many event properties that the developer can attach EventHandlers or Runnables instances so they can respond when the events are triggered. Here you focus on the OnMarker event property. The Marker property is responsible for receiving marker events (MediaMarkerEvent).

Let's begin by adding markers into our Media object. It contains a method getMarkers() that returns an javafx.collections.ObservableMap<String, Duration>. With an observable map, you can add key value pairs that represent each marker. Adding keys should be a unique identifier, and the value is an instance of Duration. For simplicity I used the closed caption text as the key for each media marker. The marker durations are those written down as you press the pause button at points in the video from recipe 17-3. Please be advised that I don't recommend doing this in production code. You may want to use a parallel Map.

After adding markers you will be setting an EventHandler into the MediaPlayer object's OnMarker property using the setOnMarker() method. Next, you will create the EventHandler instance to handle MediaMarkerEvents that are raised. Once an event has been received, obtain the key representing the text to be used in the closed caption. The instance variable closedCaption (javafx.scene.text.Text node) will simply be shown by calling the setText() method with the key or string associated to a marker.

That's it for media markers. That goes to show you how you can coordinate special effects, animations, and so on during a video quite easily.

17-5. Synchronizing Animation and Media

Problem

You want to incorporate animated effects in your media display such as scrolling text "The End" after the video is finished playing.

Solution

Use recipe 17-3 together with recipe 16-2. In recipe 17-3 response to media events and recipe 16-2 demonstrates how to use translate transition to animate text.

The following code demonstrates an attached action when an end of a media event is triggered:

```
mediaPlayer.setOnEndOfMedia(new Runnable() {
    @Override
    public void run() {
        closedCaption.setText("");
        animateTheEnd.getNode().setOpacity(.90);
        animateTheEnd.playFromStart();
    }
});
```

Shown here is a method that creates a translateTransition of a Text node containing the string "The End" that animates after an end of media event is triggered:

```
public TranslateTransition createTheEnd(Scene scene) {
    Text theEnd = TextBuilder.create()
```

```
        .text("The End")
        .font(new Font(40))
        .strokeWidth(3)
        .fill(Color.WHITE)
        .stroke(Color.WHITE)
        .x(75)
        .build();

    TranslateTransition scrollUp = TranslateTransitionBuilder.create()
        .node(theEnd)
        .duration(Duration.seconds(1))
        .interpolator(Interpolator.EASE_IN)
        .fromY(scene.getHeight() + 40)
        .toY(scene.getHeight()/2)
        .build();
    return scrollUp;
}
```

Figure 17-6 depicts the text node "The End" scrolling up after the OnEndOfMedia event is triggered.

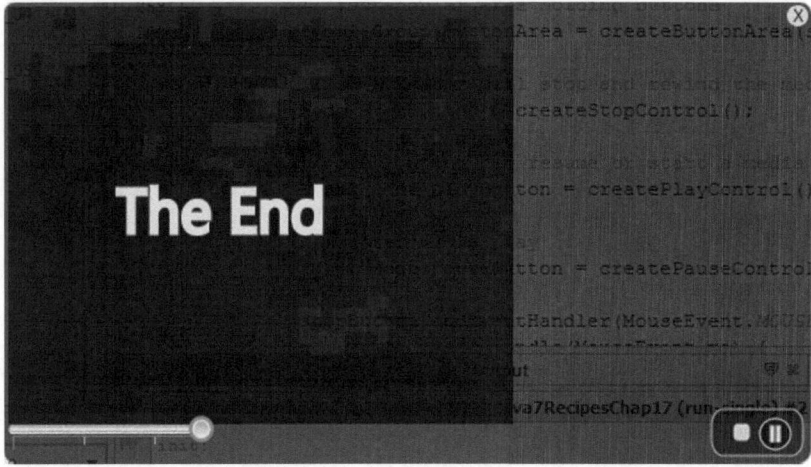

Figure 17-6. Animate The End

How It Works

In this recipe you will be able to synchronize events to animated effects. In other words, when the video reaches the end, an OnEndOfMedia property event will initiate a Runnable instance. Once initiated, a TranslateTransition animation is performed by scrolling a Text node upward with the string "The End".

So, let me describe the setOnEndOfMedia() method associated with the MediaPlayer object. Just like recipe 17-3, we simply call the setOnEndOfMedia() method by passing in a Runnable that contains our code that will invoke an animation. If you don't know how animation works, please refer to recipe 16-2.

Once the event occurs, you will see the text scroll upward. The following code snippet is from inside the `scene.setOnDragDropped()` method:

```
mediaPlayer.setOnEndOfMedia(new Runnable() {
    @Override
    public void run() {
        closedCaption.setText("");
        animateTheEnd.getNode().setOpacity(.90);
        animateTheEnd.playFromStart();
    }
});
```

For the sake of space, I trust you know where the code block would reside. If not, you may refer to recipe 17-3, in which you will notice other OnXXX properties methods. To see the entire code listing, visit the book's web site to download the source code.

To animate the text "The End" you will create a convenience `createTheEnd()` method to create an instance of a Text node and return a `TranslateTransition` object to the caller. The `TranslateTransition` returned will do the following: wait a second before playing video. Next is the interpolator in which I used the `Interpolator.EASE_IN` to move the Text node by easing in before a full stop. Last is setting up the Y property of the node to move from the bottom to the center of the Media view area.

The following code is an animation to scroll a node in an upward motion:

```
TranslateTransition scrollUp = TranslateTransitionBuilder.create()
            .node(theEnd)
            .duration(Duration.seconds(1))
            .interpolator(Interpolator.EASE_IN)
            .fromY(scene.getHeight() + 40)
            .toY(scene.getHeight()/2)
            .build();
```

Working with Servlets and Applets

The Java language provides a rich infrastructure for creation of web-based applications. Developing Java applications for the Web has become more popular throughout the years. The servlet was one of the first technologies that allowed developers to create dynamic content for the Web. Applets first appeared in the early days of Java development and they changed the concept of web development forever. These two technologies have been around for the majority of the lifetime of the Java language itself, and they are both still going strong.

Although the direct usage of the Java servlet API has decreased over time, it still remains the base for most of the web application development frameworks that are widely used today. Application frameworks such as Java Server Pages (JSP) and Java Server Faces (JSF) are built upon servlet technology. Applets have also evolved over the years from using the Abstract Windowing Toolkit (AWT) to including Java Swing, and most recently JavaFX for deploying solid Java-based applications over the Web.

This chapter will get you started developing both servlets and applets. The recipes within this chapter will teach you the basics for developing on each of these technologies, and they touch upon some of the most important concepts of each.

18-1. Setting Up a Servlet Environment

Problem

You would like to create a set up a development environment for testing and running Java Servlets using Java SE 7.

Solution

Download and install Apache Tomcat from the Tomcat web site. The version used for this book is 7.0.20, and it can be downloaded from http://tomcat.apache.org/. Select the .zip or tar.gz download format, and decompress the downloaded files within a directory on your workstation. We will refer to that directory as /JAVA_DEV/Tomcat. Set the JAVA_HOME environment variable to point to your Java runtime.

Once you have unzipped the contents of the download, you are ready to start developing servlet applications.

How It Works

You can use any Java servlet container for working with Java servlets, as long as you are using the correct JDK version for that container. For the purposes of this chapter, we will utilize one of the most commonly used containers: Apache Tomcat. The Apache Tomcat 7.0.20 release is compatible with Java 1.6 (JDK 6) and up, so it works just fine with Java SE 7.

You have a couple of options in order to set up your environment for running the examples within this chapter:

- You can install an IDE such as NetBeans or Eclipse; then install Tomcat 7.0.20 separately and register it with the IDE. Please see the IDE documentation for more details.

- You can install Tomcat 7.0.20 and set up your examples manually. This involves creating directories by hand, compiling using the `javac` command via the command line and copying files to the correct deployment directories for testing.

Because we will not cover any specific IDE in this chapter, we will default to using the second option. In order to install Tomcat 7.0.20, please download from the Tomcat site `http://tomcat.apache.org`. Once you have obtained the `.zip` or `.tar` file, unzip it to the location on your machine that you want to install Tomcat; otherwise known as `/JAVA_DEV/Tomcat` for this chapter. Next, set the `JAVA_HOME` environment variable equal to the location where Java SE 7 is installed.

■ **Note**   If you are running OS X, you may need to set the environment variable equal to the location in which OpenJDK is installed if Java 7 is not yet available on that platform.

After you perform these steps listed, you are ready to start using Tomcat. However, it is important that you configure the users by opening the `/JAVA_DEV/Tomcat/conf/tomcat-users.xml` file and create an administrative user account. To do so, enter a user account similar to the following (just be sure to include `manager-gui` and `admin-gui` as roles for the user you create):

```
<user username="your_username" password="your_password" roles="manager-gui, admin-gui"/>
```

Adding this line to the `tomcat-users.xml` configuration file will allow access to the web-based utilities that can be used for managing applications that you deploy. Just be sure to keep this file safe as all passwords are in clear text.

Last, open a command line and traverse into the `/JAVA_DEV/Tomcat/bin` directory; then execute the `startup.sh` or `startup.bat` file according to the platform on which you are running. This will cause the server to start, and once it is ready, you can open up a browser and point to `http://localhost:8080` to see the default Tomcat home page. This page gives you the ability to open up various management pages to help manage the Tomcat applications and environment.

If you have been successful in configuring the Tomcat environment and starting the server, you are ready to start developing Java servlets and applets.

18-2. Developing a Servlet

Problem

You would like to create a web page that will serve some dynamic content.

Solution

Develop a Java servlet class, and compile it to run within a Java servlet container. In the following example, a simple servlet is created that will display some dynamic content to the web page. The first listing is the servlet code that contains the functionality for the servlet:

```java
package org.java7recipes.chapter18.recipe18_02;

import java.io.IOException;
import java.io.PrintWriter;
import java.util.Date;

import javax.servlet.*;
import javax.servlet.http.*;

public class SimpleServlet extends HttpServlet {

    public void doGet(HttpServletRequest req, HttpServletResponse res)
            throws IOException, ServletException {

        res.setContentType("text/html");

        PrintWriter out = res.getWriter();

        /* Display some response to the user */

        out.println("<html><head>");
        out.println("<title>First Servlet</title>");
        out.println("\t<style>body { font-family: 'Lucida Grande', " +
                "'Lucida Sans Unicode';font-size: 13px; }</style>");
        out.println("</head>");
        out.println("<body>");
        out.println("<p>This is a simple servlet!</p>");
```

```
                out.println("</body></html>");

                out.close();
        }
}
```

Next, the web deployment descriptor is listed. This file is required for application deployment to a servlet container. It contains servlet configuration and mapping that maps the servlet to a URL. In recipe 18-4 you will learn how to omit the servlet configuration and mapping from `web.xml` to make servlet development, deployment, and maintenance easier.

```xml
<?xml version="1.0"?>
<web-app xmlns="http://java.sun.com/xml/ns/javaee"
        xmlns:xsi="http://www.w3.org/2001/XMLSchema-instance"
        xsi:schemaLocation="http://java.sun.com/xml/ns/javaee
                http://java.sun.com/xml/ns/javaee/web-app_3_0.xsd"
        version="3.0">

        <servlet>
        <servlet-name>SimpleServlet</servlet-name>
        <servlet-class>org.java7recipes.chapter18.recipe18_02.SimpleServlet</servlet-class>
        </servlet>
        <servlet-mapping>
        <servlet-name>SimpleServlet</servlet-name>
        <url-pattern>/SimpleServlet</url-pattern>
        </servlet-mapping>
<welcome-file-list>
        <welcome-file> /SimpleServlet </welcome-file>
        </welcome-file-list>
</web-app>
```

To compile the Java servlet, use the `javac` command line utility. The following line was excerpted from the command line and it compiles the `SimpleServlet.java` file into a class file. First, traverse into the directory containing the `SimpleServlet.java` file and then execute the following:

```
javac -cp /JAVA_DEV/Tomcat/lib/servlet-api.jar SimpleServlet.java
```

Once the servlet code has been compiled into a Java class file, it is ready to package for deployment.

How It Works

Java servlets provide developers the flexibility to design applications using a request-response programming model. Servlets play a key role in development of service-oriented and web application development on the Java platform. There are different types of servlets that can be created, and each of them is geared toward providing different functionality. The first type is the `GenericServlet`, which provides services and functionality. The second type, `HttpServlet`, is a subclass of `GenericServlet`, and servlets of this type provide functionality and a response that uses HTTP. The solution to this recipe demonstrates the latter type of servlet as it displays a result for the user to see within a web browser.

Servlets conform to a life cycle for processing requests and posting results. First, the Java servlet container calls the servlet's constructor. The constructor of every servlet must take no arguments. Next, the container calls the servlet `init()` method, which is responsible for initializing the servlet. Once the servlet has been initialized, it is ready for use. At that point the servlet can begin processing. Each servlet contains a `service()` method that does not have to be implemented, which handles the requests being made and dispatches them to the appropriate methods for request handling. Finally, the container calls the servlet's `destroy()` method, which takes care of finalizing the servlet and taking it out of service.

Every servlet class must implement the `javax.servlet.Servlet` interface or extend another class that does. In the solution to this recipe, the servlet named `SimpleServlet` extends the `HttpServlet` class, which provides methods for handling HTTP processes. In this scenario, a request is sent from the container to the servlet; then the servlet `service()` method dispatches the `HttpServletRequest` object and dispatches it to the appropriate method provided by `HttpServlet`. Namely, the `HttpServlet` class provides the `doGet()`, `doPut()`, `doPost()`, and `doDelete()` methods for working with am HTTP request. The `HttpServlet` class is abstract, so it must be subclassed and then an implementation can be provided for its methods. In the solution to this recipe, the `doGet()` method is implemented, and a response is written to the browser using the `PrintWriter`. Table 18-1 describes each of the methods available to an `HttpServlet`.

Table 18-1. HttpServlet Methods

Method Name	Description
doGet	Used to process HTTP GET requests. Input sent to the servlet must be included on the URL address. For example: "?myName=Josh&myBook=Java7Recipes"
doPost	Used to process HTTP POST requests. Input can be sent to the servlet within HTML form fields. See recipe 18-6 for an example.
doPut	Used to process HTTP PUT requests.
doDelete	Used to process HTTP DELETE requests.
doHead	Used to process HTTP HEAD requests.
doOptions	Called by the container to allow OPTIONS request handling.
doTrace	Called by the container to handle TRACE requests.
getLastModified	Returns the time that the HttpServletRequest object was last modified.
init	Initializes the servlet.
destroy	Finalizes the servlet.
getServletInfo	Provides information regarding the servlet.

A servlet generally performs some processing within the implementation of its methods and then returns a response to the client. The `HttpServletRequest` object can be used to process arguments that are sent via the request. For instance, if an HTML form contains some input fields that are sent to the server, those fields would be contained within the HttpServletRequest object. To learn more about sending arguments to a servlet, please refer to recipe 18-6. The HttpServletResponse object is used to send responses to the client browser. In the solution to this recipe, you can see that the HttpServletResponse object is used to set the content type of the response and to obtain a handle on the PrintWriter object. The following lines of code show how this is done, assuming that the argument name of the HttpServletResponse object is res:

```
res.setContentType("text/html");
PrintWriter out = res.getWriter();
```

A GenericServlet can be used for providing services to web applications. This type of servlet is often used for logging events because it implements the log() method. A GenericServlet implements both the Servlet and ServletConfig interfaces, and to write a generic servlet only the service() method must be overridden.

18-3. Packaging, Compiling, and Deploying a Servlet

Problem

You have written a Java servlet and would now like to package it and deploy it for use.

Solution

Compile the sources, set up a deployable application, and copy the contents into the Tomcat deployment directory. From the command line, use the javac command to compile the sources:

```
javac -cp /JAVA_DEV/Tomcat/servlet-api.jar SimpleServlet.java
```

After the class has been compiled, deploy it along with the web.xml deployment descriptor conforming to the appropriate directory structure.

QUICK START

To quickly get up and started with the packaging, compiling, and deployment of the example application for the servlet recipes in this chapter on Tomcat, follow these steps:

1) Create a single application named `SimpleServlet` by making that directory under `Tomcat/webapps`.

2) Create the `WEB-INF`, `WEB-INF/classes`, and `WEB-INF/lib` directories inside `SimpleServlet`.

3) Drag the Chapter 18 sources (beginning with the `org` directory) inside the `WEB-INF/classes` directory you created.

4) Copy the `web.xml` file that is contained within the `recipe18-02` directory into the `WEB-INF` directory you created.

5) Download the JavaMail API code from Oracle and copy the `mail.jar` file from the download into the `WEB-INF/lib` directory you created.

6) Set your `CLASSPATH` to include the `mail.jar` that you downloaded in Step 5 (see recipe 18-2 for details).

7) At the command prompt, change the directory so that you are inside the classes directory that you created in Step 2. Compile each recipe with the command `javac org\java7recipes\chapter18\recipe18_x\*.java`, where x is equal to the recipe number.

Restart Tomcat, and test the application by launching the browser to `http://localhost:8080/SimpleServlet/servlet_name`, where `servlet_name` corresponds to the servlet name in each recipe.

How It Works

In order to compile the sources, you can use your favorite Java IDE such as NetBeans or Eclipse, or you can use the command line. For the purposes of this recipe, we will use the command line. If using the command line, you must ensure that you are using the `javac` command that is associated with the same Java release that you will be using to run your servlet container. In this example, we will say that the location of Java SE 7 installation is in the following path:

`/Library/Java/JavaVirtualMachines/1.7.0.jdk/Contents/Home`

This path may differ in your environment if you are using a different operating system and/or installation location. To ensure that the Tomcat servlet container is running under the Java runtime that is located at this path, set the `JAVA_HOME` environment variable equal to this path. On OS X and *nix operating systems, the environment variable can be set by opening the terminal and typing the following:

```
export JAVA_HOME=/Library/Java/JavaVirtualMachines/1.7.0.jdk/Contents/Home
```

If you are using Windows, use the SET command within the command line to set up the JAVA_HOME environment variable:

```
set JAVA_HOME=C:\your-java-se-path\
```

Next, compile your Java servlet sources and be sure to include the servlet-api.jar that is packaged with your servlet container in your CLASSPATH. You can set the CLASSPATH by using the –cp flag of the javac command. The following command should be executed at the command line from within the same directory as the sources are located. In this case, the source file is named SimpleServlet.java.

```
javac -cp /JAVA_DEV/Tomcat/servlet-api.jar SimpleServlet.java
```

Next, package your application by creating a directory and naming it after your application. In this case, create a directory and name it SimpleServlet. Within that directory, create another directory named WEB-INF. Traverse into the WEB-INF directory and create another directory named classes. Last, create directories within the classes directory in order to replicate your Java servlet package structure. For this recipe, the SimpleServlet.java class resides within the Java package org.java7recipes.chapter18.recipe18_02, so create a directory for each of those packages within the classes directory. Create another directory within WEB-INF and name it lib, any .jar files containing external libraries should be placed within the lib directory. In the end, your directory structure should resemble the following:

```
SimpleServlet
|_WEB-INF
        |_classes
                |_org
                        |_java7recipes
                                |_chapter18
                                        |_recipe18_02
        |_lib
```

Place your web.xml deployment descriptor within the WEB-INF directory, and place the compiled SimpleServlet.class file within the recipe18_02 directory. The entire contents of the SimpleServlet directory can now be copied within the /JAVA_DEV/Tomcat/webapps directory to deploy the application. Restart the application server and visit http://localhost:8080/SimpleServlet/SimpleServlet to see the servlet in action.

18-4. Registering Servlets without WEB-XML

Problem

Registering servlets in the web.xml file is cumbersome, and you would like to deploy servlets without the need to modify web.xml at all.

Solution

Make use of the @WebServlet annotation to register the servlet, and omit the web.xml registration. This will alleviate the need to modify the web.xml each time a servlet is added to your application. The following adaptation of the SimpleServlet class that has been used in recipe 18-2 includes the @WebServlet annotation and demonstrates its use:

```java
package org.java7recipes.chapter18.recipe18_04;

import java.io.IOException;
import java.io.PrintWriter;

import javax.servlet.*;
import javax.servlet.annotation.WebInitParam;
import javax.servlet.annotation.WebServlet;
import javax.servlet.http.*;

@WebServlet(name="SimpleServlet2", urlPatterns={"/SimpleServlet2"})
public class SimpleServlet2 extends HttpServlet {

        @Override
        public void doGet(HttpServletRequest req, HttpServletResponse res)
                throws IOException, ServletException {

                res.setContentType("text/html");

                PrintWriter out = res.getWriter();

                /* Display some response to the user */

                out.println("<html><head>");
                out.println("<title>Simple Servlet 2</title>");
                out.println("\t<style>body { font-family: 'Lucida Grande', " +
                        "'Lucida Sans Unicode';font-size: 13px; }</style>");
                out.println("</head>");
                out.println("<body>");
```

```
        out.println("<p>This is another simple servlet to show you how "
            + "to deploy without listing the servlet within the "
            + "web-xml configuration file.</p>");

        out.println("</body></html>");

        out.close();
    }
}
```

■ **Note**   To display this servlet within the same application that you created in recipes 18-2 and 18-3, you will need to temporarily rename WEB.XML to something that will not be recognized by Tomcat. For instance, rename the file to old-web.xml, and then you can run the servlet using @WebServlet.

How It Works

There are a couple of different ways to register servlets with a web container. The first way is to register them using the web.xml deployment descriptor as demonstrated in recipe 18-2. The second way to register them is to use the @WebServlet annotation. The servlet 3.0 API introduced the @WebServlet annotation, which provides an easier technique to use for mapping a servlet to a URL. The @WebServlet annotation is placed before the declaration of a class, and it accepts the elements listed in Table 18-2.

Table 18-2. WebServlet Annotation Elements

Element	Description
description	Description of the servlet
displayName	Display name of the servlet
initParams	Accepts list of @WebInitParam annotations
largeIcon	Large icon of the servlet
loadOnStartup	Load on startup order of the servlet
name	Servlet name
smallIcon	Small icon of the servlet
urlPatterns	URL patterns that invoke the servlet
value	URL patterns that invoke the servlet

In the solution to this recipe, the @WebServlet annotation maps the servlet class named SimpleServlet to the URL pattern of /SimpleServlet2, and it also names the servlet SimpleServlet2.

```
@WebServlet(name="SimpleServlet2", urlPatterns={"/SimpleServlet2"})
```

The new @WebServlet can be used rather than altering the web.xml to register each servlet in an application. This provides ease of development and manageability. However, in some cases, it may make sense to continue using the deployment descriptor for servlet registration (for example, if you do not want to recompile sources when a URL pattern changes). If you look at the web.xml listing in recipe 18-2, you can see the following lines of XML, which map the servlet to a given URL, and provide a name for the servlet. These lines of XML perform essentially the same function as the @WebServlet annotation in this recipe:

```
<servlet>
<servlet-name>SimpleServlet2</servlet-name>
<servlet-class>org.java7recipes.chapter18.recipe18_04.SimpleServlet2</servlet-class>
</servlet>
<servlet-mapping>
<servlet-name>SimpleServlet2</servlet-name>
<url-pattern>/SimpleServlet2</url-pattern>
</servlet-mapping>
```

■ **Note** It is possible for you to use the same application packaging for each recipe pertaining to servlets within this chapter. That is, use the same directory structure you created within recipe 18-3, and append to it with each recipe you try. The servlet package, name, and URL pattern are different in each recipe. This makes each servlet unique, so each servlet can be mapped separately within the WEB.XML or as individual servlets with the @WebServlet annotation.

18-5. Setting Initialization Parameters

Problem

A servlet you are writing requires the ability to accept one or more parameters to be set upon initialization.

Solution 1

Set the servlet initialization parameters using the @WebInitParam annotation. The following code listing sets an initialization parameter that is equal to a String value:

```
package org.java7recipes.chapter18.recipe18_05;
```

```java
import java.io.IOException;
import java.io.PrintWriter;

import javax.servlet.*;
import javax.servlet.annotation.WebInitParam;
import javax.servlet.annotation.WebServlet;
import javax.servlet.http.*;

@WebServlet(name="SimpleServlet3", urlPatterns={"/SimpleServlet3"},
initParams={ @WebInitParam(name="name", value="Duke") })
public class SimpleServlet3 extends HttpServlet {

        @Override
        public void doGet(HttpServletRequest req, HttpServletResponse res)
                throws IOException, ServletException {

                res.setContentType("text/html");

                PrintWriter out = res.getWriter();

                /* Display some response to the user */

                out.println("<html><head>");
                out.println("<title>Simple Servlet 3</title>");
                out.println("\t<style>body { font-family: 'Lucida Grande', " +
                        "'Lucida Sans Unicode';font-size: 13px; }</style>");
                out.println("</head>");
                out.println("<body>");

                out.println("<p>This is a simple servlet!  Hello "
                                + getServletConfig().getInitParameter("name") + "</p>");

                out.println("</body></html>");

                out.close();
        }
}
```

The resulting web page will display the following text:

```
This is a simple servlet! Hello Duke
```

Solution 2

Place the init parameters inside of the web.xml deployment descriptor file. The following lines are excerpted from the web.xml deployment descriptor for the SimpleServlet application. They include the initialization parameter names and values:

```
<web-app>
<servlet>
<servlet-name>SimpleServlet3</servlet-name>
<servlet-class>org.java7recipes.chapter18.recipe18_05.SimpleServlet3</servlet-class>

<init-param>
<param-name>name</param-name>
<param-value>Duke</param-value>
</init-param>
    ...
</servlet>
    ...
</web-app>
```

How It Works

Often, there is a requirement to set initialization parameters for a servlet in order to initialize certain values. Servlets can accept any number of initialization parameters, and there are a couple of ways in which they can be set. The first solution is to annotate the servlet class with the @WebInitParam annotation as demonstrated in solution 1, and the second way to set an initialization parameter is to declare the parameter within the web.xml deployment descriptor, as demonstrated in solution 2. Either way will work, but the solution using @WebInitParam is based upon the newer Java servlet API 3.0. Therefore, solution 1 is the more contemporary approach, and solution 2 remains valid for following an older model or using an older Java servlet release.

In order to make use of the @WebInitParam annotation, it must be embedded within the @WebServlet annotation. Therefore, the servlet must be registered with the web application via the @WebServlet annotation rather than within the web.xml file. For more information on registering a servlet via the @WebServlet annotation, see recipe 18-4.

The @WebInitParam annotation accepts a name/value pair as an initialization parameter. In the solution to this recipe, the parameter name is "name" and the value is "Duke".

```
@WebInitParam(name="name", value="Duke")
```

Once set, the parameter can be used within code by calling getServletConfig().getInitialiationParameter() and passing the name of the parameter, as seen in the following line of code:

```
out.println("<p>This is a simple servlet! Hello "
                        + getServletConfig().getInitParameter("name") + "</p>");
```

The annotations have the benefit of providing ease of development and also make it easier to maintain servlets as a single package rather than jumping back and forth between the servlet and the deployment descriptor. However, those benefits come at the cost of compilation because in order to change the value of an initialization parameter using the @WebInitParam annotation, you must recompile the code. Such is not the case when using the web.xml deployment descriptor. It is best to evaluate your application circumstances before committing to a standard for naming initialization parameters.

18-6. Handling Requests and Responses

Problem

You would like to create a web form that accepts user input and supply a response based upon the input that has been received.

Solution

Create a standard HTML–based web form, and when the submit button is pressed invoke a servlet to process the end-user input and post a response. In order to examine this technique, we will look at two different pieces of code. The first code below is HTML that is used to generate the input form. Pay particular attention to the <form>and <input>tags. You will see that the action lists a servlet name, MathServlet.

```html
<html>
        <head>
        <title>Simple Math Servlet</title>
        </head>
        <body>
                <h1>This is a simple Math Servlet</h1>
                <form method="POST" action="MathServlet">
                <label for="numa">Enter Number A: </label>
                <input type="text" id="numa" name="numa"/><br><br>
<label for="numb">Enter Number B: </label>
<input type="text" id="numb" name="numb"/><br/><br/>
                <input type="submit" value="Submit Form"/>
                <input type="reset" value="Reset Form"/>
                </form>
        </body>
</html>
```

Next, take a look at the code for a servlet named MathServlet. This is the Java code that receives the input from the HTML code that is listed previously, processes it accordingly, and posts a response:

```java
package org.java7recipes.chapter18.recipe18_06;

import java.io.IOException;
import java.io.PrintWriter;
import java.util.Date;

import javax.servlet.*;
import javax.servlet.http.*;

/**
 * Simple Servlet that accepts two input parameters as Strings,
 * converts them to int values, and adds them together.
 */
public class MathServlet extends HttpServlet {

    public void doPost(HttpServletRequest req, HttpServletResponse res)
            throws IOException, ServletException {

        res.setContentType("text/html");

        // Store the input parameter values into Strings
        String numA = req.getParameter("numa");
        String numB = req.getParameter("numb");

        int solution = Integer.valueOf(numA) + Integer.valueOf(numB);

        PrintWriter out = res.getWriter();

        /* Display some response to the user */

        out.println("<html><head>");
        out.println("<title>Test Math Servlet</title>");
        out.println("\t<style>body { font-family: 'Lucida Grande', " +
                "'Lucida Sans Unicode';font-size: 13px; }</style>");
        out.println("</head>");
        out.println("<body>");

        out.println("<p>Solution: " +
                numA + " + " + numB + " = " + solution + "</p>");
        out.println("<br/><br/>");
        out.println("<a href='index.html'>Add Two More Numbers</a>");
        out.println("</body></html>");

        out.close();
    }
}
```

■ **Note** To run the example using the same application that you created in recipe 18-3, copy the index.html file into the SimpleServlet root directory, copy the <servlet> and <servlet-mapping> sections from the web.xml file that is within the recipe18_06 directory into the web.xml that is contained within the SimpleServlet application directory. After following these steps, if the application is deployed in the Tomcat/webapps directory, you should be able to browse to http://localhost:8080/SimpleServlet/index.html to see the results if Tomcat is running.

How It Works

Servlets make it easy to create web applications that adhere to a request and response life cycle. They have the capability to provide HTTP responses and also process business logic within the same body of code. The capability to process business logic makes servlets much more powerful than standard HTML code. The solution to this recipe demonstrates a standard servlet structure for processing requests and sending responses. An HTML web form contains parameters that are sent to a servlet. The servlet then processes those parameters in some fashion and then publishes a response that can be seen by the client. In the case of an HttpServlet object, the client is a web browser, and the response is a web page.

Values can be obtained from an HTML form by using HTML <input> tags embedded within an HTML <form>. In the solution to this recipe, two values are accepted as input and they are referenced by their id attributes as numa and numb. There are two more <input> tags within the form; one of them is used to submit the values to the form action, and the other is used to reset the form fields to blank. The form action is the name of the servlet that the form values will be passed to as parameters. In this case, the action is MathServlet. The <form> tag also accepts a form processing method, either GET or POST. In the example, the POST method is used because form data is being sent to the action; in this case, data is being sent to MathServlet. You could, of course, create an HTML form as detailed as you would like and then have that data sent to any servlet in the same manner. This example is relatively basic just to give you an understanding of how the processing is performed.

The <form> action attribute states that the MathServlet should be used to process the values that are contained within the form. The MathServlet name is mapped back to the MathServlet class via the web.xml deployment descriptor or the @WebServlet annotation. Looking at the MathServlet code, you can see that a doPost() method is implemented to handle the processing of the POST form values. The doPost() method accepts HttpServletRequest and HttpServletResponse objects as arguments. The values contained with the HTML form are embodied within the HttpServletRequest object. In order to obtain those values, call the request object's getParameter() method, passing the id of the input parameter that you want to obtain. In the solution to this recipe, those values are obtained and stored within local String fields.

```
String numA = req.getParameter("numa");
String numB = req.getParameter("numb");
```

Once the values are obtained, they can be processed as needed. In this case, those String value are converted into int values and then they are added together to generate a sum and stored into an int field. That field is then presented as a response on a resulting web page.

```
int solution = Integer.valueOf(numA) + Integer.valueOf(numB);
```

As mentioned previously, the HTML form could be much more complex, containing any number of `<input>` fields. Likewise, the servlet could perform more complex processing of those field values. This example is merely the tip of the iceberg, and the possibilities are without bounds. Servlet-based web frameworks such as JSP and JSF hide many of the complexities of passing form values to a servlet and processing a response. However, the same basic framework is used behind the scenes.

18-7. Setting Application-Wide Parameters

Problem

You would like to enable all servlets within your application to have the capability to communicate with the servlet container to obtain the same set of information. Furthermore, you'd like to set up some initialization parameters that can be shared by every servlet within the application.

Solution

Use a `ServletContext` object in order to allow each servlet within the application to communicate with the servlet container. Because each application has only one `ServletContext`, every servlet within the application will see the same `ServletContext`, so this is the ideal location to place initialization parameters that are intended for application-wide use. In the example that follows, application-wide parameters are set up to store an organization's e-mail address and SMTP host for sending mail. Those parameters are then used within a servlet in order to send e-mail to the organization.

The code below defines a servlet named `MailServlet` that is used for processing form values that were passed from an HTML form that is used by a client to submit feedback to an organization. The servlet sends an e-mail to the organization that contains the user feedback.

```
package org.java7recipes.chapter18.recipe18_07;

import java.io.IOException;
import java.io.PrintWriter;

import java.util.Enumeration;
import java.util.Properties;
import javax.mail.Message;
import javax.mail.Session;
import javax.mail.Transport;
import javax.mail.internet.AddressException;
import javax.mail.internet.InternetAddress;
import javax.mail.internet.MimeMessage;
import javax.servlet.*;
import javax.servlet.http.*;

/**
 * This servlet accepts input from a web form in order to send email to
```

```java
 * the servlet's owner.
 *
 * @author juneau
 */
public class MailServlet extends HttpServlet {

    public void doPost(HttpServletRequest req, HttpServletResponse res)
            throws IOException, ServletException {

        res.setContentType("text/html");
        String email = req.getParameter("email");
        String fname = req.getParameter("fname");
        String lname = req.getParameter("lname");
        String feedback = req.getParameter("feedback");

        PrintWriter out = res.getWriter();

        /* Display some response to the user */
        out.println("<html><head>");
        out.println("<title>Company Feedback</title>");
        out.println("\t<style>body { font-family: 'Lucida Grande', "
                + "'Lucida Sans Unicode';font-size: 13px; }</style>");
        out.println("</head>");
        out.println("<body>");
        if (sendMail(email, fname, lname, feedback)) {
            out.println("<p>Email sent, expect a response soon!</p>");
        } else {
            out.println("<p>There was an issue with the email, please try again.</p>");
        }
        out.println("</body></html>");

        out.close();
    }

    private boolean sendMail(String email, String fname, String lname, String feedback) {
        boolean result = false;
        try {

            // Send email here

            // servlet configuration initialization parameters

            String contextEmail =
                    getServletConfig().getInitParameter("emailAddress");
```

```
            String contextSmtp =
                    getServletConfig().getInitParameter("smtpAddress");
            //Set the host smtp address
            Properties props = new Properties();
props.put("mail.smtp.host", contextSmtp);

            // create some properties and get the default Session
Session session = Session.getDefaultInstance(props, null);
session.setDebug(false);

            // create a message
            Message msg = new MimeMessage(session);

            // set the from and to address
            InternetAddress addressFrom = new InternetAddress(email);
            msg.setFrom(addressFrom);
            InternetAddress[] address = new InternetAddress[1];
            address[0] = new InternetAddress(email);
            msg.setRecipients(Message.RecipientType.TO, address);
            msg.setSubject("***Customer Feedback ***");
            // Append Footer
            msg.setContent(feedback, "text/plain");
            // Uncomment for production
            Transport.send(msg);

            result = true;
        } catch (javax.mail.MessagingException ex) {
            ex.printStackTrace();
            result = false;
        }
        return result;

    }
}
```

The next code example demonstrates the HTML code that may be used to generate the web form for capturing the user feedback. Notice that the <form> action is the MailServlet.

```
<html>
        <head>
        <title>Send Us Feedback</title>
        </head>
        <body>
                <h1>Welcome to My Company's Feedback Form</h1>

<p>Please fill in all fields on the form below to send feedback to my company.
```

```
            </p>


                    <form method="POST" action="MailServlet">

                            <label for="email"> Email Address: </label>
                            <input type="text" id="email" name="email"/><br><br>
                            <label for="fname">First Name: </label>
                            <input type="text" id="fname" name="fname"/><br/><br/>
                            <label for="lname">Last Name: </label>
                            <input type="text" id="lname" name="lname"/><br/><br/>
                            <label for="feedback">Feedback: </label>
                            <br/>
                            <textarea cols="100" rows="20"
                            id="feedback" name="feedback">
                            </textarea>
                            <br/><br/>
                            <input type="submit" value="Submit Form"/>
                            <input type="reset" value="Reset Form"/>
                    </form>
        </body>
</html>
```

Finally, a look at the `web.xml` file, which declares the context parameters that can be utilized by any of the servlets within the application. Stop and restart Tomcat to pick up the changes in context parameter strings.

```
<?xml version="1.0" encoding="UTF-8"?>
<web-app version="2.5" xmlns="http://java.sun.com/xml/ns/javaee"
xmlns:xsi="http://www.w3.org/2001/XMLSchema-instance"
xsi:schemaLocation="http://java.sun.com/xml/ns/javaee   http://java.sun.com/xml/ns/javaee/web-
app_2_5.xsd">
<context-param>
<param-name>emailAddress</param-name>
<param-value>you@yourcompany.com</param-value>
</context-param>
<context-param>
<param-name>smtpAddress</param-name>
<param-value>smtp.yourcompany.com</param-value>
</context-param>
<servlet>
<servlet-name>MailServlet</servlet-name>
<servlet-class>org.java7recipes.chapter18.recipe18_07.MailServlet</servlet-class>
</servlet>
<servlet-mapping>
<servlet-name>MailServlet</servlet-name>
```

```
<url-pattern>/MailServlet</url-pattern>
</servlet-mapping>
<welcome-file-list>
<welcome-file> /math.html </welcome-file>
</welcome-file-list>
</web-app>
```

The user feedback form will look something like the one shown in Figure 18-1.

Welcome to My Company's Feedback Form

Please fill in all fields on the form below to send feedback to my company.

Email Address: [   ]

First Name: [   ]

Last Name: [   ]

Feedback:

[   ]

[Submit Form] [Reset Form]

Figure 18-1. *User feedback form*

How It Works

Some applications require the use of application-wide parameters that can be accessed from any servlet.
The solution to this recipe demonstrates this concept by setting up an organization's e-mail address and
SMTP host address as parameters. Application-wide parameters must be configured within the web.xml
deployment descriptor. They are set up using the <context-param> XML tag. Each <context-param> must
contain a <param-name> and <param-value> pair, which represent the name/value pair for each
parameter. In the solution to this recipe, the two parameters are set up as follows:

```
<context-param>
<param-name>emailAddress</param-name>
<param-value>you@yourcompany.com</param-value>
</context-param>
```

```
<context-param>
<param-name>smtpAddress</param-name>
<param-value>smtp.yourcompany.com</param-value>
</context-param>
```

Once configured within the deployment descriptor, these initialization parameters can be used by any of the servlets within an application by calling the servlet configuration's `getInitParameter()` method and passing the name of the parameter that you want to obtain:

```
String contextSmtp =getServletConfig().getInitParameter("smtpAddress");
```

18-8. Filtering Web Requests

Problem

You would like to invoke certain processing if a specified URL is used to access your application. For instance, if a specific URL is used to access your application, you would like to log the user's IP address.

Solution

Create a servlet filter that will be processed when the specified URL format is used to access the application. In this example, the filter will be executed when a URL conforming to the format of "/*" is used. This format pertains to any URL in the application. Therefore, any page will cause the servlet to be invoked.

```
package org.java7recipes.chapter18.recipe18_08;

import java.io.IOException;
import java.io.PrintWriter;
import java.util.Date;

import javax.servlet.*;
import javax.servlet.annotation.WebFilter;
import javax.servlet.http.*;

/**
 * Recipe 18-8
 * This filter obtains the IP address of the remote host and logs it.
 *
 * @author juneau
 */
@WebFilter("/*")
public class LoggingFilter implements Filter {
```

```
      private FilterConfig filterConf = null;

public void init(FilterConfig filterConf) {
        this.filterConf = filterConf;
    }

    public void doFilter(ServletRequest request,
            ServletResponse response,
            FilterChain chain)
            throws IOException, ServletException {
        String userAddy = request.getRemoteHost();

        filterConf.getServletContext().log("Vistor User IP: " + userAddy);

chain.doFilter(request, response);

  }

  public void destroy() {
    }
}
```

The servlet could contain any processing; the important thing to note is that this servlet is processed when a specified URL is used to access the application.

How It Works

Web filters are useful for preprocessing requests and invoking certain functionality when a given URL is visited. Rather than invoking a servlet that exists at a given URL directly, any filter that contains the same URL pattern will be invoked prior to the servlet. This can be helpful in many situations, perhaps the most useful for performing logging, authentication, or other services that occur in the background without user interaction.

Filters must implement the `javax.servlet.Filter` interface. Methods contained within this interface include `init()`, `destroy()`, and `doFilter()`. The `init()` and `destroy()` methods are invoked by the container. The `doFilter()` method is used to implement tasks for the filter class. As you can see from the solution to this recipe, the filter class has access to the `ServletRequest` and `ServletResponse` objects. This means that the request can be captured and information can be obtained from it. This also means that the response can be modified if need be. For example, including the username in the request after an authentication filter has been used.

If you want to chain filters, or if more than one filter exists for a given URL pattern, they will be invoked in the order in which they are configured in the `web.xml` deployment descriptor. It is best to manually configure the filters if you are using more than one per URL pattern rather than using the `@WebFilter` annotation. In order to manually configure the `web.xml` file to include a filter, use the `<filter>` and `<filter-mapping>` XML elements along with their associated child element tags. The following excerpt from a web.xml configuration file shows how the filter that has been created for this recipe may be manually configured within the web.xml:

```
<filter>
<filter-name>LoggingFilter</filter-name>
<filter-class>LoggingFilter</filter-class>
</filter>
<filter-mapping>
<filter-name>LogingFilter</filter-name>
<url-pattern>/*</url-pattern>
</filter-mapping>
```

Of course, the @WebFilter annotation takes care of the configuration for us, so in this case the manual configuration is not required.

18-9. Forwarding Requests to Other Web Resources

Problem

You need to redirect the browser to another URL when a specific URL within your application is visited.

Solution

Use the HttpServletResponse object's sendRedirect() method to redirect from the servlet to another URL. In the following example, when a URL that matches the /redirect pattern is used, the servlet will redirect the browser to another site:

```
import java.io.IOException;
import javax.servlet.*;
import javax.servlet.annotation.WebServlet;
import javax.servlet.http.*;

@WebServlet(name="RedirectServlet", urlPatterns={"/redirect"})
public class RedirectServlet extends HttpServlet {

@Override
    public void doGet(HttpServletRequest req, HttpServletResponse res)
            throws IOException, ServletException {
            String site = "http://www.java.net";

            res.sendRedirect(site);
    }
}
```

In this example, the servlet will redirect to the http://www.java.net web site.

How It Works

There are some cases in which a web application needs to redirect traffic to another site or URL within the same application. For such cases, the HttpServletResponse!s sendRedirect() method can be of use. The sendRedirect() method accepts a URL in String format and then redirects the web browser to the given URL. Given the fact that sendRedirect() accepts a String-based URL makes it easy to build dynamic URLs as well. For instance, some applications may redirect to a different URL based upon certain parameters that are passed from a user. Dynamic generation of a URL in such cases may look something like the following:

```
String redirectUrl = null;
If(parameter.equals("SOME STRING")
    redirectUrl = "/" + urlPathA;
else
    redirectUrl = "/" + urlPathB;
res.sendRedirect(redirectUrl);
```

The sendRedirect() method can also come in handy for creating the control for web menus and other page items that can send web traffic to different locations.

■ **Note** This simple redirect, as opposed to servlet chaining, does not pass the HttpRequest object along to the target address.

18-10. Listening for Servlet Container Events

Problem

You would like to have the ability to listen for application startup and shutdown events.

Solution

Create a servlet context event listener to alert when the application has started up or when it has been shut down. The following solution demonstrates the code for a context listener, which will log application startup and shutdown events and send e-mail alerting of such events:

```
package org.java7recipes.chapter18.recipe18_10;

import javax.servlet.ServletContextListener;
```

```java
import javax.servlet.ServletContextEvent;
import javax.servlet.annotation.WebListener;

@WebListener
public class StartupShutdownListener implements ServletContextListener  {

        public void contextInitialized(ServletContextEvent event) {
            System.out.println("Servlet startup...");
            System.out.println(event.getServletContext().getServerInfo());
            System.out.println(System.currentTimeMillis());
        sendEmail();
        }

        public void contextDestroyed(ServletContextEvent event) {
            System.out.println("Servlet shutdown...");
            System.out.println(event.getServletContext().getServerInfo());
            System.out.println(System.currentTimeMillis());
        sendEmail();
        }
}

        private void sendEmail(){
            // Email implementation
        }}
}
```

How It Works

Sometimes it is useful to know when certain events occur within the application server container. This concept can be useful under many different circumstances, but most often it would likely be used for initializing an application upon startup or cleaning up after an application upon shutdown. A servlet listener can be registered with an application to indicate when it is started up or shut down. Therefore, by listening for such events, the servlet has the opportunity to perform some actions when they occur.

To create a listener that performs actions based upon a container event, one must develop a servlet that implements the ServletContextListener interface. The methods that need to be implemented are contextInitialized() and contextDestroyed(). Both of the methods accept a ServletContextEvent as an argument, and they are automatically called each time the servlet container is initialized or shut down, respectively. To register the listener with the container, you can use the @WebListener annotation as demonstrated by the solution to this recipe, register the listener within the web.xml application deployment descriptor, or use the addListener() methods defined on ServletContext. For example, to register this listener within the web.xml, the following lines of XML would need to be added:

```xml
<listener>
<listener-class>org.java7recipes.chapter18.recipe18_10.StartupShutdownListener</listener-class>
</listener>
```

One way is not better than the other. The only time that listener registration within the application deployment descriptor (`web.xml`) would be more helpful is if you had the need to disable the listener in some cases. To disable a listener when it is registered using `@WebListener`, you must remove the annotation and recompile the code. Altering the web deployment descriptor does not require any code to be recompiled.

There are many different listener types, and the interface that the class implements is what determines the listener type. For instance, in the solution to this recipe, the class implements the `ServletContextListener` interface. Doing so creates a listener for servlet context events. If, however, the class implements `HttpSessionListener`, it would be a listener for HTTP session events. Table 18-2 shows the complete listing of listener interfaces.

Table 18-2. Servlet Listener Interfaces

Interface Class
`javax.servlet.ServletRequestListener`
`javax.servlet.ServletRequestAttrbiteListener`
`javax.servlet.ServletContextListener`
`javax.servlet.ServletContextAttributeListener`
`javax.servlet.HttpSessionListener`
`javax.servlet.HttpSessionAttributeListener`

It is also possible to create a listener that implements multiple listener interfaces. To learn more about listening for different situations, read recipes 18-11 and 18-12.

18-11. Listening for Attribute Changes

Problem

You want to be notified when an attribute has been set within a given application session.

Solution

Generate an attribute listener servlet to listen for such events as attributes being added, removed, or modified. The following class demonstrates this technique as it creates an `HttpSessionAttributeListener` and listens for attributes that are added, removed, or replaced within the HTTP session:

```java
package org.java7recipes.chapter18.recipe18_11;

import javax.servlet.ServletContext;
import javax.servlet.ServletContextEvent;
import javax.servlet.ServletContextListener;
import javax.servlet.annotation.WebListener;
import javax.servlet.http.HttpSession;
import javax.servlet.http.HttpSessionAttributeListener;
import javax.servlet.http.HttpSessionBindingEvent;
import javax.servlet.http.HttpSessionEvent;
import javax.servlet.http.HttpSessionListener;

@WebListener
public final class AttributeListener implements ServletContextListener,
        HttpSessionAttributeListener {

    private ServletContext context = null;

    public void attributeAdded(HttpSessionBindingEvent se) {

        HttpSession session = se.getSession();
        String id = session.getId();
        String name = se.getName();
        String value = (String) se.getValue();
        String message = new StringBuffer("New attribute has been added to session: \n")
                .append("Attribute Name: ").append(name).append("\n")
                .append("Attribute Value:").append(value).toString();
        log(message);
    }

    public void attributeRemoved(HttpSessionBindingEvent se) {

        HttpSession session = se.getSession();
        String id = session.getId();
        String name = se.getName();
        if (name == null) {
            name = "Unknown";
        }
        String value = (String) se.getValue();
        String message = new StringBuffer("Attribute has been removed: \n")
                .append("Attribute Name: ").append(name).append("\n")
                .append("Attribute Value: ").append(value).toString();
        System.out.println(message);
    }
```

```java
    public void attributeReplaced(HttpSessionBindingEvent se) {

        String name = se.getName();
        if (name == null) {
            name = "Unknown";
        }
        String value = (String) se.getValue();
        String message = new StringBuffer("Attribute has been replaced: \n  ")
                .append(name).toString();
        System.out.println(message);
    }

    private void log(String message) {

        if (context != null) {
            context.log("SessionListener: " + message);
        } else {
            System.out.println("SessionListener: " + message);
        }

    }

    @Override
    public void contextInitialized(ServletContextEvent event) {
        this.context = event.getServletContext();
        log("contextInitialized()");
    }

    @Override
    public void contextDestroyed(ServletContextEvent event) {
// Do something
    }

}
```

Messages will be displayed within the server log file indicating when attributes have been added, removed, or replaced.

How It Works

In some situations it can be useful to know when an attribute has been set or what an attribute value has been set to. The solution to this recipe demonstrates how to create an attribute listener in order to determine this information. To create a servlet listener, you must implement one or more of the listener interfaces. To listen for HTTP session attribute changes, implement HttpSessionAttributeListener. In doing so, the listener will implement the attributeAdded(), attributeRemoved(), and attributeReplaced() methods. Each of these methods accepts HttpSessionBindingEvent as an argument, and their implementation defines what will occur when an HTTP session attribute is added, removed, or changed, respectively.

In the solution to this recipe, you can see that each of the three methods listed in the previous paragraph contains a similar implementation. Within each method, the HttpSessionBindingEvent is interrogated and broken down into String values, which represent the id, name, and value of the attribute that caused the listener to react. For instance, in the attributeAdded() method, the Session is obtained from HttpSessionBindingEvent, and then the session ID is retrieved from that via the use of getSession(). The attribute information can be obtained directly from the HttpSessionBindingEvent using the getId() and getName() methods.

```
HttpSession session = se.getSession();
String id = session.getId();
String name = se.getName();
String value = (String) se.getValue();
```

After these values are obtained, the application can do whatever it needs to do with them. In this recipe, the attribute ID, name, and session ID are simply logged and printed:

```
String message = new StringBuffer("New attribute has been added to session: \n")
        .append("Attribute Name: ").append(name).append("\n")
        .append("Attribute Value:").append(value).toString();
log(message);
```

The body of the attributeReplaced() and attributeRemoved() methods contain similar functionality. In the end, the same routine is used within each to obtain the attribute name and value, and then something is done with those values.

There are a few different options that can be used to register the listener with the container. The @WebListener annotation is the easiest way to do so, and the only downfall to using it is that you will need to recompile code in order to remove the listener annotation if you ever need to do so. The listener can be registered within the web deployment descriptor, or it can be registered using one of the addListener() methods contained in ServletContext.

Although the example in the recipe does not perform any life-changing events, it does demonstrate how to create and use an attribute listener. In the real world, such a listener could become handy if an application needed to capture the username of everyone who logs in, or to send an e-mail whenever a specified attribute is set.

■ **Note** This listener can be used in the same application that has been used since recipe 18-2 without any need for change in the web.xml deployment descriptor.

18-12. Managing Session Information

Problem

You would like to maintain some information regarding an individual session on a per-session basis when a user visits your site.

Solution

Make use of session attributes to retain session-based information. In order to do so, use the HttpServletRequest object to obtain access to the session and then use the getAttribute() and setAttribute() methods accordingly. In the following scenario, an HTML page is used to capture a user's e-mail address, and then the e-mail address is placed into a session attribute. The attribute is then used by Java servlets across different pages of the application in order to maintain state.

The following code demonstrates what the HTML form might look like in this scenario:

```
<html>
<head>
<title></title>
<meta http-equiv="Content-Type" content="text/html; charset=UTF-8">
</head>
<body>
<h1>Provide an email address to use with this transaction</h1>
<br/>
<form method="POST" action="sessionServlet">
<input type="text" id="email" name="email"/>
<br/>
<input type="submit" value="Submit"/>
</form>
</body>
</html>
```

Next, the Java servlet with named SessionServlet using a URL pattern of /sessionServlet is initiated when the form is submitted. Any form input values are passed to SessionServlet and processed accordingly.

```
package org.java7recipes.chapter18.recipe18_12;

import java.io.*;
import javax.servlet.*;
import javax.servlet.annotation.WebServlet;
import javax.servlet.http.*;

@WebServlet(name="SessionServlet", urlPatterns={"/sessionServlet"})
```

681

```java
public class SessionServlet extends HttpServlet {
  public void doPost (HttpServletRequest req, HttpServletResponse res)
      throws ServletException, IOException {

  // Obtain he Session object

    HttpSession session = req.getSession(true);

  // Set up a session attribute

    String email = (String)
    session.getAttribute ("session.email");
    if (email == null) {
      email = req.getParameter("email");
      session.setAttribute ("session.email", email);
}

    String sessionId = session.getId();

    res.setContentType("text/html");
    PrintWriter out = res.getWriter();
    out.println("<html>");
    out.println("<head><title>Working with sessions</title></head>");
    out.println("<body>");
    out.println("<h1>Session Test</h1>");
    out.println ("Your email address is: " + email + "<br/><br/>");
    out.println ("Your session id: " + sessionId);
    out.println("<br/><br/><a href=sessionServletTwo>Go To Second Page</a>");
    out.println("</body></html>");
  }
}
```

The final code is an example of a second servlet that could be invoked by the first. This servlet also makes use of the same HTTP session attribute to show that state has been maintained:

```java
package org.java7recipes.chapter18.recipe18_12;

import java.io.*;
import javax.servlet.*;
import javax.servlet.annotation.WebServlet;
import javax.servlet.http.*;

@WebServlet(name="SessionServletTwo", urlPatterns={"/sessionServletTwo"})
public class SessionServletTwo extends HttpServlet {
  public void doGet (HttpServletRequest req, HttpServletResponse res)
      throws ServletException, IOException {
```

```
    // Obtain the Session object

        HttpSession session = req.getSession(true);

    // Obtain session attribute
        String email = (String)
session.getAttribute ("session.email");
String sessionId = session.getId() ;
        res.setContentType("text/html");
PrintWriter out = res.getWriter();
        out.println("<html>");
        out.println("<head><title>Working with sessions</title></head>");
        out.println("<body>");
        out.println("<h1>Session Test</h1>");
        out.println ("Still remembers...tracking the session...<br/><br/> " +
                    "Your email address is: " + email + "<br/><br/>");
        out.println ("Your session id: " + sessionId);
        out.println("</body></html>");
    }
}
```

In the end, the e-mail address that was entered within the original HTML form was captured and used throughout the different pages in the application.

How It Works

Since the beginning of web development, session attributes have been used to retain important information regarding a user's session. This concept holds true when developing using Java servlets as well, and servlets make it easy to set and get the attribute values. All `HttpServlet` classes must implement `doGet()` or `doPost()` methods in order to process web application events. In doing so, these methods have access to the `HttpServletRequest` object as it is passed to them as an argument. An `HttpSession` object can be gleaned from the `HttpServletRequest`, so it can be used to retrieve and set attributes as needed.

In the solution to this recipe, an `HttpSession` attribute is used to store an e-mail address. That address is then used throughout the application within different servlet classes by obtaining the session object and then retrieving the attribute value.

```
    // Obtain the Session object

        HttpSession session = req.getSession(true);

    // Set up a session attribute

        String email = (String)
        session.getAttribute ("session.email");
```

```
        if (email == null) {
            email = req.getParameter("email");
            session.setAttribute ("session.email", email);
    }
```

Any attributes will remain in the HttpSession object as long as the session remains valid. The session ID will remain consistent when traversing between pages. You can see that the solution to this recipe obtains and prints the current session ID for reference. Using attributes in the HttpSession is a good way to pass data around to maintain a session's state.

18-13. Finalization of a Servlet

Problem

There are some resources that you'd like to have your servlet clean up once the servlet is no longer in use.

Solution

The solution to the problem is twofold. First, provide code for doing any cleanup within the servlet destroy() method. Second, when there are potentially long-running methods, code them so that will become aware of a shutdown and, if necessary, halt and return so that the servlet can shut down cleanly. The following code excerpt is a small example of a destroy() method. In this code, it is being used to initialize local variables and setting the beingDestroyed boolean value to indicate that the servlet is shutting down.

```
!
/**
     * Used to finalize the servlet
     */
    public void destroy() {
        // Tell the servlet it is shutting down
setBeingDestroyed(true);
        // Perform any cleanup
        thisString = null;

    }

!
```

The code within the destroy() method may successfully achieve a full cleanup of the servlet, but if there is a long-running task, it must be notified of a shutdown. The following excerpt is a block of code that signifies a long-running task. The task should stop processing after the shutdown is indicated by the beingDestroyed value becoming true.

```
for (int x = 0; (x <= 100000 && !isBeingDestroyed()); x++) {
    doSomething();
}
```

How It Works

Finalization of a servlet can be very important, especially if the servlet is using some resources that may lead to a memory leak, making use of a reusable resource such as a database connection, or in order to persist some values for another session. In such cases, it is a good idea to perform cleanup within the servlet `destroy()` method. Every servlet contains a `destroy()` method (which may be implemented to overload default behavior) that is initiated once the servlet container determines that a servlet should be taken out of service.

The `destroy()` method is called once all the servlet's service methods have stopped running. However, if there is a long-running service method, a server grace period can be set, which would cause any running service to be shut down when the grace period is reached. As mentioned earlier, the `destroy()` method is the perfect place to clean up resources and it is also good place to help clean up after long-running services. Cleanup can be done by setting a servlet–specific local variable to indicate that the servlet is being destroyed, and having the long-running service check the state of that variable periodically. If the variable indicates that the `destroy()` method has been called, it should stop executing.

18-14. Creating an Applet

Problem

You are interested in developing an application that can be accessed from a browser but contains the functionality that can be found within a desktop application.

Solution

Develop a Java applet application. Doing so will enable you to run the application within a web browser and also allow the application to be run on the client desktop so that it has similar abilities of a standard desktop application. The following code is that of a Java applet class. This applet consists of a button and a label of text. When the user presses the button, the text changes. It is a simple example just to show you how to make a very basic applet.

```
package org.java7recipes.chapter18.recipe18_15;

import java.applet.*;
import java.awt.*;
import java.awt.event.*;

public class FirstApplet extends Applet implements ActionListener {
```

```java
Label buttonLabel;
Button messageButton;

public void init() {

    // Construct the button
    messageButton = new Button("Button");

    buttonLabel = new Label("Press Button");

    // Set the layout
    this.setLayout(new FlowLayout());

    // Add button to layout
    this.add(messageButton);
    // Add label to layout
    this.add(buttonLabel);

    // Set the action event equal to this class since it
    // implements ActionListener
    messageButton.addActionListener(this);
    this.setVisible(true);
}

/**
 * Action method for this applet.  This method will be called when this
 * class is set as an action listener.
 *
 * @param e
 */
public void actionPerformed(ActionEvent e) {
    if (this.buttonLabel.getText().equals("Press Button")) {
        this.buttonLabel.setText("Hello Java 7!");
    } else {
        this.buttonLabel.setText("Press Button");
    }
    repaint();
}
}
```

The applet shown in Figure 18-2 will result. When you press the button, the text will change.

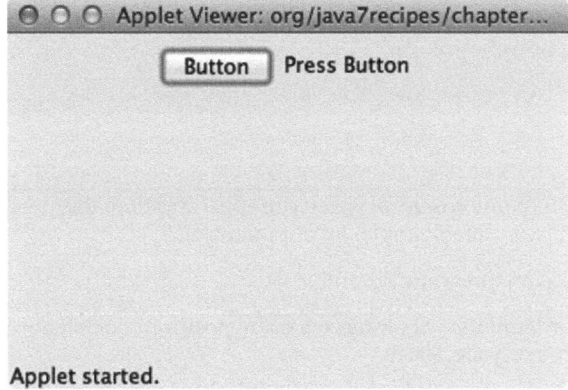

Figure 18-2. Applet with Button and Label

How It Works

Applets have been around since the beginning of Java. Some would argue that they are the cornerstones of the language itself. Although applets are not as popular now as they were in the beginning of Java, they still play an important role in the ecosystem. They are usually bound to a web page, yet they execute using the client Java runtime. Therefore, although they are a web-based technology, they make use of local resources. Applets are easy to make, and you can do a lot with them. This recipe will cover only the basics of applet development, and if you are interested in learning more, there are plenty of excellent resources about Applets to read.

Applets must either extend the abstract `Applet` class or the abstract `JApplet` class. This recipe will focus on a standard applet, which extends `java.applet.Applet`. As you can see from the example, `FirstApplet` is a subclass of `java.applet.Applet`. The `JApplet` is used for creating applets that will include Swing components. If you are interested in learning about `JApplet`, please see recipe 18-19.

Lots of functionality is obtained by subclassing the `Applet` or `JApplet` class. Specifically, all the code that coordinates the browser/Java interaction occurs behind the scenes within these abstract classes. This allows applet developers to focus on the applet design rather than how it functions within the browser and on the client machine. Applets have a life-cycle that can be traced by overriding four methods, those being: `init()`, `start()`, `stop()`, and `destroy()`. When an applet is invoked, the `init()` method is used to initialize the applet layout and components. The `init()` method is usually overridden and implemented, as demonstrated in the solution to this recipe. Looking at the example, you can see that the `init()` method contains the code necessary for building the user interface. A Button is constructed along with a Label. These two widgets are part of the AWT API, and their constructors accept a String representing the text that is displayed on the widget upon startup. The AWT API, Java's original user interface toolkit, provides graphics, windowing, and widgets that can be used to build user interfaces for Java applications. Standard applets use AWT, whereas `JApplet`s use Swing for construction of their user interface.

Following the declaration of the Button and Label widgets, the layout for the applet is set. There are many different applet layouts to choose from, and the class you use for the layout will determine how the user interface widgets are organized within the applet. This example uses the `FlowLayout`, which is arguably the easiest to work with. All widgets within a `FlowLayout` will be placed next to one another

687

horizontally until room runs out, and then they will continue to be laid out on the following line of the user interface. Thus, they flow onto the applet in a horizontal manner. Each of the different layouts is listed in Table 18-3, along with a brief description of how they work.

Table 18-3. AWT Layout Managers

Layout Manager	Description
FlowLayout	Widgets flow from left to right in one row until space runs out, and then they follow suit on the next line down (default applet layout manager).
GridLayout	Constructs a grid of widgets using rows and columns.
BorderLayout	Widgets are placed at the border of the user interface using positions such as BorderLayout.NORTH and BorderLayout.SOUTH.
CardLayout	Constructs the layout like a deck of cards. Each card usually consists of a JPanel or some other container which holds other widgets. One can then "flip" through each of the "cards", displaying the different views.
MixedLayout	Contains a nesting mixture of different layout managers.

The layout manager that you chose for your applet will determine how it looks and possibly even how functional it is. Layout managers are an important topic in Java user interface development. As you can see from the solution, the layout is set against a variable named this. The variable this refers to the class itself, and it is often the case that a small Java applet will be contained within one class, so you can refer to it using the this keyword. Next, because the layout has been set, widgets are then added to this, constructing the user interface:

```
// Set the layout
this.setLayout(new FlowLayout());

// Add button to layout
this.add(messageButton);
// Add label to layout
this.add(buttonLabel);
```

You may remember that the applet in the solution not only extends java.applet.Applet but also implements java.awt.event.ActionListener. Doing so allows the applet to handle user interface interactions such as button clicks. The method actionPerformed() must be implemented, adding functionality to the applet. In the solution to this recipe, the button sets the applet itself as the action listener because it implements the ActionListener interface. However, it is possible to set a separate ActionListener class to handle action events for the applet. By setting the action on the button to the applet itself, it means that when the button is clicked, the actionPerformed() method will be invoked.

Any number of things can occur within the actionPerformed() method; in this example, the Label text is changed. All actionPerformed() methods accept an ActionEvent argument. This ActionEvent represents the event that has triggered the call to this method. Within the implementation in this example, Label widgets are altered, but the ActionEvent argument could have been used to gain access to the event.

Last, the applet's setVisible() method is called passing a TRUE value. This will make sure that the user interface becomes visible for the user to see.

18-15. Packaging an Applet and Embedding into a Web Page

Problem

You want to embed a Java applet into a web page.

Solution 1

Compile your Java code and package it into a .jar file. Then create an HTML page that will be used to display the applet using the Invoke Deployment Toolkit (deployJava.js). Lastly, place the .jar file in the same path that is listed in the HTML <script> attributes, and then open up the HTML page to view the running applet.

When compiling your applet, include all images and other resources in a separate directory. To make things easier, use an IDE such as NetBeans to keep your applet project organized correctly. Once compiled, package the applet project within a .jar file by traversing into the base directory of your project's packages, and issuing the following command. In this case, let's call the .jar file FirstApplet.jar, and let's assume our applet code resides within a directory named projectCode, and our images and other resources reside within a directory named imagesAndResources:

```
jar cvf FirstApplet.jar projectCode imagesAndResources
```

Next, create the HTML page with embedded script references to deploy the applet:

```
<!DOCTYPE HTML PUBLIC "-//W3C//DTD HTML 4.01 Transitional//EN">
<html>
<head>
<title>Test page for launching the applet via deployJava.js</title>
</head>
<body>
<h3>Test page for launching the applet via deployJava.js</h3>
<script src="http://java.com/js/deployJava.js"></script>
<script>
        var attributes = {
codebase:   'PATH_TO_JAR',
            code:       'org.java7recipes.chapter18.recipe18_15.FirstApplet.class',
            archive:    'PATH_TO_JAR/JarFile.jar',
            width:      300,
            height:     300
        };
        var parameters = {fontSize:16}; <!-- Applet Parameters -->
        var version = "1.6"; <!-- Required Java Version -->
```

```
            deployJava.runApplet(attributes, parameters, version);
</script>
</body>
</html>
```

■ **Note** PATH_TO_JAR is a placeholder for the URI path to the .jar file in your application or HTML docbase. If your application .jar file is in the root directory of y our application, it will simply be /.

Visiting the HTML page will initiate the Java runtime on your desktop to run the applet.

Solution 2

Compile your Java code and package it into a .jar file. Then create an HTML page that will be used to display the applet using the ⟨applet⟩ tag. Looking at solution 1, you can see how to compile and package the applet and its resources into a .jar file. The difference with this solution is that it uses the ⟨applet⟩ tag within an HTML page instead of using the Invoke Deployment Toolkit to run the applet. The following HTML code demonstrates an example using the ⟨applet⟩ tag to invoke an applet named FirstApplet that is contained within a .jar file named FirstApplet.jar:

```
<!DOCTYPE HTML PUBLIC "-//W3C//DTD HTML 4.01 Transitional//EN">

<html>
<head>
<title>Test page for launching the applet via the applet tag</title>
</head>
<body>
<h3>Test page for launching the applet via the applet tag</h3>
<applet code="org.java7recipes.chapter18.recipe18_15.FirstApplet.class"
archive="/PATH_TO_JAR/FirstApplet.jar"
width=460 height=160>
</applet>
</body>
</html>
```

How It Works

When it comes to embedding an applet within an HTML page, there are a few different options. This recipe demonstrates two of those options: using the Invoke Deployment Toolkit, and using the ⟨applet⟩ tag for deployment. The same steps are necessary for compilation and packaging of an applet using each tactic. The only difference is how the applet is actually embedded within the HTML.

In order to run an applet, you first need to compile and package it appropriately. Compilation of the applet involves ensuring that any external libraries that are used by your applet are within the CLASSPATH. For more information regarding setting the CLASSPATH and compiling Java code from the command line, please refer to recipes 1-2, and 1-4. It also helps to use an IDE such as NetBeans or Eclipse to help package the applet and manage dependencies. Usually, an IDE will take care of compilation and .jar creation behind the scenes so that the developer does not have to worry about it. If you are working from the command line, the next step after compilation of the applet is to package it within a .jar file. You can do this by issuing the JDK's jar command. To package an applet, the code needs to be placed within a directory separate from any images or resources used by the applet. The jar command takes both of those directories and wraps them together into a single .jar file that can be deployed for use. In the solution to this recipe, you can see that the jar command assumes that the compiled code resides within a directory named projectCode, and the images and resources reside within a directory named imagesAndResources:

```
jar cvf FirstApplet.jar org projectCode imagesAndResources
```

Once the code has been packaged into a .jar file, it is ready for deployment. However, if your applet depends on any external libraries, their requisite .jar files will also need to be added to the HTML. Please see recipe 18-17 for more details on adding external libraries. As mentioned previously, there are a couple of options for embedding an applet within an HTML page. The first solution to this recipe shows how to make use of the Invoke Deployment Toolkit. This is essentially a JavaScript library that is used to load and run the applet. This toolkit has been around since Java 6, and it allows for deployment across many different browsers. To use this technique, first load the JavaScript file named deployJava.js, which is hosted by Oracle. It is important to note that in order to use deployJava.js, the client browser must have access to the Internet. The following line of code shows how to do this:

```
<script src="http://java.com/js/deployJava.js"></script>
```

Next, set up any attributes, parameters, and a Java version that will need to be passed to the deployJava.js script. This can be done within the <script></script> tags. The attributes will be passed as a list of values, using a name/value format. Attributes that must be set are codebase, code, archive, width, and height. You can see how this is done within the following code excerpt:

```
var attributes = {
                codebase:   'PATH_TO_JAR',
                code:       'org.java7recipes.chapter18.recipe18_15.FirstApplet.class',
                archive:    'PATH_TO_JAR/JarFile.jar',
                width:      300,
                height:     300
        };
```

The parameters are set up the same way as the attributes, within a list of name/value pairs. There may be zero or more parameters, and in solution 1 there is one:

```
var parameters = {fontSize:16};
```

Finally, set the Java runtime version that you want to use into the version variable in solution 1. Once you've done that, then you can pass the attributes, parameters, and version to the deployJava.js script.

```
deployJava.runApplet(attributes, parameters, version);
```

It should be noted that you could also use a JNLP file to deploy an applet along with the Invoke Deployment Toolkit. JNLP files are usually used to initiate Java WebStart applications or desktop Java applications that can be initiated from a web browser. In order to reference a JNLP, include the jnlp_href parameter within the parameter list. A JNLP file for the applet in the solution to this recipe may look something like the following:

```
<?xml version="1.0" encoding="UTF-8"?>
<jnlp spec="1.0+" codebase="" href="">
<information>
<title>First Applet</title>
<vendor>Java 7 Recipes Team</vendor>
</information>
<resources>
<!-- Application Resources -->
<j2se version="1.6+"
                href="http://java.sun.com/products/autodl/j2se" />
<jar href="FirstApplet.jar" main="true" />

</resources>
<applet-desc
        name="First Applet"
        main-class="org.java7recipes.chapter18.recipe18_15.FirstApplet.class"
        width="300"
        height="300">
</applet-desc>
<update check="background"/>
</jnlp>
```

Consider that the JNLP file referenced here was named FirstApplet.jnlp, it could then be referenced by the deployJava.js script by passing it as a parameter. You could then leave out the codebase and archive attributes, and use something like the following to initiate the applet via HTML:

```
<script src="http://java.com/js/deployJava.js"></script>
<script>
            var attributes = {
code:       'org.java7recipes.chapter18.recipe18_15.FirstApplet.class',
                width:      300,
                height:     300
            };
            var parameters = {fontSize:16, jnlp_href: !FirstApplet.jnlp!}; <!-- Applet
Parameters -->
            var version = "1.6"; <!-- Required Java Version -->
            deployJava.runApplet(attributes, parameters, version);
</script>
```

Use of the <applet> tag is not as universal as the Invoke Deployment Toolkit because all browsers do not recognize the <applet> tag. However, if you are working within an environment in which you know that the browser recognizes this tag, it is a viable option. The `<applet>` tag takes fewer configurations than using `deployJava.js`, so many people like to use it. The only required attributes for using the `<applet>` tag are code, archive, width, and height. Of course, you can also embed parameters into the `<applet>` tag to have them passed to the applet. The following code excerpt shows how to use the `<applet>` tag to achieve the same embedded applet result as using the `deployJava.js` script.

```
<applet code="org.java7recipes.chapter18.recipe18_15.FirstApplet.class"
archive="/PATH_TO_JAR/FirstApplet.jar"
width=460 height=160>
</applet>
```

Either option that you choose, embedding applets into web pages is quite trivial. The more complicated piece of the puzzle tends to be the packaging of the applet itself.

18-16. Creating Draggable Applets

Problem

Rather than having an applet run within a web browser, you'd like to make an applet that can be dragged off the page and run in its own window.

Solution 1

Pass the draggable parameter to the `deployJava.js` script. In this HTML code, you can see that the `draggable:true` parameter is passed to the `deployJava.runApplet` script:

```
<html>
<head>
<title>Test page for launching the applet via deployJava.js</title>
</head>
<body>
<h3>Test page for launching the applet via deployJava.js</h3>
<script src="http://java.com/js/deployJava.js"></script>
<script>
          var attributes = {
codebase:    'PATH_TO_JAR',
              code:      'org.java7recipes.chapter18.recipe18_15.FirstApplet.class',
              archive:   '/PATH_TO_JAR/FirstApplet.jar',
              width:     300,
              height:    300
          };
          var parameters = {fontSize:16, draggable:true}; <!-- Applet Parameters -->
          var version = "1.6"; <!-- Required Java Version -->
          deployJava.runApplet(attributes, parameters, version);
```

```
</script>
</body>
</html>
```

Solution 2

Pass the draggable parameter to the <applet> tag. In this HTML code, you can see that the <param name="draggable" value="true"/> is embedded within the <applet> tag:

```
<html>
<head>
<title>Test page for launching the applet via applet tag</title>
</head>
<body>
<h3>Test page for launching the applet via Applet Tag</h3>
<applet code="org.java7recipes.chapter18.recipe18_15.FirstApplet.class"
                archive="/PATH_TO_JAR/FirstApplet.jar"
                width=460 height=160>
<param name="draggable" value="true"/>
</applet>
</body>
</html>
```

After using either of the previous solutions, visit the HTML page that was created to initiate the applet. The applet can be dragged from within the browser to the desktop by holding down the Alt key while dragging the applet using the left mouse button.

How It Works

Java 6 Update 10 introduced support for draggable applets. This allows an applet to run within its own process so that it can be dragged from the browser to the desktop. Configuration for making an applet draggable is minimal; you need to pass an extra parameter via the deployJava.js script or the <applet> tag. In the solutions to this recipe, you can see that the parameter name is draggable and the value must be set to true. However, the draggable applet may not work with every browser, so it is important to test and ensure that a compliant browser is used if this feature is required.

It is also possible to override some methods within the Applet class in order to perform activities when applets are dragged from the browser. The following methods can be overridden in order to create customized functionality within an applet:

```
public boolean isAppletDragStart(MouseEvent e);
public void appletDragStarted();
public void appletDragFinished();
public void setAppletCloseListener(ActionListener l);
public void appletRestored();
```

For more information regarding custom development for draggable applets, please reference online materials.

18-17. Loading External Libraries for an Applet

Problem

You would like to load Java libraries from an external .jar for use within your applet.

Solution

If necessary, sign the .jar files and then use a comma-separated list of values for the archive attribute to include the necessary .jar files for the external libraries that the applet requires. In this example, an applet is created that generates a simple e-mail form. When the send button is pressed, an e-mail message is sent using the JavaMail API. As such, external libraries for JavaMail must be included with the applet when downloaded to the client. The following code is the applet code that is used to create the e-mail form:

```
package org.java7recipes.chapter18.recipe18_17;

import java.applet.*;
import java.awt.*;
import java.awt.event.*;
import java.util.Properties;
import javax.mail.Message;
import javax.mail.Session;
import javax.mail.Transport;
import javax.mail.internet.InternetAddress;
import javax.mail.internet.MimeMessage;

public class MailApplet extends Applet implements ActionListener {

    TextField from;
    TextField to;
    TextField smtp;
    TextArea message;
    Label mailLabel;
    Label fromLabel;
    Label toLabel;
    Label smtpLabel;
    Label blank;
    Label messageLabel;
    Button messageButton;
```

```java
public void init() {

        // Construct the widgets
        messageButton = new Button("Send");

        mailLabel = new Label("Please fill out the form below to send email.");
        fromLabel = new Label("From:");
        from = new TextField();
        toLabel = new Label("To:");
        to = new TextField();
        smtpLabel = new Label("SMTP Host:");
        smtp = new TextField();
        messageLabel = new Label("Message:");
        message = new TextArea(null,10,30);
        blank = new Label();

        // Set the layout
        this.setLayout(new GridLayout(11,2));

        // Add widgets to layout
        this.add(mailLabel);

        this.add(fromLabel);
        this.add(from);

        this.add(toLabel);
        this.add(to);

        this.add(smtpLabel);
        this.add(smtp);

        this.add(messageLabel);
        this.add(message);

        this.add(messageButton);

        // Set the action event equal to this class since it
        // implements ActionListener
        messageButton.addActionListener(this);
        this.setSize(300, 500);
        this.setVisible(true);
    }

    /**
```

```java
 * Action method for this applet.  This method will be called when this
 * class is set as an action listener.
 *
 * @param e
 */
public void actionPerformed(ActionEvent e) {
    sendMail();
    this.mailLabel.setText("Message successfully sent");
    this.mailLabel.setForeground(Color.GREEN);
    repaint();
}

private boolean sendMail() {
    boolean result = false;
    try {

        // Send email here

        String from = this.from.getText();
        System.out.println(from);
        String to = this.to.getText();
        String smtp = this.smtp.getText();
        String message = this.message.getText();

        //Set the host smtp address
        Properties props = new Properties();
        props.put("mail.smtp.host", smtp);

        // create some properties and get the default Session
        Session session = Session.getDefaultInstance(props, null);
        session.setDebug(false);

        // create a message
        Message msg = new MimeMessage(session);

        // set the from and to address
        InternetAddress addressFrom = new InternetAddress(from);
        msg.setFrom(addressFrom);
        InternetAddress[] address = new InternetAddress[1];
        address[0] = new InternetAddress(to);
        msg.setRecipients(Message.RecipientType.TO, address);
        msg.setSubject("*** Applet Email ***");
        // Append Footer
        msg.setContent(message, "text/plain");
        Transport.send(msg);
```

```
                    result = true;
                } catch (javax.mail.MessagingException ex) {
                    ex.printStackTrace();
                    result = false;
            }
            return result;

        }
    }
```

Next is the HTML named `mailApplet.html` that is used to embed the applet. Notice that there is more than one `.jar` file listed in the parameters section. This is one way to include external `.jar` files with your applet.

```html
<html>
<head>
<title>Test page for launching the applet via deployJava.js</title>
</head>
<body>
<h3>Test page for launching the applet via deployJava.js</h3>
<script src="http://java.com/js/deployJava.js"></script>
<script>
            var attributes = {
codebase:   '/PATH_TO_CODEBASE/',
                code:       'org.java7recipes.chapter18.recipe18_17.MailApplet.class',
                archive:    '/PATH_TO_JAR/MailApplet.jar, /PATH_TO_JAR/mail.jar',
                width:      300,
                height:     300
            };
            var parameters = {fontSize:16}; <!-- Applet Parameters -->
            var version = "1.6"; <!-- Required Java Version -->
            deployJava.runApplet(attributes, parameters, version);
</script>
</body>
</html>
```

When the page is visited, the simplistic e-mail applet will appear and the appropriate `.jar` files will be loaded into the local Java runtime.

How It Works

Almost any substantial applet will require the use of external libraries. As such, those external libraries will have to be included with the Java applet in order to run on a client machine. As with many other solutions in the industry, there is more than one way to include external libraries within an applet. In the solution to this recipe, the HTML code that is used to embed the applet is modified to contain a reference to any external .jar files that are required to run the code. This solution includes a reference to the mail.jar external .jar. Referencing the .jar will make it download to the client machine along with the applet .jar file. If using the <applet> tag, you can also include multiple .jar files by adding them using a comma-separated list to the archive attribute.

■ **Note** In order to run this applet, the mail.jar file should be copied into the root directory of your application (for example, webapps/SimpleServlet) or a deeper HTML directory).

18-18. Using Swing Components Within an Applet

Problem

Your application requires the use of Swing, a highly adopted Java component library, in order to contain the GUI that is required.

Solution

Use Swing components within your applet application by extending the javax.swing.JApplet class rather than the standard java.applet.Applet class. The following applet class demonstrates this functionality by using Swing components rather than AWT widgets for constructing the user interface of the MailApplet that was introduced in recipe 18-17. This solution is composed of two classes. The first class that is shown contains the actual Java Swing component code that is used to build the user interface. It extends the JPanel component and implements ActionListener for button functionality:

```
package org.java7recipes.chapter18.recipe18_18;

import java.awt.Color;
import java.awt.GridLayout;
import java.awt.event.ActionEvent;
import java.awt.event.ActionListener;
import java.util.Properties;
import javax.mail.Message;
import javax.mail.Session;
import javax.mail.Transport;
import javax.mail.internet.InternetAddress;
import javax.mail.internet.MimeMessage;
import javax.swing.JPanel;
import javax.swing.JScrollPane;

/**
```

```
 * Recipe 18_18
 *
 * This is the panel that contains the Swing components for the mail applet
 *
 * @author juneau
 */
public class SwingMailPanel extends JPanel implements ActionListener {
    javax.swing.JTextField from;
    javax.swing.JTextField to;
    javax.swing.JTextField smtp;
    javax.swing.JTextArea message;
    javax.swing.JLabel mailLabel;
    javax.swing.JLabel fromLabel;
    javax.swing.JLabel toLabel;
    javax.swing.JLabel smtpLabel;
    javax.swing.JLabel blank;
    javax.swing.JLabel messageLabel;
    javax.swing.JButton messageButton;
    javax.swing.JScrollPane scrollpane;

    public SwingMailPanel(){

        messageButton = new javax.swing.JButton("Send");

        mailLabel = new javax.swing.JLabel("Please fill out the form below to send email.");
        fromLabel = new javax.swing.JLabel("From:");
        from = new javax.swing.JTextField();
        toLabel = new javax.swing.JLabel("To:");
        to = new javax.swing.JTextField();
        smtpLabel = new javax.swing.JLabel("SMTP Host:");
        smtp = new javax.swing.JTextField();
        messageLabel = new javax.swing.JLabel("Message:");
        message = new javax.swing.JTextArea(5,20);
        message.setLineWrap(true);
        message.setWrapStyleWord(true);
        scrollpane = new JScrollPane(message);

        blank = new javax.swing.JLabel();

        // Set the layout
        this.setLayout(new GridLayout(11,2));

        // Add button to layout
        this.add(mailLabel);
```

```java
        this.add(fromLabel);
        this.add(from);

        this.add(toLabel);
        this.add(to);

        this.add(smtpLabel);
        this.add(smtp);

        this.add(messageLabel);
        this.add(scrollpane);


        this.add(messageButton);

        // Set the action event equal to this class since it
        // implements ActionListener
        messageButton.addActionListener(this);
        this.setSize(300, 500);
        this.setVisible(true);
    }

    /**
     * Action method for this applet.  This method will be called when this
     * class is set as an action listener.
     *
     * @param e
     */
    public void actionPerformed(ActionEvent e) {
        sendMail();
        this.mailLabel.setText("Message successfully sent");
        this.mailLabel.setForeground(Color.GREEN);
        repaint();
    }

    private boolean sendMail() {
        boolean result = false;
        try {


            // Send email here

            // servlet configuration initialization parameters
```

```java
        String from = this.from.getText();
        System.out.println(from);
        String to = this.to.getText();
        String smtp = this.smtp.getText();
        String message = this.message.getText();
        //Set the host smtp address
        Properties props = new Properties();
        props.put("mail.smtp.host", smtp);

        // create some properties and get the default Session
        Session session = Session.getDefaultInstance(props, null);
        session.setDebug(false);

        // create a message
        Message msg = new MimeMessage(session);

        // set the from and to address
        InternetAddress addressFrom = new InternetAddress(from);
        msg.setFrom(addressFrom);
        InternetAddress[] address = new InternetAddress[1];
        address[0] = new InternetAddress(to);
        msg.setRecipients(Message.RecipientType.TO, address);
        msg.setSubject("*** Applet Email ***");
        // Append Footer
        msg.setContent(message, "text/plain");
        // Uncomment for production
        Transport.send(msg);

        result = true;
    } catch (javax.mail.MessagingException ex) {
        ex.printStackTrace();
        result = false;
    }
    return result;

    }

}
```

The second class lists the acutal `JApplet` code itself. The `JApplet` creates a new `Runnable()` that calls the class that was previously shown to instantiate the `SwingMailPanel`:

```java
package org.java7recipes.chapter18.recipe18_18;

import javax.swing.*;
```

```java
/**
 * Recipe 18-18
 *
 * Creates a JApplet
 *
 * @author juneau
 */
public class SwingMailApplet extends JApplet {

    public void init() {

        try{
            SwingUtilities.invokeAndWait(new Runnable() {
                public void run() {
                    createGUI();
                }
            });
        } catch (Exception e) {
            System.err.println("createGUI didn't complete successfully");
        }
    }

    private void createGUI() {
        //Create and set up the content pane.
        SwingMailPanel mailPanel = new SwingMailPanel();
        // Make mailPanel visible
        mailPanel.setOpaque(true);
        // Set the content of the JApplet to mailPanel
        setContentPane(mailPanel);
    }

}
```

The resulting applet will look similar to the image shown in Figure 18-3.

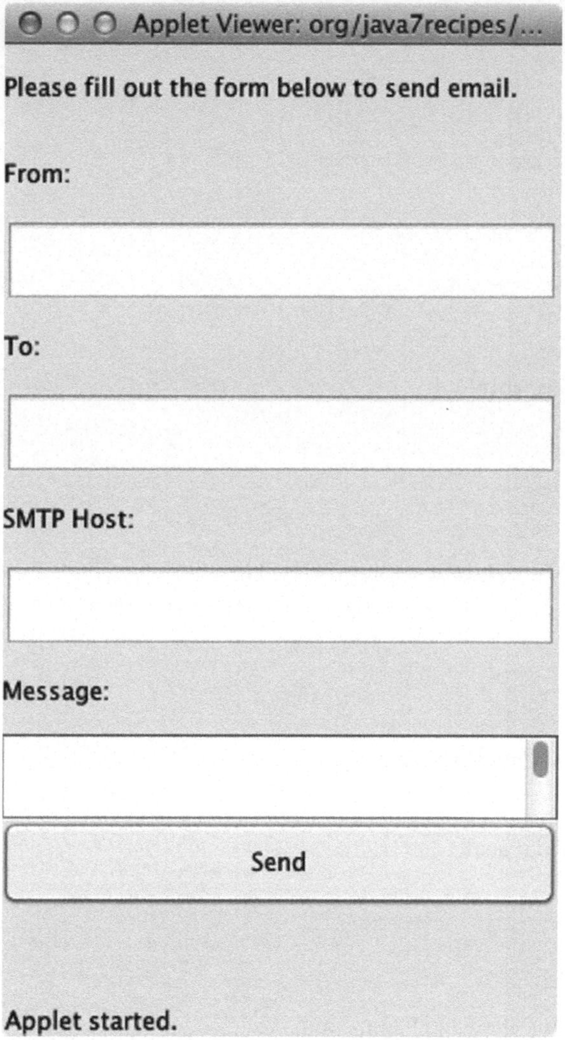

Figure 18-3. Applet composed of Swing components

How It Works

Developing applets that contain Swing components is a bit different from development using AWT because Swing components should be handled a bit differently from AWT. Swing code should always be manipulated on the event-dispatching thread. However, applets do not run on the event-dispatching thread. For this reason, they should always invoke any Swing code using the SwingUtilities.invokeAndWait method. Doing so will ensure that the Swing code is executed on the appropriate thread. Because the init() method of an applet is used to set up the layout, this is where the invokeAndWait method should be placed. Using this technique, a new `Runnable()` will be created, which then executes a given block of code on the event-dispatching thread. Typically, a separate method will be written to perform the invocation of another class that houses the Swing code. In the solution to this recipe, a class named `SwingMailPanel` subclasses the `JPanel` component and implements `ActionListener`. The code within the `SwingMailPanel` class is very similar to the code that was used within recipe 18-17, except the GUI is constructed using Swing components rather than AWT.

In the `SwingMailPanel` class, the first lines of code are declared and set up the Swing components that make up the user interface. Because the class implements the `ActionListener` interface, the button calls the class itself in order to perform its task. When the button is pressed, it will invoke the `actionPerformed()` method, which contains the code that calls the `sendMail()` method, changes the `JLabel` to display a different message, and repaints the GUI.

As mentioned previously, the most interesting code for creating the applet takes place within the `SwingMailApplet` class. As you can see from the solution, this class subclasses the `JApplet`. The `SwingUtilities.invokeAndWait` block ultimately initiates the code that instantiates the `SwingMailPanel` class to construct the user interface.

Using Swing components to construct an applet interface can significantly improve the look and feel. Although Java Swing components could be added directly to the `init()` method of an applet, it can cause issues, so it is always best to perform any Swing manipulation on the event-dispatching thread. In fact, it is possible to run entire Java Swing applications within the context of a `JApplet`. To learn more about constructing Swing applications, please refer to Chapter 14.

CHAPTER 19

Intro to Android

The Android mobile operating system has become one of the hottest mobile platforms in use. Developers of Android applications can create applications and distribute them within the Android marketplace. Android application development makes use of the Java platform, along with an Android development environment. This is a great benefit for the Android platform as it allows Android applications to make use of the wide variety of features and functionality that comes along with the Java platform.

The topic of developing Android applications can be daunting because there are a great many aspects to deal with. From the creation of the user interface screens to handling application events, Android application development is very comparable to Java Swing development or web application development. However, becoming an expert Android developer is only a matter of learning the different components that comprise an application and how to tie them together in order to make them work. This chapter will show you how to get started developing applications for the Android platform. You will learn how to set up an environment for developing applications and testing them. You will learn the basic components that are required to build an application, and you will create a nontrivial application that features some advanced layout and user interface widgets. In the end, you will have enough knowledge to begin developing applications for the Android platform, as this chapter will cover a broad aspect of Android application development.

19-1. Setting Up a Development Environment with Eclipse

Problem

You would like to develop an application for the Android mobile operating system and you need to set up a development environment.

Solution

Download and install the Eclipse IDE along with the Android Development Toolkit (ADT) plug-in. Follow these instructions:

1. Download a suitable version of Eclipse for your operating system and install it according to the instructions. To find a download that will work for you, go to http://www.eclipse.org/downloads/. If possible, install either the Eclipse Classic or Eclipse IDE for Java Developers package.

2. Install the Android software development kit (SDK). Grab the latest Android SDK by visiting http://developer.android.com/sdk/index.html. Make sure you take note of the name and location of the SDK installation directory because you may need to refer to it later.

3. Download and install the ADT plug-in for Eclipse according to the documentation that can be found at http://developer.android.com/sdk/eclipse-adt.html#installing.

4. Install the Android SDK, platform, and Android virtual device (AVD; emulator) using Eclipse's Android SDK and AVD Manager.

After following these steps to install and configure your development environment, you will be ready to develop your first Android mobile application and test it using an AVD.

How It Works

Before you can begin to develop applications for Android, you will need to set up a development environment. There are several options to choose from depending upon the IDE you want to use and the Android device that you are developing against. For the sake of maintaining an easy-to-use environment, this recipe discusses how to install the Eclipse IDE and ADT. Eclipse is the preferred IDE for beginning Android developers because it is the best-documented and arguably includes the most tools.

To begin, determine which version of Eclipse will work best for your operating system and needs, and then download a package. The preferred packages are the Eclipse Classic or the Eclipse IDE for Java Developers because they are preconfigured to be the best suited for Android development. However, just about any Eclipse package will work if configured correctly. Once downloaded, follow the installation instructions that come with the Eclipse package.

The next step is to install the Android SDK. It is best to download the latest version of the SDK to ensure that you have access to the most recent new features. To download the SDK, visit the SDK download page at http://developer.android.com/sdk/index.html and choose the correct package for your platform. Either unzip it into a directory on your machine if you are using a non-Windows environment or run the Windows installer if you are using that platform.

In order to install the ADT plug-in for Eclipse, use the Update Manager feature of the Eclipse IDE. Follow these steps to install the plug-in:

1. To begin, start Eclipse; then go to the Help menu and select Install New Software.

2. Next, click Add in the upper corner to open the Add Repository dialog box. Once it appears, add a new repository by entering **ADT Plugin** for the Name and `https://dl-ssl.google.com/android/eclipse/` for the Location; then click OK. The software that is available at the new repository will appear in the next dialog box.

3. In the Available Software dialog box, choose Developer Tools and click Next.

4. Read the software licensing form and then click Finish when complete.

5. Restart Eclipse.

Once you've successfully installed the plug-in, it will need to be configured so that it points to the SDK that you downloaded previously. To do this, open the Eclipse Preferences panel and select Android from the left panel. In the right panel, click Browse to browse to the Android SDK you downloaded. Once you have found it, click Open to populate the SDK Location.

The final steps to complete your Eclipse Android development environment are to add the components, add the platforms that you want to develop for, and create an AVD for each of the chosen platforms. You can do these things from within the Android SDK and ADT Manager, which can be found within the Eclipse Window menu option. Once the dialog box is open, you can add components that you will need for development. To do so, select Available Packages on the left menu; then expand the Android Repository option within the Packages available for download list. The Third Party Add-Ons repository can be used at some point in the future to add external libraries that can be used for development of your applications. To get started, it is recommended that you download the following components:

- **SDK Tools:** Download the most current

- **SDK Platform-Tools:** Download the most current

- **SDK Platform:** Download the platform that you want to develop against

- **Documentation**

- **Samples**

Configure an AVD for each SDK platform that you downloaded. You will use the AVDs that are configured for testing applications. To create an AVD, select the Virtual Devices menu option in the left menu within the Android SDK and ADT Manager. Click the New button in the right menu to open the Create New Android Virtual Device (AVD) dialog box. Enter a name and select a target from the pull-down list. The target list will contain the list of platforms that you have installed to develop against. Once you've entered these two fields, click the Create AVD button. You should now see the AVD that you created within the list of available AVDs. You are now ready to develop!

19-2. Creating a Basic Application

Problem

You are interested in developing a basic Android application. For example, you'd like to begin with one that will display the current date.

Solution

Create a new Android project within Eclipse. Once created, modify the Java code within the `Activity` file, named `todaysDate.java`, which Eclipse has generated for you. The code within `todaysDate.java` should be modified to look like the following:

```java
package org.java7recipes;

import java.util.Date;

import android.app.Activity;
import android.os.Bundle;
import android.widget.LinearLayout;
import android.widget.TextView;
import android.widget.LinearLayout.LayoutParams;

public class todaysDate extends Activity {
private TextView tv;
private LinearLayout layout;
    /** Called when the activity is first created. */
    @Override
    public void onCreate(Bundle savedInstanceState) {
        super.onCreate(savedInstanceState);
        doWork();
        layout = new LinearLayout(this);
        layout.setLayoutParams(new LayoutParams(LayoutParams.FILL_PARENT,
        LayoutParams.FILL_PARENT));
        layout.setOrientation(LinearLayout.VERTICAL);
        layout.addView(tv);
        setContentView(layout);
    }

        public void doWork(){
        Date todaysDate = new Date();
        tv = new TextView(this);
        tv.setText("The current date is: " + todaysDate);
    }
}
```

After you have modified the activity code to resemble this code, your Android application is ready to compile and deploy for testing. To learn more about compiling and deploying an application for testing, please see recipe 19-3.

How It Works

To create a new Android project within Eclipse, select the File menu, and then select the New and Other option. This will open the Select a Wizard dialog box, in which you should make the Android Folder and Android Project selection; then click Next. This will open up the New Android Project dialog box. In this dialog box, you need to fill in the Project Name and choose a build target; then enter an Application name, a package name (such as `org.java7recipes`), and finally the name for the activity to be created. Once all those fields are filled in, click Next button. To skip the Create Test screen, click Finish instead. In Figure 19-1, an application named Todays Date is being created.

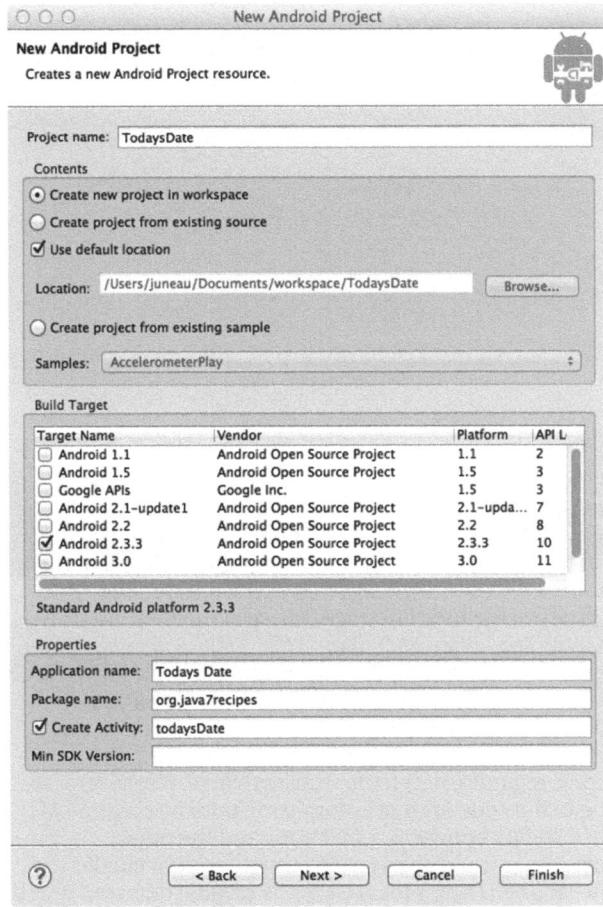

Figure 19-1. Creating a new Android project in Eclipse

After you've gone through the initial setup of an Android project, the IDE will automatically generate a Hello World view for your application, along with all the files that are required to make your application work. If you are using the Eclipse Java layout, on the left side of the Eclipse window you will see the TodaysDate project, along with all its files. Expand the project so that you can see the sources that are contained within the src folder. Also, expand the res folder and the layout folder within it so that you can see the file named main.xml. Your view should resemble that of Figure 19-2.

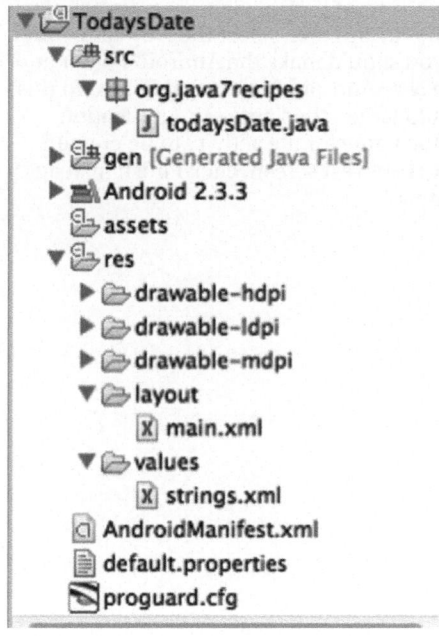

Figure 19-2. Expanded Android project within Eclipse

These todaysDate.java and main.xml files are very important. The todaysDate.java file contains the Java code that is used to create the activity, or view, of the application. This application will only contain a single activity, and it will display a line of text that will show the current date and time. The second file, main.xml, is used to build the view layout. It contains a series of XML tags that correspond to the different activities of the application, which will produce the user interface. Because there is only one activity, todaysDate.java, there is only one corresponding layout XML file.

As mentioned in the solution to this recipe, you should open up the todaysDate.java file and modify the code so that it resembles the one shown in the solution. This file contains the code for an activity within the application. An activity represents one screen within the user interface. Activities and user interface screens go hand in hand. An Activity class is implemented as a subclass of android.app.Activity. To learn more specific details regarding implementing activities, please refer to recipe 19-4. The important changes that are made to the code for this example include the addition of two global variables: one of which corresponds to a widget known as a TextView, and the other corresponds to the layout. The layout managers within Android applications are somewhat similar to those that are used in Swing development. As you can see, a new LinearLayout is created and configured within a couple of lines of code and then the TextView, tv, is added to the layout.

Finally, the layout is set as the content view, which means that it will be displayed on the screen:

```
layout = new LinearLayout(this);
layout.setLayoutParams(new LayoutParams(LayoutParams.FILL_PARENT,
                LayoutParams.FILL_PARENT));
layout.setOrientation(LinearLayout.VERTICAL);
layout.addView(tv);
setContentView(layout);
```

Next, add the doWork() method. This method contains the implementation of the activity. It creates a new java.util.Date object and then creates a new TextView widget. The text of the widget is then set to display the current date that is obtained from java.util.Date:

```
Date todaysDate = new Date();
tv = new TextView(this);
tv.setText("The current date is: " + todaysDate);
```

The custom code is now complete, and the content layout that was set in the todaysDate activity will be used to populate the view that has been laid out within the main.xml file. Those two files go hand in hand, and if you add more Activities in other applications, each one that contains a view will include a corresponding XML layout.

19-3. Compiling and Testing in an Emulator

Problem

You have developed an application for the Android mobile operating system and need to compile it and test it in your development environment.

Solution

Use the Eclipse IDE to build and compile your Android project, and then deploy the application to the emulator.

How It Works

To compile an Android project, right-click the Android project within Eclipse and choose the Run As menu option, followed by the Android Application menu option. This will compile and build a deployable Android .apk file for your application. It will then start up the corresponding AVD and deploy your application to it for testing. Once the AVD boots and loads the application, a screen that resembles Figure 19-3 will appear.

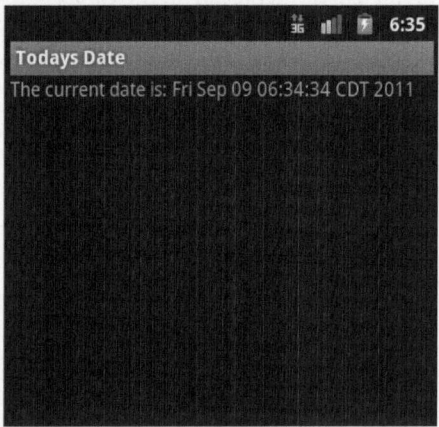

Figure 19-3. Android Todays Date application screen running within AVD

■ **Note** Be sure that you are using an emulator target platform that is compatible with the SDK version that is configured within `AndroidManifest.xml`. You will also need to ensure that the Android project properties are set to use the same SDK as the emulator target platform.

19-4. Constructing a User Interface with XML Layout

Problem

You are interested in building a nontrivial user interface for an Android application using an XML file for the layout. The application interface will contain a text box for user entry, a drop-down list that will allow a selection of text, and a button to submit the values that have been entered.

Solution

Develop the application screen, which is composed of views for each of the user interface components. The screen will consist of an `Activity` class to handle the business logic and a corresponding layout XML file to define the layout. The code for the screen's `Activity` class is shown here:

```
package org.java7recipes;

import android.app.Activity;
import android.os.Bundle;
```

```java
import android.view.View;
import android.widget.ArrayAdapter;
import android.widget.Spinner;

publicclass EnterInformation extends Activity {

        private Spinner spinner;

        /** Called when the activity is first created. */
        @Override
        publicvoid onCreate(Bundle savedInstanceState) {
                super.onCreate(savedInstanceState);
                setContentView(R.layout.enterinformation);

                spinner = (Spinner) this.findViewById(R.id.spinner);
                ArrayAdapter<CharSequence> adapter = ArrayAdapter.createFromResource(
                        this, R.array.levels_array,
                        android.R.layout.simple_spinner_item);

        adapter.setDropDownViewResource(android.R.layout.simple_spinner_dropdown_item);
                spinner.setAdapter(adapter);

        }

        publicvoid performAction(View view) {
                // Perform button action here
        }
}
```

As mentioned previously, the screen will also use an XML file to compose the overall layout. The layout XML file will look like the following:

```xml
<?xml version="1.0" encoding="utf-8"?>
<LinearLayout xmlns:android="http://schemas.android.com/apk/res/android"
    android:orientation="vertical"
    android:layout_width="fill_parent"
    android:layout_height="fill_parent"
>
        <EditText
            android:id="@+id/edittext"
            android:layout_width="fill_parent"
            android:layout_height="wrap_content"
            android:text="@string/entertext"/>
        <Spinner
            android:id="@+id/spinner"
            android:layout_width="fill_parent"
```

```
            android:layout_height="wrap_content"
            android:prompt="@string/levels_prompt"/>
        <Button
            android:layout_height="wrap_content"
        android:layout_width="wrap_content"
        android:text="@string/button"
        android:onClick="performAction" />
</LinearLayout>
```

■ **Note** This recipe discusses construction of the user interface only. For information on handling events such as button clicks, please see recipe 19-6.

■ **Note** In order to run this and the remaining examples in this chapter, merge the src and res folders from the book sources for Chapter 19 into your existing TodaysDate project. Once you've done that, then you'll only need to modify AndroidManifest.xml to modify the Activity name tag according to the example Activity class you want to run.

How It Works

Android user interfaces are constructed using a series of files that corresponds to different application screens. An application can consist of one or more different application screens, and a user will only interact with one screen at a time. A screen consists of a hierarchy of view objects. Views are drawable objects and they are the building blocks of a user interface. For instance, all user interface widgets are views; therefore, a button is a view, a text area is a view, and any other widget that is used within a screen is a view. A single screen can contain many views. Each screen within an Android application consists of a single class known as an `activity` that is used to construct the views that will be used on that screen. Hopefully by this point you are beginning to see that Android applications are constructed in a very logical and uniform fashion. Each application screen has an `Activity` class that contains its application logic. In order to build a user screen, you must create an `Activity`, which pertains to a single focused task that the user can perform. An `Activity` can be stand-alone or embedded inside other activities.

The first step to creating an activity is to create a new Java class that will become a subclass of `android.app.Activity`. In the solution to this recipe, the `Activity class` is called `EnterInformation`, and its corresponding Java file is named `EnterInformation.java`. As you can see, the class extends `android.app.Activity`, and by doing so, it inherits a number of methods. Two of the most important methods include `onCreate(Bundle)` and `onPause()`. Every Android activity must override the `onCreate(Bundle)` method; it initializes the activity because it is the first method that is called when the `Activity` class is constructed. The `onCreate(Bundle)` method is typically used to perform any necessary setup for building the layout of the screen that is associated with the activity. As you can see in solution 1, the `onCreate()` method accepts a `Bundle` argument, which pertains to the saved instance state of the activity. The first line within the `onCreate()` method should be a call to the `Activity` superclass, passing the `Bundle` as follows:

```
super.onCreate(savedInstanceState);
```

The initialization code that is contained within onCreate should call setContentView(int) to create the activity's user interface. In the solution you can see that a strange looking object is passed to the setContentView method. That object pertains to an Android layout XML file; in this case the file is named R.layout.enterinformation. You may be wondering where the R came from because this class is not listed in the imports. The R class is automatically generated when the application is compiled, and it contains the resource IDs for all the resources that are contained within the application's res directory. All resource IDs are stored within the R class, which can be used to retrieve the resource. If you look at the setContentView call within the solution, you can see that the static integer that corresponds to R.layout.enterinformation is passed to it.

■ **Note** You should never have to manually access or change the R class. The Android build process will take care of automatically generating the R class for you. The R class contains the resource IDs, which are automatically generated for each resource. The resource ID is always composed of the resource type and the resource name.

APPLICATION RESOURCES

Every Android application contains resources that are used to compose the user interface. Resources can be components such as images and strings. These resources should always be externalized from application code so that they can be independently managed. Therefore, resources are contained within XML files to make them more manageable.

All resources must be organized within the project's res directory, and they must be organized into groups that categorize them based upon type and configuration. Many different types of resources can be provided for an application, and they include the following:

- Animation Resources

    o Tween animations reside within the res/anim/ directory

    o Frame animations reside within the res/drawable/ directory

- Color-State List Resources

    o Reside within the res/color/ directory

- Drawable Resources

    o Reside within the res/drawable/ directory

- Layout Resources

o   Reside within the `res/layout/` directory

• Menu Resources

o   Reside within the `res/menu/` directory

• String Resources

o   Reside within the `res/values/` directory

• Style Resources

o   Reside within the `res/values/` directory

• Value-Type Resources

o   Reside within the `res/values/` directory

Resources can be accessed within the `Activity` class using a static integer from a subclass in the `R` class (for example, `R.layout.mylayout` or `R.string.mystring`). They can also be accessed in the XML by using a special syntax that also corresponds to the resource ID defined within the `R` class (for example, `@string/mystring`).

For more detailed information regarding application resources, please visit the online documentation at `http://developer.android.com/guide/topics/resources/index.html`.

If you are using an XML file to construct the layout for the activity's user interface, you do not need to write any more code within the `Activity` class unless you need to construct views or handle events. In the solution to this recipe, a layout XML file is used, so no further coding is required to build the layout. However, a widget called a `Spinner` is constructed within the activity as well. The `android.widget.Spinner` widget is used to represent a drop-down list of values within the user interface. The drop-down list of values can be constructed programmatically, and the strings that are contained within the drop-down list are defined within an XML resource file. This `Spinner` was added to the user interface to provide a brief introduction to working with views within Android activities. First, the `Spinner` widget is referenced using the `R.id.spinner` static integer, which corresponds to the `Spinner` tag that is located within the XML layout file (as seen in the second code listing within the solution). This reference binds the XML tag to the code.

■ **Note**   You can reference any widget that is defined within an XML layout programmatically by using the `findViewById(int)` method, and passing the resource ID for the widget you are using.

An array is then constructed using the externally defined Strings to build the drop-down list of values. It is worth noting that Android provides predefined templates for use with widgets, and often developers can make use of those templates in order to help reduce development time. Such predefined templates are used to setup the drop `ArrayAdapter` for the `Spinner` view. The complete construction of the `Spinner` view can be seen in the following code excerpt:

```
spinner = (Spinner) this.findViewById(R.id.spinner);
ArrayAdapter<CharSequence> adapter = ArrayAdapter.createFromResource(
this, R.array.levels_array,
android.R.layout.simple_spinner_item);
adapter.setDropDownViewResource(android.R.layout.simple_spinner_dropdown_item);
spinner.setAdapter(adapter);
```

The next step after creating the `Activity` class is to construct a layout XML file. An `Activity` class can have an optional corresponding layout XML file that is used to construct the layout in a visual manner. An XML file that is used for the layout is not mandatory (this will be discussed more in recipe 19-5). The layout XML file is used to organize the widgets that will be used to construct the user interface. In the solution to this recipe, there are four subviews within the XML layout. One of them is a layout object, which is used to define the manner in which its child views are positioned on the screen. The solution uses a `LinearLayout`, which aligns all children in a single direction. The orientation that is set for the layout determines in which direction the children will be aligned. The solution aligns the children vertically, which means that each child will stack one on top of the other. One can also set a width and height for the layout using the `android:layout_width` and `android:layout_height` attributes, respectively.

```
<LinearLayout xmlns:android="http://schemas.android.com/apk/res/android"
    android:orientation="vertical"
    android:layout_width="fill_parent"
    android:layout_height="fill_parent"
>
```

■ **Note** There are several layout objects that can be used within Android application screens. To see a full list of layout objects along with details regarding usage, please refer to the documentation that is available at `http://developer.android.com/guide/topics/ui/layout-objects.html`.

The tags contained within the opening and closing tags of the `LinearLayout` tag define the children; in this case they are widgets that will be displayed on the screen. Those widgets are `EditView`, `Spinner`, and `Button`, respectively. Each of these XML tags contains attributes that are used to define the widget's appearance and behavior. As you can see, each of the tags, with the exception of the `<Button>`, contains an `android:id` attribute. This declares the ID that can be referenced via the `Activity` class using the `R.id.idnumber` syntax. The `<Spinner>` tag contains the attribute `android:prompt="@string/levels_prompt"`, which refers to a string element that is contained within the `strings.xml` resource file. The `<Button>` tag contains the attributes `android:text="@string/button"` and `android:onClick="performAction"`. Similar to the `<Spinner>` tag's `android:prompt` attribute, the `android:text` attribute refers to a string element that is contained within the `strings.xml` resource file.

The android:onClick attribute specifies a method, in this case performAction, that is implemented within the corresponding Activity class that will be used as a listener for the button click. For more information regarding listeners and event handling, please refer to recipe 19-6.

The XML layout contains references to strings that have been declared within the strings.xml file for the application. Assuming that this activity is being added to the Android project, which was created in recipe 19-2, the strings.xml file should look like the following:

```xml
<?xml version="1.0" encoding="utf-8"?>
<resources>
<string name="hello">Hello World, todaysDate!</string>
<string name="app_name">Todays Date</string>
<string name="button">Press Me</string>
<string name="entertext">Enter Your Name</string>
<string name="levels_prompt">Choose a level</string>
<string-array name="levels_array">
<item>Beginner</item>
<item>Intermediate</item>
<item>Advanced</item>
</string-array>
</resources>
```

As you can see, each string element contains a name and a value, and the array element contains a list of String items. The string names can then be used within layout XML or programmatically as demonstrated in this solution.

Lastly, the Activity class must be registered with the application within the AndroidManifest.xml. To learn more about registering an activity, please see recipe 19-6. The resulting user interface screen will look similar to Figure 19-4.

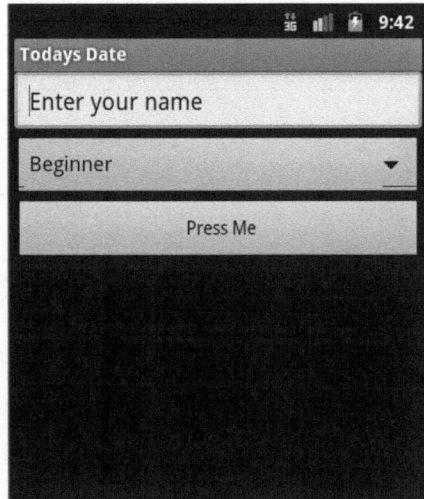

Figure 19-4. Android user interface example

■ **Note** The name of the application is "Today's Date" because this chapter assumes that you will build onto the project created in recipe 19-2. If you want to create a new Android project, please follow the steps within recipe 19-2. You could also change the string that is mapped to app_name within strings.xml, so a different name is displayed.

19-5. Constructing a User Interface Programmatically

Problem

You are interested in building a non-trivial user interface for an Android application without using an XML file for the layout. The application interface will contain a text box for user entry, a drop-down list that will allow a selection of text, and a button to submit the values that have been entered, just like the user interface that was developed in recipe 19-4.

Solution

Develop the user interface entirely within the Activity class, and do not create an XML file for the layout. The following code demonstrates how to construct the same user interface screen, which was built in recipe 19-4 by programmatically using a layout view and organizing subviews within it programmatically.

```java
package org.java7recipes;

import android.app.Activity;
import android.content.Intent;
import android.os.Bundle;
import android.view.View;
import android.widget.ArrayAdapter;
import android.widget.Button;
import android.widget.EditText;
import android.widget.LinearLayout;
import android.widget.Spinner;

publicclass EnterInformationProgrammatically extends Activity {

private LinearLayout layout;
private Button button;
private Spinner spinner;
private EditText editText;
```

```
/** Called when the activity is first created. */
@Override
    publicvoid onCreate(Bundle savedInstanceState) {
        super.onCreate(savedInstanceState);
        layout = new LinearLayout(this);
        layout.setOrientation(android.widget.LinearLayout.VERTICAL);
        button = new Button(this);
        button.setText("Press Me");

        editText = new EditText(this);
        editText.setText("Enter your name");

        spinner = new Spinner(this);
        ArrayAdapter<CharSequence> adapter = ArrayAdapter.createFromResource(
                this, R.array.levels_array,
                android.R.layout.simple_spinner_item);
        adapter.setDropDownViewResource(android.R.layout.simple_spinner_dropdown_item);
        spinner.setAdapter(adapter);

        // Add views to the layout
        layout.addView(editText);
        layout.addView(spinner);
        layout.addView(button);
        setContentView(layout);
    }
}
```

■ **Note** This recipe discusses construction of the user interface only. For information on handling events such as button clicks, please see recipe 19-6.

How It Works

It is possible to construct a user interface entirely within Java code without the need for a corresponding XML layout file. Why would you be interested in using this technique? Although defining an XML layout has the advantages of being easy to maintain and more readable, developing a layout entirely in code can provide more flexibility if the need arises. To create a user interface without XML, you need to instantiate and configure the layout programmatically within the Activity class. If using a layout object, that must be programmatically defined and each of its children must be added to it manually. If you like Java Swing, the programmatic approach may be for you because there are some close similarities between the programmatic development of Android user interfaces and the construction of a Java Swing user interface.

Looking at the code contained within the solution, you can see that
EnterInformationProgrammatically.java resembles the Activity class that was defined within recipe 19-4, except there are several more lines of code. The class extends android.app.Activity, and each of the widgets that will be used within the user interface is declared as private. The obligatory onCreate(Bundle) method is where the user interface construction takes place. The first line within the method is a call to the super class's onCreate() method, passing a Bundle that contains the saved instance state for the activity. Next, a new LinearLayout instance is created, passing the Activity class as an argument via the this keyword. After the layout is declared, its orientation is set by calling the layout's setOrientation(int), passing a static constant int value representing the type of orientation. In this case, it is android.widget.LinearLayout.VERTICAL:

```
layout = new LinearLayout(this);
layout.setOrientation(android.widget.LinearLayout.VERTICAL);
```

Next, the child views that will go within the layout are constructed. That is, each widget is now instantiated, and attributes are set accordingly. The widgets can be defined and configured in any order. First, the Button is instantiated, and its text is set.

```
button = new Button(this);
button.setText("Press Me");
```

Second, the EditText widget is instantiated, and its text is set.

```
editText = new EditText(this);
editText.setText("Enter your name");
```

Finally, the Spinner widget is instantiated and configured accordingly. If you read through recipe 19-4, you will notice that instead of passing a resource ID to the Spinner when instantiating it, the this keyword is passed. Because there is no corresponding XML layout, there is no resource ID to pass. The following code shows how the 4 is instantiated and constructed:

```
spinner = new Spinner(this);
ArrayAdapter<CharSequence> adapter = ArrayAdapter.createFromResource(
        this, R.array.levels_array,
        android.R.layout.simple_spinner_item);
adapter.setDropDownViewResource(android.R.layout.simple_spinner_dropdown_item);
spinner.setAdapter(adapter);
```

The final thing that needs to be completed is to add each of the widgets to the layout. While adding widgets to the layout, the ordering is important. The first widget that is added will be placed in the first position of the layout, and the others will follow suit according to the position in which they are added. Finally, the layout itself is passed to the setContentView() method. If you fail to do this, the user interface will be blank.

```
layout.addView(editText);
layout.addView(spinner);
layout.addView(button);
setContentView(layout);
```

That completes the programmatic construction of the user interface. The next step is to register the Activity class within the AndroidManifest.xml, which is covered in recipe 19-7. It is also important to note that the button will not do anything at this time. To learn more about adding listeners to buttons and handling events, please see recipe 19-6.

19-6. Handling Application Events and Activity Changes

Problem

You have developed an Android application user interface and would like to add some functionality to it. For instance, you created a screen that includes a button and you would like to open another application screen when that button is clicked, passing information that was obtained from the original screen.

Solution 1

Develop a listener for the button by mapping the layout XML tag to an event handling method that resides within the corresponding activity. To use this technique, your user interface must be composed of a layout XML file along with an associated `Activity` class. Once the listener is invoked, use an `Intent` to pass data to the `Activity` class for another screen. The following code excerpt shows what the XML within the layout would look like for the button:

```
!
<Button
android:layout_height="wrap_content"
android:layout_width="wrap_content"
android:text="@string/button"
android:onClick="performAction" />
!
```

In this case, a method named `performAction()` that resides within the `Activity` class will be triggered when the button is pressed. The code for the `performAction()` is as follows:

```
publicvoid performAction(View view) {
        // Perform button action here
        editText = (EditText) this.findViewById(R.id.edittext);
        Intent i = new Intent(EnterInformation.this, DisplayInformation.class);
        Bundle b = new Bundle();
        b.putString("name", editText.getText().toString());
        b.putString("level", spinner.getSelectedItem().toString());

        i.putExtra("android.intent.extra.INTENT", b);
        startActivity(i);
        }
```

Solution 2

Programmatically add an event listener to a button that is contained within the screen. Using this technique, the button functionality takes place within the screen's **Activity** class using Swing-like action listeners. The following code can be used within the **Activity** class to programmatically add an event listener to the **Button**:

```
button.setOnClickListener(new View.OnClickListener() {
publicvoid onClick(View v) {
      performAction();
   }
});
```

The performAction() method that is invoked within onClick() uses an Intent to pass data to a different Activity class. The code for performAction() is as follows:

```
public void performAction() {
        // Perform button action here
        Intent i = new Intent(EnterInformationProgramatically.this, DisplayInformation.class);
        Bundle b = new Bundle();
        b.putString("name", editText.getText().toString());
        b.putString("level", spinner.getSelectedItem().toString());

        i.putExtra("android.intent.extra.INTENT", b);
        startActivity(i);
        }
```

■ **Note** In order to run this code, add the following lines to the AndroidManifest.xml file from recipe 19-6:

<activity android:name=".DisplayInformation"

android:label="@string/app_name">

</activity>

Refer to recipe 19-7 for more information.

How It Works

Once again, there are two different ways to handle view events for a specified screen. Using the technique specified in solution 1, you can choose to use a layout XML file to configure the layout for the screen, and use the XML tag attributes to assign listeners. Note that the tag lists an `android:onClick` attribute with a listener method by the name of `performAction`. This method resides within the `Activity` class for the screen. When the button is clicked, the method is invoked and performs some work.

Using a programmatic approach, the listener can be added using the `Button` class's `setOnClickListener(OnClickListener)` method. The standard approach for adding a listener to a button in this manner is to use an anonymous inner class to use as the listener. As you can see in solution 2, a new `View.OnClickListener` class is created, and the `onClick(View)` method is implemented within it in order to perform the required activity.

What can you do within a listener method? You can do just about anything that is required to handle your event. In the `performAction` method for this recipe, the text from within the widgets on the screen is sent to another screen using an `Intent`, which is a runtime binding between the code and different classes within the application. They can be used to perform a number of operations, including starting a new activity, starting a service, and broadcasting. In this case, the `Intent` is used to start a new activity, passing data along with it. Each of the solutions in the recipe has a slightly different implementation of the `performAction()` method. In the first solution, the resource ID for each widget is used to obtain the text that has been entered into the `EditView` or selected on the `Spinner`. The second solution uses fields of the class to obtain the text from each widget. All the other functionality is the same between the two methods.

To start a new activity, instantiate a new `Intent`, passing the current `Activity` class and the `Activity` class that you want to start:

```
Intent i = new Intent(EnterInformation.this, DisplayInformation.class);
```

■ **Note**   `Intents` play an important role in Android application development. To learn more, please see the online documentation available at `http://developer.android.com/reference/android/content/Intent.html`.

ACTIVITY PROCESS LIFE CYCLE

The activity process life cycle becomes important when you have an application that contains more than one activity. Mobile devices need to maintain a close watch on system resources in an attempt to try and limit the amount of memory in use. Doing so helps to ensure that the systems do not run low on the memory required to perform background processes such as receiving phone calls. Because memory management on mobile devices is important, it is good to know how Android attempts to maintain processes. The system will attempt to keep application processes around for as long as possible, but eventually they will need to be removed in order to reallocate memory for new processes to run. An activity life cycle is used to help determine which processes are more important than others, and the less important processes will be killed first.

An activity has four states:

- Activities that are in the foreground of the screen are at the top of the stack. These are *active* activities.

- Activities that are not in focus, but still remain visible are referred to as *paused*. A paused activity is still alive and maintains state unless the system is running critically low on memory.

- Activities that are completely obscured by another activity are referred to as *stopped*. A stopped activity still retains state and information, but if it is completely hidden from the user interface, it will be killed by the system when memory is needed elsewhere.

- Activities that are paused or stopped can be dropped by the system. In order to do so, the system will ask it to finish, or simply kill it. The next time the activity is needed, it must be completely restarted and restored to its previous state.

It is important to know when an activity will be closed or needs to be restored. Sometimes such events can be critical to an application's use.

Next, create a new `Bundle` to pass the data to the new activity. The `Bundle` can contain any number of values, and in the solution to this recipe the text from both the `EditView` and `Spinner` widgets is added to the `Bundle`. The `Bundle` is then added to the `Intent` by calling the `Intent` class's `putExtra()` method. Last, the `startActivity(Intent)` method is called, passing the `Intent`.

```
i.putExtra("android.intent.extra.INTENT", b);
startActivity(i);
```

Once the screen that pertains to the `EnterInformation` activity has been filled out, and the button has been clicked, the `DisplayInformation` activity will be activated. The `DisplayInformation` activity is not very complex; it only displays a message that includes some content taken from the user in the previous screen. It uses a `TextView` widget to display the text. The code for `DisplayInformation.java` looks like the following:

```
package org.java7recipes;

import android.app.Activity;
import android.content.Intent;

import android.os.Bundle;

import android.widget.TextView;
```

```java
public class DisplayInformation extends Activity {

        private TextView textView;

    /** Called when the activity is first created. */
    @Override
    public void onCreate(Bundle savedInstanceState) {
        String displayText = null;
                super.onCreate(savedInstanceState);

        setContentView(R.layout.displayinformation);

        Intent startingIntent = getIntent();
        if (startingIntent != null) {
                Bundle b = startingIntent
                                .getBundleExtra("android.intent.extra.INTENT");
                if (b == null) {
                        displayText = "No data.";
                } else {
                        displayText = b.getString("name") + ",\n\n";
                        displayText += "You are a " + b.getString("level") + "\n\n";
                        displayText += "Android developer.\n";
                }
        } else {
                displayText = "Information Not Found.";
        }
        textView = (TextView) this.findViewById(R.id.displaytext);
        textView.setText(displayText);
    }
}
```

The corresponding layout XML file is named displayInformation.xml, and it looks like the following:

```xml
<?xml version="1.0" encoding="utf-8"?>
<LinearLayout xmlns:android="http://schemas.android.com/apk/res/android"
    android:orientation="vertical"
    android:layout_width="fill_parent"
    android:layout_height="fill_parent"
>
<TextView
android:id="@+id/displaytext"
android:layout_width="fill_parent"
android:layout_height="wrap_content" />
</LinearLayout>
```

In the end, the resulting screen will look like Figure 19-5.

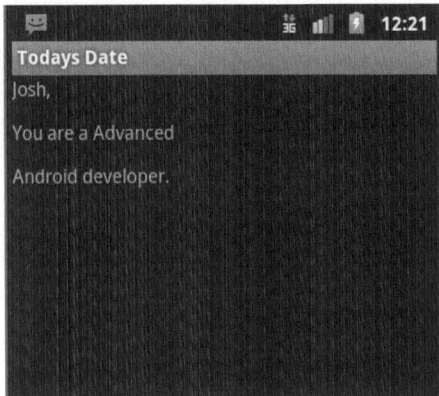

Figure 19-5. Screen corresponding to the DisplayInformation activity

This recipe only covers a small portion of what can be done with events and Intents on Android. This is a very important topic, and there is a wealth of information on them that can be found online. Please refer to the online documentation that can be found at `http://developer.android.com/reference/android/content/Intent.html` for more details.

19-7. Tying All Application Components Together

Problem

An activity has been created for your application and you would like to register it to be loaded when the application is started.

Solution

Register the activity within the `AndroidManifest.xml` file. If you'd like for the activity to be loaded at application startup, indicate that within the manifest as well. The following excerpt has been taken from the `AndroidManifest.xml` file that was created for the project from recipe 19-2. The activity being registered was created within recipe 19-4.

```
<activity android:name=".EnterInformation"
          android:label="@string/app_name">
<intent-filter>
<action android:name="android.intent.action.MAIN" />
<category android:name="android.intent.category.LAUNCHER" />
</intent-filter>
</activity>
```

How It Works

Every Android application must have an `AndroidManifest.xml` file. The file must be located in the root directory of the application. It includes information regarding the application's components, processes, permissions, and more. The manifest is read before any of the application's code is executed. As a matter of fact, the manifest is used to register `Activity` classes and determine which class is executed first when the application is started up.

All application `Activity` classes must be registered within the `AndroidManifest.xml`. In order to register an activity, embed a new `<activity>` tag within the `<application>` element of the manifest. The required `android:name` attribute should be set to the name of the class that corresponds to the activity. The tag's `android:label` attribute can be used to label the activity screen. In the solution to this recipe, the `android:label` attribute is set to `@string/app_name`, which corresponds to a string element named `app_name` that is declared within the `strings.xml` file. For normal activity registration, the `<activity>` tag is all that is required. However, if you want to register an activity as the main activity that will be launched upon application startup, an intent filter must be registered. This can be done by embedding the `<intent-filter>` tags within the `<activity>` tag, and passing the following action and category:

```
<action android:name="android.intent.action.MAIN" />
<category android:name="android.intent.category.LAUNCHER" />
```

■ **Note**   The `<activity>` tag is quite involved, and contains a great many options. For more details on using the `<activity>` tag, please see the online documentation available at:

`http://developer.android.com/guide/topics/manifest/activity-element.html`.

As mentioned previously, the manifest is used for much more than registering activities. To learn more about registering application permissions, please see recipe 19-11. To learn more about what is possible with the `AndroidManifest.xml` file, please refer to the online documentation that can be found at `http://developer.android.com/guide/topics/manifest/manifest-intro.html`.

19-8. Handling Incoming Call Events

Problem

When your users receive a phone call, the application you have written does not pause to allow the user to answer the call. You would like to make your application pause and fall into the background when a call comes in.

Solution

Create a broadcast receiver to handle the incoming phone calls. A broadcast receiver consists of two things: a `BroadcastReceiver` class, and configuration within the `AndroidManifest.xml` file. The following code demonstrates a `BroadcastReceiver` class that handles incoming phone calls:

```
package org.java7recipes;

import android.content.BroadcastReceiver;
import android.content.Context;
import android.content.Intent;
import android.os.Bundle;
import android.telephony.TelephonyManager;
import android.util.Log;

publicclass PhoneReceiver extends BroadcastReceiver {

        private PhoneReceiver application;

        @Override
        publicvoid onReceive(Context context, Intent intent) {
                Bundle extras = intent.getExtras();
                if (extras != null) {
                String state = extras.getString(TelephonyManager.EXTRA_STATE);
                if (state.equals(TelephonyManager.EXTRA_STATE_RINGING)) {
                        String phoneNumber = extras
                        .getString(TelephonyManager.EXTRA_INCOMING_NUMBER);
                }
                }
        }
}
```

Register the receiver within the `AndroidManifest.xml` file. The following excerpt from the `AndroidManifest.xml` demonstrates how to register the receiver. These tags should be nested within the `<application>` tags. Please refer to the source files for a full example.

```
!
<receiver android:name=".PhoneReceiver">
<intent-filter>
<action android:name="android.intent.action.PHONE_STATE" />
<action android:name="android.provider.Telephony.SMS_RECEIVED" />
</intent-filter>
</receiver>
!
```

When the application is started, it should now be paused when an incoming call event occurs. If a Short Message Service (SMS) message is received, it will be displayed within the top menu bar while the application is running.

How It Works

Your application is the most important piece of software running on an Android device. Well, you may think that is the case, but unfortunately it is not. The most important software running on the device may not have any interaction with your application at all. Of course, we are talking about the capability for the Android device to communicate via phone or SMS services. Ultimately, mobile devices are most useful for communication, and applications that do not pause or allow the user to exit and take action upon a received phone call or SMS message are usually frowned upon. It is important to build your application so that it is aware of any incoming phone calls or messages and takes the appropriate action to allow users to act upon them.

The solution to this issue is the broadcast receiver. *Broadcast receivers* are components that respond to system-wide announcements. They have no user interface; instead they act as a transparent gateway for other components to perform tasks. For instance, the system may broadcast any number of announcements. They may include an incoming phone call or SMS message, low battery, or a screen being turned off. Any broadcast receivers will be notified of such announcements, and then they can perform a task such as pausing an application to allow the user to take a phone call.

TYPES OF BROADCASTS

There are two main types of broadcasts that can be received. Those types are as follows:

Normal Broadcasts: Completely asynchronous broadcasts. All receivers are run in an undefined order. Sent via `Context.sendBroadcast.`

Ordered Broadcasts: Delivered to one receiver at a time. Each receiver can execute and then propagate a result or abort the broadcast. Sent via `Context.sendOrderedBroadcast`. Receivers can be run in a specified order by setting the `android:priority` attribute within the corresponding intent filter. If two or more receivers contain the same priority number, they will be executed in any order.

Broadcasts are delivered as `Intent` objects, and a `Broadcast Receiver` acts as a listener for those Intents. In order to create a broadcast receiver class, you must extend the `android.content.BroadcastReceiver` class. The `onReceive(Context, Intent)` method must be implemented within a `BroadcastReceiver` class. Its purpose is to receive any broadcasts and act upon them accordingly. In the solution to this recipe, the receiver's main objective is to listen for incoming phone calls or SMS messages. When a call comes in, the broadcast receiver's `onReceive()` method is called and the `Intent` is passed into it. The first line of the method gets the broadcasted announcement by calling the `Intent`'s `getExtras()` method, and a `Bundle` is obtained. The `Bundle` can then be interrogated to determine the type of broadcast that has been made. To check for broadcasts pertaining to telephony, the `TelephonyManager.EXTRA_STATE` state is parsed. If the state equals `TelephonyManager.EXTRA_STATE_RINGING`, a task is performed. In the solution, the incoming phone number is captured. All this can be seen within the following code excerpt taken from the solution's `onReceive()` method:

```
Bundle extras = intent.getExtras();
if (extras != null) {
String state = extras.getString(TelephonyManager.EXTRA_STATE);
if (state.equals(TelephonyManager.EXTRA_STATE_RINGING)) {
        String phoneNumber = extras
                        .getString(TelephonyManager.EXTRA_INCOMING_NUMBER);
}
}
```

■ **Note** Although broadcasts to the system use `Intent` objects, they are separate from those `Intent` objects that are used for starting activities.

Just like an `Activity` class, a `BroadcastReceiver` class must be registered in the `AndroidManifext.xml` file. A `<receiver>` tag is used to register a broadcast receiver, and each Intent action that the receiver will be listening for is embedded within the `<intent-filter>` tag. In the solution, the `android:name` attribute of the `<receiver>` tag specifies the name of the corresponding receiver class. Two Intent actions are filtered with the receiver: phone calls and SMS. The corresponding action names are `android.intent.action.PHONE_STATE` and `android.provider.Telephony.SMS_RECEIVED`, respectively.

The topic of broadcast receivers is immense, and entire chapters can be written on the topic. This recipe only covers a small aspect of what broadcast receivers are capable of doing. To learn more about broadcast receivers, please see the online documentation that can be found at `http://developer.android.com/reference/android/content/BroadcastReceiver.html`.

19-9. Building a Tabbed User Interface

Problem

You would like to design a user interface that can make it easy to switch between two or more application screens.

Solution

Develop a tabbed user interface and designate a tab for each application screen. To do so, create a new `Activity` class that extends the `android.app.TabActivity` class. This activity will be used to construct the tabbed user interface. For this example, a tabbed interface will be developed for the application that has been created using the previous recipes in this chapter. The following code is from the TabContainer.java file, which is the implementation for the TabActivity class named TabContainer:

```java
package org.java7recipes;

import android.app.TabActivity;
import android.content.Intent;
import android.content.res.Resources;
import android.os.Bundle;
import android.widget.TabHost;

public class TabContainer extends TabActivity {
    /** Called when the activity is first created. */
    @Override
    public void onCreate(Bundle savedInstanceState) {
        super.onCreate(savedInstanceState);
        setupTabs();
    }

    private void setupTabs(){
        setContentView(R.layout.tabs);

        Resources res = getResources(); // Resource object for obtaining drawables
        TabHost tabHost = getTabHost();
        TabHost.TabSpec spec;
        Intent intent;

        // Create an Intent to launch an Activity for the tab
        intent = new Intent().setClass(this, EnterInformation.class);

        // Initialize a TabSpec for each tab, and then add to tabhost
        spec = tabHost.newTabSpec("enterInformation").setIndicator("Information",
                            res.getDrawable(R.drawable.enterinformation))
                    .setContent(intent);
        tabHost.addTab(spec);

        intent = new Intent().setClass(this, todaysDate.class);
        spec = tabHost.newTabSpec("todaysDate").setIndicator("Todays Date",
                        res.getDrawable(R.drawable.main))
                    .setContent(intent);
        tabHost.addTab(spec);

        intent = new Intent().setClass(this, VisitSite.class);
        spec = tabHost.newTabSpec("visitSite").setIndicator("Visit java.net",
                        res.getDrawable(R.drawable.visitsite))
                    .setContent(intent);
```

```
        tabHost.addTab(spec);

        tabHost.setCurrentTab(0);
    }

}
```

The next step is to provide a new drawable XML file for each of the activities for which you want to create a tab. These drawable XML files must reside within the `res/drawable/` directory in the application. The following code shows what one of these XML files will look like. One should be created for each activity that is going to be contained within a tab. The following code is contained within a file named `enterinformation.XML`, which resides within the `res/drawable/` directory:

```xml
<?xml version="1.0" encoding="utf-8"?>
<selector xmlns:android="http://schemas.android.com/apk/res/android">
<!-- When selected, use grey -->
<item android:drawable="@drawable/group-selected"
        android:state_selected="true" />
<!-- When not selected, use white-->
<item android:drawable="@drawable/group-deselected" />
</selector>
```

After creating a new drawable XML file for each tab, create the main tab layout XML file within the `res/layout/` directory. This file will be used to construct the XML layout for the tabbed user interface. The following code is taken from a file named `tabs.xml` which resides within the `res/layout/` directory:

```xml
<?xml version="1.0" encoding="utf-8"?>
<TabHost xmlns:android="http://schemas.android.com/apk/res/android"
    android:id="@android:id/tabhost"
    android:layout_width="fill_parent"
    android:layout_height="fill_parent">
<LinearLayout
        android:orientation="vertical"
        android:layout_width="fill_parent"
        android:layout_height="fill_parent"
        android:padding="5dp">
<TabWidget
        android:id="@android:id/tabs"
        android:layout_width="fill_parent"
        android:layout_height="wrap_content" />
<FrameLayout
        android:id="@android:id/tabcontent"
        android:layout_width="fill_parent"
        android:layout_height="fill_parent"
        android:padding="5dp" />
</LinearLayout>
</TabHost>
```

Lastly, register the new `TabActivity` class within the `AndroidManifest.xml` file. After doing so, the complete manifest file should look as follows:

```xml
<?xml version="1.0" encoding="utf-8"?>
<manifest xmlns:android="http://schemas.android.com/apk/res/android"
        package="org.java7recipes" android:versionCode="1" android:versionName="1.0">


        <application android:icon="@drawable/icon" android:label="@string/app_name">
                <activity android:name=".TabContainer" android:label="@string/app_name"
                        android:configChanges="keyboardHidden|orientation"
                                        android.theme="@android:style/Theme.NoTitleBar"
                        android:launchMode="singleTop">
                        <intent-filter>
                                <action android:name="android.intent.action.MAIN" />
                                <category android:name="android.intent.category.LAUNCHER" />
                        </intent-filter>
                </activity>
                <activity android:name=".todaysDate" android:label="@string/app_name">


                </activity>
                <activity android:name=".EnterInformation"
                        android:label="@string/app_name">
                </activity>
                <activity android:name=".VisitSite"
                        android:label="@string/app_name">
                </activity>
                <activity android:name=".EnterInformationProgrammatically"
                        android:label="@string/app_name">

                </activity>
                <activity android:name=".DisplayInformation" android:label="@string/app_name">

                </activity>
                <receiver android:name=".PhoneReceiver">
                        <intent-filter>
                        <action android:name="android.intent.action.PHONE_STATE" />
                        <action android:name="android.provider.Telephony.SMS_RECEIVED" />
                        </intent-filter>
                </receiver>
        </application>
        <uses-permission android:name="android.permission.READ_PHONE_STATE" />
        <uses-permission android:name="android.permission.INTERNET" />
</manifest>
```

The resulting tabbed interface should resemble that shown in Figure 19-6.

Figure 19-6. Tabbed user interface

How It Works

Tabbed user interfaces make it easy to navigate applications, especially on devices with smaller screens because the tabs do not take a lot of real estate. Developing a tabbed user interface is an easy task, but it does require the manipulation of a few different files. The tabbed interface itself must have its own `Activity` class and corresponding layout XML file. Each activity that is going to reside within a tab must also have its own corresponding drawable XML file.

To begin implementing the tabbed user interface, create a drawable XML file for each activity that you want to load into a tab. These files are known as a state-list drawables. A *state-list drawable* is an object that is defined in XML, which uses different images to represent the same graphic, depending upon the state of the corresponding object. In other words, these drawable files represent the tabs along with the images and text to load onto each tab. Intricate applications load different images on tabs depending if they are the currently selected tab or not. In the solution to this recipe, the drawable XML for the `EnterInformation Activity` class is shown, and you can see that different images are referenced depending upon the selection state of the tab. The excerpt below shows the lines of XML that enable this functionality:

```
<!-- When selected, use grey -->
<item android:drawable="@drawable/group-selected"
        android:state_selected="true" />
<!-- When not selected, use white-->
<item android:drawable="@drawable/group-deselected" />
```

The `android:drawable` attributes of the `<item>` tags are set equal to a drawable element correlating to an image that is located in the `res/drawable/` directory. Images with the names of `group-selected.png` and `group-deselected.png` reside within the `res/drawable/` directory, and the `android:drawable` attribute maps the tab state to those images. Designate one of the images as selected by adding the `android:state_selected="true"` attribute and value to it.

An `Activity` class that will be used for creating a tab container must extend the `android.app.TabActivity` class. The resulting `Activity` class will contain the `onCreate(Bundle)` method just like every other activity. Per the specification, the `onCreate()` method will be initiated prior to loading the user interface on the screen, and it is used to build the elements of the user interface. In the solution to this recipe, another method named `setupTabs()` is called within the `onCreate()` method. The tab builder implementation takes place within `setupTabs()`. Taking a look at the code, the layout XML which corresponds to the tab view is loaded within the first line of the `setupTabs()` method. Next, a `Resources` instance is obtained for working with the resource files that correspond to the different activities, which will be placed within the tabs. A `TabHost` instance is also obtained for working with the tabs. A couple of other variables are also declared for later use:

```
setContentView(R.layout.tabs);

Resources res = getResources();
TabHost tabHost = getTabHost();
TabHost.TabSpec spec;
Intent intent;
```

For the creation of each tab, a new `Intent` is created; passing the class of the corresponding activity that is to be loaded into the tab. In this excerpt, an `Intent` is created for the `EnterInformation` activity that was developed in recipe 19-4:

```
intent = new Intent().setClass(this, EnterInformation.class);
```

Next, a `TabSpec` object is initialized for each tab. The `TabSpec` is created to define the different properties for each tab. When creating the `TabSpec`, pass a string value, which can be used to identify the tab. The text and icon for the tab are set next by calling the `setIndicator(CharSequence, Drawable)` method, passing a `CharSequence` of text that will be displayed on the tab, as well as the resource ID for the drawable that was created for the activity. Finally, set the content of the tab by passing the `Intent` that was created previously. Once these steps have been taken, the `TabSpec` can be added to the `TabHost`. Although this seems like a lot of steps to complete, it is done within two lines of code. The following code excerpt sets up the `TabSpec` for the `EnterInformation` activity and adds it to the `TabHost`:

```
spec = tabHost.newTabSpec("enterInformation").setIndicator("Information",
                res.getDrawable(R.drawable.enterinformation))
                .setContent(intent);
tabHost.addTab(spec);
```

Follow these steps for each tab that you want to create. The last line of the `setupTabs()` method sets the index for the tab that will be loaded first:

```
tabHost.setCurrentTab(0);
```

Similar to other activities, the `TabActivity` class must have a corresponding layout XML file. This file should be placed within the `res/layout/` directory and it is responsible for defining the layout structure of the tab interface. In the solution to this recipe, a file named `tabs.xml` is created for this purpose. A

<TabHost> container is at the root of all tabbed user interfaces, and the actual layout for the individual tabs should be nested within it. The tab layout in the solution to this recipe uses a LinearLayout to organize the content of the tabbed user interface. Within the <LinearLayout> tags, a <TabWidget> tag is used to represent the actual tabs that will be pressed by the user to navigate between activities, and a <FrameLayout> tag is used to represent the content of the tabs.

After all the XML files and the TabActivity class have been created, the tabbed user interface is just about ready. The last piece of the puzzle is to add the Activity class to the manifest. The TabContainer activity has a couple of additional attributes specified within the <activity> tag. Particularly, the android:configChanges attribute lists the configuration changes that you would like for the activity to handle itself. This attribute allows you to override the default system configuration changes such as the screen orientation change. In the solution, this attribute is set to android:configChanges="keyboardHidden|orientation", which specifies that the activity will handle the keyboard accessibility and also what happens when the user rotates the device. This attribute allows for customization, and it can be used with any activity. The other attribute that we have not yet discussed in this chapter is android:launchMode. For the TabController activity, it is set to a value of "singleTop". This attribute handles the way in which the activity is launched. Specifying "singleTop", which basically allows only one instance of the activity to be created. This is important with the TabController activity because you do not want more than one set of tabs on the screen. To see other useful attributes that can be used with the <activity> tag, please refer to the online documentation that can be found at: http://developer.android.com/guide/topics/manifest/activity-element.html.

After the tabbed interface has been configured and registered in the manifest, the application is ready to run. There are more interfaces that can be useful for laying out application user interfaces, including the Grid Layout and Table Layout. For a list of the others, as well as examples, please see the online documentation at: http://developer.android.com/resources/tutorials/views/index.html.

19-10. Embedding Web Pages into an Application View

Problem

You would like to embed an active web page to your application.

Solution

Develop an activity that creates a WebView, and load the web page into it. The following Java class contains an activity that instantiates a WebView:

```java
package org.java7recipes;

import android.app.Activity;
import android.os.Bundle;
import android.view.Window;
import android.webkit.WebChromeClient;
import android.webkit.WebView;
import android.webkit.WebViewClient;
import android.widget.Toast;
```

```
publicclass VisitSite extends Activity {

private WebView webview;

/** Called when the activity is first created. */
@Override
publicvoid onCreate(Bundle savedInstanceState) {
        super.onCreate(savedInstanceState);
        webview = new WebView(this);
        // Add progress bar
        getWindow().requestFeature(Window.FEATURE_PROGRESS);
        // Enable Javascript
        webview.getSettings().setJavaScriptEnabled(true);
        final Activity activity = this;
        webview.setWebChromeClient(new WebChromeClient() {
        publicvoid onProgressChanged(WebView view, int progress) {
                activity.setProgress(progress * 1000);
        }
});
webview.setWebViewClient(new WebViewClient() {
// Handle errors accordingly
publicvoid onReceivedError(WebView view, int errorCode,
                           String description, String failingUrl) {
        Toast.makeText(activity, "Error Received:" + description,Toast.LENGTH_SHORT).show();
}
});
webview.loadUrl("http://www.java.net");
setContentView(webview);
}
}
```

After adding this activity to the AndroidManifest.xml, the window would look similar to Figure 19-7.

Figure 19-7. WebView within a TabLayout

How It Works

A WebView is an Android view that displays web pages. It uses WebKit for rendering and includes the functionality to navigate the web. By default, the WebView does not enable any browser-like widgets, and functionality such as JavaScript is turned off. When you use a vanilla WebView, it will load a web page and display it, and that is all. However, the WebView is very customizable and can be adjusted to create a fully capable web browser if needed.

In the solution to this recipe, a standard WebView is created within an Activity class named ViewSite, which will include no browser-like widgets such as the back and forward buttons. A progress bar is added to the activity by obtaining a handle on the window and then setting the Window.FEATURE_PROGRESS feature. This will overlay the WebView.

```
getWindow().requestFeature(Window.FEATURE_PROGRESS);
```

Next, JavaScript is enabled on the WebView by obtaining the WebSettings class for the view by calling the getSettings() method and passing true to the setJavaScriptEnabled() method. There are many other useful settings that can be set within the WebSettings class. For complete documentation regarding the WebSettings class, please see the online documentation available at http://developer.android.com/reference/android/webkit/WebSettings.html. The code to enable JavaScript within the WebView is as follows:

```
webview.getSettings().setJavaScriptEnabled(true);
```

Next, a WebChromeClient subclass is created and set. A WebChromeClient subclass is used when an event occurs that may impact the browser UI. In this case, when loading the specified web page, the progress bar is updated to reflect the progress:

```
final Activity activity = this;
webview.setWebChromeClient(new WebChromeClient() {
publicvoid onProgressChanged(WebView view, int progress) {
        activity.setProgress(progress * 1000);
}
});
```

■ **Note** Creating and setting a WebChromeClient can take care of providing specified functionality when browser specific events occur. For more information on using the WebChromeClient class, please see the online documentation available at

http://developer.android.com/reference/android/webkit/WebChromeClient.html.

The next code block creates and sets a WebViewClient, which is called when events occur that could impact the loading of a specified web page, such as JavaScript errors. You can customize the functionality of a WebViewClient by implementing specific methods depending upon the events you are trying to handle. In the solution, we want to display a message when errors occur, so the onReceivedError(WebView, int, String, String) method is implemented, and text is created within the method implementation for displaying the message. After the text is created, it is displayed to the user within a Toast object. A Toast is a view for displaying a message to a user. For more information pertaining to using Toasts, please see the online documentation that can be found at http://developer.android.com/reference/android/widget/Toast.html.

```
webview.setWebViewClient(new WebViewClient() {
// Handle errors accordingly
publicvoid onReceivedError(WebView view, int errorCode,
                           String description, String failingUrl) {
      Toast.makeText(activity, "Error Received:" + description,Toast.LENGTH_SHORT).show();
}
});
```

■ **Note** Creating and setting a `WebViewClient` can take care of handling events that impact the loading of web pages. There are a great number of events that can be handled using a `WebViewClient` such as a malformed URL or a failed SSL handshake. For complete details on using a `WebViewClient`, please see the online documentation available at `http://developer.android.com/reference/android/webkit/WebViewClient.html`.

Finally, the activity loads the URL for the `WebView` to display and sets the content view. In this case, the URL is `http://www.java.net`.

```
webview.loadUrl("http://www.java.net");
setContentView(webview);
```

The last thing that needs to be done to enable a `WebView` to access the Internet is to grant permissions to your application for doing so. If you fail to grant permissions to your application for accessing the Internet, your `WebView` will be unable to display any web content. For information regarding granting these permissions to your application, please see the next recipe, 19-11.

Quite a bit is going on here that has not yet been discussed within the context of this chapter. The `WebView` class is complex because it enables the developer to customize `WebView` instances in many different ways. This recipe barely scratches the surface of what can be achieved by using a `WebView` within your Android application. For complete documentation on using `WebViews`, please see the online documentation available at `http://developer.android.com/reference/android/webkit/WebView.html`.

19-11. Granting Application Device Permissions

Problem

You need to grant your application-specific privileges on a mobile device. For instance, you want to embed a web browser into your application and you need to provide the ability for your application to access the Internet.

Solution

Add the appropriate permissions to the `AndroidManifest.xml` file. For instance, if you want to allow your application the ability to access the Internet, add the following tag to the manifest:

```
<uses-permission android:name="android.permission.INTERNET" />
```

How It Works

Upon creation, a basic Android application has no permissions granted to it. This is a safety feature so that the application will be unable to do anything that may adversely affect the user experience or the device on which the application is running. Permissions can be added to the `AndroidManifest.xml` file to enable protected features on a per-application basis. To specify permissions for an application, a series of one or more `<uses-permission>` tags can be added to the manifest declaring the permissions that the application requires. The package installer then grants the requested permissions to the application at install time. There are no security checks that will be displayed to the user at application runtime. Either the application is granted the permissions at install time, or it is not. If a permission failure occurs, a `java.lang.SecurityException` will be thrown.

■ **Note** You can view the permissions that Android has granted to your application by going to the Settings->Applications screen on an Android device and selecting an application.

Any number of permissions can be specified within the manifest in order to provide more functionality to an application. However, it is important that only the permissions required for the application to run normally are specified. Specifying more permissions than are needed can cause a device run in an unsecured state, allowing bad things to happen.

■ **Note** For a complete set of permissions that can be used within an Android application, please see the online documentation available at `http://developer.android.com/reference/android/Manifest.permission.html`.

CHAPTER 20

JavaFX on the Web

JavaFX provides new capabilities to interoperate with HTML5. The underlying web page–rendering engine in JavaFX is the popular open-source API called Webkit. Webkit is also used in Google's Chrome and Apple's Safari browsers. HTML5 is the new standard markup language for rendering content in web browsers. HTML5 content consists of JavaScript, CSS, Scalable Vector Graphics (SVG), and new HTML element tags.

The relationship between JavaFX and HTML5 is important because they complement one another by drawing from each of their individual strengths. For instance, JavaFX's rich client APIs coupled with HTML5's rich web content create a user experience resembling a web application with the characteristics of desktop software. This new breed of applications is called RIAs.

In this chapter, we will cover the following:

- Embedding JavaFX applications in an HTML web page

- Displaying HTML 5 content

- Manipulating HTML5 content with Java code

- Responding to HTML events

- Displaying content from the database

20-1. Embedding JavaFX Applications in a Web Page

Problem

You hope to get promoted out of your cubicle into an office with windows by impressing your boss by creating a proof of concepts using JavaFX with your existing web development skills.

Solution

Create a Hello World application using the NetBeans IDE 7.1 or later by using its new project wizard to create an application to run in a browser. Shown following are steps to follow to create a Hello World JavaFX application that is embedded in an HTML web page:

> ■ **Note** For in-depth JavaFX deployment strategies refer to Oracle's deploying JavaFX Applications: http://download.oracle.com/javafx/2.0/deployment/deployment_toolkit.htm.

Here are the steps to follow in running the new project wizard:

1. Select New Project in the File menu of the NetBeans IDE version 7.1 or later. Figure 20-1 highlights the menu option in the NetBeans File menu.

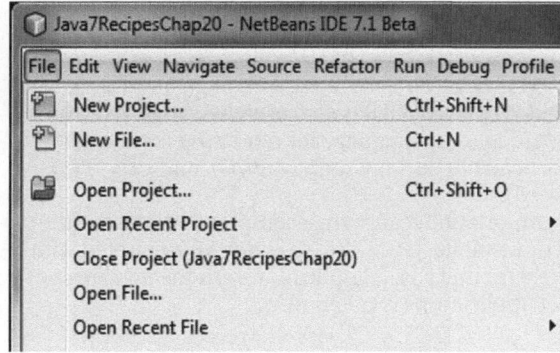

Figure 20-1. Creating a new JavaFX project

2. Select JavaFX in the Categories section under Choose Project, as shown in Figure 20-2. Next, select JavaFX Application under Projects. Then click Next to proceed.

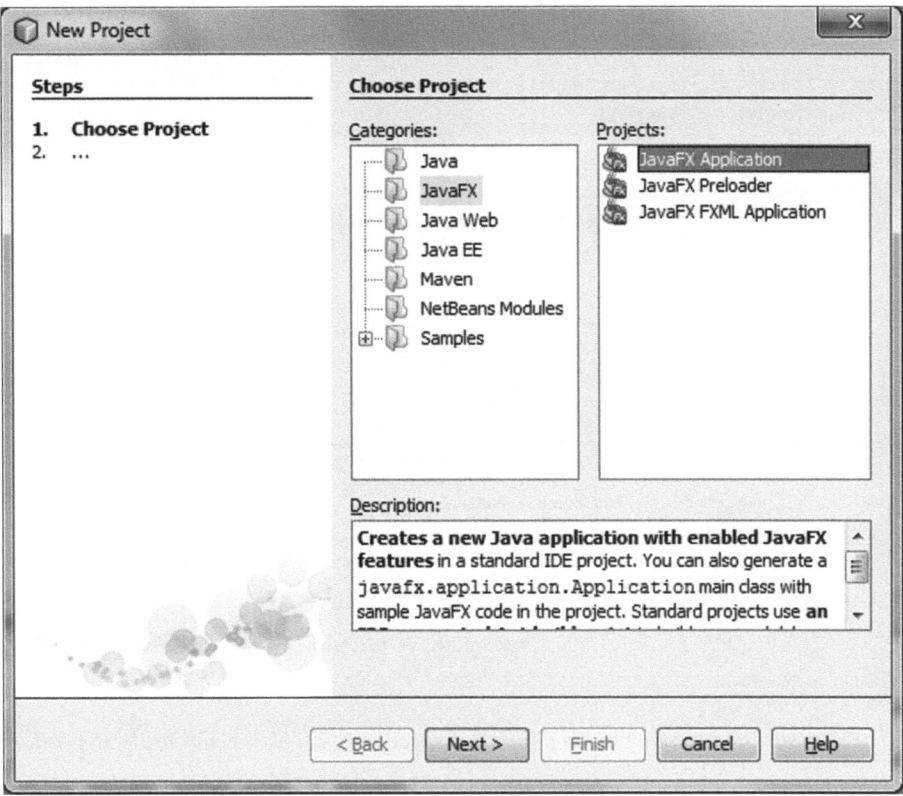

Figure 20-2. New Project dialog box

3. Create a project by specifying a name and selecting the check box to allow the wizard to generate a main class called MyJavaFXApp.java. Figure 20-3 shows a New JavaFX application wizard that specifies the project name and location. When you finish, click the Finish button.

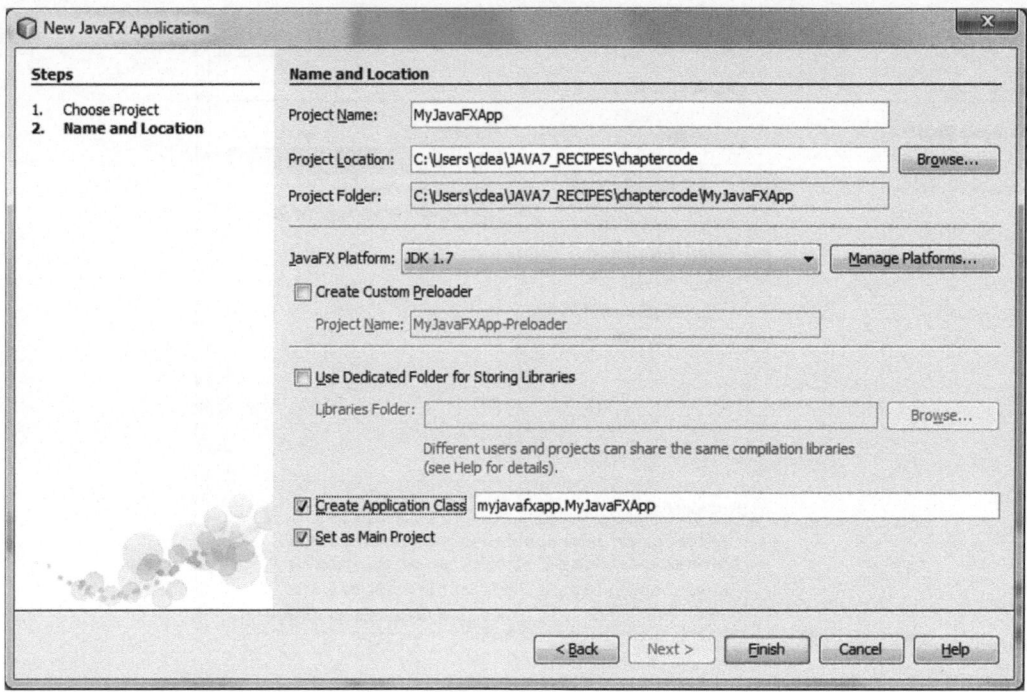

Figure 20-3. New JavaFX Application dialog box, in which you specify Project Name and Project Location

4. Once your new project has been created, you modify project properties. To modify the properties, right-click the project and select Properties via the popup menu. Figure 20-4 shows the project created with a main JavaFX file named MyJavaFXApp.java.

Figure 20-4. MyJavaFXApp.java project

5. Go into the project's properties, as shown in Figure 20-5. Select Sources in the categories option area. Next, check the Source/Binary Format option to point to JDK 7.

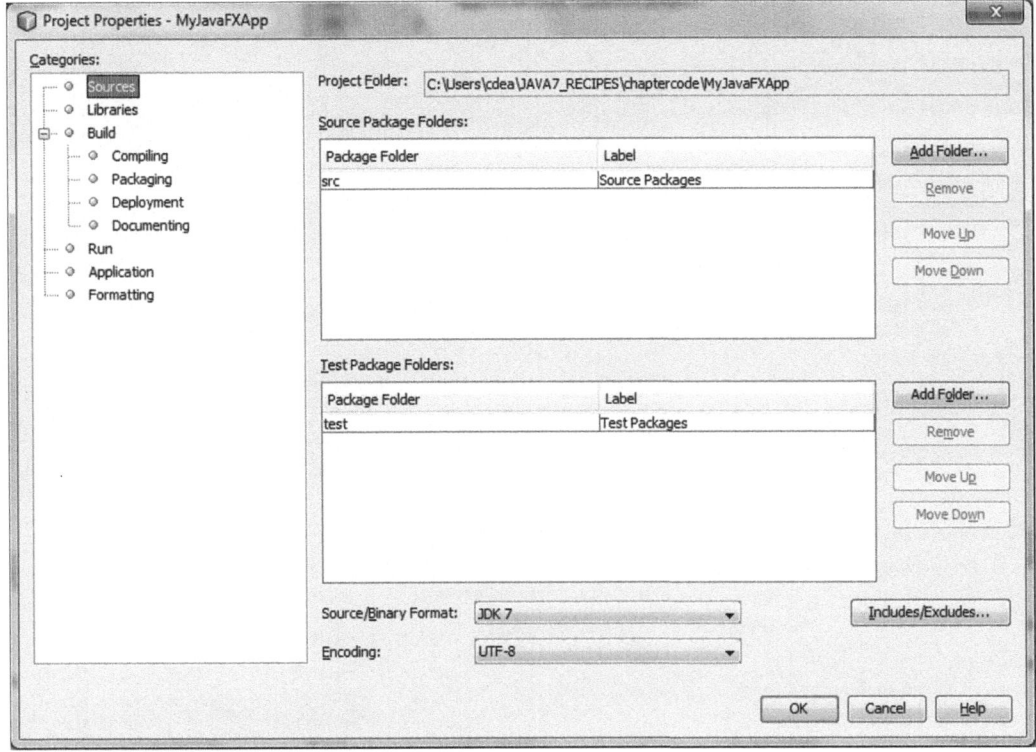

Figure 20-5. Project Properties MyJavaFXApp dialog window

6. Select the Run option in the Categories list shown in Figure 20-6. Select the
    in Browser radio button option. Then click the OK button.

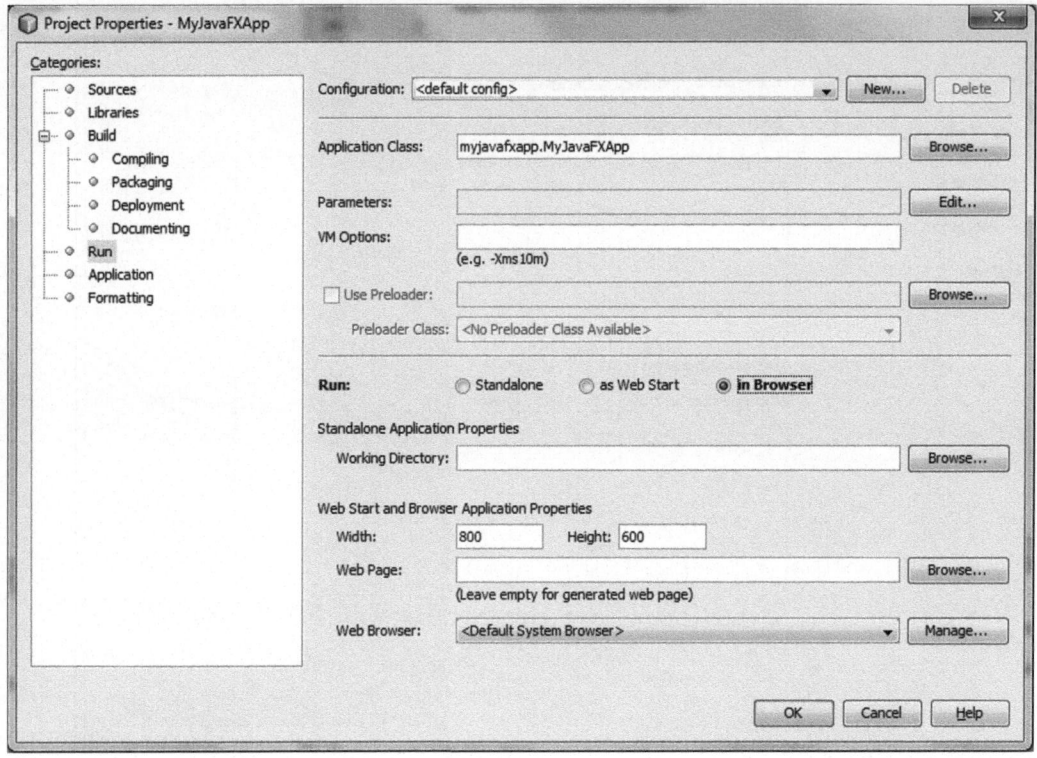

Figure 20-6. *Setting up the Run option in Browser*

7. Run and test the project by clicking the Run button on the toolbar or the F6 key. Figure 20-7 depicts the resulting Hello World application running in a browser.

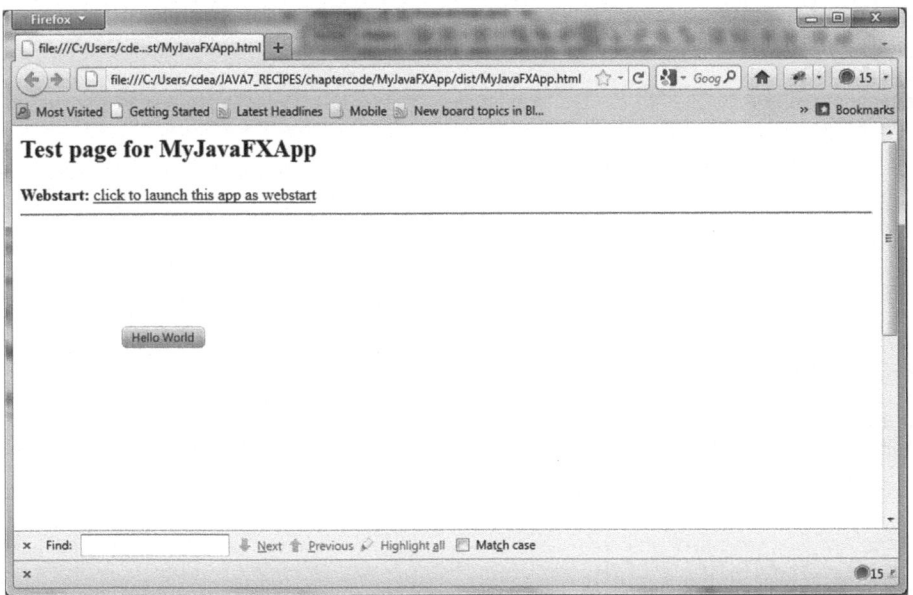

Figure 20-7. The MyJavaFXApp Hello World application running inside a browser

How It Works

To create an embedded JavaFX application inside an HTML page, you use the NetBeans IDE. Although there are different deployment strategies, such as Webstart and Standalone modes, here you use the NetBeans new project wizard to automatically deploy as a local web page containing your JavaFX application in your browser. For in-depth JavaFX deployment strategies, refer to Oracle's Deploying JavaFX Applications: `http://download.oracle.com/javafx/2.0/deployment/deployment_toolkit.htm`.

Following is the code generated by this solution. You will notice the JavaFX classes being used; for example, Stage, Group, and Scene classes.

■ **Note** You can drag the imports and body of code from another code file for this recipe into the body of your new main project class, changing the name on the class definition line, as appropriate.

Following is the source code when the NetBeans' wizard generates a new project to create a JavaFX application embedded in a HTML web page:

```
package myjavafxapp;

import javafx.application.Application;
import javafx.event.ActionEvent;
```

```
import javafx.event.EventHandler;
import javafx.scene.Group;
import javafx.scene.Scene;
import javafx.scene.control.Button;
import javafx.stage.Stage;

/**
 *
 * @author cdea
*/
public class MyJavaFXApp extends Application {

    /**
     * @param args the command line arguments
     */
    public static void main(String[] args) {
        Application.launch(args);
    }

    @Override
    public void start(Stage primaryStage) {
        primaryStage.setTitle("Hello World");
        Group root = new Group();
        Scene scene = new Scene(root, 300, 250);
        Button btn = new Button();
        btn.setLayoutX(100);
        btn.setLayoutY(80);
        btn.setText("Hello World");
        btn.setOnAction(new EventHandler<ActionEvent>() {

            public void handle(ActionEvent event) {
                System.out.println("Hello World");
            }
        });
        root.getChildren().add(btn);
        primaryStage.setScene(scene);
        primaryStage.show();
    }
}
```

In Step 1, you initiate a new project (shown in Figure 20-7). In Step 2, you select the standard JavaFX application to be created. After selecting the project type, you will be specifying the name of the project. Make sure you click the Create Application Class check box to allow the wizard to generate the MyJavaFXApp Java file. Once you have clicked Finish, your newly created application will appear in the projects tab. Next, you will take Step 5 in changing project properties.

In Step 5 you will be changing two categories: Sources and Run. In the Sources category, make sure the Source/Binary Format is set to JDK 1.6 or later. After updating the Sources category, you will be changing how the project will run (Step 6) through the Run category. In Step 6, after selecting the in Browser radio button option, you will notice the Width and Height below the working directory field. To use your own custom web page, you click the browse button to select an existing HTML file, but in this recipe you can leave it blank to allow the wizard to generate a generic HTML page. Assuming that you are done with your settings, click OK to close the Project Properties dialog window.

Last, you will run your embedded JavaFX web application (Step 7). To run your application you will want to make sure this project is set as the main project by selecting in the menu Run -> Set Main Project ->MyJavaFXApp. Once you are initiating a run, your browser will launch, containing a generic web page with your JavaFX application. You'll also notice that a convenient link allows you to launch the application as a Webstart application (not embedded).

20-2. Displaying HTML5 Content

Problem

You are so engrossed with a project for work that you often miss your kid's soccer games. What you need is a clock application to keep track of the time.

Solution

Create a JavaFX based-application containing an analog clock that was created as HTML5 content. Use JavaFX's WebView API to render HTML5 content in your application.

The following source code is a JavaFX application displaying an animated analog clock. The application will load an SVG file named clock3.svg and display the contents onto the JavaFX Scene graph:

```
package org.java7recipes.chapter20.recipe20_02;
import java.net.URL;
import javafx.application.Application;
import javafx.scene.Scene;
import javafx.scene.paint.Color;
import javafx.scene.web.WebView;
import javafx.stage.Stage;

/**
 *
 * @author cdea
 */
public class DisplayHtml5Content extends Application {
    private Scene scene;
    @Override public void start(Stage stage) {
        // create the scene
        stage.setTitle("Chapter 20-2 Display Html5 Content");
        final WebView browser = new WebView();
        URL url = getClass().getResource("clock3.svg");
        browser.getEngine().load(url.toExternalForm());
        scene = new Scene(browser,590,400, Color.rgb(0, 0, 0, .80));
        stage.setScene(scene);
        stage.show();
    }
```

```
        public static void main(String[] args){
            Application.launch(args);
        }
}
```

This JavaFX code will load and render HTML5 content. Assuming that you have a designer who has provided content such as HTML5, it will be your job to render assets in JavaFX. The following code represents an SVG file named clock3.svg that is predominantly generated by the powerful tool Inkscape, which is an illustrator tool capable of generating SVG. In the following code, notice hand-coded JavaScript code (inside the CDATA tag) that will position the second, minute, and hour hands of the clock based on the current time of day. Because all the logic (from setting the time to animating the hands) is inside this file, things are self contained, which means any HTML5 capable viewer can display the file's contents. So when debugging, you can easily render content in any HTML5-compliant browser. Later in this chapter, we will demonstrate JavaFX code that can interact with HTML5 content.

Shown here is a pared-down version of the SVG analog clock. (To obtain the file's source code, download the code from the book's web site.) This is anSVG analog clock created in Inkscape (clock3.svg):

```
<svg
    xmlns:dc="http://purl.org/dc/elements/1.1/"
    xmlns:cc="http://creativecommons.org/ns#"
    xmlns:rdf="http://www.w3.org/1999/02/22-rdf-syntax-ns#"
    xmlns:svg="http://www.w3.org/2000/svg"
    xmlns="http://www.w3.org/2000/svg"
    xmlns:xlink="http://www.w3.org/1999/xlink"
    xmlns:sodipodi="http://sodipodi.sourceforge.net/DTD/sodipodi-0.dtd"
    xmlns:inkscape="http://www.inkscape.org/namespaces/inkscape"
    width="300"
    height="250"
    id="svg4171"
    version="1.1"
    inkscape:version="0.48.1 "
    sodipodi:docname="clock3.svg" onload="updateTime()">

<script>

<![CDATA[
var xmlns="http://www.w3.org/2000/svg"

function updateTime()
{
  var date = new Date()

  var hr = parseInt(date.getHours())
  if (hr > 12) {
    hr = hr - 12;
  }
  var min = parseInt(date.getMinutes())
  var sec = parseInt(date.getSeconds())
  var pi=180
```

```
  var secondAngle = sec * 6 + pi
  var minuteAngle = ( min + sec / 60 ) * 6 + pi
  var hourAngle   = (hr + min / 60 + sec /3600) * 30 + pi

  moveHands(secondAngle, minuteAngle, hourAngle)
}

function moveHands(secondAngle, minuteAngle, hourAngle) {

  var secondHand = document.getElementById("secondHand")
  var minuteHand = document.getElementById("minuteHand")
  var hourHand = document.getElementById("hourHand")

  secondHand.setAttribute("transform","rotate("+ secondAngle + ")")
  minuteHand.setAttribute("transform","rotate("+ minuteAngle +")")
  hourHand.setAttribute("transform","rotate("+ hourAngle + ")")

}

]]>

</script>
<defs id="defs4173">
... // beginning of SVG code
... // Main clock code

<g id="hands" transform="translate(108,100)">
<g id="minuteHand">
<line stroke-width="3.59497285" y2="50" stroke-linecap="round" stroke="#00fff6" opacity=".9"
/>
<animateTransform attributeName="transform" type="rotate" repeatCount="indefinite"
dur="60min" by="360" />
</g>

<g id="hourHand">
<line stroke-width="5" y2="30" stroke-linecap="round" stroke="#ffcb00" opacity=".9" />
<animateTransform attributeName="transform" type="rotate" repeatCount="indefinite" dur="12h"
by="360" />
</g>
<g id="secondHand">
<line stroke-width="2" y1="-20" y2="70" stroke-linecap="round" stroke="red"/>
<animateTransform attributeName="transform" type="rotate" repeatCount="indefinite" dur="60s"
by="360" />
</g>
</g>

    ... // The rest of the Clock code: shiney glare, black button cover (center) on top of
arms

</svg>
```

Figure 20-8 depicts a JavaFX application, rendering the SVG file `clock3.svg` displaying an analog clock.

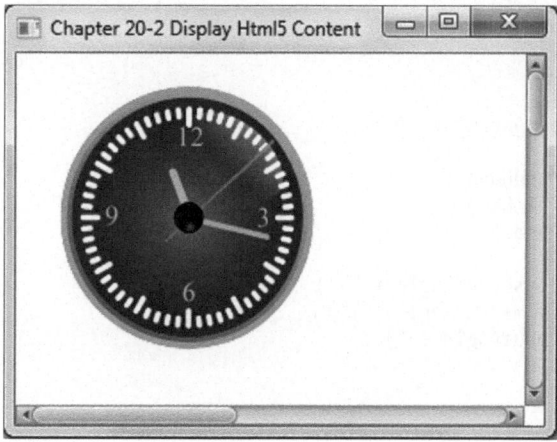

Figure 20-8. Analog clock

How It Works

In this recipe, you will be creating an analog clock application that will take existing HTML5 content to be rendered onto the JavaFX Scene graph. HTML5 allows the use of SVG content to be shown in browsers. SVG is similar to JavaFX's Scene graph, in which nodes can be scaled at different sizes while preserving details. To manipulate SVG or any HTML5 elements, you will be using the JavaScript language. Depicted in Figure 20-8 is a JavaFX application displaying an animated analog clock. To learn more about SVG, visit `http://www.w3schools.com/svg/default.asp`. Before running this example, make sure the `clock3.svg` file is located in the build path. In NetBeans you may need to perform a clean and build before running the application that will copy the resource (`clock3.svg`) to the build path. You may also want to manually copy the `clock3.svg` file to reside in the build path co-located where the `DisplayHtml5Content.class` file is located if you are running application on the command line.

In software development you will undoubtedly experience working with a designer where he/she will use popular tools to generate web content that will be wired up to an application's functions. To create an analog clock, I enlisted my daughter, who is quite proficient with the open-source tool Inkscape. Although Inkscape was used to generate the content for this recipe, I will not go into details regarding the tool because it is beyond the scope of this book. To learn more about Inkscape, please visit `http://www.inkscape.org` for tutorials and demos. To model the Designer and Developer Workflow, she created a cool looking clock and I added JavaScript/SVG code to move the clock's hour, minute, and second hands. Inkscape allows you to create shapes, text, and effects to generate amazing illustrations. Because SVG files are considered as HTML5 content ,you will be able to display SVG drawings inside of an HTML5-capable browser. In this scenario, you will be displaying the analog clock in JavaFX's `WebView` node. You can think of a `WebView` node as a mini browser capable of loading URLs to be displayed. When loading a URL you will notice the call to `getEngine().load()` where the `getEngine()` method will return an instance of `javafx.scene.web.WebEngine` object. So, the `WebView` object is implicitly creating one `javafx.scene.web.WebEngine` object instance per `WebView` object. Shown here is the JavaFX's `WebEngine` object loading a file `clock3.svg`:

```
final WebView browser = new WebView();
URL url = getClass().getResource("clock3.svg");
browser.getEngine().load(url.toExternalForm());
```

You are probably wondering why the JavaFX source code is so small. The code is small because its job is to instantiate an instance of a `javafx.scene.web.WebView` that instantiates a `javafx.scene.web.WebEngine` class and passes a URL. After that, the `WebEngine` object does all the work by rendering HTML5 content just like any browser. When rendering the content, notice that the clock's arms move or animate; for example, the second hand rotates clockwise. Before animating the clock, you have to set the clock's initial position by calling the JavaScript `updateTime()` function via the `onload` attribute on the entire SVG document (located on the root `svg` element). Once the clock's arms are set, you will add SVG code to draw and animate by using the line and animate transform elements, respectively. Shown here is a SVG code snippet to animate the second hand indefinitely:

```
<g id="secondHand">
<line stroke-width="2" y1="-20" y2="70" stroke-linecap="round" stroke="red"/>
<animateTransform attributeName="transform" type="rotate" repeatCount="indefinite"
dur="60s" by="360" />
</g>
```

On a final note, if you want to create a clock like the one depicted in this recipe, visit `http://screencasters.heathenx.org/blog` to learn about all things Inkscape. Another impressive and beautiful display of custom controls that focuses on gauges and dials is the Steel Series by Gerrit Grunwald. To be totally amazed, visit his blog at `http://harmoniccode.blogspot.com`.

20-3. Manipulating HTML5 Content with Java Code

Problem

You are an underpaid developer, and your boss refuses to let you relocate to the cube next to the window. You must find a way to determine the weather without leaving your workspace.

Solution

Create a weather application that fetches data from Yahoo's weather service. The following code implements a weather application that retrieves Yahoo's weather information to be rendered as HTML in a JavaFX application:

```
package org.java7recipes.chapter20.recipe20_03;

import javafx.animation.*;
import javafx.application.Application;
import javafx.beans.property.*;
import javafx.beans.value.*;
import javafx.concurrent.Worker.State;
import javafx.scene.*;
import javafx.scene.web.*;
```

```
import javafx.stage.Stage;
import javafx.util.Duration;
import org.w3c.dom.*;

/**
 * Shows a preview of the weather and 3 day forecast
 * @author cdea
 */
public class ManipulatingHtmlContent extends Application {
    String url = "http://weather.yahooapis.com/forecastrss?p=USMD0033&u=f";
    int refreshCountdown = 60;

    @Override public void start(Stage stage) {
        // create the scene
        stage.setTitle("Chapter 20-3 Manipulating HTML content");
        Group root = new Group();
        Scene scene = new Scene(root, 460, 340);

        final WebEngine webEngine = new WebEngine(url);

        StringBuilder template = new StringBuilder();
        template.append("<head>\n");
        template.append("<style type=\"text/css\">body {background-
color:#b4c8ee;}</style>\n");
        template.append("</head>\n");
        template.append("<body id='weather_background'>");

        final String fullHtml = template.toString();

        final WebView webView = new WebView();

        IntegerProperty countDown = new SimpleIntegerProperty(refreshCountdown);
        countDown.addListener(new ChangeListener<Number>() {
            @Override
            public void changed(ObservableValue<? extends Number> observable, Number
oldValue, Number newValue){
                // when change occurs on countDown call JavaScript to update text in
HTMLwebView.getEngine().executeScript("document.getElementById('countdown').innerHTML =
'Seconds till refresh: " + newValue + "'");
                if (newValue.intValue() == 0) {
                    webEngine.reload();
                }
            }
        });
        final Timeline timeToRefresh = new Timeline();
        timeToRefresh.getKeyFrames().addAll(
                new KeyFrame(Duration.ZERO, new KeyValue(countDown, refreshCountdown)),
                new KeyFrame(Duration.seconds(refreshCountdown), new KeyValue(countDown, 0))
        );

        webEngine.getLoadWorker().stateProperty().addListener(new ChangeListener<State>() {
            @Override
```

```
            public void changed(ObservableValue<? extends State> observable, State oldValue,
State newValue){
                System.out.println("done!" + newValue.toString());
                if (newValue != State.SUCCEEDED) {
                    return;
                }
                // request 200 OK
                Weather weather = parse(webEngine.getDocument());

StringBuilder locationText = new StringBuilder();
                locationText.append("<b>")
                        .append(weather.city)
                        .append(", ")
                        .append(weather.region)
                        .append(" ")
                        .append(weather.country)
                        .append("</b><br />\n");

                String timeOfWeatherTextDiv = "<b id=\"timeOfWeatherText\">" +
weather.dateTimeStr + "</b><br />\n";
                String countdownText = "<b id=\"countdown\"></b><br />\n";
                webView.getEngine().loadContent(fullHtml + locationText.toString() +
                        timeOfWeatherTextDiv +
                        countdownText +
                        weather.htmlDescription);
                System.out.println(fullHtml + locationText.toString() +
                        timeOfWeatherTextDiv +
                        countdownText +
                        weather.htmlDescription);
                timeToRefresh.playFromStart();
            }
        });

        root.getChildren().addAll(webView);

        stage.setScene(scene);
        stage.show();
    }

    public static void main(String[] args){
        Application.launch(args);
    }
    private static String obtainAttribute(NodeList nodeList, String attribute) {
        String attr = nodeList
                .item(0)
                .getAttributes()
                .getNamedItem(attribute)
                .getNodeValue()
                .toString();
        return attr;
    }

    }
```

```
    private static Weather parse(Document doc) {

        NodeList currWeatherLocation =
doc.getElementsByTagNameNS("http://xml.weather.yahoo.com/ns/rss/1.0", "location");

        Weather weather = new Weather();
        weather.city = obtainAttribute(currWeatherLocation, "city");
        weather.region = obtainAttribute(currWeatherLocation, "region");
        weather.country = obtainAttribute(currWeatherLocation, "country");

        NodeList currWeatherCondition =
doc.getElementsByTagNameNS("http://xml.weather.yahoo.com/ns/rss/1.0", "condition");
        weather.dateTimeStr = obtainAttribute(currWeatherCondition, "date");
        weather.currentWeatherText = obtainAttribute(currWeatherCondition, "text");
        weather.temperature = obtainAttribute(currWeatherCondition, "temp");

        String forcast = doc.getElementsByTagName("description")
                            .item(1)
                            .getTextContent();
        weather.htmlDescription = forcast;

        return weather;
    }

}
class Weather {
    String dateTimeStr;
    String city;
    String region;
    String country;
    String currentWeatherText;
    String temperature;
    String htmlDescription;

}
```

Figure 20-9 depicts the weather application that fetches data from the Yahoo Weather service. In the third line of displayed text, you'll notice that Seconds till refresh: 31 is a countdown in seconds until the next retrieval of weather information. The actual manipulation of HTML content occurs here.

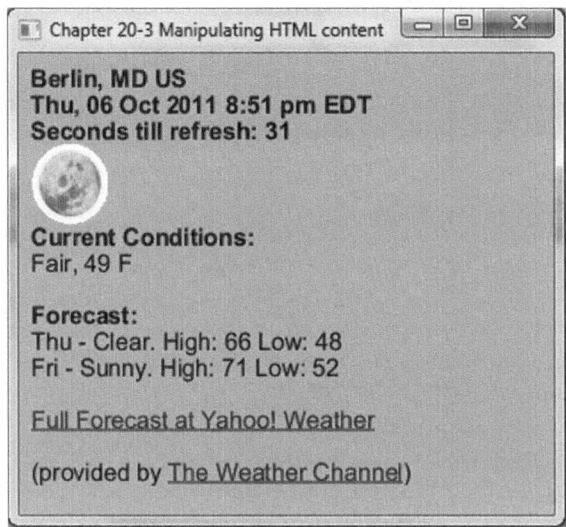

Figure 20-9. Weather application

The following is output to the console of the HTML that is rendered onto the `WebView` node:

```
<head>
<style type="text/css">body {background-color:#b4c8ee;}
</style>
</head>
<body id='weather_background'><b>Berlin, MD US</b><br />
<b id="timeOfWeatherText">Thu, 06 Oct 2011 8:51 pm EDT</b><br />
<b id="countdown"></b><br />

<img src="http://l.yimg.com/a/i/us/we/52/33.gif"/><br />
<b>Current Conditions:</b><br />
Fair, 49 F<BR />
<BR /><b>Forecast:</b><BR />
Thu - Clear. High: 66 Low: 48<br />
Fri - Sunny. High: 71 Low: 52<br />
<br />
<a
href="http://us.rd.yahoo.com/dailynews/rss/weather/Berlin__MD/*http://weather.yahoo.com/foreca
st/USMD0033_f.html">Full Forecast at Yahoo! Weather</a><BR/><BR/>
(provided by <a href="http://www.weather.com" >The Weather Channel</a>)<br/>
```

How It Works

In this recipe you will be creating a JavaFX application able to retrieve XML information from Yahoo's weather service. Once the XML is parsed, HTML content is assembled and rendered onto JavaFX's `WebView` node. The `WebView` object instance is a graph node capable of rendering and retrieving XML or any HTML5 content. The application will also display a countdown of the number of seconds until the next retrieval from the weather service.

When accessing weather information for your area through Yahoo's weather service, you will need to obtain a location ID or the URL to the RSS feed associated with your city. Before I explain the code line by line, I will list the steps to obtain the URL for the RSS feed of your local weather forecasts.

1. Open browser to `http://weather.yahoo.com/`.

2. Enter city or ZIP code and press Go button.

3. Click the small orange colored RSS button near the right side of the web page (under "Add weather to your website").

4. Copy and paste the URL address line in your browser to be used in the code for your weather application. For example, I used the following RSS URL web address: `http://weather.yahooapis.com/forecastrss?p=USMD0033&u=f`.

Now that you have obtained a valid RSS URL web address, let's use it in our recipe example. When creating the `ManipulatingHtmlContent` class, you will need two instance variables: `url` and `refreshCountdown`. The `url` variable will be assigned to the RSS URL web address from Step 4. The `refreshCountdown` variable of type `int` is assigned 60 to denote the time in seconds until a refresh or another retrieval of the weather information takes place.

Like all our JavaFX examples inside of the `start()` method, we begin by creating the `Scene` object for the initial main content region. Next, we create a `javafx.scene.web.WebEngine` instance by passing in the `url` into the constructor. The `WebEngine` object will asynchronously load the web content from Yahoo's weather service. Later we will discuss the callback method responsible for handling the content when the web content is done loading. The following code line will create and load a URL web address using a `WebEngine` object:

```
final WebEngine webEngine = new WebEngine(url);
```

After you create a `WebEngine` object, you will be creating an HTML document that will form as a template for later assembling when the web content is successfully loaded. Although the code contains HTML markup tags in Java code, which totally violates the principles of the separation of concerns, I inlined HTML by concatenating string values for brevity. To have a proper MVC-style separation, you may want to create a separate file containing your HTML content with substitution sections for data that will change over time. The code snippet that follows is the start of the creation of a template used to display weather information:

```
StringBuilder template = new StringBuilder();
template.append("<head>\n")
   .append("<style type=\"text/css\">body {background-color:#b4c8ee;}</style>\n")
   .append("</head>\n")
   .append("<body id='weather_background'>");
```

Once you have created your web page by concatenating strings, you will create a `WebView` object instance, which is a displayable graph node that will be responsible for rendering the web page. Remember from recipe 20-2, in which we discussed that a `WebView` will have its own instance of a `WebEngine`. Knowing this fact, we only use the `WebView` node to render the assembled HTML web page, not to retrieve the XML weather information via a URL. In other words, the `WebEngine` object is responsible for retrieving the XML from Yahoo's Weather service to be parsed and then fed into the `WebView` object to be displayed as HTML. The following code snippet instantiates a `WebView` graph node that is responsible for rendering HTML5 content:

```
final WebView webView = new WebView();
```

Next, you will create a countdown timer to refresh the weather information being displayed in the application window. First, you will instantiate an `IntegerProperty` variable, `countdown,` to hold the number of seconds until the next refresh time. Second, you will add a change listener (`ChangeListener`) to update the HTML content dynamically using JavaFX's capability to execute JavaScript. The change listener also will determine whether the countdown has reached zero. If so, it will invoke the `webEngine`'s (`WebEngine`) `reload()` method to refresh or retrieve the weather information again. The following is the code that creates an `IntegerProperty` value to update the countdown text within the HTML using the `executeScript()` method:

```
IntegerProperty countDown = new SimpleIntegerProperty(refreshCountdown);
countDown.addListener(new ChangeListener<Number>() {
    @Override
    public void changed(ObservableValue<? extends Number> observable, Number oldValue,
Number newValue){

webView.getEngine().executeScript("document.getElementById('countdown').innerHTML =
'Seconds till refresh: " + newValue + "'");
                if (newValue.intValue() == 0) {
                    webEngine.reload();
                }
            }
}); // addListener()
```

After implementing your `ChangeListener`, you can create a `TimeLine` object to cause change on the `countdown` variable, thus triggering the `ChangeListener` to update the HTML text depicting the seconds until refresh. The follow code implements a `TimeLine` to update the `countDown` variable:

```
final Timeline timeToRefresh = new Timeline();
timeToRefresh.getKeyFrames().addAll(
    new KeyFrame(Duration.ZERO, new KeyValue(countDown, refreshCountdown)),
    new KeyFrame(Duration.seconds(refreshCountdown), new KeyValue(countDown, 0))
);
```

In summary, the rest of the code creates a `ChangeListener` that responds to a `State.SUCCEEDED`. Once the `webEngine` (`WebEngine`) has finished retrieving the XML, the change listener (`ChangeListener`) is responsible for parsing and rendering the assembled web page into the `webView` node. The following code parses and displays the weather data by calling the `loadContent()` method on the `WebView`'s `WebEngine` instance:

```
                if (newValue != State.SUCCEEDED) {
                    return;
                }
                Weather weather = parse(webEngine.getDocument());

                ...// the rest of the inlined HTML

                String countdownText = "<b id=\"countdown\"></b><br />\n";
                webView.getEngine().loadContent(fullHtml + location.toString() +
```

```
                              timeOfWeatherTextDiv +
                              countdownText +
                              weather.htmlDescription);
```

To parse the XML returned by the `webEngine`'s `getDocument()` method, you will interrogate the `org.w3c.dom.Document` object. For convenience, I created a `parse()` method to walk the DOM to obtain weather data and return as a `Weather` object. See Javadocs and Yahoo's RSS XML Schema for more information on data elements returned from weather service.

20-4. Responding to HTML Events

Problem

You begin to feel sorry for your other cube mates who are also oblivious to the outside world. A storm is approaching and you want to let them know to take their umbrella before leaving the building.

Solution

Add a Panic Button to your weather application that will simulate an e-mail notification. A Calm Down button is also added to retract the warning message.

The following code implements the weather application with additional buttons to warn and disregard a warning of impending stormy weather:

```
@Override public void start(Stage stage) {

...  // template building
```

This code will add HTML buttons with the `onclick` attributes set to invoke the JavaScript `alert` function:

```
        template.append("<body id='weather_background'>");
        template.append("<form>\n");
        template.append("  <input type=\"button\" onclick=\"alert('warning')\" value=\"Panic
Button\" />\n");
        template.append("  <input type=\"button\" onclick=\"alert('unwarning')\"
value=\"Calm down\" />\n");
        template.append("</form>\n");
```

The following code is added to the `start()` method to create the warning message with opacity set as zero to be invisible:

```
        // calls the createMessage() method to build warning message
        final Text warningMessage = createMessage(Color.RED, "warning: ");
        warningMessage.setOpacity(0);

        ... // Countdown code
```

Continuing inside of the start() method, this code section is added to update the warning message after weather information was retrieved successfully:

```
webEngine.getLoadWorker().stateProperty().addListener(new ChangeListener<State>() {
    public void changed(ObservableValue<? extends State> observable, State oldValue,
State newValue){
        System.out.println("done!" + newValue.toString());
        if (newValue != State.SUCCEEDED) {
            return;
        }
        Weather weather = parse(webEngine.getDocument());
        warningMessage.setText("Warning: " + weather.currentWeatherText + "\nTemp: "
+ weather.temperature + "\n E-mailed others");

        ... // the rest of changed() method
}); // end of addListener method
```

This code sets the OnAlert property, which is an event handler to respond when a the Panic or Calm Down button is pressed:

```
webView.getEngine().setOnAlert(new EventHandler<WebEvent<String>>(){
    public void handle(WebEvent<String> evt) {
        warningMessage.setOpacity("warning".equalsIgnoreCase(evt.getData()) ? 1d :
0d);
    }
}); // end of setOnAlert() method.

root.getChildren().addAll(webView, warningMessage);

stage.setScene(scene);
stage.show();

} // end of start() method
```

The following method is code that you will add as a private method that is responsible for creating a text node (javafx.scene.text.Text) to be used as the warning message when the user presses the Panic Button:

```
private Text createMessage(Color color, String message) {
    DropShadow dShadow = DropShadowBuilder.create()
                            .offsetX(3.5f)
                            .offsetY(3.5f)
                            .build();
    Text textMessage = TextBuilder.create()
                .text(message)
                .x(100)
                .y(50)
                .strokeWidth(2)
                .stroke(Color.WHITE)
                .effect(dShadow)
                .fill(color)
```

```
                        .font(Font.font(null, FontWeight.BOLD, 35))
                        .translateY(50)
                        .build();
            return textMessage;
    }
} // end of the RespondingToHtmlEvents class
```

Figure 20-10 shows our weather application displaying a warning message after the Panic Button has been pressed. To remove the warning message, you can press the Calm Down button.

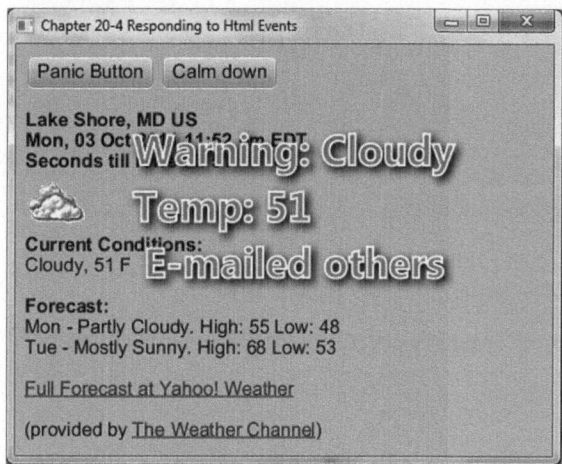

Figure 20-10. Weather application displaying warning message

How It Works

In this recipe you will add additional features to the weather application (from recipe 20-3) that responds to HTML events. The application you will be creating is similar to the previous recipe, except you will be adding HTML buttons on the web page to be rendered onto the WebView node. The first button added is the Panic Button that, when pressed, displays a warning message stating the current weather condition and a simulated e-mail notification to your cube mates. To retract the warning message you will also add a Calm Down button.

■ **Note**   Because the code is so similar to the previous recipe, I will point out the additions to the source code without going into great detail.

To add the buttons, you will use the HTML tag `<input type="button"!>` with an `onclick` attribute set to use JavaScript's `alert()` function to notify JavaFX of an alert event. Shown here are the two buttons added to the web page:

```
        StringBuilder template = new StringBuilder();
        ...// Header part of HTML Web page
        template.append("<form>\n");
        template.append("  <input type=\"button\" onclick=\"alert('warning')\" value=\"Panic
Button\" />\n");
        template.append("  <input type=\"button\" onclick=\"alert('unwarning')\"
value=\"Calm down\" />\n");
        template.append("</form>\n");
```

When the web page renders allowing you to press the buttons, the onclick attribute will call JavaScript's alert() function that contains a string message. When the alert() function is invoked, the web page's owning parent (the webView'sWebEngine instance) will be notified of the alert via the WebEngine's OnAlert attribute. To respond to JavaScript's alerts, you will add an event handler (EventHandler) to respond to WebEvent objects. In the handle() method, you will simply show and hide the warning message by toggling the opacity of the warningMessage node (javafx.scene.text.Text). The following code snippet toggles the opacity of the warning message based on comparing the event's data (evt.getData()) that contains the string passed in from the JavaScript's alert() function. So, if the message is "warning," the warningMessage opacity is set to 1; otherwise, set to 0 (both of type double).

```
webView.getEngine().setOnAlert(new EventHandler<WebEvent<String>>(){
    public void handle(WebEvent<String> evt) {
        warningMessage.setOpacity("warning".equalsIgnoreCase(evt.getData()) ? 1d : 0d);
    }
});
```

Please see the Javadocs for additional HTML web events (WebEvent).

20-5. Displaying Content from the Database

Problem

You want to keep up on the latest news monitoring the local legislature and science regarding the detrimental effects of the lack of light in small cubical work areas.

Solution

Create a JavaFX RSS reader. The RSS feed location URLs will be stored in a database to be later retrieved. Listed here are the main classes used in this recipe:

- javafx.scene.control.Hyperlink
- javafx.scene.web.WebEngine
- javafx.scene.web.WebView
- org.w3c.dom.Document
- org.w3c.dom.Node

- `org.w3c.dom.NodeList`

This recipe will be using an embedded database called Derby from the Apache group at `http://www.apache.org`. As a requirement, you will need to download the Derby software. To download the software, visit `http://db.apache.org/derby/derby_downloads.html` to download the latest version containing the libraries. Once downloaded, you can unzip or untar into a directory. To compile and run this recipe, you will need to update the classpath in your IDE or environment variable to point to Derby libraries (`derby.jar` and `derbytools.jar`). When running the example code you can type into the text field a valid RSS URL and then hit the enter key to load your new RSS headlines. After loading is complete the headline news is listed to the upper right frame region. Next, you will have an opportunity to choose a headline news article to read fully by clicking on a view button beneath it.

The following code implements an RSS reader in JavaFX:

```
package org.java7recipes.chapter20.recipe20_05;

import java.util.*;
import javafx.application.Application;
import javafx.beans.value.*;
import javafx.collections.ObservableList;
import javafx.concurrent.Worker.State;
import javafx.event.*;
import javafx.geometry.*;
import javafx.scene.*;
import javafx.scene.control.*;
import javafx.scene.input.*;
import javafx.scene.layout.*;
import javafx.scene.paint.Color;
import javafx.scene.web.*;
import javafx.stage.Stage;
import org.w3c.dom.Document;
import org.w3c.dom.Node;
import org.w3c.dom.NodeList;


/**
 * Display Contents From Database
 * @author cdea
 */
public class DisplayContentsFromDatabase extends Application {

    @Override public void start(Stage stage) {
        Group root = new Group();
        Scene scene = new Scene(root, 640, 480, Color.WHITE);
        final Map<String, Hyperlink> hyperLinksMap = new TreeMap<>();


        final WebView newsBrief = new WebView(); // upper right
        final WebEngine webEngine = new WebEngine();
        final WebView websiteView = new WebView(); // lower right

        webEngine.getLoadWorker().stateProperty().addListener(new ChangeListener<State>() {
```

```java
            public void changed(ObservableValue<? extends State> observable, State oldValue,
State newValue){
                if (newValue != State.SUCCEEDED) {
                    return;
                }

                RssFeed rssFeed = parse(webEngine.getDocument(), webEngine.getLocation());

                hyperLinksMap.get(webEngine.getLocation()).setText(rssFeed.channelTitle);

                // print feed info:
                StringBuilder rssSource = new StringBuilder();
                rssSource.append("<head>\n")
                        .append("</head>\n")
                        .append("<body>\n");
                rssSource.append("<b>")
                        .append(rssFeed.channelTitle)
                        .append(" (")
                        .append(rssFeed.news.size())
                        .append(")")
                        .append("</b><br />\n");
                 StringBuilder htmlArticleSb = new StringBuilder();
                for (NewsArticle article:rssFeed.news) {

                    htmlArticleSb.append("<hr />\n")
                        .append("<b>\n")
                        .append(article.title)
                        .append("</b><br />")
                        .append(article.pubDate)
                        .append("<br />")
                        .append(article.description)
                        .append("<br />\n")
                        .append("<input type=\"button\" onclick=\"alert('")
                            .append(article.link)
                            .append("')\" value=\"View\" />\n");
                }

                String content = rssSource.toString() + "<form>\n" +
htmlArticleSb.toString() + "</form></body>\n";
                System.out.println(content);
                newsBrief.getEngine().loadContent(content);
                // write to disk if not already.
                DBUtils.saveRssFeed(rssFeed);
            }
        }); // end of webEngine addListener()

        newsBrief.getEngine().setOnAlert(new EventHandler<WebEvent<String>>(){
            public void handle(WebEvent<String> evt) {
                websiteView.getEngine().load(evt.getData());
            }
        }); // end of newsBrief setOnAlert()
```

```
// Left and right split pane
SplitPane splitPane = new SplitPane();
splitPane.prefWidthProperty().bind(scene.widthProperty());
splitPane.prefHeightProperty().bind(scene.heightProperty());

final VBox leftArea = new VBox(10);
final TextField urlField = new TextField();
urlField.setOnAction(new EventHandler<ActionEvent>(){
    public void handle(ActionEvent ae){
        String url = urlField.getText();
        final Hyperlink jfxHyperLink = createHyperLink(url, webEngine);
        hyperLinksMap.put(url, jfxHyperLink);
        HBox rowBox = new HBox(20);
        rowBox.getChildren().add(jfxHyperLink);
        leftArea.getChildren().add(rowBox);
        webEngine.load(url);
        urlField.setText("");
    }
}); // end of urlField setOnAction()

leftArea.getChildren().add(urlField);

List<RssFeed> rssFeeds = DBUtils.loadFeeds();
for (RssFeed feed:rssFeeds) {
    HBox rowBox = new HBox(20);
    final Hyperlink jfxHyperLink = new Hyperlink(feed.channelTitle);
    jfxHyperLink.setUserData(feed);
    final String location = feed.link;
    hyperLinksMap.put(feed.link, jfxHyperLink);
    jfxHyperLink.setOnAction(new EventHandler<ActionEvent>() {
            public void handle(ActionEvent evt) {
                webEngine.load(location);
            }
        }
    );
    rowBox.getChildren().add(jfxHyperLink);
    leftArea.getChildren().add(rowBox);

} // end of for loop


// Dragging over surface
scene.setOnDragOver(new EventHandler<DragEvent>() {
    @Override
    public void handle(DragEvent event) {
        Dragboard db = event.getDragboard();
        if (db.hasUrl()) {
            event.acceptTransferModes(TransferMode.COPY);
        } else {
            event.consume();
        }
    }
```

```
        }); // end of scene.setOnDragOver()

        // Dropping over surface
        scene.setOnDragDropped(new EventHandler<DragEvent>() {

            @Override
            public void handle(DragEvent event) {
                Dragboard db = event.getDragboard();
                boolean success = false;
                HBox rowBox = new HBox(20);
                if (db.hasUrl()) {
                    if (!hyperLinksMap.containsKey(db.getUrl())) {
                        final Hyperlink jfxHyperLink = createHyperLink(db.getUrl(),
webEngine);

                        hyperLinksMap.put(db.getUrl(), jfxHyperLink);
                        rowBox.getChildren().add(jfxHyperLink);
                        leftArea.getChildren().add(rowBox);
                    }
                    webEngine.load(db.getUrl());
                }
                event.setDropCompleted(success);
                event.consume();
            }
        });  // end of scene.setOnDragDropped()

        leftArea.setAlignment(Pos.TOP_LEFT);

        // Upper and lower split pane
        SplitPane splitPane2 = new SplitPane();
        splitPane2.setOrientation(Orientation.VERTICAL);
        splitPane2.prefWidthProperty().bind(scene.widthProperty());
        splitPane2.prefHeightProperty().bind(scene.heightProperty());

        HBox centerArea = new HBox();

        centerArea.getChildren().add(newsBrief);

        HBox rightArea = new HBox();

        rightArea.getChildren().add(websiteView);

        splitPane2.getItems().add(centerArea);
        splitPane2.getItems().add(rightArea);

        // add left area
        splitPane.getItems().add(leftArea);

        // add right area
        splitPane.getItems().add(splitPane2);
        newsBrief.prefWidthProperty().bind(scene.widthProperty());
        websiteView.prefWidthProperty().bind(scene.widthProperty());
        // evenly position divider
```

```
        ObservableList<SplitPane.Divider> dividers = splitPane.getDividers();
        for (int i = 0; i < dividers.size(); i++) {
            dividers.get(i).setPosition((i + 1.0) / 3);
        }

        HBox hbox = new HBox();
        hbox.getChildren().add(splitPane);
        root.getChildren().add(hbox);

        stage.setScene(scene);
        stage.show();


    } // end of start()

    private static RssFeed parse(Document doc, String location) {

        RssFeed rssFeed = new RssFeed();
        rssFeed.link = location;

        rssFeed.channelTitle = doc.getElementsByTagName("title")
            .item(0)
            .getTextContent();

        NodeList items = doc.getElementsByTagName("item");
        for (int i=0; i<items.getLength(); i++){
            Map<String, String> childElements = new HashMap<>();
            NewsArticle article = new NewsArticle();
            for (int j=0; j<items.item(i).getChildNodes().getLength(); j++) {
                Node node = items.item(i).getChildNodes().item(j);
                childElements.put(node.getNodeName().toLowerCase(), node.getTextContent());
            }
            article.title = childElements.get("title");
            article.description = childElements.get("description");
            article.link = childElements.get("link");
            article.pubDate = childElements.get("pubdate");

            rssFeed.news.add(article);
        }

        return rssFeed;
    } // end of parse()

    private Hyperlink createHyperLink(String url, final WebEngine webEngine) {
        final Hyperlink jfxHyperLink = new Hyperlink("Loading News...");
        RssFeed aFeed = new RssFeed();
        aFeed.link = url;
        jfxHyperLink.setUserData(aFeed);
        jfxHyperLink.setOnAction(new EventHandler<ActionEvent>() {
            public void handle(ActionEvent evt) {
                RssFeed rssFeed = (RssFeed)jfxHyperLink.getUserData();
                webEngine.load(rssFeed.link);
```

```
            }
        });
        return jfxHyperLink;
    } // end of createHyperLink()

    public static void main(String[] args){
        DBUtils.setupDb();
        Application.launch(args);
    }
}
class RssFeed {
    int id;
    String channelTitle = "News...";
    String link;
    List<NewsArticle> news = new ArrayList<>();

    public String toString() {
        return "RssFeed{" + "id=" + id + ", channelTitle=" + channelTitle + ", link=" + link
+ ", news=" + news + '}';
    }
    public RssFeed() {
    }
    public RssFeed(String title, String link) {
        this.channelTitle = title;
        this.link = link;
    }
}
class NewsArticle {
    String title;
    String description;
    String link;
    String pubDate;

    public String toString() {
        return "NewsArticle{" + "title=" + title + ", description=" + description + ",
link=" + link + ", pubDate=" + pubDate + ", enclosure=" + '}';
    }

}
```

The following code is an exerpt from DBUtils.java showing the saveRssFeed() method which is responsible for persisting RSS feeds:

```
    public static int saveRssFeed(RssFeed rssFeed) {
        int pk = rssFeed.link.hashCode();

        loadDriver();

        Connection conn = null;
        ArrayList statements = new ArrayList();
        PreparedStatement psInsert = null;
```

```
        Statement s = null;
        ResultSet rs = null;
        try {

            // database name
            String dbName = "demoDB";

            conn = DriverManager.getConnection(protocol + dbName
                    + ";create=true", props);

            rs = conn.createStatement().executeQuery("select count(id) from rssFeed where id
= " + rssFeed.link.hashCode());

            rs.next();
            int count = rs.getInt(1);

            if (count == 0) {

                // handle transaction
                conn.setAutoCommit(false);

                s = conn.createStatement();
                statements.add(s);

                psInsert = conn.prepareStatement("insert into rssFeed values (?, ?, ?)");
                statements.add(psInsert);
                psInsert.setInt(1, pk);
                String escapeTitle = rssFeed.channelTitle.replaceAll("\'", "''");
                psInsert.setString(2, escapeTitle);
                psInsert.setString(3, rssFeed.link);
                psInsert.executeUpdate();
                conn.commit();
                System.out.println("Inserted " + rssFeed.channelTitle + " " + rssFeed.link);
                System.out.println("Committed the transaction");
            }
            shutdown();
        } catch (SQLException sqle) {
            sqle.printStackTrace();
        } finally {
            // release all open resources to avoid unnecessary memory usage

            // ResultSet
            close(rs);

            // Statements and PreparedStatements
            int i = 0;
            while (!statements.isEmpty()) {
                // PreparedStatement extend Statement
                Statement st = (Statement) statements.remove(i);
                close(st);
            }
```

```
        //Connection
        close(conn);

    }

    return pk;
}
```

In Figure 20-11, our JavaFX reader displays three frames. The left column shows a text field at the top to allow the user to enter new urls and RSS feed sources as hyperlinks underneath. The upper-right frame contains the headline, an excerpt of the article, and a view button that renders the article's web page in the bottom frame (lower-right region).

Figure 20-11. *JavaFX RSS reader*

Shown here is an example of output of the HTML to be rendered in the new headlines region (upper-right frame). You will also see the html view button responsible for notifying the application to load and render the entire article in the lower right frame region:

```
<head>
</head>
<body>
<b>Carl's FX Blog (10)</b><br />
<form>
<hr />
<b>
JavaFX Forms Framework Part 2</b><br />Mon, 03 Aug 2009 18:36:02 +0000<br />Introduction
This is the second installment of a series of blog entries relating to a proof of concept
for a JavaFX Forms Framework. Before I specify the requirements and a simple design of the
FXForms Framework, I want to follow-up on comments about tough issues relating to enterprise
application development and JavaFX. If you recall [...]<img alt="" border="0"
src="http://stats.wordpress.com/b.gif?host=carlfx.wordpress.com&amp;blog=6443320&amp;post=33
9&amp;subd=carlfx&amp;ref=&amp;feed=1" width="1" height="1" /><br />
<input type="button" onclick="alert('http://carlfx.wordpress.com/2009/08/03/javafx-forms-
framework-part-2/')" value="View" />

... // the rest of the headlines

</form></body>
```

How It Works

To create an RSS reader, you will need to store feed locations for later reading. When adding a new RSS feed, you will want to locate the little orange iconic button and drag the URL address line into your JavaFX RSS reader application. I find that the drag metaphor works on my FireFox browser. However, if dragging doesn't work I've provided a text field to allow you to cut-and-paste the URL. Once the URL is entered you will hit the enter key to initiate the loading of the headline news. For example you can visit Google's technology news RSS at:

http://news.google.com/news?pz=1&cf=all&ned=us&hl=en&topic=tc&output=rss.

Figure 20-12 depicts the orange RSS icon in the upper left.

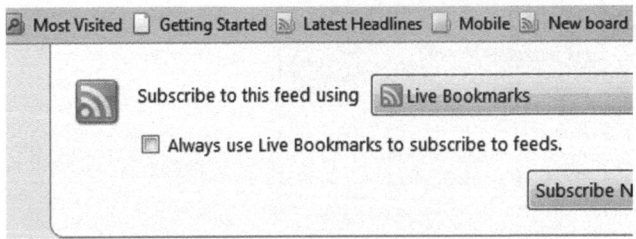

Figure 20-12. RSS icon

Once the URL is accepted via drag-n-drop or text field, the JavaFX RSS reader application will save the URL location to a database. The RSS application consists of three frame regions: the RSS feed title column (left), headline news (upper right), and web site view (lower right). To display the news headlines, click the hyperlinks to the left. To show the entire article in the lower-right frame, click the

View button below the headline in the upper-right frame. Before running the code, the application will require the jar libraries `derby.jar` and `derbytools.jar` included into your project classpath. These libraries allow you to save RSS URLs to an embedded JDBC database.

Similar to what you did in recipe 20-3, you retrieve news information from the Internet. The RSS retrieved will be using version 2.0. RSS is an XML standard providing really simple syndication, thus the acronym RSS. Now enough with the acronyms; let's jump into the code, shall we?

In our `start()` method, you will create a 640 by 480 white scene display area. Next, you will create a map (`TreeMap`) containing `Hyperlink` objects as values and keys representing the URL location (`String`) to the RSS feed. As before when displaying HTML content, you will need to create `WebViews`. Here you will create two `WebViews` and one `WebEngine`. The two `WebViews` will render HTML for the news headline frame region and the viewing of the entire article region (lower right). The single `WebEngine` is responsible for retrieving the RSS feed when the user clicks the left frame region containing the RSS hyperlinks.

To support the feature that allows the user to enter an RSS feed you will need to create a text field that is able to save and render the headline news. Below is the code snippet to save an RSS URL and to add an address as a new hyperlink to the list of feeds.

```
final VBox leftArea = new VBox(10);
final TextField urlField = new TextField();
urlField.setOnAction(new EventHandler<ActionEvent>(){
    public void handle(ActionEvent ae){
        String url = urlField.getText();
        final Hyperlink jfxHyperLink = createHyperLink(url, webEngine);
        hyperLinksMap.put(url, jfxHyperLink);
        HBox rowBox = new HBox(20);
        rowBox.getChildren().add(jfxHyperLink);
        leftArea.getChildren().add(rowBox);
        webEngine.load(url);
        urlField.setText("");
    }
}); // end of urlField setOnAction()
```

After a user has clicked on a hyperlink the news retrieval is initiated. Once a successful retrieve has occurred on the `webEngine` (`WebEngine`) object, you will need to add a `ChangeListener` instance to respond when the state property changes to `State.SUCCEEDED`. With a valid state of `State.SUCCEEDED`, you will begin to parse the XML DOM returned from the `WebEngine`'s `getDocument()` method. Again, I provided a convenience method called `parse()` to interrogate the `Document` object representing the RSS news information.

```
RssFeed rssFeed = parse(webEngine.getDocument(), webEngine.getLocation());
```

Next, you will create an HTML page that will list the channel tile and the number of total news headlines returned. After creating the HTML to display the RSS channel title and number of articles, you will iterate over all the news headlines to build record sets or rows. Each row will contain an HTML button labeled View to notify the `WebEngine` object of an alert containing the URL of the article. When the `WebEngine` object is notified, the `OnAlert` property will contain an event handler to render the entire article in the frame in the lower-right split region. After the web page is assembled, you will call the `newsBrief` object's `getEngine().loadContent()` method to render the page. Once rendered you will save the URL `rss Feed` (`RssFeed`) object to the database by invoking the `DBUtils.saveRssFeed(rssFeed)`. As a convenience, the `saveRssFeed()` method will check for duplicates and not save them. The following code loads the web page to be rendered and saves the newly added rssFeed URL:

```
newsBrief.getEngine().loadContent(content);
// write to disk if not already.
DBUtils.saveRssFeed(rssFeed);
```

As in the previous recipes, you will be responding to HTML WebEvents when the new headline View button is pressed, which calls a JavaScript's alert() function. Shown following is the code snippet to handle a web event (WebEvent) containing a string of the URL that links to the entire article to be viewed in the frame to the lower right region:

```
newsBrief.getEngine().setOnAlert(new EventHandler<WebEvent<String>>(){
        public void handle(WebEvent<String> evt) {
            websiteView.getEngine().load(evt.getData());
        }
    });
```

When creating the headlines region (upper right) containing HTML buttons to render the article's web page, you will notice the alert() function containing the URL to be loaded and rendered in the lower bottom split frame region. Shown following is an example of HTML generated for an headline news containing a View button that can notify the web engine's OnAlert web event (WebEvent).

```
    <input type="button" onclick="alert('http://carlfx.wordpress.com/2009/08/03/javafx-
forms-framework-part-2/')" value="View" />
```

One last thing to point out is that the RSS application has missing features. One feature that comes to my mind is the ability to delete individual RSS hyperlinks on the left column region. A workaround is to remove all links by deleting the database on the file system. Because Derby is an embedded database, you can delete the directory containing the database. The JavaFX RSS application will re-create an empty database if one doesn't exist. Hopefully, you can add new features to enhance this fun and useful application.

CHAPTER 21

E-mail

E-mail notification is part of today's enterprise systems. Java enables e-mail notification by offering its Mail API. Using this API you can send e-mail communications in response to an event (say a completed form or a finalized script). You can also use the Email API to check an IMAP or POP3 mailbox. In all, sending and receiving e-mail using the Email API has become pretty straightforward.

For the recipes in this chapter, please make sure that you have set up your firewall to allow e-mail communication; most of the time, firewalls will allow outbound communications to e-mail servers without an issue, but if you are running your own local SMTP (e-mail) server, you may need to configure your firewall to allow the e-mail server to operate correctly.

■ **Note**　If you are using the J2EE JDK, the JavaMail API is included as part of the EE download. If you are using the J2SE, you will need to download and install the JavaMail API.

21-1. Installing JavaMail

Problem

You want to install JavaMail for use by your application in sending e-mail notifications.

Solution

Download JavaMail from the JavaMail web site. Currently, the download you need is found at

`http://www.oracle.com/technetwork/java/javamail/`.

Once downloaded, unzip and add the JavaMail `.jar` files as dependencies from your project (both `mail.jar` and `lib\*.jar`).

How It Works

The JavaMail API is included in the J2EE SDK, but if you are working with the J2SE SDK you will need to download and add the JavaMail API to your J2SE project. By downloading and adding the dependencies, you get access to the robust Email API that allows you to send and receive e-mails.

21-2. Sending an E-mail

Problem

You need your application to send an e-mail.

Solution

Using the `Transport()` methods, you can send an e-mail to specific recipients. In this solution, an e-mail message is constructed and sent through the smtp.somewhere.com server:

```java
    private void start() {
        Properties properties = new Properties();
        properties.put("mail.smtp.host", "smtp.somewhere.com");
        properties.put("mail.smtp.auth", "true");

        Session session = Session.getDefaultInstance(properties, new
MessageAuthenticator("username","password"));

        Message message = new MimeMessage(session);
        try {
            message.setFrom(new InternetAddress("someone@somewhere.com"));
            message.setRecipient(Message.RecipientType.TO, new
InternetAddress("someone@somewhere.com"));
            message.setSubject("Subject");
            message.setContent("This is a test message", "text/plain");
            Transport.send(message);
        } catch (MessagingException e) {
            e.printStackTrace();
        }
    }

    class MessageAuthenticator extends Authenticator {
        PasswordAuthentication authentication = null;

        public MessageAuthenticator(String username, String password) {
            authentication = new PasswordAuthentication(username,password);
        }

        @Override
        protected PasswordAuthentication getPasswordAuthentication() {
            return authentication;
        }
    }
```

How It Works

The JavaMail API starts by creating a `Properties` object that works as a standard `Map` object (in fact, it inherits from it), in which you put the different properties that might be needed by the JavaMail service. In this example, you put the hostname ("`mail.smtp.host`" property) and that the host requires authentication ("`mail.smtp.auth`", "`true`"). After the `properties` object is configured, you fetch a `javax.mail.Session` that will hold the connection information for the e-mail message.

When creating a `Session`, you can specify the login information if the service requires authentication. This might be necessary when connecting to an SMTP service that is outside of your local area network. To specify the login information, you have to create an `Authenticator` object, which will contain the `getPasswordAuthentication()` method. In this example, there is a new class called `MessageAuthenticator`, which extends the `Authenticator` class. By making the `getPasswordAuthentication()` method return a `PasswordAuthentication` object, you can specify the username/password used for the SMTP service.

The `Message` object represents an actual e-mail message and exposes e-mail properties such as `From`/`To`/`Subject` and `Content` properties. After setting these properties, you call the `Transport.send()` static method to send the e-mail message.

▪Tip If you don't need authentication information, you can call the `Session.getDefaultInstance(properties, null)` method, passing a `null` for the `Authenticator` parameter.

21-3. Attaching a File to an E-mail Message

Problem

You need to attach a file to an e-mail message.

Solution

Creating a message that contains different parts (a multipart message) is what allows you to send attachments such as files and images. You can specify the body of the e-mail message and also specify an attachment. Messages that contain different parts are referred to as Multipurpose Internet Mail Extensions (MIME) messages. They are represented in the `javax.mail` API by the `MimeMessage` class. The following code creates such a message:

```
Message message = new MimeMessage(session);
message.setFrom(new InternetAddress(from));
message.setRecipient(Message.RecipientType.TO, new InternetAddress(to));
message.setSubject("Subject");

// Create Mime "Message" part
MimeBodyPart messageBodyPart = new MimeBodyPart();
messageBodyPart.setContent("This is a test message", "text/plain");
```

781

```
// Create Mime "File" part
MimeBodyPart fileBodyPart = new MimeBodyPart();
fileBodyPart.attachFile("attach.txt");

// Put Parts together in a Multipart Message
Multipart multipart = new MimeMultipart();
multipart.addBodyPart(messageBodyPart);
multipart.addBodyPart(fileBodyPart);

// Set the content of the message to be the MultiPart
message.setContent(multipart);
Transport.send(message);
```

How It Works

Within the JavaMail API you can create a Multipurpose Internet Mail Extensions (MIME) e-mail. This type of Message allows it to have different body parts. In the example, you create a plain text part (which contains the text that the e-mail displays), and an attachment part, which holds the attachment you are trying to send. Depending on the type of attachment, the Java API will choose an appropriate encoding for the attachment part. Once these two parts are created, they are combined by creating a MultiPart object, and adding each individual part (the plain text and the attachment) to it. Once the MultiPart object has all the parts, it is assigned as the content of the MimeMessage and sent (just like recipe 21-2).

21-4. Sending E-mail to a Group

Problem

You want to send the same e-mail to multiple recipients.

Solution

Use the setRecipients() method from the Mail API to send e-mail to multiple recipients. The setRecipients() method allows for specifying more than one recipient at a time. For example:

```
// Main send body
    message.setFrom(new InternetAddress("someone@somewhere.com"));
    message.setRecipients(Message.RecipientType.TO, getRecipients(emails));
    message.setSubject("Subject");
    message.setContent("This is a test message", "text/plain");
    Transport.send(message);

// ------------------


    private Address[] getRecipients(List<String> emails) throws AddressException {
        Address[] addresses = new Address[emails.size()];
        for (int i =0;i < emails.size();i++) {
```

```
            addresses[i] = new InternetAddress(emails.get(i));
        }
        return addresses;
    }
```

How It Works

By using the `setRecipients()` method of the `Message` object, you can specify multiple recipients on the same message. The `setRecipients()` method accepts an array of `Address` objects. In this recipe, because you have a collection of Strings, you create the array as the size of the collection and create `InternetAddress` objects to fill the array with. Sending e-mails using multiple e-mail addresses (as opposed to individual e-mails) is much more efficient because only one message is sent from your client to the target mail servers. Each target mail server will then deliver to all recipients that it has mailboxes for. For example, if sending to five different `yahoo.com` accounts, the `yahoo.com` mail server will only need to receive one copy of the message and it will deliver it to all the `yahoo.com` recipients specified in the message.

■Tip If you want to send bulk messages, you might want to specify the Recipient Type as BCC, so that the e-mail received doesn't show everyone else that might have gotten the e-mail. To do so, specify `Message.RecipientType.BCC` in the `setRecipients()` method.

21-5. Checking E-mail

Problem

You need to check if a new e-mail has arrived in an e-mail account.

Solution

Use `javax.mail.Store` to connect, query, and retrieve messages from an Internet Message Access Protocol (IMAP) e-mail account. For example, the following code connects to an IMAP account, retrieves the last five messages from that IMAP account, and marks those five messages as "read".

```
Session session = Session.getDefaultInstance(properties, null);
Store store = session.getStore("imaps");
    store.connect(host,username,password);
    System.out.println(store);
    Folder inbox = store.getFolder(folder);
    inbox.open(Folder.READ_WRITE);
    int messageCount = inbox.getMessageCount();
    int startMessage = messageCount - 5;
    int endMessage = messageCount;
    if (messageCount < 5) startMessage =0;
```

```
    Message messages[]  = inbox.getMessages(startMessage,endMessage);
    for (Message message : messages) {
boolean hasBeenRead = false;
for (Flags.Flag flag : message.getFlags().getSystemFlags()) {
if (flag == Flags.Flag.SEEN) {
hasBeenRead = true;
break;
    }
}
message.setFlag(Flags.Flag.SEEN, true);
System.out.println(message.getSubject() + " "+ (hasBeenRead? "(read)" : "") +
message.getContent());

    }
    inbox.close(true);
```

How It Works

A `Store` object allows you to access e-mail mailbox information. By creating a store and then requesting the "Inbox" folder, you have access to the messages in the main mailbox of your IMAP account. With the folder object, you can request to download the messages from the inbox. To do so, you use the `getMessages (start, end)` method. The inbox also provides a `getMessageCount()` method, which allows you to know how many e-mails are in the inbox. Keep in mind that the messages start at index 1.

Each message will have a set of flags that can then tell whether the message has been read (`Flags.Flag.SEEN`) or whether the message has been replied to (`Flags.Flag.ANSWERED`). By parsing the `SEEN` flag, you can then process messages that haven't been seen before.

To set a message as being seen (or answered), you can call the `message.setFlag()` method. This method allows you to set (or reset) e-mail flags. If setting message flags, you need to open the folder as `READ_WRITE`, which allows you to make changes to e-mail flags; and you will need to call `inbox.close(true)` at the end of your code, which will tell the JavaMail API to flush the changes to the IMAP store.

■**Tip** For IMAP over SSL, you would want to use `session.getStore("imaps")`. This creates a secure IMAP store.

21-6 Monitoring an E-mail Account

Problem

You want to monitor when e-mails arrive at a certain account and want to process them depending on their content.

Solution

Begin with recipe 21-5. Then add IMAP flag manipulation to create a robust e-mail monitor for your application. The following example checks the subject of new messages and deals with them appropriately. The example uses message flags to delete processed messages so they need not be read twice. Messages that can't be processed are marked as read but left in the server for troubleshooting by a human.

```java
private void checkForMail() {
        System.out.println("Checking for mail");
        Properties properties = new Properties();
        String username = "username";
        String password = "password";
        String folder = "Inbox";
        String host = "imap.server.com";

        try {
            Session session = Session.getDefaultInstance(properties, null);
            Store store = session.getStore("imaps");
            store.connect(host,username,password);
Folder inbox = store.getFolder(folder);
            inbox.open(Folder.READ_WRITE);
int messageCount = inbox.getMessageCount();
            Message messages[]  = inbox.getMessages(1,messageCount);
            for (Message message : messages) {
                boolean hasBeenRead = false;
                if
(Arrays.asList(message.getFlags().getSystemFlags()).contains(Flags.Flag.SEEN)) {
                    continue;                        // not interested in "seen" messages
                }
                if (processMessage(message)) {
                    System.out.println("Processed :"+message.getSubject());
                    message.setFlag(Flags.Flag.DELETED, true);
                } else {
                    System.out.println("Couldn't Understand :"+message.getSubject());
                    // set it as seen, but keep it around
                    message.setFlag(Flags.Flag.SEEN, true);
                }
            }
            inbox.close(true);
        } catch (MessagingException e) {
            e.printStackTrace();
        }
    }

    private boolean processMessage(Message message) throws MessagingException {
        boolean result = false;

        String subject = message.getSubject().toLowerCase();
        if (subject.startsWith("subscribe")) {
            String emailAddress = extractAddress (message.getFrom());
            if (emailAddress != null) {
```

```
                subscribeToList(emailAddress);
                result = true;
            }

        } else if (subject.startsWith("unsubscribe")) {
            String emailAddress = extractAddress (message.getFrom());
            if (emailAddress != null) {
                unSubscribeToList(emailAddress);
                result = true;
            }
        }

        return result;
    }


    private String extractAddress(Address[] addressArray) {
        if ((addressArray == null) || (addressArray.length < 1)) return null;
        if (!(addressArray[0] instanceof InternetAddress)) return null;
        InternetAddress internetAddress = (InternetAddress) addressArray[0];
        return internetAddress.getAddress();
    }
}
```

How It Works

After connecting to the IMAP server, the example requests all messages received. The code skips over the ones that are marked as SEEN. To do so, the recipe uses the `Arrays.AsList` to convert the array of system message flags into an `ArrayList`. Once the list is created, it is a matter of querying the list to see whether it contains the `Flag.SEEN` enum value. If it's present, the recipe skips to the next item.

When a message is found that has not been read, the message is then processed by the `processMessage()` method. The method subscribes or unsubscribes the sender of the message depending on the start of the subject line (This is akin to a mailing list, where sending a message with the subject of "subscribe" adds the sender to the mailing list.)

After determining the command to execute, the code proceeds to extract the sender's e-mail from the message. To do so, the `processMessage()` calls the `extractEmail()` method. Each message contains an array of possible "From" addresses. These `Address` objects are generic because the `Address` object can represent Internet or newsgroup addresses. After checking that the `Address` object is indeed an `InternetAddress`, you cast the `Address` object as `InternetAddress` and call the `getAddress()` method, which contains the actual e-mail address.

Once the e-mail address is extracted, the recipe calls subscribe or unsubscribe, depending on the subject line. If the message could be understood (meaning that the message was processed), the `processMessage()` method returns `true` (if it couldn't understand the message, it returns `false`). In the `checkForMail()` method, when the `processMessage()` method returns `true`, the message is flagged for deletion (by calling `message.setFlag(Flags.Flag.DELETED, true)`; otherwise, the message is just flagged as "Seen". This will allow the message to still be around if it wasn't understood or deleted if it was processed. Finally, to commit the new flags on the messages (and expunge deleted messages), you need to call the `inbox.close(true)` method.

CHAPTER 22

XML Processing

XML APIs have always been available for the Java developer, usually supplied as third-party libraries that could be added to the runtime classpath. However, in Java 7, you will find that the Java API for XML Processing (JAXP), Java API for XML Binding (JAXB), and even the Java API for XML Web Services (JAX-WS) have been included in the core runtime libraries.

The most fundamental XML processing tasks that you will encounter involve only a few use cases: writing and reading XML documents, validating those documents, and using JAXB to assist in marshalling/unmarshalling Java objects. This chapter provides recipes for these common tasks.

■ **Note** The source code for this chapter's examples is available in the `org.java7recipes.chapter22` package. Please see the introductory chapters for instructions on how to find and download this book's sample source code.

22-1. Writing an XML File

Problem

You want to create an XML document to store application data.

Solution

To write an XML document, use the `javax.xml.stream.XMLStreamWriter` class. The following code iterates over an array of `Patient` objects and writes their data to an `.xml` file. This sample code comes from the `org.java7recipes.chapter22.DocWriter` example:

```
import javax.xml.stream.XMLOutputFactory;
import javax.xml.stream.XMLStreamException;
import javax.xml.stream.XMLStreamWriter;
!
public void run(String outputFile) throws FileNotFoundException, XMLStreamException,
IOException {
    Patient[] patients = new Patient[3];
    patients[0].setId(BigInteger.valueOf(1));
    patients[0].setName("John Smith");
    patients[0].setDiagnosis("Common Cold");
    patients[1].setId(BigInteger.valueOf(2));
    patients[1].setName("Jane Doe");
    patients[1].setDiagnosis("Broken Ankle");
    patients[2].setId(BigInteger.valueOf(3));
    patients[2].setName("Jack Brown");
    patients[2].setDiagnosis("Food Allergy");
    XMLOutputFactory factory = XMLOutputFactory.newFactory();
    try (FileOutputStream fos = new FileOutputStream(outputFile)) {
        XMLStreamWriter writer = factory.createXMLStreamWriter(fos, "UTF-8");
        writer.writeStartDocument();
        writer.writeCharacters("\n");
        writer.writeStartElement("patients");
        writer.writeCharacters("\n");
        for(Patient p: patients) {
            writer.writeCharacters("\t");
            writer.writeStartElement("patient");
            writer.writeAttribute("id", String.valueOf(p.getId()));
            writer.writeCharacters("\n\t\t");
            writer.writeStartElement("name");
            writer.writeCharacters(p.getName());
            writer.writeEndElement();
            writer.writeCharacters("\n\t\t");
            writer.writeStartElement("diagnosis");
            writer.writeCharacters(p.getDiagnosis());
            writer.writeEndElement();
            writer.writeCharacters("\n\t");
            writer.writeEndElement();
            writer.writeCharacters("\n");
        }
```

```
        writer.writeEndElement();
        writer.writeEndDocument();
        writer.close();
    }
}
```

The previous code writes the following file contents:

```
<?xml version="1.0" ?>
<patients>
    <patient id="1">
        <name>John Smith</name>
        <diagnosis>Common Cold</diagnosis>
    </patient>
    <patient id="2">
        <name>Jane Doe</name>
        <diagnosis>Broken ankle</diagnosis>
    </patient>
    <patient id="3">
        <name>Jack Brown</name>
<diagnosis>Food allergy</diagnosis>
</patient>
</patients>
```

How It Works

Java 7 provides several ways to write XML documents. One model is the Simple API for XML (SAX). The newer, simpler, and more efficient model is the Streaming API for XML (StAX). This recipe uses StAX defined in the `javax.xml.stream` package. Writing an XML document takes only five steps:

1.   Create a file output stream.

2.   Create an XML output factory and an XML output stream writer

3.   Wrap the file stream in the XML stream writer.

4.   Use the XML stream writer's write methods to create the document and write XML elements.

5.   Close the output streams.

Create a file output stream using the `java.io.FileOutputStream` class. You can use a `try-block` to open and close this stream. Learn more about the new `try-block` syntax in Chapter 6.

The `javax.xml.stream.XMLOutputFactory` provides a static method that creates an output factory. Use the factory to create a `javax.xml.stream.XMLStreamWriter`.

Once you have the writer, wrap the file stream object within the XML writer instance. You will use the various write methods to create the XML document elements and attributes. Finally, simply close the writer when you finish writing to the file. Some of the more useful methods of the `XMLStreamWriter` instance are these:

- `writeStartDocument()`

- `writeStartElement()`

- `writeEndElement()`

- `writeEndDocument()`

- `writeAttribute()`

After creating the file and `XMLStreamWriter`, you always should begin the document by calling the `writeStartDocumentMethod()` method. Follow this by writing individual elements using the `writeStartElement()` and `writeEndElement()` methods in combination. Of course, elements can have nested elements. You have the responsibility to call these in proper sequence to create well-formed documents. Use the `writeAttribute()` method to place an attribute name and value into the current element. You should call `writeAttribute()` immediately after calling the `writeStartElement()` method. Finally, signal the end of the document with the `writeEndDocument()` method and close the `Writer` instance.

One interesting point of using the `XMLStreamWriter` is that it does not format the document output. Unless you specifically use the `writeCharacters()` method to output space and new-line characters, the output will stream to a single unformatted line. Of course, this doesn't invalidate the resulting XML file, but it does make it inconvenient and difficult for a human to read. Therefore, you should consider using the `writeCharacters()` method to output spacing and new-line characters as needed to create a human readable document. You can safely ignore this method of writing additional whitespace and line breaks if you do not need a document for human readability. Regardless of the format, the XML document will be well formed in that it is adheres to correct XML syntax.

The command-line usage pattern for this example code is this:

```
java org.java7recipes.chapter22.DocWriter <outputXmlFile>
```

Invoke this application to create a file named `patients.xml` in the following way:

```
java org.java7recipes.chapter22.DocWriter patients.xml
```

22-2. Reading an XML File

Problem

You need to parse an XML document, retrieving known elements and attributes.

Solution 1

Use the `javax.xml.stream.XMLStreamReader` interface to read documents. Using this API, your code will pull XML elements using a cursor-like interface similar to that in SQL to process each element in turn. The following code snippet from `org.java7recipes.DocReader` demonstrates how to read the `patients.xml` file from the previous recipe:

```java
public void cursorReader(String xmlFile)
throws FileNotFoundException, IOException, XMLStreamException {
    XMLInputFactory factory = XMLInputFactory.newFactory();
    try (FileInputStream fis = new FileInputStream(xmlFile)) {
        XMLStreamReader reader = factory.createXMLStreamReader(fis);
        boolean inName = false;
        boolean inDiagnosis = false;
        String id = null;
        String name = null;
        String diagnosis = null;

        while (reader.hasNext()) {
            int event = reader.next();
            switch (event) {
                case XMLStreamConstants.START_ELEMENT:
                    String elementName = reader.getLocalName();
                    switch (elementName) {
                        case "patient":
                            id = reader.getAttributeValue(0);
                            break;
                        case "name":
                            inName = true;
                            break;
                        case "diagnosis":
                            inDiagnosis = true;
                            break;
                        default:
                            break;
                    }
```

```
                    break;
            case XMLStreamConstants.END_ELEMENT:
                String elementname = reader.getLocalName();
                if (elementname.equals("patient")) {
                    System.out.printf("Patient: %s\nName: %s\nDiagnosis: %s\n\n",id, name,
                    diagnosis);
                    id = name = diagnosis = null;
                    inName = inDiagnosis = false;
                }
                break;
            case XMLStreamConstants.CHARACTERS:
                if (inName) {
                    name = reader.getText();
                    inName = false;
                } else if (inDiagnosis) {
                    diagnosis = reader.getText();
                    inDiagnosis = false;
                }
                break;
            default:
                break;
        }
    }
    reader.close();
    }
}
```

Solution 2

Use the XMLEventReader to read and process events using an event-oriented interface. This API is called
an iterator-oriented API as well. The following code is much like that of Solution 1, except that it uses the
event-oriented API instead of the cursor-oriented API. This code snippet is also available from the same
org.java7recipes.DocReader class used in Solution 1:

```
public void eventReader(String xmlFile)
        throws FileNotFoundException, IOException, XMLStreamException {
    XMLInputFactory factory = XMLInputFactory.newFactory();
    XMLEventReader reader = null;
    try(FileInputStream fis = new FileInputStream(xmlFile)) {
        reader = factory.createXMLEventReader(fis);
        boolean inName = false;
        boolean inDiagnosis = false;
        String id = null;
        String name = null;
```

```java
        String diagnosis = null;

        while(reader.hasNext()) {
            XMLEvent event = reader.nextEvent();
            String elementName = null;
            switch(event.getEventType()) {
                case XMLEvent.START_ELEMENT:
                    StartElement startElement = event.asStartElement();
                    elementName = startElement.getName().getLocalPart();
                    switch(elementName) {
                        case "patient":
                            id =
startElement.getAttributeByName(QName.valueOf("id")).getValue();
                            break;
                        case "name":
                            inName = true;
                            break;
                        case "diagnosis":
                            inDiagnosis = true;
                            break;
                        default:
                            break;
                    }
                    break;
                case XMLEvent.END_ELEMENT:
                    EndElement endElement = event.asEndElement();
                    elementName = endElement.getName().getLocalPart();
                    if (elementName.equals("patient")) {
                        System.out.printf("Patient: %s\nName: %s\nDiagnosis: %s\n\n",id, name,
diagnosis);
                        id = name = diagnosis = null;
                        inName = inDiagnosis = false;
                    }
                    break;
                case XMLEvent.CHARACTERS:
                    String value = event.asCharacters().getData();
                    if (inName) {
                        name = value;
                        inName = false;
                    } else if (inDiagnosis) {
                        diagnosis = value;
                        inDiagnosis = false;
                    }
                    break;
            }
```

```
        }
    }
    if(reader != null) {
        reader.close();
    }
}
```

How It Works

Java 7 provides several ways to read XML documents. One way is to use StAX, a streaming model. It is better than the older SAX API in that it allows you to both read and write XML documents. Although StAX is not quite as powerful as a DOM API, it is an excellent and efficient API that is less taxing on memory resources.

StAX provides two methods for reading XML documents: a cursor-oriented API and an iterator-based, event-oriented API. The event-oriented, iterator API is preferred over the cursor API at this time because it provides XMLEvent objects with the following benefits:

- The XMLEvent objects are immutable and can persist even though the StAX parser has moved on to subsequent events. You can pass these XMLEvent objects to other processes or store them in lists, arrays, and maps.

- You can subclass XMLEvent, creating your own specialized events as needed.

- You can modify the incoming event stream by adding or removing events, which is more flexible than the cursor API.

To use StAX to read documents, create an XML event reader on your file input stream. Check that events are still available with the hasNext() method, and read each event using the nextEvent() method. The nextEvent() method will return a specific type of XMLEvent, which corresponds to the start and stop elements, attributes, and value data in the XML file. Remember to close your readers and file streams when finished with those objects.

You can invoke the example application like this, using the patients.xml file as your <xmlFile> argument:

```
java org.java7recipes.chapter22.DocReader <xmlFile>
```

22-3. Transforming XML

Problem

You want to convert an XML document to another format, for example HTML.

Solution

Use the `javax.xml.transform` package to transform an XML document to another document format.

The following code demonstrates how to read a source document, apply an Extensible Stylesheet Language (XSL) transform file, and produce the transformed, new document. Use the sample code from the `org.java7recipes.chapter22.TransformXml` class to read the `patients.xml` file and create a `patients.html` file. The following snippet shows the important pieces of this class:

```
import javax.xml.transform.TransformerConfigurationException;
import javax.xml.transform.TransformerException;
import javax.xml.transform.TransformerFactory;
import javax.xml.transform.Transformer;
import javax.xml.transform.Source;
import javax.xml.transform.stream.StreamResult;
import javax.xml.transform.stream.StreamSource;
!
public void run(String xmlFile, String xslFile, String outputFile)
        throws FileNotFoundException, TransformerConfigurationException, TransformerException
{
    InputStream xslInputStream = new FileInputStream(xslFile);
    Source xslSource = new StreamSource(xslInputStream);
    TransformerFactory factory = TransformerFactory.newInstance();
    Transformer transformer = factory.newTransformer(xslSource);
    InputStream xmlInputStream = new FileInputStream(xmlFile);
    StreamSource in = new StreamSource(xmlInputStream);
    StreamResult out = new StreamResult(outputFile);
    transformer.transform(in, out);
    !
}
```

How It Works

The `javax.xml.transform` package contains all the classes you need to transform an XML document into any other document type. The most common use case is to convert data-oriented XML documents to user-readable HTML documents.

Transforming from one document type to another requires three files:

- An XML source document

- An XSL transformation document that maps XML elements to your new document elements

- A target output file

The XML source document is, of course, your source data file. It will most often contain data-oriented content that is easy to parse programmatically. However, people don't easily read XML files, especially complex, data-rich files. Instead, people are much more comfortable reading properly rendered HTML documents.

The XSL transformation document specifies how an XML document should be transformed into a different format. An XSL file will usually contain an HTML template that specifies dynamic fields that will hold the extracted contents of a source XML file.

In this example's source code, you'll find two source documents:

- `resources/patients.xml`

- `resources/patients.xsl`

The `patients.xml` file is short, containing the following data:

```xml
<?xml version="1.0" encoding="UTF-8"?>
<patients>
    <patient id="1">
        <name>John Smith</name>
        <diagnosis>Common Cold</diagnosis>
    </patient>
    <patient id="2">
        <name>Jane Doe</name>
        <diagnosis>Broken ankle</diagnosis>
    </patient>
    <patient id="3">
        <name>Jack Brown</name>
        <diagnosis>Food allergy</diagnosis>
    </patient>
</patients>
```

The `patients.xml` file defines a root element called `patients`. It has three nested `patient` elements. The `patient` element contains three pieces of data:

- Patient identifier, provided as the `id` attribute of the patient element

- Patient name, provided as the `name` subelement

- Patient diagnosis, provided as the `diagnosis` subelement

The transformation XSL document (`patients.xsl`) is quite small as well, and it simply maps the patient data to a more user-readable, HTML format using XSL:

```xml
<?xml version="1.0" encoding="UTF-8"?>
<xsl:stylesheet xmlns:xsl="http://www.w3.org/1999/XSL/Transform" version="1.0">
<xsl:output method="html"/>
<xsl:template match="/">
```

```
<html>
<head>
    <title>Patients</title>
</head>
<body>
    <table border="1">
        <tr>
            <th>Id</th>
            <th>Name</th>
            <th>Diagnosis</th>
        </tr>
        <xsl:for-each select="patients/patient">
        <tr>
            <td>
        <xsl:value-of select="@id"/>
            </td>
            <td>
        <xsl:value-of select="name"/>
            </td>
            <td>
        <xsl:value-of select="diagnosis"/>
            </td>
            </tr>
        </xsl:for-each>
    </table>
</body>
</html>
        </xsl:template>
        </xsl:stylesheet>
```

Using this stylesheet, the sample code transforms the XMLinto an HTML table containing all the patients and their data. Rendered in a browser, the HTML table should look like the one in Figure 22-1.

Id	Name	Diagnosis
1	John Smith	Common Cold
2	Jane Doe	Broken ankle
3	Jack Brown	Food allergy

Figure 22-1. A common rendering of an HTML table

The process for using this XSL file to convert the XML file to an HTML file is straightforward, but every step can be enhanced with additional error checking and processing. For this example, refer to the previous code in the solution section.

The most basic transformation steps are these:

1. Read the XSL document into your Java application as a Source object.

2. Create a Transformer instance and provide your XSL Source instance for it to use during its operation.

3. Create a SourceStream that represents the source XML contents.

4. Create a StreamResult instance for your output document, which is an HTML file in this case.

5. Use the Transformer object's transform() method to perform the conversion.

6. Close all the relevant streams and file instances as needed.

If you choose to execute the sample code, you should invoke it in the following way, using patients.xml, patients.xsl, and patients.html as arguments:

```
java org.java7recipes.chapter22.TransformXml <xmlFile><xslFile><outputFile>
```

22-4. Validating XML

Problem

You want to confirm that your XML is valid, conforming to a known document definition or schema.

Solution

Validate that your XML conforms to a specific schema by using the javax.xml.validation package. The following code snippet from org.java7recipes.chapter22.ValidateXml demonstrates how to validate against an XML schema file:

```
import java.io.File;
import java.io.IOException;
import javax.xml.XMLConstants;
import javax.xml.transform.Source;
import javax.xml.transform.stream.StreamSource;
import javax.xml.validation.Schema;
import javax.xml.validation.SchemaFactory;
import javax.xml.validation.Validator;
import org.xml.sax.SAXException;
!
```

```
public void run(String xmlFile, String validationFile) {
    boolean valid = true;
    SchemaFactory sFactory =
            SchemaFactory.newInstance(XMLConstants.W3C_XML_SCHEMA_NS_URI);
    try {
        Schema schema = sFactory.newSchema(new File(validationFile));
        Validator validator = schema.newValidator();
        Source source = new StreamSource(new File(xmlFile));
        validator.validate(source);
    } catch (SAXException | IOException | IllegalArgumentException ex) {
        valid = false;
    }
    System.out.printf("XML file is %s.\n", valid ? "valid" : "invalid");
}
!
```

How It Works

The `javax.xml.validation` package provides all the classes needed to reliably validate an XML file against a variety of schemas. The most common schemas that you will use for XML validation are defined as constant URIs within the `XMLConstants` class:

- `XMLConstants.W3C_XML_SCHEMA_NS_URI`

- `XMLConstants.RELAXNG_NS_URI`

Begin by creating a `SchemaFactory` for a specific type of schema definition. A `SchemaFactory` knows how to parse a particular schema type and prepares it for validation. Use the `SchemaFactory` instance to create a `Schema` object. The `Schema` object is an in-memory representation of the schema definition grammar. You can use the `Schema` instance to retrieve a `Validator` instance that understands this grammar. Finally, use the `validate()` method to check your XML. The method call will generate several different exceptions if anything goes wrong during the validation. Otherwise, the `validate()` method returns quietly, and you can continue to use the XML file.

■ **Note** The XML Schema was the first schema to receive "Recommendation" status from the World Wide Web consortium (W3C) in 2001. Competing schemas have since become available. One competing schema is the Regular Language for XML Next Generation (RELAX NG) schema. RELAX NG may be a simpler schema, and its specification also defines a non-XML, compact syntax. This recipe's example uses the XML schema.

Run the example code using the following command-line syntax, preferably with the sample `.xml` file and validation files provided as `resources/patients.xml` and `patients.xsl`, respectively:

```
java org.java7recipes.chapter22.ValidateXml <xmlFile><validationFile>
```

22-5. Creating Java Bindings for an XML Schema

Problem

You would like to generate a set of Java classes (Java bindings) that represent the objects within an XML schema.

Solution

The JDK provides a tool that can turn schema documents into representative Java class files. Use the `<JDK_HOME>/bin/xjc` command-line tool to generate Java bindings for your XML schemas. To create the Java classes for the `patients.xsd` file from section 22-3, you could issue the following command from within a console:

```
xjc -p org.java7recipes.chapter22 patients.xsd
```

This command will process the `patients.xsd` file and create all the classes needed to process an XML file that validates with this schema. For this example, the `patients.xsd` file looks like the following:

```
<?xml version="1.0" encoding="UTF-8"?>
<xs:schema xmlns:xs="http://www.w3.org/2001/XMLSchema" elementFormDefault="qualified">
<xs:element name="patients">
<xs:complexType>
<xs:sequence>
<xs:element maxOccurs="unbounded" name="patient" type="Patient"/>
</xs:sequence>
</xs:complexType>
</xs:element>
<xs:complexType name="Patient">
<xs:sequence>
<xs:element name="name" type="xs:string"/>
<xs:element name="diagnosis" type="xs:string"/>
</xs:sequence>
<xs:attribute name="id" type="xs:integer" use="required"/>
</xs:complexType>
</xs:schema>
```

Executed on the previous xsd file, the xjc command creates the following files in the
org.java7recipes.chapter22 package:

- ObjectFactory.java

- Patients.java

- Patient.java

How It Works

The JDK includes the <JDK_HOME>/bin/xjc utility. The xjc utility is a command-line application that
creates Java bindings from schema files. The source schema files can be of several types, including XML
Schemas, RELAX NG, and others.

The xjc command has several options for performing its work. Some of the most common options
specify the source schema file, the package of the generated Java binding files, and the output directory
that will receive the Java binding files.

You can get detailed descriptions of all the command line options by using the tools' -help option:

```
xjc -help
```

A Java binding contains annotated fields that correspond to the fields defined in the XML Schema
file. These annotations mark the root element of the schema file and all other subelements. This is useful
during the next step of XML processing, which is either unmarshalling or marshalling these bindings.

22-6. Unmarshalling XML to a Java Object

Problem

You want to unmarshall an XML file and create its corresponding Java object tree.

Solution

JAXB provides an unmarshalling service that parses an XML file and generates the Java objects from the
bindings you created in recipe 22-4. The following code can read the file patients.xml from the
org.java7recipes.chapter22 package to create a Patients root object and its list of Patient objects:

```
public void run(String xmlFile, String context)
        throws JAXBException, FileNotFoundException {
    JAXBContext jc = JAXBContext.newInstance(context);
    Unmarshaller u = jc.createUnmarshaller();
```

```
        FileInputStream fis = new FileInputStream(xmlFile);
        Patients patients = (Patients)u.unmarshal(fis);
        for (Patient p: patients.getPatient()) {
            System.out.printf("ID: %s\n", p.getId());
            System.out.printf("NAME: %s\n", p.getName());
            System.out.printf("DIAGNOSIS: %s\n\n", p.getDiagnosis());
        }
    }
}
```

If you run the sample code on the `resources/patients.xml` file and use the
`org.java7recipes.chapter22` context, the application will print the following to the console as it iterates
over the `Patient` object list:

```
ID: 1
NAME: John Smith
DIAGNOSIS: Common Cold

ID: 2
NAME: Jane Doe
DIAGNOSIS: Broken ankle

ID: 3
NAME: Jack Brown
DIAGNOSIS: Food allergy
```

■ **Note**   The previous output comes directly from instances of the Java `Patient` class that was created from
XML representations. The code does not print the contents of the XML file directly. Instead, it is printing the
contents of the Java bindings after the XML has been marshalled into appropriate Java binding instances.

How It Works

Unmarshalling an XML file into its Java object representation has at least two criteria:

- A well-formed and valid XML file

- A set of corresponding Java bindings

The Java bindings don't have to be autogenerated from the `xjc` command. Once you've gained some
experience with Java bindings and the annotation features, you may prefer to create and control all
aspects of Java binding by handcrafting your Java bindings. Whatever your preference, Java's
unmarshalling service utilizes the bindings and their annotations to map XML objects to a target Java
object and to map XML elements to target object fields.

Execute the example application for this recipe using this syntax, substituting `patients.xml` and `org.java7recipes.chapter22` for the respective parameters:

```
java org.java7recipes.chapter22.UnmarshalPatients <xmlfile><context>
```

22-7. Building an XML Document with JAXB

Problem

You need to write an object's data to an XML representation.

Solution

Assuming you have created Java binding files for your XML schema as described in recipe 22-4, use a `JAXBContext` instance to create a `Marshaller` object. Use the `Marshaller` object to serialize your Java object tree to an XML document. The following code demonstrates this:

```java
public void run(String xmlFile, String context)
        throws JAXBException, FileNotFoundException {
    Patients patients = new Patients();
    List<Patient> patientList = patients.getPatient();
    Patient p = new Patient();
    p.setId(BigInteger.valueOf(1));
    p.setName("John Doe");
    p.setDiagnosis("Schizophrenia");
    patientList.add(p);

    JAXBContext jc = JAXBContext.newInstance(context);
    Marshaller m = jc.createMarshaller();
    m.marshal(patients, new FileOutputStream(xmlFile));
}
```

The previous code produces an unformatted but well-formed and valid XML document. For readability, the XML document is formatted here:

```xml
<?xml version="1.0" encoding="UTF-8" standalone="yes"?>
    <patients>
    <patient id="1">
        <name>John Doe</name>
        <diagnosis>Schizophrenia</diagnosis>
    </patient>
    </patients>
```

■ **Note** The getPatient() method in the previous code returns a List of Patient objects instead of a single patient. This is a naming oddity of the JAXB code generation from the XSD schema in this example.

How It Works

A Marshaller object understands JAXB annotations. As it processes classes, it uses the JAXB annotations to provide it the context it needs for creating the object tree in XML.

You can run the previous code from the org.java7recipes.chapter22.MarshalPatients application using the following command line:

```
java org.java7recipes.chapter22.MarshalPatients <xmlfile><context>
```

The context argument refers to the package of the Java classes that you will marshal. In the previous example, because the code marshals a Patients object tree, the correct context is the package name of the Patients class. In this case, the context is org.java7recipes.chapter22.

## CHAPTER 23

Networking

Today, writing an application that does not communicate over the Internet in some fashion is rare. From sending data to another machine, to scraping information off remote web pages, networking plays an integral part in today's computing world. Java makes it easy to communicate over the network using the New I/O (NIO) and More New I/O Features for the Java Platform (NIO.2) APIs. Java SE 7 brought forth a few new features, enabling easier multicasting among other things. With the addition of these new features, the Java platform contains a plethora of programming interfaces to help accomplish network tasks.

This chapter will not attempt to cover every networking feature that is part of the Java language. It will only provide a handful of recipes that were thought to be the most useful for a broad base of developers. You will learn about a few of the standard networking concepts such as sockets and some new concepts that were introduced with the release of Java SE 7. If you find this chapter interesting and would like to learn more about Java networking, a vast amount of resources can be found online. Perhaps the best place to go for learning more about it is the Oracle documentation that can be found at `http://download.oracle.com/javase/tutorial/networking/index.html`.

23-1. Defining a Network Connection to a Server

Problem

You need to establish a connection to a remote server.

Solution

Create a **Socket** connection to the remote server using its name and port number where the server is listening for incoming client requests. In the following example class, a **Socket** connection to a remote server is created. The code then sends a textual message to the server and receives a response. In the example, the server name that the client is attempting to contact is named "**server-name**", and the port number is **1234**.

■ **Tip**   To create a connection to a local program running on the client machine, set the "server-name" equal to "127.0.0.1". This is done within the source listing for this recipe. Usually local connections such as this are used for testing purposes only.

```java
public class SocketClient {

    public static Socket socket = null;
    public static PrintWriter out;
    public static BufferedReader in;

    public static void main(String[] args) {
        createConnection("127.0.0.1", 1234);
    }

    public static void createConnection(String host, int port) {

        try {
            //Create socket connection
            socket = new Socket(host, port);
            // Obtain a handle on the socket output
            out = new PrintWriter(socket.getOutputStream(),
                    true);
            // Obtain a handle on the socket input
            in = new BufferedReader(new InputStreamReader(
                    socket.getInputStream()));
            testConnection();
            System.out.println("Closing the connection...");
            out.flush();
            out.close();
            in.close();
            socket.close();
            System.exit(0);
            } catch (UnknownHostException e) {
            System.out.println(e);
            System.exit(1);
            } catch (IOException e) {
            System.out.println(e);
            System.exit(1);
        }
    }

    public static void testConnection() {
        String serverResponse = null;
        if (socket != null && in != null && out != null) {
            System.out.println("Successfully connected, now testing...");

            try {
```

```
                    // Send data to server
                    out.println("Here is a test.");
                    // Receive data from server
                    while((serverResponse = in.readLine()) != null)
                    System.out.println(serverResponse);
                    } catch (IOException e) {
                    System.out.println(e);
                    System.exit(1);
                }
            }
        }
}
```

If testing this client against a server that successfully accepts the request, you will see the following result:

```
Successfully connected, now testing...
```

■ **Note** This program will do nothing on its own. To create a server-side socket application that will accept this connection for a complete test, please see recipe 23-2. If you attempt to run this class without specifying a server host that is listening on the provided port, you will receive an exception: `java.net.ConnectException:` `Connection refused`.

How It Works

Every client/server connection occurs via a *socket*, which is an endpoint in a communication link between two different programs. Sockets have port numbers assigned to them, which act as an identifier for the Transmission Control Protocol/Internet Protocol (TCP/IP) layer to use when attempting a connection. A server program that accepts requests from client machines typically listens for new connections on a specified port number. When a client wishes to make a request to the server, it creates a new socket utilizing the hostname of the server and the port on which the server is listening and attempts to establish a connection with that socket. If the server accepts the socket, then the connection is successful.

This recipe discusses the client side of the socket connection, so we will not go into the details of what happens on the server side at this time. However, more information regarding the server side of a connection will be covered in recipe 23-2. The example class in the solution to this recipe is representative of how a client-side program attempts and establishes connections to a server-side program. In this recipe, a method named `createConnection()` is used to perform the actual connection. It accepts a server hostname and port number, which will be used to create the socket. Within the `createConnection()` method, the server hostname and port number are passed to the `Socket` class constructor, creating a new `Socket` object. Next, a `PrintWriter` object is created using the `Socket` object's output stream, and a `BufferedReader` object is created using the `Socket` object's input stream.

```
//Create socket connection
socket = new Socket(host, port);
// Obtain a handle on the socket output
out = new PrintWriter(socket.getOutputStream(),
```

```
                            true);
// Obtain a handle on the socket input
in = new BufferedReader(new InputStreamReader(
                        socket.getInputStream()));
```

After creating the socket and obtaining the socket's output stream and input stream, the client can write to the `PrintWriter` in order to send data to the server. Similarly, to receive a response from the server, the client reads from the `BufferedReader` object that was created. The `testConnection()` method is used to simulate a conversation between the client and the server program using the newly created socket. To do this, the `socket`, `in`, and `out` variables are checked to ensure that they are not equal to `null`. If not, then the client attempts to send a message to the server by sending a message to the output stream using `out.println("Here is a test.")`. A loop is then created to listen for a response from the server by calling the `in.readLine()` method until nothing else is received and printing out the messages that are received.

The `java.net.Socket` class is true to the nature of the Java programming language. It enables developers to code against a platform-independent API in order to communicate with network protocols that are specific to different platforms. It abstracts the details of each platform from the developer, and provides a straightforward and consistent implementation for enabling client/server communications.

23-2. Listening for Connections on the Server

Problem

You would like to create a server application that will listen for connections from a remote client.

Solution

Set up a server-side application that makes use of `java.net.ServerSocket` to listen for requests on a specified port. The following Java class is representative of one that would be deployed onto a server, and it listens for incoming requests on port 1234. When a request is received, the incoming message is printed to the command line and a response is sent back to the client.

```java
package org.java7recipes.chapter23.recipe23_2;

import java.io.BufferedReader;
import java.io.IOException;
import java.io.InputStreamReader;
import java.io.PrintWriter;
import java.net.ServerSocket;
import java.net.Socket;

public class SocketServer {

public static void main(String a[]) {
        final int httpd = 1234;
        ServerSocket ssock = null;
        try {
            ssock = new ServerSocket(httpd);
```

```
                System.out.println("have opened port 1234 locally");

                Socket sock = ssock.accept();
                System.out.println("client has made socket connection");

        communicateWithClient(sock);

System.out.println("closing socket");
} catch (Exception e) {
System.out.println(e);
} finally {
try{
ssock.close();
} catch (IOException ex) {
System.out.println(ex);
}
}
}

    public static void communicateWithClient(Socket socket) {
        BufferedReader in = null;
        PrintWriter out = null;

        try {
            in = new BufferedReader(
                    new InputStreamReader(socket.getInputStream()));
            out = new PrintWriter(
                    socket.getOutputStream(), true);


            String s = null;
            out.println("Server received communication!");
            while ((s = in.readLine()) != null) {
                System.out.println("received from client: " + s);
                out.flush();
                break;
            }
        } catch (Exception e) {
            e.printStackTrace();
        } finally {
            try {
                in.close();
                out.close();
            } catch (IOException ex) {
                ex.printStackTrace();
            }
        }
    }
}
```

Executing this program along with the client that was built in recipe 23-1 would result in the following output from the `SocketServer`:

```
have opened port 1234 locally
client has made socket connection
received from client: Here is a test.
closing socket
```

■ **Note** To run the two recipes so that they work with each other, first start the `SocketServer` program so that the client can create a socket using the port that is opened in the server program. After the `SocketServer` is started, initiate the `SocketClient` program to see the two work together.

■ **Caution** This `SocketServer` program opens a port on your machine (1234). Be sure that you have a firewall set running on your machine, otherwise you will be opening port 1234 to everyone. This could result in an attack on your machine. Open ports create vulnerabilities for attackers to break into machines, like leaving a door in your house open. Note that the example in this recipe has a minimal attack profile because the server is run through only one pass and will print only a single message from the client before the session is closed.

How It Works

In order for a client application to connect to a server application, the server application must be listening for connections and then processing them somehow. You cannot simply run a client against any given host and port number combination because doing so would likely result in a refused connection. The server-side application must do three things: open a port, accept and establish client connections, and then communicate with the client connections in some way. In the solution to this recipe, the `SocketServer` class does all three of them.

Starting with the `main()` method, the class begins by opening a new socket on port 1234. This is done by creating a new instance of `ServerSocket` and passing a port number to it. The port number used must not conflict with any other port that is currently in use on the server. It is important to note that ports below 1024 are usually reserved for operating system usage, so port numbers should be chosen above that range. If you attempt to open up a port that is already in use, the `ServerSocket` will not successfully be created, and the program will fail. Next, the `ServerSocket` object's `accept()` method is called, returning a new `Socket` object. Calling the `accept()` method will do nothing until a client attempts to connect to the server program on the port that has been set up. The `accept()` method will wait idly until a connection is requested and then it will return the new `Socket` object bound to the port that was set up on the `ServerSocket`. This socket also contains the remote port and hostname of the client attempting the connection, so it contains the information on two endpoints and uniquely identifies the TCP connection.

At this point, the server program can communicate with the client program, and it does so using the PrintWriter and BufferedReader objects. In the solution to this recipe, the communicateWithClient() method contains all the code necessary to accept messages from the client program, sends messages back to the client, and then returns control to the main() method that closes the ServerSocket. A new BufferedReader object can be created by generating a new InputStreamReader instance using the socket's input stream. Similarly, a new PrintWriter object can be created using the socket's output stream. Notice that this code must be wrapped in a try-catch block in case the creation of these objects is not successful.

```
in = new BufferedReader(
                new InputStreamReader(socket.getInputStream()));
out = new PrintWriter(
                socket.getOutputStream(), true);
```

Once these objects have been successfully created, the server can communicate with the client. To do so, a loop is created, reading from the BufferedReader object (the client input stream), and then sending messages back to the client using the PrintWriter object. In the solution to this recipe, the server closes the connection by issuing a break, which causes the loop to end and control returns to the main() method.

```
out.println("Server received communication!");
while ((s = in.readLine()) != null) {
System.out.println("received from client: " + s);
out.flush();
break;
}
```

In a real-life server program, the server would most likely listen endlessly without using a break to end communication. To handle multiple concurrent clients, each client connection would spawn a separate Thread to handle communication. The server would do something useful with the client communication as well. In the case of an HTML server, it would send back an HTML message to the client. On an SMTP server, the client would send an e-mail message to the server, and the server would then process the e-mail and send it. Socket communication is used for just about any TCP transmission, and both the client and servers create new sockets to perform a successful communication.

23-3. Bypassing TCP for InfiniBand to Gain Performance Boosts

Problem

Your application deployed on Linux or Solaris requires the ability to move data very quickly and efficiently, and you need to remove all bottlenecks that could slow things down.

Solution

Make use of the Sockets Direct Protocol (SDP) to bypass TCP, a possible bottleneck in the process. In order to do so, create an SDP configuration file and set the system property to specify the configuration file location.

■ **Note** The SDP was added to the Java SE 7 Release for applications deployed in the Solaris or Linux operating systems only. SDP was developed to support stream connections over InfiniBrandfabric, which both Solaris and Linux operating systems support. The Java SE 7 release supports the 1.4.2 and 1.5 versions of OpenFabrics Enterprise Distribution (OFED).

This configuration file is an example of one that could be used to enable the use of SDP:

```
# Use SDP when binding to 192.0.2.1
bind 192.0.2.1 *

# Use SDP when connecting to all application services on 192.0.2.*
connect 192.0.2.0/24    1024-*

# Use SDP when connecting to the http server or a database on myserver.org
connect myserver.org    8080
connect myserver.org    1521
```

The following excerpt is taken from the terminal. It is the execution of a Java application named SDPExample, specifying the SDP system property:

```
% java -Dcom.sun.sdp.conf=sdp.conf -Djava.net.preferIPv4Stack=true  SDPExample
```

How It Works

Sometimes it is essential that an application be as fast as possible while performing network communications. Transfers over the TCP protocol can sometimes decrease performance, so bypassing TCP could be beneficial. In JDK 7, support for the SDP is included for certain platforms. The SDP is a protocol that supports stream connections over InfiniBand fabric. Both Solaris and Linux include support for InfiniBand, so SDP can be useful on those platforms.

No programmatic changes need to be made to an application in order to support SDP. The only two differences for using SDP are that you must create an SDP configuration file, and the JVM must be told to use the protocol by passing a flag when running the application. Because the implementation is transparent, applications can be written for any platform, and those that support SDP can merely include the configuration file and bypass TCP.

The SDP configuration file is a text file that is composed of **bind** and **connect** rules. A **bind** rule indicates that the SDP protocol transport should be used when a TCP socket binds to an address and port that match the given rule. A **connect** rule indicates that the SDP protocol transport should be used when an unbound TCP socket attempts to connect to an address and port that match the given rule. The rule begins with either the **bind** or **connect** keyword indicating the rule type, followed by the hostname or IP address, and a single port number or range of port numbers. Per the online documentation, a rule has the following form:

```
("bind"|"connect")1*LWSP-char(hostname|ipaddress)["/"prefix])1*LWSP-char("*"|port)↩
["-"("*"|port)]
```

In the rule format shown here, **1*LWSP-char** means that any number of tabs or spaces can separate the tokens. Anything contained within square brackets indicates optional text, and quotes indicate literal text. In the solution to the recipe, the first rule indicates that SDP can be used for any port (* indicates a wildcard) on the IP address of 192.0.2.1, a local address. Each local address that is assigned to an InfiniBand adaptor should be specified with a bind rule within the configuration file. The first connect rule within the configuration file specifies that SDP should be used whenever connecting to the IP address of 192.0.2.*, using a port of 1024 or greater.

```
connect 192.0.2.0/24     1024-*
```

This rule uses some special syntax that should be noted. Specifically, the /24 suffix of the IP address indicates that the first 24 bits of the 32-bit IP address should match against a specified address. Because each portion of an IP address is 8 bits, this means that the 192.0.2 should match exactly, and the final byte can be any value. The dash -* within the port identifier specifies the range of 1024 or greater because the wildcard character is used.The third and fourth connect rules within the configuration file specify that SDP should be used with the hostname of myserver.org and a port of 8080 or 1521.

Next, in order to enable SDP, the –Dcom.sun.sdp.conf property should be specified along with the location to the SDP configuration file when starting the application. Also, in the solution you will notice that the property -Djava.net.preferIPv4Stack is set to true, this indicates that the IPv4 address format will be used. This is necessary because IPv4 addresses mapped to IPv6 are currently not available in the Solaris OS or under Linux.

Although the SDP is only available under Solaris or Linux, it is a nice addition to the JDK for users of those platforms. Any performance booster is always viewed as a bonus, and the solution to this recipe certainly falls into that category.

23-4. Broadcasting to a Group of Recipients

Problem

You would like to broadcast datagrams to zero or more hosts identified by a single address.

Solution

Make use of datagram multicasting using the DatagramChannel class. The DatagramChannel class provides the ability for more than one client to connect to a group and listen for datagrams that have been broadcasted from a server. The following sets of code demonstrate this technique using a client/server approach. The class demonstrates a multicast client.

■ **Note** The following code may not function as expected using the OpenJDK platform on OS X. It has been tested successfully using Windows 7 and Oracle's official Java SE 7 Release.

```
package org.java7recipes.chapter23.recipe23_4;

import java.io.IOException;
import java.net.DatagramPacket;
import java.net.DatagramSocket;
import java.net.InetAddress;
```

```java
import java.net.InetSocketAddress;
import java.net.NetworkInterface;
import java.net.SocketAddress;
import java.net.StandardProtocolFamily;
import java.net.StandardSocketOptions;
import java.nio.ByteBuffer;
import java.nio.channels.CompletionHandler;
import java.nio.channels.DatagramChannel;
import java.nio.channels.MembershipKey;

public class MulticastClient {
    public MulticastClient(){

    }

    public static void main (String[] args){
        try {
            // Obtain Supported network Interface
            NetworkInterface networkInterface = NetworkInterface.getByName("en1");

            // Address within range
            int port = 5239;
            InetAddress group = InetAddress.getByName("226.18.84.25");

            final DatagramChannel client = DatagramChannel.open(StandardProtocolFamily.INET);

            client.setOption(StandardSocketOptions.SO_REUSEADDR, true);
            client.bind(new InetSocketAddress(port));
            client.setOption(StandardSocketOptions.IP_MULTICAST_IF, networkInterface);

            System.out.println("Joining group: " + group + " with network interface " +
networkInterface);
            // Multicasting join
            MembershipKey key = client.join(group, networkInterface);
            client.open();



        // receive message as a client
        final ByteBuffer buffer = ByteBuffer.allocateDirect(4096);
        buffer.clear();
        System.out.println("Waiting to receive message");
        // Configure client to be passive and non.blocking
         // client.configureBlocking(false);
        client.receive(buffer);
        System.out.println("Client Received Message:");
buffer.flip();
        byte[] arr = new byte[buffer.remaining()];
        buffer.get(arr, 0, arr.length);

        System.out.println(new String(arr));
        System.out.println("Disconnecting...performing a single test pass only");
```

```
                client.disconnect();

        } catch (IOException ex) {
            ex.printStackTrace();
        }
    }

}
```

Next, a server class can be used to broadcast datagrams to the address that multicast clients are connected to. The following code demonstrates a multicast server:

```
package org.java7recipes.chapter23.recipe23_4;

import java.io.IOException;
import java.net.DatagramPacket;
import java.net.DatagramSocket;
import java.net.InetAddress;
import java.net.InetSocketAddress;
import java.nio.ByteBuffer;
import java.nio.channels.DatagramChannel;

public class MulticastServer extends Thread {

    protected DatagramSocket socket = null;
    protected ByteBuffer message = null;


    public MulticastServer() {
    }

    public static void main(String[] args) {

        MulticastServer server = new MulticastServer();
        server.start();

    }

    public void run() {

        try {

            // send the response to the client at "address" and "port"
            InetAddress address = InetAddress.getByName("226.18.84.25");
            int port = 5239;

            DatagramChannel server = DatagramChannel.open().bind(null);
ByteBuffer message = ByteBuffer.wrap("Hello to all listeners".getBytes());
            server.send(message, new InetSocketAddress(address, port));

            server.disconnect();
```

```
        } catch (IOException e) {
            e.printStackTrace();

        }
    }   }
}
```

The server will have the ability to broadcast a message to each client that is a member of the group.

How It Works

Multicasting is the ability to broadcast a message to a group of listeners in a single transmission. A good analogy of multicasting is radio. Thousands of people can tune into a single broadcast event and listen to the same message. Computers can do similar things when sending messages to listeners. A group of client machines can tune into the same address and port number to receive a message that a server broadcasts to that address and port. The Java language provides multicasting functionality via datagram messaging. Datagrams are independent, nonguaranteed messages that can be delivered over the network to clients. (Being *nonguaranteed* means that the arrival, arrival time, and content are not predictable.) Unlike messages sent over TCP, sending a datagram is a nonblocking event, and the sender is not notified of the receipt of the message. Datagrams are sent using the User Datagram Protocol (UDP) rather than TCP. The ability to send multicast messages via UDP is one benefit over TCP, as long as the ordering, reliability, and data integrity of the message are not mission critical.

Java facilitates multicast messaging via the `MulticastChannel` interface. Classes that implement the `MulticastChannel` interface have multicasting enabled and can therefore broadcast to groups and receive group broadcasts. One such class is the `DatagramChannel`, which is a selectable channel for datagram-oriented sockets. In the solution to this recipe, both a client and a server program are used to communicate via multicast messaging, and the `DatagramChannel` class is used in both sides of the communication. A `DatagramChannel` must be configured in a specific way if it is to be used for accepting multicast messages. Specifically, there are options that need to be set on the `DatagramClient` that is opened. We will discuss those options shortly. The following steps are required for creating a client for receiving multicast messages.

1. Open a `DatagramChannel`.

2. Set the `DatagramChannel` options that are required multicast.

3. Join the client to a multicast group and return a `MembershipKey` object.

4. Open the client.

In the solution to this recipe, the client application begins by obtaining a reference to the network interface that will be used for receiving the broadcast messages. Setting up a `NetworkInterface` is required for multicasting. Next, a port number is chosen, as well as a multicasting IP address. The group or registered listeners will use the IP address in order to listen for broadcasts. The port number must not be in use, or an exception will be thrown. For IPv4 multicasting, the IP address must range from 224.0.0.0 to 239.255.255.255, inclusive. This port and IP address will be the same that is used by a server to broadcast the message. Next, a new `DatagramChannel` is opened using `StandardProtocolFamily.INET`. The choices for opening a `DatagramChannel` are either `StandardProtocolFamily.INET` or `StandardProtocolFamily.INET6`, corresponding to IPv4 and IPv6, respectively. The first option that is set on the `DatagramChannel` is `StandardSocketOptions.SO_REUSEADDR`, and it is set to `true`. This indicates that multiple clients will be able to "reuse" the address or use it at the same time. This needs to be set for a multicast to occur. The client is then bound to the port using a new `InetSocketAddress` instance. Last, the StandardSocketOptions.IP_MULTICAST_IF option is set to the network interface that is used. This option represents the outgoing interface for multicast datagrams sent by the datagram-orientedsocket.

■ **Note** In OpenJDK, java.net.StandardSocketOptions is a valid class. However, in the official Oracle Java SE 7 release, the class name might be java.net.StandardSocketOption. Change the code accordingly, depending upon which platform you are using.

```
client.setOption(StandardSocketOptions.SO_REUSEADDR, true);
client.bind(new InetSocketAddress(port));
client.setOption(StandardSocketOptions.IP_MULTICAST_IF, networkInterface);
```

Once these options have been set, and the port has been bound to the DatagramChannel, it is ready to join the group of listeners. This can be done by calling the DatagramChanneljoin(InetAddress, NetworkInterface) method, passing the group address and network interface that will be used by the client. As a result, a java.nio.channels.MembershipKey object is produced, which is a token that represents the membership of an IP multicast group. Last, the DatagramChannelopen() method is called, which opens the channel to listen for broadcasts. At this point, the client is ready to receive multicast messages and it waits for a message to be received.

```
MembershipKey key = client.join(group, networkInterface);
client.open();
```

The next lines of code within the client take care of receiving messages from the server. In order to receive a broadcasted message, a ByteBuffer is created and then eventually passed to the DatagramChannel's receive() method. Once the receive() method is called, the client will pause until a message is received. You can disable this feature by calling the DatagramChannel configureBlocking(boolean) method and passing a false value. Next, the ByteBuffer is converted to a String value and printed out by repositioning the buffer index at 0 using the flip() method, and then pulling the text starting at index 0 to the last index into a byte[]. Finally, be sure to disconnect the client when finished. That wraps it up for the client code portion.

■ **Note** In the example to this recipe, a single pass is performed, and the client is then disconnected. For extended listening, a loop with a timeout configured and tests for an ending state would be required.

The server code is fairly basic. You can see that the MulticastServer class extends Thread. This means that this server application could be run in a thread separate from other code within an application. If there were another class that initiated the MulticastServer class' run() method, it would run in a thread separate from the class that initiated it. The run() method must exist within any class that extends Thread. For more information regarding threading and concurrency, refer to Chapter 8.

The bulk of the server code resides within the run() method. A new InetAddress object is created using the same IP address that the client registered with in order to join the multicast group. The same port number is also declared within the server code, and these two objects will be used later in the code block to send the message. A new DatagramChannel is opened and bound to null. The null value is important because by setting the **SocketAddress** equal to **null**, the socket will be bound to an address that is assigned automatically. Next, a **ByteBuffer** is created that contains a message that will be broadcast to any listeners. The message is then sent using the **DatagramChannel**'s **send(ByteBuffer, InetSocketAddress)** method. The **send()** method in the solution accepts the message as a **ByteBuffer** object, as well as a new **InetSocketAddress** that is created by using the address and port, which was declared at the beginning of the block. Told you we'd get back to those!

```
server.send(message, new InetSocketAddress(address, port));
```

At this point, the client would receive the message that was sent by the server. As for the client that is demonstrated in the solution to this recipe, it would then disconnect. Normally in a real-world scenario, a different class would most likely initiate the server, and its **run()** method would contain a loop that would continue to execute until all messages have been broadcast or the loop was told to stop. The client would probably not disconnect until after a user initiated a shutdown.

23-5. Generating and Reading from URLs

Problem

You would like to generate URLs programmatically within your application. Once the URLs have been created, you'd like to read data from them for use within your application.

Solution

Make use of the **java.net.URL** class in order to create a URL. There are a few different ways to generate a URL depending upon the address you are attempting to work with. This solution demonstrates a few different ways to create URL objects, along with comments indicating the differences. Once the URL objects have been created, one of the URLs is read into a **BufferedReader** and printed out to the command line.

```
import java.io.BufferedReader;
import java.io.IOException;
import java.io.InputStreamReader;
import java.net.MalformedURLException;
import java.net.URL;

public class GenerateAndReadUrl {

    public static void main(String[] args) {
        try {
            // Generate absolute URL
            URL url1 = new URL("http://www.java.net");
            System.out.println(url1.toString());
            // Generate URL for pages with a common base
            URL url2 = new URL(url1, "search/node/jdk7");

            // Generate URL from different pieces of data
            URL url3 = new URL("http", "java.net", "search/node/jdk7");
```

```
            readFromUrl(url1);

        } catch (MalformedURLException ex) {
            ex.printStackTrace();
        }
    }

    /**
     * Open URL stream as an input stream and print contents to command line.
     *
     * @param url
     */
    public static void readFromUrl(URL url) {
        try {
            BufferedReader in = new BufferedReader(
                    new InputStreamReader(
                    url.openStream()));

            String inputLine;

            while ((inputLine = in.readLine()) != null) {
                System.out.println(inputLine);
            }

            in.close();
        } catch (IOException ex) {
            ex.printStackTrace();
        }
    }
}
```

Running this program will result in the printing of HTML from the URL resource identified as `url1` to the command line.

How It Works

The creation of URLs within Java code is fairly straightforward thanks to the **java.net.URL** class, which does all of the heavy lifting for you. A URL is a character string that points to a resource on the Internet. Sometimes it is useful to create URLs within Java code so that you can read content from, or push content to, the Internet resource that the URL is pointing to. In the solution to this recipe, a few different URL objects are created, demonstrating the different constructors that are available for use.

The easiest route to use for creating a URL is to pass the standard readable URL String for a resource that is located on the Internet to the **java.net.URL** class to create a new instance of the URL. In the solution, an absolute URL is passed to the constructor to create the `url1` object.

```
URL url1 = new URL("http://www.java.net");
```

Another useful way to create a URL is to pass two arguments to the URL constructor and create a relative URL. Relative URLs are useful for basing upon the context of another URL. For instance, if a particular site has a number of different pages, you could create a URL pointing to one of the subpages relative to the URL of the main site. Such is the case with the **url2** object in the solution to this recipe.

```
URL url2 = new URL(url1, "search/node/jdk7");
```

As you can see, the path **search/node/jdk7** is relative to the URL that is known as **url1**. In the end, the human-readable format of the **url2** object would be represented as **http://www.java.net/search/node/jdk7**. There are a couple more constructors for creating URL objects that take more than two arguments. Those constructors are as follows:

```
new URL (String protocol, String host, String port, String path);
new URL (String protocol, String host, String path);
```

In the solution, the second of the two constructors shown here is demonstrated. The protocol, hostname, and path of the resource are passed to the constructor to create the **url3** object. These last two constructors are usually most useful when generating a URL dynamically.

23-6. Parsing a URL

Problem

You would like to programmatically gather information from a URL within your application.

Solution

Parse the URL using the built-in URL class methods. In the following example class named **ParseUrl**, a URL object is created and then parsed using the built-in URL class methods to gather information regarding the URL. After the information has been retrieved from the URL, it is printed to the command line and then used to create another URL.

```
import java.net.MalformedURLException;
import java.net.URL;

public static void main(String[] args) {
URL url1 = null;
URL url2 = null;
try {
        // Generate absolute URL
        url1 = new URL("http://www.apress.com/catalogsearch/result/?q=juneau");

        String host = url1.getHost();
        String path = url1.getPath();
        String query = url1.getQuery();
        String protocol = url1.getProtocol();
        String authority = url1.getAuthority();
        String ref = url1.getRef();

        System.out.println("The URL " + url1.toString() + " parses to the following:\n");
        System.out.println("Host: " + host + "\n");
        System.out.println("Path: " + path + "\n");
```

```
            System.out.println("Query: " + query + "\n");
            System.out.println("Protocol: " + protocol + "\n");
            System.out.println("Authority: " + authority + "\n");
            System.out.println("Reference: " + ref + "\n");

            url2 = new URL(protocol + "://" + host + path + "?q=java");

        } catch (IOException ex) {
            ex.printStackTrace();

        }
    }
```

When this code is executed, the following lines will be displayed:

```
The URL http://www.apress.com/catalogsearch/result/?q=juneau parses to the following:

Host: www.apress.com

Path: /catalogsearch/result/

Query: q=juneau

Protocol: http

Authority: www.apress.com

Reference: null
```

How It Works

When constructing and working with URLs within an application, it is sometimes beneficial to have the ability to extract information pertaining to a URL. This can be easily done using the URL built-in class methods that can be called upon a given URL to return Strings of information. Table 23-1 shows the different accessor methods available within the URL class for obtaining information.

Table 23-1. Accessor Methods for Querying URLs

Method	URL Information Returned
getAuthority()	Authority component
getFile()	File name component
getHost()	Hostname component
getPath()	Path component
getProtocol()	Protocol identifier component

Method	URL Information Returned
getRef()	Reference component
getQuery()	Query component

Each of these accessor methods returns a String value that can be used for informational purposes or for constructing other URLs dynamically, as was done in the example. If you take a look at the results from the solution to this recipe, you can see the information that was obtained regarding the URL via the accessor methods listed in Table 23-1. Most of the accessors are self-explanatory. However, a couple of them could use further explanation. The `getFile()` method returns the file name of the URL. The file name is the same as the result of concatenating the value returned from `getPath()` with the value returned from `getQuery()`. The `getRef()` method may not be very straight forward. The reference component that is returned by calling the `getRef()` method refers to the "fragment" that may be appended to the end of a URL. For instance, a "fragment" is indicated using the pound character (#), followed by a String that usually corresponds to a subsection on a particular web page. Given the URL such as the following, `recipe23_7` is what would be returned using the `getRef()` method.

`http://www.java7recipes.org/chapters/chapter23#recipe23_7`

Although not always needed, the ability to parse a URL to obtain information can come in very handy at times. Because the Java language has helper methods built into the `java.net.URL` class, it makes gathering information pertaining to URLs a piece of cake.

Index

■ L